RUSSIA AND THE
INDEPENDENT STATES

Expanded Reference Edition

Edited by

DANIEL C. DILLER

CONGRESSIONAL QUARTERLY INC.

WASHINGTON, D.C.

Printed in the United States of America

Photo credits: x, xi, 15, 16, 26, 31, 41, 46, 57, 74, 192, 311, 315, 317, Library of Congress; xiii, 56, 102, 104, 111, 112, 122, 123, 129 (top and bottom), 131, 132, 133, 134 (top), 168, 173, 174, 183, Russian Information Agency-Novosti; xii, 74, 312, John F. Kennedy Library; xii, xiii, 73, 87, 89, 124, 127, 134 (bottom), 136, 142, 145, 163, 205, 318, AP/Wide World Photos; 75, U.S. Navy; 91, 223, White House; 109, Gene Draschner; 149, 212, U.S. Department of Defense; 176 (left and right), Tass; 195, United Nations; 200, Hopi-Pressefoto—Bernhard J. Holzner; 216, 229, 298, R. Michael Jenkins; 219, International News Photo; 233, U.S. Department of Agriculture; 237, David Valdez-White House; xii, xiii, 297, 305, 307, 309, 310, 313, 320, Novosti.

Contributing writers: Dan Berg, Joel Levin, Jerry Orvedahl, Ron de Paolo, Sharon Werning

Cover design: Ben Santora
Maps (except frontispiece): William J. Clipson

Library of Congress Cataloging-in-Publication Data

Diller, Daniel C., 1959-
    Russia and the independent states / Daniel C. Diller.
      p.   cm.
    Includes bibliographical references and index.
    ISBN 0-87187-617-5 : (soft cover). -- ISBN 0-87187-862-3 :
      (hard cover)
    1. Former Soviet republics--History. 2. Commonwealth of
Independent States. 3. Soviet Union--History. 4. Russia--History.
I. Title.
DK293.D55   1992
947--dc20   92-33273
                                               CIP

CONTENTS

MAPS, BOXES, TABLES, AND FIGURES

PREFACE

Russia and the Independent States is published close on the heels of one of the most momentous events of the twentieth century. Over the course of a year and a half the world's last great empire was torn asunder by centuries-old national animosities and aspirations, the failure of the Soviet economic system, and a pervasive cynicism that rotted the foundations of Soviet political culture.

The ramifications of the Soviet empire's demise radiate throughout the world. On an individual level, employees of defense-related corporations in small-town America, sugar-cane growers in Cuba, and diamond merchants in South Africa are among millions of people affected by the breakup of the Soviet Union. On an epic scale, the international communist movement was dealt a knockout, the bipolar balance of power was shattered, and the omnipresent threat of massive nuclear war between the superpowers was vastly reduced.

Across the lands of the former Soviet Union the transformations are no less dramatic. The collapse left a tangled web of economic, political, and social interrelationships that will take the fifteen newly independent states decades to resolve.

The expanded reference edition of *Russia and the Independent States* combines current analysis with extensive background to place the causes and implications of the revolution of 1991-1992 in historical context. The chronological format of Part I, topical arrangement of Part II, and regional focus of Part III provide different perspectives on the continuum of Russian, Soviet, and post-Soviet eras.

Students of history will find *Russia and the Independent States* an invaluable reference source as well as a highly readable textbook. The appendix includes biographies of more than sixty influential leaders of the past and present; a detailed chronology of milestones from 1900 to the present; selected historic documents; and a bibliography of authoritative information sources. A thorough index facilitates research. The maps in this volume were custom-drawn to illuminate the textual discussions.

The discussions that led to this text began in early 1991, several months after Congressional Quarterly published *The Soviet Union,* third edition. The breakneck pace of change in the USSR persuaded us of the need for a fourth edition. By the time the project was under way, the country had dissolved and the book had been renamed *Russia and the Independent States.* Despite the change in title, this text draws heavily on its predecessors. The sections on early Russian and Soviet history and the chronology through 1990 appeared in the third edition of *The Soviet Union.* The balance of the material, however, was drafted anew in mid-to-late 1992 in light of the seminal events that had taken place.

This book was produced by a talented team of editors and writers to whom I am greatly indebted. Associate editor Jerry Orvedahl gracefully shepherded the project throughout all its phases, oversaw the selection and acquisition of photographs and maps, and applied his own expertise of Russia and the independent states as the writer of Chapter 7. Associate editor John Moore, who was indispensable to this book and all three editions of *The Soviet Union,* provided sage advice and skillful editing. Contributing writers Dan Berg, Joel Levin, Ron de Paolo, and Sharon Werning brought a wealth of knowledge and insight about the former Soviet Union to the book. This text also reflects the efforts of those who established a legacy with the three editions of *The Soviet Union.*

1910 | **1920** |

Domestic Events

1918—Tsar Nicholas II and his family are murdered by Bolsheviks.

1918—Bolsheviks sign the Treaty of Brest-Litovsk with Germany, ending Russian participation in World War I.

1917—Russian Revolution results in the overthrow of the tsar and the seizure of power by the Bolsheviks.

1921—Lenin initiates the New Economic Policy, promoting limited free enterprise as a means to rebuild the Soviet economy.

1918–1920—Bolshevik Red Army defeats opposing White forces in the Russian Civil War.

1928—Stalin introduces the First Five-Year Plan, which ends the New Economic Policy and calls for rapid industrial expansion and the reorganization of peasants into collectives.

1922—Union of Soviet Socialist Republics is declared.

Leaders

1917—V.I. Lenin heads Bolsheviks and Russia as the chairman of the Council of the People's Commissars.

1922—Joseph Stalin becomes general secretary of the Communist party.

1924—Lenin dies; a power struggle between Joseph Stalin, Leon Trotsky, and others follows.

World Events

1914–1918—World War I; Great Britain, France, Russia, and (beginning in 1917) the U.S. battle the Central Powers led by Germany and Austria-Hungary.

1919—Versailles Treaty settles World War I issues, imposes reparations on the defeated Central Powers, and creates the League of Nations.

1929—Stock market crash in the United States signals beginning of the Great Depression.

1930

1940

1950

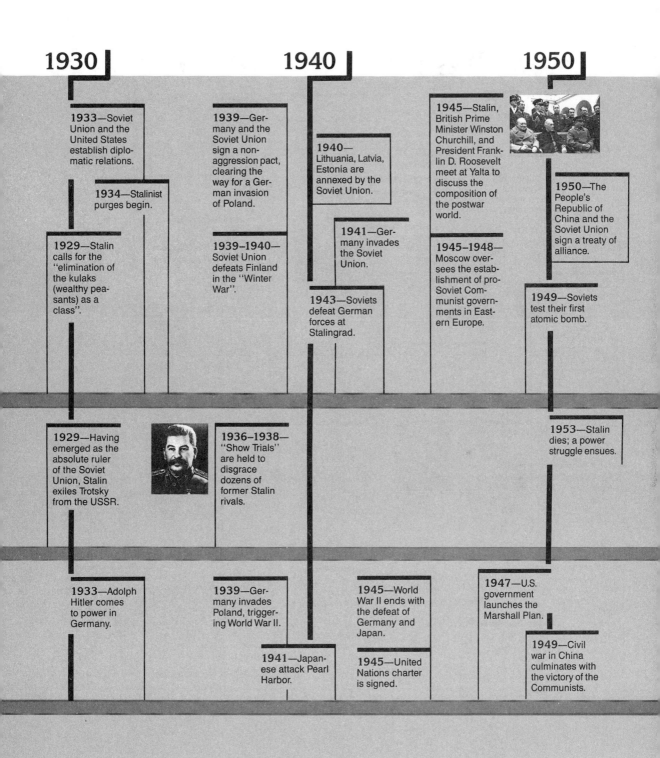

1933—Soviet Union and the United States establish diplomatic relations.

1934—Stalinist purges begin.

1929—Stalin calls for the "elimination of the kulaks (wealthy peasants) as a class".

1939—Germany and the Soviet Union sign a non-aggression pact, clearing the way for a German invasion of Poland.

1939–1940—Soviet Union defeats Finland in the "Winter War".

1940—Lithuania, Latvia, Estonia are annexed by the Soviet Union.

1941—Germany invades the Soviet Union.

1943—Soviets defeat German forces at Stalingrad.

1945—Stalin, British Prime Minister Winston Churchill, and President Franklin D. Roosevelt meet at Yalta to discuss the composition of the postwar world.

1945–1948—Moscow oversees the establishment of pro-Soviet Communist governments in Eastern Europe.

1950—The People's Republic of China and the Soviet Union sign a treaty of alliance.

1949—Soviets test their first atomic bomb.

1929—Having emerged as the absolute ruler of the Soviet Union, Stalin exiles Trotsky from the USSR.

1936–1938—"Show Trials" are held to disgrace dozens of former Stalin rivals.

1953—Stalin dies; a power struggle ensues.

1933—Adolph Hitler comes to power in Germany.

1939—Germany invades Poland, triggering World War II.

1941—Japanese attack Pearl Harbor.

1945—World War II ends with the defeat of Germany and Japan.

1945—United Nations charter is signed.

1947—U.S. government launches the Marshall Plan.

1949—Civil war in China culminates with the victory of the Communists.

1960

1956—Soviet forces crush the Hungarian revolution.

1956—Nikita Khrushchev delivers his 'Secret Speech' denouncing Stalin at the Twentieth Soviet Communist Party Congress.

1960—Paris summit is undermined by the downing of an American U-2 spy plane over Soviet territory.

1961—Khrushchev meets President John F. Kennedy at Vienna summit.

1953—Secret police chief Lavrentii Beria is arrested, tried, and executed on the orders of Stalin's successors, who fear his power and ruthlessness.

1957—Soviets launch *Sputnik*, the world's first space satellite.

1961—Soviet cosmonaut Yuri Gagarin becomes the first person in space.

1959—Khrushchev visits the U.S.

1970

1968—Soviets invade Czechoslovakia to put down 'Prague Spring' liberalization movement.

1975—Moscow cancels the U.S.-Soviet trade pact after the U.S. Congress links trade privileges to freer Jewish emigration.

1972—Brezhnev meets President Richard Nixon in Moscow to sign the first Strategic Arms Limitation Treaty.

1957—Khrushchev overcomes a challenge to his authority by rivals known as the ''anti-party group.''

1964—Khrushchev is ousted by his colleagues; Leonid Brezhnev is chosen general secretary.

1977—Brezhnev is elected president, becoming the first Soviet leader to be head of state and general secretary at the same time.

1955—Nikita Khrushchev becomes pre-eminent leader of the Soviet Union.

1953—Korean War ends after three years of fighting.

1962—Cuban missile crisis.

1964—U.S. Congress passes the Gulf of Tonkin Resolution supporting presidential discretion in the use of force in Vietnam.

1969—U.S. astronauts land on the moon.

1973—Paris Peace Agreement is signed, ending the U.S. combat role in Vietnam.

1956—Great Britain, France, and Israel invade Egypt during the Suez crisis.

1967—Israel defeats Arabs in the Six-Day War.

1980

1990

1985—Mikhail Gorbachev discusses arms control with President Ronald Reagan in Geneva.

1987—Gorbachev and Reagan sign the INF Treaty.

1991—Failed hard-line coup hastens dissolution of Soviet Union into fifteen sovereign states.

1989—Soviet troops complete their withdrawal from Afghanistan.

1983—Soviet warplanes shoot down a Korean Airlines passenger jet that had strayed into Soviet airspace.

1989—Multi-candidate elections for the new Congress of People's Deputies are held in the Soviet Union.

1992—Commonwealth of Independent States formed by eleven of the fifteen former Soviet republics.

1979—Soviets invade Afghanistan to prop up a pro-Soviet government.

1986—Chernobyl nuclear disaster causes severe environmental damage.

1990—Communist Party of the Soviet Union renounces its monopoly on power.

1982—Brezhnev dies; Yuri Andropov succeeds him.

1985—Chernenko dies; Mikhail Gorbachev succeeds him.

1991—Gorbachev resigns.

1984—Andropov dies; Chernenko succeeds him.

1991—UN-sanctioned coalition drives Iraq from Kuwait.

1981—Martial law is declared by the Polish government in an effort to suppress the Solidarity labor movement.

1989—Eastern European Communist regimes fall.

1979—Iranian Revolution brings Ayatollah Ruhollah Khomeini to power.

1990—East Germany and West Germany reunify.

1992—Interethnic warfare in the former Yugoslav Federation escalates.

INTRODUCTION

On December 25, 1991, Soviet president Mikhail S. Gorbachev resigned, bringing an end to the Soviet Union. Minutes after Gorbachev's televised announcement, the red Soviet flag with its hammer and sickle was replaced on the Kremlin flagpole by the Russian tricolored flag. The huge Eurasian nation, which was the wellspring of the international communist movement and the Western world's main adversary, ceased to exist. It was replaced by fifteen nations that had been union republics under the Soviet system.

Eleven of these new countries agreed to form an entity that came to be known as the Commonwealth of Independent States (CIS). But it was soon clear that the CIS was not to be a smaller version of the Soviet Union or even an effective confederation. The CIS merely provided a forum for coordinating some policies and resolving some disputes. The fifteen nations of the former Soviet Union moved toward establishing their own national governments and identities.

The largest of the new states was Russia, which had dominated the Soviet Union politically, economically, and culturally. In Russia, the first among equals in the CIS, a new leadership under popularly elected president Boris N. Yeltsin advanced a reform program based on the free market and democracy. The Communist party had been banned and the dismantling of the central economic apparatus was well under way. After seventy-four years of building communism, Russia had completely abandoned its official ideology and its government embraced what appeared to be very Western economic and political institutions.

Fall of the Soviet Union

In 1985 when Mikhail Gorbachev came to power, a prediction that internal forces would cause the demise of the Soviet Union in less than seven years would have been dismissed as unlikely at best and ridiculous at worst. Although the Soviet Union was suffering from numerous economic maladies and scholars long had acknowledged the explosive potential of nationalism among the USSR's 169 ethnic groups, the country also was a model of stability and central government control.

The Communist party and its bureaucracy dominated virtually every facet of Soviet life. The Committee for State Security (KGB) and other security organs were pervasive in society and had successfully squelched most dissent. The command economy was inefficient, wasteful, and overcentralized, but it appeared to be limping along at a pace sufficient to produce jobs and the basic necessities of life for the Soviet people. The Soviet economy in 1985 was not close to collapse. In international affairs, the Soviet Union had established a reputation as a superpower. Its international ambitions were backed up by a huge nuclear arsenal and conventional military force. Despite its troubles, the Soviet system appeared solid and secure.

The Soviet leadership, however, had recognized the need for reforms. Gorbachev had come to power in part because he represented a more energetic younger generation willing to seek innovative solutions to the nagging problems plaguing Soviet society. More than any other factor, the declining state of the economy was the catalyst for reform. Economic growth had declined sharply during the late 1970s and early 1980s, and the USSR suffered from chronic agricultural production shortfalls, a lack of technological sophistication in most industries, unacknowledged inflation, growing environmental problems, and labor shortages in regions where most industry was located. Only in military production could the Soviet Union compete with the West, but high rates of defense spending weakened the general state of the economy by siphoning off investment from other areas.

Gorbachev's Reforms

Mikhail Gorbachev took power in 1985 unwilling to accept economic stagnation. Yet despite his pronouncements advocating a major economic reconstruction, Gorbachev's initial strategy was cautious and seemed to reflect the need to consolidate his political power. He tried to improve economic performance by enforcing greater labor discipline, giving factory managers more autonomy, and introducing more sophisticated technology into the workplace.

Along with his mild economic reforms, Gorbachev launched his policy of glasnost (openness). Glasnost had many elements, including more open and honest news coverage by the Soviet media and greater freedom of expression and speech for Soviet artists and common citizens. The policy was designed to put pressure on conservative bureaucrats to accept economic change by allowing the Soviet people and press to criticize abuses of power and unimaginative or timid leadership. It also was intended to facilitate a wider dissemination of information throughout the Soviet Union and overcome the severe social malaise that afflicted the USSR by giving the Soviet people a bigger say in how the country was managed. Gorbachev apparently believed that his economic reforms could not succeed without glasnost.

But the policy contained inherent risks. Once Soviet citizens felt free to chastise corrupt regional officials and party bureaucrats in the central government, criticisms of the Communist party and the Soviet leadership could not be far behind. Moreover, moves to make society more open and less repressive risked encouraging dissidents and igniting the ambitions of various ethnic groups. Dynamic nationalism in the non-Russian republics was not a force the Kremlin wanted to unleash, given the large number of nationalities, their varying demands, and the costs and risks of putting down domestic protests by force.

Considering these possibilities, Gorbachev's approach was risky. He could have continued to try to improve the Soviet economy at the margins as previous Soviet leaders had done and as he had tried to do during his first year in power. Even if conservative bureaucrats remained capable of blocking serious economic restructuring, he had reason to hope that additional limited reforms—such as cutting Soviet defense spending and foreign aid in conjunction with a détente with the West, opening up the Soviet Union to more foreign investment, and significantly increasing the size of private farming plots—would provide a boost without jeopardizing the central role of the Communist party or the stability of the country.

Failure of Reforms

Beginning in 1987 Gorbachev and his increasingly radical economic advisers responded to the economy's failure to improve by accelerating glasnost, introducing democratic elections, and launching farther-reaching economic reforms. The Soviet leadership sanctioned limited private enterprise activities, sought greater Soviet involvement in the international economy, and demanded that enterprises and farms become self-financing. Yet these moves were criticized by many experts in the West and liberals in Russia as too cautious to bring real change to the Soviet economy.

Gorbachev's plan was accompanied by a continuing economic decline that made the Soviet people increasingly restless. Their patience with steps that were seen as threatening their traditional state-provided economic security diminished as their standard of living dropped, lines at stores grew, and consumer items became increasingly scarce.

By 1990 the experiment with communism begun in Russia in 1917 appeared to have failed. The Soviet economy was in shambles, and Marxist-Leninist ideology—the basis of Soviet politics, economics, and historical interpretation—had been abandoned by all but a few die-hard conservatives. Responding to angry accusations from conservative party members at the Twenty-eighth Party Congress in June 1990, Aleksandr Yakovlev, a close Gorbachev adviser, said: "A decision of this congress . . . cannot change the fact that the volume of labor production in South Korea is ten times that of the North, nor the fact that people in West Germany live far better than people in the East." The Communist party had come to be seen as a cynical anachronism whose actions mainly benefited its elite few, not the Soviet people. Even V. I. Lenin, the revered founder of the Soviet state, was not immune to criticism by Soviet journalists and historians. Gorbachev and his reformist colleagues had hoped to orchestrate a gradual reform of Soviet society from the top, but change had developed its own uncertain momentum that the government could not stop.

Ethnic Unrest

As the Soviet economy collapsed, a parallel collapse of Soviet central authority over its internal empire was taking place. During Soviet rule, the Kremlin leadership advanced the myth that the USSR's myriad nationalities were bonded by communism into a fraternal confederation. The union was imposed on most non-Russian minorities by the Soviet Red Army, just as the tsars had used force to attach neighboring nations in Europe and Asia to the Russian empire. Gorbachev's liberalizations had inadvertently opened the way for ethnic groups to pursue their dormant aspirations. Nationalist movements in republics on the Soviet periphery agitated for greater sovereignty or outright independence from Moscow.

Meanwhile, the loosening of coercive controls brought to the surface ethnic rivalries and tensions that had been suppressed under a uniform adherence to Marxism-Leninism. In 1990 Moscow was forced to interpose troops between Armenians and Azeris in the Transcaucasian region. Violence on a smaller scale erupted in Central Asia, the Baltics, and within the non-Russian areas of the Russian Federation itself. In March of that year Lithuania officially declared itself independent of Moscow, setting off a crisis that would last for a year and a half. Gorbachev tried to hold Lithuania and the Baltic states within the union, fearing that a successful secession would encourage an avalanche of demands from independence movements in other republics.

Gorbachev hung his hopes for saving the Soviet Union on a union treaty. This treaty would have redefined the relationship between the republics and the central government, allowing the local governments to exercise autonomy over most affairs while Moscow would play a coordinating role and carry out military and foreign policies.

By the time the treaty was ready to be signed in August 1991, the Soviet Union was in disarray. Gorbachev long had been beset by critics from the left and the right. Liberals saw him as too timid on reform and too willing to continue using repressive measures to hold the country together. Conservatives saw him as someone who was willing to destroy the cherished foundations of Soviet communism. Most Soviet citizens saw him as a leader who had opened up society but failed to deliver on his promises, especially in the economic sphere. The economy was mired in a depression; republic governments, including Yeltsin's Russian government, were openly ignoring the decisions of the central government; ethnic unrest was growing unabated; independence movements in the republics were increasing in strength; and rumors of a coup by conservative Communist party leaders or the military were commonplace.

The Coup

A day before the union treaty was to be signed, on August 19, 1991, conservative party leaders tried to overthrow the Gorbachev government. Gorbachev was detained at his country home in the Crimea and some military units were mobilized in support of the coup. The plotters announced over the national media that Gorbachev was ill and that they had formed the "State Committee for the State of Emergency in the USSR" through which they would govern the country.

Although the coup had many of the trappings of past Communist power plays, it was carried out with little nerve or skill. Boris Yeltsin vigorously rallied the people of Moscow behind his efforts at resistance. As the democratically elected president of the Russian Federation, he quickly became the focal point for popular opposition to the coup. Yeltsin denounced the putsch as a crude and illegitimate attempt by hardliners to undermine democracy and the rule of law in the Soviet Union. Although he had many well-publicized disagreements with Gorbachev, Yeltsin demanded the Soviet president be restored to power.

Tens of thousands of Russians formed a human barrier around the Moscow "White House," the home of the Russian Federation's government and Yeltsin's stronghold. Key Soviet military units and leaders defected to Yeltsin's side. The coup leaders, having failed to move decisively in the hours immediately after seizing the government, backed down in the face of populist opposition. They declined to order an assault on the White House that would have been bloody and was uncertain of success. On August 21 the coup plotters, realizing their position was untenable, tried to save themselves by proposing a deal with Gorbachev, but the Soviet leader angrily refused.

With the collapse of the coup, Yeltsin was revered as a hero. He and his democratic and reform-minded supporters assumed a dominant role in Soviet politics. Yeltsin placed many of the functions of the former Soviet Union under the control of the Russian republic. Gorbachev returned to his position as president of the USSR, but power had clearly been transferred to the republic governments, most of which declared their independence soon after the failed coup. Gorbachev was weakened by the fact that he had appointed many of the plotters to office.

End of an Era

During the four months between the coup and his resignation Gorbachev struggled without success to put the union treaty back on track. Yeltsin, meanwhile, asserted the authority of Russia, while exploring possibilities for creating some type of cooperative arrangement among the other republics.

On December 1, 1991, the people of Ukraine, the Soviet Union's second most populous and important republic, voted overwhelmingly to endorse independence. The vote removed any hope that the Soviet Union could be salvaged. On December 8 Russia, Ukraine, and Belarus proclaimed the Commonwealth of Independent States. Eight other republics joined the CIS on December 21. Lithuania, Latvia, Estonia, and Georgia declined (in the fall of 1992 Azerbaijan withdrew).

Although the success or failure of the CIS depends on one's expectations of its potential, the CIS has failed to accomplish the three most ambitious tasks it might have addressed: constructing a coordinated defense policy, solidifying mechanisms through which the tightly linked economies of the former Soviet Union would continue to support one another, and constructing an effective response to ethnic conflicts. Russia's decision in May 1992 to establish its own defense force indicated that a CIS military force had ceased to be a viable alternative. Although the CIS has attempted economic coordination, most of the economic agreements between the republics have been accomplished on a bilateral basis. Currencies and armies have become symbols of national sovereignty for the new nations.

International Transformation

International relations have been dominated since World War II by the bipolar military balance and ideological competition between the United States and its allies and the Soviet Union and its bloc of Marxist client states. The Soviet Union appeared to most in the West as a blustering, aggressive, imperial colossus that constantly threatened surrounding nations, ignored human rights, and pursued an unceasing military buildup.

During Gorbachev's tenure, Soviet foreign policy was completely realigned according to the principles of "new thinking." This approach aimed at extricating the Soviet Union from costly regional conflicts, cutting foreign aid and defense spending, encouraging foreign trade and investment, concluding major arms agreements, and improving the USSR's international image.

In 1987 the Soviet government made major concessions that led to the Intermediate Nuclear Forces (INF) Treaty with the United States. In 1988 Gorbachev announced that the USSR would unilaterally cut a half-million troops from its armed forces. In 1989 Moscow withdrew its forces from Afghanistan and began working with the United States to end regional conflicts. Most dramatically, however, the Soviet leadership allowed revolutions to take place in Eastern Europe that effectively broke up the Warsaw Pact military alliance and deprived Moscow of its Eastern European empire.

The Soviets recognized that Eastern Europe was not a typical empire. Since the 1970s it had been an economic drain on the Soviet Union. Yet the Soviets felt obliged to continue dominating the region because of its role as a buffer between the Soviet Union and Western Europe.

But in 1988 Gorbachev encouraged Soviet-style economic and political reforms in Eastern Europe, and by 1989 he had made it clear that the Soviet Union no longer would use force to prop up communist governments. After the Soviet guarantee was removed, the East European communists could not resist the demands of their people. With the exception of Nicolae Ceausescu's regime in Romania, the governments of Eastern Europe gave up their power peacefully when massive protests demonstrated that they could not hold on to it.

As the USSR turned inward to focus on its domestic troubles, it de-emphasized the international geopolitical struggle with the West and rejected Marxist-Leninist ideology as a significant factor in foreign policy making. Consequently, nations that had looked to the Soviet Union as a source of economic and military aid were forced to repair relations with neighbors or with the West.

The dramatic foreign policy changes could be seen in the Soviet response to the Iraqi invasion of Kuwait in August 1990. Previously, almost any nation or group that threatened the interests of the West would receive Soviet support, encouragement, or sympathy. The Soviet Union did not cooperate with the West in combating terrorism and rarely condemned terrorist acts against Western citizens, saying they were regrettable but understandable. Although the West had more to lose than the Soviets from the Iraqi invasion and Moscow was a major Iraqi arms supplier, the Kremlin quickly joined the United States in condemning Baghdad and agreed to impose an arms embargo against the Iraqis.

The breakup of the Soviet Union has reduced even further the possibility of conflict between East and West. Yeltsin has stated his intent to pursue not only cooperation, but also active friendship with the Soviet Union's former enemies. The Soviet army contained 4 million troops in 1990. But under the Yeltsin government's plan, the Russian military would have no more than 1.5 million troops by 1995.

Russia and the other former Soviet states are in great need of financial and technical assistance that the West could provide. Russian foreign policy under Yeltsin has been aimed at building international support for his domestic reforms, reducing or eliminating costly commitments made during the Soviet era, and advancing Russia as a responsible and important member of the international community.

Where once the main objectives of American policy toward the Soviet Union were containment of its expansion and maintenance of the military balance, objectives in the post-Soviet era have become helping democracy and the free market to survive and codifying rapid arms cuts and military reductions through far-reaching agreements.

Yet while the revolution in the Soviet Union has transformed the international situation for the better, it has also opened a new, unpredictable era in world politics. Fears of an instant nuclear holocaust arising out of a superpower confrontation have been replaced by fears of nuclear proliferation and the emergence of a vast area of instability and ethnic conflict that will have implications for the security of Europe, the Middle East, and East Asia.

A Continuing Revolution

On January 2, 1992, the Yeltsin government implemented a major liberalization of prices—the first step in a radical plan to create a free-market economy. During the first three quarters of 1992, the government made progress in implementing the plan, despite some setbacks. But the already weak economy, strained by the shock of the reform measures, fell further into depression. Moreover, there were signs during the summer that Yeltsin had to backtrack in deference to conservative opposition.

The task of reviving the economy is complicated by the severed links between the interdependent states of the former Soviet Union and the ongoing ethnic and political conflicts in those states. Attacks and discrimination against Russians in the non-Russian republics have fueled Russian nationalism in Russia. At the same time, seemingly intractable territorial, religious, and tribal disputes between ethnic groups—long suppressed under Soviet rule—have erupted in open warfare. In Moldova Russian communist holdovers in the trans-Dniester region declared their secession, prompting fighting between Moldovan troops and Russian separatists. Violence between Azerbaijan and Armenia over the disputed Nagorno-Karabakh region has escalated, and no measures to stop the bloodshed have enjoyed success. In Georgia and Tajikistan, civil wars have seriously disrupted travel and trade. These conflicts have killed thousands of people, created hundreds of thousands of refugees, and raised the specter that outside countries such as China, Iran, Turkey, or Romania could become involved.

A few republican leaders must also confront accusations that they are using dictatorial methods of the past to accomplish their programs. In Russia, for example, Yeltsin got the Russian parliament to agree to postpone the planned elections for regional administrators, effectively leaving his personal appointees in place until late 1992. He also wanted to impose emergency rule in the ethnically troubled region of Chechen-Ingushetia in southern Russia, and he assumed the post of prime minister at the beginning of November 1991, effectively becoming both head of state and head of the government. In Georgia, president Zviad Gamsakhurdia was ousted in January 1992 after accusations that he had been running the government in an autocratic manner.

The future does not seem bright to most Russians. Even in the fourteen other republics, where independence was greeted with jubilation by many citizens, optimism has deteriorated as the economic depression has deepened. The Soviet system, though repressive, undemocratic, and anti-nationalist, had at least offered security, predictability, and guaranteed employment.

The economy appears to be in a helpless decline, and the chaos in the former Soviet Union is more widespread than at any time since World War II. Street crime and organized crime are rampant in many cities and the new states must deal with severe environmental degradation without sufficient funds or expertise for clean-up. Most people expect conditions to get worse before they get better.

But from a different perspective, the future of Russia and the independent states may not be grim. Russia and most of the other states are heavily industrialized societies with educated populations and large reserves of natural resources. They are receiving the support and encouragement of the international community and international lending institutions. If the people have the patience to let reforms work, many of the states of the former Soviet Union can emerge as prosperous and secure members of the world community.

It is possible that Boris Yeltsin will survive in power and his economic reform program will gradually lift Russia out of its economic and political troubles. But history suggests that even if Russian democracy survives, the process of its institutionalization will be turbulent. Yeltsin's position is not fully secure. Though he enjoys the enthusiastic support of liberals and intellectuals, his popularity among the general public has weakened as living standards have fallen. During the summer of 1992, a public opinion poll showed that fewer Russians trusted Yeltsin than his conservative vice president, Aleksandr Rutskoy, who has sharply denounced Yeltsin's reforms.

The small but real possibility exists of a military

coup or an antigovernment conspiracy by Russian conservatives or nationalists. In some ways Yeltsin is less vulnerable to a coup than Gorbachev had been. In particular he enjoys the legitimacy of being elected president in a popular vote. After his forthright stand during the August 1991 coup attempt, he also is regarded by many as a national hero. But in other ways, Yeltsin is more vulnerable than Gorbachev. A coup could be undertaken against him in the name of Russian nationalism, a concept enjoying much more popularity in Russia in late 1992 than a return to communism enjoyed in the Soviet Union in August 1991. In addition, in 1991, the Yeltsin-led Russian government was an authoritative and powerful structure capable of inspiring loyalty and offering an alternative to the coup leaders. In 1992, no such structure exists if some combination of conservatives moves against Yeltsin.

Russia's historical experience with revolution would suggest that more change, and possibly upheaval, can be expected. In March 1917 the initial revolution that overthrew the tsar was followed seven months later by another revolution that brought the Bolsheviks to power. After a bloody civil war that consolidated the Bolsheviks' control, Joseph Stalin took charge of the country. He gradually established one of the most repressive regimes in world history.

Like the first Russian revolution, the second Russian revolution has progressed in stages. During the late 1980s, Mikhail Gorbachev instituted far-reaching reforms that propelled Soviet society into a new era. The failed coup ended Gorbachev's efforts to manage change and led to the Soviet breakup. Now the world watches to see if Yeltsin and Russian democracy can survive. The second Russian revolution is an ongoing affair that is not necessarily in its last stage.

PART I

RUSSIAN AND SOVIET HISTORY

CHAPTER **1**

IMPERIAL RUSSIA
AND THE REVOLUTION

The early history of Russia—from 1000 B.C. to the mid-fifteenth century A.D.—was a chronicle of foreign invasion and domination. The Slavic agricultural tribes that inhabited the southern Russian steppes lived between East and West and were conquered by peoples from both Asia and Europe.

From about 1000 B.C. to 700 B.C. the Cimmerians (about whose origins little is known) ruled southern Russia. They were replaced by the Scythians, a central Asian nomadic tribe that dominated until the end of the third century B.C. when it gave way to another group of Asian nomads, the Sarmatians. Around A.D. 200 the Goths, a Germanic tribe, replaced the Sarmatians. The Goths in turn were defeated by the Huns around A.D. 370, reinstituting the pattern of Asian domination. The Huns were ousted by yet another Asian tribe, the Avars, in A.D. 558. Avar rule lasted about a hundred years.

The centuries of invasion caused considerable migration among the Slavs, breaking up the original tribe into three groups. These were the West Slavs: Poles, Czechs, Slovaks, and Lusatians; the South Slavs: Serbs, Croats, Macedonians, Slovenes, Montenegrins, and Bulgars; and the East Slavs: the Russians, Ukrainians, and Belorussians.

While suffering invasion, the Slavs became adept at assimilating the ways of their foreign rulers. They benefited from exposure to foreign influences, notably trade with Greek colonies in southern Russia. By the mid-eighth century A.D. the East Slavs had established several independent city-states that were attractive targets for roving bands of Viking and Asian warriors. The need for joint protection led to consolidation of these city-states and the establishment of the first Russian state.

Establishing a Russian State

Scandinavian Vikings, known as Varangians to the Slavs, played an important role in the development of Russian civilization during the ninth and tenth centuries. Varangian merchants used Russia as a trading route to the Byzantine Empire centered in Constantinople. They developed contacts with the East Slavs and eventually became rulers of a united Russian state. Historians have offered three explanations of how the Scandinavians came to rule Russia. The Varangians may have been invited by the East Slavs to be their rulers in return for guaranteeing order, they may have shared power with local Slav leaders in an effort to create a stable state in which trade would flourish, or they may have established their rule over the Slavs by force. Disagreements also surround the word "Rus," from which "Russia" is derived. Some historians and philologists believe "Rus" is of Scandinavian origin, while others maintain it was the name of a place in southern Russia.

Kievan Period

Around A.D. 862 a Dane named Rurik assumed control over a united Russian state and settled in Novgorod, a trading town about three hundred miles northeast of present-day Moscow. His successor, Oleg, transferred the seat of power south to Kiev, located on the Dnepr River. Oleg established himself as a prince, brought the neighboring eastern Slavic tribes under his sway, and extracted tribute from them. Trade and culture flourished in the relatively liberal Kievan state as subsequent princes expanded the boundaries of their domain until the eleventh century, when the state reached from the Baltic Sea to the Black Sea and from near the Russian town of Nizhny Novgorod to present-day Romania.

The Scandinavian rulers, instead of imposing a foreign culture upon their subjects, adopted the local language and customs. Kievan Russia witnessed a tremendous growth of culture, art, architecture, language, and law. Cultural and social development was strongly influenced by the state's relations with the Byzantine Empire, although contacts also were developed with western states. Prince Vladimir, who ruled from about 980 to 1015, established friendly relations with the Byzantine Empire to the south and adopted Byzantine Christianity for himself and his pagan subjects around 988.

The establishment of the Russian Orthodox Church turned Russia away from Western Europe and the influence of the Roman Church, a development that would contribute greatly to Russia's isolation. The conversion of the country gave rise to a written language, based on the Cyrillic alphabet developed by St. Cyril and his brother, St. Methodius. Both were holy men from Moravia (now in central Czechoslovakia) who ministered to the Slavs in the second half of the ninth century. The institution of uniform religion, language, and customs and the consolidation of an empire created the idea of a separate Russian state and a sense of national identity that withstood the subsequent years of disintegration and domination.

Appanage Period

The Kievan state survived until the Mongol invasion, which began in 1236. However, the central authority of the grand prince of Kiev was weakened by the division of the state into principalities—a process of inheritance established by Yaroslav, who ruled from 1036 to 1054. Under this system, each principality was headed by one of Yaroslav's sons.

The most important princedom was Kiev, and, according to Yaroslav's awkward system, it was to be ruled by each of his sons on a rotating basis. The system soon created tension and acrimony among the various uncles and nephews and gave rise to Appanage Russia, a period during which princes ruled their individual lands (appanages). Civil war characterized the two hundred years following the death of Yaroslav. Kiev also declined because changing East-West trade routes sapped its commercial strength, while continual foreign aggression—culminating in the Mongol invasion—undermined its tenuous cohesion.

Among the greatest of the appanage princes was Alexander of Novgorod, who warded off attacks on Russia from the West. In 1240 he defeated Swedish invaders on the banks of the Neva River. From this battle he took the name Alexander Nevsky. He also fought the Teutonic Knights, Germanic crusaders dedicated to expansion and Roman Catholicism. They were routed by Alexander's troops April 5, 1242, at a battle on the ice of Lake Peipus in Estonia. This defeat of European invaders, long enshrined in Russian folklore, was depicted in Russian director Sergei Eisenstein's famous 1938 film, *Alexander Nevsky*.

Mongol Period

The composition of thirteenth-century Russia—consisting of dozens of informally related city-states—contributed to the Mongols' victory. Skilled and experienced soldiers, the invaders overcame the various Russian princes, who failed to fashion a joint defense. By 1242 all of Russia was under Mongol domination. The Mongols (called Tatars by Russian historians) secured the loyalty of the grand prince and through him collected tribute from the other appanage princes.

During the Mongol domination of Russia, Moscow was established as the center of the state. Kiev had been destroyed during the invasion, and by

1315 the grand prince ruled from Tver, located about a hundred miles northwest of Moscow. In the early fourteenth century, Yuri, the prince of Moscow, undertook a campaign to win the title of grand prince. After several years of battle and intrigue, Ivan Kalita, the younger brother of Yuri (who was killed by a Tver enemy), was named grand prince by the Mongol khan in 1328. Ivan expanded his territory by buying up appanages and villages from bankrupt princes. He also convinced Metropolitan Theognost, the head of the Russian Church, to live in Moscow, making it the religious capital of the state.

Ivan's grandson, Grand Prince Dmitry, attempted to overthrow the Mongol lords, and on September 8, 1380, his army defeated Mongol forces at the battle of Kulikovo field. From then on the Mongols' authority in Russia steadily weakened, even though they reestablished military control of Russia in 1382. Finally, in 1480, Ivan III, also known as Ivan the Great, refused to recognize the authority of the Mongols. With their empire falling apart, the Mongols failed in a half-hearted effort to perpetuate their control over the Russians.

Muscovite Russia

Under Ivan the Great and his son Basil III, the last independent appanages were brought under Moscow's control. Ivan in 1472 married Sophia, a niece of the last Byzantine emperor, and began to refer to himself as tsar (derived from Caesar).

The power and authority of the Moscow tsar was established definitively under Basil III's son, Ivan IV, better known as Ivan the Terrible. Crowned tsar in 1547 at the age of sixteen, Ivan for several years relied on the advice of a group of liberal-minded advisers, the Chosen Council. He also sought the approval of the *zemsky sobor,* an assembly of landholders. As he grew older, however, he began to suspect the boyars—the descendants of the appanage princes, who now formed the hereditary nobility—of plotting against him. Ivan in 1565 established his personal domain, the *oprichnina* (from the Russian word for "apart"), and gave land to trusted followers, the *oprichniki*. The oprichniki, described

by some historians as the first political police force, were assigned the task of eliminating anyone who opposed the tsar. In the reign of terror that lasted until 1572, thousands perished and whole towns—Novgorod, for example—were leveled.

Relative calm was restored under Ivan's son Fëdor I, who ruled from 1584 to 1598. Russia again was thrown into turmoil, however, when Fëdor died without an heir and his brother-in-law and close adviser, Boris Godunov, seized power, ushering in a period of dynastic confusion that became known as the "Time of Troubles."

Boris Godunov was elected tsar by a special session of the zemsky sobor. His rule soon was beset with crises. In 1601-1603, drought and famine decimated the population. At the same time, it was rumored that Godunov had had a hand in the death of Prince Dmitry, the younger brother of Tsar Fëdor. Moreover, some suspected that another child had been murdered in Dmitry's place and that the "real" Dmitry would reappear and claim the throne.

A young man claiming to be Prince Dmitry gathered an army, with Polish assistance, and invaded Russia in October 1604. His campaign gained popular support, and, after Godunov died in April 1605 and his wife and son Fëdor II were murdered, the False Dmitry ascended the throne. His disdain for the Russian people and reliance on Polish advisers soon eroded his support among the nobility, and he was overthrown in May 1606. The leader of the coup, Basil Shuisky, a boyar prince, named himself tsar. A second False Dmitry arose during Basil's reign and almost succeeded in gaining the throne. Basil was overthrown in 1610, and during the next three years the country was ruled by a group of seven boyars.

Basil Shuisky's desperation to defend his throne against the second False Dmitry led him to form an alliance with Sweden. In return for some Russian territory along the Baltic and a Russian promise to fight with the Swedish against the Poles, Sweden provided Basil with troops that helped defeat the second False Dmitry. In 1609, however, the king of Poland, Sigismund III, attacked Russia at the request of the supporters of the second False Dmitry. Basil Shuisky was deposed, and the Poles occupied

Moscow. The Muscovites invited the Polish king's son, Ladislas, to become tsar, but negotiations stalled over the details of the arrangement. Meanwhile the Swedes had invaded Russia from the northwest to oppose the expansion of Polish power and to punish Moscow for its failure to live up to its alliance responsibilities.

The Russian state faced a dire situation. Its capital was occupied, it had no clear leader, and it was forced to contend with two invading powers. In 1612, however, the Russian people rallied behind a nationalist movement led by the Russian Orthodox Church to rid the country of foreign armies and reestablish a national government. Patriarch Hermogen, concerned about the spread of Catholicism in the Polish-occupied territories, rallied disparate segments of Russian society against the Poles. By the end of the year the Russians had driven the Poles from Moscow. A special zemsky sobor elected Michael Romanov tsar in early 1613. He was crowned, at the age of sixteen, on July 21, 1613. Although civil strife continued until 1618, the administration of Russia was back in Russian hands. Michael, the grand-nephew of Anastasia, Ivan the Terrible's first wife, was the first member of the Romanov line that would rule Russia until the Russian revolution of 1917.

Rise and Fall of the Romanovs

Michael Romanov took the throne of a country in turmoil. As historian Nicholas V. Riasanovsky wrote in *A History of Russia:*

The treasury was empty, and financial collapse of the state appeared complete. In Astrakhan, Zarutsky [a cossack leader] ... rallied the cossacks and other malcontents, continuing the story of pretenders and social rebellion so characteristic of the Time of Troubles. Many roaming bands, some of them several thousand strong, continued looting the land. Moreover, Muscovy remained at war with Poland and Sweden, which had seized respectively Smolensk and Novgorod as well as other Russian territory and promoted their own candidates to the Muscovite throne.

Tsar Michael moved quickly to quiet domestic unrest. His armies broke the rebel movement in the countryside. He reached an agreement with the Swedes in 1617 that returned Novgorod to Russian control and made a truce with Poland in 1618. The truce gave the Poles control over the town of Smolensk and other areas in western Russia. After the truce expired in 1632 the war began anew, but it ended in 1634 with a treaty that again recognized Polish authority in western Russia.

To restore Moscow's financial stability, Tsar Michael levied new taxes and arranged loans generating sufficient funds to keep the country from bankruptcy. Nevertheless, financial problems were to plague the tsars for several decades.

Michael's successor, his son Alexis, ruled from 1645 to 1676. He oversaw the Ukraine's unification with Moscow in 1654 after the Ukrainians broke with their Polish rulers. His armies put down a large peasant rebellion, led by Stepan Razin in 1670. Tsar Fëdor III, Alexis's elder son from his first marriage, assumed the throne in 1676 and died six years later at the age of twenty, without leaving an heir.

Peter the Great

Peter I (1672-1725), known as Peter the Great, transformed Russia into a leading European power during the first quarter of the eighteenth century. Peter was the son of Tsar Alexis I and his second wife. The leading boyars named the ten-year-old Peter tsar after the death of his half-brother, Tsar Fëdor III. But a faction backing Fëdor's incompetent older brother Ivan, and led by Ivan's sister Sophia, rebelled and forced the boyars to appoint Ivan and Peter co-tsars. Under this arrangement Sophia became regent. She attempted to claim the throne for herself in 1689, but the church hierarchy and the boyars backed Peter, and Sophia's coup failed. She was sent to a convent, leaving Peter in control of the country, although, technically, Ivan remained co-tsar until he died in 1696. Peter was aided in running the government by his mother, Natalia Narishkina, until her death in 1694.

At this time, Russia was an extremely backward and isolated nation with few diplomatic and commercial links to foreign countries. Peter, who toured Western Europe on a diplomatic mission early in his reign, was impressed with Western culture and its technological advances. Taking Western Europe as his model, Peter launched a campaign to modernize Russian society. He reorganized the army and created a navy, built ports, expanded manufacturing and mining operations, updated the Russian calendar, modified the Cyrillic alphabet, introduced Roman numerals, mandated compulsory education for gentry children, oversaw the publication of Russia's first newspaper, and imported European teachers and technicians to advance Russian education and science.

Peter also restructured Russia's system of government by creating a new system of provinces and establishing a Senate to handle state financial, legal, and administrative matters. Government ministries *(collegia)* were created to administer commerce, income, war, manufacturing, and other activities. Peter, however, remained an absolute ruler, and no proposal from the Senate or collegia could be implemented without his approval.

He also reformed the traditional system of service to the state by introducing the Table of Ranks (the *chin*) under which a member of the gentry entered service in the military or the government at the bottom and worked his way up through a series of levels, instead of receiving a certain rank based on family influence. Nongentry Russians who entered service were made members of the gentry class for life if they reached a certain rank.

Peter pursued an active foreign policy designed to defeat Russia's old enemies and expand its territory. During his reign, Russia was almost constantly at war with either the Swedes, Turks, or Persians. In "The Great Northern War," waged against Sweden from 1700 until 1721, Russia acquired territories bordering the Gulf of Finland, including St. Petersburg, as well as Estonia and Latvia. After the defeat of the Swedes, the Senate conferred upon Peter the title of emperor (which subsequently was used interchangeably with tsar), and the Russian Empire formally was established. The capital was moved from Moscow to St. Petersburg in 1712.

Although Peter's modernization campaign and activist foreign policy strengthened his nation, they nevertheless were the source of much suffering and

Peter I, "The Great"

discontent in Russia. His foreign wars forced two generations of Russians to endure the hardships of eighteenth-century military service, and the army and navy required large amounts of capital that Peter could obtain only through oppressive taxes. Peasant uprisings against taxes and conscription led to mass executions, and Peter maintained an active secret police organization to guard against subversion.

In addition, some of Peter's reforms were resented by the Russian people as arbitrary attacks on Russian customs in favor of distrusted Western culture. For example, he forced noblemen to pay a tax if they wanted to keep their traditional Russian beards, and he outlawed the manufacture of traditional Russian garments. Peter's reforms also extended to the Russian Orthodox Church. In 1721 he decreed that the head of the church would be a layman, thus infuriating clergy who felt deprived of control over religious affairs.

Peter died February 8, 1725, without designating

a successor. Over the next thirty-seven years, Russia was governed by six monarchs, none of whom was effective. In the absence of a strong tsar, the gentry class was able to advance its interests.

In 1736 the lifetime term of gentry service to the crown, which the gentry hated, was reduced to twenty-five years, and in 1762 service was canceled altogether. At the same time, the peasant serfs who farmed the gentry's fields had many of their rights taken away. Serfs no longer could gain their freedom through service in the military. Moreover they could not buy land or engage in commerce without the permission of their landlord. The serfs had become little more than the personal property of their gentry masters, who could whip them, sell them, or deport them to Siberia.

Catherine the Great

Catherine II (1729-1796), known as Catherine the Great, was a princess from the small German state of Anhalt-Zerbst, who married Peter, a grandson of Peter the Great, in 1745. She spent the next seventeen years carefully forming alliances among

Catherine II, "The Great"

members of the imperial court. Her husband ascended to the throne as Tsar Peter III in 1762, but before the year was over she cooperated with conspirators who murdered her husband and placed her on the throne.

Although she was well versed in democratic thought associated with the Enlightenment (she carried on a celebrated correspondence with Voltaire), Catherine remained a staunch supporter of absolute monarchy in Russia. Mindful that as a foreigner and an usurper her place on the Russian throne was not secure, she cultivated the favor of the gentry. She contributed to the continuing degradation of the serfs by giving away to her supporters thousands of acres of state land. The peasants working the lands were included in the gifts.

A rebellion of serfs in 1773-1775, led by Emelyan Pugachev, ultimately was crushed, but it alarmed Catherine and her gentry supporters. In response she divided Russia's twenty provinces into fifty in a scheme designed to bring greater central control over the countryside.

Gentry privilege was broadened by the 1785 Charter of the Nobility, which guaranteed a trial by a jury of noble peers and freed the gentry from taxation, conscription, and corporal punishment. It also reaffirmed the gentry's 1762 exemption from military or civil service to the state.

Catherine's foreign policy was designed to expand Russia's southern and western boundaries. In the south, the empress's army and navy defeated the Turks in 1774 and gained control over part of the Black Sea coastline. By 1783 Russian forces had captured the Crimea.

To the west, Catherine joined with other European powers in partitioning the Polish empire. The acquisitions from Poland brought millions of non-Russians and their lands into the Russian empire.

Weakened by years of internal strife and civil war, Poland was a likely prospect for domination by her powerful neighbors. In 1772 Russia, Prussia, and Austria divided among themselves about one-third of Poland's territory. Russia received part of what is now Belarus. In 1792 a second partition awarded Russia most of the rest of Belarus and western Ukraine. The Poles rose in rebellion against the loss of their territory but were defeated by the Russian and Prussian armies in 1795. To punish the rebels, the remaining parts of their homeland were divided among Russia, Prussia, and Austria. Poland, as a state, no longer existed.

Catherine died in 1796, and her son Paul took control of one of the world's mightiest powers. During his five years on the throne, Paul codified the law of succession to require primogeniture in the male line (Peter the Great had declared that the emperor had the right to name his successor) and displayed a liberal attitude toward the serfs, reducing the number of days each week a serf was required to work his master's lands. Nevertheless, Paul continued to give the gentry state lands along with the peasants who lived on them. In foreign affairs, he made war against revolutionary France and later entered into a Russian-French coalition. His extreme disdain for the gentry, who had supported his mother's claims to a throne he considered rightfully his, led to a coup in 1801. Paul was murdered and his son, the twenty-three-year-old Alexander, was made emperor.

Alexander I

Alexander I (1777-1825), who had received a liberal education, appeared ready early in his reign to apply the principles of the Enlightenment to his rule. He increased the powers of the Senate, which had been moribund for several years; tightened and improved the administration of the ministerial departments; and promoted education. He approved a plan to permit the gentry to release serfs from bondage, although few serf owners took advantage of it.

Alexander's reforms, however, were not far-reaching, and domestic policy frequently took a back seat to foreign affairs. Alexander's apprehension over Napoleon Bonaparte's aggressive empire building caused Alexander to break the treaty his father had negotiated with France. A war with France followed in which the French and their Spanish allies defeated a coalition made up of Russia, Great Britain, Sweden, Prussia, and Austria. The Treaty of Tilsit, signed in 1807, severely weakened Prussia and left France and Russia as the only two major powers on the continent. Tensions between the two simmered for five years, culminating in Napoleon's ill-fated invasion of Russia.

The French emperor assembled an army of seven hundred thousand men, many of whom were conscripts from his European empire. Napoleon hoped to break Russian defenses in a decisive battle, but the Russian strategy was to avoid major confrontation. Instead Russian forces executed a scorched-earth retreat ahead of Napoleon's Grand Army. Napoleon followed deep into Russia, stretching his supply lines beyond their limits. The one major confrontation of the campaign, the September 7, 1812, Battle of Borodino outside Moscow, resulted in tens of thousands of casualties on both sides. The battle weakened the invasion force but did not check its drive on the Russian capital. That month Napoleon reached and occupied Moscow after the Russians had set it on fire.

Napoleon hoped to pressure Alexander into a negotiated settlement, but the Russian tsar declined to make peace. Napoleon's troops remained in Moscow five weeks before the onset of winter and the scarcity of food and supplies forced Napoleon to order a retreat. On its way out of Russia, the Grand Army had to contend with the Russian winter, disease, short rations, and attacks from Russian troops and partisans. Less than a quarter of Napoleon's force survived.

After forming a coalition with Austria, Sweden, and Great Britain, the Russians pursued Napoleon's army into France. The coalition's forces defeated Napoleon at the decisive Battle of Nations, fought near Leipzig in October 1813. They then occupied Paris March 31, 1814, and Napoleon was banished to Elba.

Alexander represented Russia at the 1814-1815 Congress of Vienna, the momentous gathering of European leaders that redrew the map of the continent in the wake of Napoleon's defeat. The decisions of the Congress were implemented despite Napoleon's retaking of the French throne in March 1815. He assembled an army but was defeated by the British and Prussians at the Battle of Waterloo, June 18, 1815, and was banished permanently to the South Atlantic island of St. Helena.

The Congress of Vienna created a smaller Poland with Tsar Alexander as its constitutional monarch. Prussia emerged as a restored major power, Austria received much of northern Italy, Belgium and Holland were joined in a kingdom, and Switzerland and Germany were awarded constitutions. In addition, Norway was taken from Denmark and given to Sweden. The Congress compensated the Danes with German lands.

Although Alexander was preoccupied with Napoleon during the first fifteen years of his reign, he also engaged in wars on his empire's southern and northern frontiers. His response to a request for help from the small nation of Georgia led to the 1804-1813 war against Georgia's neighbor, Persia, and the 1806-1812 Russo-Turkish war. In both, the Russian armies won and Russian rule was extended over Georgia. In the north, a war with Sweden in 1809 resulted in the Russian occupation of Finland, which Alexander ruled as grand duke.

The moves toward domestic liberalism that characterized Alexander's early rule did not extend to his later years. The emperor investigated and, according to some historians, gave his approval to a proposal for a Russian constitutional monarchy, but the plan was never implemented.

Alexander's disavowal of his earlier liberal tendencies provoked animosity among a small group of aristocratic army officers who, familiar with the democratic changes sweeping Europe, established a secret society in St. Petersburg that aimed to establish a constitutional monarchy in their homeland. When Alexander died suddenly in December 1825 without an heir, the country temporarily was left leaderless while the late emperor's brothers, Constantine and Nicholas, each claimed that the other was the rightful heir. Although Constantine was the older brother, he had renounced his claim to the throne when he married a commoner. In the ensuing confusion, the army officers in St. Petersburg attempted to seize power. Their supporters, however, were quickly defeated by government troops. The leaders of the rebellion, thereafter known as the Decembrists, were tried and either executed or exiled to Siberia by the government of the new emperor, Nicholas I. Although there had been many coups and coup attempts in Russian history, the Decembrist revolt was significant because it was the first to be driven by revolutionary principles.

The Decembrist revolt had two results: It ushered in an era of repression under the new emperor, and it served as an important symbolic event for the generations of Russian revolutionaries who matured during the nineteenth and early twentieth centuries.

Nicholas I

Nicholas I (1796-1855) was determined to preserve the social and political status quo in Russia and reassert complete control over the lives of his subjects. He greatly expanded the censorship apparatus to block the influx of Western ideas, placed restrictions on the curriculum of Russian universities, prohibited foreign travel by most citizens, and was intolerant of liberalism among military officers and civil servants. To enforce his policies, he gave his political police force the responsibility to monitor anything that might be a threat to the established order. The secret police frequently abused their power, and many Russian citizens were killed or sent into exile.

Although Nicholas was wary of the upheaval that could be caused by a continuation of serfdom, he believed revolution was more likely to be stimulated by the granting of concessions to the serfs. He therefore staunchly supported the privileges of the gentry and made no significant moves toward ending serfdom.

Nicholas adopted a similarly conservative outlook toward international affairs. His defense of the status quo reached beyond Russian borders. He ordered his armies to put down revolutions in Poland (1830-1831) and Hungary (1849). Russian troops also intervened in 1848 to curb increasing Romanian nationalist activities. He even considered dispatching his armed forces to restore order during the revolutions in France in 1830 and 1848.

Nicholas's foreign policy led to disaster for Russia in the Crimean War (1853-1856). War broke out between Russia and Turkey in October 1853 over a dispute about religious rights in the Holy Land. The tsar not only sought to protect the rights of Orthodox Christians in the Holy Land, but he also hoped to enhance Russian power in the Black Sea region and Russian influence over the Ottoman Empire, which he believed was crumbling. Turkey soon was joined by two powerful allies, Great Britain and France, whose troops laid siege to Sevastopol, Russia's naval base in the Crimea. After nearly a year, the Russians were forced to forsake Sevastopol in September 1855 and accept defeat. The Treaty of Paris, signed March 30, 1856, obliged Moscow to withdraw all its forces from the Black Sea and abandon its claim as the protector of the Orthodox peoples in the Ottoman Empire.

Despite the generally repressive atmosphere that prevailed in Russia during Nicholas's reign, the cultural life of the nation flourished. The years 1820 to 1860 are known as Russia's "Golden Age," especially in literature. The early years of this Golden Age were marked by the writings of Aleksander Pushkin and Nikolai Gogol, as well as the work of several lesser poets and novelists. In later years, the leading Russian writers included Ivan Turgenev, Fëdor Dostoevsky, and Leo Tolstoy.

Alexander II

Tsar Nicholas I died in March 1855, before the end of the Crimean War. His son Alexander II (1818-1881) presided over the conclusion of the war and the signing of the Treaty of Paris. Alexander attempted, with some success, to improve Russia's tarnished international image.

He took advantage of the Franco-Prussian War of 1870 to unilaterally void the provisions of the Paris Treaty that restricted Russian activities in the Black Sea region. Russia's standing as a military power improved after it won the Russo-Turkish War of 1877-1878. The peace treaty ending the war granted Russia dominion over Bulgaria, but a conference of European powers at Berlin took much of the territory away from Russia.

In the East, Russia's expansion was unhampered by European political considerations. The tsar's armies established Moscow's dominion over the Caucasus and central Asia, and his diplomats received land concessions from the Chinese, including the area around Vladivostok, which was founded in 1858.

Alexander's most pressing concerns, however, were domestic. Although he was not a liberal crusader, he did recognize that certain changes were necessary for the welfare of Russia. Early in his reign he undertook a series of reforms that dramatically altered Russian society.

The primary question that had to be addressed was what to do about serfdom. Few members of the gentry could afford to maintain vast numbers of serfs, and the changing Russian economy required new types of laborers that serfdom could not provide efficiently. For their part, the serfs in the early nineteenth century began to seek freedom. Between 1800 and 1860, there were more than fifteen hundred peasant rebellions. Almost five hundred had occurred between 1854 and 1860. Emancipation was the only remedy likely to quell the unrest. The Crimean War also contributed to the perception that serfdom should be abolished because the ill-educated, docile serf, who lacked a political and economic stake in the country, had fought poorly. Finally, an increasing number of Russians objected to serfdom on moral grounds. *(Development of serfdom, box, p. 20)*

By 1860 there was a growing consensus in favor of emancipation, but substantial disagreement existed over how it should be done. The powerful landholding class would have to be compensated for the loss of their serfs, while the serfs had to be given enough land and resources to make a living. Landowners also functioned as Russia's local political authority. If serfdom were abolished some type of local government would have to be created to fill the administrative vacuum that would be left. With the strong support of Tsar Alexander, gentry committees began to study the issue in 1858.

On March 3, 1861, Alexander signed an imperial order freeing an estimated forty million serfs. Under the terms of the emancipation, the gentry class gave up about half of its land for which it was reimbursed by the government. This land was given to the serfs to work as their own, although legal title to it was held collectively by a system of village communes. The serf household was obligated to accept its land

The Development of Serfdom

Serfdom in Russia had its roots in the Kievan period, but the institution developed gradually over many centuries. At the dawn of Kievan Russia in the ninth century, most peasants were free farmers of land owned by the nobility. Frequent economic calamities—droughts, poor harvests, famines—compelled peasants to borrow money from their landlords. Many were unable to repay the loans, however, and they became perpetually indebted to their landlords. Peasants who fell into this plight were required to work for their creditors or supply them with a specified amount of goods every year. In the process they were transformed from free peasants into the gentry's serfs.

Over the centuries, landlords' control of the peasants grew. By the fifteenth century, a peasant could become free of his master only on a specified day each year—some time near the feast of St. George, late in the fall—if he had paid off his debts.

The plight of the peasantry deteriorated further during the Muscovite period (fifteenth, sixteenth, and seventeenth centuries). Landlords were empowered to govern and tax their subjects. The peasants also fell victim to the tsars' practice of awarding vast tracts of state lands *(pomesties)* to the service gentry, the men who performed administrative chores for the ruler and served in his armies. The peasants who occupied the state land granted to the gentry became serfs.

When they resisted by escaping to outlying regions, the government outlawed peasant migration.

The legal code of 1649, the *Ulozhenie,* lengthened to an indefinite time the period during which an escaped serf had to be returned to his master (it had been five years) and stiffened penalties for providing refuge to fugitive serfs. By the end of the seventeenth century buying and selling serfs was common.

In the eighteenth century the position of the serfs continued to decline as the power of the gentry grew. Millions of peasants passed into serfdom as the emperors and empresses expanded on the practice of giving state land to their supporters. Decrees prohibited serfs from owning land, signing government contracts, or escaping servitude by joining the army. Landlords, in contrast, were given authority to exile errant serfs to Siberia and to shift serfs from one estate to another. Because the government did not effectively reach past the district level, landlords also functioned as local judges and tax collectors in charge of their serfs. In 1741 serfs were not among the Russians required to pledge loyalty to the tsar, and a criminal code of 1754 designated serfs as gentry property.

Catherine the Great (who ruled from 1762 to 1796) established serfdom in the Ukraine, continued the practice of giving generous grants of land and peasants to her favorites, and prohibited serfs from complaining to the empress or her government about their treatment by landlords. By 1800 landlords had complete control over the lives of their serfs.

allotment and assume the taxes on the land and a redemption payment to the government that was extended over a forty-nine-year period.

Although emancipation bolstered the self-respect of the serfs, its terms were not generous enough to substantially improve the lives of many of them. The redemption payments were high, and the land each serf had been forced to purchase averaged only about six or seven acres. Consequently, the emancipated peasants had little excess income with which to purchase more land. The emancipation order also did not provide the peasants with other crucial resources needed to improve their lot, such as timber and pasture lands and water rights. The financial burden imposed by emancipation led to a short but intense wave of peasant revolts that died down by the following year.

Additional reforms followed the emancipation of the serfs. In 1864 Alexander introduced provincial and district assemblies known as *zemstvos* to administer local affairs. Zemstvo representatives were chosen through a complicated electoral system that divided representatives among the classes. Although the peasants received significant representation, the gentry class dominated the provincial zemstvos and had slightly more representatives at the district level. The zemstvos met once a year and selected committees that served continuously. Although the responsibilities of the zemstvos and their committees were limited primarily to local finances, public health, road maintenance, and education, they improved conditions in Russia and gave the Russian people some experience with representative government.

In 1864 Alexander also instituted legal reforms. The administration of justice was made a separate branch of government, jury trials were introduced, freedom of speech was given to courtroom lawyers, and equal treatment before the law was guaranteed for all citizens. Alexander's reforms eventually extended to the military as well. General conscription was expanded to all Russians (it previously had applied only to peasants), and the term of service was lowered from twenty-five years to six. This created a huge military reserve and was an important factor in the improvement of Russian military strength in the post-Crimean War period.

Rise of Radicalism

During the second half of the nineteenth century, radical movements among Russian intellectuals flourished. Although Alexander's reforms addressed some major popular concerns, Russian revolutionary groups sought the overthrow of the tsar and the establishment of various types of governments. Since the failed Decembrist revolt of 1825, the Russian revolutionary movement had developed into several distinct branches, yet it remained an upper-class phenomenon, centered in the universities and the drawing rooms of Moscow and St. Petersburg. Indeed, Tibor Szamuely, in *The Russian Tradition,* has pointed out that the paradox of Russian radicalism was that the Russian people were regarded as too backward and uneducated to make the right choices about their own and their country's welfare. It was the job of the intellectual to force them in revolutionary directions that would re-create Russian society for the better.

As early as the 1840s two main intellectual movements had appeared, the Slavophiles and the Westerners. The Slavophiles were nationalists who sought a return to the Russian state as it existed before the introduction of Western ideas under Peter the Great and his successors. Their ideal was an isolated nation based on the peasant commune, a purified Orthodox Church, and an autocracy free of bureaucratic interference. The Westerners advocated a secular, rational approach to Russian development based on increased use of Western technology, thought, and social structures (though many Westerners rejected capitalism). They claimed that Russia was like the nations of Western Europe but had failed to keep up with the West's pace of political and economic modernization. Their inspiration was Peter the Great, who had sought to westernize Russia in the eighteenth century.

A third intellectual group that rose to prominence in the 1840s was the Petrashevtsi. Named after Mikhail Petrashevsky, at whose home they met secretly, the Petrashevtsi followed the teachings of the French utopian socialist Charles Fourier. They were responsible for the spread of socialist literature among the intelligentsia, an activity that, coupled with their general opposition to the government of Nicholas I, led to the arrest and sentencing to death of some of the group's members, including the great novelist Fëdor Dostoevsky. The death sentences were reduced to prison terms at the last minute.

The intellectual movements of the 1840s were superseded in the 1850s by the rise of populism *(narodnichestvo).* Its most influential advocate was Aleksandr Herzen (1812-1870), a Westerner and moderate revolutionary who adopted some Slavophile elements into his social philosophy. He embraced socialism but adapted it to Russian conditions, arguing that socialism would spring from a peasant revolution and would be based on the traditional Russian communal village. Herzen's views, contained in *Kolokol* (The Bell), a journal he published during his exile in Europe from 1857 until 1867, found an eager audience among the educated class.

Another Westerner, Mikhail Bakunin (1814-1876), advocated a more radical path than Herzen. Bakunin called for a violent revolution that would abolish the Russian Church and state and establish a society in which no class would be allowed to dominate. In place of the Russian centralized state Bakunin envisioned political authority being held by self-governing communes. Like Herzen, Bakunin spent much of his life in exile in the West. He participated in the 1848 revolution in Europe and later became a leader of the anarchists in the early international socialist movement. He helped establish the First International Workingmen's Association in 1864, but his opposition to Karl Marx's concept of state socialism eventually led to his expulsion from the organization. *(Marx, box, p. 34)*

As the tide of revolution rose in Russia, the ideas of Bakunin, Herzen, and other radical intellectuals were adopted by those committed to the immediate overthrow of the state. Herzen's populism was taken up by Nikolai Chernyshevsky (1828-1889), whose novel *What Is to Be Done?* outlined his vision of Russia under a socialist system. In it, he postulated the existence of the "new men," an elite corps of intellectuals who selflessly would strive to improve conditions for the people. Borrowing from Herzen, Chernyshevsky argued that Russia should forgo capitalist development and step directly into socialism. But unlike Herzen, who expected that the change to socialism would come about peacefully, Chernyshevsky exhorted his followers to pull down the existing system. Chernyshevsky's ideas enjoyed wide popularity among Russian radicals and made a lasting impression on the generations of revolutionaries who followed him. In 1902, when Lenin wrote a pamphlet describing his blueprint for the development of the Bolshevik party, he chose to call it "What Is to Be Done?"

Numerous conspiratorial groups and radical cliques regularly discussed the problems of Russia and ways to resolve them. These groups, however, took little direct action until 1873, when thousands of students decided to work among the peasants in a movement known as "going to the people." Lasting for several years, the exercise was a failure. Most of the students agreed with Bakunin's assessment that the peasants were ready for revolution and could be converted to socialism and radicalism. In most cases, however, the students met with indifference; in others, the student propagandists were handed over to the police. By 1877 the disillusioned students had returned to the cities.

The failure of "going to the people" convinced many radicals that the revolutionary movement required an elite group of leaders to tear down the tsarist system and re-create Russian society in the name of the "people." The leading proponent of this concept was Peter Tkachev (1844-1886), an exiled Russian radical who would have a profound influence on Lenin's approach to revolution.

In the autumn of 1876, several disparate radical groups that included many anarchists and socialists formed a central organization, Land and Liberty *(Zemlya i Volya)*. Among other goals, Land and Liberty was dedicated to the overthrow of the government through any means, the end of private land ownership, the redistribution of land among the peasants, and self-determination for national minorities.

In January 1878 the pace of radical activity quickened. A revolutionary named Vera Zasulich failed in her attempt to assassinate the governor of St. Petersburg. Although she was caught red-handed, the jury at her trial refused to convict her. The stunned government immediately ordered that all political crimes would be tried by special tribunals.

By 1879 Land and Liberty had split into two groups, one that wanted to prepare the people for revolution and another dedicated to an immediate reign of terror. The latter group, The Will of the People *(Narodnaya Volya)*, decided to throw the government into disarray by killing Alexander II. After several unsuccessful attempts on the tsar's life—including a February 5, 1880, bomb blast that killed eleven servants and destroyed the dining room in the Winter Palace—the terrorists achieved their goal March 1, 1881. A revolutionary assassin killed Alexander (and himself) with a homemade hand grenade.

Alexander III

The son of Alexander II, Tsar Alexander III (1845-1894) was determined to reestablish law and order and reassert the complete authority of the autocracy. He initiated a series of measures designed to destroy Russian revolutionary activity. Police were given broad authority to arrest and imprison troublemakers, and some revolutionaries were banished to Siberia. Many intellectuals who avoided arrest went into self-imposed exile in Europe. In addition, student associations were banned and university curriculums were strictly controlled to prevent the discussion of liberal ideas. The tsar's government reinforced its efforts against revolutionary activity by increasing its support of the gentry and the Orthodox Church. Among other moves, the government established a bank to extend credit to the nobility, restricted the access of the lower classes to secondary education, and forced many subjects of the Russian empire to convert to Orthodox Christianity.

Alexander III was an ardent Russian nationalist who had been greatly influenced by Konstantin Pobedonostsev (1827-1907), his former tutor. After 1880 Pobedonostsev served as head of the Holy Synod, the managing council of the Orthodox Church. He was a conservative intellectual who preached the virtues of autocracy and Russian nationalism, while criticizing science, secular rationalism, and any deviation from Orthodox religious beliefs. Alexander's desire to advance Russian nationalism and his dislike of Jews and other minorities caused him to support an intense "Russification" program. Minorities endured discrimination, and Russian authorities suppressed local culture, language, and religion in the non-Russian regions of the empire.

Jews suffered most from Russification. Government-organized pogroms in Russian cities resulted in many Jewish deaths and the mass destruction of Jewish property. Most Jews were required to stay in the Pale of Settlement, an area roughly corresponding to the Ukraine and Belorussia, where Jews traditionally had settled. In 1891 the government forcibly removed twenty thousand Jews from Moscow to the Pale. The government also restricted the number of Jews who could be admitted to secondary schools and universities. As a result of this persecution, more than a million Jews emigrated from Russia during the late nineteenth century.

In foreign affairs, Alexander III made one major move. Russia's alliance with Austria-Hungary and Germany, formed in the early 1870s, dissolved over conflicts between Moscow and Vienna in the Balkans. Germany attempted to maintain a secret Berlin-Moscow connection to offset growing French power, but this arrangement fell apart in 1890. Casting about for new European allies, Russia negotiated an alliance with France, which had loaned Russia large sums to advance industrialization. By 1894 Russia and France faced an alliance of Austria-Hungary, Germany, and Italy.

Industrialization

Although the government's reactionary and ethnocentric policies blocked political and social development, the reign of Alexander III saw the beginning of an industrial revolution in Russia. Under the direction of the minister of finance, Count Sergei Witte (1849-1915), the governments of Alexander III and his son Nicholas II created a climate of investment that spurred the development of Russian industry.

Russia had begun the process of industrialization well after most other European nations. When Peter the Great assumed control of the government, Russia had just twenty factories. By the time of his death thirty-six years later, there were more than two hundred, about 40 percent of which were state owned. Peter promoted the establishment of metallurgical and textile factories to furnish guns and clothing to his armed forces.

The progress of industrialization slowed after Peter. Metallurgy and textile production continued to be the dominant industries. The pace of industrial growth began to accelerate again in the nineteenth century. In 1800 there were about twelve hundred Russian factories; by midcentury, their number had more than doubled. Between 1850 and 1860 the number of factories devoted to machine building increased fivefold.

Russian industrial expansion continued steadily during the early years of the reign of Alexander III. Much of the expansion was fueled by foreign investment, which rose from one hundred million rubles in 1880 to nine hundred million by 1900. In 1892 Russian industrial development was placed in the hands of the new finance minister, Sergei Witte. He

The Romanov Dynasty

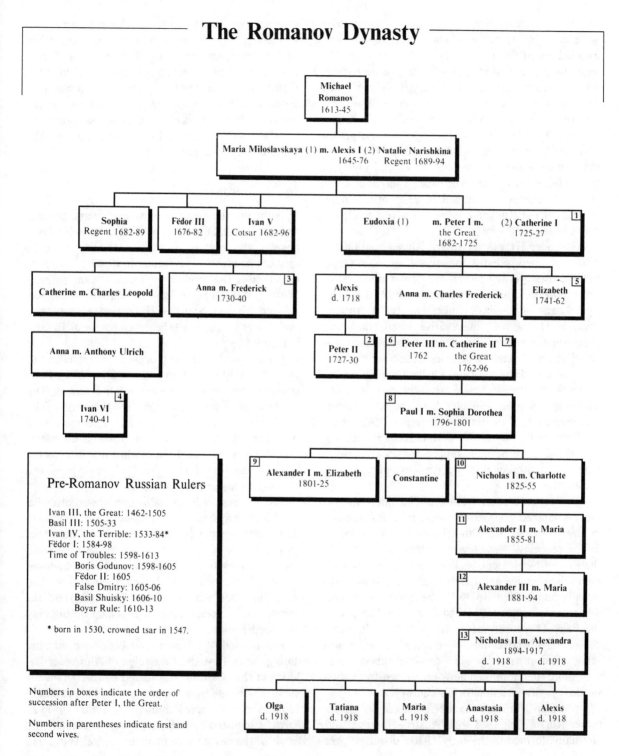

Michael Romanov
1613-45

Maria Miloslavskaya (1) m. Alexis I (2) Natalie Narishkina
1645-76   Regent 1689-94

Sophia
Regent 1682-89

Fëdor III
1676-82

Ivan V
Cotsar 1682-96

Eudoxia (1)   m. Peter I m.   (2) Catherine I |1|
the Great   1725-27
1682-1725

Catherine m. Charles Leopold

Anna m. Frederick |3|
1730-40

Alexis
d. 1718

Anna m. Charles Frederick

Elizabeth |5|
1741-62

Anna m. Anthony Ulrich

Peter II |2|
1727-30

|6| **Peter III m. Catherine II** |7|
1762   the Great
1762-96

Ivan VI |4|
1740-41

|8|
Paul I m. Sophia Dorothea
1796-1801

|9|
Alexander I m. Elizabeth
1801-25

Constantine

|10|
Nicholas I m. Charlotte
1825-55

|11|
Alexander II m. Maria
1855-81

|12|
Alexander III m. Maria
1881-94

|13| **Nicholas II m. Alexandra**
1894-1917
d. 1918   d. 1918

Olga
d. 1918

Tatiana
d. 1918

Maria
d. 1918

Anastasia
d. 1918

Alexis
d. 1918

Pre-Romanov Russian Rulers

Ivan III, the Great: 1462-1505
Basil III: 1505-33
Ivan IV, the Terrible: 1533-84*
Fëdor I: 1584-98
Time of Troubles: 1598-1613
    Boris Godunov: 1598-1605
    Fëdor II: 1605
    False Dmitry: 1605-06
    Basil Shuisky: 1606-10
    Boyar Rule: 1610-13

* born in 1530, crowned tsar in 1547.

Numbers in boxes indicate the order of succession after Peter I, the Great.

Numbers in parentheses indicate first and second wives.

Source: Adapted from Nicholas V. Riasanovsky, *A History of Russia*, 3d ed. (New York: Oxford University Press, 1977)

continued to encourage foreign investment, increased the state's investment in industry, balanced the state's budget, and launched an ambitious railroad construction program that included the Trans-Siberian Railroad. In the 1890s Russia's growth rate averaged a booming 8 percent a year with the steel, coal, chemical, textile, and oil industries leading the way. Meanwhile, the state-owned railroad system doubled in size between 1895 and 1905.

In the 1880s, a series of labor laws were passed that mandated some government protection for industrial workers. The legislation outlawed the use of women and children for night work in the textile industry, limited to eight hours the working days of twelve- to fifteen-year-old factory hands, and established regulations guaranteeing regular pay for employees. By 1900 the estimated two million Russian workers received additional protection. Factories with more than twenty employees could not require adults to work more than eleven and a half hours daily or ten hours nightly on Saturdays and on the day before holidays. Work was forbidden on Sundays and holidays. Adolescents were permitted to work only ten hours a day, children only nine. In 1903 a law made employers liable for job-related injuries. Despite the improvement of conditions in the workplace, most Russian workers still lived in squalor.

Ironically Witte's success at promoting rapid industrialization contributed to unrest and revolutionary activity. To raise capital for investment and technology, the government imposed severe taxes on the peasants and bought their grain at deflated prices to earn large profits by selling it on the world market. The plight of the peasant during the half century following emancipation in 1861 was complicated by a rural population boom that by 1905 had reduced an average peasant's share of communal land by a third. The deterioration of conditions in the countryside led to famines and frequent peasant revolts.

In the cities, industrialization had created a budding proletarian class that numbered between two million and three million by 1905. Some revolutionary groups, such as the Bolsheviks, targeted their propaganda on the workers, who began to develop a class consciousness. Finally, since the Russian industrial expansion was financed largely by foreign and state capital, no significant entrepreneurial class developed that could pressure the autocracy for liberal reforms, respond to the needs of workers, or at least deflect worker criticism from the state. Under the system of state ownership that developed, discontented workers would blame the government. Although the surge of industrialization had made Russia a stronger, more advanced nation, it had contributed to peasant unhappiness and had created a working class that was ripe to be influenced by revolutionaries.

Nicholas II

Tsar Alexander III died from a stroke in 1894 and was succeeded by his son, Nicholas II, the last Russian tsar. Nicholas expanded his father's conservative policies, restricting the authority of local zemstvo assemblies and imposing widespread press censorship. Pogroms against Jews and violent harassment of other non-Orthodox denominations intensified as religious persecution and Russification, begun under Alexander III, reached new heights.

Nicholas's conservative policies, the constant threat of famine, and the dreadful living conditions of peasants and workers rallied the disparate liberal and radical movements decimated by the repression of the 1880s. By the early 1900s liberals, many of whom were from the rising professional class, had established the Union of Liberation. In 1905 they created the Constitutional Democratic party. The party's members, who were known as the "Kadets" from the Russian initials for "constitutional democrat," were devoted to the establishment of a constitution, basic civil liberties, and equality for all minorities and classes. The radicals split into two major units, the Marxist-oriented Russian Social Democratic Labor party, which hoped to use the workers as a base of power, and the populist Socialist Revolutionaries, a group that was committed to a peasant revolution that would bring self-determination for minority groups, universal suffrage, civil liberties, and improvement of the peasants' economic conditions.

Tsar Nicholas II and Tsarina Alexandra with their entourage

At its 1903 gathering, the Social Democratic Labor party split into two branches, the "majoritarians" (Bolsheviks) and the "minoritarians" (Mensheviks). The Bolsheviks, led by V. I. Lenin (whose real name was Vladimir Ilich Ulyanov), preferred a concentrated party guided by an elite group of dedicated revolutionaries. The Mensheviks envisioned a more broadly based organization. Yuli Martov, a Menshevik leader, wrote that his group believed that "unlimited democracy [is] the only political form in which the social emancipation of the proletariat can be prepared and realized." The Mensheviks and Bolsheviks also differed on the timing of a socialist revolution. The Mensheviks were loyal to the theories of George Plekhanov (1857-1918), who has been called the "father of Russian Marxism." He maintained that before Russia could achieve socialism, it would have to go through a period of capitalism that would create a large worker class and other conditions necessary to sustain a socialist society. The Bolsheviks, however, claimed that its elite group of revolutionaries could lead Russian society directly to socialism, bypassing the capitalist stage of development that Plekhanov (and Marx) believed was necessary.

Russo-Japanese War

The Russo-Japanese War of 1904-1905 increased domestic opposition to Nicholas's rule. The war resulted from the mutual ambitions of the Russians and Japanese to dominate Manchuria and Korea in an era of waning Chinese strength. To the surprise of the tsar's government and most of the world, the Japanese defeated the Russians. The key event of the war came on May 27, 1904, when the Japanese navy decimated the Russian Baltic fleet, which had sailed to the Pacific, in the battle of the Tsushima Strait. Although Russia was considered a more powerful nation, the Japanese had surpassed the Russians in naval technology and benefited from British support and shorter supply and communication lines. Japan also maintained a high degree of morale and national cohesion, while the war quickly became unpopular with the Russian people. The war ended in September 1905 with the signing of the Treaty of Portsmouth (New Hampshire), which was mediated by President Theodore Roosevelt. Count Sergei Witte served as the Russian negotiator and secured relatively favorable terms given his nation's clear defeat. The treaty, however, obliged Russia to cede southern Sakhalin Island and Port Arthur to Japan, recognize Japan's protectorate over Korea, and remove its forces from Manchuria.

The military humiliation at the hands of what was perceived as an inferior power seriously weakened the prestige of the tsar's government. Moreover, the government's apparent inefficiency in prosecuting the war, the higher taxes necessitated by the war, and the loss of many Russian lives for distant objectives that had little meaning to the average peasant or worker increased the revolutionary activities of the people. Demands mounted for the establishment of a legislative assembly and civil rights as workers went on strike and students demonstrated in the cities.

Revolution of 1905

The series of events known as the Revolution of 1905 began on "Bloody Sunday," January 22, 1905. A large group of nonrevolutionary workers, demonstrating peacefully for moderate reforms in front of the tsar's Winter Palace in St. Petersburg, was fired upon by the police. Hundreds were killed and wounded. Although Nicholas had been away from the palace at the time, the violent police reaction shattered the ideal that a sacred bond existed between the Russian people and a paternalistic tsar who would look after their welfare. Consequently, many traditionally loyal working people who had supported the tsar joined the socialists and other groups calling for radical changes. Bloody Sunday also stunned the Kadets and other moderate liberals who began cooperating more closely with the radical opposition. The anti-tsarist revolution became a broad social movement that included workers, peasants, national minorities, intellectuals, members of the bourgeoisie, and, for the first time, members of the armed forces.

Strikes, disturbances, and mutinies continued until August, when Nicholas announced the creation of an elective *Duma* (representative assembly) to advise the tsar. The proposal satisfied few in the opposition, and the revolutionaries organized a general strike that paralyzed the country from October 20 to October 30. In particular, railroad and communication services were almost totally shut down. The strike forced Tsar Nicholas and his ministers on October 30 to issue a manifesto mandating a Duma empowered to propose and enact legislation and guaranteeing all Russians civil rights, including freedom of the press, speech, and assembly.

This program won the approval of the liberals and the disdain of the radicals, thus splitting the opposition. Disturbances continued, but the government had blunted the momentum of the revolution. In addition, the armies returning from the Far East remained loyal to the tsar. After troops prevailed over dissidents in several days of bloody street fighting in Moscow in December, the revolution was effectively ended.

Duma Period

Although Nicholas had agreed to establish a Duma, he continued to espouse absolutist principles and tried to avoid relinquishing any power. To this end he and his advisers devised several means through which they could limit the power of the new Duma. The government issued a list of "fundamental laws" that the Duma could not change and announced that the tsar at any time could dissolve the Duma, arrange new elections, and issue legislation in the interim. Under the fundamental laws, the tsar would have sole authority over foreign and military policy, succession to the throne, ministerial appointments, pardons, and internal court affairs. In addition his finance minister would be responsible for currency issues and foreign loans. To further insulate itself, the government secured a large loan from France and allowed the Duma to control only 60 percent of the state budget. Finally the tsar's council of state, an advisory body, was transformed into an upper house with equal power to the Duma so that it could function as a conservative legislative counterweight to the Duma's liberal and radical membership.

The first Duma met May 10, 1906. The tsar and his advisers expected the peasants to vote for conservative representatives who would support the crown, but instead they elected a reform-minded majority. Behind the leadership of the Kadets, the party that won the most seats (38 percent), the Duma demanded land redistribution. The tsar refused, and after a period of bitter debate, he dissolved the Duma in July. Its Kadet members crossed into Finland, where they reconvened and issued a call urging Russian citizens to deny the government tax payments and military service until the Duma was brought back into session. The government declared the Kadets who rebelled ineligible for office in future Dumas and set up new elections.

The second Duma, which opened in March 1907, was even more radical than the first. It was dissolved in July of that year. Nicholas and his advisers realized that the original election laws would not produce a cooperative Duma. They therefore changed the laws to enhance the representation of the wealthier and more conservative groups. As a result the third Duma (1907-1912) served out its full term and was largely supportive of the tsar's government. The fourth Duma (1912-1916) was conservative but displayed greater independence from the tsar. Both Dumas had moderate and radical members who were able to voice their concerns in the assembly, and the bodies advanced some reforms, particularly in the area of improving conditions for workers and peasants.

World War I

Popular dissatisfaction with the imperial government simmered from 1905 until 1914. Radicals continued to agitate, workers struck, and terrorists succeeded in assassinating some government officials. The assassination on September 14, 1911, of Peter Stolypin, prime minister since 1906, was a particularly hard blow to Nicholas's government. Stolypin's land reform policies had substantially improved the lot of the Russian peasantry, thereby complicating the task of radical agitators who sought to convince the peasants to support a revolution. Historians suspect, however, that Stolypin's assassin was actually employed by officials whom the prime minister had alienated. The tsar's agents, meanwhile, sought to infiltrate and disrupt revolutionary societies. *(Stolypin, box, p. 29)*

The burgeoning political, economic, and cultural transformation of Russia was interrupted when World War I broke out in August 1914. Russia fought with France and Great Britain against Germany and Austria-Hungary. Its initial goals were to block German and Austrian ambitions in the Balkan states and fulfill its mutual defense obligations to France. However, the tsar's government soon added the acquisition of the Turkish Straits and Constantinople to its list of objectives.

At the beginning of the war the Russian people rushed to support the tsar and his army, believing unprovoked Austro-German aggression necessitated a common effort for national defense. The populace was encouraged by early successes, but a series of military disasters on the German front dashed morale. The government's ineptitude contributed to an excessively high rate of Russian casualties. By 1915 German armies had captured Poland and penetrated into Russia. Arms and munitions were in short supply or completely unavailable. Food was scarce, and the mood of the people toward the government was hostile.

Nicholas had left St. Petersburg in September 1915 to take personal charge of his armies. In his absence, the government was run by Tsarina Alexandra, who for several years had relied heavily on the counsel of Grigory Rasputin, a strange Siberian

Stolypin: Tsarist Minister

As prime minister of Russia from 1906 until 1911, Peter Stolypin built a reputation as an efficient, innovative, and ruthless servant of Tsar Nicholas II. Historians have called him imperial Russia's last effective prime minister.

Although the tsar's creation of a Duma in 1905 had temporarily relieved the threat of a popular revolution, radical intellectual groups and terrorists still operated against the government. Determined to break the radical opposition, Stolypin launched a "pacification" campaign in 1906. He shut down more than two hundred newspapers, backed an aggressive police campaign to infiltrate radical organizations, and established summary courts-martial, under which a suspect could be arrested, tried, and executed on the same day. More than a thousand persons were executed on the order of these courts.

Stolypin's pacification policy achieved its goals by 1908. Many revolutionaries fled the country, several leading revolutionary groups were destroyed, and terrorism was dramatically reduced.

While suppressing the opposition, Stolypin also tried to eliminate the causes of societal discontent, particularly among the peasantry. He aspired to create a free, educated class of peasant land owners that would be economically productive, loyal to the tsar, and immune to revolutionary appeals. To this end, he initiated a program of agrarian reform in the fall of 1906. The Stolypin Land Reforms, also known as the "wager on the strong," provided for the partitioning of commune lands into plots owned by individual commune members. Stolypin's government also allowed peasants to buy state-owned land, created the Peasant Land Bank, and encouraged peasant migration to remote virgin farmland.

The implementation of Stolypin's reform program was cut short by his death and the onset of World War I, but many peasants responded to the program enthusiastically. Given its scope and promising beginning, its full implementation might have changed the course of Russian history.

Stolypin's proclivity to create enemies eventually brought his downfall. Those on the radical left despised him for his ruthless suppression of revolutionary activity, while those on the right feared and resented his power. Even the tsar came to dislike Stolypin, in part because he frustrated the tsarina's unmerited promotions of her favorites to high government positions.

On September 14, 1911, Stolypin was assassinated by a man named Dmitry Bogrov while attending an opera in Kiev with the tsar. Bogrov was apprehended at the scene and labeled a terrorist, but there is evidence that he was a police agent.

monk whom the tsarina credited with relieving her son's hemophilia. Rasputin and the tsarina alienated the members of the Duma, on the left and the right. Rasputin, "the mad monk," was assassinated December 30, 1916, by a group of conservatives in the hope that his elimination would restore confidence in the government. By that time, however, the Russian people had so many grievances with the government, it is unlikely that any reform or change in personalities at court could have slowed the revolution. *(Rasputin, box, p. 30)*

The Revolution of 1917

The Russian Revolution began spontaneously in March 1917 in Petrograd, which had been renamed from the Germanic St. Petersburg during the war. A severe shortage of bread led to enforced rationing and long lines at shops. The prospect of hunger and even starvation led to demonstrations and strikes. On March 8 a huge crowd that included many women marched in the streets to demand government action to end the bread shortages. The march was broken up by police, but over the next two days the demonstrations grew.

The government ordered troops to restore order on March 11, but instead of putting down the riots, the soldiers stood by passively or even joined them. The defection of the local army garrisons to the side of the demonstrators caused the government to crumble. Tsar Nicholas II abdicated March 15 in favor of his brother, Michael, who handed power to

Rasputin: Rakish Adviser

Grigory Rasputin, the strange mystic who wielded enormous influence over Tsarina Alexandra, was a peasant. He was born around 1872 in Pokrovokoe, a village in Siberia, to a family named Novykh. He was given the name Rasputin—in Russian, "dissolute"—by villagers who witnessed his early lecherous behavior. After his marriage to a local woman, Rasputin spent his early adulthood in religious wandering.

During these travels across Russia he fashioned a personal brand of religion, which included his belief that sexual indulgence was part of the process of religious rapture. Most commentators believe that Rasputin's endorsement of uninhibited sexual activity was a convenient justification for indulging his own sexual appetite.

In 1903 Rasputin arrived in St. Petersburg. He persuaded members of the royal circle that he was a clairvoyant and soon became their spiritual adviser. In 1905 he was introduced to the royal family. Presenting himself simply as a holy man, Rasputin won the admiration and respect of the tsarina through his reported ability to improve the health of her son, Alexis, a hemophiliac and heir to the throne.

Over the next several years he became one of the tsarina's favorites, advising her on spiritual and, even-tually, political matters. He considered himself the voice of the Russian peasantry; the tsarina, some think, considered him the voice of God.

As Rasputin's influence grew, he was besieged by petitioners seeking the favor of the royal family and the government. The constant flow of visitors to his home in St. Petersburg facilitated his debauchery. He allegedly seduced many of the more attractive female petitioners. Reports of his sexual exploits were circulated widely in St. Petersburg, but the tsarina dismissed them as gossip.

Opposition to Rasputin grew among conservatives at court after Tsar Nicholas II in September 1915 assumed field command of his troops fighting in World War I. Nicholas's departure from St. Petersburg left the tsarina, with Rasputin at her side, in virtual control of the country. As reports of Rasputin's scandalous excesses increased, a group of conspirators hatched a plot to assassinate him in the hope of preserving the monarchy.

According to historical accounts, the group included Vladimir Purishkevich, a conservative Duma member; Prince Feliks Yusupov, a wealthy nobleman; and Grand Duke Dmitry Pavlovich, the tsar's first cousin. On the night of December 30, 1916, during a visit to Yusupov's home, Rasputin was poisoned and, when the poison seemed to have no effect, shot.

---

the "Provisional Government" formed by the Duma two days before. The revolution in Petrograd spread quickly throughout Russia. In most locations tsarist governors and representatives were replaced without bloodshed.

The Provisional Government

The Provisional Government, which initially was led by Prince Georgy Lvov, operated from an inherently weak position. Because it included representatives from several groups that had little in common but their opposition to the tsar, it had difficulty reaching a consensus on policy. The Provisional Government also found it impossible to satisfy the great expectations of the Russian people who be-lieved that the revolution would remedy all that was wrong with their nation. In addition the Provisional Government was regarded as a temporary arrangement that would govern Russia until a permanent constituent assembly could be elected. Perhaps the most significant weakness of the Provisional Government's position, however, was that it had to share authority with local assemblies known as *soviets*.

Soviets were grass-roots councils that had been formed throughout the country in neighborhoods, villages, factories, and army posts. They were modeled after the first soviet, which had been formed in St. Petersburg during the October strike of 1905. This soviet had been a committee of elected representatives from various factories that coordinated the strike. After the general strike, the government

Bystanders scramble for cover as government machine gunners fire at revolutionists in Petrograd, 1917.

arrested the members of the St. Petersburg Soviet, including its most famous leader, Leon Trotsky, who was banished to Siberia but escaped to Europe.

On March 12, 1917, revolutionaries reconstituted the St. Petersburg Soviet as the Petrograd Soviet of Workers' and Soldiers' Deputies. In the early days of the revolution thousands of soviets were established across Russia to provide revolutionary forums and administer local affairs. The power of the Petrograd Soviet, however, extended to national affairs because it had influence over soldiers and workers in important industries in Petrograd and other large cities. It quickly became a partner of and competitor to the Provisional Government. The Petrograd Soviet lent support to the Provisional Government in return for some say in the running of the state.

The Provisional Government immediately proclaimed full equality before the law for all Russians and guaranteed freedom of speech, assembly, press, and religion. Unions and strikes were permitted, and new labor laws inaugurated eight-hour days for some workers. The Provisional Government also mandated changes in local government that made it

more egalitarian and promised greater autonomy to ethnic minorities.

Although these actions were popular, the Provisional Government failed to assert control over the country or address its two most pressing problems—the economy and the war. The steep decline of the economy was exacerbated by food shortages and the destruction and dislocations caused by the fighting on Russian territory. The government's most fateful decision was to continue the war, despite the dismal state of Russian morale, the lack of supplies, and the decimated transportation system. The Provisional Government had taken modest steps toward establishing a more just society, but the Russian people expected these steps after the revolution. What they wanted was progress toward peace and prosperity.

Peasants formed an overwhelming majority in the armed forces, and with the promise of coming land redistribution, more than one million men simply left the army between March and October to ensure receiving their share of the land. Peasants began to take action against landowners because they felt the Provisional Government was moving too slowly on land reform. Owners who refused to sell their land to peasants at deflated prices were subject to attack. The government was besieged by owners' pleas for help. Little was forthcoming, as the government did not have adequate means to enforce order in the countryside, and it hoped to defer action on land redistribution until a constituent assembly could be elected.

Industrial workers, meanwhile, were rapidly joining the revolutionary ranks. Because they were centered in urban areas and were better organized, these workers had aided the revolution and were among the first to see benefits from it. But things still were not moving fast enough for them, and, as the economic picture rapidly declined, many were forced out of work. With increasing hunger in the cities came increasing violence and protests.

Bolsheviks Seize Power

On April 16, 1917, after ten years of exile in Switzerland, Lenin arrived in Petrograd intending to radicalize the revolution. Lenin's return had been aided by the Germans, who hoped that he would intensify revolutionary activity in Russia and thereby weaken the Russian war effort. Lenin, however, was not working for the Germans and ultimately expected that the international socialist revolution would engulf Germany as well as Russia.

In Petrograd Lenin issued what came to be known as his "April Theses," a radical Bolshevik strategy that surprised many of his colleagues. Lenin urged his party not to support the Provisional Government or the war effort. He also advocated transferring government power to the soviets (although Lenin did not press for the immediate achievement of this objective, since the Bolsheviks were not well represented in the soviets at this time). Many moderate liberals and socialists denounced Lenin's approach, but the Bolshevik party gradually grew in strength.

Meanwhile, the unpopularity and weakness of the Provisional Government were becoming increasingly apparent. In June, despite the Provisional Government's protests, the Ukraine took action to establish its independence. In early July an offensive against Germany, which the government hoped would turn the tide of the war, stalled. Russian forces were left more exhausted and vulnerable to attack than they had been before. Responding to a sense of impending national calamity, citizens in Petrograd on July 16 and 17 staged massive demonstrations against the government in what became known as the "July Days." Minister of War Aleksandr Kerensky dispersed the two-day riot and arrested some radical leaders. Lenin was forced to flee to Finland. Calm was restored to the capital, but the demonstrations had revealed the vulnerability of the government and the revolutionary mood of the people.

On July 21 Prince Lvov resigned as premier. It took more than two weeks for the disorganized and contentious leaders of the Provisional Government to form a new ruling coalition. On September 7 Kerensky was named premier of a somewhat more leftist government composed primarily of Kadets, Socialist Revolutionaries, and Mensheviks.

In September, the Provisional Government faced its first serious counterrevolutionary challenge. Gen. Lavr Kornilov, the recently appointed commander in chief of the Russian Army, attempted a military coup that became known as the "Kornilov affair." A simple, hard-working man with little capacity for political nuance, Kornilov was convinced the Petrograd Soviet was the source of all Russia's problems. He initiated what most historians now regard as a comedy of errors that contributed to the disintegration of the military and the Provisional Government.

After Prime Minister Kerensky sanctioned the use of troops to put down domestic unrest, Kornilov believed that he had been authorized to take over the government. The general dispatched troops to the capital ostensibly to combat dissent but in reality to ensure military control of the government and the removal of the Petrograd Soviet. After an intermediary urged Kerensky to cede to Kornilov, Kerensky became convinced that Kornilov's efforts were really a conspiracy. He dismissed Kornilov, who refused to give up control of the army, and ordered more troops to the capital.

In the meantime, the Petrograd Soviet and other

socialist organizations acted quickly by mobilizing and arming the generally sympathetic workers in Petrograd and the nearby sailors from Kronstadt naval base. It took little effort to disband the arriving Kornilov soldiers once they were convinced their efforts were counterrevolutionary. Kornilov and other officers were arrested, and several government ministers who had cooperated with him were dismissed.

Although the Provisional Government survived, Kerensky had been forced to appeal to the Bolsheviks for help. He also had released Leon Trotsky and other important radical leaders from prison. Kerensky's reliance on the left cost him the support of the right and many moderates, while strengthening the reputation of the Bolsheviks, who were regarded by many as the defenders of the revolution. This perception was significant since the Bolsheviks' opponents had attempted to portray them as disloyal because of their opposition to the war with Germany. In addition, the Kornilov affair increased support for the Bolsheviks because it seemed to confirm their warnings about the threat of counterrevolutionary activity and the need to expand on the revolution.

The attempted coup also weakened the military. Purges and other moves against men and groups within the army that had supported Kornilov caused the situation at the front to deteriorate further. Desertions increased, and many of the men who remained were embittered, disillusioned, and physically incapable of continuing the war.

The Bolsheviks wasted little time in taking advantage of the disorganized situation. They obtained a majority of the seats in the Petrograd Soviet in September, and by October, Trotsky became its chairman. The Bolsheviks gained popularity largely because they were the only Russian political group that promised the workers, peasants, and soldiers what they wanted—land redistribution, an end to food shortages, and an immediate withdrawal from the war. The Bolsheviks expressed their commitment to these objectives through the simple slogan "land, bread, and peace." They also were popular with the non-Russian minorities because they promised to establish the right of self-determination.

Lenin secretly returned to Petrograd from Finland October 23 and urged his followers to seize power. "History will not forgive us if we do not take power now," he pleaded. His longtime lieutenants Grigory Zinoviev and Lev Kamenev, however, wanted to postpone the coup to further strengthen support among the masses. After some initial hesitation the Bolsheviks occupied government offices November 7, 1917, as soldiers stood by refusing to defend the Provisional Government. The next day the Bolsheviks took over the Winter Palace after facing weak resistance from troops defending it and placed under arrest those members of the Provisional Government who remained behind after Kerensky and other government leaders escaped the city. The Bolshevik takeover often is called the "Great October Revolution" in the Soviet Union because in 1917 the Julian calendar was still in use in Russia, making the date of the revolution October 25 instead of November 7. The Gregorian, or Western, calendar was adopted January 31, 1918.

The Bolsheviks had accomplished one of the most dramatic political feats in history. At the time of the tsar's overthrow, they were a well-organized, but relatively small party with little influence over the Provisional Government. By November the party had grown more than ten times, acquired substantial support from urban workers and soldiers, and seized power in Petrograd with relatively little bloodshed.

Establishing Bolshevik Rule

The Bolsheviks on November 9, 1917, established the Council of People's Commissars as the highest ruling body in the country. Lenin assumed the chairmanship of the council. Other prominent Bolsheviks in the government included Leon Trotsky, commissar for foreign affairs, and Joseph Stalin, who was assigned responsibility for national minority groups. In March 1918 the party changed its name from the "Russian Social Democratic Labor party, Bolshevik" to the "Communist party, Bolshevik." The Russian Soviet Federated Socialist Republic was created by the first Soviet constitution, which the Fifth All-Russian Congress of Soviets adopted July 10, 1918.

The Philosophy of Karl Marx: Foundation of a Revolution

Karl Marx (1818-1883), the philosopher who gave his name to the system of social, economic, and political thought embraced by Russian revolutionaries, was born in the German Rhineland city of Trier. He studied history and philosophy at the universities of Bonn and Berlin, where he was exposed to the writings of the German philosopher Georg Wilhelm Friedrich Hegel (1770-1831). Throughout his life Marx witnessed the misery and exploitation that accompanied the Industrial Revolution in Europe. These impressions influenced the development of his radical socialist philosophy.

In 1842 Marx began editing a Cologne-based political journal, *Rheinische Zeitung*. The authorities closed the publication in 1843, and Marx moved to Paris to work as an editor of *Deutsch-Franzosische Zeitung*. In 1845 his revolutionary ideas led to his expulsion from France. Marx and his wife, Jenny von Westphalen, took refuge in Brussels. While there he and his colleague and frequent financial supporter, Friedrich Engels (1820-1895), wrote the *Communist Manifesto*. A blueprint for the Communist League, a small group of European radicals, the *Manifesto* called on the oppressed mass of workers, the proletariat, to liberate itself from capitalist enslavement. It ended with the rallying cry:

The proletarians have nothing to lose but their chains. They have a world to win. Working men of all countries, unite!

Shortly after publication of the *Manifesto* in 1848, Marx returned to Cologne and again published a newspaper, until the German government expelled him the following year. He settled in London, where he spent the rest of his life.

Marxist Theory

The philosophy outlined in the *Manifesto* and Marx's other writings centered on the struggle between social classes. Adapting an idea developed by Hegel, Marx argued that class struggle occurred in cycles: an existing situation (the thesis) inevitably was challenged by a new idea (the antithesis), and the exchange (the dialectic) between thesis and antithesis resulted in something new (the synthesis). According to Marx, throughout history the continuous cycle of thesis, antithesis, and synthesis spurred the evolution of social and economic organization from slavery to feudalism to capitalism.

Marx maintained that labor alone created value. Under capitalism, however, the owners of businesses and factories received profits from the unpaid labor time of those who possessed only their work skills. In Marx's view this inherently exploitive arrangement would become increasingly unendurable for workers as competition forced owners to squeeze greater profits out of them to accumulate more capital. Simultaneously, as capital became concentrated in fewer and fewer hands, small owners would be driven out of business, swelling the ranks of the working class.

Many socialist thinkers had predicted that a peaceful evolution toward socialism (a system where the means of production are owned commonly by society) would occur in industrialized na-

The victory of communism in Russia generally is attributed to the opportunism and organizational brilliance of Lenin and Trotsky and to the Bolsheviks' ability to appeal to the Russian people during a time of national unrest created by a failing economy and Russian military losses in World War I. The Bolsheviks were able to remain in power because they were better organized than their opponents and because they established their own type of totalitarianism that eliminated dissent and challenges to their rule. The Bolsheviks capitalized on the mistakes of their opponents but appropriated popular policies of other parties when it suited their needs. In particular they adopted the agrarian policies of the Socialist Revolutionaries in an effort to increase peasant support for their regime during their first months in power.

In November 1917 the Bolsheviks firmly controlled Petrograd, but they still were struggling to establish their authority over the rest of the country.

tions. Marx, however, believing that economic conditions more than any other factor were responsible for political behavior, reasoned that the pressures created by the exploitation of the working class would inevitably produce a violent upheaval. The unrest would culminate in a proletarian revolution in which workers would overthrow capitalist governments and establish socialist states. Eventually Marx believed that these socialist states would achieve the final (and to Marx the highest) form of society, communism. At this point dialectic tension would end.

Marx envisioned a communist society as one in which all classes would be eliminated and property would be owned commonly by all citizens. Under such a system there would be no exploitation of labor, unemployment would be eliminated, goods would be abundant and fairly distributed according to need, and citizens would be motivated to work hard for the benefit of the whole society. Because Marx thought of political power as a means through which one class oppressed another, he expected state institutions to "wither away." He also expected the bonds between workers in different countries would transcend national identities and loyalties. Consequently, a major cause of war would be eliminated with the establishment of communism.

The radical revolutions that swept Europe in 1848 were not communist inspired, a fact that disappointed Marx. But he continued to promote revolution from London, helping to establish with the radical Russian émigré Mikhail Bakunin the First International Workingmen's Association in 1864 and maintaining a network of revolutionary contacts.

Marx also devoted himself to his major scholarly effort, *Das Kapital,* the first volume of which was published in 1867.

Russia's Revolutionary Potential

Marx believed that a society had to pass through the capitalist stage before it could reach socialism. Because Russia had barely entered the industrial age and remained backward and largely agricultural, Marx initially put it low on the list of countries ripe for socialist revolution. He looked instead to the industrialized nations—Germany, France, Great Britain, and the United States—for signs of impending upheaval.

Late in his life, however, Marx became interested in Russia's revolutionary potential. He devoted much time to the study of Russia's language, history, and culture and followed closely the activities of its revolutionary intellectuals. Engels complained to Marx that his preoccupation with conditions in Russia was delaying completion of *Das Kapital.* By the 1870s, the establishment of communism was debated in Russia's radical circles. The revolutionary Populists, members of *Narodnaya Volya,* argued that socialism was uniquely suited to Russia because Russian society was based on the village commune, a primitive communist organization. Under this favorable circumstance, Russia could skip over the capitalist development phase and directly proceed to socialism. In the preface to a new Russian edition of the *Communist Manifesto* published in 1882, Marx and Engels agreed with this analysis of Russia's revolutionary potential.

To achieve this authority, they needed the support, or at least the acquiescence, of the army. Russia's defeats at the hands of the Germans and the Kornilov affair created disarray in the army that aided Bolshevik efforts to gain control of it. The Bolsheviks appealed to the class consciousness of the soldiers who had not already deserted. This propaganda was somewhat successful. Many soldiers, however, threw in their lot with Lenin's government simply out of loyalty to the Russian state or a desire

to continue their military careers under whoever happened to be in power. Consequently, although a significant number of soldiers eventually would join units that would fight against the new government in the coming civil war, the Bolsheviks succeeded in co-opting enough of the army to prevent a military coup. On January 28, 1918, Lenin and his colleagues decided to abandon the structure of the old tsarist army and replace it with a new "Red Army" based on socialist principles.

Lenin's efforts to bring all of Russia under Bolshevik authority centered on gaining control of the local soviets. Since the Bolsheviks were not well represented in many city and rural soviets, they resorted to tactics ranging from political campaigning and propaganda to intimidation and the use of armed force. The struggle for control of the soviets in many large cities, including Moscow, was bloody. By the end of the year, the Bolshevik government controlled most major population centers, although many rural areas remained outside their complete authority. Lenin bolstered his government's popularity by reaffirming its intention to redistribute gentry land, establish worker control of industry (which Lenin did within twenty days of taking power), and negotiate a peace settlement with the Germans.

The peace terms eventually accepted by Bolshevik negotiators were harsh. Trotsky and other leaders initially refused to accept the treaty, but they relented after Lenin threatened to resign if it were not approved. The Treaty of Brest-Litovsk, signed on March 3, 1918, obligated Russia to recognize the independence of Estonia, Latvia, Lithuania, Poland, and the Ukraine and to recognize German influence over them. The relinquishment of these lands meant that the Russian empire would lose about one-quarter of its population and arable land, one-third of its manufacturing capacity, and nearly three-quarters of both its iron and coal production. German troops or local non-Russian authorities, however, controlled much of the area given up by Russia, so the treaty primarily recognized political realities that the Bolsheviks were not in a position to change.

Politically, the new government faced a challenge from the Constituent Assembly elected November 25, 1917. Although the Bolsheviks had taken over complete control of the government, they felt obligated to continue paying lip service to democracy. Consequently, they allowed elections to take place for the Constituent Assembly that had been promised by the Provisional Government. The Bolshevik party, however, won only 170 out of 707 seats in the assembly. Behind strong peasant support, the Socialist Revolutionaries won 370 seats, an absolute majority. The Constituent Assembly met for the first time on January 18, 1918, and immediately challenged Bolshevik policies. The next day Lenin ordered the body to dissolve. The Socialist Revolutionaries protested, but the Bolsheviks suffered no major repercussions from their disbandment of the assembly. From then on, opposition to Bolshevik rule would come only from outside the central government.

War Communism

The Bolshevik seizure of power did not end social strife in Russia. From 1918 until early 1921 Lenin and his fellow Bolsheviks faced challenges from several domestic armies seeking their overthrow, non-Russian minorities seeking national liberation, and foreign forces seeking a variety of objectives. The Bolsheviks also had to contend with an economy devastated by World War I and indignation from some segments of society over the harsh terms of the Brest-Litovsk treaty. In this uncertain atmosphere, the Bolsheviks launched a series of policies that came to be known as "War Communism."

War Communism sought to construct a communist society and economic system in the shortest possible time and to mobilize all available resources for the fight against the anti-Bolsheviks. It aimed to achieve these goals by establishing a planned economy based on state ownership of the means of production, eliminating markets, compensating workers according to their needs, and extending egalitarian principles to all aspects of life.

The government, therefore, rapidly took over businesses and factories. By 1920 all production and distribution enterprises employing ten workers or more were controlled by the state. The Bolsheviks also nationalized banks, foreign trade, and all land; repudiated the tsar's foreign debts; outlawed strikes; seized private property; and replaced Russia's inflated currency with a system of barter. To silence domestic critics they dissolved all other political parties and established a political police force—the Extraordinary Commission to Combat Counterrevolution, Sabotage, and Speculation (Cheka). They also initiated compulsory military training and free education and declared a separation of church and state. (Secret police, box, p. 50)

War Communism brought about a direct, violent struggle between the new regime and the peasants. To gain peasant loyalty, the Bolsheviks had advocated a general land redistribution. Under War Communism, however, they initiated a plan to transform the peasants into farm workers under a large-scale, centralized system of agricultural production. Peasants resisted this, and the government temporarily acceded to some of their wishes. Meanwhile the food shortages that had contributed to the 1917 revolutionary upheaval in Russia continued under Bolshevik rule. As the food situation grew more desperate (in part because of the ongoing civil war), the government directed "food requisition detachments" to get food from the countryside any way they could. In theory the peasants were to be compensated for their grain with manufactured goods. But often they were given nothing, and the items that they did receive were likely to be of poor quality or of little use to them. The requisitioned food was transported to the cities, where its distribution was overseen by a growing central bureaucracy.

Lenin's draconian policies in the countryside led to fighting between the peasants and government agents sent to requisition food. The Bolsheviks further enflamed the situation by enlisting the poorer peasants as informers and requisitioners against the wealthier peasants, who were known as *kulaks*. Although the government's use of terror did not approach the magnitude used by Joseph Stalin during the 1930s, some hundred thousand kulaks were killed or sent to labor camps for resisting Bolshevik policies.

The effect of the government's food requisition policies was to alienate much of the peasantry and induce them to either produce less or hide surplus grain, since any food they produced beyond their immediate needs was likely to be requisitioned. Consequently, the food crisis in Russia continued throughout the War Communism period. From 1920 to 1922 the frequent food shortages escalated into an outright famine that killed as many as five million people.

War Communism was almost as unsuccessful in the cities. The Bolsheviks' monetary and industrial policies worsened the deteriorating economy they had inherited. Industrial workers protested economic conditions through absenteeism and illegal strikes. In 1921, with the civil war won, Lenin called a retreat from War Communism and instituted the New Economic Policy (NEP).

Civil War

The most pressing problem facing the new regime during the period of War Communism, however, was the civil war. The war pitted the Bolshevik Red Army against various anti-Bolshevik (White) forces. The White armies were made up of soldiers from the tsar's army, monarchists, conservatives, liberals, Socialist Revolutionaries, Mensheviks, and most other political and social groups. Many people took up arms against the Bolsheviks in an idealistic attempt to restore democratic principles that the Bolsheviks had rejected in disbanding the Constituent Assembly. Others had been angered by the loss and humiliation of the Treaty of Brest-Litovsk. Still others sought personal power or a restoration of the old tsarist order. Because of their wide political differences, the leaders of the White forces could not agree on a program beyond the overthrow of the Bolshevik government. This factor hampered their ability to recruit soldiers and weakened the morale of their troops.

The war began in the summer of 1918 when a military front was established by White forces under Gen. Aleksandr Kolchak in western Siberia. Soon other White armies formed in the Baltic region, the Caucasus, and the far north near Murmansk. Thus, the White forces challenged Bolshevik rule in central Russia from widely distant bases on the nation's periphery.

Tsar Nicholas II and his family were among the war's early casualties. After the March 1917 revolution, they had been sent into internal exile at Ekaterinburg. On July 16, 1918, as White forces loyal to the tsar approached the town, local Bolsheviks with the support of Lenin killed the tsar, his wife, and their five children to prevent them from becoming a rallying point for the White armies.

In October 1919 White forces appeared to have the upper hand. Separate White armies reached the outskirts of Petrograd and penetrated to within 250 miles of Moscow (the Bolsheviks had moved the capital to Moscow in March 1918 for greater security). The Bolsheviks, however, stopped the advance of the White armies, and they went on the offensive. By April 1920 the Red Army had routed the White forces and had executed or chased into exile most of the White generals. The last active White army, under the leadership of Gen. Peter Wrangel, had retreated to the Crimea. Wrangel's troops abandoned the fight in November.

Several factors contributed to the Bolsheviks' victory. Foremost among these was their success at creating an army. They used conscription and patriotic appeals to build their Red Army into an effective, unified fighting force of several million troops under the command of Trotsky, who had become minister of war in 1918 after resigning as foreign minister. By 1919 the Red Army was larger than the various White armies arrayed against it. The Bolsheviks also had the advantages of interior lines of communication, control of most of the important railroad lines, and the ability to concentrate their forces against whichever White army was most threatening at the time. The divided White forces suffered from poor coordination caused by the great distances between armies and the personal rivalries of their generals. In addition, the leaders of the White forces refused to back progressive land reform or autonomy for non-Russian states that had been part of the tsar's empire. Had White leaders adopted more enlightened policies in these two areas, they likely would have increased their support among peasants and ethnic minorities—two large societal groups that tended to be dissatisfied with Bolshevik rule.

Foreign Intervention

The civil war between the Red and White armies was accompanied by armed intervention by Russia's erstwhile World War I allies. When the Bolsheviks withdrew Russia from the war against the Central Powers, the Western Allies were alarmed that Germany would be able to transfer hundreds of thousands of troops from the eastern to the western front. They also were concerned that the Germans would seize massive stockpiles of Allied war supplies stored in the northern Russian cities of Archangel and Murmansk. After diplomatic efforts failed to convince the Bolsheviks to reenter the war, the Allies began transporting troops to Russia in March 1918 to protect their supplies from the Germans and explore the opportunities for reestablishing the eastern front. Great Britain, France, Italy, the United States, and Japan landed small contingents in northern Russia or around Vladivostok in the Far East.

At first Lenin did not object to the intervention since it strengthened Russia's bargaining position with the Germans. Soon after the Treaty of Brest-Litovsk was concluded, however, Lenin came to regard the Allied forces as a threat. During 1918 the Allies ignored Bolshevik protests and began building up their garrisons in Russia.

Soviet politicians and historians pointed to the Allied intervention as evidence of the capitalist world's innate hostility toward the socialist experiment in Russia. From the beginning the Allies disliked and feared the Bolshevik government, which had urged workers in industrialized nations to revolt. Western leaders clearly preferred that such a government be replaced. Contrary to Soviet contentions, however, Allied governments initially saw the intervention primarily as a necessary war measure.

In May an incident in Siberia involving a brigade of Czechoslovak soldiers accelerated the movement toward civil war and greater Allied intervention. The forty-five-thousand-man brigade had been formed by Czechoslovaks living in Russia who wanted to fight on the side of the Allies. With Russia's withdrawal from the war, they were no longer needed on the eastern front. The Bolsheviks and Allies agreed on arrangements to transport the Czechoslovaks to the western front by traveling to Vladivostok on Russian trains, and then being transported to France on Allied ships. During their journey east, a fight between the Czechoslovak brigade and a group of Hungarian prisoners, who were being returned to Hungary under the provisions of the Treaty of Brest-Litovsk, led to a Bolshevik order to disarm the Czechoslovaks. The brigade, which was a match for any fighting force of comparable size in Russia at the time, ignored the order, took over the Trans-Siberian Railroad, and began to cooperate with Allied forces who had landed in Vladivostok. The ease with which the Czechoslovaks resisted the Bolsheviks and the growing strength of the Allied forces in Russia encouraged the establishment of White armies. The brigade's success and the spontaneous anti-Bolshevik uprisings that occurred also convinced some Allied leaders that the Bolshevik government was vulnerable.

On November 11, 1918, World War I ended with the Allies victorious. The defeat of Germany removed all justification for the Allies' intervention in Russia, but by this time the Bolsheviks' anticapitalist propaganda, ambitions in eastern Europe, repudiation of the tsar's debts, and nationalization of foreign-owned industry had convinced some Allied leaders that they should attempt to overthrow the new Bolshevik government. The Allied forces in Russia, therefore, funneled material and financial support to the White armies, although the size of the Allied contingents was reduced. The one intervening nation to go beyond material support of the White armies was Japan, which sent a large contingent of soldiers to occupy parts of Siberia in the hope of permanently expanding its own empire in the Far East.

The Allied intervention never escalated into a large-scale cooperative effort to overthrow the Bolsheviks. The populations of the Allied countries, who had just lived through the most brutal war in history, were in no mood to support large military operations in Russia. Moreover, it was not clear that the White forces could win or that Allied aid would further their cause, since Allied participation in their efforts enabled the Bolsheviks to portray the White armies as puppets of foreign invaders. Finally, several prominent Allied leaders, including President Woodrow Wilson, doubted the legality and wisdom of the intervention. Consequently, when the defeat of the White armies appeared likely in late 1919, the Allies began withdrawing their remaining troops. Except for the Japanese, who remained in Siberia until 1922, all Allied forces had left Russia by the end of 1920.

In 1920 Russia faced a different foreign challenge. Poland had taken advantage of the Red Army's struggle with White forces in 1919 to occupy certain disputed areas to its east that were claimed by Russia. In April 1920 Polish forces under Gen. Joseph Pilsudski attempted to extend these gains by invading the Ukraine. In May, after Pilsudski had reached Kiev, the Red Army counterattacked, driving the Poles all the way back to Warsaw by July. Lenin and Trotsky hoped to establish a communist government in Poland and perhaps touch off a revolution in Germany. The French, however, came to Poland's aid with military supplies and a small contingent of troops. The rejuvenated Poles successfully counterattacked in August and forced the Red Army back into Russia. Both sides agreed to an armistice October 12, 1920. The Treaty of Riga, signed March 1921, gave Poland control of the disputed border regions in the Ukraine and Belorussia, which had been Poland's original objective in 1919.

Creating the USSR

Before coming to power in 1917, the Bolsheviks had supported the concept of national self-determination for the minorities of the Russian empire. On November 15, 1917, a week after seizing power, the Bolsheviks issued "The Declaration of the Rights of the Peoples of Russia," which proclaimed the right of non-Russian ethnic groups to form independent states. For Lenin and his colleagues, however, this was a theoretical statement, not a government policy. They did not intend to allow states that had long been a part of the Russian empire to secede.

When local authorities in the Ukraine and Finland responded to the popular will by moving to establish their countries' independence in December, the Bolsheviks condemned their actions. In January 1918 the Bolsheviks invaded the Ukraine to stop its independence movement. The same month they helped pro-Bolshevik Finns overthrow the Finnish government and establish a new regime based on the Bolshevik model. Latvia and Lithuania, which were occupied by German forces, and Estonia,

Kronstadt Rebellion

The Kronstadt rebellion in early 1921 was a dramatic climax to anti-Bolshevik unrest following the civil war. Terrible conditions in the countryside and strikes and demonstrations in Petrograd over food shortages caused sailors stationed at the nearby Kronstadt naval base to question the leadership of the Bolsheviks. The sailors adopted a platform that called for secret ballot elections, guarantees of civil rights, release of political prisoners, freedom for peasants to use their land however they wished, and an end to the Communist party's monopoly on power.

On March 2 the sailors rebelled by establishing a Provisional Revolutionary Committee to govern the naval base and work for the adoption of their platform. They hoped their rebellion would rally workers and peasants throughout the country to oppose Bolshevik leadership. The nationwide revolution, however, did not materialize.

After the chairman of the Soviet Central Executive Committee, Mikhail I. Kalinin, failed to settle the situation at the Kronstadt base with a personal visit, the government prepared to take the base by force. On March 18 government forces led by Leon Trotsky attacked Kronstadt. The attackers overcame the sailors' resistance, and some fifteen thousand people who surrendered were executed without a trial.

The rebellion had failed, but it succeeded in shaking up Lenin and his colleagues. Although the Bolshevik leaders called the rebellion the work of counterrevolutionary forces, they knew that the Kronstadt sailors were among the staunchest supporters of the revolution and previously had fought bravely against forces threatening the Bolshevik regime. The Kronstadt rebellion, therefore, was a sign that the dictatorship of the proletariat established by the Bolsheviks was being opposed by the class of people it was designed to represent. In response the Bolsheviks passed resolutions strengthening their monopoly on power and outlawing factionalism within the party. They then launched the New Economic Policy, which relaxed economic controls and allowed limited private enterprise.

which came under German occupation early in 1918, also declared their independence despite protests from the Bolshevik government.

The Treaty of Brest-Litovsk of March 1918 temporarily deprived Russia of control over the Baltic states, the Ukraine, and Finland, since it obligated the Bolsheviks to recognize German predominance in these areas. When World War I ended in November 1918 with the defeat of Germany by the Western allies, the Bolsheviks immediately repudiated the Brest-Litovsk treaty. As they fought against the White forces in the Russian civil war, they also moved to reestablish control over the non-Russian areas of the tsarist empire. Consequently, the ethnic minorities' fight for independence became entangled in the civil war. Although both the Whites and the Bolsheviks appealed to the minorities for help, neither advocated a program that would guarantee the independence of the non-Russian peoples. As a result members of the various ethnic groups fought on both sides of the civil war, although more sided with the Whites.

After the Bolsheviks defeated the White armies, the Baltic states and Finland remained independent. The Red Army, however, quickly reestablished control over the Ukraine and the Transcaucasia region, which had given much aid to the White forces. The Bolsheviks initiated a program in these areas to suppress local culture and language that resembled the policy of Russification implemented under Alexander III and Nicholas II. By 1920 the Bolsheviks had established theoretically independent "Soviet Socialist Republics" in Belorussia, the Ukraine, Armenia, Azerbaijan, and Georgia. These republics, however, did not possess sovereign powers, and during the early 1920s Moscow increasingly deprived them of autonomy over their local affairs.

On December 30, 1922, the Bolshevik government formally established the Union of Soviet Socialist Republics (USSR). It consisted of the Russian, Belorussian, Ukrainian, and Transcaucasian republics. A constitution ratified January 31, 1924, formalized this arrangement. By 1929 the Turkmen, Uzbek, and Tajik republics were added to the USSR, and the Transcaucasian republic was split into the Armenian, Azerbaijan, and Georgian republics.

New Economic Policy

In 1921 the civil war had ended, and Bolshevik rule no longer was threatened by foreign or domestic armies. Yet the miserable economic conditions in Russia and the restlessness of recently discharged soldiers had led to numerous peasant rebellions, urban demonstrations, and strikes. Industrial production continued to decline, goods of all types were in short supply, the Russian currency had lost most of its value, and a thriving black market had developed. An open rebellion in March by the sailors of Kronstadt naval base, who previously had been strong supporters of the Bolsheviks, further emphasized the growing discontent in Russia. Lenin and his colleagues maintained control of the country by force, but they felt vulnerable to the same sort of revolutionary upheaval that had brought them to power. *(Kronstadt rebellion, box, p. 40)*

In this atmosphere, Lenin proclaimed the New Economic Policy as a way to ease the nation's financial woes. The NEP, launched in March 1921, was a dose of free enterprise, designed to rebuild the Russian economy after years of revolution, war, and famine by replacing coercion with market incentives. In announcing it, Lenin said, "We are in a condition of such poverty, ruin, and exhaustion of the productive powers of the workers and the peasants, that everything must be set aside to increase production."

Under the NEP, compulsory surrender of agricultural produce was replaced by a tax, leaving farmers free to sell their surplus on the open market. Peasants also were allowed to lease land and hire farm laborers. In the cities, control of small factories reverted to private owners, and individuals were allowed to engage in retail trade. The government, meanwhile, tried to induce foreign companies to invest in the country's industrialization process. Despite the NEP's permissiveness, Lenin was careful to maintain party control of the country's economic "commanding heights": heavy industry, transportation, foreign trade, wholesale commerce, and banking.

The NEP succeeded in stabilizing the country and revitalizing the economy. By 1928 production in

Lenin and Stalin confer in 1922.

most industries had recovered to pre-World War I levels. This revitalization was accompanied by an increase in prosperous peasants and small business owners.

The Bolsheviks and World Revolution

The men who led the Russian Revolution considered themselves to be the vanguard of an international socialist movement that would sweep through the rest of the industrialized world. George Vernadsky noted in his *History of Russia* that

Uprisings did actually occur in a few nations, but their achievements were short-lived: the Communist government of Bela Kun in Hungary lasted from March 21 until August 1, 1919, and a Bavarian Soviet government, founded on April 7, 1919, held power for an even shorter period. Revolutions were also planned for England and the United States, though in these countries the "plans" could hardly have been more than vague hopes.

In March 1919 the Soviet leadership had brought together the First Congress of the Third International in Moscow, a meeting of communist parties and groups from the international community. The organization of these parties and groups, which was dominated by the Russians, became known as the "Comintern." The goal of the Comintern was "the overthrow of capitalism, the establishment of the dictatorship of the proletariat and of the International Soviet Republic for the complete abolition of classes, and the realization of socialism."

Despite the Comintern's encouragement of international revolution and its dissemination of communist propaganda, it was clear to the Soviet leaders by 1922 that widespread revolution in the capitalist states was not likely to occur. Moscow therefore sought recognition from and commercial relations with the capitalist world as a means of establishing Soviet legitimacy and improving the Soviet economy.

On April 16, 1922, the Soviet Union and Germany signed the Treaty of Rapallo establishing commercial ties. In 1924 diplomatic recognition was extended to the Soviet state by several nations—Great Britain, France, China, Mexico, Greece, Austria, Denmark, Sweden, Norway, and Italy. The United States, however, did not offer diplomatic recognition to the Soviet regime until November 1933.

The Soviets established relations with their southern and eastern neighbors as well, negotiating treaties with Afghanistan, Persia, and Turkey. In China, the Soviets urged the local Communists to support Chiang Kai-shek's nationalist forces. Once Chiang had the upper hand, however, he purged the Chinese Communists and sent the Russian advisers back to Moscow.

Lenin's Death

Unlike his successors, Lenin never held the official title of party leader, governing instead from the post of chairman of the Council of People's Commissars. Nevertheless, from 1917 to 1922 he was the unchallenged head of the Communist party and the Soviet state.

On May 26, 1922, Lenin suffered a paralytic stroke. He partially recovered and resumed some of his duties, but he had a second stroke on December 16 that greatly reduced his ability to function as the leader of his nation and party. He suffered a third and final stroke on March 9, 1923. As Lenin deteriorated he remained the nation's revered figurehead, but Joseph Stalin, Leon Trotsky, and other leading Bolsheviks took over the tasks of running the country.

After Lenin's death on January 21, 1924, the state honored him by building a mausoleum in Red Square to house his embalmed remains and by changing the name of the former Russian capital from Petrograd to Leningrad. His death opened a succession battle that would take several years to settle.

CHAPTER 2

STALIN ERA

When Lenin died no rules existed on how his successor as preeminent leader of the Soviet Union should be chosen. Lenin had hoped that his colleagues would forswear power struggles and institute a system of collective rule, but he realized that this was unlikely to happen. Strokes that impaired his health in 1922 already had precipitated competition for power among his lieutenants, especially Leon Trotsky and Joseph Stalin. In letters unsealed after Lenin's death in 1924, he cautioned the party against factionalism and recommended that Stalin be removed as general secretary of the party. Lenin's warnings, however, failed to prevent a power struggle or block the accumulation of power in Stalin's hands. *(Lenin's "Testament," box, p. 44)*

Trotsky had been Lenin's right-hand man during the revolution and had organized the victorious Red Army in the civil war. Trotsky, however, also had clashed bitterly with Lenin at times and was a Jew—two factors that became weapons against him. In fact, Stalin alone among the contenders for power had never had a major public conflict with Lenin. Stalin also occupied the strongest institutional position of any of the contenders for power. He had been named general secretary in 1922 and from this position had built a power base as he ran the daily affairs of the party. Stalin's development of innumerable contacts in the non-Russian republics during his tenure as commissar for nationalities also contributed to his power.

Grigory Zinoviev and Lev Kamenev, the influential party leaders in Petrograd and Moscow, respectively, were the other top Bolsheviks in contention for party leadership after Lenin died. Both had

clashed with Lenin but retained their standing in the party. Lenin had mentioned one other man, Nikolai Bukharin, as a possible successor. Bukharin, one of the party's leading theoreticians and the editor of *Pravda,* however, was never seriously considered by the other leaders.

To fill the vacuum after Lenin's death, Stalin, Zinoviev, and Kamenev, all members of the Politburo, formed a triumvirate, although Stalin was clearly the most powerful of the three. This group occupied the political center and was challenged by groups on the left and right. The "left" faction was led by Leon Trotsky, who charged that the New Economic Policy (NEP), which was launched in 1921, was a retreat from socialism because it allowed limited free enterprise and foreign investment. Trotsky also maintained that a socialist society could not be constructed in the Soviet Union unless socialist revolutions occurred in other countries that would provide each other with economic and political support. The "right" faction, led by Bukharin, supported the NEP as a way to gain the trust of the peasantry and achieve economic recovery. Bukharin also asserted that socialism could be achieved in the Soviet Union without further international revolution. He urged cooperation with noncommunist groups abroad, including western European Social Democratic parties. In the center Stalin and his followers backed the NEP as a repugnant but necessary tool to further socialism in the Soviet Union. They also adopted the middle position that while socialism could be built in the Soviet Union alone, its final victory could not be achieved without socialist revolutions in foreign countries.

Lenin's "Testament"

In December 1922 and January 1923, Lenin wrote to the Twelfth Soviet Party Congress scheduled to be held in the spring. In his letters the ailing father of the Bolshevik Revolution proposed organizational changes (including an expansion of the Central Committee from fifty to one hundred members) to preserve a unified collective leadership, and he offered judgments of his potential successors. The letters, particularly two written on December 24 and January 4, became known as his "Testament."

In the December 24 letter he warned against a split in the party and cited the strengths and weaknesses of the prospective candidates for succession without making clear who he favored to hold the top leadership posts. He wrote that Joseph Stalin "has boundless power . . . and I am not sure whether he will always be capable of using that power with sufficient caution." The January 4 letter, however, recommended that Stalin be removed as general secretary of the Communist party. Lenin wrote:

Stalin is too coarse, and this fault, though quite tolerable in relations among us communists, becomes intolerable in the office of General Secretary. Therefore I suggest to the comrades that they think of a way of transferring Stalin from this position and assigning another man to it who differs from Comrade Stalin only in one superiority: more tolerant, more loyal, more polite and more considerate of his comrades, less capricious, and so on.

The letters, however, were not read at the congress. Lenin had sealed them and stipulated that only he could open them unless he had died, in which case only his wife, Nadezhda Krupskaya, could open them. During the congress, Lenin remained alive but too ill to function—a situation he had not anticipated when he gave instructions for disposition of the letters. Consequently, the delegates to the congress did not learn of Lenin's objections to Stalin.

Lenin died in January 1924. The following May, Krupskaya carried out her husband's wishes and gave the letters to the Central Committee so that they could be read by the delegates to the upcoming Thirteenth Soviet Party Congress. Party leaders thus learned of Lenin's appraisal of Stalin, and the general secretary's removal became a topic of discussion among the delegates. By this time, however, Stalin had further solidified his position as party leader by cultivating supporters throughout the party. With the aid of his powerful allies, Grigory Zinoviev and Lev Kamenev, he was able to minimize the damage of Lenin's criticism and hold on to power.

In the power struggle of the 1920s, Stalin, a master of the political switch, maneuvered to extend his personal control over the party membership and eliminate his rivals. Stalin used his alliance with Zinoviev and Kamenev to weaken the position of Trotsky and other powerful party leaders on the left. In 1926 Zinoviev and Kamenev, who long had been wary of Stalin's growing power, formed an anti-Stalin alliance with Trotsky. Stalin countered by joining with the right to discredit Zinoviev and Kamenev. Finally, when the left was defeated, Stalin attacked Bukharin and the right wing. By 1927 Stalin had achieved clear preeminence and had engineered the expulsion of most of his rivals from the party. In 1929, after Trotsky was banished from the Soviet Union, Stalin's power over the country was unchallenged.

Although Lenin and other early Soviet leaders had endorsed terror as a political weapon and believed that an iron-fisted rule was necessary for the establishment and development of the Soviet state, Stalin exercized power with a ruthlessness that far surpassed that of his fellow Bolsheviks. He established dictatorial authority over every aspect of Soviet society and instituted policies that resulted in the execution or imprisonment of millions of Soviet citizens.

In foreign affairs, the Stalin era saw the German invasion of the Soviet Union during World War II, the eventual defeat of Germany and Japan by the Soviet-British-American alliance, the creation of Soviet satellites in Eastern Europe after the war, and the onset of hostile relations between the Soviet Union and its former allies in the West.

Prewar Foreign Policy

The foreign policy trend begun after the civil war—developing Soviet contacts with foreign governments—continued under Stalin's one-man rule. Originally intended to lend legitimacy to the regime, this policy in the late 1920s and 1930s was designed to preserve peace and enhance Soviet security while Moscow achieved an economic and social transformation of the Soviet Union.

In 1928 Stalin had fully endorsed Bukharin's concept of "socialism in one country." By this Bukharin and Stalin meant that world revolution was not so essential to the construction of socialism in Russia as Lenin and many other Bolshevik leaders had believed. Stalin and Bukharin maintained that the Soviet Union could build a socialist society regardless of the progress of the revolutionary movement elsewhere. Moreover, because Stalin saw the Soviet Union as surrounded by capitalist enemies that would exploit opportunities to overthrow the Soviet Communist regime, resources had to be devoted to strengthening the Soviet Union instead of financing revolutionary movements abroad. The theory of "socialism in one country" provided a theoretical basis for expanding relations with capitalist countries, which no longer were regarded as being threatened by imminent revolution.

Nevertheless, this did not mean that Stalin and his colleagues had abandoned the concept of world revolution or Soviet support for it. The Comintern, established in 1919 to foment world revolution, continued to receive the enthusiastic backing of the Soviet Union until 1943, when Stalin dissolved it as a concession to his World War II allies, the United States and Great Britain.

Soviet foreign policy during the 1920s and 1930s, therefore, was full of contradictions. Moscow expanded its contacts with capitalist nations, even while Soviet leaders remained wary of an anti-Soviet capitalist alliance and worked for the eventual demise of the capitalist structure. In *Expansion and Coexistence,* Adam B. Ulam noted an additional contradiction in the Soviets' position: By 1933 the increasing instability in the capitalist world, which

Moscow had hoped would lead to an era of revolution, threatened Soviet security.

The historical irony of the situation facing Soviet policymakers at the end of 1933 consisted in the fact that the fulfillment of many long-standing Soviet hopes in international politics promised not successes but a terrible danger to the Soviet Union. The League of Nations and the Versailles settlement had been the object of unremitting Soviet propaganda attacks ever since 1919. Now the League had been rendered even more ineffective since Japan and Germany were turning their backs on it. The Versailles settlement was crumbling, with Germany openly rearming and advancing far-reaching claims in other directions. The great crisis of the world economy had come to pass, but its political consequences were seen in the growth and successes of fascist movements rather than communist ones. The rising level of international tension threatened new wars, but the targets of Japanese and German militarism might become not the other capitalist powers but the Soviet Union. Seldom has an ideology played a comparable trick on its devotees as did communism in 1933: all the major desiderata of its philosophy of international relations were fulfilled, and their sum total promised disaster for the Soviet Union.

In the Far East, Japan embarked on a program of expansion, occupying southern Manchuria in 1929. China could do little more than protest to the powerless League of Nations. Emboldened, the Japanese in 1932 seized northern Manchuria, threatening the Soviet-controlled Chinese Eastern Railway. Moscow, preoccupied with collectivization and industrialization, had no desire for a war with the Japanese and, in 1935, sold the railroad to the Tokyo-controlled Manchurian government. To prevent Japanese expansion into Mongolia and Siberia, however, the Soviets patched up their differences with China's nationalist leader, Chiang Kai-shek, and supplied his armies with materiel and advisers. Soviet-Japanese tensions continued to build through the 1930s, resulting in clashes in 1938 and 1939 on the Manchurian-Mongolian border.

In Europe, the Soviet Union faced the prospect of a rearmed Germany led by a virulently anticommunist Nazi dictator, Adolf Hitler, who publicly proclaimed his desire to expand German borders. To meet the threat Stalin sought improved

Joseph Stalin and German foreign minister Joachim von Ribbentrop look on as Soviet foreign minister Viacheslav Molotov signs the nonaggression pact in August 1939.

relations with the West and his eastern European neighbors. Responding to growing German and Japanese power, the United States recognized the Soviet Union in 1933. In 1934 the Soviet Union joined the League of Nations. The following year, Moscow concluded military alliances with France and Czechoslovakia. The Soviets' fears of fascist animosity were confirmed in November 1936 when Germany and Japan signed an "Anti-Comintern Pact" that stated the signatories' opposition to international communism. Italy and Spain signed the pact in 1937 and 1939, respectively.

Moscow's alliance with Czechoslovakia required the Soviet Union to aid the Czechs, provided France also offered assistance. French acquiescence in Hitler's seizure of the Sudetenland, a section of Czechoslovakia densely populated by Germans, relieved the Soviets of any responsibility to defend their Czech allies. However, the French and British capitulation to Hitler—the Soviets had not been invited to participate at the September 1938 Munich conference that sealed Czechoslovakia's fate—

made Stalin and his colleagues question the value of the Soviet-French alliance. Stalin had felt similar disillusionment with the West in 1936, when he had tried unsuccessfully to obtain Western cooperation in aiding the Republican forces in Spain against the fascists, who were supported by Germany and Italy.

After appeasing German ambitions in Czechoslovakia, Great Britain and France were determined to take a stand against potential Nazi aggression toward Poland. The two Western allies guaranteed Polish independence but excluded the Soviet Union from participating in their declaration of support for Poland. During 1939 the Soviets continued negotiations with Great Britain and France on forming a united front against Hitler, but Stalin let it be known that he was open to the possibility of concluding an agreement of mutual neutrality with Germany.

On August 23, 1939, while Hitler's armies secretly prepared to invade Poland, Germany and the Soviet Union signed a ten-year nonaggression pact—sometimes called the Molotov-Ribbentrop

Pact after the Soviet and German foreign ministers who negotiated it. The agreement included a promise that each partner would remain neutral toward the other and a secret protocol that carved up Poland between them and designated spheres of influence in the Baltic region.

In signing the pact, the Soviet leadership almost certainly understood that Hitler would invade Poland. Stalin may have calculated, however, that the agreement was the only way to avoid war between his nation and Nazi Germany. He also may have believed that the pact would allow the Soviet Union to sit on the sidelines while Germany and the Western allies waged a devastating war that would leave the Soviet Union as the dominant power in Europe. In case Germany did have ambitions to attack the Soviet Union, the pact at least would provide Stalin time to bolster Soviet defenses. Finally, the agreement offered the obvious dividend of giving the Soviets control of lands in eastern Poland and securing German acquiescence for Soviet domination of Finland and the Baltic region.

The treaty assured Hitler and his generals that they could invade Poland without fear that the Soviet Union would declare war. German armies launched a blitzkrieg into Poland on September 1, prompting Great Britain and France to declare war on Germany September 3. Within three weeks the German army had captured Warsaw. The Soviet Army, meanwhile, occupied eastern Poland.

The Soviet Union remained neutral during 1940 and early 1941, a period that saw virtually all of Europe, including France, come under the occupation of Germany and its allies. Great Britain struggled for survival as the only major power that continued to oppose Nazi Germany.

Meanwhile Moscow pursued its ambitions in the Baltic region. Soviet forces invaded Finland in November 1939. To the surprise of the Soviets and most Western observers the Finnish army fought effectively against the Soviet invaders. The Soviets did not subdue their small neighbor until March 1940. The Red Army's poor showing in Finland may have helped convince German generals that the Soviet Union could be defeated quickly. In the summer of 1940 Soviet forces occupied the independent Baltic states of Latvia, Lithuania, and Estonia with little resistance. Moscow set up puppet governments that facilitated the annexation of these nations into the Soviet Union in August.

Domestic Policy

Stalin's reign in the years leading up to World War II was dominated by three programs—forced collectivization of agriculture, rapid industrialization of the economy, and the great purges. This period was a dark time in Soviet history when millions of people were imprisoned in labor camps or killed in pursuit of greater social discipline, the achievement of a socialist economy, and the elimination of all real or imagined opponents of Stalin's totalitarian rule.

During the 1920s the successes of the NEP raised fears among the Communist party leadership that private enterprise was gaining a foothold in Soviet society. In addition, Soviet leaders believed that the development of heavy industry had received inadequate attention and resources under the NEP. In response, the government in 1928 announced the First Five-Year Plan, calling for industrial projects to be financed by the production of agricultural collectives. The plan represented the first attempt by a society to use large-scale, centralized planning and social ownership of the means of production as a basis for national economic advancement.

Collectivization

During the 1920s agricultural production had increased at a rate too slow to supply the rapidly growing needs of the Soviet Union. By encouraging peasants to produce more, the NEP had helped Soviet agricultural production to recover to pre-World War I levels by 1925. Yet Soviet agriculture remained inefficient because the land was broken into millions of small, poorly equipped farms. Production also was held below its potential by peasant dissatisfaction with the artificially low prices at which the state offered to buy surplus grain. It appeared that if Moscow wanted further increases in production it would have to offer the peasants greater material incentives. Devoting more resources to agricultural production, however, would deprive the industrial sector of the economy of the funds required for the rapid advancement envisioned by Stalin and many of his colleagues. The Soviet leadership, therefore, hoped to increase production at a low cost by collectivizing peasants into larger, more efficient farms under state control that could better take advantage of emerging technology.

Collectivization, however, was not popular in the countryside, especially among the *kulaks,* the wealthier peasants who had taken advantage of conditions under the NEP to increase their land holdings and incomes. The kulaks, who had been targets of oppression during the period of War Communism, staunchly opposed collectivization, high taxes, and any government interference in their affairs. To break the kulaks, Moscow enlisted the support of the poorest peasants, who were promised a share of the kulaks' land and assets once agriculture was collectivized. This led to violence in the countryside between rich and poor peasants.

In December 1929 Stalin declared a new policy of "eliminating the kulaks as a class." Party workers, police, and army units were sent into rural areas to aid in the fight against the kulaks, but this campaign quickly turned into a broader push toward collectivization that engulfed the entire peasantry. Peasants who fought back (and many who did not) were shot, sent to labor camps, or forced to resettle in remote areas. As many as five million peasants were sent to Siberia during the drive for collectivization.

The chaos in the countryside, however, was too much even for Stalin. On March 2, 1930, he published an article in *Pravda* entitled "Dizziness with Success," in which he denounced the excesses of collectivization and blamed them on overzealous local party officials. The article temporarily stalled the collectivization drive, but later in the year it began anew. By 1932 more than 60 percent of peasant households had been collectivized, and by 1938 the number exceeded 90 percent.

Many peasants had resisted collectivization by destroying their assets before they could be confiscated for collective farms. They butchered and ate their livestock, burned their crops, and broke their farm implements. By 1934 Soviet livestock had been reduced to less than half the number that existed in 1928. The lack of implements and draft animals and the chaos in rural society caused agricultural production to decline sharply. This decline created a devastating famine centered in the Ukraine, the northern Caucasus, and parts of Russia. The government denied the existence of the famine and stood by while an estimated five million to ten million peasants died.

Industrialization

In tandem with the radical reconstruction of agriculture, Stalin sought to greatly expand the Soviet Union's industrial capacity. This effort was outlined in the first three five-year plans. These plans were highly ambitious blueprints of economic activity that devoted a large percentage of resources to industrial investment. They were formulated by Gosplan, the Soviet state planning commission, under the supervision of Stalin and other Soviet leaders. The First Five-Year Plan was launched in 1928 and was declared completed December 31, 1932, nine months ahead of schedule. The second ran from 1932 to 1937, and the third ran from 1937 until it was interrupted in 1941 by the German invasion of the Soviet Union.

By concentrating Soviet resources on the development of heavy industry, Stalin intended to end his nation's economic backwardness and reduce its military vulnerability. The success of his agricultural program also depended on industrialization, since boosting agricultural productivity would require large-scale production of mechanized farm implements and the gasoline to run them. He also hoped rapid industrialization would achieve dramatic successes that would demonstrate to the world the superiority of socialism.

The First Five-Year Plan did not produce economic miracles, but it was a partial success. Industrial growth rates averaged a strong 12 percent annually. Industries created or greatly expanded during this period included machine building, electric power, automobiles, chemicals, agricultural machines, and aviation. Despite the high growth rates, the output of many key products, including iron, steel, coal, and grain, failed to reach their targets. In addition, the plan was frequently out of balance. For example, the production of certain raw materials could not keep up with some industries, and often the lack of technicians needed to repair or install equipment slowed the pace of whole enterprises.

The second and third five-year plans continued the push toward expansion of heavy industry, but they lowered output targets slightly and put more emphasis on the qualitative improvement of goods. Like the First Five-Year Plan, they failed to achieve many of the optimistic goals set by the planners, while dramatically advancing Soviet industry beyond where it had been. The Soviets also greatly expanded their production of electricity and improved the national infrastructure by building new roads, bridges, and rail lines. In the thirteen years of the "era of five-year plans" the Soviet Union succeeded in catching up to the industrialized capitalist nations in most areas of industry. This progress was crucial to the Soviet Union's survival in World War II.

Nevertheless, rapid industrialization was accomplished at great cost to the Soviet people. Most consumer goods were scarce, and many products were rationed. Housing, sanitation, and water projects also received inadequate attention to meet the nation's growing needs during the era of five-year plans. These problems were made particularly acute by the growth of the Soviet urban population. In 1926 only 18 percent of Soviet citizens lived in the cities. By 1940 this figure had risen to 33 percent, as peasants were recruited or forced to take jobs in industry.

While the peasants in the countryside were enduring forced collectivization, workers in the cities lost their freedom to choose their jobs and faced miserable and often dangerous working conditions. Stalin attempted to motivate workers by publicizing the exploits of Stakhanovites, workers with incredibly high outputs who got their name from a coal miner who set production records. The production levels of Stakhanovites in every industry increased the expectations of factory managers, planners, and Soviet leaders, who set higher production targets for all workers. Under this system, many average laborers were punished for not meeting their quotas. Soviet workers had little chance to improve their lot. They had been deprived of the right to strike, and their trade unions were not allowed to challenge industry managers.

To increase industrial production, Stalin also provided economic rewards and incentives to party leaders, bureaucrats, skilled laborers, and factory managers. Citizens with special talents, such as athletes, musicians, writers, and artists, also were rewarded. Stalin thus subverted the old Bolshevik notion that all Soviet citizens should receive equal economic and social benefits. He created an elite class that owed its success to the Soviet state and the Communist party, and therefore could be counted on to support the regime's programs.

The Purges

While his government was extending its control over the Soviet economy and the lives of Soviet citizens, Stalin moved against his political enemies, real and imagined. The purge of the Communist party began in the late 1920s and early 1930s with several trials of groups of minor officials who were accused of sabotage, counterrevolutionary activities, and plotting with foreign agents. These trials were accompanied by partywide purges designed to expel party members who were inefficient in their work or unenthusiastic about party policies.

These purges, however, were merely a preliminary to the bloodbath that was to follow. On December 1, 1934, Sergei Kirov, the party leader in Leningrad, was assassinated. Kirov's murder was used by Stalin as a pretext for mass arrests and executions that marked the beginning of what became known as the "Great Purge." During the rest of the decade, an estimated eight million citizens were arrested on suspicion of disloyalty to the state and other political charges. Most of those arrested were sent to labor camps. *(Secret police, box, p. 50)*

The main events of the purge era were the so-

Secret Police under Stalin: Feared Tool of Repression

The Bolsheviks who seized power in November 1917 declared themselves eager to erase all remnants of the tsarist era. But they retained one leftover from the monarchy—the secret police. The early Bolshevik secret police organs, like the tsar's police, ruthlessly suppressed dissent to ensure that the regime remained in power. The use of terror was legitimized by Lenin, who wrote in a letter on the Soviet criminal code: "The law should not abolish terror. . . . The paragraph on terror should be formulated as widely as possible, since only revolutionary consciousness of justice and revolutionary conscience can determine the conditions of its application in practice."

Dzerzhinsky and the Cheka

Feliks Dzerzhinsky, the first head of the Soviet security police, was born in Vilnius (now in Lithuania) in 1877. The son of Polish aristocracy, he became a terrorist and revolutionary at an early age. He established his revolutionary credentials by leading a series of unsuccessful raids against the tsar's security forces, the Okhrana. He was arrested for the first time in 1897, two months before he turned twenty, for these raids and for distributing pamphlets demanding release of political prisoners. Sentenced to five years' hard labor in Siberia, he escaped before two years had passed.

As William Corson and Robert Crowley describe in *The New KGB: Engine of Soviet Power,* Dzerzhinsky became a "convict celebrity" by the time he was recaptured. He escaped several more times from the Okhrana, until his final release before the 1917 revolution. In 1906, during one period of freedom, he had a fateful meeting in Stockholm with two other revolutionaries—Lenin and Stalin. Dzerzhinsky lived to serve both men as head of the Soviet security service. It was Dzerzhinsky, in fact, who urged the Bolsheviks to establish the "Extraordinary Commission to Combat Counterrevolution, Sabotage, and Speculation." The Bolsheviks' Council of People's Commissars established the security service on December 20, 1917, just six weeks after taking over the state. Its acronym, VChK, was soon shortened to ChK, or "Cheka," which means "linchpin" in Russian. Dzerzhinsky cele-

brated the Cheka's birth with two Americans, Louise Bryant and John Reed.

To combat tsarists and rival revolutionary factions, the Bolsheviks gave the Cheka immense powers. During the Russian civil war the Chekists were free to arrest, imprison, torture, and execute those they judged to be enemies of the revolution. By 1921 the Cheka was thirty thousand strong, had its own armed force, was responsible for protecting Soviet borders and maintaining domestic peace, and had begun to set up an international spy network.

After the civil war ended, Lenin and his colleagues wished to create a less repressive security service that would focus its efforts on counterrevolution and espionage. Toward this end the Cheka was replaced February 7, 1922, by the Main Political Administration (GPU), part of the People's Commissariat of Internal Affairs (NKVD). Unlike the Cheka, the GPU was not granted the legal authority to judge and punish those it arrested. Dzerzhinsky headed the GPU, retaining his place as security chief. In 1924 Stalin also gave him responsibility for the Soviet economic program. Dzerzhinsky became a candidate member of the Politburo and backed Stalin in his succession fight with Trotsky.

Stalin and the NKVD

Joseph Stalin, building on Lenin's willingness to use terror, oversaw the most brutal application of secret police activity in Soviet history. In 1990, the Soviet government released a report that said 786,098 people were shot by state authorities between 1930 and 1953. The total did not include millions of people who died in labor camps, starved during artificial famines, or were executed by other means.

During the 1930s Politburo members and common Soviet citizens alike feared a visit from the secret police that could end in arrest, torture, internal exile, or execution. Many of the victims seemed to be chosen arbitrarily. The dictator's paranoid personality disposed him to order the arrest of individuals for slight provocations or suspicious behavior. Moreover, the general climate of terror and distrust and the existence of a huge police apparatus created conditions that inevitably led to widespread abuses. In *Russia's Failed Revolutions,* however, Adam B. Ulam asserts that terror should not be ascribed entirely to Stalin's derangement:

To look for an explanation of the terror of the 1930s in just Stalin's irrational characteristics is to postulate that he was entirely mad, an assumption that his ability to retain absolute power for twenty-five years renders quite absurd. ... It is more reasonable to assume that terror on such a scale was the product of a deliberate design. ... Terror was part of the educational campaign to convince the nation that all horrors which attended forced collectivization, such as the famine which claimed five million lives, that all the privations and sufferings consequent upon hurried industrialization resulted not from the government's policies, but from sabotage from the people's enemies. Terror, in brief, was necessary not only to make the people obey but, even more so, also to make them believe.

Dzerzhinsky died in 1926 and was succeeded by Viacheslav Menzhinsky, another Pole. During Menzhinsky's tenure the GPU adopted increasingly repressive techniques and oversaw the brutal drive to collectivize the peasantry. Menzhinsky, however, was frequently ill, and the day-to-day administration of the GPU was handled by his chief assistant, Genrikh Yagoda, a close ally of Stalin. In 1932 the GPU became a separate organization, the United State Political Administration (OGPU). Soon after, the OGPU was absorbed by the NKVD. When Menzhinsky died in office in 1934, he was replaced as head of the NKVD by Yagoda.

In *KGB: Inside the World's Largest Intelligence Organization,* Brian Freemantle asserts that Yagoda, a trained pharmacist, first developed the security service's facilities and research on "methods of extermination." Stalin apparently directed Yagoda to arrange the murder of Sergei Kirov, a potential rival of Stalin's. After Kirov's assassination in 1934, which Stalin passed off to the public as a conspiracy, Yagoda was charged with finding the culprits. Dozens of men were charged with the crime and executed. The killing of Kirov's "murderers" marked the opening of the Stalinist purges. Yagoda eventually became a victim. He was dismissed in 1936, charged with "abusing his office," and shot in 1938.

Yagoda's successor, Nikolai Yezhov, directed the bloodiest phase of the Great Purge. While publicly charged with curbing the NKVD's "excesses," he reigned over the greatest period of terror in Soviet history. The period bears his name—the *Yezhovshchina*. Most top-ranking Soviet political and military leaders were killed, and millions of citizens were sent to labor camps in Siberia. Less than five feet tall, Yezhov became known as the "bloody dwarf." Accounts of his fate differ. Stalin removed him from office in 1938. Freemantle claims he was shot. Others say he was first sent to a mental hospital where he either committed suicide or was murdered.

Beria Era

Yezhov was succeeded by Lavrenty Beria, an ally of Stalin and a fellow Georgian. An early Chekist, he entered intelligence work in 1921. During the late 1920s he developed a notorious reputation while serving in the GPU in Georgia. Stalin appointed him party leader in Transcaucasia in 1931 despite the objections of local officials. In 1938 Stalin named Beria to replace Yezhov as head of the NKVD. Soviet dissident historian Roy Medvedev wrote in *Let History Judge:*

Letters and reports about Beria's crimes and moral corruption reached Stalin from many Party members in Transcaucasia. But Stalin, for all his suspiciousness, favored Beria, and put the punitive organs of the entire country under a man who had long ago lost any trace of conscience or honor.

However, in 1938-1939 not many people knew Beria for what he really was, so the replacement of Ezhov [Yezhov] by Beria was received as a hopeful sign. And in fact, right after Ezhov's replacement, mass repression was discontinued for a while. Hundreds of thousands of cases then being prepared by the NKVD were temporarily put aside. A special commission was even appointed to investigate NKVD activity. ... Soon Beria and his men resumed the repression. Admittedly, the mass scale of 1937-38 was not approached. But Stalin had begun to use terror, and he could not stop; arrests and shooting accompanied him to the last days of his life.

Yezhov had terrorized his NKVD officers and decimated their ranks. Beria tempered the internal purges, though he did not stop them, and reinitiated intelligence work abroad. During World War II Be-
Continued

ria's secret police were assigned additional responsibilities, including deportation and destruction of ethnic groups living in the Soviet Union, and guarding
the front-line Russian troops to prevent retreat and
desertion. Beria became a candidate Politburo member in 1939, deputy premier in charge of security in
1941, and a full Politburo member in 1946.

By the time Stalin died in 1953, Beria controlled
Soviet espionage activities, the labor camps, the
militia, and more than a quarter-million troops. A
candidate to succeed Stalin until other Politburo
members turned on him, Beria was convicted of
"criminal antiparty and antistate activities" and shot
in 1953. Over the next three years at least eighteen of
his secret police associates suffered a similar fate.

During Beria's tenure, the security service underwent additional name changes. The People's Commissariat of State Security (NKGB) was established

in February 1941 but was dismantled that June, after
the German invasion. It was reestablished in April
1943, and in 1946 it became the Ministry of State
Security (MGB).

An associate of Beria, Viktor Abakumov, was
named head of the MGB. He was succeeded by
Semen Ignatiev in 1951. Beria replaced Ignatiev
when the MGB and Ministry of Internal Affairs
(MVD) merged in 1953. The Committee for State
Security (KGB) was established in March 1954.

After Beria's execution, the security organs became directly responsible to the Politburo. The Communist party wished to ensure that its security organs
would not be used against members of the regime in
the future. The party's efforts to control the KGB
were largely successful. It functioned as the regime's
instrument of repression against dissidents, spies, and
other enemies of the party.

---

called "show trials" held to disgrace former high-
ranking government and party officials. The first
show trial, begun on August 19, 1936, resulted in
the conviction of sixteen Bolshevik leaders for treasonous activities. The defendants included Grigory
Zinoviev and Lev Kamenev, Stalin's former allies
on the Politburo. All sixteen were executed. The
accused were not given any rights to due process of
law, and confessions and testimony that implicated
other high-ranking officials were extracted by coercion and torture.

A second show trial was held in January 1937, at
which seventeen other Soviet leaders were found
guilty. In March 1938 a third show trial convicted
an additional twenty-one former leaders, including
Nikolai Bukharin. Of the fifty-four men tried in the
show trials, fifty received death sentences and were
executed.

The purge extended to every area of Soviet society. It was carried out by the People's Commissariat
of Internal Affairs (NKVD), the political police,
headed by Nikolai Yezhov. Yezhov himself disappeared in 1938 and was replaced by Lavrenty Beria.
The purge hit the military particularly hard. Three
of the five Soviet marshals, including Mikhail Tuk-

hachevsky, a Civil War hero, were removed, as well
as 13 of the army's 15 commanders, 57 of its 85
corps commanders, 110 of its 195 division commanders, and 70 percent of all officers holding the
rank of colonel or above.

The effects of the purge also were severe at the
top levels of government. Only 37 percent of the
members of the 1934 Central Committee survived
the purges. Among Lenin's original Politburo, only
Stalin and Leon Trotsky remained alive in 1939.
Trotsky, who had been exiled from the Soviet Union
in 1929, was assassinated in 1940 in Mexico, presumably on Stalin's orders.

Although there is no historical consensus about
what motivated Stalin to conduct the purges of the
1930s, many historians believe that the Soviet leader's paranoid personality disposed him to eliminate
anyone who conceivably could challenge his leadership or threaten his own safety. In addition Stalin
may have seen the purges as a way of providing
scapegoats for his own mistakes. As he disgraced
and killed his prominent Bolshevik rivals, Stalin
portrayed himself in the mass media as the infallible
protector of the communist movement and the Soviet people. He also oversaw the rewriting of Soviet

Nazi Invasion Plan

The German army may have been more successful in its 1941 campaign had Nazi leaders developed a plan to exploit the anti-Russian and anticommunist sentiments of the Soviet people. In some areas of the western Soviet Union, especially the non-Russian republics, the German armies were greeted initially as liberators. Many members of minority groups hoped that the Germans would break Moscow's hold on their regions and allow them to establish their own independent nations. Similarly, some Russian peasants hoped that the Germans would sanction the division of the fields, livestock, and assets of collective farms, thereby allowing them to fulfill their ambitions of farming their own land.

The Nazis, however, sure that their invasion force quickly would smash all resistance and intending not just to defeat the Soviet Union, but also to strip conquered areas of anything of value and eventually resettle them, largely ignored the grievances of Soviet minorities and peasants. More important, the Nazi assault and occupation were brutal.

Hitler had told his generals three months before the invasion that "The war against Russia will be such that it cannot be conducted in a knightly fashion. This struggle is one of ideologies and racial differences and will have to be conducted with unprecedented, unmerciful, and unrelenting harshness. . . . The commissars are the bearers of ideologies directly opposed to National Socialism [Nazism]. Therefore the commissars will be liquidated. German soldiers guilty of breaking international law . . . will be excused. Russia has not participated in the Hague Convention and therefore has no rights under it." Although some of Hitler's generals objected to this directive, which became known as the "Commissar Order," it was widely implemented.

The Germans' inhumane treatment of prisoners of war and the civilian population, their failure to address the political aspirations of Soviet minorities, and their exploitation of the peasantry hardened Soviet resistance against them and fueled a Soviet partisan movement behind German lines that harassed the occupiers. The lightly armed partisans attacked German supply columns and rear units with surprising effectiveness.

Meanwhile, Joseph Stalin shrewdly had chosen to rally the Soviet people behind the cause of defending Mother Russia and other Slavic lands—a cause dearer to the hearts of most Russians than the defense of the socialist movement and the Soviet state. The fight against Germany became known in the Soviet Union as the "Great Patriotic War."

---

history to further reinforce his preeminent position.

In 1936, under Stalin's direction, the government formulated a new constitution to replace the document adopted in 1924. It purported to guarantee civil rights for all Soviet citizens, including the rights to work, rest, vote, and receive medical care and education. It also declared that women and members of minority groups would enjoy equal rights. The constitution stipulated, however, that only one political organization, the Communist party, was allowed to exist.

World War II

On June 22, 1941, Hitler renounced the Soviet-German nonaggression pact signed less than two years before and turned the fury of his armies on the Soviet Union. Stalin reportedly was stunned by the German surprise attack, which pressed into the Soviet Union along a wide front. Instead of rallying the people against the invaders, he went into seclusion for several days. He also had ignored reports from Western and Soviet intelligence sources that indicated Germany might be preparing for a massive assault.

Hitler had held ambitions of invading Russia for many years. He believed its vast lands and abundant natural resources made it ideal for German colonization and exploitation. Moreover, the defeat of the Soviet Union would be a mortal blow to the ideology of communism, which the Nazis hated, and it would eliminate the only rival to German power on the European continent. *(Nazi invasion plan, box, p. 53)*

In 1941 Hitler and his generals temporarily had abandoned plans for invading Great Britain because of the difficulty that a large invasion force would have crossing the English Channel, particularly given the strength of the British navy. They also believed that Great Britain would be easier to deal with diplomatically and militarily if they first conquered the Soviet Union. Some Nazis even believed that since the British also opposed the international communist movement, they might be persuaded to join Germany in its fight against the Soviet Union.

With most of the continent securely under German domination, Hitler was able to concentrate 175 divisions along the Soviet border. German generals hoped that Soviet defenses would crumble under the pressure of a massive blitzkrieg. The German campaign was designed to defeat the Soviets before late 1941, when the Russian winter would bring mud, snows, and cold that favored the defenders. Many Western military observers privately estimated after the attack that the Germans' chances of defeating the Russians in a single campaign were good. The German high command was so confident of a swift victory that it made no preparations to supply its troops with cold-weather gear, assuming the fighting would not last into winter.

The Germans made rapid progress throughout the summer. They surrounded Leningrad (which would endure a two-and-a-half-year siege costing the lives of more than a million Russians), pushed Soviet armies back toward Moscow, and captured Kiev. Despite achieving these objectives, the German army could not defeat the Soviet Union before winter. The expanse of Soviet territory not only forced German tanks and troops to cover vast distances, it also stretched German supply lines to their limits. More important, the Soviet people rallied to the defense of their nation. Directed by Stalin, who had recovered from his initial indecisiveness, they managed to mobilize millions of troops, convert domestic industries to military production, and transfer many manufacturing plants to the safety of the remote Ural Mountain region. In addition an April 1941 nonaggression treaty with Japan enabled Mos-

cow to shift some army units protecting the Soviet Far East to the European theater after the attack. Nevertheless the German offensive reached the suburbs of Moscow before it stalled, and the Soviets prepared to move the seat of government east in the event the Germans captured the city. *(World War II, map, p. 55)*

In December 1941, with the German army effectively halted by the onset of winter, the Red Army launched its first major counteroffensive. Both sides suffered heavy casualties, but the Soviets dislodged the Germans from some of their advance positions and forced the Germans to concentrate on the fight at hand instead of preparations for a new spring offensive.

The Tide Turns

In the summer of 1942 Hitler ordered an attack designed to capture the industrial regions of the South and eventually the oil-rich Caucasus. By August the Germans had driven beyond the Don River to the city of Stalingrad (now Volgograd). The Soviets' determination to hold the city at all costs led to an epic battle that was the turning point in the war between Germany and the Soviet Union.

To reach Stalingrad, German forces had extended their already stretched supply lines to the limit. During the fall of 1942, as the Germans engaged the Soviets in a desperate house-to-house battle for the city, the Soviets reinforced units in the region and prepared to take advantage of the overextended German lines. On November 19, 1942, the Soviets launched a counterattack that broke through German lines to the north and south of Stalingrad. The two pincers of the Soviet attack quickly linked up west of the city, trapping Gen. Friedrich Paulus's Sixth Army—nearly three hundred thousand troops—in Stalingrad. Hitler, unwilling to accept his army's dire position, ordered Paulus to stay in Stalingrad and fight instead of attempting to break out of the encirclement. Totally surrounded, capable of receiving only minimal supplies by air drop, and still fighting against pockets of Soviet troops within Stalingrad, the German Sixth Army was doomed. The battle at Stalingrad lasted

THE EASTERN FRONT,
WORLD WAR II

0   100   200   300
Miles

▨ Western Soviet border, 1938

▦ Western Soviet border, June 1941

– – – Line of deepest German
advance, 1941–1942

Arctic Ocean

Petsamo

Murmansk

Archangel

SWEDEN

NORWAY

FINLAND

Petrozavodsk

HELSINKI

Leningrad

Tikhvin

UNION OF
SOVIET
SOCIALIST
REPUBLICS

ESTONIA

Novgorod

Pskov

Kalinin

★MOSCOW

LATVIA

Tula

Baltic Sea

LITHUANIA

Smolensk

Vilnius

EAST
PRUSSIA

Minsk

Orel

Voronezh

BERLIN ★

Kursk

GERMANY

WARSAW ★

POLAND

Kharkov

Stalingrad

Kiev

★ PRAGUE

Lvov

Caspian
Sea

CZECHOSLOVAKIA

Krivoy
Rog

Rostov

VIENNA ★

Mozdok

AUSTRIA

BUDAPEST ★

Kishinev

Sea of
Azov

HUNGARY

ROMANIA

Odessa

BESSARABIA

Novorossisk

Caucasus

Mountains

YUGOSLAVIA

BUCHAREST
★

Sevastopol

ITALY

Black Sea

BULGARIA

TURKEY

ALBANIA

GREECE

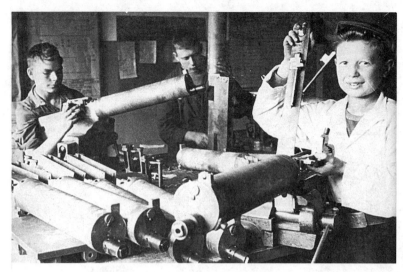

Russian youths assemble machine guns behind the front lines.

until February 1943, when the exhausted remnants of Paulus's force surrendered.

The defeat at Stalingrad placed the Germans on the defensive for the rest of the war. Although hundreds of thousands of Soviet soldiers were killed or wounded as the Red Army slowly drove back its enemy during 1943 and 1944, the Soviets were better able to replace their losses than the Germans. By January 1945 Soviet troops had recaptured all Soviet territory and secured most of Eastern Europe. Meanwhile American, British, and French forces had successfully invaded France and were driving on Germany from the West. The Germans could not withstand this two-front assault and were pushed relentlessly back toward Berlin. Great Britain and the United States agreed to allow Soviet troops to capture the German capital. In late April 1945 the Soviets carried the fight into Berlin, and Hitler committed suicide. On May 8 the Allies declared that German resistance had ended.

Grand Alliance

German and Japanese aggression led to the Grand Alliance among the Soviet Union, Great Britain, and the United States. However, the three allies did not enter the war simultaneously. Hitler's invasion of the Soviet Union in June 1941 ended Soviet neutrality and led to a practical alliance between Moscow and London. The United States joined the Allies after the December 7, 1941, Japanese attack on Pearl Harbor, Hawaii. During the war the United States and Great Britain shipped 11 billion dollars in aid to the Soviet Union to support the Soviet war effort.

Joseph Stalin, President Franklin D. Roosevelt of the United States, and Prime Minister Winston Churchill of Great Britain met twice to discuss alliance strategy—at Tehran in December 1943 and at Yalta in February 1945. For Stalin the most important issue at the first meeting was the establishment of a second front in France by Great Britain and the United States, a proposal he had urged on his allies at every opportunity after the German invasion of the Soviet Union. Although British and American troops had captured Sicily and invaded the Italian mainland earlier in 1943, Stalin believed that only a major landing in France could relieve pressure on the Red Army, which had born the brunt of the fighting against Germany since 1941. Stalin got his wish June 6, 1944, when Allied forces invaded Normandy on the French coast.

The Yalta summit dealt with the joint war effort and the administration of a liberated Europe. When the "Big Three" met at Yalta, Germany was almost defeated. Churchill and Roosevelt sought Soviet

British prime minister Winston Churchill, U.S. president Franklin D. Roosevelt, and Soviet premier Joseph Stalin meet at the 1945 summit conference at Yalta, in the Soviet Crimea.

participation in the war against Japan, an agreement on the occupation of Germany, and Soviet guarantees that the nations of Eastern Europe would be able to decide their own future through popular elections. Stalin agreed to a provisional plan for the partition of Germany into four occupation zones, with the Soviet Union, the United States, Great Britain, and France each administering one zone. Stalin also pledged to enter the war against Japan and gave his Western allies ambiguous assurances that elections would be held in Eastern Europe. In return, Stalin received Roosevelt and Churchill's reluctant approval for Soviet annexation of parts of eastern Poland, for which Poland was to be compensated with German lands to its west.

In the late 1940s, after the Soviet Union had set up communist dictatorships in Eastern Europe, Western politicians and scholars began criticizing the Yalta agreement and Roosevelt in particular for failing to ensure democratic governments in Eastern Europe. Stalin, however, was in a strong bargaining position at Yalta. He argued that the Soviet Union had fought Germany for three years before the allies established a second front in France and that the devastation inflicted upon the Soviet Union by

the Germans justified a dominant Soviet role in postwar Eastern Europe. Stalin's most potent card, however, was the simple fact that the Red Army occupied Eastern Europe. Unless the Western allies were willing to go to war against the Soviet Union to liberate the countries of the region, there was little they could do to force the Soviets to grant free elections. Roosevelt and Churchill therefore endorsed the vague agreement on Eastern Europe and hoped that the Soviets would wish to maintain good will with the West by allowing pluralistic governments in the region.

Alliance leaders met once more, at Potsdam in late July and early August 1945. This time the summit's participants were Stalin, President Harry S. Truman, and Churchill (halfway through the summit Churchill was replaced by a new prime minister, Clement R. Attlee). As the conference began, Truman was informed that the planned test of an atomic bomb in New Mexico had been successful. Armed with this powerful new weapon, Truman reasoned, the United States had less need to be conciliatory toward Moscow. The leaders discussed the Soviet Union's planned entry into the war against Japan and the arrangements for convening war crime trials in Europe. The Potsdam conference, however, focused on Germany. Truman informed Stalin that, contrary to understandings reached at Yalta, the Americans favored a plan under which German war reparations would be extracted by the Allies from their individual zones of occupation. Stalin objected that the Soviet zone in eastern Germany, which was largely agricultural, could not support reparations as large as the industrialized areas of western Germany. Truman's position on reparations also indicated to Stalin that the Americans were willing to exclude Moscow from participating in the administration of the three western zones. After the Potsdam conference the wartime Allies seemed to move inevitably toward the partition of Germany.

After the fighting in Europe ended in May 1945, the focus of the Allied war effort switched to the Far East. Although at Yalta Roosevelt had secured a promise from the Soviets to declare war on Japan once Germany was defeated, by the time of the Potsdam conference, U.S. leaders saw Soviet involvement against Japan as a mixed blessing. Truman and his advisers wanted to end the war quickly, in part to prevent the Soviet Union from being part of an Asian peace settlement. On August 6, two days before the Soviets were to enter the war, U.S. forces dropped an atomic bomb on Hiroshima with devastating effects. Three days later a second bomb was dropped on Nagasaki.

Truman claimed that the atomic attacks were necessary to bring an end to the war so American lives would not be lost in an invasion of Japan. However, historical evidence suggests that the Japanese, economically and militarily broken, might soon have surrendered even if the atomic bombs were not dropped. Documents and the memoirs of American policy makers indicate that in addition to securing a quick end to the war, Truman's decision to order the atomic attacks was motivated in part by a desire to demonstrate the power of the atomic bomb to the Soviets. The American leadership hoped that the bomb would make Stalin more compliant on other issues, including the fate of Eastern Europe.

As agreed, the Soviet Union entered the war

against Japan August 8 and its forces proceeded to occupy parts of Manchuria, the Kuril Islands, and the Japanese section of Sakhalin Island, prizes the Soviets had been promised at Yalta if they joined the fight against Japan. The Japanese formally surrendered to the United States September 2, 1945. The Soviets maintained control of the territories they captured, but the United States refused to accede to Moscow's post-Yalta demand that it have a role in the postwar administration of Japan.

Effects of the War

Estimates of the casualties suffered by the Soviet Union during World War II range as high as twenty million to twenty-five million. In addition to lives lost, the war caused widespread destruction. The Red Army practiced a scorched-earth policy during its retreats; the German forces followed similar practices when they quit Soviet territory. In *A History of Russia,* Nicholas Riasanovsky described the devastation:

Much of the Soviet Union became an utter wasteland. According to official figures—probably somewhat exaggerated as all such Soviet figures tend to be—Soviet material losses in the war included the total or partial destruction of 1,700 towns, 70,000 villages, 6,000,000 buildings, 84,000 schools, 43,000 libraries, 31,000 factories and 1,300 bridges. Also demolished were 98,000 kolkhozes [collective farms] and 1,876 sovkhozes [agricultural factories]. The Soviet economy lost 137,000 tractors and 49,000 combine-harvesters as well as 7,000,000 horses, 17,000,000 head of cattle, 20,000,000 hogs and 27,000,000 sheep and goats.

The war evoked a strong wave of nationalist feeling in Russia. Stalin came to be directly associated with the war effort, and he portrayed himself as leading the Red Army to victory over the invaders. As a result Stalin and the Communist party emerged from the war more powerful than ever.

Many Soviet experts in the West believe that World War II also profoundly affected Soviet foreign policy during the postwar era. According to this theory, the devastating effects of the war on the Soviet homeland disposed the Kremlin to adopt a conception of security that emphasized the achievement of Soviet military superiority and Soviet domination (or at least the neutralization) of contiguous states. The war also probably contributed to the Soviets' adoption of an offensive military doctrine designed to take any fight to enemy soil. Although other factors were involved in the Soviet Union's military buildup during the postwar era and its struggle to control Eastern Europe, it is likely that the experience of World War II did contribute to the push for these objectives.

Cold War

When World War II ended in Europe, the Red Army occupied Albania, Czechoslovakia, Poland, Yugoslavia, Bulgaria, Romania, and Hungary. By 1948 all these countries had established communist regimes (although a rift with the Soviets caused the Yugoslav Communists to adopt an independent course in 1948). East European governments were not governed directly by the Soviet Union. Instead, indigenous communists with close ties to Moscow took power. Soviet military might remained in the background as the ultimate guarantor of the new communist regimes in Eastern Europe. The Red Army also occupied eastern Germany and Austria. The Soviets in 1949 set up the communist-ruled German Democratic Republic (East Germany). In 1955 the Kremlin withdrew its troops from Austria in return for a pledge by the Austrian government to remain neutral.

The Soviet domination of Eastern Europe—in violation of Stalin's pledges at Yalta to allow free elections—was accomplished with relative ease. Although British and American leaders were alarmed by the rise of communist states in Eastern Europe, there was little they could do to convince or pressure the Soviets to allow free elections. For Moscow, there was no higher foreign policy priority after World War II than establishing Soviet control over Eastern Europe and ensuring that Germany would remain either weak or divided. The Soviets believed their intense suffering during the war at the hands of German invaders justified the creation of sympathetic communist governments on their borders that would provide a long-desired

buffer zone between the Soviet Union and the West.

The Soviet expansion of influence in Eastern Europe and elsewhere and disagreements over specific postwar issues such as German reparations and reconstruction, international custody of atomic weapons, and Poland's borders brought on an era of Allied-USSR animosity, the so-called Cold War. The question of who or what was responsible for the Cold War has been one of the most debated topics among scholars of postwar history. It is likely, however, that nothing could have prevented the Cold War given that the Soviet Union and the Western allies interpreted their interests so differently, espoused competing ideologies, saw each other correctly as the main threat to their security, and were rivals for influence and power in many parts of the world.

Even during the war the Soviet Union and the Western allies had never completely trusted each other. Although they fought a common enemy, they continued to be suspicious of each other's motives and philosophies. Many leaders in both the West and the Soviet Union regarded their ally as only slightly less malevolent than their common enemy.

There also were many differences over strategy between Moscow and the West, most notably Moscow's anger with what it perceived as unnecessary delays in the opening of a second front in France. In May 1942 Churchill had promised the Soviets in a memorandum that Great Britain was "making preparations for a landing on the continent in August or September 1942." However, in November the Allies landed forces in North Africa, intending eventually to attack Italy through Sicily. Instead of relieving the Soviets, the North African campaign actually may have made their task more difficult. Fewer than fifteen German divisions were occupied in North Africa, while Soviet troops faced nearly two hundred divisions. The commitment of Allied troops and supplies to North Africa negated the possibility of an Allied landing in France, thereby allowing the Nazis to send troops that had been stationed in France to the eastern front. Many Soviet leaders suspected Great Britain and the United States of intentionally holding back an invasion while the massive armies of Germany and the Soviet Union destroyed each other. Meanwhile Stalin insinuated that he might be open to a separate peace with Germany to pressure the Western allies to establish a second front and send larger amounts of war materiel to the Soviet Union.

Nevertheless, during the war the Soviet-British-American alliance endured. After the war, however, relations between the Western allies and the Soviet Union chilled rapidly. The Soviets refused to join the newly established United Nations Atomic Energy Commission and only reluctantly agreed to remove their forces from northern Iran after the United States issued veiled threats of military intervention. Churchill warned of the hazards of growing Soviet domination of Europe in a historic March 5, 1946, speech at Westminster College in Fulton, Missouri. In the speech, Churchill popularized the term "iron curtain," which he said had "descended across the continent."

Expansion and Containment

After the war Moscow's foreign policy appeared to be designed to consolidate its control over regions within its sphere of influence while using diplomatic, economic, subversive, and military means to make inroads into areas outside its sphere. The United States under President Truman initiated a policy of opposing Soviet expansion. As a result a contest of resources, ideologies, and wills developed between the two camps for influence in numerous nations around the world.

The Truman administration's views on Soviet behavior and its corresponding policy prescriptions were set forth in an article in the July 1947 issue of *Foreign Affairs*. Signed "X," the article was written by George F. Kennan, a State Department Soviet expert who became U.S. ambassador to Moscow in 1952. Kennan declared that "we are going to continue for a long time to find the Russians difficult to deal with" and argued that "the main element of any United States policy toward the Soviet Union must be that of a long-term, patient but firm and vigilant containment of Russian expansive tendencies." The term "containment" came to describe longstanding U.S. policy toward the Soviet Union.

Several months before Kennan's article appeared, President Truman and his advisers had taken action to block communist expansion in Greece and Turkey. He proposed March 12, 1947, that the United States assume responsibility for aiding the democratic governments in those countries from an impoverished Great Britain. At the time, the Greeks were engaged in a civil war that pitted government troops against Communist forces, and the Turks were facing mounting pressure from the Soviet Union. In proposing the aid plan, the president outlined to Congress what became known as the Truman Doctrine. He said:

I believe that it must be the policy of the United States to support free peoples who are resisting attempted subjugation by armed minorities or by outside pressures. ... The seeds of totalitarian regimes are nurtured by misery and want. ... The free peoples of the world look to us for support in maintaining their freedoms. If we falter in our leadership, we may endanger the peace of the world—and we shall surely endanger the welfare of this Nation.

Despite fears in Congress that direct U.S. aid would undercut the United Nations and worsen relations with the Soviet Union, a four hundred million dollar assistance program was approved. The Truman Doctrine had become U.S. policy.

To bolster European economies, the United States in June 1947 proposed the European Recovery Program, known as the Marshall Plan after its chief architect, Secretary of State George C. Marshall. The original plan included 17 billion dollars in grants and loans to rebuild industry and agriculture in war-torn Europe; aid totaled 10.25 billion dollars over three years. The purpose of this aid was not primarily humanitarian. The Truman administration sought to create strong democracies in Western Europe that would resist communism and become economic and security partners of the United States.

Although Marshall Plan assistance was offered to all European states, including the Soviet Union and its satellites, the United States attached conditions to the offer that made it impossible for Moscow to accept. Instead, the Soviet-bloc countries in October

1947 formed the Communist Information Bureau (Cominform), the successor to Comintern, the propaganda organization abolished in 1943. Dominated by Moscow, the Cominform was designed to orchestrate communist policy in Europe. Its early cohesion was damaged in 1948, when Marshal Josip Broz Tito, the Yugoslav leader, broke with the Soviet Union to follow a communist line independent of Moscow's direction.

Western opposition to the Soviet Union was consolidated by the April 4, 1949, signing of the North Atlantic Treaty, establishing a mutual defense pact among the United States and its Western allies: Belgium, Canada, Denmark, France, Great Britain, Iceland, Italy, Luxembourg, the Netherlands, Norway, and Portugal. In 1955 the Soviets would counter the Western alliance by establishing the Warsaw Pact, a Soviet-led alliance of Eastern European nations.

East-West tensions increased in June 1948 when the Soviets blocked land transport of Allied supplies into West Berlin, the Allied-administered section of the former German capital deep inside the Soviet zone in eastern Germany. Stalin hoped that the blockade would cause the West to abandon the city, or at least to make concessions on the political and economic status of the divided Germany. Instead, the Allies mounted an airlift to supply the estimated 2.5 million West Berliners under their jurisdiction, while the United States moved sixty nuclear-capable B-29 bombers to Europe. The tense situation threatened war, but the Soviets were unwilling to risk a confrontation with a nuclear-armed United States by attempting to stop the airlift. Thwarted, the Soviets ended the blockade in May 1949. The same month the Western Allies established the Federal Republic of Germany, with the seat of the new government in Bonn. The Soviets responded in October 1949 with the establishment of the German Democratic Republic in their occupation zone.

The previous month, on September 23, 1949, Moscow announced that its scientists had successfully exploded an atomic bomb. Although it would take the Soviets several years to develop a significant operational nuclear capability and it would not be until the 1960s that they achieved nuclear parity

with the United States, the end of the American nuclear monopoly increased the self-confidence of the Soviets, gave them a claim to the status of superpower, and contributed to the atmosphere of confrontation that existed between the two countries.

Also in September 1949, the victory of Chinese Communist forces, led by Mao Zedong, over the nationalist followers of Chiang Kai-shek seemed to confirm the fears of many Western leaders that Soviet-inspired communist subversion was a grave and pervasive international threat. In actuality, although Moscow had given moral support to Mao's forces, it had provided them with little material aid and had continued to recognize Chiang as the legitimate ruler of China during the civil war. There also were indications that Stalin saw Mao as a rival and was uncomfortable with the idea of a strong, unified China on the Soviet Union's southern border, even if it were led by a communist regime. Nevertheless, after Mao's victory, the Soviets hailed the creation of a communist state and signed a thirty-year Sino-Soviet mutual aid pact on February 14, 1950. The displays of affection between Chinese and Soviet leaders and their close cooperation on many issues greatly disturbed Western leaders, who feared the Sino-Soviet alliance was the beginning of a communist monolith that would challenge and threaten the West. The United States refused to recognize Communist China and instead established ties with the nationalist government established by Chiang on Formosa (now Taiwan).

Korean War

The Cold War turned hot in Korea in 1950. The Asian nation had been divided between occupying forces at the end of World War II, the Red Army in the North and U.S. forces in the South. As in Germany, reunification efforts failed and separate governments were established.

On June 24 (June 25 Korean time), 1950, the Soviet-backed Communist North Koreans attacked South Korea. The following day, President Truman, seeking to aid South Korea and discourage further communist aggression, called an emergency session of the UN Security Council to consider the Korean crisis. By coincidence the Soviets were boycotting the Security Council to protest the exclusion of Communist China from the United Nations. Consequently, their representative was not present to veto a resolution passed by the council condemning the invasion and asking UN members to "render every assistance" to South Korea. President Truman ordered U.S. troops into Korea June 27, the same day that the Security Council passed a second resolution specifically requesting military assistance from UN members to halt North Korean aggression.

The Soviet role in the invasion beyond supplying North Korea with its military equipment is unclear. Although the Soviets likely knew the attack would take place and perhaps hoped to reap benefits from it, it is not certain that they ordered, or even directed, the invasion. North Korean leader Kim Il-Sung had displayed aggressive intentions toward the South and was capable of acting on his own. Moreover, Moscow had reduced sharply the number of Soviet military advisers in North Korea between 1948 and 1950. It was probable that Stalin believed the Americans would do little to defend South Korea, since they had not sent troops to prevent a Communist victory in China, an infinitely larger strategic prize. In addition, in a January 12, 1950, speech, Secretary of State Dean Acheson had outlined an anticommunist defensive perimeter in Asia that excluded South Korea. The speech and subsequent administration actions supporting it may have helped convince Stalin that the North Koreans could attack South Korea without risking U.S. intervention.

The American-led UN forces drove the North Koreans back into their own territory during the fall of 1950. The entry of China into the conflict in November, however, forced the UN army to retreat.

Fighting eventually bogged down near the border between North and South Korea. The war continued until the signing of an armistice July 27, 1953.

Soviet Postwar Economy

While directing Soviet foreign policy in the postwar years, Stalin also had overseen the reconstruction of his damaged country. In 1946 the government revealed the terms of the Fourth Five-Year Plan, a blueprint for the rebuilding of Soviet industry, particularly the production of farm machinery and trucks, iron and steel, coal, electrical power, timber, and cement. The plan also devoted a high percentage of resources to defense. Moscow declared the plan fulfilled in four years and three months. The concentrated investment in heavy industry, however, was accomplished at the expense of agriculture, housing, and consumer goods.

Peasants suffered the most under Stalin's reconstruction plan. Collective farms were forced to pay increasingly heavy taxes, while the prices they received from the government for grain remained low. Consequently, as before the war, many peasants left their farms to resettle in urban areas during this period.

The living standard of the average Soviet citizen improved under the Fifth Five-Year Plan, which ran from 1951 to 1955. Although the plan again emphasized heavy industry, wages increased and more consumer goods became available. Economic conditions in the countryside still lagged behind those in the cities, and housing space remained a problem.

Stalin would not live to see the completion of this plan or the end of the Korean War. On the night of March 1, 1953, he reportedly suffered a large brain hemorrhage. He died at the age of seventy-three on March 5, without leaving a clear plan of succession.

CHAPTER **3**

KHRUSHCHEV ERA

When Joseph Stalin died on March 5, 1953, no Soviet leader was in a position to assume the role of preeminent leader of the USSR. Stalin's lieutenants announced that they would institute a collective leadership. Behind the scenes, however, a struggle for power already had begun.

Georgy Malenkov appeared to be Stalin's most likely successor. Stalin had endorsed Malenkov by naming him the main speaker at the Nineteenth Soviet Party Congress in 1952. After Stalin's death Malenkov emerged as both chairman of the Council of Ministers (prime minister) and first secretary of the Central Committee Secretariat. These strong institutional positions could have made him first among equals in a collective leadership or perhaps even could have enabled him to eliminate his rivals. Only a few weeks later, however, Malenkov resigned his Secretariat duties after his colleagues protested the publication in *Pravda* of a picture of Stalin, Malenkov, and Mao in which the images of other Soviet and Chinese leaders had been removed. This weakened Malenkov's position and opened the way for Nikita S. Khrushchev to become de facto first secretary because he was the only Presidium (Politburo) member also in the Central Committee Secretariat.

Another key figure in the succession struggle was Lavrenty Beria, the powerful head of the Soviet secret police, who, after Malenkov, was considered Stalin's next most likely successor. Malenkov, Khrushchev, and their colleagues on the Presidium feared Beria and believed that his control of the vast secret police network gave him a weapon that could threaten not only their positions but also their lives. The Soviet leadership therefore conspired against Beria. He was arrested in July 1953 and charged with "criminal antiparty and antistate work" and with being a British agent. After a short trial on December 17, he was found guilty and executed.

Beria's demise left Malenkov and Khrushchev as the main rivals for leadership. Their power struggle centered on the question of how to allocate industrial resources. On August 8, 1953, Malenkov had announced a moderate shift in resources away from heavy industry and toward consumer goods. This shift was not a radical departure from Stalin's economic policies, because heavy industry would remain the leading component of the Soviet economy. The Soviet leadership, fearful that public impatience with food shortages and with the seemingly endless subordination of consumer needs to rapid industrialization would lead to unrest, endorsed Malenkov's program, which aimed at producing more and better food, housing, medical care, and household items.

By late 1954, however, the Soviet leadership began to have doubts about the redistribution of resources. Khrushchev became the leader of a growing faction that favored a reconcentration on heavy industry and the military, while Malenkov remained a proponent of increasing the quality and quantity of consumer goods. The debate over industrial priorities came to a climax in early 1955 when Khrushchev had garnered enough support for his position not only to reverse the shift of resources to consumer goods, but also to use the issue as a lever to demote Malenkov. After Khrushchev castigated Malenkov's views at a Central Committee meeting, Malenkov was accused of administrative inexperience and forced to resign as chairman of the Council of Ministers. He was replaced by Khrushchev ally Nikolai Bulganin. Malenkov's demotion left Khrushchev in control of the government and the party. Although Khrushchev was not an unchallenged leader as Stalin had been, he dominated Soviet foreign and domestic policy until his ouster in 1964.

De-Stalinization

After Stalin's death the Soviet collective leadership had cautiously begun dismantling some of the more oppressive manifestations of Stalin's rule. This process came to be known as "de-Stalinization." During this time Soviet political activity gradually returned to more normal operation, and daily life for the citizenry became less repressive. Khrushchev declared that government organizations must operate during traditional business hours, a departure from the secretive midnight meetings common during Stalin's regime. The Soviet leadership allowed greater freedom of movement within the Soviet Union, moderately eased controls on artistic expression, relaxed labor discipline, and rehabilitated some of the victims of Stalin's purges.

The most important aspect of this thawing process was the regime's repudiation of terror. Khrushchev and his colleagues recognized that Stalin's terror tactics had stifled initiative in Soviet society because scientists, artists, educators, party workers, enterprise managers, military officers, and other leaders were afraid of the consequences of being judged wrong or disloyal by Stalin. The Soviet leadership also realized that because terror had been used widely against top leaders in the government and party, their own lives would constantly be in danger if the system were not changed. The party signaled its repudiation of terror on April 4, 1953, by exonerating the physicians implicated in the "Doctors' Plot," a fictitious conspiracy by nine prominent Moscow doctors who allegedly sought to murder certain Soviet leaders. After their arrest in 1952, the doctors had been tortured on Stalin's orders to obtain their confessions. Two of them had died during their ordeal. Historians have speculated that the nine doctors' arrest was part of a plan by Stalin to launch another purge. The new regime

subsequently announced that "strict Leninist legality" would be observed and that arbitrary arrests would end. Soon thousands of prisoners held in Stalin's forced labor camps—the Gulag—were released and officially rehabilitated.

The arrest of Beria and many of his top aides resulted in the enhancement of party control over the secret police. This did not eliminate secret police abuses of power, but it did reduce the arbitrary nature of their activities. After Beria's execution, Soviet leaders also took action to protect themselves from the terror that had prevailed during the Stalin era. Under Stalin an ousted leader was likely to be killed to eliminate any possibility that he might one day make a comeback that could threaten his rivals. Khrushchev and his colleagues instituted an unwritten rule that leaders who came into disfavor or lost a power struggle simply would be demoted or retired.

Kremlin leaders initially were careful not to go too far with de-Stalinization because they all had held powerful posts under Stalin and could implicate themselves with a harsh attack on the abuses of the late dictator. In addition, they did not want to risk weakening the Communist party's preeminent position in society by instituting widespread reforms too fast.

Foreign Affairs

De-Stalinization also extended to foreign affairs as the Soviet leadership abandoned Stalin's unequivocally hostile attitude toward the West and demonstrated a willingness to explore possibilities for cooperation. In 1954 Khrushchev had shown his determination to pursue friendlier international relations by joining the United Nations International Labor Organization (ILO) and the United Nations Educational, Scientific, and Cultural Organization (UNESCO). The following year, the Soviets agreed to remove their forces occupying Austria, thus recognizing Austria's neutrality and independence. Lenin and Stalin had not recognized neutrality as an ideological option. A nation could not be neutral; it was either friendly or an enemy, socialist or imperialist. In return for these moves by the Kremlin, leaders of the United States, France, and Great

Britain agreed to participate in a week-long summit with the Soviets at Lake Geneva, Switzerland. Khrushchev and Bulganin attended, meeting President Dwight D. Eisenhower of the United States. It was the first trip to the West by a top Soviet leader.

The Geneva summit began July 18, 1955. Four items were on the agenda: the reunification of Germany, European security, disarmament, and improvement of East-West relations. An overriding external objective of Khrushchev's was to rid West Berlin of the continued Allied military presence.

During the meeting, President Eisenhower proposed an "open skies" arrangement to the Soviets. Under such a system the two nations would "give to each other a complete blueprint of our military establishments" and "provide within our countries facilities for aerial photography to the other country." Although the Soviets refused to rise to Eisenhower's bait, the meeting did result in the "spirit of Geneva," generally equated with a desire on both sides to seek accommodation and avoid confrontation. The four powers directed their foreign ministers to continue the talks in October, though the ministers' talks made little progress on key issues.

Khrushchev took his next step in revising Stalinist foreign policy at the July 1955 Central Committee session. Khrushchev made known his intent to seek a reconciliation with Yugoslavia's leader Josip Broz Tito. This was in marked opposition to Stalin's foreign minister Viacheslav Molotov, a powerful member of the post-Stalin leadership who believed concessions to Tito would undermine East-bloc unity. Molotov's views on Yugoslavia found little support in the Central Committee and his influence began declining.

Also in 1955, the Soviets formed the Warsaw Pact to offset the North Atlantic Treaty Organization (NATO) and the rearming of West Germany. While Yugoslavia did not join the pact, relations between the countries did improve, with past animosity between the two blamed on Stalin.

"Secret Speech"

At the Twentieth Soviet Party Congress in February 1956 Khrushchev dramatically transformed de-Stalinization from a cautious, incremental policy into a vigorous campaign of denunciation against Stalin's methods and the dictator himself. By focusing his attack directly on Stalin, Khrushchev hoped to avoid any responsibility for events such as the Great Purge, in which he had played a role.

Khrushchev had the honored responsibility of delivering the main Central Committee report at the congress. In his speech, delivered on February 14, Khrushchev boldly challenged the world view of many party members. He renounced bedrock Marxist-Leninist doctrines such as the inevitability of war among capitalist states and the eventual revolutionary overthrow of those systems. He declared that the danger of nuclear war dictated the prudent strategy of peaceful coexistence, and that international socialist goals could be achieved peaceably.

The most striking aspect of Khrushchev's performance at the congress, however, was his so-called Secret Speech of February 24, which attacked Stalin and began the process of unrestrained de-Stalinization. In the speech, Khrushchev portrayed Stalin as a ruthless tyrant responsible for the deaths of thousands of loyal high-ranking Communist party members and innumerable innocent Soviet citizens. Khrushchev charged that Stalin used violence "not only toward everything which opposed him, but also toward that which seemed to his capricious and despotic character contrary to his concepts." The party leader accused Stalin of being not only ruthless, but also irresponsible in his failure to prepare the nation for the devastating 1941 Nazi invasion. Khrushchev said that unlike Lenin, who "had always stressed the role of the people as the creator of history," Stalin had systematically constructed his own personality cult—a pervasive, self-glorifying portrayal of himself in the mass media—as the unrivaled and perfect hero-leader of the Soviet Union. Khrushchev claimed that by doing this Stalin had distorted history, set himself above the party and the principle of collective leadership, and deviated from Leninist precepts. Khrushchev's Secret Speech was not published in the Soviet Union, but it was distributed to party members in the Soviet Union and abroad. A copy was leaked to the West, and on June 4, 1956, the U.S. State Department published the complete text.

Although the Secret Speech marked the first time a Soviet leader had publicly and explicitly condemned Stalin's abuses of power, Khrushchev's presentation of the facts was neither complete nor perfectly objective. He made no mention of the role he had played in building Stalin's personality cult and executing his orders. In addition, the speech portrayed Lenin as a saintly and judicious father figure while failing to acknowledge that he also had gained near dictatorial power and had advocated the use of terror as a necessary tool in the fight for socialism.

Khrushchev was able to take such a bold step because he had developed a strong contingent of allies among the delegates to the congress, primarily through numerous party personnel replacements in the republics and regions since Stalin's death. Scholars still debate Khrushchev's motives for making these sensational revelations at the congress. Khrushchev said years later that he was trying to preclude recurrence of "such phenomena in the future" and to reinvigorate Leninist "norms" in the party. It is likely, however, that the speech was intended partly to strengthen Khrushchev's hand against rivals in the Soviet leadership.

1956 Foreign Policy Crises

Khrushchev's Secret Speech had unintended consequences in Eastern Europe, where Soviet domination generally was resented. Eastern Europeans took his denunciation of Stalin as a signal that they would have greater freedom over their affairs. In 1956 Communist party control broke down in Poland and Hungary. In late June, Polish workers in Poznan, emboldened by Khrushchev's speech and a growing anticommunist attitude among the Polish people, rioted. They demanded improved living and working conditions, more consumer goods, and government reform. Only the arrival of Polish army units reestablished order.

The riot split the Polish Communist party between those who wanted to pursue reforms and those who wanted to maintain a Stalinist hard line.

The apparent victory in October of the reformers under Wladyslaw Gomulka caused concern in the Kremlin. A delegation including Molotov, Lazar Kaganovich, Khrushchev, and Anastas Mikoyan went hurriedly to Warsaw on October 19 to confer with Polish leaders. Gomulka and his colleagues persuaded the Soviets that they did not plan a split with the Soviet Union, and the Soviet delegation returned to Moscow the following day. Further negotiations produced concessions on both sides, including a Polish promise to support Soviet foreign policy and the Soviet cancellation of more than two billion rubles of Polish debt.

Soviet Invasion of Hungary

The upheaval in Poland encouraged reformers in Hungary, where the brutality of the Hungarian regime had created a revolutionary mood among the public and divisions within the Communist party. Hungarian students began mass demonstrations in Budapest on October 20, demanding formation of a new government by former premier Imre Nagy, a liberal Communist party member. The protests turned violent October 23 as the Hungarian people rose in a genuine popular revolt driven by local revolutionary committees. Soviet tanks helped restore order in Budapest, but the Soviets acceded to the replacement of the hard-line communist regime with one headed by Nagy. Soviet forces began withdrawing from Budapest on October 30. That day Nagy inflamed the uprising by appealing for the support of Hungary's "fighters for freedom," by pledging an end to the one-party system, and by calling for Hungary's withdrawal from the Warsaw Pact. This demonstrated to the Soviets that the Hungarian revolt was going far beyond the limited change that they had decided to permit in Poland.

On November 4, eight Soviet military divisions struck at Budapest and other Hungarian cities in an effort to suppress the rebellion. Hungarian resistance fighters fought fiercely but were overwhelmed by superior Soviet firepower. About three thousand Hungarians were killed and another two hundred thousand fled to Austria. Nagy took refuge in the Yugoslav embassy. After receiving a guarantee

EASTERN EUROPE, 1956

0   100   200   300
Miles

Soviet client states

Independent communist states

NORWAY

SWEDEN

FINLAND
HELSINKI

OSLO ★

STOCKHOLM

Tallinn

ESTONIA

Gulf of Finland

Leningrad

★ MOSCOW

LATVIA
Riga

UNION OF
SOVIET
SOCIALIST
REPUBLICS

DENMARK

Baltic Sea

LITHUANIA
Vilnius

Minsk

BELORUSSIA

COPENHAGEN

RSFSR

NETH.

★ Bonn

WEST
GERMANY

BERLIN ★

EAST
GERMANY

WARSAW ★

POLAND

Kiev

UKRAINE

FRANCE

BERN
★

SWITZ.

PRAGUE

CZECHOSLOVAKIA

VIENNA ★

AUSTRIA

BUDAPEST ★

HUNGARY

MOLDAVIA

Kishinev

Sea of
Azov

ROMANIA

ITALY

★ ROME

YUGOSLAVIA

BELGRADE ★

BUCHAREST ★

Black Sea

BULGARIA
★ SOFIA

Tyrrhenian Sea

TIRANA ★

ALBANIA

GREECE

Aegean
Sea

TURKEY

★ ANKARA

Ionian Sea

ATHENS ★

Western Schools of Thought on Khrushchev's Power Structure

Nikita S. Khrushchev's tenure as Communist party first secretary was characterized by policy inconsistency and ambiguity. The frequent shifting of priorities between competing programs such as agrarian reform and building military strength made coherent policy impossible. While Khrushchev vocally supported agricultural reform, capital investments for farming lagged far behind those for heavy industry. In cultural areas, official leniency one day was offset by suppression of dissidents the next.

On defense and foreign policy issues, Khrushchev's statements were less inconsistent with his actions than they were in some other areas. They often changed, however, from steps toward détente with the West to steps certain to provoke confrontation, which made Soviet international conduct volatile and unpredictable.

Pressure Factor

Did changes in Khrushchev's individual priorities adequately explain these reversals and inconsistencies? Were the decisions Khrushchev's alone to make, or was he forced to bend to pressures applied by his colleagues and influential institutions? There are two broad schools of thought among Western analysts with regard to these questions, though in recent years distinctions between the two have blurred somewhat.

The first school is generally referred to as the "conflict school." Carl Linden and certain other early Kremlinologists believed Khrushchev was a reformer who fought an uphill battle against powerful bureaucrats opposed to major reforms or concessions to the citizenry that might unleash uncontrollable consequences. Policy decisions, according to this school, resulted either from Khrushchev's defeat on certain issues or his attempts to outmaneuver or compromise with his opponents to ward off defeat. Accordingly, inconsistent, ambivalent policy flowed from Khrushchev's battles to implement at least parts of his reforms.

Scholars subscribing to this view have argued that the events of 1960—particularly his harsh response to the U-2 spy incident—were evidence of Khrushchev's weakening position. The conflict school also has cited the removal of several Khrushchev allies in 1960-1961 from their posts on the Presidium (Politburo) and Central Committee as evidence that serious divisions existed among the top leaders.

The opposing school of thought maintained that

---

from newly installed Communist party leader Janos Kadar that he could leave the country, Nagy was arrested on November 22 and executed by Soviet authorities.

Kadar accepted Soviet direction in forming a new government that closely followed the Soviet line. He was faced with the task of rebuilding a country crippled by violence and strikes that continued through the winter. Meanwhile, the Soviets came under worldwide condemnation. The United States, while declining to intervene directly in Hungary, mounted a propaganda campaign in the United Nations and elsewhere against the Soviet action.

After the Hungarian revolt was crushed, Tito again broke with Moscow. This further discredited Khrushchev and his attempts to reconcile with Yugoslavia. It also kept the opposition, led by Molotov, in a better position from which to maintain support.

Suez Crisis

International condemnation of the Soviet invasion of Hungary would have been more severe had not the world's attention been focused on events in the Middle East. Egyptian president Gamal Abdel Nasser had advocated a nonaligned stance for his country since coming to power in 1952. His opposition to imperialism had brought him into conflict with the Western alliance, particularly Great Britain and France. In 1955 his purchase of Soviet weapons through Czechoslovakia alarmed U.S.

Khrushchev was not inherently a reformer. According to Merle Fainsod, Khrushchev was an "essentially conservative transitional figure," willing to experiment with reforms but without necessarily calculating their consequences. Fainsod viewed Khrushchev as a typical national leader who avoided hard policy choices by reacting to events as they occurred instead of developing and promoting a coherent policy course.

This school viewed Khrushchev's inconsistency as being similar to Lenin's. Policy ambivalence was not the result of political battles within the top party leadership; instead it was largely attributed to Khrushchev's changing perceptions of his own policies and the needs of the Soviet Union. Accordingly, this school did not see the 1960-1961 Presidium and Central Committee personnel changes as a political move against Khrushchev engineered by his rivals. Khrushchev himself may have had a hand in removing his own Presidium allies. According to Jerry Hough, this school of thought interprets the "reduction in the number of Central Committee secretaries on the Presidium . . . as an attempt to prevent the Secretariat from dominating the Presidium and thereby to strengthen the position of the one individual (Nikita Khrushchev) who headed the three major collective institutions below the level of the Presidium—the Central Committee Secretariat, the Council of Ministers, and the Bureau of the Central Committee for the RSFSR [Russian Soviet Federated Socialist Republic]."

Role of the Majority

In synthesizing the views of the two schools, Hough asserts that the real issue was whether Khrushchev had to have a majority in the Presidium to push through his policies. The abrupt changes in those policies may have indicated that Khrushchev was not always forced to act according to the wishes of a collective leadership. In *How the Soviet Union Is Governed,* Hough said:

In judging the structure of power in the Khrushchev period, we must ultimately rely upon our sense of the nature of committee politics and the meaning of different patterns of policy outcomes that emerge. . . . The natural outcome of a divided collective committee is deference to the key individual interests of most of the respective members (logrolling, if you will), compromise on the major issues dividing the committee, and (except in rare cases) gradualism and even conservatism in the change of major policy.

The leadership was not divided in 1964 when it engineered a major policy shift: Khrushchev's removal.

leaders and solidified his reputation as an anti-Western maverick. In July 1956 after the United States withdrew funding for the Aswan High Dam, the centerpiece of Nasser's economic development program, he nationalized the Suez Canal.

The move led the British and French to begin planning a military action against Egypt. Not only was the Suez Canal Company a British- and French-owned enterprise, but also Egyptian control of the canal threatened Europe's oil supply. In late October, Israeli, French, and British forces attacked Egypt and captured the canal. Eisenhower condemned the action of his allies and applied economic and diplomatic pressure to force them to end their intervention. On November 7 Great Britain and France announced that they would withdraw; Israel did the same the following day. The crisis had bolstered Nasser's standing in the Middle East, confirmed Egyptian control of the Suez Canal, temporarily fractured the Western alliance, and provided Moscow (which pledged financial support for the Aswan High Dam) with an opportunity to increase its influence in Egypt and the Middle East.

Domestic Difficulties

Many of Khrushchev's domestic programs were begun not because of their soundness but because of his hard lobbying work and an outwardly jovial personality that masked what some have called a violent cleverness. Western observers have said Khrushchev was the last "true believer." He took

Marxism-Leninism seriously and was convinced of the likelihood of rapid industrial, technological, and societal advancement. He believed in the possibility of perfecting a "new Soviet man" and of the Soviet Union's ability to overtake the West economically in a matter of decades.

Virgin Lands and Decentralization

Khrushchev addressed the Soviet Union's long-standing agricultural troubles by initiating his celebrated Virgin Lands program in 1954. He chose Leonid I. Brezhnev to carry out the risky venture of cultivating for grain millions of acres of previously unplanted (virgin) land in Central Asia and Siberia. By 1960 more than one hundred million acres had been opened for planting. After several years of famines and poor harvests, the program succeeded in temporarily relieving the agrarian crisis, but it failed to solve the underlying problem of low agriculture productivity. The Soviets were forced in the early 1960s to begin buying large quantities of grain from Canada, Australia, and the United States.

Industrial difficulties led to a decision at the December 1956 Central Committee meeting to further centralize the country's economic planning machinery. Khrushchev objected, but the Supreme Soviet nonetheless approved the move February 12, 1957. The next day, Khrushchev counterattacked with a plan to decentralize economic power.

Western analysts have questioned why, if Khrushchev controlled the leadership and opposed the changes, he waited until February to move against his opponents. Three possible reasons stand out: the satellite countries were, by February, under control; the Virgin Lands program had brought in a good harvest; and Khrushchev had developed a plan behind which he believed the Central Committee would rally. In short, Khrushchev was in a much better political position in February to launch his attack.

Khrushchev's counterprogram was designed to weaken the power of the highly centralized economic ministries that had flourished under Stalin by abolishing most of them and placing much of their industrial responsibilities in the hands of new regional economic councils—or *sovnarkhozes*. Khrushchev employed the Supreme Soviet in his effort to line up support among regional officials. It was not a difficult task because decentralization would directly benefit these officials at the expense of entrenched urban industrial administrators. Khrushchev, however, apparently did not fully comprehend the power of these bureaucrats. They supported Khrushchev's opponents on the Presidium in an effort to overthrow him.

Antiparty Group

Since besting Malenkov, Khrushchev had maneuvered to strengthen his position by undermining the authority of weaker rivals. In 1955 he succeeded in demoting Lazar Kaganovich, one of Stalin's top aides, from deputy prime minister to a minor governmental position, although he remained a Presidium member. Khrushchev also had continuously lobbied against Molotov.

At the Twentieth Party Congress Khrushchev's control was greatly strengthened—and his opponents' guard raised further—when 133 new members of the Central Committee were named. Many of these could trace their elevation to earlier associations with Khrushchev. Full Presidium membership did not change, though five new candidate members were chosen who appeared also to owe their promotions to Khrushchev.

After Khrushchev's Secret Speech he stepped up attacks on Stalin's "Old Guard." Molotov, Kaganovich, Malenkov, and Kliment Voroshilov were accused of attempting to thwart Khrushchev's proposal to disclose Stalin's crimes. Dmitry Shepilov replaced Molotov as foreign affairs minister. Kaganovich was relieved from his minor post as chairman of the State Committee on Labor and Wages and named to a still lower ministerial job. Molotov and Kaganovich, however, remained on the Presidium.

In June 1957 Khrushchev's growing circle of powerful enemies, which would come to be known as the "antiparty group," decided to oust him. When it came time for the showdown, Mikoyan, Mikhail Suslov, and Aleksei Kirichenko were the only full Presidium members openly supporting

Khrushchev. The other members opposed Khrushchev either because of his policies or his efforts to have them demoted. Spearheaded by Malenkov, Molotov, Shepilov, and to a lesser degree Bulganin (in whose office the group met), the antiparty group called for Khrushchev's resignation. The group tried to announce the resignation immediately, so as to present the Central Committee, which was dominated by Khrushchev's supporters, with a fait accompli. Khrushchev, however, refused to resign. He astutely demanded that his fate be decided by the Central Committee, a body that did have the formal authority to rule on such matters, though it had become a rubber stamp for the decisions of the Presidium. The Presidium met in almost continuous session for several days, hoping to forestall a Central Committee meeting, but regional officials swarmed upon Moscow, rallied behind Khrushchev, and demanded a plenum.

Firm support for Khrushchev among both the Central Committee and candidate Presidium members blocked the "resignation." The rising young Central Committee members from the republics likely saw themselves as beneficiaries if Khrushchev retained his position and as direct losers if he did not.

After the situation settled, Khrushchev took aim at his opponents. Malenkov, Kaganovich, Molotov, and Shepilov were accused of "antiparty, factional methods in an attempt to change the composition of the party's leading bodies." All four lost their Presidium and Central Committee memberships and their governmental posts. Other conspirators also were demoted or removed immediately, although Bulganin was not ousted from the Presidium until 1958 and Voroshilov did not resign his posts until 1960.

Khrushchev promoted those officials who had supported him in his fight against the antiparty group, and the Presidium swelled to fifteen members. He rewarded not only numerous lower-level supporters, but also Marshal Georgy Zhukov, who was promoted to full membership in the Presidium from candidate status. Zhukov, however, lasted only four months. The strong-willed World War II hero was removed both from the Presidium and as de-

fense minister amidst accusations of political deficiency and of "surrounding himself with sycophants and flatterers." Khrushchev and other party leaders had objected to several Zhukov moves that appeared to limit party control of the military. His ouster marked yet another instance of a Soviet leader eliminating a perceived source of competition for power. In 1958 Khrushchev replaced Bulganin as chairman of the Council of Ministers. The man who had been a party worker all his career now was head of the government as well.

Khrushchev did not slow down his efforts to bring about a thoroughly industrialized, equally competitive superpower after his 1957 successes. In fact, after 1957 Khrushchev was able to pursue his policies more freely. For the most part, his domestic initiatives failed; and, as with many of his foreign adventures, they became known as Khrushchev's "hare-brained schemes."

U.S.-Soviet Relations

The Soviet invasion of Hungary and the Suez crisis had damaged the good will built up between the superpowers at the Geneva conference in 1955. During 1957 tense relations continued as Moscow announced a series of scientific accomplishments that caused alarm in the United States. On August 26, 1957, the Soviets disclosed that they had tested successfully an intercontinental ballistic missile (ICBM). On October 4 they announced that they had placed into orbit *Sputnik I*, a 184-pound satellite. *Sputnik II*, weighing more than eleven hundred pounds and carrying a dog named Laika, was launched November 3. Not until January 31, 1958, did the United States launch its first satellite, a thirty-pound cylinder. The Soviet space shots lent credence to Moscow's claims that it had developed ICBMs capable of carrying nuclear warheads. Although the United States had clear nuclear superiority during this period, the notion that a "missile gap" had developed in favor of the Soviet Union became a popular American concern. Proponents of a U.S. weapons buildup used the fictitious gap to lobby for greater defense spending. Khrushchev, aware of his country's continuing strategic vulnerability, played up the idea that Soviet scientists were making great strides in military technology.

Meanwhile, Khrushchev's political intrigues had enabled him to assume complete control over Soviet foreign affairs. He attempted to walk the line between two conflicting policies: peaceful coexistence with the United States and the West and the militant expansion of communist influence and power around the world. The Eisenhower administration responded by continuing U.S. efforts to contain communist expansion, while exploring opportunities for improved relations.

Superpower Summitry and the U-2 Incident

In 1959 superpower relations warmed considerably. Vice President Richard Nixon visited the Soviet Union from July 22 to August 2. He and Khrushchev discussed superpower relations, West Berlin, and the status of the Eastern-bloc nations. They also held an unlikely public debate on the quality of life in their respective nations that captured the world's attention. *(Kitchen Debate, box, p. 73)*

In September Khrushchev became the first top Soviet leader to visit the United States. He and President Eisenhower conferred cordially at the Camp David presidential retreat in Maryland. Khrushchev also visited rural Iowa and Eisenhower's farm at Gettysburg, Pennsylvania, all the while projecting an image of a benign, grandfatherly leader who wanted to end the hostility between East and West. The summit visit did not produce significant agreements, but it created expectations on both sides that further summit diplomacy could resolve the major issues of contention between the United States and the Soviet Union. This optimism came to be known as the "spirit of Camp David." The two leaders agreed to participate in a multilateral summit meeting scheduled for May 1960, to be followed by an Eisenhower visit to the Soviet Union.

The summit meeting was torpedoed, however, by the May 5, 1960, disclosure that the Soviets had shot down an American U-2 spy plane over their territory. The United States had been making the routine flights since 1956, with the planes flying at seventy thousand feet to elude Soviet air defenses. But in

May a recently developed Soviet ground-to-air missile reportedly hit the U-2, forcing the pilot, Francis Gary Powers, to bail out. Powers, an ex-Air Force flyer employed by the Central Intelligence Agency, was captured, and the Soviets retrieved the wreckage of the spy plane. After some initial denials of responsibility, Eisenhower admitted May 9 that the flights occurred with his full knowledge and support.

The reaction from Moscow was threatening. Khrushchev warned Turkey, Pakistan, and Norway that "if they allow others to fly from their bases to our territory we shall hit at those bases." He added May 11 that Powers would be tried "severely as a spy." In regards to Eisenhower's scheduled June 10 visit to the USSR, Khrushchev withdrew the invitation, saying, "The Russian people would say I was mad to welcome a man who sends spy planes over here like that."

The summit meeting in Paris, attended by Eisenhower, Khrushchev, British prime minister Harold Macmillan, and French president Charles de Gaulle, opened May 16 and quickly broke down into mutual recrimination. Khrushchev condemned the U-2 surveillance missions, while Eisenhower defended the overflights as an essential precaution against surprise attack. Nevertheless, Eisenhower claimed, "These flights were suspended after the recent incident and are not to be resumed."

The conference ended in deadlock. The Soviets tried Powers and, on August 9, sentenced him to ten years in prison. He was released February 10, 1962, in exchange for the Soviet "master spy" Rudolph Abel, who was apprehended by U.S. authorities in 1957 and sentenced to a thirty-year prison term. Several strange circumstances surrounding the U-2 incident have led a few observers to speculate that the United States may have intentionally used it to subvert the developing superpower diplomacy. These circumstances include the survival of the plane, which was expected to disintegrate if struck by a Soviet missile; the treatment of Powers (who had willingly confessed the nature and details of his operation to the Soviets) as a hero by the CIA upon his return; and the muted questioning of Powers by the Senate Armed Services Committee after CIA chief John McCone secretly briefed the committee.

The Nixon-Khrushchev "Kitchen Debate"

Premier Khrushchev and Vice President Nixon visit a U.S. trade exhibition in Moscow, July 1959. Leonid I. Brezhnev, who would succeed Khrushchev as party leader five years later, looks on.

An unlikely public give-and-take session between Soviet premier Nikita S. Khrushchev and U.S. vice president Richard Nixon made worldwide headlines when Nixon visited Moscow from July 22 to August 2, 1959.

The trip was a follow-up to a visit to the United States earlier in the summer by Nixon's Soviet counterpart, First Deputy Premier Frol R. Kozlov. After arriving in the Soviet capital, Nixon quickly found himself defending actions of his government at home. The previous week Congress had passed a "captive nations" resolution, and President Dwight D. Eisenhower had issued a declaration calling on Americans to "study the plight of the Soviet-dominated nations and to recommit themselves to the support of the just aspirations of those captive nations." Khrushchev condemned the resolution as "rude" interference in "our internal affairs" and added that "the camp of the socialist countries has never before been so solid and powerful as now."

The most publicized event of Nixon's visit, however, was his informal discussion with Khrushchev, which took place on July 24 before reporters at a U.S. trade exhibition. It was soon dubbed the "Kitchen Debate" because part of the colloquy occurred near a display of an American home, complete with a kitchen. Viewing the model home, Khrushchev said, "You think the Russian people will be dumbfounded to see this? But I tell you all our modern homes have equipment of this sort, and to get a flat you have only to be a Soviet visitor, not a citizen."

To which Nixon replied: "We do not claim to astonish the Russian people. We hope to show our diversity and our right to choose. We do not wish to have decisions made at the top by government officials who say that all homes should be built in the same way. Would it not be better to compete in the relative merits of washing machines than in the strength of rockets? Is this the kind of competition you want?" Khrushchev: "Yes, that's the kind of competition we want, but your generals say we must compete in rockets."

President Kennedy greets Premier Khrushchev in Vienna, June 1961, as Andrei Gromyko steps from the car.

Khrushchev returned to the United States in September 1960 to attend a meeting of the heads of government of the eighty-two members of the United Nations. Ostensibly there to help reopen disarmament negotiations, Khrushchev used the gathering to promote a plan to replace UN General Secretary Dag Hammarskjöld of Sweden, whom the Soviets charged was a "willing tool" of the Western powers. The Soviet plan called for replacing Hammarskjöld with a three-member executive committee representing three UN groups: the Western powers, the socialist states, and the neutral countries. The Soviet proposal garnered little support among world leaders. The heated debate was punctuated by Khrushchev's shouted interruptions and desk-pounding (with his fists and, in a celebrated incident, his shoe). His plan a failure, Khrushchev returned to Moscow October 13.

Germany and Berlin

Despite the failure of the summit meeting the previous year, Khrushchev was eager to meet and size up the new U.S. president, John F. Kennedy, elected in November 1960. A Kennedy-Khrushchev meeting was arranged for June 3-4, 1961, in Vienna. President Kennedy said afterward on June 6 that their "most somber talks" mainly dealt with Germany and Berlin. Khrushchev had made plain his determination to sign a peace treaty with East Germany, a move long interpreted in Washington as part of the Soviet effort to force Western powers out of West Berlin. Kennedy, in press conferences in June and July, stressed the "real intent" of the Soviets to dislodge the Western powers and on July 25 called for an immediate buildup of U.S. and NATO forces. Khrushchev replied, in speeches August 7, 9, and 11, with threats of Soviet mobilization

CHERRY PICKER

OXIDIZER TRAILERS

2 FUEL TRAILERS

METALLURG ANOSOV

UEL TRAILERS

MISSILE ERECTOR

DIVNOGORSK

BRATSK

A U.S. Navy reconnaissance photo of Cuba's Mariel Naval Port, taken November 2, 1962, confirms that Soviet nuclear weapons are being removed from Cuba.

and boasts that Moscow could build a hundred-megaton nuclear bomb.

Then, with no advance warning, the East German regime August 13 began sealing off the sector border between East and West Berlin to stem the flow of East Germans to the West. (Nearly three million East German citizens had emigrated to the West since the end of World War II.) The Soviets and East Germans ignored the protests of the Western allies. Within a few months, the East Germans had built a mortar and barbed-wire wall running along the entire sector border, effectively stopping the transit of refugees from East to West. But Khrushchev's hopes for Western concessions in response to his actions failed, and the Berlin Wall came to symbolize communist oppression.

Cuban Missile Crisis

Another serious confrontation between Washington and Moscow developed in 1962 over a Soviet move to deploy missiles carrying nuclear warheads in Cuba. Since the successful revolution in 1959, Cuban leader Fidel Castro had moved his government solidly into the Soviet sphere of influence. In January 1962, at Washington's urging, Cuba was expelled from the Organization of American States. Cuba's economic isolation in the Western Hemisphere led to increased Soviet shipments of arms and goods to the island nation, a development that was viewed with increasing alarm in Washington.

On October 22, 1962, President Kennedy stunned the nation by announcing that aerial reconnaissance photos revealed that the Soviets secretly were building launching sites in Cuba for medium- and intermediate-range ballistic missiles capable of reaching many U.S. cities. The "secret, swift and extraordinary buildup" of a nuclear capability in Cuba, the president said, "is a deliberately provocative and unjustified change in the status quo which cannot be accepted by this country."

Kennedy announced the imposition of "a strict

quarantine of all offensive military equipment under shipment to Cuba," adding that "ships of any kind bound for Cuba, from whatever nation or port, will, if found to contain cargoes of offensive weapons, be turned back." Kennedy said, "Any nuclear missile launched from Cuba against any nation in the Western Hemisphere" would be regarded "as an attack by the Soviet Union on the United States requiring a full retaliatory response upon the Soviet Union." The president called on Khrushchev "to halt and eliminate this clandestine, reckless and provocative threat to world peace."

An estimated twenty-five Soviet-bloc vessels were moving toward Cuba as the U.S. Navy quarantine officially began October 24. The Soviets recalled several ships that might have been challenged and on October 27 Kennedy received two letters from Khrushchev broaching a compromise. The first letter was conciliatory, offering to remove the weapons from Cuba. The second letter proposed in return the removal of U.S. intermediate-range ballistic missiles from bases in Turkey. The missiles in Turkey were obsolete and had already been scheduled for removal, but Kennedy refused to consider removing them in return for Moscow's removal of the missiles in Cuba. Khrushchev wrote again October 28, agreeing to dismantle the Cuban missiles without demanding any reciprocal U.S. move in Turkey. President Kennedy announced November 20 that "all known offensive missile sites in Cuba have been removed." He declared the quarantine lifted.

What Kennedy saw as Khrushchev's "statesmanlike decision" to remove the Cuban missiles appeared differently to many hard-line communists. They viewed it as the leader of the world's socialists backing down to the leader of the capitalist camp. The Chinese in particular lost whatever faith they had retained in Moscow's ability to lead the struggle against imperialism. At home the Cuban missile crisis eroded Khrushchev's support in the party. Some members considered his decision to back down a betrayal, while others questioned the party leader's judgment in initiating such a risky scheme.

After the crisis, U.S.-Soviet relations did improve slightly as Moscow and Washington cooperated on several arms control measures. Most notably the two superpowers along with Great Britain signed the 1963 Partial Nuclear Test Ban Treaty, which banned nuclear weapons tests in the atmosphere, in outer space, and under water. That year the superpowers also established a "hot line" between their two capitals to facilitate communication during international crises. Nevertheless, the U.S.-Soviet nuclear arms race continued throughout the decade.

Sino-Soviet Relations

Soviet aid to the Chinese Communists prior to their victory over the nationalists was inconsistent and often came with strings attached. But in 1950, when Chinese Communist leader Mao Zedong went to Moscow and signed a treaty of friendship and alliance with the Soviet Union, old Sino-Soviet animosities appeared to be buried. Western observers saw the new relationship as a logical union of two communist powers. In fact, the similarities in ideologies obscured fundamental differences and did nothing to halt numerous Soviet efforts to interfere in internal Chinese politics.

Strategic Differences

After 1950 Chinese leaders perceived the United States as attempting to surround China, cut it off from the world, and replace its communist regime with the government of Chiang Kai-shek on Taiwan. There were U.S. troops all around China: on Taiwan, in Japan, in the Philippines, and in South Korea. There were U.S. advisers in South Vietnam and British troops in Burma and Malaysia. Mao and his colleagues saw the Sino-Soviet alliance and Soviet atomic weapons as the ultimate guarantors of Chinese security against the West.

Khrushchev, eager to maintain the image of a monolithic Communist bloc led by the Soviet Union, pacified his radical Asian allies with aid and promises of nuclear protection in the event of an attack on China. The Chinese, however, preferred the prospect of relying on their own power and pressed Moscow to supply them with the technology to produce atomic weapons. The Soviets complied in a secret agreement signed in 1957. But the Kremlin's refusal to risk a nuclear confrontation with the United States during the Quemoy crisis of 1958 and its repudiation of the secret nuclear weapons technology agreement in 1959 led Beijing to believe that it could not depend on Moscow. The Chinese continued with their own nuclear program, which, ironically, would produce a bomb tested October 16, 1964, a day after Khrushchev's ouster was announced.

Ideological Differences

Khrushchev's performance at the Twentieth Soviet Party Congress in 1956 sent shock waves through China. While some communist governments embraced the concepts of peaceful coexistence and de-Stalinization, China considered Khrushchev's movement to be heretical. The Chinese had endorsed a never-ending struggle against the imperialist camp, and they found much to criticize in the unthinkable notion of peaceful coexistence. Moreover, Khrushchev's Secret Speech was a condemnation of one-man, totalitarian rule that many Chinese Communists viewed as an attack on Mao. The Chinese at first responded to Khrushchev's actions by moderately relaxing censorship. The intensity of the resulting criticism of the government and party caught the regime unawares, however, and the lid on free expression was quickly slammed shut. The Chinese then challenged Soviet ideological preeminence by asserting that Moscow was revisionist, that peaceful coexistence with the West was impossible, and that Khrushchev had violated the basic tenets of Leninist orthodoxy.

Some of the trouble between the countries stemmed from the personal animosity that developed between Khrushchev and Mao. After Stalin's death, Mao saw himself as the successor to the ideological throne of communism. It soon became obvious that Khrushchev and the other Soviet leaders were not interested in relinquishing the crown. The Soviets also viewed the Chinese as too backward to represent the cutting edge of international communism.

In 1958 with the decision to launch the Great Leap Forward—"a great revolutionary leap toward the building of socialism"—the Chinese tried to solve all their problems at once. They claimed that Beijing, not Moscow, was the true center of the world communist movement. They asserted that, faced with U.S. encirclement and Soviet abandonment, they would modernize on their own. Announcing that Mao had discovered a shortcut to achieving a communist society, the Chinese espoused the principle of "self-reliance." Mao explained that no longer would the Chinese "lean to one side" (rely on Moscow) but would "walk on two legs."

The Soviets heaped scorn on the Great Leap Forward (which soon stumbled) and chided the Chinese for claiming to understand Lenin better than his own countrymen. As the 1960s began, the war of words was confined to ideology and attacks were indirect. The Soviets criticized China's ally Albania, instead of China itself, as "adventurist" and "infantile" for its insistence on direct confrontation with the West. In turn, China castigated Yugoslavia, in place of the Soviet Union, for its "revisionist" views toward peaceful coexistence.

In July 1960 the Soviets retaliated against the Chinese verbal abuse by recalling all their technicians in China and suspending their cooperative scientific and technical ventures. The Chinese continued to accuse Khrushchev of being soft on imperialism.

In 1962 the Soviets refused to help China in its war with India, and Khrushchev responded to U.S. pressure to withdraw the missiles the Soviets had placed in Cuba. Beijing denounced both moves as "retreats." During the last years of Khrushchev's reign, Chinese and Soviet polemics became increasingly direct and accusatory. Khrushchev himself became the primary focus of Chinese attacks. Western observers finally began to acknowledge that the Sino-Soviet dispute was more than a temporary rift or a personality conflict between Khrushchev and Mao.

The Fall of Khrushchev

The men surrounding Khrushchev in the Kremlin tired of his inconsistent and overly optimistic plans.

Amidst plan reversals, perceived foreign policy humiliations, and fears for personal power, party leaders soon joined in an effort to remove Nikita Khrushchev.

The Soviet Communist party goals of the Seven-Year Plan (so called because the Sixth Five-Year Plan, 1956-1960, was scuttled in 1958) proved impossible to achieve. The goals included an 83 percent jump in housing investment, a 70 percent increase in agricultural production, and a 100 percent hike in productivity on collective farms. Certain areas of the Soviet economy performed well. The heavy industry sector continued to grow, and the Soviets achieved more scientific firsts, including the April 12, 1961, spaceflight of Yuri Gagarin, the first human to be launched into space. Yet in most areas the Soviet economy achieved only modest gains that failed to meet the ambitious targets of Soviet planners.

In addition, Kremlin leaders feared that aspects of de-Stalinization at home—particularly reductions in censorship and restrictions on the flow of information—would provoke unrest. State control over the arts eased after Khrushchev's 1956 Secret Speech, although the thaw never resulted in more than a modicum of artistic freedom. Moreover, in early 1957 Khrushchev had backed off somewhat from his aggressive denunciation of Stalin. The official Soviet position had become that Stalin was guilty of making mistakes and violating legal norms, but that he was a devoted Communist party member who strove faithfully for the cause of socialism. Relaxed censorship was applied selectively. For example, in 1958 Khrushchev prevented the publication in the Soviet Union of Boris Pasternak's *Doctor Zhivago*.

At the Twenty-second Soviet Party Congress in October 1961, however, Khrushchev renewed his assault on Stalin. On October 30, following Khrushchev's lead, the delegates unanimously voted to remove Stalin's remains from Lenin's mausoleum on Red Square to a less prominent spot near the Kremlin wall. Thereafter the Soviet regime attempted to remove all traces of Stalin's influence from Soviet society. Schoolbooks containing nearly thirty years of Stalin-dominated Soviet history were rewritten. Towns and streets bearing Stalin's name were re-

named, including Stalingrad, which became Volgograd. Khrushchev personally oversaw the publication in 1962 of Alexander Solzhenitsyn's harsh portrait of Stalin's labor camps, *One Day in the Life of Ivan Denisovich*. This reinvigorated assault on Stalin made Khrushchev's colleagues nervous.

Khrushchev's attempt to reorganize the party and government in 1962 was probably the domestic initiative that most damaged his standing. This reorganization was a bifurcation, or split, of most of the lower party and governmental organs into two independent structures. One was industrial (or urban), the other agricultural (or rural). Important regions of the country were given sections of both. The industrial regional party committees and soviets, which had subordinate units in areas roughly equivalent to U.S. cities or counties, supervised nearly all the population in the cities and those involved with industry and construction efforts. The agricultural counterpart supervised rural citizenry and institutions, as well as institutions in cities that were closely related to agriculture. The bifurcation failed largely because it created needless confusion and threatened or diminished the jobs of many powerful bureaucrats and administrators.

For several years prior to 1964, Khrushchev's supporters as well as opponents became increasingly alarmed over the loss of Soviet international prestige, a loss they attributed to Khrushchev. In relations with the noncommunist world, Khrushchev pursued policies, such as placing missiles in Cuba, that resulted in Soviet humiliation. Within the socialist world, his opponents charged, he presided over and promoted the Sino-Soviet split, thereby relinquishing Moscow's position as unqualified leader of the communist movement and turning an important ally into a hostile, ideological rival.

Khrushchev Removed

Khrushchev was forced to surrender leadership of the state and the party at the October 14, 1964, session of the Central Committee. His actual ouster presumably occurred the day before at a meeting of the Presidium. It was announced October 15 that the Central Committee granted Khrushchev's "request to be relieved of his duties ... in view of his advanced age and deterioration of his health." In fact, Khrushchev's health was fine. His ouster was the result of a carefully planned plot by his fellow members on the Presidium. Khrushchev, political scientist Adam Ulam has written, "was too unpredictable and too arbitrary to be tolerated as head of the regime. He had ceased to be respected and trusted and was not feared enough—a fatal combination for the head of a totalitarian state."

American president Lyndon B. Johnson broadcast a message October 18, 1964, in which he said, "We do not know exactly what happened to Nikita Khrushchev. ... We do know that he has been forced out of power by his former friends and colleagues. Five days ago he had only praise in Moscow. Today we learn only of his faults." The president disclosed that at an October 16 White House meeting the Soviet ambassador, Anatoly Dobrynin, assured Johnson that the new regime planned "no change in basic foreign policy."

Unlike 1957 when Khrushchev was able to outflank his opponents by taking his case to the Central Committee, in 1964 the Presidium members prevented him from making a similar appeal. It is not known who was the driving force behind the coup, which occurred without warning. Leonid Brezhnev, a close associate of Khrushchev, was named first secretary of the Communist party, and Aleksei Kosygin assumed the premiership.

The seventy-year-old Khrushchev, who was vacationing at his dacha on the Black Sea coast when he was summoned back to Moscow October 13, dropped from sight. Supported by a government pension, he lived in enforced obscurity outside Moscow until he died September 11, 1971. During this period he wrote his memoirs, which were smuggled out of the Soviet Union. They were published in the West in two volumes—*Khrushchev Remembers* in 1970 and *The Last Testament* in 1974.

CHAPTER **4**

BREZHNEV ERA

An oligarchy took control of the Soviet Union after ousting party leader Nikita S. Khrushchev in October 1964. In contrast to Khrushchev's unpredictable and gregarious approach to governing, the oligarchy emphasized stability and collective decision making. During the second half of the 1960s the new leadership would preside over a chronically troubled economy, an acceleration of the Soviet military buildup, unrest in Czechoslovakia, an increasingly bitter dispute with the People's Republic of China, and the first tentative steps toward détente with the West. Relations between the United States and the Soviet Union became an increasingly important barometer of the climate of international affairs worldwide. Little was left outside the reach of superpower involvement.

The men who replaced Khrushchev moved quickly to do away with domestic programs instituted during their predecessor's years at the top. They dismantled Khrushchev's regional economic councils, designed to decentralize state authority by allowing local jurisdictions some say over regional matters. In addition they ended Khrushchev's confusing bifurcation of the party and government bureaucracies into industrial and agricultural units. Within two years they also had reversed Khrushchev's program of de-Stalinization. Among other actions, the new leadership curbed public criticism of Stalin. At a November 3, 1967, ceremony marking the fiftieth anniversary of the Bolshevik Revolution, Brezhnev referred to Stalin's reign of terror as "temporary setbacks and errors."

While the new leaders de-emphasized the kind of individual dominance that Khrushchev personified,

one of them—Leonid I. Brezhnev—gradually emerged as the leading figure in fact as well as title. During Brezhnev's eighteen-year regime (1964-1982) the Soviet Union built itself into a military superpower with client states around the world. But the USSR's success in the military sphere was not matched in other areas of Soviet society. The living standard of Soviet citizens fell and internal dissent grew as the aging Brezhnev leadership resisted change into the 1980s.

Internal Politics

Brezhnev did not dominate the regime immediately after Khrushchev's ouster. The Presidium was a heterogeneous group, and Brezhnev had only one close ally, Andrei Kirilenko. Brezhnev had limited influence within the Council of Ministers because Premier Aleksei Kosygin ran the government apparatus. Brezhnev's public role as foreign policy spokesman also was limited by Kosygin, who was primarily responsible for relations with noncommunist countries. Mikhail Suslov was another independent and influential figure who had the potential to erode or supersede Brezhnev's authority. Suslov was seen by his colleagues as the defender of the rights of the oligarchy against individual leadership, something uppermost in the leaders' minds. Nikolai Podgorny, who was widely regarded in the West as the third-ranking leader in the Kremlin, was primarily responsible for party organization. In December 1965 he succeeded Anastas Mikoyan as chairman of the Presidium of the Supreme Soviet (president). If Brezhnev faltered, Podgorny would have been a logical alternative to assume the position of general secretary.

Other Politburo members were allies of Brezhnev rivals, were vulnerable party elders (such as Mikoyan), or were personal protégés of Khrushchev who were on the way out. Less important candidate Politburo members also were waiting to gravitate toward the leader who proved the strongest.

In the wake of Khrushchev's ouster, Petr Shelest was promoted to the Politburo, a move that benefited his associate Podgorny. Aleksandr Shelepin, who had provided the "muscle" for the Khrushchev ouster through his contacts in the Committee for State Security (KGB), also was rewarded with a Politburo seat.

Shelepin initially was the main threat to Brezhnev. He was young and ambitious and had a foothold in both the Council of Ministers (as deputy premier) and the Secretariat. Shelepin was chairman of the Party-State Control Commission, and he had well-placed personal associates below him.

Despite all these rivals for power, during the first eighteen months after Khrushchev's ouster Brezhnev managed to extend his power base in a number of ways. It was inevitable that some of Khrushchev's cronies would be replaced. These removals opened slots that Brezhnev filled to his advantage, although he sometimes was forced to compromise. One change that benefited Brezhnev was the promotion of his close associate, Konstantin U. Chernenko, to the post of secretary of the General Department of the Central Committee in 1965.

Twenty-third Party Congress

At the Twenty-third Party Congress, convened in March 1966, Brezhnev and Kosygin demonstrated that they were the leading policy makers in the regime. Nikolai Podgorny's power was diluted when the congress replaced him on the Secretariat with Andrei Kirilenko. As head of the party, Brezhnev was responsible for party matters and relations with other communist countries and parties. He delivered the opening speech at the congress on March 29. Kosygin oversaw economic planning and relations with the noncommunist world. He presented the

government's new five-year plan covering the years 1966 to 1970. It included ambitious targets for growth of national income, but Kosygin declared that, because of "mistakes and miscalculations" under Khrushchev's seven-year plan (1959-1965), the growth targets for some industries were set "lower than had formerly been envisioned."

The Twenty-third Party Congress gave its blessing to the moderate course backed by Brezhnev and Kosygin. Although the needs of consumers were not ignored, the economic program adopted at the congress clearly emphasized defense production and heavy industry. The congress also endorsed the new leadership's promotion of stricter artistic and ideological controls. The end of Khrushchev's "thaw" was marked by the trial in February 1966 of two dissident writers, Andrei Siniavsky and Yuli Daniel. The two were convicted of writing articles critical of the Soviet regime and sentenced to several years of internal exile. The congress approved of the treatment of Siniavsky and Daniel and attacked the somewhat relaxed censorship of the Khrushchev years as harmful to the state and the party.

The congress halted the process of de-Stalinization. The Soviet leadership agreed that discussions of Stalinist crimes must end. Since the current leaders had derived their power from Stalin, attacking him would raise questions about the legitimacy of their own rule. Still, Brezhnev was cautious not to completely rehabilitate or associate himself with Stalin, and the Soviet leadership generally discouraged any kind of discussion about Stalin, good or bad. The new regime's desire to curtail de-Stalinization was symbolized by its readoption of the Stalin-era titles for the top policy-making group in the party and the party leader. The policy-making Presidium reverted to its former name, the Politburo, and the designation of the party chief was changed from first secretary to general secretary (both titles had been changed at the Nineteenth Party Congress in 1952).

Brezhnev Consolidates Power

Brezhnev's power increased as the positions of Shelepin and Podgorny were weakened. Shelepin's downfall came about after rumors surfaced in 1965 that Brezhnev might be replaced. Shelepin's associates were believed to have started the rumors, and the other Politburo members resented this type of leak. Brezhnev rivals and allies joined to form a coalition against Shelepin. He was stripped of his deputy-premiership in December 1965 and over the next ten years gradually lost the rest of his power as his associates were demoted. Despite this erosion, Shelepin retained enough influence for some time to help instigate anti-Brezhnev confrontations whenever Brezhnev was vulnerable on an issue. He was not removed from the Politburo until 1975.

Brezhnev's other top rival, Podgorny, also was neutralized in stages. Opportunistic fence-sitters deserted Podgorny as Brezhnev's strength became more apparent. Podgorny's stand on several important issues also had hurt his image among many colleagues. In particular, he had offended the military by urging cuts in defense spending and arguing for increased investment in consumer goods industries. During the 1970s Podgorny remained an influential figure, but he was no longer a serious threat to Brezhnev's authority. In 1977 he was removed from the Politburo, and Brezhnev replaced him as president.

By the April 1973 session of the Central Committee of the Communist party, Brezhnev was firmly in control. Brezhnev's power had eclipsed Kosygin's, and the party boss was clearly first among equals. At this meeting, two men thought to be hard-line conservatives critical of Brezhnev's opening to the West—Petr Shelest, former first secretary of the Ukrainian Communist party, and Gennadii Voronov, former president of the Russian Soviet Federated Socialist Republic—were dropped from the Politburo. The Central Committee on April 27 endorsed "entirely and without reservation" the policy of détente with the West that bore Brezhnev's personal imprint. The Central Committee also cited the "important role played personally by Leonid Brezhnev."

The meeting's most important result, however, was the selection of new full members of the Politburo: Yuri V. Andropov, head of the KGB (the first secret police chief in the Politburo since Lavrenty Beria's ouster in 1953), Foreign Minister Andrei Gromyko, and Defense Minister Andrei Grechko. That all three new Politburo members were responsible for some part of the Kremlin's foreign policy apparatus pointed toward a greater emphasis on international affairs within the Soviet leadership.

Evidence suggests that, during most of his years in power, Brezhnev was the only member of the Secretariat who was also a member of the Defense Council (renamed from Khrushchev's Supreme Military Council). This dual membership gave him significant power. The Politburo tacitly agreed to let the Defense Council, a small Politburo subcommittee, dominate military policy. This arrangement created a subelite that other Politburo members were unable to challenge because they lacked information and expertise on most defense issues that did not have to do with broad questions of foreign policy or resource allocation. One important political disadvantage for Brezhnev in the Defense Council arrangement was that a small number of members (perhaps as few as three) could block a Brezhnev policy within the council. He had to reach an accommodation with these colleagues before a defense issue was brought to the Politburo.

Rules of the Oligarchy

The Brezhnev oligarchy was self-contained, self-renewing, and conscious of the barriers between itself and the rest of the party. Even Politburo members based outside Moscow such as Vladimir Shcherbitsky, Grigory Romanov, and Dinmukhamed Kunaev, the party bosses in the Ukraine, Leningrad, and Kazakhstan, respectively, were generally less influential and excluded from some important matters because they were not always able to attend weekly meetings or receive routine information about impending decisions. The simple circumstance of being based outside of Moscow was a disadvantage.

The Politburo also was divided informally between a changing group of four or five superelite members and the remainder. The top echelon always included the general secretary, the premier, the president, and the leaders of the Secretariat, which included at various times Andropov, Brezhnev, Chernenko, Kirilenko, Kosygin, Podgorny, Suslov, and Nikolai Tikhonov.

Brezhnev and the post-Khrushchev oligarchs strove for stability, order, routine, and predictability. Their sense of political decorum made it unacceptable to publicly air any internal Politburo disputes, as had happened occasionally under Khrushchev. The leaders wanted to protect the exclusivity of the Politburo and Secretariat's decision-making prerogatives and to limit influence and pressure from below. The Politburo leaders usually punished violators of these unwritten rules, such as apparently occurred with Shelepin's removal. The leadership was suspicious and resentful of members who tried to use public opinion for personal advantage. Even Brezhnev was not immune to criticism when he took independent actions that his colleagues believed sidestepped collective rule.

In Brezhnev's quest for scientific decision-making processes, he employed social science experts and other specialists to a greater degree than any previous Soviet leader. The power and influence of these experts on the policy-making process, however, was circumscribed. They provided information and analyses to decision makers but rarely were included in policy-making discussions.

Economic Policy

Whether because he truly believed it best or because he found it politically expedient, Brezhnev advocated two "first priorities" in resource allocation: the military and agriculture. Brezhnev "threw money" at the chronic Soviet agriculture problem. Because the leadership feared the implications of food shortfalls created by bad weather and poor management, Brezhnev's spending continued despite unspectacular results.

Similarly, the established 3 to 4 percent growth rate for defense spending remained sacrosanct. Despite changes in Politburo personnel over time, the Politburo consensus on military issues and priorities did not change much during the Brezhnev era. Brezhnev's political credentials and military contacts enabled him to benefit from a shift of priorities to the military. He knew many military leaders, most of whom disliked Khrushchev; he never uselessly criticized the military and publicly always appeared supportive of it.

Although the Soviet Union had spent a large percentage of its resources on the military during the Khrushchev years, the premier had made moves during the late 1950s and early 1960s to increase consumer production (particularly in the agricultural sector) at the expense of defense. After Khrushchev's ouster, the Soviet leadership reaffirmed the military's priority over national resources. This readjustment pleased conservative leaders who believed Khrushchev had been too liberal. In addition to meeting the perceived military threats from the United States, Western Europe, and China, Soviet military power brought the nation superpower status and influence in foreign relations. Military strength, therefore, became indispensable to the prestige of the Soviet nation and its leadership.

In the Eighth Five-Year Plan (1966-1970), the Soviet leadership tried to satisfy everyone. Through the late 1960s, it largely succeeded. The standard of living rose, and most industries experienced healthy growth. Good weather and the continued expansion of land under cultivation aided agricultural production.

In the 1970s, however, inefficiency and bad weather combined to reduce agricultural production, creating the need to import more food. Adverse demographic trends (a low birthrate in European Russia and high rates of alcoholism and infant mortality) slowed the increase in the labor force, especially in areas where most industry was located. Raw materials, including oil, became more difficult and expensive to extract. As a result of these developments, economic growth rates began to decline. The Soviets were no longer able to depend on extensive growth (wider exploitation of natural and human resources) to achieve economic expansion.

Faced with a tight budget, the Soviet leaders made small cuts in industrial investment and more severe cuts in consumer investment. As the economy continued to decline in the late 1970s, the regime was forced to make even larger cuts in industrial investment. More alarming for the Soviets, they were falling farther behind the West in the development of industrial and agricultural technology. Between 1976 and 1980 the Soviet economy grew by just 2.3 percent per year, according to CIA estimates. *(Economy under Brezhnev, p. 172)*

Foreign Policy

The newly installed Brezhnev leadership endorsed the Khrushchev-era policy of peaceful coexistence. The twin legacies of Khrushchev's foreign policy were a slowly improving relationship with the United States and an increasingly bitter quarrel with the People's Republic of China. Moscow's dealings with both nations would be colored by the growing conflict in Vietnam.

Khrushchev's successors continued the improvement of superpower relations that had begun in 1962 after the Cuban missile crisis. The United States and Soviet Union had agreed in June 1963 to the installation of a hot line between Washington and Moscow to provide immediate communication that would lessen the chance of an accidental nuclear war. On June 10, Kennedy had introduced a new and friendlier tone in U.S. policy toward the Soviets in a speech at American University. This in turn had elicited an amicable response from Moscow.

Kennedy had announced in his American University speech that the United States, the Soviet Union, and Great Britain would begin talks on a partial nuclear test ban treaty. The treaty, which banned nuclear weapons tests in the atmosphere, outer space, and under water, was initialed in Moscow July 25 and ratified by the Senate September 24. Negotiations begun in 1963 resulted in a large American wheat sale to the Soviets in 1964. Other 1964 symbols of comity included efforts to increase East-West trade; cutbacks in the production of fissionable uranium by the United States and the Soviet Union; a slight easing of the requirements for passage between East and West Berlin; and a U.S.-Soviet accord signed February 22 that modestly expanded educational, cultural, scientific, and technical exchanges. By 1965, however, superpower relations were once again strained, largely because of the escalating conflict in Vietnam.

Vietnam Dilemma

American involvement in Vietnam in the mid-1960s posed a dual problem for Soviet leaders. Their hopes for a continuing rapprochement with the United States were jeopardized by Washington's increasing role in a war against their socialist ally, North Vietnam. Too much aid to the North Vietnamese and Communist guerrilla forces in South Vietnam could set back bilateral relations with the United States or even cause a superpower confrontation; too little support for the Vietnamese Communists would bring condemnation from China and offer evidence that Moscow had surrendered leadership of the socialist movement.

The optimal solution to the Soviets' Vietnam problem would have been a negotiated peace settlement limiting the U.S. presence in Indochina, while enhancing Soviet influence in North Vietnam. To obtain such a settlement, however, Moscow needed to convince the independent-minded North Vietnamese to accept major concessions that likely would halt, or at least delay, progress toward their goal of a united Vietnam. Soviet representatives, indeed, had urged Hanoi to go to the bargaining table. But in the wake of U.S. air attacks against North Vietnamese targets on February 7, 1965, Soviet hopes for concessions were reduced. The bombing raids, a response to an assault by Communist guerrillas on the U.S. base at Pleiku, South Vietnam, came while Premier Kosygin was on a state visit to Hanoi, the North Vietnamese capital.

On his way home from Hanoi, Kosygin stopped at Beijing and requested access to Chinese air bases to facilitate shipment of Soviet supplies to North Vietnam. Beijing declined. The *Beijing Review* said in a November 1965 article that "if we were to take united action on the question of Vietnam with the new leaders of the CPSU [Communist Party of the Soviet Union] who are pursuing the Khrushchev revisionist line, wouldn't we be helping them to bring the question of Vietnam within the orbit of Soviet-U.S. collaboration?" The verbal fireworks continued into 1966.

These untimely air attacks and the subsequent bombing campaign against North Vietnam that began later in February reduced Soviet flexibility. As the war progressed, the Soviets increased their aid to North Vietnam and intensified their condemnations of U.S. behavior in Southeast Asia.

Relations between the USSR and North Vietnam were stable and pragmatic during this period. Hanoi maneuvered to obtain as much aid as possible from Moscow, and Kremlin leaders were forthcoming. Their investment in Vietnam was considerable, yet Southeast Asia was not an area of vital interest for the Soviets in the mid-1960s. Building Soviet influence in Indochina was less important to Moscow than using the situation in Vietnam against the United States and China.

By supplying aid to the North Vietnamese, the USSR deepened the quagmire in which the United States found itself. The Soviet Union was careful not to offer weapons or assistance that could have produced a confrontation with the United States. But because U.S.-Soviet relations had cooled considerably since 1964, Moscow did not stand to lose much by supporting Hanoi. U.S. involvement in Vietnam also enabled the Soviet Union to portray the United States to the Third World as an aggressive power willing to use massive force against a small nation to protect its neocolonialist interests.

The Vietnamese conflict also gave the Soviet Union an opportunity to outcompete China in a Third World arena. The North Vietnamese primarily were interested in obtaining material aid, and the USSR's capacity for delivering economic assistance and quality arms was far greater than China's. Also, Beijing's rejection of the Soviets' plan for a united effort against the United States in Vietnam made Chinese accusations that Soviet leaders were not selflessly concerned with Vietnam's struggle sound hypocritical. Finally, Moscow hoped its support of Vietnam would not only solidify its reputation as a defender of Third World national liberation movements, but also produce a cooperative relationship with North Vietnam that would limit Chinese influence in the entire region.

India-Pakistan Conflict

The outbreak of major hostilities between India and Pakistan in August 1965 gave Premier Kosygin a chance to play the statesman and increase Soviet prestige and good will in the subcontinent. The dispute between India, which had established ties with Moscow, and Pakistan, a friend of Beijing, was mediated by Kosygin in January 1966. Meeting at Tashkent in Uzbekistan, the two sides agreed to withdraw their forces to positions held before August 5, 1965. Kosygin's diplomatic intervention blocked Chinese participation in the resolution of a conflict in which Beijing had a strong regional interest.

The dispute between India and Pakistan over Kashmir had flared intermittently since the partition of the state in 1947, following India's and Pakistan's independence from Great Britain. Fighting in Kashmir continued for more than a year before a cease-fire agreement was negotiated to go into effect January 1, 1949. India was left in control of about two-thirds of the area of Kashmir, while Pakistan was given control of the other one-third.

In August 1965 India broke the cease-fire line with Pakistan, and full-scale Indian-Pakistani hostilities followed. As fighting continued, the United States and Great Britain halted all military aid shipments to both nations. In September, India and Pakistan accepted a UN Security Council resolution demanding a cease-fire. The USSR then stepped in and arranged the January negotiating session.

War between India and Pakistan again broke out December 3, 1971, but the Indians, fortified by Soviet military aid and a new twenty-year friendship treaty, easily defeated the Pakistanis, who were backed by the Chinese.

Six-Day War

On June 5, 1967, Israel began the third major Arab-Israeli war by invading its Arab neighbors. During the conflict, referred to as the Six-Day War, Israel destroyed a substantial part of the armed forces of Egypt, Jordan, and Syria. In addition, large amounts of Arab territory were captured— land that Israel did not relinquish after the fighting

Soviet premier Aleksei Kosygin and President Lyndon B. Johnson meet in Glassboro, New Jersey, with, from left, U.S. secretary of state Dean Rusk, Soviet foreign minister Andrei Gromyko, and Soviet ambassador Anatoly Dobrynin.

stopped. The UN Security Council June 6 unanimously adopted a resolution calling for a cease-fire. A truce went into effect June 10.

Israel's decisive victory stunned the Arabs and their Soviet backers and left Israel in a position of strength in the Middle East. Despite Soviet and American pressure, Israel announced that it would remain in the newly occupied territories until decisive progress toward a permanent settlement had been made.

The Six-Day War was an important event for Soviet influence in the region. Before the war, the Soviets had worked to create an anti-Western alliance among the Arabs. The Soviets, however, lost prestige by not providing the Arabs with much assistance during the Six-Day War. In fact, the Soviet decision to back a cease-fire while Israel was in Arab territories angered the Arabs. The only significant measure that Moscow and its East European allies took was severance of diplomatic ties with Israel.

Despite the Arabs' disappointment with Moscow during the fighting, in the long run the Six-Day War boosted Soviet influence among the Arabs. Egypt, charging that U.S. aircraft had contributed to its

defeat, severed diplomatic relations with Washington, as did six other Arab states. While U.S. support for Israel soured U.S. relations with the Arab states, the Soviets solidified their position as the chief benefactor and arms supplier of the Arabs. Partially to make up for its inaction during the war, Moscow rebuilt the armed forces of Egypt, Syria, and Jordan.

Glassboro Summit

Premier Kosygin traveled to New York in 1967 to join the UN debate on the Middle East. While in the United States, Kosygin met with President Johnson on June 23 and 25 in Glassboro, New Jersey. Both the nature of the meeting and the site of the impromptu summit conference were in dispute (Kosygin officially was visiting the United Nations, not the United States). The meeting site at Glassboro State College was selected because it allowed Johnson and Kosygin to meet halfway between UN headquarters and the White House.

Neither side claimed major gains as a result of the ten hours of meetings, but the sessions produced a new, although short-lived, feeling of international good will—christened the "spirit of Glassboro." The first session at Glassboro lasted more than five hours and dealt with the Middle East, Vietnam, and the nonproliferation of nuclear arms. After the second meeting it was announced that progress had been made on the nonproliferation issue but that vast differences still existed over the Middle East and Vietnam. The two world leaders termed the meetings "useful," agreed to meet again sometime, and instructed their foreign policy personnel to continue the talks.

Non-Proliferation Treaty

The Non-Proliferation Treaty, signed July 1, 1968, was the culmination of more than four years of negotiations at the eighteen-nation Disarmament Conference in Geneva and at the United Nations. The treaty called upon the nuclear powers not to disseminate nuclear devices to nonnuclear nations for at least twenty-five years and to engage in discussions aimed at halting the arms race. It also pledged nonnuclear nations not to seek to acquire such devices and encouraged cooperation in the peaceful use of nuclear energy. France and the People's Republic of China, both of which possessed nuclear weapons, refused to sign the treaty. India, which detonated a nuclear device in May 1974, also refused to sign, as did at least six nations possessing advanced nuclear facilities: Israel, Spain, Argentina, Brazil, Pakistan, and South Africa.

President Johnson submitted the treaty to the Senate for ratification July 9, and, in the short-lived spirit of good will prevailing after the Glassboro summit, the Senate Foreign Relations Committee took the unprecedented step of beginning consideration of the treaty within twenty-four hours of its submission. After the Soviet invasion of Czechoslovakia in August 1968, however, calls arose to postpone ratification to signal U.S. condemnation of the Soviet move. The Senate decided to hold off consideration until the next session. Presidential candidate Richard Nixon stated during the 1968 presidential race that he strongly opposed ratification at that time for fear of condoning the Czechoslovakian invasion. But in January he called on the Senate to approve the treaty, promising to "implement it in

my new administration." The Senate ratified the treaty March 13.

Invasion of Czechoslovakia

Soviet troops, accompanied by forces from four Warsaw Pact nations—Poland, Hungary, East Germany, and Bulgaria—invaded Czechoslovakia August 20-21, 1968, to stem a liberal democratic movement that, according to Moscow, threatened Czechoslovak socialism. The Soviets reported that the intervention was requested by the "party and government leaders of the Czechoslovak Socialist Republic." In their statement, however, Czechoslovak leaders asserted that the invasion occurred "without the knowledge of the President of the Republic, the Chairman of the National Assembly, the Premier or the First Secretary of the Czechoslovak Communist Party Central Committee." The invasion, the Czechoslovak statement continued, was "contrary not only to the fundamental principles of relations between Socialist states," but also "contrary to the principles of international law." The statement appealed to the Czechoslovaks "to maintain calm and not to offer resistance to the troops on the march. Our army, security corps and people's militia have not received the command to defend the country."

Development of the Crisis

In June 1967 the Fourth Congress of Czechoslovak Writers adopted a vigorous denunciation of government censorship in literature, culture, and politics. The government expelled from the Communist party the leaders of the anticensorship movement. Afterward, however, it exhibited a more liberal attitude in foreign relations by signing August 4, 1967, a two-year trade pact with West Germany, despite objections from the Soviets and the East Germans.

The most important development occurred in January 1968 when Alexander Dubcek, a reform-minded Slovak, took over the post of party first secretary from the more orthodox Antonin Novotny. During the "Prague Spring" of 1968, Dubcek and other Czechoslovak leaders repeatedly affirmed

Soviet tanks line a street off Old Town Square in Prague following the August 1968 invasion of Czechoslovakia.

their intention of moving the country toward "democratic socialism," as contrasted with the party-controlled socialism of the Soviet Union. The Central Committee of the Czechoslovak Communist party April 15 adopted a program, "Czechoslovakia's Road to Socialism," designed to ensure freedom of speech, the press, assembly, and religion, as well as greater freedom for the country's four noncommunist political parties. Gen. Ludvik Svoboda, who was elected president March 30 following the forced resignation of Novotny from that office, said in May, "We are starting out to create a new type of socialist democracy, a democracy which will lend support to the full development of the human personality."

The first threat of Soviet military intervention developed when Soviet troops, which had moved into Czechoslovakia in June to engage in Warsaw Pact maneuvers, stayed behind when the exercises were completed.

Moscow July 19 summoned the Czech leadership to the Soviet Union to discuss Czechoslovakia's "democratic socialism." The Czechs declined but agreed to meet with the Soviet Politburo July 29-August 1 at the Czechoslovak border town of Cierna. The Soviet delegation consisted of party chief Brezhnev, Premier Kosygin, President Podgorny, and eleven other Politburo members. Czechoslovakia's representatives included sixteen officials of the party and the government, led by Dubcek. Faced with Czechoslovak determination, the Soviets appeared to back down and agreed to remove their troops from Czechoslovakia. The troop withdrawal was announced and an apparent compromise was confirmed at an August 3 meeting in Bratislava attended by representatives of the Communist parties of the Soviet Union, Czechoslovakia, Bulgaria, East Germany, Hungary, and Poland.

Yet the relaxation of tension did not last. After three weeks, the Soviet Union August 16 resumed criticism of the Czechoslovak press. Also on August 16, Dubcek pleaded with the Czechoslovak people not to push liberalization too far or too fast. "We need order in our country," he said, "so that we can be given freedom of action in our democratization process." Four days later, an estimated 400,000 troops, three-fourths of whom were Soviet soldiers, entered Czechoslovakia to put down the "counter-revolution."

The invaders promptly arrested Dubcek and other members of the government. They were flown to Moscow, where, under pressure, they agreed to crack down on liberalization. Dubcek remained in power until April 1969, when he was replaced as first secretary by Gustav Husak, a pro-Soviet hardliner, who dismantled what remained of the liberalization movement.

Widespread Condemnation

World reaction to the invasion of Czechoslovakia was severe. Though most of Moscow's satellites supported the move, the two mavericks of Eastern Europe, Romania and Yugoslavia, were critical. Romanian strongman Nicolae Ceausescu charged that the invasion was "a great mistake and a grave danger to peace in Europe, to the fate of socialism in the world."

The Communist parties of France and Italy condemned the Soviet action, as did the governments of France, Britain, Italy, India, Canada, and other nations. The Chinese said the invasion was a "shameless act" comparable to Hitler's occupation of the Sudetenland and U.S. involvement in Vietnam. President Johnson said the invasion "shocks the conscience of the world. The Soviet Union and its allies have invaded a defenseless country to stamp out a resurgence of ordinary human freedom."

The Brezhnev Doctrine

In the wake of the international furor over the invasion of Czechoslovakia, the Kremlin formulated a theory, quickly termed the Brezhnev Doctrine, to justify Soviet interference in the affairs of other communist states. The Brezhnev Doctrine was outlined in an article, "Sovereignty and the International Duties of Socialist Countries," published in *Pravda* September 26, 1968:

The weakening of any of the links in the world socialist system directly affects all the socialist countries. Thus, with talk about the right of nations to self-determination the anti-socialist elements in Czechoslovakia actually covered up a demand for so-called neutrality and Czechoslovakia's withdrawal from the socialist community. However, the implementation of "self-determination" of that kind or, in other words, the detaching of Czechoslovakia from the socialist community would have come into conflict with Czechoslovakia's vital interests and would have been detrimental to the other socialist states. Such "self-determination," as a result of which NATO troops would have been able to come up to the Soviet borders, while the community of European socialist countries would have been rent, would have encroached, in actual fact, upon the vital interests of the peoples of these countries and would be in fundamental conflict with the right of these peoples to socialist self-determination.

Brezhnev reiterated the argument in a speech to the Fifth Congress of the Polish Communist party, November 13, 1968, and in a speech in Moscow made October 28, 1969, to a delegation of Czechoslovak officials. He told his Polish audience that "when the internal and external forces hostile to socialism seek to revert the development of any socialist country toward the restoration of the capitalist order, when a threat to the cause of socialism in that country, a threat to the security of the socialist community as a whole emerges, this is no longer a problem of the people of that country but also a common problem, a concern of all socialist countries."

Rise and Fall of Détente

The invasion of Czechoslovakia in August 1968 was a setback to East-West relations. Nevertheless,

President Richard Nixon, Soviet president Nikolai Podgorny, and General Secretary Leonid Brezhnev toast the signing of an agreement on cooperation in science and technology, May 24, 1972, the Grand Kremlin Palace.

in the months that followed leaders in the West made moves to improve relations with Moscow. A new administration in Washington, headed by Richard Nixon, a famous cold warrior, embarked on a course that led to a dramatic series of U.S.-Soviet summit meetings and several agreements on the limitation of nuclear weapons.

After its initial successes, however, the Nixon administration's policy of détente came under increasing attack in the United States, with critics charging that the Soviets got the best of the bargain and demanding that in return for Western cooperation on trade and arms control Moscow should ease its tight emigration restrictions and improve human rights in the USSR. The succeeding administrations of Gerald R. Ford and Jimmy Carter tried to build on the successes of Nixon's détente, particularly in the area of arms control. But by the late 1970s, relations between the superpowers had become strained. The Soviet invasion of Afghanistan in December 1979 ended détente and ushered in a period of U.S.-Soviet animosity and confrontation.

Détente's Accomplishments

Détente sought to limit tensions between the superpowers and create a stable international atmosphere that would reduce the risk of war and allow for cooperative actions that were in the interest of both the Soviet Union and the West. In the early 1970s détente focused on stabilizing the situation in Europe and concluding arms control agreements.

In 1970 West Germany signed agreements with the Soviet Union and Poland that recognized post-World War II borders. This agreement was followed in 1971 by an agreement between the four powers responsible for Berlin (the Soviet Union, the United States, France, and Great Britain) regarding the administration of the divided city. The Soviet Union pledged to refrain from interfering with communication and transportation to West Berlin, and all the parties vowed not to attempt to change the status of the city. In addition, the treaty allowed West Berliners to travel with West German passports and receive West German consular protection abroad, although the four powers did not recognize West Berlin as part of West Germany. In December 1972, the two Germanies signed a treaty that recognized their postwar separation.

In arms control the United States and the Soviet Union concluded several agreements limiting the growth of nuclear weapons. Strategic Arms Limitation Talks (SALT) began in November 1969. By 1972 the superpowers had reached agreement on limiting defensive antiballistic missile (ABM) systems. In May President Nixon became the first president ever to visit Moscow when he traveled there for a summit that included the signing of the SALT I treaty. The treaty provided for limitations on the deployment of ABMs. An accompanying executive agreement restricted each side's offensive weapons to the number already under construction or deployed when the agreement was signed. The executive agreement also placed limitations on the number of missile-carrying submarines that could be constructed.

There was speculation immediately preceding Nixon's trip that the Soviets might withdraw their invitation as a result of his decision to thwart a North Vietnamese offensive by increasing air attacks on supply lines in North Vietnam and mining Haiphong harbor and six other ports in the north. That the Kremlin, North Vietnam's main arms supplier, went through with the summit was taken as a sign in the West that Moscow was as eager as Washington to conclude the arms pact and improve relations. Soviet leaders were motivated to hold the summit in part because of the warming relationship between the United States and China (Nixon had visited Beijing earlier in the year). The Soviets feared a Sino-American détente would result in anti-Soviet cooperation between their two rivals.

Superpower relations continued to improve during 1973 and 1974, despite President Nixon's preoccupation with the Watergate scandal that led to his resignation in August 1974. Brezhnev visited the United States in June 1973, and Nixon returned to Moscow in June 1974. These summits produced scientific, cultural, and commercial agreements and pledges to accelerate the pace of arms control.

Waning of Détente

Throughout the early period of détente, arms control had overshadowed progress made by the United States and Soviet Union on establishing better trade relations. As a result of the 1972 summit, the two countries established a Joint United States-USSR Commercial Commission, and Moscow bought millions of tons of American grain in a purchase financed by U.S. credits. On October 18, 1972, the United States and Soviet Union signed a three-year trade pact that would greatly expand commercial relations between the two countries and provide for the Soviets' repayment of their World War II lend-lease debts to the United States. Implementation of the trade agreement hinged on congressional approval of most-favored-nation (MFN) status (nondiscrimination in customs matters) for Soviet production. If MFN status was not granted, the pact would not enter into force, and the Soviet Union, in accordance with the second agreement, would not have to repay the balance of its lend-lease debt of 722 million dollars.

The granting of MFN status to the Soviet Union ran into strong resistance in Congress. Many members objected to the Soviet's backing of the Arabs in the 1973 Arab-Israeli war and Moscow's levying of an exit fee—reportedly up to thirty thousand dollars—on Jews wishing to emigrate from the Soviet Union who held advanced academic degrees. Moscow justified the fees as reimbursement for the state's investment in education, the benefits of which would be lost through emigration. But the effect of the fee was to block the emigration of most Soviet Jews to Israel.

In December 1974, Congress passed the Jackson-Vanik amendment. This legislation made extension of MFN status to the Soviet Union conditional on the liberalization of Soviet emigration policies. The Jackson-Vanik amendment disillusioned Brezhnev and the Soviet leadership. Détente was not paying off so well in their view that they would permit what they considered to be interference in their internal affairs. On January 14, 1975, the Soviets informed the United States that they were rejecting the terms of trade contained in the Jackson-Vanik amendment and accordingly would not put into force the 1972 trade agreement.

The demise of the trade accord did not end détente, but thereafter the U.S.-Soviet relationship gradually deteriorated. Continued harsh treatment of dissidents in the Soviet Union, the USSR's ongoing military buildup, North Vietnam's conquest of South Vietnam in 1975, and Moscow's backing of a Marxist faction in Angola that came to power in 1976 with the help of tens of thousands of Cuban troops discredited détente in the eyes of many American policy makers. Nevertheless the United States and Soviet Union continued to negotiate on arms control. In 1979 Carter and Brezhnev signed the SALT II treaty at a summit in Vienna. The treaty placed limits on the growth of the strategic nuclear arsenals of the superpowers.

The treaty immediately ran into opposition in the U.S. Senate. Opponents claimed that it gave the Soviets unfair advantages and rewarded Moscow despite continued Soviet-backed communist aggression in the Third World and human rights abuses in the Soviet Union. Carter countered that the treaty placed few limits on weapons the United States was planning to build, while restricting the Soviets in some important areas. He also said that he would continue pressuring the Soviet Union to improve its human rights record. In a major defeat for the policy of détente, the Senate Armed Services Committee on December 20, 1979, voted 10-0 to recommend rejection of the SALT II treaty. Within a week the treaty's demise became inevitable when Soviet forces invaded Afghanistan to prop up a pro-Soviet government there. The invasion destroyed what support was left for détente in the United States. (*Afghanistan invasion, p. 204*)

Assessment of Détente

At the heart of détente's demise were the divergent Soviet and American conceptions of what détente meant and what it was supposed to accomplish. The principal American architects of détente, President Nixon and his national security adviser and eventual secretary of state, Henry A. Kissinger, have stated that they saw détente as a way to complement containment of the Soviet Union by slowing the arms race and reducing the risk of confrontation. Most members of Congress and the American public, however, saw détente in more ambitious terms. They hoped that it would lead to an end to superpower arms competition, Soviet adventurism in the Third World, and human rights abuses in the USSR. As a result, American attitudes concerning cooperating with the Soviet Union in areas such as trade and cultural exchanges became linked with assessments of the Soviet regime's domestic and international behavior.

These expectations were bound to produce disillusionment in the United States. For while the Soviet Union welcomed the relaxation of tensions and the increase in trade with the West, it had no intention of allowing the West to make demands that affected its internal affairs or its recruitment of and support for allies and clients.

The Soviets saw no contradiction between détente and the continuation of their worldwide struggle against capitalism. A Soviet publication on foreign policy published during the height of détente declared:

It may be asked whether peaceful coexistence signifies a certain conciliation between socialism and capitalism? Does it mean recognition of the capitalist order? Does it represent the curtailment of the struggle against imperialism?

On no account!

Peaceful coexistence is one of the principal forms of the struggle against imperialism.

Consequently, détente with the West did not dissuade the Soviets from supporting wars of national liberation in such places as Angola and Ethiopia or helping allies such as the Vietnamese and the Cubans to carry out aggressive military operations in the Third World.

When Ronald Reagan took office as president in January 1981, the policy of détente had been thoroughly discredited in the United States and had little appeal for the Soviet leadership. Most Americans, including Reagan, believed that the United States could not engage in a détente with a partner that was perceived as internally corrupt, openly aggressive, and obsessed with its own security. For their part, the Soviets believed that the United States was uncommitted to détente (as demonstrated by the Senate's refusal to ratify the SALT II treaty), bent on interfering in Soviet internal affairs, and unwilling to grant them room to pursue legitimate Soviet national security objectives. Reagan's subsequent anti-Soviet rhetoric ended any faint Soviet hopes that the United States would resume détente and made the Soviet leadership increasingly pessimistic about the usefulness and likelihood of improving U.S.-Soviet relations.

Crisis in Poland

Both sides saw the events surrounding the imposition of martial law in Poland in December 1981 as confirming their opinion of their former partner in détente.

A political crisis was triggered in Poland July 1, 1980, when the government removed subsidies from the price of meat. Scattered strikes erupted throughout Poland to protest the price hikes. Workers at the Lenin shipyard in Gdansk, Poland's largest, took over the yard August 14. On August 17 the strikers formed an Interfactory Strike Committee, and its leader, thirty-seven-year-old unemployed electrician Lech Walesa, announced the group's terms for negotiations. In addition to demands for increased wages and reduced meat prices, the committee called for the formation of independent labor unions, relaxed government censorship, and the right to strike.

After some reluctance, the Polish Communist party, led by First Secretary Edward Gierek, agreed to negotiate with the strikers. The settlement reached August 30 permitted workers to form unions free of government interference, reduced official censorship, allowed churches and other groups access to the government-controlled news media, and freed imprisoned dissidents who had supported the strike. In addition, the government vowed to increase wages, upgrade medical services, and improve supplies of basic foods.

After strikers returned to work, the party announced September 6 that Gierek had been ousted.

Ironically, Gierek had been named first secretary in 1970 after labor unrest caused the downfall of his predecessor, Wladyslaw Gomulka. The new Polish leader, Stanislaw Kania, formerly the head of the country's security forces, pledged to honor the strike settlement and vowed to retain Poland's close ties with the Soviet Union.

The situation remained tense for the remainder of 1980 as the strike committee, which took the name Solidarity, accused the Kania regime of failing to fulfill the terms of the settlement. Speculation arose that the Soviet military might intervene in Poland to strengthen Warsaw's control. President Carter on December 3 warned the Soviets that any intervention in Poland's affairs would have "most negative consequences" and that U.S.-Soviet relations would be "directly and adversely affected."

The problem facing the Kremlin was considerable. If Soviet forces were not sent into Poland, Moscow feared that the momentum of liberalization would threaten the Warsaw government and perhaps spread to other Soviet satellites and into the Soviet Union itself. Faced with similar situations in Hungary in 1956 and Czechoslovakia in 1968, Soviet armies invaded and occupied these countries. In late December, during the last weeks of the Carter administration, the White House reported that Soviet "preparation for possible intervention in Poland appears to have been completed."

In his Twenty-sixth Party Congress speech February 23, 1981, Brezhnev, discussing Poland, reiterated the Brezhnev Doctrine. He said the Soviet Union would always stand up for Poland and would "not leave her in the lurch." In Brezhnev's words: "Let no one have any doubt about our common determination to secure our interests and defend the people's socialist gains."

Moscow stepped up the pressure on the Polish leadership with a June 5 letter stressing measures to block counterrevolution and a July 21 message calling on the Polish Communist party "to resolutely rebuff anarchy and counterrevolution." Warsaw Pact maneuvers were held in early September in the Soviet Union near the Polish border.

In the midst of the tense fall of 1981, Polish

Communist party leader Kania was purged and replaced by the prime minister, Gen. Wojciech Jaruzelski. Under Jaruzelski's leadership, the Polish Politburo November 28 ordered the legislature to enact a law banning strikes, thus reversing one of the key elements of the government-Solidarity agreement of August 1980. On December 12 Solidarity leaders met in Gdansk to discuss proposals calling for free elections and the establishment of a new government. After the meeting, most top Solidarity officials, including Walesa, were arrested and detained. The government declared martial law, closed the border, and cut off all communications to and from Poland and within Poland itself.

Imposition of martial law provided the first major test of President Reagan's handling of U.S.-Soviet relations. In an address televised from the White House, Reagan announced December 23 that the United States would take "concrete political and economic measures" against Moscow if the Polish crackdown continued. Reagan added, "The Soviet Union, through its threats and pressures, deserves a major share of blame for the developments in Poland."

Reagan suspended U.S. government shipments of food to Poland, withdrew its line of export credit insurance with the Export-Import Bank, halted Polish airline service in the United States, and withdrew Poland's permission to fish in U.S. waters. Reagan said, "These actions are not directed against the Polish people. They are a warning to the government of Poland that free men cannot and will not stand idly by in the face of brutal repression."

On December 29 Reagan announced sanctions aimed directly at the Soviet Union. Charging that the "Soviet Union bears a heavy and direct responsibility for the repression in Poland," the president suspended new export licenses for high-technology items, including oil and gas equipment; postponed talks on a maritime pact and a grain agreement; restricted Soviet access to U.S. ports; and withdrew Soviet air service privileges. The president, however, declined to cancel U.S.-Soviet talks on limiting nuclear weapons in Europe.

Stagnation under Gerontocracy

The Soviet Union under Brezhnev was characterized by its domestic stability. Although dissidence grew and the Soviet people became increasingly disgruntled with economic conditions, Soviet society remained calm due to several factors.

First, the KGB aggressively repressed dissident individuals and groups. This repression had little in common with the systematic mass arrests under Joseph Stalin that sent hundreds of thousands of Soviets to labor camps. Instead it was directed almost exclusively against dissidents who openly criticized or challenged the regime. Dissidents risked being harassed, losing privileges, having their access to education or career advancement blocked, and in extreme cases, being arrested or deported. Second, the Communist party remained in total control of the nation's political, military, and economic institutions. Party members pervaded all institutions of Soviet government and society. They promoted the party's interests and guarded against activities that could undermine the party's authority (and by extension their own privileges). Third, Soviet authorities maintained strict censorship rules. Soviets could voice complaints with specific problems, such as local corruption or defects in a particular consumer item, but the censors did not allow Soviet journalists, artists, and citizens to express dissatisfaction with the ruling regime or the Soviet system. Finally, the Soviet people had become used to the conditions in their country. Although citizens routinely complained and joked to one another about the hassles of life, most had witnessed a very gradual improvement in the standard of living since World War II. As long as conditions appeared to be improving over the long run, few Soviets were willing to risk the consequences of dissent. Moreover, their tolerance for the Communist party's dictatorial rule was reinforced by Russia's long tradition of autocracy.

Brezhnev and his colleagues had succeeded in pacifying Soviet society and protecting their own power and the privileges of Communist party members. The late 1970s and early 1980s witnessed a virtual cessation of turnover in the Soviet leadership. With few exceptions, only leaders who died or

Brezhnev Politburo

Below is a list of the full members of the Politburo as of January 1, 1982. The age of each member is in parentheses following his name.

Arvid Pel'she (82)
Mikhail Suslov (79)
Nikolai Tikhonov (76)
Andrei Kirilenko (75)
Leonid Brezhnev (75)
Dmitry Ustinov (73)
Andrei Gromyko (72)
Konstantin Chernenko (70)
Dinmukhamed Kunaev (69)
Yuri Andropov (67)
Viktor Grishin (67)
Vladimir Shcherbitsky (63)
Grigory Romanov (58)
Mikhail Gorbachev (50)

became seriously ill were replaced. As a result, the average age of Soviet leaders rose dramatically. At the beginning of 1982, eleven of the fourteen full Politburo members were at least sixty-seven years old. The average age of Politburo members was seventy (almost seventy-two if the fifty-year-old Mikhail S. Gorbachev were excluded from the calculation). The Soviet Union had become a gerontocracy—a nation governed by old men. Brezhnev, who was frequently ill, had turned over the daily management of the party and state to other leaders, but he still possessed the authority and the energy to block initiatives that he opposed and advance the general outlines of policies that he preferred.

This political stagnation at the top contributed to a stagnation of the Soviet economy and society as the job security and advancing age of prominent Soviet leaders sapped their ability and will to address the Soviet Union's problems. The conservative leadership refused to consider meaningful changes, especially those that held the risk of causing public dissatisfaction, such as price reforms.

Under Brezhnev's policy of "respect for cadres"

(personnel), party and government figures had become intertwined in a web of personal corruption. In return for unswerving loyalty, Brezhnev had adopted a hands-off policy in the republics and localities. As a result, local political elites wielded unchallenged power. This contributed to rising doubts in Soviet society about the efficacy of socialist leadership, and ultimately, of socialism itself.

The developing malaise in Soviet society manifested itself in numerous ways. A high rate of alcoholism had led to widespread absenteeism from work and drunkenness on the job. Soviet laborers, who did not have access to quality consumer goods and were not rewarded for hard work with higher wages, displayed little enthusiasm for their jobs. Meanwhile the Soviet black market flourished. As much as 18 percent of consumer expenditures went to the "second economy," where Soviets could find scarce items if they were willing to pay high prices. Black market entrepreneurs stole items subject to frequent shortages, such as gasoline and medical supplies, and sold them at inflated profits. Standing in line for coveted consumer items that one did not need, then selling them on the street for a large profit became a common practice. Many service industry workers such as plumbers, cab drivers, and doctors engaged in "moonlighting"—selling their services in their off hours for black market prices. Because services provided by the state were so poor and undependable, moonlighters rarely had to look hard to find extra work.

During the Brezhnev period evidence also existed of growing alienation among Soviet youth. Many young people, starved for entertainment and witnessing the apathy and corruption in adult society, turned to petty crime, black market activities, alcohol, and drugs. Few youths embraced higher socialist ethics, preferring nonconformist diversions such as Western fashions and rock music, which developed a huge following in the Soviet Union, despite the leadership's efforts to discourage their popularity.

Most troublesome, however, was the general decline of the Soviet economy. During the Khrushchev and early Brezhnev years, the Soviet leadership had depended on extensive growth to propel economic expansion. As resources became more difficult to extract and environmental problems became more acute the Soviets could no longer rely on a wider exploitation of their natural riches. The economy had to be made more efficient. But the Brezhnev leadership continued to hope that minor adjustments in central planning could get the economy moving without recourse to significant decentralization, price reforms, increases in worker incentives, and other radical measures.

The Soviet economic system had a bias toward imbalances and chronic shortages because the transportation infrastructure was often unreliable. The large central planning bureaucracy also made coordinating supplies and deliveries difficult. This inefficiency contributed to falling growth rates and hampered the Soviet leadership's efforts to allocate resources effectively.

The USSR's foreign economic relations also were problematic. The Soviet economy produced low-quality goods that did not meet world standards. Consequently, the Soviet Union could earn the hard currency needed to trade for food and technology only by exporting raw materials and natural resources. Its inconvertible ruble hindered its participation in the world economy, and the subsidies it provided to its allies were a huge drain on its budget.

Hampered by a string of bad harvests in the early 1980s (despite continued high investment in agriculture), Soviet economic growth fell below 2 percent per year for the years 1981 to 1985. The Soviet Union's international trade position also suffered as the growth of oil revenues slowed in the early 1980s and nations imposed sanctions against the USSR in response to the invasion of Afghanistan and the suppression of unrest in Poland. The continuing restrictions on exports of high technology to the Soviet Union by the United States and other Western nations were particularly damaging to Moscow.

Consequently, in the early 1980s, an unusual and ironic situation had developed in the Soviet Union. Despite the USSR's abundant natural resources, well-educated population, huge industrial base and land mass, and tremendous military power, the Soviet people had to endure an intractable housing shortage, shoddy consumer goods, inadequate food

supplies, and a standard of living that in many areas of the country approached Third World levels. Real per capita consumption, perhaps the best measure of living standards, had steadily declined during the early 1980s. Male life expectancy had declined from sixty-six years to sixty-two years during the Brezhnev era, while the infant mortality rate had increased to almost twice the rate in the United States.

On November 10, 1982, Brezhnev died of a heart attack at the age of seventy-five. Two days later the Communist party announced the selection of Yuri V. Andropov as the new general secretary.

Brezhnev had held the post of general secretary for eighteen years, a term exceeded only by Joseph Stalin's twenty-nine years. Although Brezhnev's "cult of personality" did not reach the extent of Stalin's or even Khrushchev's, he did systematically promote himself during the latter years of his regime. His writings were widely published, he was frequently quoted in the Soviet media, and his picture appeared on billboards and at official events. In 1976 he was named a marshal of the Soviet Union and his military service during World War II was glorified. In 1977 he pushed weakened rival Nikolai Podgorny out of the presidency and assumed the ceremonial position himself. Brezhnev was buried in front of the Kremlin Wall in a distinguished spot behind the Lenin mausoleum.

After Mikhail Gorbachev came to power in 1985, however, Brezhnev's official reputation came under attack. At first the criticism was indirect and suggestive, but by 1987 Brezhnev and his cronies were being blamed by name for much of what was wrong with Soviet society. After watching a film on Bolshevik history with a Soviet audience in 1988, *Washington Post* reporter David Remnick observed, "When the film showed Brezhnev in action, the snide laughter in the theater was reminiscent of the way college audiences after Watergate would chortle at films of Richard Nixon's "Checkers speech," in which the 1952 vice-presidential candidate defended himself against charges of a secret political fund." Whether this appraisal of Brezhnev was fair or not, he had become a symbol in the Soviet Union of inefficient, unimaginative, and corrupt leadership.

CHAPTER **5**

GORBACHEV COMES TO POWER

Leonid I. Brezhnev's death in 1982 ended years of stagnant leadership and precipitated a long-delayed succession crisis. Would the Kremlin opt for another aging leader who would continue muddling through? Or would it choose a younger man prepared to institute change? Sixty-eight-year-old Yuri V. Andropov was selected to succeed Brezhnev as general secretary. Although he displayed reformist tendencies, his policies produced only minor results before he died in February 1984. Andropov was succeeded by seventy-three-year-old Konstantin U. Chernenko, a close associate of Brezhnev. Chernenko, who was in ill health, was widely perceived to be a transitional leader who did little to advance reforms during his thirteen months in power. Upon Chernenko's death in March 1985, Mikhail S. Gorbachev and a younger generation claimed the helm.

Andropov's Rule

On November 12, 1982, two days after Leonid Brezhnev's death, Yuri Andropov was chosen to succeed him as general secretary of the Soviet Communist party. Within two months, Andropov appeared to be firmly in control of the Soviet Union. From 1967 to 1982 Andropov had headed the country's intelligence and internal security agency, the Committee for State Security (KGB). As head of the KGB, Andropov had overseen a systematic and effective campaign to suppress Soviet dissidents. He became a candidate member of the Politburo in 1967 and a full member six years later. In May 1982, Andropov had resigned as KGB head to become a member of the Secretariat, a better stepping-stone to the general secretaryship. On the Secretariat he succeeded his patron Mikhail Suslov as the top party ideologist. Nevertheless, he retained close ties to the KGB, and it was a major institutional force behind his rise to power.

Western analysts were impressed with Andropov's apparent intelligence and sophistication. They suggested that he was selected over Brezhnev's personal favorite, Konstantin Chernenko, because Andropov had the support of the military, the KGB, and leading party technocrats who believed Chernenko was incapable of the vigorous leadership necessary to deal with the country's severe economic and social problems. Most Western experts believed that the support of Foreign Minister Andrei Gromyko and Defense Minister Dmitry Ustinov was decisive in Andropov's elevation and that the choice of Andropov seemed to indicate the Soviet leadership's preference for tightly controlled reform in both domestic and foreign policy.

When Andropov was selected as general secretary, former U.S. ambassador to the Soviet Union Malcolm Toon said that "Some measure of reform might be palatable to the old guard . . . if carried out under the watchful eye of Andropov." He could, "in the view of the conservatives, be relied upon to use the same ruthlessness he applied to his KGB responsibilities in making sure reforms would not seriously damage the role of the party and thus would not get out of hand," Toon wrote in the *Christian Science Monitor* November 17, 1982.

Any economic reform, however, would risk offending many members of the Communist party bureaucracy. Most Soviet leaders recognized the need for changes, but a shake-up of the procedures or structure of the party bureaucracy likely would infringe on the fiefdoms of powerful national and regional party potentates.

Nevertheless, Andropov proposed a limited decentralization of the party apparatus and economic planning system in an effort to invigorate the economy. His proposals drew strong opposition not only from corrupt elements of the party bureaucracy worried about their jobs, but also from many orthodox Communists who feared that even modest changes in the Soviet system could become uncontrollable and eventually threaten the Communist party's authority over Soviet society.

The Soviet Union's position in international affairs complicated Andropov's efforts to improve the economy. A confrontational administration in Washington had launched a military buildup that the Soviets believed they had to match. In addition, the Soviets were spending large amounts of money to support the governments of client states around the world. Meanwhile Soviet oil export revenues—the USSR's main source of hard currency—had peaked, and subsidies and aid to the failing economies of Eastern Europe had become a tremendous economic drain. China remained stridently hostile toward the Soviet Union, necessitating, in the Kremlin's view, the deployment of hundreds of thousands of troops along the Chinese border. And the Soviet military was bogged down in an expensive war in Afghanistan that continued to damage Moscow's reputation in the Third World and showed no signs of ending.

If Andropov was going to initiate change he had to act quickly, for the new Soviet leader was in dubious health. Andropov's kidneys failed only four months into his tenure, and after this setback he had to use a dialysis machine at least twice a week. In September 1983 Andropov became seriously ill. He made a partial recovery after doctors removed one of his kidneys in October. From that point, Andropov was confined almost all the time to a specially equipped apartment inside a government hospital.

Despite his poor health, Andropov was able to run the country. He did not govern in the manner of an interim leader willing to follow his predecessor's policies until a new leader was ready to take over. He pressed his moderate reform package with mixed success and placed his stamp on foreign policy and personnel decisions.

Economic Reform

Until his health failed in the fall of 1983, Andropov devoted himself primarily to attempts at revitalizing the sluggish Soviet economy. He openly criticized the party and government bureaucracies for blocking change and encouraged frank debates among economists and national leaders about how to get the economy moving. The centerpiece of his economic plan was his campaign to reduce corruption, inefficiency, and alcoholism. Though significant for its acknowledgment of these problems, the campaign did little to improve low Soviet labor productivity.

Andropov also advocated giving manufacturing and agricultural enterprises more autonomy and introducing incentives for productive workers. In July 1983 he announced a series of economic experiments in selected enterprises designed to test his proposals and reduce central bureaucratic controls. Ministries were to have less control of daily decisions at enterprises, and enterprise managers were given control of funds used to reward employees for hard work. The profitability of the enterprises involved in the experiment was made an important factor in their operation. Managers' salaries were linked to profits, and fulfillment of production quotas was based on the number of items produced by the enterprise that were sold, instead of on how many items the enterprise produced. In 1984 the Soviet leadership labeled the experiment a success and extended it to additional enterprises, but the Kremlin was unwilling to introduce these reforms on a large scale.

Andropov and his colleagues also were unwilling to substantially cut the Soviet defense budget. If Andropov had suggested large-scale reductions in Soviet military spending, he would have risked losing the support of the military. Another factor working against cuts in the military budget was the continuing defense buildup by the United States.

President Ronald Reagan's March 1983 call for the development of a space-based anti-missile weapons system (the Strategic Defense Initiative, or SDI) that would render the Soviet strategic nuclear arsenal "impotent and obsolete" also contributed to Soviet unwillingness to spend less on defense, particularly in the area of weapons technology research. The Soviets feared that an aggressive American SDI program would widen the technological gap between the superpowers.

Personnel Changes

After his health setback in the fall of 1983, Andropov shifted his attention to personnel changes. He retired scores of party and government officials because of their age or ineffectiveness. He promoted Mikhail Gorbachev and numerous lower-level officials who supported reforms. These younger men shared Andropov's concern about the Soviet Union's economic weakness, and they set the stage for future general secretary Gorbachev's more rapid, extensive personnel changes and economic initiatives.

At the time of Brezhnev's death, full Politburo membership had dwindled to ten, giving Andropov the opportunity to influence the appointment of as many as five new members. His first top-level change was announced November 22, 1982, when Geidar Aliev was elevated to full member of the Politburo. Aliev was a fifty-nine-year-old KGB career officer whom Andropov had appointed to oversee the drive against corruption in Azerbaijan in the late 1960s. Viktor Chebrikov, who succeeded Andropov as KGB head, was named a candidate Politburo member in December 1983. Mikhail Solomentsev and Vitaly Vorotnikov, never close allies of Brezhnev, were promoted to full Politburo membership at a Central Committee plenum in December 1983. The plenum also approved the appointment of Yegor Ligachev to the Central Committee Secretariat.

East-West Relations

In an inaugural-style address before the Central Committee November 22, 1982, Andropov said: "The policy of détente is by no means a past stage. The future belongs to this policy." Few leaders in either the United States or the Soviet Union, however, expected relations to improve quickly. Immediately after Brezhnev's death President Reagan and other administration officials had stressed their desire for better superpower relations. But explicit or implicit in these statements was the caveat that any improvement would require some change in Soviet behavior. "It takes two to tango," President Reagan quipped at a news conference the day after Brezhnev's death.

In a meeting with *Washington Post* editors and reporters November 12, Secretary of State George P. Shultz outlined the steps the Soviet Union had to take before better relations could be established: Soviet withdrawal from Afghanistan, Vietnamese withdrawal from Cambodia, relaxation of tensions in Poland, and progress toward arms reductions. Andropov, in his speech to the Central Committee November 22, countered that "statements in which the readiness for normalizing relations is linked with the demand that the Soviet Union pay with preliminary concessions in different fields do not sound serious, to say the least. We shall not agree to this."

The same day Reagan proposed the deployment of a hundred MX intercontinental ballistic missiles in Wyoming. The administration hoped that the threat of deployment would move Kremlin leaders to engage in meaningful arms reduction talks. Moscow denounced the MX decision, saying that it violated existing arms agreements and insisting that the USSR would find "an effective way to reply to Washington" if such provocations continued.

The arms issue that dominated Andropov's reign, however, was the North Atlantic Treaty Organization's (NATO) deployment of intermediate-range nuclear missiles in Europe. During the late 1970s the Soviets had deployed about 350 intermediate-range SS-20 missiles. Most of the SS-20s were targeted on Western Europe, and each carried three highly accurate warheads. In December 1979, NATO agreed to deploy 108 intermediate-range Pershing II missiles in Germany and 464 ground-launched cruise missiles (GLCMs) in five West European countries to counter the SS-20s. NATO

Soviet general secretary Yuri Andropov, pictured here with Finnish president Mayno Koyvisto in June 1983, impressed most Western leaders with his sophistication.

leaders also adopted a "dual track" policy under which its deployment plan could be waived if U.S.-Soviet negotiations removed the SS-20 missile threat to Western Europe. Preventing the deployment of the NATO missiles, scheduled for late 1983, became one of Andropov's highest priorities.

The Kremlin pressured and cajoled Western European governments to oppose the deployments, while offering various arms control options short of NATO's demand that the USSR remove its SS-20s. The Soviets also conducted a sophisticated propaganda campaign aimed at undermining support for the deployments among the people of Western Europe. The Soviet tactics failed to break the resolve of the NATO nations to go ahead with the deployments, which began on schedule in November 1983.

As they had threatened to do if the deployments took place, the Soviets withdrew their negotiating team from the Intermediate-range Nuclear Forces (INF) talks in Geneva on November 23. The Soviets also refused to continue other major arms control negotiations, including the Strategic Arms Re-

duction Talks (START) in Geneva. Arms control negotiations between the superpowers would not resume until 1985.

KAL Incident

On September 1, 1983, a Soviet warplane shot down a South Korean Boeing 747 that passed over Soviet territory, killing all 269 people aboard. Korean Air Lines Flight 007, one of thousands of commercial flights that skirt Soviet air space in the North Pacific each year, had deviated three hundred miles from its assigned course on the last leg of its flight from New York to Seoul. The Soviets initially denied that their pilot had destroyed the plane and refused to permit the United States and Japan to search the waters where the plane went down. On September 6 they admitted downing the plane but claimed that the Soviet pilot was forced to fire on the plane (which they accused of being engaged in espionage), after it failed to acknowledge warning signals. The incident undermined Soviet antimilitaristic propaganda and plunged already declining U.S.-Soviet relations to one of their lowest points since the Cuban missile crisis.

A crisis atmosphere surrounded the incident. President Reagan said on September 5 that the attack was "an act of barbarism, born of a society which wantonly disregards individual rights and the value of human life and seeks constantly to expand and dominate other nations." The United States accused the Soviets of knowingly shooting down an unarmed civilian aircraft and then failing to acknowledge or apologize for the act. The Soviets accused the United States of using the plane for a spy mission and of manipulating public opinion in support of militaristic policies.

After extensively reviewing the evidence, including tapes of intercepted voice transmissions of the Soviet pilots, U.S. intelligence experts concluded that the pilots and the Soviet air defense personnel with whom they were in contact during the incident did not know that the plane was a civilian airliner. Moreover, the United States admitted that an RC-135, an American electronic reconnaissance plane that is the military's version of the Boeing 747, was flying a routine mission outside Soviet airspace within seventy-five miles of the path of KAL 007. Nevertheless the investigation by the International Civil Aviation Organization, an affiliate of the United Nations, concluded that the Soviets "did not make exhaustive efforts to identify the aircraft through inflight visual observations."

Despite Moscow's refusal to take responsibility for the attack, the United States imposed only minor sanctions against the USSR. Reagan suspended a bilateral transportation agreement and talks on opening a U.S. consulate in Kiev. Many other nations temporarily restricted civil aviation with the Soviet Union to protest the incident.

Andropov's Death

Andropov acted quickly to foster change, and if he had had more time he might have achieved more of his goals. His last public appearance was August 18, 1983, when he received a delegation of nine U.S. senators, at which time he declared a unilateral moratorium on the deployment of Soviet antisat-

ellite weapons. Sen. Patrick Leahy, D-Vt., and several other senators said they were impressed with Andropov.

Andropov continued to run the country from his closely guarded hospital apartment. In responding to various arms control proposals and in appointing or removing personnel, Andropov relied on the telephone. He also was visited almost daily by Politburo member Mikhail Gorbachev. But by the end of January 1984 his condition had deteriorated markedly. According to most accounts, at that time the government came to a standstill. He died February 9, 1984, less than fifteen months after he became general secretary.

Chernenko "Interregnum"

Konstantin Chernenko's selection as Andropov's successor disappointed many Soviets who privately regarded him as an uneducated professional bureaucrat who rose to positions of power solely because of his association with Leonid Brezhnev. This evaluation of the man was truthful in many respects but incomplete.

Chernenko had depended on Brezhnev for advancement. He also was uneducated relative to many of his colleagues and was not experienced in foreign policy or defense matters. Chernenko had other qualities, however, that made his selection less of an aberration. He was a skilled party functionary, a loyal team player, and a leader who knew his limitations. He could be expected to submit to collective leadership and to defer to better informed Politburo members on issues outside his expertise.

Chernenko was not chosen primarily for his personal qualities, however, but because he was likely to function as a transitional leader. The old guard was not yet ready to turn power over to the next generation. They wanted a leader who could be trusted to protect the positions of Brezhnev-era appointees and return stability to a bureaucracy shaken by Andropov's personnel changes. The younger, more reform-minded leaders, however, wanted to avoid promoting anyone who would obstruct change in the party hierarchy for many years. West-

General Secretary Konstantin Chernenko addresses a combined meeting of the Council of Nationalities and Council of Union of the Supreme Soviet, April 11, 1984.

ern scholars have suggested Chernenko was chosen precisely because of his old age and poor health rather than in spite of them. The younger and more progressive leaders promoted by Andropov could accept Chernenko because he would not be around long, while the old guard could cling to their positions and influence a little longer and possibly prepare for retirement. Indeed, not a single member of the Politburo or Secretariat lost his job under Chernenko.

Although Chernenko's selection as general secretary made sense from the perspective of Soviet internal politics, he was not what the ailing Soviet economy and society needed. He did not possess the strength or will to implement the reforms necessary to substantially improve the lives of Soviet citizens.

To his credit, Chernenko endorsed most of the limited reforms Andropov had been able to push through the system during his fifteen-month tenure. Chernenko called for the decentralization of selected areas of the economy and greater labor discipline and productivity. But he did not aggressively promote or build on these reforms as Andropov might have done had he lived longer. In some cases,

most notably his reversal of Andropov's order to reduce the bureaucracy by 20 percent, Chernenko actively worked against reform. In addition, Chernenko offered only a few relatively minor domestic initiatives of his own. He backed education reform, a land reclamation project, better representation in constitutional bodies such as the Supreme Soviet, and elimination of some duplication of economic tasks by parallel party and government bodies.

Despite Chernenko's lack of foreign policy experience, his regime succeeded in renewing the arms control dialogue with the United States that had been silenced during Andropov's short tenure. Chernenko's speeches and writings signaled his support for détente, but his health was too uncertain, his expertise too suspect, and anti-Reagan sentiment in Moscow too strong for him to make many significant changes in the relations between the superpowers. Moreover, during 1984 the Soviets had sought to avoid any action that might contribute to a Reagan-Republican landslide in the November national elections. Thus, even if Chernenko had desired to significantly improve U.S.-Soviet relations (which is doubtful), he probably could not have done so.

What he did do was support a return to the Geneva arms control negotiations following Reagan's election. The real architect of this pragmatic shift may have been Foreign Minister Gromyko, who was reported to have taken over foreign policy formulation under Chernenko. But Chernenko's backing was critical to the speed with which the policy was implemented and the support it received in Moscow. Only eight days after Reagan's election, Anatoly Dobrynin, then ambassador to the United States, indicated that the Soviet Union was interested in holding umbrella talks on strategic and intermediate-range nuclear weapons and on weapons in space. The combined talks initially had been proposed by the United States in 1983, but now the Soviets sought to make the proposal their own. On November 22 the superpowers announced that Gromyko and Secretary of State Shultz would meet in Geneva in January to lay the groundwork for the arms control talks.

Gorbachev Takes Control

On March 10, 1985, Chernenko died of heart failure at the age of seventy-three. The next day the announcement that Mikhail Gorbachev had been chosen as general secretary came just four hours after Chernenko's death was disclosed to the public. The speed of Gorbachev's selection indicated that the decision had been made before Chernenko's death. In his acceptance speech to the Central Committee, Gorbachev set priorities for his government. Foremost among these were economic revitalization and arms control. Gorbachev announced the Politburo's decision to go ahead with the U.S.-Soviet arms talks scheduled to begin in Geneva on March 12, despite the official mourning period for Chernenko.

Gorbachev would accomplish much during 1985. He met with an American president at the first superpower summit to be held in six years and placed his personal stamp on arms control negotiations. He overhauled the Kremlin leadership, replacing older officials with men of his own generation. And he initiated several bureaucratic and economic reforms that aimed at reinvigorating Soviet society.

During Gorbachev's first year in power, however, he distinguished himself from past Soviet leaders more through his style of leadership than through the policies he promoted. From the day he took power he projected an image different from his three aging predecessors. He exploited his relative youth, presenting himself as a vigorous leader capable of improving the Soviet way of life. He frequently appeared in public with his wife and other family members and startled Soviet people with his penchant for wading into crowds of citizens to shake hands.

There was little hint during Gorbachev's first year of how far his reforms eventually would go. Gorbachev appeared to be a more energetic and engaging version of Andropov, his former patron. He reemphasized Andropov's anticorruption and anti-alcohol campaigns and continued Andropov's efforts to create a split in the Western alliance. In an interview published in the September 9, 1985,

issue of *Time* magazine, Gorbachev's pragmatic comments about the need to improve the economy and social conditions of his country demonstrated his realism. Yet he also claimed confidence in the Marxist-Leninist ideology that had pervaded Soviet life for decades, saying that the Soviet Union's rise to the status of "a major world power . . . has attested to the strength and the immense capabilities of socialism."

New Faces in the Kremlin

The most noticeable change made by Gorbachev during 1985 was the replacement of dozens of party and government personnel. The *Washington Post* reported January 26, 1986, that Gorbachev had replaced 45 of 159 regional party first secretaries and 4 of 15 first secretaries of republics. In addition, 19 of 59 government ministers were replaced, while 37 of 113 seats on the Council of Ministers changed hands.

Many of Gorbachev's targets for retirement were holdovers from the Brezhnev era. The Soviet press increasingly referred to Brezhnev as an unnamed "former leader" who allowed corruption to flourish among party and government officials. Meanwhile, Gorbachev rehabilitated many associates of Nikita Khrushchev. No longer anonymous, Khrushchev was "unambiguously extolled as a major contributor to victory in the Soviet-Nazi war," Sidney I. Ploss noted in the spring 1986 issue of *Foreign Policy*. Ploss also cited the criticism of Joseph Stalin in the Soviet press as another indicator of Gorbachev's bias toward reform.

The most visible evidence of Gorbachev's bloodless purge was the transformation he engineered in the Politburo. Just one month after gaining power, Gorbachev added three new members: Yegor Ligachev, party secretary in charge of high-level appointments and ideology; Nikolai Ryzhkov, initially charged with setting economic reform policy and later named premier; and Viktor Chebrikov, head of the KGB. Like Gorbachev, all three to some degree had been protégés of Andropov and had supported his economic reforms and discipline campaign.

Five Leaders on a Train

During the last years of the Brezhnev regime, a joke about Leonid Brezhnev and past Soviet leaders circulated in the Soviet Union.

As the story goes, the top Soviet leaders since the Bolshevik revolution are traveling in the same compartment on a train somewhere in the USSR. Suddenly the train stops without explanation in the middle of nowhere.

Vladimir Lenin rises from his seat and declares, "I'll get the train moving." He goes forward to the locomotive, where he lectures the engineer on his duty to the Soviet state and the international communist movement. But the train does not move.

After Lenin returns to his seat, Joseph Stalin sneers, "You people don't know how to deal with the Russian mentality." He then marches to the locomotive, where he shoots the engineer. Naturally the train does not budge.

Stalin returns to his seat, and Nikita Khrushchev takes up the challenge. He argues, "We must not hold the engineer's past mistakes against him." He enters the locomotive, where he rehabilitates the engineer by propping him up at the controls, but still the train does not move.

After Khrushchev returns, Brezhnev says, "I have an easy solution to our troubles. We'll pull the blinds and imagine that the train is moving." The train remains motionless, but everyone remarks how fast it is going.

After Mikhail Gorbachev came to power and began encouraging open discussion of the Soviet Union's problems, the story came to have a new ending: Finally a disgusted Gorbachev climbs to the top of the train and shouts, "Look everybody, the train is not moving." The passengers are so surprised and excited by his honesty that they no longer care about making progress toward their destination. "Finally," they say, "we have a leader who speaks the truth."

Gorbachev also replaced Foreign Minister Andrei Gromyko with Eduard Shevardnadze. Gromyko, who had presided over the postwar course of U.S.-Soviet relations during twenty-eight years as foreign minister, was named president of the Soviet Union at a July 2, 1985, session of the Supreme Soviet. Many analysts saw Gromyko's elevation to this ceremonial post as a way of gracefully retiring him.

Shevardnadze had made a name for himself by weeding out corruption when he served as party secretary in his native republic of Georgia. Although he had no previous foreign policy experience, he quickly impressed Western observers as a capable diplomat whose relaxed demeanor was in keeping with Gorbachev's own style of leadership.

At the same July 1985 session of the Supreme Soviet, Grigory Romanov, the Leningrad party chief and Brezhnev protégé who was thought to have posed the greatest challenge to Gorbachev's rise to power, was retired from the Politburo. Ryzhkov replaced Nikolai Tikhonov, the eighty-year-old Soviet premier, in October. Moscow party chief Viktor Grishin, another member of the old guard, was replaced in December by Boris Yeltsin. Yeltsin was promoted to candidate Politburo status just one week before the Twenty-seventh Party Congress in February 1986.

Gorbachev's Early Economic Agenda

From the time he came to power, Gorbachev called for economic change. But the "radical" changes he claimed were necessary to revive the economy, reinvigorate the bureaucracy, and improve worker productivity did not take place with any great speed. Western observers noted that during his first months in power his calls for reform were not accompanied by concrete plans.

Gorbachev needed time to consolidate power. Moving too rapidly on economic reform could foster dissatisfaction among many members of the elite. He needed to effect a wider turnover in personnel before he could launch more serious economic reforms.

In the meantime, Gorbachev focused on implementing Andropov's program to combat alcoholism and poor labor discipline. On May 16, 1985, the Soviet government announced that alcohol production was being cut, liquor store hours were being shortened, and the legal drinking age was being raised from eighteen to twenty-one. Gorbachev also used moral appeals to encourage workers to improve their job performance and introduced limited monetary incentives to reward productive employees.

This early gradualist approach can be attributed in part to sharp differences in the party and government elite about the best way to modernize the economy. Gorbachev's careful beginning also could have been due to the hope of the leadership (including Gorbachev) that the economy was suffering primarily from the mismanagement and corruption of the Brezhnev years. If this were true, they reasoned, a little "fine-tuning" might be all that was needed to jump-start the economy.

The Twelfth Five-Year Plan adopted in 1985 under Gorbachev's supervision set ambitious goals for growth. The plan called for 4 percent growth per year from 1986 through 1990. This growth was to be achieved through improved worker productivity and the introduction of more high technology machines into factories and farms. Toward this goal, the plan greatly expanded investment in high technology research, development, and production.

Foreign Policy

Upon becoming general secretary, Gorbachev took an active interest in foreign policy making. He displayed a pragmatic willingness to advance arms control negotiations with the United States, while simultaneously focusing on improving relations with other countries. He also appeared to be more adept than any of his predecessors at competing with the United States for world public opinion.

The new general secretary began scaling back foreign adventures, though under Gorbachev the Soviets did not abandon policy designed to extend their international influence. Soviet efforts to gain footholds in sub-Saharan Africa, Latin America, and Asia had proved costly and had yielded few benefits. Gorbachev and his colleagues likely decided that needs closer to home were more pressing. Soviet troops in Afghanistan launched a series of

offensives against U.S.-supported resistance forces in 1985, but Gorbachev told the Supreme Soviet in November that he was seeking a political settlement of the six-year war there and the eventual withdrawal of Soviet forces. In 1986 he called Afghanistan a "bleeding wound."

The Kremlin launched an ambitious diplomatic offensive to improve its standing around the world. The Soviets worked toward a reconciliation with Japan that culminated in a trip by Foreign Minister Shevardnadze to Tokyo in January 1986. The trip marked the first time a Soviet foreign minister had visited Japan in ten years. Enemies during World War II, the two countries have never signed a peace treaty because of a dispute over four northern Japanese islands that were occupied by the Soviets at the end of World War II. Although the visit did not produce a resolution of the territorial dispute, it opened the way for moderately improved relations between the two countries.

Gorbachev also continued to improve relations with China, a process initiated by Andropov. Yet the "three obstacles" identified by China to complete normalization of relations remained: the presence of Soviet troops along the border separating the two nations, the Soviet presence in Afghanistan, and the occupation of Cambodia by Moscow's ally Vietnam.

On May 22, 1986, Gorbachev and Prime Minister Rajiv Gandhi of India signed a major economic agreement. It outlined a new fifteen-year economic and technical cooperation program and provided for 1.2 billion dollars in Soviet credits for construction of industrial and energy projects in India.

The Kremlin's foreign policy in the Middle East had mixed results. To improve its standing among the moderate Arab nations, the Soviet Union established diplomatic relations with the sultanate of Oman and the United Arab Emirates. But a diplomatic setback followed in mid-January 1986, when civil war broke out in Soviet-backed South Yemen. Although the rebellion was settled by early February with the installation of another Moscow-supported leader, the incident clearly caught the Kremlin by surprise and unprepared to control its closest ally in the region.

U.S.-Soviet Summitry

Superpower relations during 1985 centered around the summit scheduled for November in Geneva. President Reagan had proposed the summit to Gorbachev on March 12, 1985, through a letter delivered by Vice President George Bush, who was attending the funeral of Konstantin Chernenko. Gorbachev accepted the invitation July 3.

The Geneva summit would be the first meeting between the leaders of the United States and the Soviet Union since June 1979, when President Jimmy Carter met Leonid Brezhnev in Vienna to sign the SALT II treaty setting limits on both countries' strategic arsenals. In agreeing to go to Geneva, Reagan had put aside his earlier distrust of summits. During his first term he adopted a confrontational tone toward the Soviet Union and dismissed summitry, saying that the Soviets had used past meetings to extract arms control agreements that put the United States at a disadvantage.

After much media buildup, the summit (November 19-21) produced mixed reviews and ambivalence. The two leaders agreed to further meetings, and both welcomed the beginning of a new dialogue between the superpowers. However, the summit produced no visible progress on major issues. Those who evaluated the summit as positive expressed satisfaction that Reagan and Gorbachev had conversed amiably and planned to continue talking. This in itself, they said, was a great accomplishment. Those who saw the summit as a disappointment pointed out that arms control, regional, and human rights issues remained unresolved.

In a joint communiqué released at the end of the summit, Reagan and Gorbachev described their discussions as "frank and useful" while acknowledging that "serious differences remain on a number of critical issues."

Despite Reagan's last-minute attempt to give high priority to regional conflicts involving the Soviets, arms control issues dominated the meeting. The two leaders pledged to accelerate efforts for an arms reduction agreement in the ongoing Geneva arms talks and singled out two possible areas for early progress: a 50 percent cut in nuclear weapons and a separate agreement to cut intermediate-range forces based in Europe. In both areas, superficial similarities between the U.S. and Soviet positions masked profound disagreements over what weapons the negotiations should cover.

No concrete arms control accords were signed at the summit, but numerous cultural exchange agreements were reached, as were agreements calling for regular high-level meetings, new consulates, air flights, and other cooperative arrangements. The leaders also made tentative plans for a Gorbachev visit to Washington in 1986 and a Reagan trip to Moscow for a third meeting in 1987.

Road to Reform

When Foreign Minister Gromyko nominated Gorbachev for the post of general secretary, he told his colleagues in the Central Committee, "Comrades, this man has a nice smile, but he has got iron teeth." Indeed Gorbachev was the first Soviet leader since Khrushchev with a "nice smile." His outgoing style created a more human image of the Soviet Union abroad and reassured many Soviet citizens that the leadership was interested in their welfare. But he also had the "iron teeth" associated with past Soviet leaders. He was a skillful and aggressive politician who sought to increase Soviet advantages abroad and enhance his own power at home.

As 1986 began almost no one anticipated the economic and social upheaval that would engulf the Soviet Union during the coming years. Gorbachev's first steps toward reform had been cautious, even predictable. He had staunchly upheld the validity of Marxist ideology and the necessity of Communist party control of society. Only in the area of personnel had he taken dramatic steps.

Gorbachev, however, apparently recognized that reversing the malaise in Soviet society required radical change. Through 1986 and 1987 his reform goals became increasingly ambitious and daring. Limited free market characteristics were introduced into the economy, controls on information were loosened, the Soviet press and public were encouraged to debate candidly society's problems, and the Soviet Union made concessions in arms control that

Mikhail Gorbachev's reforms angered and adversely affected many people. Some citizens with complaints pitched tents and lived just off Red Square in protest of government policies.

led to a December 1987 treaty with the United States eliminating intermediate-range nuclear weapons. By 1988 Gorbachev's reforms had progressed so far that many of the "reformers" he had helped to promote in 1985 had been ousted or remained as the more conservative members within the leadership.

With a mandate for change, a knack for flexibility, and a large measure of political savvy, Gorbachev gradually expanded his reforms. He did not follow a carefully scripted plan. Instead, he continually adapted his reform program to accommodate the political realities of the moment.

Perestroika

Perestroika, or "restructuring," is the umbrella concept for Gorbachev's entire reform program, meaning the decentralization of political and economic decision making, increased openness, modernization based on technological restructuring, and a new foreign policy that emphasized international interdependence. This word, however, is used most often in reference to the restructuring of the Soviet economy.

When the concept of perestroika first was intro-

duced at the April 1985 Central Committee plenum, Gorbachev spoke mainly about economic improvements. Using phraseology that had been employed by Andropov, Gorbachev talked in broad, general terms about "basic restructuring" of the economy and "perfection of the economic mechanism." His watchword was "acceleration" *(uskorenie)* of social and economic development, which would be accomplished in the long run by technological modernization. In the short run, he called for an "activization of the human factor," which meant a return to Andropov's emphasis on improving labor productivity through reduced corruption, inefficiency and alcoholism. The policies adopted during Gorbachev's first year reflected this limited definition of perestroika.

The Twenty-seventh Party Congress in February 1986 was a watershed event in the refinement of the meaning of perestroika. Gorbachev for the first time talked about perestroika with reference to far-reaching institutional changes in the economy. In contrast to his earlier optimism about the economy's ability to modernize itself, he called for a "radical reform." He stressed that the perfection of economic management procedures alone would not be enough to turn the economy around. He spoke approvingly of

Lenin's New Economic Policy (NEP) and talked about revitalizing the "political economy" and creating new conceptions of property. From this point on, he referred to perestroika as a "revolutionary" change, implying that he would go beyond Andropov's disciplinarian emphasis and even Khrushchev's reorganization and decentralization of the economic planning apparatus.

At the same time, he acknowledged the political obstacles to economic change, alluding to "functionaries" in the party and state bureaucracies who were resisting change. At the party congress, Gorbachev replaced 41 percent of the full (voting) members of the Central Committee—not as many as he had wanted, but still a significant turnover.

The Twenty-seventh Party Congress therefore opened the way for reformers to challenge long-held assumptions about Soviet socialism. Emboldened by Gorbachev's words, the reformers went to work during late 1986 and early 1987 to give shape to Gorbachev's broad parameters for change.

The culmination of many months of debate and negotiation was the June 1987 Central Committee plenum on the economy. There Gorbachev laid out his plan to decentralize the economy and to experiment with limited market forces. He spoke in favor of legalizing small-scale private and cooperative businesses, and he stated that enterprises must become self-financing.

Subsequently the perestroika debate challenged other central tenets of socialism, such as bans on private property and income equality. Gorbachev also sought greater Soviet involvement in the international economy. Yet despite the significance of Gorbachev's economic reforms compared with those initiated under previous Soviet leaders, his reforms fell far short of the economic overhaul that most Western observers believed was necessary to turn around the Soviet economy. Liberals, such as Russian republic president Boris Yeltsin, criticized Gorbachev for implementing "half measures."

Glasnost

Glasnost, or "openness," stems from the old Russian word *glas,* meaning "voice" or "vote."

Sovietologist Jerry Hough interprets glasnost in his 1988 book, *Russia and the West: Gorbachev and the Politics of Reform,* as a call for a more open society that does not necessarily advocate an undercutting of the authority of the leadership. In his book *Perestroika,* Gorbachev states that the functions of glasnost are twofold: to facilitate an open search for truth and to ensure the accountability of the government to the people.

Gorbachev introduced this concept into the political discourse in early 1985. He maintained that glasnost was inextricably linked with perestroika because economic reforms would not work unless they were supported by broad public participation and enthusiasm. As Gorbachev had noted, public apathy was widespread; a sense of inertia pervaded most economic and social institutions. At the same time, the power of the corrupt and intransigent bureaucracy to block or stall significant changes would have to be broken. Glasnost, by allowing public and media pressure to focus on corruption, inefficiency, and elite privileges, was to serve as the means to overcome the entrenched bureaucracy.

The concept of glasnost changed in tandem with changes in the meaning of perestroika. In early 1985, when Gorbachev's emphasis was on routing corruption and fostering discipline, glasnost focused mainly on exposing abuses in the state bureaucracy and wastefulness in the economic sector. The glasnost campaign reinforced Gorbachev's emphasis on establishing accountability in government and encouraging individuals to evaluate and criticize their leaders. Televised call-in shows, for example, encouraged public oversight of ministry bureaucrats, while the press was instructed to publish letters from the public condemning abuses of power by officials. Also, glasnost was intended to stimulate public interest in the economy and society—thus encouraging people to work harder and more efficiently.

The Chernobyl nuclear disaster in April 1986 marked a turning point in the glasnost campaign because it illustrated to the Soviet leadership why freer information was important. Defects in the reactor had been allowed to exist without the knowledge of higher-level officials, and the government's tight control on information about the disaster brought severe international condemnation and domestic apprehension. More important, after Chernobyl, Soviet writers began to link the disaster with overall shortcomings in the Soviet economic system. Sweeping historical questions still were prohibited, but the scope of discussion broadened to include some critical reappraisal of the past.

By this time, Gorbachev had buttressed his authority among the political elite with his sweeping personnel changes. He realized, however, that he needed additional allies for his reform program, particularly among the intelligentsia. In 1986 Gorbachev moved to take over the leadership of most cultural institutions, including the all-union film maker's union and such publications as *Literaturnaya Gazeta* and *Sovetskaya Kultura*. In January 1987, he named fellow reformer Aleksandr Yakovlev a candidate member of the Politburo and soon afterward gave him responsibility for the social sciences, culture, and the media. In the following year, taboos on what could be discussed in the media disappeared one after another. By early 1989 it was becoming easier to define what was unacceptable under glasnost than what was acceptable.

Concurrently, glasnost was used to accomplish a much deeper de-Stalinization than Khrushchev had ever attempted. In 1986, public discussion began to open up about the defects of Stalin's personality, and by 1988, most Stalinist institutions were under intense scrutiny. Gorbachev encouraged the full-scale discrediting of the old system to make room for the new. Although in 1988 and 1989 certain topics were still off limits, such as the meaning of the Bolshevik Revolution and the person of Lenin, by 1990 even those taboos had been broken.

Finally, Gorbachev was counting on glasnost to stimulate public initiative that would advance economic and societal reforms. He hoped people would become more involved in political and civic activities, thereby accepting responsibility for improving the life of the nation. This strategy, however, presented the Soviet leadership with the problem of determining how much political participation was desirable because a rising tide of political activism could threaten the Communist party's monopoly on power.

A Soviet helicopter flies over the Chernobyl nuclear reactor.

New Thinking

Gorbachev introduced "new thinking" (*novoe myshlenie*) in foreign and military policy in 1987 and 1988. This policy rejected the notion that peaceful coexistence was only a breathing spell in the competition between the socialist and capitalist camps, urged the abandonment of exporting revolution, and de-emphasized the military threat to the Soviet Union from the West. It also sought to make the USSR a participant in the economic and political affairs of the world community.

Gorbachev believed new thinking, like glasnost, was necessary for perestroika to be successful. While glasnost was required to create an energetic, critical, and motivated domestic population, new

Speaking before the Council of Europe in Strasbourg, France, on July 6, 1989, Mikhail Gorbachev states that the Soviet Union will not interfere with the reform movements in Eastern Europe.

the Twenty-seventh Party Congress in February 1986. There he introduced the doctrine of "reasonable sufficiency." This doctrine called for the USSR to avoid matching every U.S. military program. Instead, tough procurement decisions would be made according to what was absolutely necessary for national security.

New thinking expanded on this concept by rejecting offensive military doctrine in favor of less expensive and less threatening defensive weapons and tactics. This reorientation was motivated by cost considerations as well as by the realization that offensive doctrine was counterproductive because it pushed opposing nations into defensive alliances and caused them to conduct their own military buildups.

In addition, new thinking emphasized the existence of common human interests in a complex, interconnected world. It abandoned the old antagonism between opposing systems based on class interests and declared a commitment to adhere to international legal norms and standards of human rights.

One of the earliest and most tangible signs of Gorbachev's new thinking was his December 1988 UN speech, in which he promised to demobilize five hundred thousand troops. The most dramatic of the changes brought about by new thinking was the collapse of Communist governments in Eastern Europe in 1989. Although one can argue that the changes in Eastern Europe had less to do with Gorbachev than events in that region, Gorbachev declined to respond to the instability in Eastern Europe with force, as Khrushchev had done in Hungary in 1956 and Brezhnev had done in Czechoslovakia in 1968. As early as 1988, Gorbachev's remarks appeared to indicate that the Soviet Union would not stand in the way of revolutionary change in Eastern Europe.

Demokratizatsia

By January 1987, it was clear that perestroika faced serious opposition from the bureaucracy. Although Gorbachev had carried out purges in many key party and government institutions and had promoted many of his supporters, the strongest resistance to his reforms was rising from the lower levels

thinking was needed to secure a long-term period of peace in foreign policy. This would allow the Soviet Union to redirect spending from military to consumer purposes. It also would permit the USSR to gain entrance into international financial institutions and to be eligible for foreign loans. Finally, it would allow the country to obtain needed technology from the West to boost its sagging economy.

The foundation of new thinking was a redefinition of the concept of national security. Gorbachev had taken the first step toward this redefinition at of the bureaucracies. Glasnost in the newspapers and freer cultural expression were not capable of removing the "dead wood" from the system. Moreover, public support for perestroika centered more on exposing the ills of the previous system than on creating a new one.

To address these problems, Gorbachev initiated a far-reaching political reform called *demokratizatsia* (democratization). In an important speech at the January 1987 Central Committee plenum, Gorbachev directly linked political reform with economic reform. "The business of restructuring," he stated, "has turned out to be more difficult . . . than we had imagined earlier." Party leaders had become immune to public criticism and had participated in the widespread corruption pervading Soviet society. Hence, Gorbachev argued, a "profound democratization" of the political system was needed so that people could once again take charge of their own destinies.

To accomplish this, he proposed sweeping electoral reforms whereby members of all soviets (elected councils ranging from the local to the all-union level) would be elected on multi-candidate ballots. He assured the Central Committee that democratization would activate latent social energies and stimulate public interest in perestroika. As freely elected bodies, the soviets would return to their rightful places as the instruments of the people's power. Gorbachev also proposed that multi-candidate elections be extended to party positions as well, including the first secretaries of the republican central committees. The latter idea was extremely controversial and was not approved by the plenum.

Gorbachev developed the specifics of his political reform at the specially convened Nineteenth Party Conference in June-July 1988 (the first party conference in nearly fifty years). In his opening speech to the conference delegates, Gorbachev stated that during the Brezhnev years ministries and departments had begun to dictate their will in the economy and in politics. It was exceptionally important, he argued, to create a uniform system of public and state control subordinate to elected bodies. Furthermore, Gorbachev observed that the party's role had grown through the years to include economic management, and this had hindered it from fulfilling its vanguard role in society.

Gorbachev's solution was to separate the functions of the party and the state. The party would return to its Leninist origins and be freed from its economic-administrative duties. It would concentrate instead on key areas of domestic and foreign policy.

On the national level, Gorbachev advocated the resurrection of a full-time working parliament to replace the rubber-stamp body of the past. Specifically, Gorbachev proposed the creation of an entirely new legislative body: a 2,250-member Congress of People's Deputies (CPD), which would elect a much smaller, full-time Supreme Soviet. Elections to these bodies would make high-level party and state officials more accountable to the people, and those officials who did not win in the elections would have to, according to Gorbachev, "draw the appropriate conclusions" (step down from their positions). At the conference, Gorbachev also proposed the creation of a powerful new post—the chairman of the Supreme Soviet. This new chairman would assume many of the duties that had been reserved for the Communist party general secretary since the Brezhnev era. Gorbachev's plan for multi-candidate elections extended below the national level. As he stated, the soviets should be rejuvenated "from the bottom to the top."

Another of Gorbachev's themes at the conference was the need to develop a "socialist law-governed state." Too often, he argued, laws were arbitrarily ignored by officials. Ministerial departments and party agencies were accustomed to changing, repealing, and suspending legislation at will. The restoration of the legitimate organs of people's rule—the soviets—was to be accompanied by a new respect for legislation.

Although these proposals represented the most radical political reforms in the Soviet Union since the revolution, they were not intended to undermine party influence in policy making. Instead, they were designed to improve and streamline the policy-making process. How could this be done? First, the elections could weed out the opponents of perestroika. Second, by subjecting party officials to competitive processes, the party could gain an added measure of legitimacy before the people. Third, the newly elected legislators could become a sounding board for the rising tensions in the USSR by debating public issues. Fourth, by separating party and state functions, the policy-making process could become more effective and less cumbersome.

But Gorbachev was adamant about retaining the party's "leading role" in Soviet political life while transferring "all power" to the soviets. He recommended, therefore, that the first secretaries of the appropriate party committees run for the posts of chairmen of the soviets. According to him, this would raise the prestige of the soviets by investing them with the authority of the party. At the same time it would increase the public's control over the party secretaries. Gorbachev probably in part made this suggestion so that he could run for the chairmanship of the Supreme Soviet while remaining general secretary.

Throughout 1988 and 1989, these resolutions and principles were put into action. Gorbachev streamlined the top party structure in September-October 1988. He reorganized the twenty-two Central Committee Secretariat departments into nine departments under the jurisdiction of six commissions—presumably to reduce their involvement in day-to-day affairs. He also eliminated party economic departments on all levels to remove the party from economic decision making. Also in 1988, he retired conservative Politburo members Andrei Gromyko and Mikhail Solomentsev, among others, and reassigned Committee for State Security (KGB) chief Viktor Chebrikov and "second secretary" Yegor Ligachev to less powerful positions as the heads of the Secretariat's legal and agricultural commissions, respectively. The Central Committee apparatus (bureaucracy) was trimmed, and the apparatus at the regional and republican levels was reduced by about 30 percent. Perhaps most significant, in 1988 Gorbachev also assumed Gromyko's position as chairman of the Supreme Soviet Presidium, or de facto head of state, a move that indicated a more complete consolidation of power by the general secretary.

The March 1989 elections to the new CPD were a turning point in the development of demokratizatsia, although an unexpected one. Com-munist party members won 87.6 percent of the seats in the CPD. After the elections, Gorbachev skillfully used defeats of Communist party candidates to weed out a number of conservative party officials from the Central Committee and lower-level party organizations. The composition of both the CPD and Supreme Soviet made both bodies relatively pliable for Gorbachev, and he had been elected by an overwhelming margin to the new powerful post of Supreme Soviet chairman. But the elections nevertheless were disturbing for the party, which had expected to dominate the voting more completely. Party officials at all levels had suffered surprising defeats, despite evidence of electoral rigging. Gorbachev himself acknowledged in July 1989 that public dissatisfaction was expressed in the defeat of a number of party and state officials.

In late 1989, moreover, turnover in lower-level party personnel began to accelerate as a result of grass-roots discontent. Resignations by and dismissals of first secretaries of regional party committees occurred frequently throughout 1989 and into early 1990. In addition, the Bolshevik slogan "all powers to the soviets" assumed new meaning on the national level. The newly elected CPD actively debated the most serious issues of Soviet life in televised sessions, while Soviet citizens, mesmerized, watched members challenge even Gorbachev.

The Supreme Soviet also demonstrated its independence. It rejected nine out of seventy-one ministerial nominees in the first real confirmation hearings ever held in the Soviet Union. In October 1989, it blocked emergency legislation proposed by the USSR Council of Ministers that would ban strikes for more than a year. In that same month, the Supreme Soviet voted to abolish the reservation of 750 seats in the CPD for public organizations such as the Communist party. Perhaps most significant, during the fall sessions of the Supreme Soviet and the CPD, the new Inter-regional Group of Deputies (a group of about two hundred reformers in the parliament) called for debates on revoking Article 6 of the USSR Constitution (which guarantees the Communist party's leading role in society).

As 1989 progressed, public opinion polls revealed

the sinking prestige of the Communist party. Other events indicated a comparative rise in the influence of the national legislature. Striking coal miners in Vorkuta, for example, declared in the summer that their faith in the Communist party, government ministries, and trade unions was gone; instead they were relying on the Supreme Soviet for assurances on government promises.

Until 1990, Gorbachev continued to insist on the party's indispensable "unifying and inspirational role" in Soviet political life. By January of that year, however, it appeared that his personal position as head of both party and state was in danger. The CPD could remove him as chairman of the Supreme Soviet, and the Central Committee likewise could remove him as general secretary (or, it could force his resignation as Supreme Soviet chairman by recalling him as a representative of the Communist party in the Congress).

In February 1990, Gorbachev made two significant changes: He persuaded the Central Committee to revoke Article 6 of the USSR Constitution guaranteeing the Communist party's leading role in society, and he pushed through a proposal for an executive presidency. The proposal granted to the president many of the powers that had been vested in the Supreme Soviet Presidium—the powers to declare martial law and issue binding decrees, for example. It also granted the president new powers, including the power to request the parliament to dismiss the Council of Ministers and the USSR procurator-general (the highest-ranking state prosecutor)—and under certain circumstances, the right to ask the CPD to call new elections to the Supreme Soviet. In addition, new consultative bodies were to be created. The Council of the Federation was to oversee nationalities policy, and the Presidential Council was to serve as the president's personal "cabinet."

These changes went beyond Gorbachev's early conception of demokratizatsia in several ways. First, they represented the final acknowledgment of a complete separation between the party and the state. The way was clear for a multi-party political system and, with it, genuine parliamentary factions. Second, they represented a tentative move toward a Western-style separation of powers among the executive, judicial, and legislative branches. In December 1989, for example, the CPD passed legislation to create a quasi-independent constitutional court, the Committee for Constitutional Oversight, to rule on the constitutionality of legislation. Third, they exhibited an openness to experimenting with other countries' democratic practices. Whereas Soviet ideologists traditionally had condemned Western democracies, now leading Soviet theoreticians were calling for democratic features of foreign governments to be incorporated into the Soviet system. And finally, the 1990 constitutional amendments provided for a popular election of the head of state. Gorbachev was elected by the CPD as president in 1990 for a five-year term, but beginning in 1995 the president was to be elected directly by the people.

Many observers, however, doubted not only that Gorbachev would be a viable candidate for reelection in 1995, but that he could even stay in power for five years until his term ended. Most Soviet citizens saw him as a leader who opened up Soviet society, but failed to deliver on his promises, especially in the economic sphere. Gorbachev had been successful in initiating a reform program that would transform Soviet society. But by the beginning of the new decade, it appeared that he had lost control of the process, as he was forced to respond to a seemingly unending string of political, economic, and social crises.

CHAPTER **6**

THE SECOND RUSSIAN REVOLUTION

During his first five years in power, Mikhail S. Gorbachev took dramatic steps toward destruction of the totalitarian regime in the USSR. Under his leadership, the pervasive repression that once haunted Soviet streets was removed. He unleashed the forces of political pluralism—in the first multicandidate elections in more than seventy years, in renunciation of the Communist party's monopoly on power, and in elections that transformed reformers and secessionists into officeholders. The Soviet people were allowed to explore uncharted territory on their television screens, in their movie houses, on their stages, and in their literature. Gorbachev initiated cautious economic reforms that encouraged some free enterprise. Finally, he guided the transformation of Soviet relations with the West from confrontation to cooperation.

Yet, despite these successes, Gorbachev in 1990 seemed to be a leader caught in his own devices. By articulating and implementing his program of perestroika, glasnost, demokratizatsia, and new thinking, he had set in motion forces that could block or reverse the process of his reforms. Gorbachev faced what seemed to be an unending succession of economic, political, and ethnic crises that threatened to rip apart the Soviet Union.

Permanent Crisis

Though Gorbachev was hailed in foreign lands as a visionary reformer and peacemaker who was leading his country away from the repression and inter-

national confrontation of the Brezhnev era, Soviet citizens grew increasingly disillusioned and impatient with his reforms. After many years of cradle-to-grave security, most Soviets were hesitant to accept the economic risks of perestroika, which could threaten their job security, guaranteed wages, and medical and social security benefits.

The Soviet Union entered perestroika without the benefit of an entrepreneurial foundation. Moreover, many Soviet citizens regarded with suspicion those who attempted to "pull ahead" of their neighbors. This attitude was evident in the widespread public antipathy to the lucrative cooperative movement, a form of small-group private enterprise encouraged by Gorbachev in which the workers in the business share the profits.

The Soviet people may have been more willing to bear the risks and disadvantages inherent in perestroika if immediate economic gains could have been achieved. But the initiation of reforms plunged the economy into a near-crisis situation. As store shelves became bare, the population grew increasingly weary of unfulfilled promises of long-term prosperity. Gorbachev and his advisers found themselves trapped in a paradox. Prosperity was not likely without more changes, while the population's willingness to accept further reforms depended upon achieving an improvement in the standard of living.

The difficulty of introducing controversial reforms such as decontrolling prices was demonstrated by the announcement in May 1990 of a proposed hike in the price of bread that would take place in July. Panic buying ensued, and store shelves were quickly cleared of foodstuffs. The Supreme Soviet reacted to the panic buying by overwhelmingly rejecting the plan.

The piecemeal economic reform program advanced by Gorbachev showed no signs of improving economic conditions. Nevertheless, the Soviet leadership rejected the Polish strategy of "shock therapy," in which prices and wages were decontrolled virtually overnight. Hence the fear of widespread public unrest in the face of the government's dwindling legitimacy delayed the transition to market forces—the only measure likely to reverse the slide of the Soviet economy.

Gorbachev's program also was threatened by the possibility of a conservative backlash, by party hardliners, the military, or both. This threat received much attention in the Western media. Hard-line party officials were the most resistant to Gorbachev's reforms, as perestroika for them meant the loss of their privileges, job security, and prestige. Even if no overt coup occurred, party bureaucrats still in place had the power to resist or sabotage reforms from within the system.

Much of the professional military (and security apparatus) also was unhappy with Gorbachev's reforms. The officer corps experienced humiliation with the "loss" of Eastern Europe and with the falling prestige of the military in Soviet society. It also became increasingly disillusioned by the growing number of deserters and draft evaders, the impending defense budget cuts, the lack of housing for demobilized troops, the ethnic violence among draftees, and the increasing public criticism of the armed forces.

By 1990 ethnic upheaval in the Soviet Union, which generations of Soviet leaders suppressed, had become an everyday reality. Azerbaijan's blockade of Armenia in late 1989, for example, led to widespread violence and hardship. Unrest in Baku in January 1990 caused stoppages in the oil production facilities located there. When Gorbachev imposed a state of emergency in Azerbaijan, its parliament threatened to secede from the USSR. Even the peaceful secession drives in the Baltic states created serious social divisions in the other republics, espe-cially the Russian republic. Lithuania had declared its independence and Latvia and Estonia had announced "transition periods" leading to independence.

When the forces of political liberalization and economic decentralization were unleashed in Eastern Europe, they did not stop until those countries had achieved a complete break from Moscow and a measure of political pluralism. It appeared that unless Gorbachev was willing to resort to the wholesale use of armed force, many of the Soviet Union's own republics would follow Eastern Europe's lead to independence.

Yeltsin Eclipses Gorbachev

The summer of 1990 was a critical period for Mikhail Gorbachev. Although he had won an important victory in March of that year with his election as USSR president, he was facing mounting economic and nationalist pressures. Gorbachev tried to walk the middle line between reformers and conservatives. The reformers generally favored greater republican autonomy and moves toward a market economy and democratic governance. The conservatives, though motivated by diverse factors, generally wanted to preserve the union, the USSR's command economy, and the power of the Communist party. This tactic had worked before for Gorbachev, who had been able to portray himself as a moderate facing extremism.

The country, however, had become highly polarized. Most citizens and politicians were dissatisfied with Gorbachev, even if they believed he was the only moderate alternative. At each end of the political spectrum, visible and decisive leaders began to dominate the discourse. Viktor Alksnis and Nikolai Petrushenko, known as the "Black Colonels," had become spokesmen for the conservatives by attacking certain Soviet policies, such as Moscow's acceptance of the loss of Eastern Europe. On the reformist side, Boris Yeltsin, ex-Politburo member from Sverdlovsk, had taken a dramatic stand for reform. In the months that followed, Gorbachev attempted to pacify both sides. As his centrist strategy became increasingly less useful, Gorbachev leaned to the right, thus helping Yeltsin to emerge as his most viable competitor for power.

Twenty-eighth Party Congress

The Twenty-eighth Congress of the Communist Party of the Soviet Union (CPSU), held in July 1990, was a turning point in the distribution of power between Gorbachev and Yeltsin. Before perestroika, party congresses, which brought together several thousand delegates from all regions of the Soviet Union, were carefully orchestrated events. The Twenty-eighth Party Congress, however, was to be the setting for genuine decision making and political drama.

Most of the delegates were extremely conservative. Before the Congress, Gorbachev had tried to persuade the Central Committee to require delegates to be selected in multicandidate elections. His efforts failed, however, and most delegates were chosen according to the old method of using prearranged lists drawn up by party leaders.

Consequently, the business of the Congress took on a conservative slant. Delegates demanded that top party officials publicly defend their actions over the previous five years. This resulted in a series of bitter accusations against party leaders that they had presided over the loss of Eastern Europe, the destruction of socialism, and the implementation of economic reforms that betrayed Soviet workers. Delegates also refused to support the depoliticization of the armed forces and instead adopted a compromise resolution to retain the party's control of the military.

For the first time in the party's history, the general secretary was elected by a vote of the Congress rather than chosen behind closed doors by the CPSU Central Committee. Despite the strength of conservative delegates, Gorbachev did not face serious opposition and was reelected on July 10 by a vote of 3,411 to 1,116. Gorbachev also prevailed in the election for deputy general secretary. His candidate, Ukrainian president Vladimir Ivashko, defeated prominent hard-liner Yegor Ligachev 3,109 to 776. In addition, all top government officials (except for President Gorbachev) were removed from the Politburo. Its membership was expanded to include the first party secretaries of the fifteen republics. At the time, most observers concluded that this move signified the diminution of the party's policy-making role and the transfer of power to Gorbachev's Presidential Council, an advisory body created earlier that year.

The most dramatic moment of the Congress, however, belonged to Boris Yeltsin, who had recently been elected president of the Russian Republic. On July 12 he marched to the podium and turned in his Communist party membership card. He stated that as RSFSR president "I can only subordinate myself to the will of the people and its elected representatives." He then walked out of the hall to the jeers of most delegates. Soon afterward, reformers Anatoly Sobchak and Gavriil Popov announced their decisions to leave the CPSU as well.

In this way, the Congress drew the final dividing line between those who continued to believe that the party must manage reform of the Soviet Union, and those, like Yeltsin, who had decided that the Communist party was unreformable and that change could come only through other means.

The "War of Laws"

As Moscow's influence was waning, the prestige of the republican governments was increasing. By the spring of 1990 most republics had held elections to local and republic-level soviets, or councils. Reformers in Russia had united behind the coalition group "Elections '90" and had taken control of city councils in Moscow and Leningrad. A similar result occurred in Kiev. Nationalist movements had come to power in the Baltic republics, Armenia, Georgia, and western Ukraine.

Reformers saw these electoral successes as evidence that they could coordinate their activities to wrest greater control over policy making from Moscow. In Russia, for example, reformers held a founding congress of the Movement for Democratic Russia in October 1990, an effort designed to create an umbrella group for all democratic movements in the republic. This group was to become the most active reformist movement in Russia. Reformers in the republics openly challenged Moscow's legitimacy and capacity to represent republican and local interests. Some called for the dissolution of the USSR Congress of People's Deputies, charging—as did Moscow mayor Gavriil Popov—that it was merely a vehicle for "endless speeches and paperwork."

The republics' primary tactic in challenging Moscow was to defy the center's legislative authority. By October 1990, fourteen republics had passed declarations of either independence or sovereignty over USSR laws. Gorbachev had decreed in August 1990 that the Russian declaration of sovereignty was "null and void." The USSR Supreme Soviet reaffirmed the supremacy of its laws until a new union treaty was signed.

The RSFSR declaration of sovereignty was particularly important in prompting Gorbachev to take serious action to replace the original 1922 union treaty with a new document. The negotiations between the center and the republics were conducted under Gorbachev's leadership and thus produced a draft that fell short of devolving the powers the republics had demanded with their declarations of sovereignty. The Baltics and Georgia declared their refusal to sign the treaty under any circumstances. In October 1990 the Ukrainian Supreme Soviet—under pressure from university students on a two-week hunger strike—decided to postpone signing the treaty until after a new Ukrainian constitution was signed.

Throughout this highly uncertain period, the republics and Moscow waged a "war of laws." This was a situation in which the republics—after issuing sovereignty declarations—passed various laws that conflicted with all-union legislation, often leading to political stalemate. One example of this occurred in November when a USSR government resolution freed prices on many luxury items such as jewelry, furs, and video equipment. When Russia, Azerbaijan, and Kazakhstan proclaimed the USSR law nonbinding on their territory, most stores closed and waited for further instructions.

The RSFSR's powerful position in the union allowed Yeltsin to repeatedly defy the central government. He concluded bilateral agreements with other republics without Moscow's approval and, in a dramatic move at the end of 1990, announced that the RSFSR parliament had voted to reduce the republic's contribution to the all-union 1991 budget by about 80 percent. This shocked the all-union government and provoked an accusation by Gorbachev that Russia's arrogant "economic populism" could throw the USSR deeper into chaos.

The Baltics continued their tenacious campaign against Moscow's rule. Although Lithuania had suffered a three-month economic blockade by Moscow in response to its March declaration of independence, it and Latvia and Estonia continued to seek membership in several international organizations as a means of validating their reemerging independent foreign policies. They applied for—but were denied four times—observer status at the Conference on Security and Cooperation in Europe (CSCE) negotiations being held throughout 1990.

The "war of laws" was replicated on lower levels as well. Many of the USSR's twenty autonomous republics (subunits of the fifteen union republics) declared sovereignty in the summer and fall of 1990, and several other autonomous formations did the same.

Some of the disputes turned violent. The Georgian Supreme Soviet, for example, rejected declarations of sovereignty by the Abkhaz Autonomous Republic and the South Ossetian Autonomous Oblast (or region). On December 11 it voted to abolish the latter as a distinct territorial region within Georgia and, in so doing, touched off violence and bloodshed.

Consequently, a paradoxical situation was emerging. Challenges from the grass roots were met by resistance from their juridical authorities, and these higher-level bodies usually managed to retain power through control of administrative, state, and party structures. No one, it seemed, was running the USSR, and this paralysis of power deepened the crisis atmosphere enveloping the country.

An Uneasy Compromise

To make matters worse, the Soviet economy was continuing to deteriorate. Despite its enhanced powers, the USSR Supreme Soviet had failed to take the lead in drafting effective economic legislation. In May, Prime Minister Nikolai Ryzhkov had submitted a proposal to the USSR Supreme Soviet calling for the introduction of significant market reforms. This plan, as economist Edward Hewett notes, was a "major improvement over previous efforts." However, a central feature of the proposal was its call for dramatic price increases on bread, other food, and consumer goods, which many Soviet leaders feared would destabilize the already restless society. Therefore, the Soviet parliament had rejected Ryzhkov's proposal and had ordered him to come up with a better plan by the fall.

Meanwhile, Yeltsin was riding the wave of popularity stemming from his election as president of the Russian republic in May 1990. Shortly after assuming his post, Yeltsin boldly promised to create a market economy in 500 days. He had adopted a plan for market reform developed by Grigory Yavlinsky, a young progressive economist who had been working in the Ryzhkov government.

In the face of the defeat of Ryzhkov's plan and the threat of the RSFSR's introducing a market economy on its own, Gorbachev moved to work out a compromise with Yeltsin. Gorbachev agreed to set up a commission to develop a program for economic reform, and it was expected that the group would rely heavily on Yeltsin's "500-day plan." Most analysts heralded the agreement as evidence that Gorbachev had shifted back toward the liberal side of the spectrum. The compromise decreased political tensions between Gorbachev and Yeltsin, but it did not eliminate them.

Working for the most part independently of each other, the two groups prepared fundamentally different proposals. Ryzhkov and his advisers drafted a revised version of their previous proposal. It provided for the retention of power by the center in conjunction with consumer price increases and wage hikes. The Shatalin Group (as it came to be known for its director, Stanislav Shatalin, a reformist economist on Gorbachev's Presidential Council) called for rapid privatization of state assets with a delay in the introduction of price increases. Its most important feature was a provision whereby the republics

would delegate powers to the center, instead of the reverse. In particular, the plan called for the republics and local governments to hold all authority to tax; financing for the central government would come either from republican contributions or from specific taxation powers granted by the republics.

Gorbachev, however, refused to support either plan. Instead, he appointed economist Abel Aganbegyan to develop a compromise proposal. This "Presidential Plan," which Gorbachev presented to the Soviet parliament in October, was basically the Shatalin Plan stripped of specifics on key issues and its timetable for implementation. In contrast to the Shatalin Plan, the Presidential Plan did not call for the reconstitution of the union based on support from the republics. Instead, it relied on the existing government to implement presidential decrees. The Soviet legislature approved the Presidential Plan without much opposition, but this approval had marginal value as the plan was little more than a statement of intent.

At approximately the same time, the Supreme Soviet granted Gorbachev his request for emergency economic powers to halt the nation's slide into social and economic chaos. In requesting increased authority, Gorbachev pointed out that there was a "serious crisis in executive power" and warned later that he might have to introduce presidential rule in some places. The resolution passed by the legislature gave the president special powers for eighteen months to enact polices on wages, prices, and the budget as well as to "strengthen law and order."

Meanwhile, the RSFSR Supreme Soviet took a different tack: it decided to implement the original 500-day plan on its own. In a direct challenge to Gorbachev, Yeltsin declared that his plan would include protective measures to "insulate the Russian people from the economic and social consequences of the union program." Concurrently, he called for Prime Minister Ryzhkov's resignation and the abolition of most central government structures.

By the fall of 1990 then, the temporary Gorbachev-Yeltsin alliance was over, the battle between the center and the republics waged on, and the country was no closer to unified leadership than it had been half a year earlier.

A Coming Dictatorship?

Although many reformers had been encouraged by Gorbachev's apparent embrace of market economics and his compromise with Yeltsin in the summer, events during the fall of 1990 dashed hopes for coordinated economic and social reform. Conservative leaders became bolder in their pronouncements. Their calls for stability and the preservation of the old order played on the fears of the Soviet people, who saw little evidence that the economy was improving. Many Soviets had grown tired of the upheaval caused by reforms and yearned for the order, stability, and security of the past.

At two important meetings in November 1990, conservatives signaled to Gorbachev that they were willing to challenge him. The first was a private assembly on November 13 of one thousand military officers. During this five-hour meeting, officers rose

Mikhail Gorbachev was under pressure from conservative forces when he appointed Boris Pugo as minister of internal affairs on December 2, 1990. One month later, troops under Pugo's command spearheaded a crackdown in the Baltic states.

one after another to complain about draft evasion and desertion, the declining prestige of the military, and their poor living conditions. After the meeting, Lieutenant Colonel Alksnis demanded that Gorbachev show results within thirty days or be forced from office. Alksnis also proposed that power be transferred to a committee of national salvation.

The second meeting was a November 16 session of the USSR Supreme Soviet at which Gorbachev delivered his "state of the union" address. Following his presentation, the deputies angrily pronounced their dissatisfaction with Gorbachev's accounting and demanded that the president put forth specific proposals for restoring public confidence. After working feverishly all night, Gorbachev announced his plan the next day. It was centered around another sweeping governmental reorganization. The Presidential Council would be abolished and replaced with a Security Council, the Council of Ministers would be transformed into a cabinet subordinate directly to the president, and a new vice-presidential post would be introduced. In addition to creating his own security council overseeing the military and security forces, Gorbachev would set up a network of presidential representatives to enforce Moscow's orders around the country. A week later at a press conference, Gorbachev announced his intention to use these augmented powers to hold the country together. He argued that attempts to break up the USSR could result in bloodshed.

Both the centralization of powers specified in the reorganization plan and the personnel changes that followed worried reformers. On December 2, 1990, Gorbachev replaced the generally liberal Vadim Bakatin as USSR minister of internal affairs with Boris Pugo, a hard-line former first secretary of the Latvian Communist party. Gorbachev reportedly had been persuaded by "Soyuz"—the right-wing group of parliamentary deputies headed by Alksnis—to appoint Pugo.

On December 11 KGB Chief Vladimir Kryuchkov warned that extremist groups supported from overseas were pushing the country toward chaos. He announced that the KGB was committed to preserving the unity of the USSR. In a later speech he said Western economic contacts were attempts to exert "overt and covert pressure on the USSR" and issued a thinly veiled warning to foreign businesses to stay away from the Soviet Union. Furthermore, fifty-three top military officers and industrialists urged Gorbachev to consider direct presidential rule to "put an end to the chaos" and prevent disintegration of the state. In response, Gorbachev told the USSR Congress of People's Deputies on December 19 that he was willing to impose a state of emergency or presidential rule in regions where there was a "serious threat to the security of the state or to people's lives."

Shevardnadze Resigns

By December 1990 many proreform Soviet leaders believed that Gorbachev had given in to conservative pressures and a right-wing crackdown would be hard to prevent or resist. Foreign Minister Eduard Shevardnadze was one such person. On December 20 he stunned the world with his dramatic announcement to the USSR Congress of People's Deputies that he was resigning. In what he called the "shortest and the most difficult speech" of his life, Shevardnadze warned that a dictatorship was approaching. "No one knows what this dictatorship will be like," he added, nor "what kind of dictator will come to power and what order will be established." He said he was resigning to protest the onset of dictatorship and to encourage democrats to resist the reactionary forces that were stirring in the country. In a later interview, he stated that he could not support the use of force to restore order.

Many observers considered Shevardnadze to have been Gorbachev's most important adviser during his years as leader of the Soviet Union. Shevardnadze had guided the Soviet disengagement from Eastern Europe, the arms talks with the West that led to significant reductions in nuclear weapons, and the end of the cold war. He also had directed the Soviet Union's policy of siding with the U.S.-led coalition against Iraq during the Persian Gulf crisis. For doing so, he had been severely criticized by some conservatives and military leaders.

Shevardnadze's resignation seemed to shock the Soviet president. Shevardnadze had not told Gorba-

Eduard Shevardnadze, confidant of Mikhail Gorbachev and architect of the new thinking in Soviet foreign policy, stuns everyone with his resignation from the Foreign Ministry.

chev of his decision, and in a speech later in the day Gorbachev said that he "personally disapproved" of the surprise move. He also stated that he had planned to nominate Shevardnadze for the post of vice president. Finally Gorbachev appealed to his audience not to panic or "grow hysterical" about the serious situation the country was facing.

At this defining moment, Gorbachev had a choice to make: he could either cast his lot with the reformers or be placed firmly in the conservative camp. By refusing to resist the mounting hard-line pressures, Gorbachev made a symbolic move to the right.

Instead of Shevardnadze, Gorbachev nominated for vice president the former trade union head Gennady Yanayev, a colorless bureaucrat steeped in Communist party discipline. Later in January Gorbachev appointed Valentin Pavlov to replace Nikolai Ryzhkov as prime minister. Pavlov had served in the USSR government as minister of finance. He too was considered a conservative.

Crackdown in the Baltics

During January 1991 Gorbachev's shift to the right was evidenced by the central government's military crackdown in the Baltics. On January 2 special Interior Ministry forces called the "Black Berets" seized the press building in Riga. On January 7 the Defense Ministry announced that elite paratroop units were being sent to enforce the military draft in the Baltics, as well as in Moldavia, Armenia, Georgia, and parts of Ukraine. On January 11 Soviet army troops took control of the Lithuanian press center and national guard headquarters. Then on January 13 Soviet troops stormed the radio and television station in Vilnius, Lithuania, killing fourteen people and injuring more than one hundred sixty others. The military commander in the region announced that he had been acting on the orders of the National Salvation Committee of Lithuania, group of conservative party and military persons intent on holding the union together. On January 20 the Black Berets took over Latvia's Interior Ministry, killing four persons and wounding ten. A similar announcement was made: the All-Latvian Committee of National Salvation had taken over the Latvian government.

In the aftermath of the Lithuanian attack, Interior Minister Boris Pugo and Defense Minister Dmitry Yazov denied that orders to use force against civilians had come from Moscow. Waiting more than thirty-six hours to comment on the raid, Gorbachev also denied that he had known of or sanctioned the assault. He placed the blame on the local commander in Vilnius, Maj. Gen. Vladimir Uskhopchik, saying, "The manner of defense was decided by the commandant. I learned only in the morning." Nevertheless, he blamed leaders of the Lithuanian parliament for bringing on the attack and did not disavow the killings. About a week later, he did express sympathy for the victims but still refused to condemn the attacks.

Gorbachev's precise role in the crackdown is still unknown, but it seemed that he either approved the raids in an attempt to reverse republic efforts to gain independence or he had become hostage to right-wing forces in control of the military and KGB. Adherents of the latter view speculate that late in 1990 the security forces went to Gorbachev and warned that if he did not let them restore order he would face deposal. Neither interpretation was reassuring. Either Gorbachev was fully in control of the country and had decided to use force to hold the

A Soviet army officer, flanked by a militia member (left) and a soldier (right), checks the papers of two army enlistees (center). Joint militia-army patrols, begun in January 1991, search for deserters and draft dodgers.

union together, or he had lost control and hard-line security forces had free rein.

Not surprisingly, the military moves further polarized the Soviet people. Immediately after the incident, Yeltsin traveled to the Baltics. In Tallinn on January 13 he signed a mutual security pact with the three Baltic republics. The next day in a radio address from Moscow he appealed to Russian soldiers not to fire on civilians. A week later he criticized Gorbachev before the RSFSR Supreme Soviet, charging that Gorbachev was planning to establish presidential rule throughout the USSR with the national salvation committees as his agents. Conservatives criticized Gorbachev too. Colonel Alksnis argued that Gorbachev had planned the takeover of the Baltic governments but in the face of world reaction had blamed the military.

Television footage of the crackdown provoked strong condemnation from the world community. The European Parliament suspended delivery of $1.5 billion in food and technical assistance in response to the attacks. U.S. President George Bush said that the violence was "deeply disturbing," but he avoided taking action that would derail U.S.-Soviet relations. The Group of Seven (G-7) major industrialized nations, including the United States, put on hold a proposal to grant the USSR associate status in the World Bank and International Monetary Fund.

Conservative Resurgence

As the winter wore on, this "turn to the right" continued. In a hastily announced decree in January, Prime Minister Pavlov's cabinet announced that after January 22 fifty- and hundred-ruble notes would no longer be legal tender. This was necessary, Pavlov said, to combat speculation, corruption, and forgery. He later contended that the move had been necessary to thwart a Western bankers' plot to destabilize the economy. A provision of the decree allowed a central intergovernmental commission to monitor compliance in the republics and even to take over the banks there, a measure that some thought might be invoked to force the breakaway republics into submission.

Another ominous decree soon followed. As of February 1, central television announced, the military would be joining police patrols to "combat crime" in large cities. Many thought that this was a precautionary step for the impending price increases. At roughly the same time, Gorbachev authorized the KGB and police to search domestic and foreign businesses without warning to root out economic sabotage and corruption. As did the joint patrol decree, this order increased foreboding among the Soviet people, further discredited the government, and caused foreign businesses to delay plans for investment.

A renewed conservatism was apparent in foreign policy as well. When the American-led coalition launched its air war against Iraq in January, Gorbachev implied that the United States had not tried hard enough to achieve a diplomatic solution to the confrontation. Later, the new foreign minister, Aleksandr Bessmertnykh, said that military actions conducted by the coalition might be exceeding the United Nations mandate. Then without consulting Washington, Moscow presented a peace plan on February 21 that positioned the Soviet Union as mediator between Iraq and the United States. With this move, the Soviets distanced themselves from full cooperation with the anti-Iraq coalition and tried to preserve their traditional role as protector of the Arab world.

Union Treaty

During the spring of 1991 Gorbachev and his advisers focused on negotiations to conclude a new union treaty that would preserve the Soviet Union. The draft version written the previous year had been passed by the USSR Congress of People's Deputies in December 1990, but negotiations had been proceeding slowly. Gorbachev had been unwilling to accept the possibility that not all the republics would sign the treaty and, although he had made some concessions on republican autonomy, he had not removed from the revised treaty provisions guaranteeing the primacy of federal laws over republican laws.

To gain support for the new draft and obtain a

The Birth of a Labor Movement

In what was the worst labor unrest in the USSR since the 1920s, coal miners in the Far North, Siberia, Ukraine, and Central Asia went on strike in July 1989 to express their opposition to the government. In defiance of the USSR's long-standing tradition of worker quiescence, the miners began their strike over a shortage of soap, but their demands quickly expanded to include economic and political concerns. They demanded local control over their mines, free trade unions, and the abolition of the leading role of the Communist party. In a stunning victory for the miners, the government conceded to their demands, though it did not follow through on all of its promises to improve working and living conditions.

These strikes illustrated that the old "social contract" between the workers and the state was breaking down. The miners no longer trusted the government to provide for their basic needs. This declining trust led to the creation of independent trade unions. Although the official trade union (the AUCCTU) responded to the labor unrest by decentralizing and creating a looser confederation of unions in October 1990, most workers regarded this as mere window dressing. Unofficial trade unions organized during this period, but most remained small and disconnected from the emerging political parties.

Significantly, the strikes also had shown that Soviet workers saw a connection between their economic welfare and the political environment. During a one-day strike held on July 11, 1990, to protest the government's failure to fulfill its promises of a year ago, one miner explained their action this way: "It is now clear to all of us that without political change, there is no hope for [our] economic demands."

The miners gained experience in local management and governance through the strikes. They set up strike committees on the local level that in some regions eventually forced local government officials to resign. These committees then became de facto municipal governments that continued to exist after the strikes ended.

In March 1991 these local organizations played a major role in coordinating another devastating nationwide miners' strike. As strikes in the energy sector had been declared illegal, these committees adopted a sophisticated "rolling strike" strategy whereby mines would strike consecutively in order to circumvent the ban and avoid the loss of pay. The strikes came to a halt in April 1991, when Yeltsin transferred the mines from all-union to Russian jurisdiction. This action was a milestone in Yeltsin's attempt to wrest control from Gorbachev's central government. It pushed Gorbachev to concede to extensive decentralization of power to the republics in the proposed union treaty.

Soon afterward, the rise of the labor movement as a powerful force in Soviet politics became evident in places other than the coal mines, notably in Belorussia. Spurred to action by consumer price increases, enterprises across Belorussia staged a general strike in April 1991. A hundred thousand workers gathered in

popular mandate for a renewed union, Gorbachev scheduled an all-union referendum on whether the union should be preserved as a "renewed federation of equal sovereign republics." The referendum was held on March 17, 1991, with 76 percent of voters favoring the proposal.

While the Soviet government heralded the vote as evidence that the Soviet people favored preserving the union as a federal state, the referendum was not a complete success. Only nine of the fifteen republics took part in the referendum (the RSFSR, Ukraine, Belorussia, Azerbaijan, and the five Central Asian republics). These were the same republics that had been participating in the union treaty negotiations. In a show of defiance, the Baltic republics held their own referendums in February and early March. A substantial majority in each voted in favor of independence. Although Ukraine and Russia did hold the all-union referendum, they both ran concurrent polls as counterweights to the all-union measure. Ukraine garnered an 80 percent approval margin for its own referendum on sovereignty; this

By March 1991 Ukrainian miners were demanding political rather than economic change. The sign reads: Demands:
1. Abolition of the USSR Supreme Soviet as an institution of legal authority. 2. Abolition of presidential authority.
3. Political and economic sovereignty of Ukraine. 4. Cessation of payments to the center.

Lenin Square in Minsk to call for the resignation of the Belorussian government. The republican government was forced to the negotiating table to discuss the economic and political demands of the striking workers.

The birth of the labor movement is ironic because socialism was supposed to satisfy the workers and meet their basic needs. As the labor unrest in the former Soviet Union demonstrated, socialism had satisfied neither the economic needs nor the political aspirations of workers. Under conditions of continuing economic hardship, the labor movement is bound to play a vital role in shaping the future of Russia and the newly independent states.

contrasted with a 70 percent approval vote for the all-union measure. The RSFSR held a referendum asking whether a popularly elected presidency should be instituted. It received overwhelming support, and Yeltsin was elected to this post on June 12 with 60 percent of the vote. Several weeks later Georgia held a plebiscite on independence and reported 98 percent support for it.

During the spring the Soviet Union experienced growing labor unrest, which underscored the fragile nature of the government's support. In March 1991 coal miners across the country went on a month-long strike to demand the resignation of Gorbachev and his government. Soon after, Belarus—traditionally a bastion of conservatism—was swept by a wave of general labor unrest protesting the introduction of steep consumer price hikes. Just a few weeks earlier, Belorussian voters had approved the all-union referendum by 83 percent; now workers were calling for the resignation of Soviet authorities. The general strike began over economic concerns but quickly expanded to include demands for the resignation of the Soviet and Belorussian leaderships.

Some analysts have contended that these work stoppages shocked Gorbachev into recognizing the crippling potential of prolonged labor unrest and prompted him to seek yet another compromise with Yeltsin. A major breakthrough came on April 23 when Gorbachev and the leaders of nine republics met at Novo-Ogarevo to hammer out their differences over the union treaty. The result was an accord in which Gorbachev essentially acknowledged that the remaining six republics would not be part of a future union. He promised the nine republics increased powers, including the right to control their own property and exports.

The revised union treaty was sent to the republican parliaments for approval in June, and within a month eight out of nine signed the treaty. As before, Ukrainian deputies postponed their approval, but the others decided to sign the treaty anyway, hoping that Ukraine would agree to it later. The signing date was set for August 20.

Meanwhile, conservative forces were demonstrating their distress over the union treaty and Gorbachev's accommodations with the left. Border posts in the three Baltic republics were attacked by Black Beret troops beginning in mid-May; attacks continued intermittently during the summer. On July 31, on the eve of the Bush-Gorbachev summit in Moscow, unknown assailants tried to foil the meeting by attacking eight border guards at a Lithuanian post.

On June 17, USSR Prime Minister Pavlov asked the Supreme Soviet to increase his cabinet's authority, a move that many interpreted as an effort to usurp Gorbachev's power. Indeed Pavlov had not consulted Gorbachev about the plan, and conservatives took the opportunity to speak in its favor and to criticize Gorbachev. Although the legislature eventually rejected Pavlov's proposal, this move was a sign that conservatives were worried about power passing to the republics. An open letter published the next month in the conservative newspaper *Sovetskaya Rossiya* confirmed the depth of their sentiments. In a document entitled "A Word to the People," Communist party officials and senior military officers appealed to the Soviet people to preserve the USSR at all costs.

The Coup

The prospect that the union treaty would soon be signed and a growing sense among conservatives that if they did not assert themselves soon their cause would be lost led to a right-wing coup against Gorbachev's government in mid-August 1991. Western observers had been predicting for more than a year that some type of coup attempt in the Soviet Union was likely. These expectations were heightened on August 16, several days before the coup, when former Gorbachev ally Aleksandr Yakovlev resigned from the CPSU, warning that a "Stalinist group in the party leadership was getting ready for a party and state coup." Yet when the coup came, it nevertheless shocked Soviets and Westerners alike. Its brevity—three days in length—did not detract from its significance. The failed coup ensured and hastened the end of the Soviet Union.

Emergency Committee Takes Power

Shortly after 6:00 a.m. on Monday, August 19, 1991, TASS made an announcement that was chillingly reminiscent of the pre-Gorbachev years: "For reasons of health" Mikhail Gorbachev could not fulfill his duties as president, and USSR vice president Gennady Yanayev was assuming power as acting president. The announcement also declared that a state of emergency would become effective in certain parts of the country and that a State Committee for the State of Emergency in the USSR had been formed to lead the country out of crisis. A series of decrees banned the independent press, established a curfew, and prohibited demonstrations.

At 9:00 a.m. military vehicles started moving toward the center of Moscow. Tanks and armored personnel carriers positioned themselves along the main roads, on the squares, and outside important government buildings. In the Baltics, Gen. Fyodor Kuzmin, the top military leader in the region, declared that he was assuming control of Latvia, Lith-

On the morning of August 19, tanks take up position on Red Square (top) and in front of the Russian White House (bottom). Muscovites, who are just beginning to gather in defense of the White House, clamber aboard one of the first tanks to arrive and question the tank crew about its intentions. The farm tractor behind the tank will become part of an impromptu barricade.

uania, and Estonia on behalf of the Emergency Committee. Soviet warships blockaded Estonia's port in Tallinn and Black Beret troops in Latvia and Lithuania seized television and radio stations. Military personnel also entered Leningrad, and in smaller cities the local KGB closed independent radio stations.

Later in the day the coup plotters revealed themselves at an anachronistic press conference. The members of the eight-man Emergency Committee were Yanayev, KGB Chairman Kryuchkov, Prime Minister Pavlov, Interior Minister Pugo, Defense Minister Yazov, Communist party Central Committee Secretary Oleg Baklanov, and lesser-known Central Committee members Vasily Starodubtsev and Aleksandr Tizyakov. Yanayev stated that the situation had "gone out of control in the USSR" and that the group had no alternative but to take resolute action to stem the slide into disaster. The committee, he continued, was determined to restore law and order immediately.

The press conference had been convened to win public support, but it had the opposite effect. The dour committee, clad in colorless suits, appeared as a throwback to the Brezhnev era. Moreover, Yanayev's unconvincing performance did little to heighten the Soviet people's confidence in or fear of the coup leaders. He trembled as he spoke and was obviously nervous.

The same evening, the committee appealed to the USSR Council of Ministers for support. At a secret session held at 6:00 p.m., Pavlov presented his case for emergency measures, and afterward thirty or so ministers spoke in favor of the coup. According to Environment Minister Nikolai Vorontsov, only three ministers objected to the new regime.

Most analysts agreed that the putsch had been prompted by Gorbachev's plan to sign the new union treaty on August 20. The treaty symbolized everything the conservatives opposed: the secession of six republics, the transfer of central ministerial functions to the republics, and the demise of the Soviet Union in its existing form. The Emergency Committee's appeal to the Soviet people warned of "extremist forces" that were intent on liquidating the USSR. That Gorbachev was at his dacha in the Crimea made the plotters' task easier.

Reaction and Resistance

As Muscovites woke to hear short bulletins on the television and radio stating that Gorbachev had been relieved of office, several thousand of them braved the rains to confront the soldiers sitting on their tanks. Meanwhile, Yeltsin took the lead in harnessing public resistance to the takeover. Late in the morning, he had held a press conference in front of the Russian republic's parliament building (known as the "Russian White House") in which he demanded that Gorbachev be released. In a highly symbolic moment, Yeltsin stood on top of a tank in front of the parliament and delivered a virulent speech to the assembled resisters, condemning the "rightist, reactionary, anticonstitutional coup." He also called for a general strike and issued a decree declaring that he was assuming control of the RSFSR and ordering officials to obey the RSFSR government, not the Emergency Committee.

Citizens from throughout the city made their way to the Russian White House to defend it. By nightfall barricades made of tree limbs, buses, furniture, and concrete chunks had been erected around the building. Thousands of people decided to stay up all night to act as "human shields" in its defense.

The second day of the coup, August 20, was the most tense and decisive. By then almost fifty thousand people had gathered at the White House. As Yeltsin's government held forth inside the building with its "war room" ham radio and printing press, former foreign minister Shevardnadze addressed the crowd outside. He got an enthusiastic response when he stated that if Gorbachev was party to the plot, he would have to be tried.

Around the country, journalists reported similar public defiance. In Leningrad, Ukraine, and Moldavia, hundreds of thousands of people joined in protest. In the Siberian town of Novokuznetsk, mines emptied out in support of Yeltsin, and in many cities across Russia, local councils voted to defy the Emergency Committee and obey Yeltsin. Top leaders of Ukraine, Moldavia, and Kazakhstan joined Yeltsin in denouncing the coup.

Despite the drama of public resistance, the So-

A Botched Coup

The conspirators who tried to seize power in August 1991 faced open defiance from the Soviet public that may have brought about the failure of the coup even if it had been skillfully executed. But the poor planning of the conspirators and their incompetent performance during the coup did much to undermine their chances of success. The plotters committed numerous mistakes that virtually doomed the putsch from the start.

First and probably most important, the plotters failed to arrest or otherwise silence Boris Yeltsin. Yeltsin had flown back to Moscow from Kazakhstan on August 18, the day before the coup. He would have been easy to detain at the airport. The coup leaders also could have orchestrated a quick attack on the Russian White House soon after the coup began to ensure that Yeltsin would not be able to rally Muscovites against the coup. The opportunity for a quick and simple assault faded away on the first day of the coup as thousands of citizens went to the Russian White House to form a human barrier against attack and some military units defected to Yeltsin.

Second, although the plotters took some steps to censor the media, they failed to completely control it. Western journalists had virtually unimpeded access to Moscow streets and were able to broadcast footage of the coup as it was unfolding. The independent Russian radio station "Ekho Moskvy" circumvented an order to stop broadcasting by setting up an office in the Russian White House. Liberal and independent Russian publications continued to operate in spite of the Emergency Committee's ban on all but nine national newspapers. All of Leningrad's newspapers but one reportedly appeared on the second day of the coup, and the liberal *Moscow News* distributed news using fax machines located across Moscow. The continued operation of news organizations opposed to the coup reinforced the impression that the plotters were headed for failure.

Third, the plotters overestimated the loyalty of military officers to the Emergency Committee. In Leningrad, for example, the regional military commander ordered one thousand troops approaching the city in tanks not to enter the city. In Moscow, Lieutenant General Pavel Grachev and Yevgeny Shaposhnikov, chief of the air force, defected to Yeltsin's side. These and other mutinies by officers and whole units undermined the coup plotters' confidence and emboldened the resisters.

Fourth, the plotters let three hours elapse between the announcement of the coup and the movement of military vehicles in Moscow. To many observers, this delay was interpreted as a sign that the coup's leaders were indecisive and perhaps locked in disagreement. In fact, some reports suggest that Prime Minister Pavlov's behavior at the Monday Council of Ministers meeting indicated that he had been drinking heavily. The next day he was hospitalized because of "high blood pressure." Several of his colleagues said that this was Pavlov's way of trying to back out of the coup.

By all accounts, the coup was not the streamlined decisive action typical of previous Soviet intrigues. Gorbachev's reforms had created a society that would stand up to the use of force and fight to retain its hard-won freedoms. Coupled with the tragicomic behavior of the coup plotters, the putsch could not help but fail.

By August 20 it was clear that at least some military units would not support the coup.

Armored personnel carriers file past the Ukraine Hotel as they move out of Moscow on August 21.

viet military was the key to the success or failure of the coup. Already the day before in Moscow, three units that had been sent to surround Yeltsin's stronghold had defected to Yeltsin's cause. On the second night of the event, soldiers continued to fly their Russian tricolor flags atop their tanks as they joined masses of ordinary people shielding the Russian parliament. Throughout the night, reports circulated that troops would soon attempt to storm the White House, but no assault was made.

The Coup Fails

The decisive moment of the coup came at 8:00 p.m. on August 20, when armed forces chief of staff Mikhail Moiseyev ordered a halt to troops moving toward the Russian parliament. According to Russian defense chief Gen. Konstantin Kobets, three battalions of KGB troops were supposed to have led the attack on the building after midnight; as Kobets stated, Moiseyev's action thwarted this plan.

From that point onward, the coup quickly disintegrated. On the morning of August 21, the collegium of the Defense Ministry decided to withdraw its troops. As troops and armored cars began leaving Moscow, residents gathered on the street to cheer on the departing soldiers. Later in the day, Defense Minister Yazov, KGB Chief Kryuchkov, and two other collaborators flew to the Crimea to bargain with President Gorbachev.

Gorbachev was released from house arrest that day and flew back to Moscow with a Russian governmental delegation dispatched by Yeltsin to accompany him home. The following morning Gorbachev held a press conference in which he described the circumstances of his detainment. He stated that on Sunday, August 18, members of the Emergency Committee had arrived unexpectedly at his dacha in the Crimea. He said that he had attempted to phone Moscow but discovered that the lines had been cut. According to Gorbachev, the delegation demanded that he hand over his presidential powers to Vice President Yanayev and offered him the opportunity to join the Emergency Committee. He refused and was placed under house arrest.

Although Gorbachev used the press conference to distance himself from the failed coup, he disappointed many viewers by reaffirming his loyalty to the Communist party. He suggested only that the party's reactionary members be driven out and

Boris Yeltsin humiliates Gorbachev before the Russian republic's parliament on August 23.

urged his viewers to do everything to ensure that the party reforms itself and "becomes a vital force for perestroika."

This stubborn faith in the CPSU contributed to Gorbachev's declining influence. On August 23 he addressed the Russian republic's parliament and faced a scornful, heckling audience calling him to account for his refusal to outlaw the CPSU, even in the face of betrayals by its top leadership. The Russian parliament also derided him for having originally appointed the coup plotters to office. Yeltsin publicly humiliated Gorbachev by forcing him to read the minutes from the Council of Ministers session at which Gorbachev's former ministers had condoned the coup.

Under this pressure, Gorbachev soon afterward resigned from his position as CPSU general secretary and called on the Central Committee to dissolve itself. He also ordered the party's property to be nationalized.

The coup plotters were arrested and charged with state treason. Three top leaders of the old order committed suicide: former chief of staff of the armed forces Marshal Sergei Akhromeyev, Interior Minister and coup plotter Boris Pugo, and Nikolai Kruchina, the CPSU official in charge of party finances.

In a symbolic conclusion to the failed putsch, a crowd of ten thousand citizens gathered outside KGB headquarters to topple the iron statue of Feliks Dzerzhinsky, the founder of the first Soviet secret police. As fireworks went off, the statue came down.

End of the Soviet Union

In the four months following the coup, the Soviet Union gradually disintegrated. The skeleton central government lost its remaining shred of legitimacy and collapsed, the Communist party was banned from most republics, and the fifteen republics declared their independence. Simultaneously, the newly independent states moved to establish a new form of cooperation, as most of them joined in forming the Commonwealth of Independent States.

Republics Gain Independence

At the time of the coup, only Lithuania had formally declared its full independence and Latvia, Estonia, Armenia, and Georgia had announced transition periods leading to independence. After the failed coup, however, the republics seized the opportunity to make their final breaks with the center. On August 20—the second day of the coup—Estonia

On the morning of August 23, Boris Yeltsin addresses a crowd of Muscovites at the base of the statue of Feliks Dzerzhinsky, the first head of the Soviet secret police and an icon of the discredited communist regime (top). The graffiti-stained statue, located across from KGB headquarters, bears the inscription "Lenin, executioner of Russia." Later that evening, a jubilant crowd, flush from its victory over the coup plotters two days earlier, witnesses the removal of Dzerzhinsky's statue.

declared that it was an independent and democratic state. Latvia made a similar announcement a day later. Before the end of the month, twelve republics (all but Kazakhstan, the RSFSR, and Turkmenistan) had declared their independence. The three remaining republics did the same over the next few months.

Although independence had been declared, international diplomatic recognition of all the new countries did not come immediately. Denmark, Norway, and Finland recognized the Baltic states immediately; the European Community followed on August 27. The United States, however, delayed complete recognition of the Baltics until September 2, because the Bush administration wanted to wait until the USSR recognized them first. On September 17 the Baltic states were accepted into the United Nations General Assembly.

Diplomatic recognition of the other republics by the United States came more slowly. The United States was hoping that the republics would agree to combine in a loose federation. It therefore delayed recognition to avoid hastening the disintegration of the Soviet Union. Full diplomatic recognition of the other twelve former republics finally came at year's end after Gorbachev had resigned and the union had dissolved. At that time Russia inherited the USSR's seat on the United Nations Security Council.

Yeltsin Moves Ahead

The failed coup was followed by a rapid dismantling of the power structure that had ruled the Soviet Union for seventy-four years. In a series of adroit moves, Yeltsin capitalized on the reformist sentiment engendered by the coup and took bold steps to bury the old system.

First, Yeltsin swiftly and unilaterally seized control of the central government and party apparatus. As early as the second day of the coup, Yeltsin appointed himself commander in chief of the Soviet military. In another decree issued the next day, Yeltsin placed all enterprises located on the territory of the RSFSR under the control of the Russian government.

He continued this trend by reversing the temporary appointments to the defense and security ministries that Gorbachev had made after his return from the Crimea. Yeltsin named air force head Yevgeny Shaposhnikov as the new USSR defense minister and dismissed Leonid Kravchenko as head of the state television company. He placed the Soviet radio and television network and the communications lines run by the KGB under the Russian government's control. He also transferred authority over USSR State Bank to the RSFSR.

By November 15 Yeltsin declared that 80 percent of the former Soviet government had been shut down. At the end of the year, he announced that the Russian government was taking over the Soviet Foreign Ministry building, the KGB, and all Soviet embassies abroad, as the USSR government had run out of funds to operate them.

Yeltsin appointed presidential representatives to ensure that his reforms were implemented in the provinces. These envoys were to expose local decisions that violated republican laws, but they were ordered not to violate local laws. Yeltsin also appointed "governors" to replace leaders of regional councils that had supported the coup. The governors were originally scheduled to run for election in December 1991 but were later given permission to stay in place until December 1992.

In June 1991 Yeltsin had already taken a dramatic step with his ban on party activities at workplaces in Russia, but immediately after the coup he issued a decree outlawing party activities in the military and security forces stationed on Russian territory. He also suspended activities of the Russian Communist party despite Gorbachev's strenuous objections. Party offices were closed and archives were sealed. In November 1991 Yeltsin signed an edict permanently banning the activities of the CPSU on Russian territory. Most of the other republics did likewise. In the Baltic states where the CPSU had split much earlier, the pro-Moscow Communist parties were banned. In Ukraine, Armenia, and Moldavia the party was banned and its assets seized. By contrast, in Uzbekistan the party simply changed its name and remained in power.

The flag of the Russian Federation is raised over the Kremlin on the evening of December 25, 1991.

CIS Is Born

During the fall of 1991, even as the republics declared their independence, the possibility remained that the Soviet Union (minus the Baltic states) might somehow reconstitute itself in a confederal arrangement along the basic lines of the union treaty. Both Yeltsin and Gorbachev backed some type of confederation.

Persuading Ukraine to sign the treaty appeared to be the key to confederation. That republic had scheduled presidential elections and a referendum in December to ratify its independence declaration. Ukrainian leaders refused to negotiate on the treaty until after the referendum. Furthermore, although it

had initialed a draft of a treaty on economic cooperation, Ukraine surprised the other eight republics by refusing to sign the final document. In the meantime, the Ukrainian parliament overwhelmingly passed legislation to establish its own republican army. Nationalist passions were diminishing hopes that Ukraine would sign on to plans for a renewed form of the union.

Ukraine's position was troubling for both Gorbachev and Yeltsin. Gorbachev declared, "I cannot think of a Union without Ukraine. I cannot think of it and cannot imagine it." Yeltsin—who had surpassed Gorbachev in leading the negotiation process—urged Ukraine and the other former republics to join the economic community and conclude a political treaty.

The results of the December 1 vote in Ukraine gave the former republic a powerful bargaining chip in its determination to secede from the USSR. Leonid Kravchuk won election as president with 62 percent of the vote, and almost 90 percent of the voters supported Ukrainian independence. Buttressed by this victory at the polls, Ukraine made it clear that it would not sign a new union treaty.

As a compromise solution, the leaders of the three Slavic republics (Russia, Ukraine, and Belarus) met in Minsk to discuss the formation of a loose confederation. On December 8 Yeltsin, Kravchuk, and Belarus president Stanislav Shushkevich announced the creation of the Commonwealth of Independent States (CIS). They stated that the USSR "as a subject of international law and a geopolitical reality" was ceasing to exist. Instead of a separate union government, "coordinating bodies" would be created to oversee common interests in defense, foreign policy, and the economy.

The agreement was a politically astute adjustment on the part of Yeltsin. Although he and Gorbachev had been united in their common quest for a renewed union, the Ukrainian referendum had demonstrated that this hope was extremely unlikely. Rather than waste political capital in an attempt to preserve the union, Yeltsin endorsed the creation of a looser commonwealth. He explained, "We found the only possible formula for a community of members of the former union. This may be the last chance."

Gorbachev rejected the right of the three republics to declare the end of the USSR and called the termination of all-union legal norms "illegal and dangerous." He also seemed indignant about the speed with which the document had appeared and that he had not been invited to join the discussions. Leaders of the Central Asian republics also felt slighted at their exclusion but did agree to join the CIS several days later. The Central Asian republics, Armenia, Azerbaijan, and Moldova (which had changed its name from Moldavia upon declaring independence) were officially admitted into the CIS at a meeting in Alma-Ata on December 21. The vestiges of the all-union Kremlin government were reduced to irrelevance.

On Christmas Day, December 25, Gorbachev resigned as Soviet president, stating that his resignation had been brought on by the creation of the CIS. In a brief farewell address he hailed the end of the cold war and stressed that mankind was now living in "a new world." At the same time, he emphasized that he had not changed his position on the necessity of preserving the union but that developments had taken "a different course." In a symbolic move, Gorbachev then signed a decree relinquishing his position as commander in chief of the Soviet armed forces and transferring his control of the Soviet nuclear arsenal to Yeltsin. Then the red hammer-and-sickle Soviet flag that had flown over the Kremlin for years was lowered, and the white, blue, and red Russian flag was raised. The Soviet Union was officially no more.

PART II

THE COMMONWEALTH TODAY

CHAPTER 7

THE COMMONWEALTH

An empire spanning eleven time zones, that took the tsars and commissars four centuries to consolidate, splintered into fifteen sovereign states over the course of a year and a half. The empire fell victim to centuries-old national identities that, in the end, proved stronger than the countervailing forces of Soviet political culture and central Muscovite power. Nationalism—a sense of historical community based on a common culture, tradition, language, and customs—is a major factor complicating relations both within and among the newly independent states as they grapple with the task of disentangling an ancient empire.

The Soviet Union was home to more than 130 national groups professing a half dozen different religions. After the collapse of the empire, 15 of those groups became the titular head of their own independent state, leaving no fewer than 115 distinct groups as minorities. Some of the larger of these minority groups, such as the Tatars and Chechens, are agitating for greater autonomy, even for outright independence.

The diaspora that took place during seventy-five years of communist rule has weakened the internal stability of the new states. Soviet leaders encouraged migration as a means of diluting parochialism and promoting a sense of Soviet citizenship. An estimated forty-three million people now live outside of their titular state. For example, tens of thousands of Christian Armenians live within the borders of Moslem Azerbaijan and approximately twenty-five million Russians live outside Russia. Sixty percent of the population of Alma-Ata (capital of Kazakhstan) and 34 percent of the population of Tashkent

(capital of Uzbekistan) are Russian. Ukraine is 20 percent Russian, and Kazakhs are not a majority in their own country. The division of the Soviet Union, therefore, has created conditions where long suppressed ethnic rivalries can flourish within the newly independent states.

While the former Soviet republics wrestle with their internal cohesiveness, they must simultaneously conduct international relations among themselves despite mutual antagonisms that in many instances are centuries old. Sentiment is so strong and of such long standing that antagonism toward a neighboring national group is sometimes a defining characteristic of a group's national identity. Warfare has broken out between Russians and Moldovans, Azeris and Armenians, and Georgians and Ossetes. Several other national groups appear to be on the brink of war.

In addition to maintaining ethnic peace, the fifteen new states face a wide array of daunting economic and political tasks as they attempt to disentangle. These tasks include the reconfiguration or dissolution of a common currency and banking structure; the establishment of new trade patterns; the equitable division of the military and military-industrial complex; the refocusing of foreign policy; the maintenance of a transportation and communications network; and the establishment of new political structures and practices. The highly centralized nature of decision making in the tsarist empire, a characteristic that was magnified by Soviet communism, complicates the task of dissolution.

The mechanism for resolving these questions is the Commonwealth of Independent States (CIS), a

Ukrainian president Leonid Kravchuk, Chairman of the Supreme Soviet of Belarus Stanislav Shushkevich, and Russian president Boris Yeltsin applaud the founding of the Commonwealth of Independent States on December 9, 1991.

structure described by veteran journalist and Soviet watcher Strobe Talbott as "a misnomer wrapped in a contradiction inside a political fiction." There is some question whether the commonwealth is up to the challenge.

The Commonwealth Structure

The CIS was formed in great haste by signatories who had varying degrees of commitment to the new organization. Of the original fifteen Soviet republics, four—Georgia, Estonia, Latvia, and Lithuania—refused to participate in the commonwealth, instead preferring to conduct relations on a bilateral basis with each of the new states individually. The remaining eleven joined the CIS between December 8 and December 21, 1991, some with much trepidation. They all signed a joint accord that contained the general principles on which the CIS was to be based. The accord left many questions unanswered and created extremely weak institutions for resolving future problems.

The fourteen articles of the accord adopted by the commonwealth states were composed of princi-

pled phrases about human rights, respect for minorities and borders, and promises to cooperate in spheres as diverse as foreign policy and health care. But the phrasing was intentionally rendered ambiguous to accommodate differences of opinion among the signatories about the purpose, structure, and prospects for the commonwealth. Was it to be a temporary structure to ease the transition from empire to independent states? Or was it to be a permanent entity? If the commonwealth was to be permanent, was it to take the form of a confederation, with limited central powers? Or was it to be looser still, with ad hoc coordinating bodies? Opinions were so disparate and unyielding that had an attempt been made to iron out these issues, Ukraine, Moldova, and Azerbaijan—the least enthusiastic of the signatories—would likely have opted out of the commonwealth.

Disagreement over these most fundamental issues came to the fore on the very day the document was signed by the non-Slavic members in Alma-Ata, December 21, 1991. The president of Uzbekistan, upon signing the document, commented that henceforth all former Soviet citizens would be citizens of the CIS. Leonid Kravchuk, the president of Ukraine, who was seated across the table, immediately rebuked him: "There will be no commonwealth citizenship, as the commonwealth is not a state."

The signatories went to great lengths to emphasize that the commonwealth was a mutually beneficial arrangement of independent states. The word selected for the arrangement, *sodruzhestvo,* is the same used to translate "British Commonwealth" into Russian, and implies an even looser relationship than *soobshchestvo,* which is used to translate "European Community." The very term "commonwealth," then, indicated the signatories' intentions to create a loose arrangement. Similarly, the signatories referred to Minsk (capital of Belarus) as the "coordination center" of the commonwealth, rather than as the "capital."

The exchange that took place between Kravchuk and President Islam A. Karimov of Uzbekistan in Alma-Ata in December was indicative of a regional split in perceptions of the CIS. The five Central Asian states, when they were still republics of the Soviet Union, had been supportive of Gorbachev's attempts to maintain the union. As independent states they were still supportive of a central government entity and were in favor of maintaining many unifying features, such as a common military and currency.

Central Asian support for a central unifying structure can be traced to the social and economic benefits that association with Moscow had brought to the region. Prior to tsarist domination of the region, the Kazakhs, Kyrgyz, Tajiks, Turkmen, and Uzbeks had been nomadic peoples, largely illiterate and with a poorly developed sense of nation. In socioeconomic terms, they were the least developed people in the empire, and the advancements they made in education, health care, and economic opportunity were significant. The Central Asian states also recognize that their economies are tightly integrated with the Russian economy. Consequently, though many Central Asians harbor anti-Russian sentiment and have stated their preference for independence, there is also strong backing for maintaining close ties with Moscow.

The Ukrainians, Georgians, Belarus, and the Baltic peoples, however, perceive themselves as having gained no benefit from their historical association with Russia. To the contrary, they blame Russia for retarding their development and had attempted to break away from Russian domination amid the chaos of the Russian civil war. Upon formation of the commonwealth they fiercely defended the prerogatives of sovereignty, jealously guarding from the beginning their right to defend their borders, issue their own currencies, form their own militaries, establish their own visa systems, and regulate their own trade. The Georgians and Baltic nations shunned the nascent commonwealth altogether.

The Russian government, led by President Boris Yeltsin, initially leaned toward the Central Asian conceptualization of the commonwealth as a centralized coordinating body. But Russia was forced to react to events in other states—notably Ukraine—and modify its positions accordingly. The reconfiguration of the Soviet military is illustrative of the commonwealth's disunity of purpose and the ramifications of that disunity for formerly Soviet institutions.

The Military

The mighty Soviet military, defender of the Soviet state and pillar of communist mythology, found itself in December 1991 without a state to defend, an ideology to profess, or a civilian leadership to obey. The Red Army—already distressed by the "loss" of Eastern Europe, drastic budget cuts, lack of adequate housing, treaty-mandated troop and equipment reductions, and an awesome display of American military prowess in the Gulf war—was in the words of Harriet Fast Scott, a respected American commentator on the former Soviet military, "demoralized, discontented, and drifting, divided along generational and ethnic lines, drowning in recriminations, and fearful of the future." Without a clear chain of command or raison d'etre, the military was wracked by the same centrifugal forces at work in society at large.

The Soviet military was never the ethnically homogenizing institution that it was touted to be. In theory, it was supposed to draft people of all nationalities and transform them into *Homo Soveticus,* teaching them the values of communist internationalism. In practice, the ethnic schisms within the military exacerbated nationalist tensions in general and anti-Russian sentiment in particular. The officer corps of this international army was 80 percent ethnic Russian, with the percentage rising to 95 at the highest ranks.

Conscripts, long subject to hazing from older soldiers, began in the late 1980s to face serious harassment on the basis of nationality: conscripts from the Baltic republics were assaulted and sometimes killed by Russian conscripts in retaliation for the independence drives of the Baltic republics; Chechens and Tatars assaulted Russian conscripts; and numerous other ethnic groups vented ancient hatreds upon one another. A commission appointed in 1990 by Mikhail Gorbachev reported that 6,000 to 10,000 military personnel died between 1986 and 1989, most of them as a result of hazing and ethnic rivalry. These conditions gave rise to *zemlyaks,* ethnic mafias within military units that protected their members against other ethnic groups. Military discipline among conscripts deteriorated as the union disintegrated under nationalist recriminations. Said one officer, "When I lead my men on a run, I'm expecting to be shot from behind at any time."

In 1991 approximately 360,000 conscripts either deserted or evaded the draft. In many cases the Soviet government was too weak to enforce its laws, as some republic governments tried to shield their citizens from Soviet military recruiters. Thirty percent of those drafted in 1991 failed to appear for military service, and an increasing number of those who did report opposed being stationed outside their home regions.

Morale and discipline among the largely Russian officer corps was little better as the material advantages and prestige of the profession dissipated. Russian officers still stationed in Eastern Europe were no longer protected from hostile publics by fraternal communist governments. Many could not leave their bases without being verbally or even physically assaulted by the local populace. With the collapse of the Soviet Union, Russian officers stationed in the former republics found themselves in nearly identical circumstances: living in foreign countries, surrounded by hostile people who viewed them as occupiers. In July 1992, fearing that his troops might become the target of violence, the highest ranking officer stationed in the Baltics ordered all soldiers to carry their weapons whenever they leave base. Whereas a Soviet officer's uniform had been a source of pride, many officers no longer leave their bases without changing to civilian clothes.

Officers' pay, perquisites, and housing had been above average in the Soviet Union. But as the economy deteriorated and troops were withdrawn from Eastern Europe, the officers' standard of living fell sharply. According to Col. Valery Ochirov, former deputy chairman of the now defunct Supreme Soviet Committee for Defense and Security Affairs, 175,000 officers and warrant officers were without housing *even before* the first of 555,000 troops (including 143,000 officers and warrant officers) began streaming home from Hungary, Czechoslovakia, Mongolia, and Germany. Those officers still in Germany have 185,000 dependents who also require housing. Housing for retired officers is equally scarce; as many as 150,000 recently demobilized officers lack apartments. One Western analyst has speculated that as many as one million ex-military personnel could be homeless within the next few years.

Command Structure. This fractured military became the stepchild of an equally fractured commonwealth. In early December 1991, Russia's Boris Yeltsin and top officers, including then chief of the general staff Vladimir Lobov, proposed two alternative command structures. Their preferred arrangement was the establishment of a collegial military leadership body on which each of the independent states would be represented by an elected or appointed officer. This arrangement implied that, with the possible exception of small national guards in each state, virtually the entire former Soviet military would remain under a unified command. Realizing that this arrangement varied only slightly from the old Soviet military structure, save for equal representation on a general staff-like body,

Lobov and Yeltsin floated an alternative proposal: a structure resembling NATO in which certain military units in each state would be "earmarked" as subordinate to the commonwealth's unified command, and other "nonearmarked" units would be subordinate to their respective national commands.

These proposals were discussed at the inaugural meeting of the Council of the Heads of State, a coordinating body established by the commonwealth accord. At that December 30, 1991, meeting, some leaders, notably Kazakhstan's Nursultan Nazarbayev, were receptive to Yeltsin's proposals. Other leaders were uneasy with either alternative; and Ukraine, Moldova, and Azerbaijan vetoed both alternatives outright. Ukraine's Kravchuk and others argued that the military had been an instrument of Russian imperial domination and that, given the continued preponderance of Russians in the highest ranks, a unified CIS military would perpetuate that domination. Kravchuk would settle for nothing short of total sovereignty in defense matters. The vague terms of Article 6 of the accord—"Members of the commonwealth will preserve and support common military and strategic space under a common command"—were empty rhetoric from the start.

The chasm between the Russian and Kazakh position on the one hand and the Ukrainian, Moldovan, and Azeri position on the other was so vast that little attempt was made to bridge it. Kravchuk had little room to compromise, even if he had desired to do so. The Ukrainian parliament had criticized him for signing the CIS accord and had ratified it only after passing an amendment that negated Article 6 and claimed Ukrainian authority over all conventional forces on Ukrainian territory. Other amendments to the accord passed by the Ukrainian parliament rejected a coordinated foreign policy, open borders among commonwealth member states, and a unified currency. The other ten signatories to the commonwealth agreement, whose parliaments had ratified it without amendment, did not seek a "conference committee" to standardize the accord. Thus, not only were the vague terms of the accord open to different interpretations, but the signatories had not even ratified the same agreement.

Black Berets haul down the Hammer and Sickle at their base in Vecsmiqravis, near Riga. Thousands of formerly Soviet troops still remain in the Baltics.

Before the accord was two weeks old, four other states—Armenia, Azerbaijan, Moldova, and Turkmenistan—had joined Ukraine in decreeing that all conventional weaponry and personnel on their territories were nationalized. Belarus followed suit on January 11, followed by several of the Central Asian states. By March 16, 1992, Russia was the only state that had not created its own defense ministry.

While most of the commonwealth states were claiming custody of the troops, bases, and equipment within their borders, nonmembers Estonia, Latvia, and Lithuania were demanding that all former Soviet military personnel evacuate immediately but leave much of their equipment behind. On January 5 the presidents of the Baltic states issued a joint demand that all ex-Soviet troops leave the region. The Baltic Military Command of the CIS responded with a statement that, due to the extreme shortage of housing in Russia and other complications, the pullout of the 100,000 troops stationed there would take at least three years. After several weeks of tense discussions, an agreement was reached between the CIS and Baltic states under which troops would begin leaving Lithuania at the end of February and Latvia in March. But the agreement included no timetable or projected completion date and was soon moribund. The Baltic states continued through the first half of 1992 to agitate for a quicker drawdown and for as much as $200 billion in reparations for the environmental and property damage caused by Soviet forces. They held referendums on the subject, asked Western states to apply diplomatic pressure on Russia, and in August brought their case to the United Nations, but their efforts achieved little immediate progress.

Of the commonwealth states that proclaimed custody of former Soviet forces on their territory, only Ukraine moved aggressively to implement its proclamation. Kravchuk replaced the commanders of the Kiev, Odessa, and Carpathian military districts with trusted officers and severed communications between those districts and the central CIS authorities. Then on January 4 he demanded that all former Soviet troops in Ukraine—many of them ethnic Russians and other nationalities—take an oath of allegiance to Ukraine or leave the country. According to Ukrainian defense minister Konstantin Morozov, roughly 80 percent took the oath during the ensuing two months. More than one thousand left Ukraine and still others stonewalled, neither leaving nor taking the oath.

Azerbaijan and Moldova were not so assertive as Ukraine but concurred that a unified military, even in the short term, was undesirable. Their reluctance was based partly on historical animosity toward the Russians and partly on political disputes: Azerbaijan accused Russia of siding with Armenia in their war over Nagorno-Karabakh, and Moldova accused Russia of siding with the Russian minority in the trans-Dniester region. Therefore, those two states advocated an immediate dissolution and dismemberment of the military.

All states except Ukraine, Moldova, and Azer-baijan agreed at the second meeting of the Council of the Heads of State on February 14 to continued unified CIS command over troops on their territory for an interim period of unstated length. They further agreed to jointly fund the CIS military, though Russia shouldered the burden alone during the first quarter of the year.

Despite this agreement for continued cooperation in the short term, the long-term prospects for a common defense effort were dim. Marshal Yevgeny Shaposhnikov, who had been a highly vocal proponent of a centralized CIS defense establishment, acknowledged at a February 18 press conference that a unified military command was unworkable without a centralized political authority. Bowing with regret to the commonwealth's intractable disunity, Shaposhnikov called for a negotiated devolution of military forces over a three-year period.

On March 20 the third convening of the Council of the Heads of State failed to reach agreement on any significant issue, military or otherwise. By May 7, 1992, Yeltsin too had given up hope of ever cementing an agreement with the fractious states on a permanently unified military structure. On that day he signed legislation establishing a Russian ministry of defense and appointing himself commander in chief.

By the time of the fourth summit of the Council of the Heads of State, on May 15, 1992, the commonwealth was so moribund that only six heads of state bothered to attend in person, though all sent representatives. In a tacit admission that the CIS military was defunct, the presidents of Russia, Armenia, Kazakhstan, Uzbekistan, and Turkmenistan joined a representative of the president of Tajikistan in signing a collective security pact. The signatories agreed to come to one another's defense if attacked. The other five commonwealth states declined to participate even in this collective security pact.

The Black Sea Fleet. The potentially explosive rift between Russia and Ukraine over the 350-ship Black Sea Fleet demonstrated the difficulties of maintaining a common CIS defense effort. Ukraine's drive to create its own defense establishment out of former Soviet units stationed on its territory led to intense dialogue with Russia through the winter and spring of 1992. The issue was complicated by ultranationalists in both states who forced their respective presidents to more extreme positions than they otherwise might have adopted.

At the inaugural December 30, 1991, meeting of the Council of the Heads of State, Yeltsin declared the entire fleet belonged to the CIS, while Kravchuk claimed a large share of it for Ukraine. They agreed to discuss the issue further. It was five days later, on January 4, 1992, that Kravchuk demanded that all military personnel in the country, including the ninety thousand sailors of the fleet, take an oath of allegiance to Ukraine. Yeltsin reiterated his position on January 8 that the fleet should be a CIS command. But under nationalist pressure before an audience of Russian workers the next day Yeltsin stated belligerently that "the Black Sea Fleet was, is, and will be Russia's." At this point, however, Yeltsin still hoped to maintain a common CIS defense. Unwilling to see the commonwealth unravel over this issue, he retreated from his opening position and agreed on January 11 that Ukraine should receive a portion of the fleet to be determined through negotiations.

The next three months were filled with incendiary statements, decrees, and counterdecrees from both sides. Neither president could show much flexibility without jeopardizing his domestic political base. Kravchuk was particularly vulnerable because he had been chief of ideology in Ukraine under the communist regime and as such his nationalist credentials were suspect. Yeltsin, too, had problems. Russian vice president Aleksandr Rutskoy, a former military officer whom Yeltsin had selected as a running mate so as to co-opt him, was building a base of support among right-wing nationalists by championing their causes.

Rutskoy enraged Ukraine on April 3 when, during a fact-finding mission in Crimea, the home of the Black Sea Fleet, he berated sailors who had sworn allegiance to Ukraine. Kravchuk retaliated three days later with "Decree on Urgent Measures to Build the Ukrainian Armed Forces." Kravchuk created a paper Ukrainian navy, appointed Rear Admiral Boris Kozhin head of the navy, and dis-

patched the ethnic Ukrainian to Sevastopol to set up a headquarters and take command of the fleet. On April 7 Yeltsin retaliated by issuing a decree claiming Russian administrative jurisdiction over the fleet, though it was to remain under CIS operational command. Commonwealth fleet commander Igor Kasatonov, an ethnic Russian, implored commonwealth leaders to find a political resolution to the quarrel and not place the military in a position in which it did not know to whom it was responsible.

With tension reaching a dangerous level, Kravchuk and Yeltsin spoke personally by telephone on April 9 and agreed to suspend all decrees and begin negotiations. The talks between Russia and Ukraine over the fleet began April 29, 1992, and continued through the spring and into the summer. But once Yeltsin formally established the Russian military on May 7, the issue of CIS control of the fleet became moot.

The status of Crimea itself was a complicating factor in the dispute. Ukraine has controlled the region as an autonomous republic since 1954, but ethnic Russians are 67 percent of the population, and on May 21, 1991, the Russian parliament proclaimed the 1954 transfer unconstitutional by a vote of 136-18. On May 5, 1992, the parliament of the Crimean Autonomous Oblast (region), which was furious that it was being circumvented by Ukraine and Russia in negotiations over the Black Sea Fleet, voted 118-28 in favor of independence from both Ukraine and Russia.

Late in the summer, both Kravchuk and Yeltsin sought to resolve—or at least temporarily table—the issue. The Crimean dispute was overshadowing other serious problems, such as the economy, and the nationalist overtones of the dispute were weakening both leaders politically vis-à-vis their right-wing opponents. On August 6 the two leaders met at Kravchuk's dacha in Mukhalatka on the Black Sea coast. After daylong talks, the two leaders emerged hailing an agreement that essentially postponed the issue until 1995. The fleet was to be removed from commonwealth control and transferred to a joint Russian-Ukrainian command for three years, at which time the division of the fleet would be discussed. In the interim, a new command structure would be established and each leader would appoint a co-fleet commander. The status of Crimea was delicately avoided.

When the remainder of the former Soviet military is divided among the states, the loyalties and desires of individual soldiers will be at least as important as their geographic location or the decrees of heads of state. The preceding discussion of the Black Sea Fleet, with its emphasis on high state politics, understates the schisms that will take place at the unit level. For example, one of the units that Kravchuk nationalized in his sweeping proclamation was a bomber wing in western Ukraine. That unit, like most in the former Soviet military, was multiethnic: the pilots and officer corps were largely Russian; and the maintenance technicians and support personnel represented many ethnic groups. On February 12 the ethnic Russian crews of six SU-24 bombers defected to Smolensk, in Russia. Ukraine demanded the return of planes and crews on the grounds of desertion. A similar event occurred in late July when a ship of the Black Sea Fleet, commanded by an ethnic Ukrainian, left its commonwealth-controlled port without authorization, hoisted the Ukrainian flag, and fled to the Ukrainian port of Odessa. Ukraine refused to return the ship. When the states implement their proclamations of suzerainty over military forces on their territory, this scenario could be replayed over and over as each soldier weighs his or her loyalties.

The dispute over the fleet highlights the structural weakness of the CIS. The accord signed on December 21 established two bodies that would coordinate the commonwealth: the "Council of the Heads of State" and the "Council of the Heads of Government." The councils, composed respectively of the presidents and prime ministers of the states, meet only infrequently. These bodies were given a vague mandate to establish ad hoc working groups to resolve specific problems such as the disposition of the Black Sea Fleet. But no formal, permanent forum for conducting business was established because Ukraine, Azerbaijan, and Moldova refused to be tied into a permanent structure. Thus, the states must resort to clumsy, inefficient high-level sum-

mits or must conduct their business through decrees, which can excite public sentiments and complicate delicate negotiations.

The existence of parallel CIS and republic military structures claiming sovereignty over the same conventional forces placed the military—itself badly fractured—in limbo. With several different entities claiming jurisdiction over it, the military was in effect responsible to none. The commonwealth agreement had placed Marshal Shaposhnikov in command of all military forces but had not clarified his relationship to civilian authorities.

In the spring of 1992, amid this chaos, seemingly everyone with physical proximity to military equipment claimed "ownership" and began to sell it. Among those putting arms up for sale were senior commonwealth military officers, division commanders, base commanders, individual officers, conscripts, military academies, city governments, and defense-manufacturing enterprises.

Commercial arrangements with dubious mandates sprang up at the highest levels of the commonwealth army and navy. A joint stock company called the Military Exchange Section claimed the right to sell army property at a 10 percent commission. The Conversion Housing International Concern tried to peddle two hundred army plants and storage areas over which it claimed jurisdiction. In the navy, Admiral Igor Makhonin, chief of the former Soviet Navy's Rear Services Directorate, entered a complicated commercial venture called Navikon that began trying to sell nuclear powered submarines and ships for scrap in the West. It was not clear on whose authority Makhonin was operating.

Small-time operations existed as well. A division commander in the Far East sold four of his division's "Grad" rocket launchers to Azerbaijanis, presumably for use in their war with Armenia. The commander of a cadet air school near St. Petersburg wrote off four of his unit's training aircraft as inoperable and sold them to Swedish interests. The city of Ulyanovsk sold four Antonov 124 military cargo planes, and Omsk was reportedly selling tanks for scrap. At the state level, Kazakhstan was reportedly marketing advanced SU-24 fighter-bombers.

Many small arms, sold by conscripts who had reported them as lost or stolen, were fueling warfare in the Transcaucasus and Moldova.

Nuclear Weapons. The awesome responsibility of nuclear arms inclined the states to closer cooperation than they exhibited over conventional weaponry. A separate addendum to the commonwealth accord was signed by the four states that housed Soviet nuclear warheads—Ukraine, Belarus, Kazakhstan, and Russia. The leaders of those states agreed to maintain a unified command and control system pending disposition of the weapons. Yeltsin was in sole possession of the launch codes and presumably could have launched the weapons without interference from the other leaders, but the addendum stipulated that Yeltsin would not employ the weapons without prior agreement of the other three signatories. On December 30, at the first meeting of the Council of the Heads of State, the four nuclear powers agreed to consult the other commonwealth member states before using the weapons, but those states would not have a veto power. At the end of January Yeltsin revealed that a telephone hotline had been established linking the four leaders.

Belarus, Kazakhstan, and Ukraine agreed to ship all tactical nuclear weapons (short-range weapons designed for use on a battlefield) within their borders to Russia by July 1, 1992. Those weapons were not to become part of the Russian arsenal but were to be dismantled under joint supervision. The Kazakhs and Belarus were well ahead of schedule; all of their tactical weapons were removed to Russia by the end of January 1992. The Ukrainians began transporting their warheads but temporarily ceased transfers March 12, complaining that they were not receiving adequate assurances that the weapons were in fact being destroyed. After reassurances from Russia and the establishment of a bilateral commission to oversee the process, the operation resumed on April 16 and was completed a short time later.

The issue of strategic nuclear arms (long-range weapons capable of striking other nations), which are more difficult to transport or decommission, was

All tactical nuclear weapons such as this SCUD-B have been removed from Belarus, Kazakhstan, and Ukraine.

more controversial. As with tactical arms, Ukraine and Belarus renounced any desire to maintain a strategic arsenal and agreed to formulate a timetable for removing them to Russia for dismantling. But Nazarbayev defiantly announced that as long as Russia had nuclear weapons, so would Kazakhstan. That attitude was a curiosity: Russian-Kazakh relations were among the warmest of all the ex-Soviet states. It is possible that he believed retaining nuclear warheads would "buy" Kazakhstan more attention—meaning more trade, aid, and investment—from the West. Whatever his initial motivation, by May 1992 Nazarbayev had reversed his stance and agreed to cede Kazakhstan's strategic nuclear weapons. A timetable developed by the CIS military called for the withdrawal of all strategic nuclear weapons from Ukraine by 1994, from Belarus by 1995-1996, and from Kazakhstan by 1998-1999.

The Economy

The states that were most opposed to a unified military structure were equally opposed to centralized economic decision-making bodies for the same reason: participation in them would mean ceding a measure of sovereignty to the other states, principally Russia. Because the Russian economy was large relative to those of the other commonwealth states, any monetary, fiscal, budgetary, or pricing policy adopted by Moscow would have a tremendous impact outside of Russia's borders. For example, if Russia—the only state with the capacity to print rubles—were to run the printing presses nonstop to cover a budget shortfall, the ensuing inflationary pressures would extend to the other states that used rubles. That reality left the former Soviet republics with two alternative means of retaining control over their own economies: they could demand equal voting status with Russia on centralized coordinating economic bodies; or they could abandon the ruble for national currencies. The former alternative meant the abdication of some sovereignty and was unacceptable to Ukraine and other states.

Disagreement among the signatories on such basic economic issues as whether to maintain a single currency led to vague terms in the commonwealth accord. Article 7 stated: "The parties recognize that the spheres of their mutual activities conducted on a mutual basis through common coordinating institutions of the commonwealth embrace . . . cooperation in forming and developing a common economic space, common European and Eurasian markets, in the sphere of customs and policy."

The Historical Legacy. Whether the states were inclined to maintain central economic coordination or not, their economies were almost inextricably intertwined by historical, geographic, demographic, and political factors. Vladimir I. Lenin and the early Bolsheviks made a conscious decision after the Russian civil war to bind the farflung states together in a web of economic interrelationships. This policy furthered the political goal of preventing any one republic or region from becoming autarkic.

One way in which the Soviets promoted economic integration was by relying on enormous manufacturers of intermediate products. Rather than construct a nationwide network of medium-size manufacturers of a given product, they established a small number of large industrial combines that would then serve end users across the country. This practice tied the farflung republics together, but it placed an enormous strain on the transportation system.

The economic potential of tsarist Russia and the Soviet Union always was hampered by the geographic dispersal of the three primary economic inputs: labor resources, capital stock, and raw materials. This problem was becoming even more severe and raised questions about the viability of the commonwealth states' economies.

Because the Slavic region was more developed socioeconomically—more urbanized and with a more skilled work force—the bulk of the tsarist, and later, Soviet, capital stock was situated there. But with urbanization and socioeconomic development come natural demographic changes in which birthrates fall, the population ages, and the population growth slows until finally it stabilizes. The more advanced Slavic areas of Belarus, Ukraine, and Russia—where the capital stock is located—are farther along this demographic path and consequently have proportionately fewer people entering the labor force than is the case in Central Asia. The Central Asian states, characterized by less urbanization and socioeconomic development, have booming rates of population growth.

Raw materials, which are worthless without labor and capital equipment, are concentrated primarily in the Russian heartland of Siberia, far from the labor resources of Central Asia or the factories of European Russia, Ukraine, or Belarus. As the more accessible of these resources are exhausted, less accessible resources must be exploited, at greater cost and difficulty, to maintain production.

This "triangular distribution" of economic inputs was a topic of much debate both within the Soviet Union and among Western observers during the past two decades. When the Soviet republics became independent states—potentially with their own import/export regulations, customs duties, tax structures, and restrictions on labor and capital flows—the situation became infinitely more complex than it had been.

One other Soviet legacy also necessitates cooperation among the newly independent states. The Soviet federal system, which was based loosely on ethnic considerations, often split regions that on economic grounds should have been administered as a whole. For example, the Fergana Basin, one of the richest farming and uranium mining regions in the former Soviet Union, was divided between Kyrgyzstan, Uzbekistan, and Tajikistan. The Donetsk Basin, an important coal mining region, was split between Ukraine and Russia. To achieve maximum economic efficiency, those neighboring states will have to cooperate closely on such issues as irrigation and transportation.

The centripetal force of these historical, geographic, and demographic factors are forcing many of the former republics to cooperate in order to maintain the "common economic space" mentioned in Article 7.

Russia Takes the Lead. By November 1991 the Soviet economy was dangerously unstable. Inflation was running at 400 percent per month, the Soviet Bank for Foreign Economic Affairs (Vneshekonombank) froze hard currency accounts because it was nearly bankrupt, and the Soviet State Bank (Gosbank) also ran out of money. On December 19, President Yeltsin signed decrees under which Russia assumed the functions of the Soviet central government, including the two banks. Under instructions from the Russian government, Vneshekonombank continued to freeze all hard currency accounts and Gosbank pursued a tight monetary policy to keep inflation under control. These policies crippled foreign trade in Ukraine and elsewhere. The Russian government had made difficult choices concerning what was in its own economic interests, but in doing so it was taking all of the former Soviet republics along for the ride. The other former republics were powerless to influence the Russian government's policy.

Russia's neighbors were equally affected by Russian price reforms. At the December 30, 1991, meeting of the Council of the Heads of State, Ukraine's Kravchuk and President Stanislav S. Shushkevich of Belarus implored Yeltsin to postpone, moderate, or at least discuss the price reform that Russia was scheduled to implement on January 2. They argued that if prices were freed in Russia but not elsewhere, it would be prohibitively expensive to import Russian products into the other states. Yeltsin refused to alter his course. Kravchuk and Shushkevich were forced against their will to follow Russia's lead and free prices on a broad range of products in their countries.

Despite three meetings of the Council of the Heads of State, no agreement could be reached on an interbank union to coordinate monetary and fiscal policies. By early spring Ukraine and most other states, angered at Russia's unilateral policy formulations, had given up on achieving agreement and begun laying the groundwork for their own national banking systems. Estonia introduced its own currency, the kroon, in June; Latvia issued its own ruble in July; and Azerbaijan started issuing the manat in August. At the end of the summer Lithuania, Tajikistan, Ukraine, Belarus, and Uzbekistan were preparing to introduce their own currencies.

The commonwealth countries did achieve some success, in the short run at least, at keeping vital infrastructures operating. A Council and Railway Coordinating Center was established that kept the railway network in operation; a similar arrangement aimed at keeping civil aviation operational; and all but Ukraine and Moldova signed a customs agreement that took effect April 9. This last agreement was vital for maintaining trade between and through the signatory states.

Under pressure from Western creditors, the states also had some success at servicing the Soviet Union's foreign debt. Twelve of the fifteen Soviet republics agreed in principle in October 1991 to jointly assume responsibility for the Soviet $68 billion debt. The Baltic states, claiming that they had been occupied nations, refused to participate. After difficult negotiations, subsequent agreement apportioned shares of the debt among the agreeing parties; Russia was to be responsible for servicing 51 percent of the total debt, Ukraine for 16 percent, and the other former republics for 33 percent. That arrangement, however, was in danger of unraveling. Ukraine and other states threatened to renounce their shares of the debt unless progress was made in apportioning shares of Soviet assets, such as diamond and gold reserves, hard currency accounts, and foreign property.

Internal Political Dynamics

Any assessment of the prospects or efficacy of the commonwealth depends on one's expectations, and the expectations vary widely not only among the new states but also within them. The preceding discussion of the policy positions and attitudes of Russia and the independent states with regard to commonwealth cooperation on military and economic issues is based on the attitudes of the presidents and parliamentary majorities of the countries. But this approach belies wide disagreement within each country over the proper role of the commonwealth as well as over the nature and extent of political and economic reform within each state.

In Russia, for example, President Yeltsin must work with the Russian Congress of People's Deputies, which is splintered into three identifiable coalitions each of which is composed of several factions. The Coalition of Support for Reform, which has roughly 300 deputies and firmly supports Yeltsin's policies, includes Democratic Russia (73 deputies); United Republican Faction (68 deputies); Free Russia (66 deputies); and Radical Democrats (47 deputies). An opposition coalition, Russian Unity, includes nationalists and unreconstructed communists whose only shared plank is opposition to Yeltsin's reforms and handling of commonwealth affairs. Russian Unity's factions include the Agrarian Alliance (149 deputies); Communists of Russia (59 deputies); Russia (54 deputies); and Home Country (54 deputies).

The Russian parliament's third coalition, Centrist Bloc, with 164 deputies, generally supports what Yeltsin has accomplished so far, but it questions Yeltsin's long-term goals. Its support of the Yeltsin government is more tenuous than that of the Coalition of Support for Reform. The two principal factions comprising Centrist Bloc are Industrial Union (73 deputies) and New Generation-New Policies (52 deputies). A similar splintering of interests and outlooks exists in all of the independent states. *(See the country profiles for the internal political dynamics of each state.)*

Geography

The geographic distribution of national groups across the former Soviet Union is even more important to the future of the region than is the geographic distribution of economic inputs. For historical and political reasons, the state boundaries do not coincide with national frontiers. Consequently, Russia and the independent states must address two contradictory principles that have bedeviled Europe throughout the twentieth century and that played a major role in the outbreak of both world wars: the right to national self-determination and the inviolability of existing borders.

When the Bolsheviks came to power in 1917 they inherited from the tsars a patchwork mosaic of more than 130 national groups. The Bolsheviks attempted to superimpose on this mosaic a federal political structure. But the intermingling of these peoples over the centuries made it impossible in most areas to draw political boundaries that corresponded exactly to national frontiers. In some instances where this would have been possible, the Bolsheviks declined to do so. The Bolsheviks could more easily control national groups if they were split between two or more federated bodies.

The diaspora of some national groups—particularly Ukrainians and Russians—during seventy-five years of communist rule further complicated the situation. More than 25 million Russians (17.4 percent of all members of that national group) live outside of Russia, and more than 6 million Ukrainians (15.3 percent of that group) live outside of Ukraine. The composition of the former Soviet republics illustrates the extent of the ethnic intermingling:

• Armenia: 93% Armenian, 3% Azeri, 2% Kurd, 2% Russian, 1% other

- Azerbaijan: 83% Azeri, 6% Russian, 6% Armenian, 6% other
- Belarus: 78% Belarus, 13% Russian, 4% Polish, 3% Ukrainian, 2% other
- Estonia: 62% Estonian, 28% Russian, 7% other
- Georgia: 69% Georgian, 9% Armenian, 5% Azeri, 3% South Ossetian, 14% other
- Kazakhstan: 40% Kazakh, 38% Russian, 6% German, 5% Ukrainian, 11% other
- Kyrgyzstan: 53% Kyrgyz, 22% Russian, 13% Uzbek, 3% Ukrainian, 2% German, 7% other
- Latvia: 52% Latvian, 34% Russian, 5% Belarus, 3% Ukrainian, 2% Pole, 4% other
- Lithuania: 80% Lithuanian, 9% Russian, 7% Polish, 4% other
- Moldova: 65% Moldovan, 14% Ukrainian, 13% Russian, 4% Gaugaz, 2% Bulgarian, 2% Jews, 2% other
- Russia: 82% Russian, 4% Tatar, 3% Ukrainian, 12% other
- Tajikistan: 62% Tajik, 24% Uzbek, 7% Russian, 7% other
- Turkmenistan: 72% Turkmen, 9% Russian, 9% Uzbek, 11% other
- Ukraine: 73% Ukrainian, 22% Russian, 1% Belarus, 4% other
- Uzbekistan: 71% Uzbek, 11% Russian, 5% Tajik, 4% Kazakh, 9% other

Many of the Russian diaspora are first- or second-generation migrants who retain ties to their native region. They now find themselves in foreign states where they are often unwelcome. Right-wing nationalists in Russia, including Vice President Rutskoy and Defense Minister Pavel Grachev, are inflaming relations with the other independent states by championing the cause of their fellow nationals living in neighboring states. Both of these factors— poorly drawn borders and the diaspora of people— are destabilizing the former Soviet Union.

Border Disputes

The principles of self-determination and inviolability of borders are in many cases mutually exclusive: if a cohesive national group living in a border region is permitted to exercise its right of self-determination through a referendum, it may well vote for independence or incorporation into a neighboring political entity, thus redrawing the map. Conversely, if existing borders are held inviolable, then a national group living on a border may be denied its right to self-determination.

The U.S. government considered this dilemma when it was considering granting diplomatic recognition to the newly independent states. American recognition was based on the inviolability of existing borders and respect for minority rights—*not* on the right of national self-determination. The commonwealth accord, however, recognized the "inalienable right to self-determination."

There are literally dozens of borders that could be challenged on ethnic or historical grounds, not only among the former Soviet republics but also between former republics and states neighboring the former Soviet Union. The dissolution of the USSR potentially jeopardized much of the territorial settlement of World War II, in which the USSR had annexed portions of Finland, Czechoslovakia, Germany, Poland, and Romania. It will be up to the Soviet successor states of Lithuania, Belarus, Ukraine, Moldova, and Russia to defend the postwar borders. To date, there has been little enthusiasm among any of the states that lost territory after the war to reopen the issue of borders, but it is a possibility in the future.

Among the former Soviet republics borders are very much at issue. Warfare broke out in three areas: Ossetia, trans-Dniester Moldova, and Nagorno-Karabakh. All three disputes were due in part to the capriciousness of Soviet mapmakers and a desire on the part of the inhabitants to redraw the map.

Ossetia. The Ossetes, Persian-speaking descendants of a Scythian tribe, straddle the Caucasus Mountains. The area was annexed by Russia between 1801 and 1806. In the 1930s the fiercely independent Ossetes were deliberately divided into two separate administrative units by Joseph Stalin so as to weaken them politically. North Ossetia was made an autonomous republic within the Russian

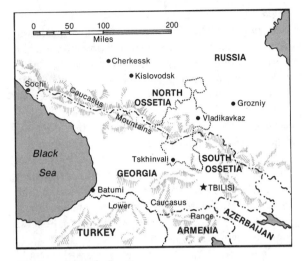

North and South Ossetia

Federation and South Ossetia was made an autonomous oblast (region) within the Georgian Republic. The border separating them was wholly artificial.

South Ossetians, long resentful of their subordination to the Georgians, sought unification with North Ossetia within the Russian Federation. Their guerrilla war against Georgia—replete with blockades, hostage-taking, and artillery barrages—claimed 250 lives in the latter half of 1991. The insurrection forced 23,000 Georgians in South Ossetia to flee to Georgia. Retaliatory pogroms against Ossetians in Georgia forced at least 50,000 to flee to North Ossetia, where they organized and radicalized their fellow nationals.

Early in 1992 South Ossetians voted overwhelmingly for unification with Russia in a referendum. The Georgian leadership, headed by former Soviet foreign minister Eduard Shevardnadze, denounced the referendum as null and void. The Georgian National Guard and irregulars continued to enforce a months-old economic blockade under a state of emergency declared by the Georgian leadership. All rail traffic, road traffic, and communications were severed.

In the meantime, prounification demonstrations in North Ossetia grew so large that in mid-June 1992 the Russian government declared a state of emergency and dispatched a motorized regiment of Russian antiriot troops to the region. Fighting erupted immediately upon the troops' arrival in the North Ossetian capital of Tskhinvali. A crowd of 1,000 civilians tried to seize the troops' vehicles and weapons, which they wanted to send to the South Ossetians. Four people were killed and twelve wounded when the Russian soldiers defended themselves.

The Ossetians gradually gained allies in Russia after repeated requests for reunification. On June 15, 1992, Russia's parliamentary speaker, Ruslan Khasbulatov, threatened to begin deliberations in parliament on forcibly annexing South Ossetia from Georgia. Once again, Yeltsin needed to resolve the conflict before ultranationalists in Russia exploited the issue to his detriment. Discussions held in mid-July by officials from Russia, Georgia, and North and South Ossetia led to the establishment of a peacekeeping force. Each participant contributed two hundred troops, who took up positions between the combatants on July 14. Despite their efforts, sporadic fighting continues, with no end in sight.

Trans-Dniester Moldova. The Moldavian Soviet Socialist Republic was created by Stalin at the close of World War II largely from land seized from Romania. Its western border is not based on ethnic boundaries. The people of present day Moldova and Romania are linguistically and historically one nation. Many Moldovans favor reincorporation into Romania, but sizable Ukrainian and Russian minorities are violently opposed. These two minority groups are concentrated in a thin strip of land between the Dniester River and the Ukrainian border. A third minority, the Gaugauzi, seek their own sovereign state in what is now southern Moldova.

After the collapse of the August coup and Moldova's proclamation of independence, the so-called trans-Dniester Russians declared their own separatist state, the Dniester SSR. They began forming paramilitary detachments and established a semiprofessional Dniester Republican Guard. From September through December 1991 these forces laid siege to police stations throughout the region, demanding that the police either accept the authority of the Dniester SSR or cross the river to Moldova. Great restraint on the part of the Moldovan government limited casualties to only six deaths in three months of confrontation.

Fighting escalated in 1992, however, and outside parties were drawn into the fray. The Dniester SSR received vocal support from Russian vice president Rutskoy, who personally attended a proindependence rally in the breakaway republic on April 5. While there, he advocated Russian military intervention to protect the Russian minority, just as—in his analogy—the United States had invaded the Caribbean island of Grenada in 1983 to protect U.S. citizens. Rutskoy's statements contradicted the Yeltsin government's policy of noninvolvement, but Yeltsin could not repudiate his vice president without angering right-wing nationalists in Russia.

The trans-Dniester Russians also received support from the Don, Kuban, and Ural cossacks, who resurrected their centuries-old tradition of sending volunteers to assist fellow Russians. The Romanian government objected to both Rutskoy's statements and to the cossack development, and it offered economic assistance and limited military aid to Moldova.

The trans-Dniester Russians had the tacit support of the local military commander, Lt. Gen. Gennady Yakovlev, commander of the Soviet Fourteenth Army. His army was headquartered in the Dniester capital of Tiraspol. An ethnic Russian, Yakovlev accepted the title "Chief of Defense and Security of the Dniester SSR" and did little to prevent irregulars in Tiraspol from pillaging army depots. Trucks, armored vehicles, sophisticated machine guns, and ammunition were looted for use against Moldovan forces.

On April 1 Yeltsin signed a decree putting the Fourteenth Army directly under his control, but discipline had so deteriorated that elements of that army ignored orders from Yeltsin and the CIS central command. At the end of June, units of the Fourteenth Army, comprising largely Russian and Ukrainian troops, openly joined the Dniester irregulars. These renegade troops had the public support of Russian defense minister Grachev. Moldova and Romania held the Yeltsin government

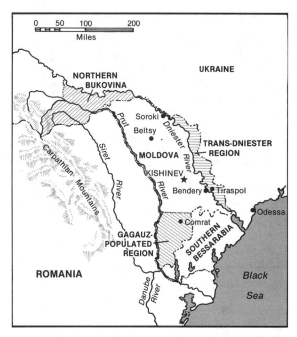

Trans-Dniester Moldova

responsible for the soldiers' actions, though the Russian government had little control over events. Moldova's president, Mircea Snegur, threatened to declare war on Russia.

The fighting continued into the summer, finally ebbing in late July when a joint Moldovan-Russian peacekeeping force moved into the region. To further reduce tensions, the Russian government agreed to consider withdrawing the Fourteenth Army, but, for lack of military housing anywhere in Russia, was unable to do so. By August the fighting had ebbed, but the underlying issue of Romanian-Moldovan unification remained.

The Ukrainian government, which is publicly neutral in the Dniester dispute, is deeply disturbed by the effect the issue is having on the national consciousness of ethnic Romanians living within Ukraine. At the close of World War II, when the Soviet Union seized present day Moldova from Romania, it also annexed the historically Romanian regions of southern Bessarabia and northern Bukovina, which Moscow appended to Ukraine. Now, the Romanian minorities in those two regions are agitat-

Nagorno-Karabakh

ing for closer ties with—even incorporation into—a greater Romania.

Nagorno-Karabakh. Centuries of pogroms, fleeing refugees, and enforced relocations left the lower Caucasus region a mosaic of Christian Armenians and Moslem Azeris. The intermingling was such that the Soviet federal system imposed between 1920 and 1923 could not have followed national frontiers; it was inevitable that some Azeris would end up in Armenia and vice versa. However, the Soviets could have created more ethnologically pure political units than they did. As was the case with the Ossetes, the Armenian population was deliberately divided so as to weaken it politically.

The autonomous region of Nagorno-Karabakh is a predominantly Armenian-populated enclave located entirely within the borders of Azerbaijan. In 1988 Armenians in the region began demonstrating for unification with their ethnic and religious brethren. Azerbaijan responded by blockading Nagorno-Karabakh, starving it of food and fuel. Anti-Armenian pogroms in Azeri towns and anti-Azeri pogroms in Armenian towns left many dead and created a half-million refugees. The ethnically heterogeneous city of Baku began to resemble Beirut.

The Soviet federal system also had created Nakhichevan, an Azeri-populated region within Armenia. Though Nakhichevan was wholly enveloped by Armenia, it was nonetheless made administratively subordinate to Azerbaijan. When all power resided in Moscow, that territorial-administrative arrangement was no more than an anomaly, but with the dissolution of the empire, Nakhichevan became part of a sovereign country with which it was not contiguous.

Four years of war between Armenians and Azeris has resulted in two thousand dead and thousands more wounded. Deployments of Soviet (and then CIS) troops, Italian mediation, and talks sponsored by the Conference on Security and Cooperation in Europe have all failed to stop the fighting. The CIS military found itself in a position analogous to that of U.S. Marines in Beirut in the early 1980s. It was caught in the crossfire between rival factions, but it had no mandate to move decisively against the warring parties. The military wanted to pull out of the Caucasus altogether but agreed on June 1 to postpone the final withdrawal from Armenia and Georgia after receiving pleas from those governments to stay.

The Russian Diaspora

The events of the trans-Dniester crisis did not go unnoticed by Russia's neighbors, all of which had their own Russian minorities. The former Soviet military had fractured along ethnic lines, with Russian troops supporting their fellow nationals in a separatist movement. And high-ranking officials of the Russian government had openly advocated military intervention in behalf of transnational Russians. Those developments justifiably concerned the Baltic and Central Asian states, which have significant Russian minorities.

Unlike in Moldova, in the Baltic states and all of Central Asia save Kazakhstan, the Russian minorities are not concentrated in compact regions that are contiguous with a border. Rather, they are concentrated in urban areas. *(See Table 7-1.)* Nonetheless, Russians are in some places being discriminated against culturally, economically, and

politically. This is a major source of friction between Russia and its neighbors.

The Baltics. In 1939, just before the Soviet
annexation of Estonia, the population of that country was 88 percent Estonian. Under Soviet rule, the
communist government attempted to dilute the nationalist and separatist tendencies of the Baltic peoples by encouraging Russians and other nationals to
migrate to the Baltics. By 1989 Estonians were 61.5
percent of their country's population; the analogous
percentages for Latvia and Lithuania were 52.0 and
79.6, respectively. The Estonian and Latvian governments were concerned that fifty years of russification threatened to annihilate the cultures of
their small nations.

Out of concern for their national identity, those
two states drafted laws that in effect denied citizenship to many resident Russians. Citizenship is an
essential prerequisite for the exercise of basic civil
and political rights. The rights to vote, to have
political representation, to receive due process of
law, to own property, and even to work are tenuous
or nonexistent without citizenship.

In September 1991 the Estonian parliament began debating proposed citizenship legislation
drafted by a parliamentary commission. The proposal conceived of three categories of residency:

1. Those who had been citizens of Estonia prior to
   June 16, 1940, when the country was annexed by
   the USSR, would be granted automatic citizenship. Their descendants, either through maternal
   or paternal lineage, would also be granted automatic citizenship.
2. Those who emigrated to Estonia after March 30,
   1991—the start of the transition period to full
   independence—could apply for naturalized Estonian citizenship or remain in the country as resident aliens. If they chose the former, they would
   have to live in Estonia for ten years, take a
   loyalty oath, and pass an Estonian-language proficiency test.
3. Those who emigrated between June 16, 1940,
   and March 30, 1991, would also be given the
   option of applying for naturalized citizenship,

**Table 7-1   Ethnic Russians as a Percentage of Capital
City Populations**

Capital City	Country	Russian Population (%)
Yerevan	Armenia	1.9
Baku	Azerbaijan	18.0
Minsk	Belarus	20.0
Tallinn	Estonia	41.2
Tbilisi	Georgia	10.0
Alma-Ata	Kazakhstan	59.1
Bishkek	Kyrgyzstan	55.8
Riga	Latvia	47.3
Vilnius	Lithuania	20.2
Kishinev	Moldova	26.4
Moscow	Russia	89.6
Dushanbe	Tajikistan	32.8
Ashkhabad	Turkmenistan	32.4
Kiev	Ukraine	20.9
Tashkent	Uzbekistan	34.0

Note: Figures are from the 1989 Soviet census.

but if they did, the state would waive the ten-
year residency requirement and the language
test.

Conservative Estonian nationalists bitterly protested the third category. They argued that waiving
the language test for all who had settled in Estonia
during the Soviet occupation would negate the goal
of preserving the native language and culture.

Within weeks the commission submitted a new
draft to parliament that merged the second and
third categories. Anyone who had moved to Estonia
after June 16, 1940, would have to meet the ten-
year residency requirement, pass the language test,
and take a loyalty oath. In the meantime they would
be considered resident aliens and would be denied
the rights and protections afforded by citizenship.
According to the 1989 Soviet census, only 12.2
percent (19,790 of 162,714) of the ethnic Russians
living in the Estonian capital knew the native language.

The Latvian and Lithuanian draft laws were similar to Estonia's in intent and content. These developments angered Russian conservatives. Rutskoy,
who enraged Moldova and Ukraine with his defense
of ethnic Russians in trans-Dniester and Crimea,

unleashed his fury on the Baltic states. He was joined by other conservatives in the parliament who advocated delaying the withdrawal of troops from the Baltic region until the treatment of the Russian minorities improved. In June 1992, Defense Minister Grachev intoned ominously that any infringement on "the honor and dignity" of ethnic Russians would invite "the most ironhanded measures, including the use of armed force." That threat presumably applied equally to the Baltic states, Ukraine, Moldova, and Georgia.

The Russian minorities in Central Asia have fared better than their counterparts in the Baltic states. Though tensions between ethnic Russians and Central Asians are not uncommon, Central Asians tend to be less hostile than the Baltic peoples toward ethnic Russians. Over time, it is possible that the Russian minority in northern Kazakhstan—which is compact and contiguous with the border—will seek unification with Russia, but for now no major movement toward this end has been organized.

A Complicating Factor. During the 1940s and 1950s Joseph Stalin ordered the deportation of entire national groups from their historical homelands. Crimean Tatars, Volga Germans, Meshketian Georgians, Chechens, Ingushis, Kalmyks, Karachai, and Balkars were deported en masse from their native lands to Central Asia and Siberia. They were accused, in most cases unjustly, of aiding and abetting Nazi occupation forces during the war.

Those displaced peoples agitated for decades for the return of their traditional homelands. They received a sympathetic ear from the Yeltsin government. In October 1991 the Russian parliament passed the Law on the Rehabilitation of Victims of Political Repression. This law acknowledged that the mass deportations of the Stalin era had been unlawful, and it agreed in principle that the grievances of displaced groups should be addressed.

The law, however, complicated the tasks of creating a workable Federation Treaty and resolving border disputes, because the lands vacated by the displaced nationalities had been inhabited by other groups that did not want to leave. For example,

while the North Ossetians are clamoring for unification with the South Ossetians, who are in a guerrilla war with Georgia, deported Ingushis are trying to reclaim portions of North Ossetia. While Ukraine and Russia debate jurisdiction over Crimea—and the Crimeans are claiming independence from both—Tatars deported from Crimea by Stalin are seeking redress of that forty-year-old injustice. These are only two of many such confusing situations.

The Russian Federation

The Russian government's difficulties were not limited to relations with neighboring states. It had problems at home as well. Russia, stretching from Vladivostok in the east to St. Petersburg in the west, encompassed more than a hundred nationalities. The national consciousness that shook apart the USSR also threatened the cohesion of Russia itself.

Twenty of the one hundred nations within Russia were granted limited powers of self-government under the Soviet federal system. Many of the residents of these autonomous Soviet socialist republics (ASSRs) and autonomous oblasts (AOs) were dissatisfied with Muscovite rule. Their complaints about exploitative economic relationships and stifled cultural and social expression mirrored the complaints brought against Moscow by the republics. Sentiment for independence from Russia is acute in Tatarstan and Chechen-Ingushetia, two regions where anti-Russian feelings are centuries-old.

The atomization of political authority did not stop with ASSRs and AOs. Krais, okrugs, and cities—subdivisions of ASSRs and AOs in the Soviet federal system—began agitating for their own independence or autonomy in a seemingly endless display of entropy. Koryasky Nagorye, an okrug on the Kamchatka Peninsula, declared itself a sovereign republic. The Yamalo-Nenetsk okrug, a subdivision of the Tyumen oblast, declared itself a sovereign state as well. The Karachai-Cherkessia oblast, on the Russian-Georgian border, devolved into four sovereign states: the republics of Karachai, Abaza, Cherkessia, and Cossack Zelenchuk-Urup. Vorkuta, a city in the Komi region, declared its independence. The Yeltsin government did not recognize these or any of the many other declarations of sovereignty.

Yeltsin did acknowledge that a new agreement would have to be negotiated with the autonomous regions if the territorial integrity of Russia was to be maintained. After eighteen months of negotiations, eighteen of the twenty former ASSRs and AOs signed a new federation treaty on April 1, 1992. The treaty granted greater political and economic autonomy while preserving a single, federal state. Tatarstan and Chechen-Ingushetia refused to accede to the treaty.

Tatarstan. The Turkic-speaking Tatars, living at the confluence of the Volga and Kama rivers 500 miles east of Moscow, were descendants of the Mongol tribe that ruled Russia from 1240 to 1480. Ivan the Terrible annexed the region in 1552, and the fiercely independent Tatars have been ruled from Moscow ever since. During the Russian civil war they attempted to break away from Moscow, but the Red Army crushed their rebellion.

The present-day population of Tatarstan is 49 percent Tatar and 43 percent Russian. The region is heavily industrialized and sits astride oil and natural gas pipelines that originate in Tyumen. For these reasons, as well as because of historical attachments, Moscow is unwilling to lose control of Tatarstan.

The Tatar parliament unanimously declared independence on August 30, 1991. The declaration was ratified by 67 percent of the population in a March 1992 referendum. The Russian minority, which is concentrated in five districts and the capital of Kazan, largely voted against the referendum.

The majority of Tatarstan residents, as well as the region's leadership, recognize that it would be impracticable to sever ties with Russia completely. Their goal is to be recognized by Russia as a sovereign state, and then to enter into a confederation with Russia as an equal partner.

Chechen-Ingushetia. The Chechens and Ingushis are neighboring Moslem peoples who were lumped together in the autonomous republic that bears their names. In the winter of 1991-1992 the republic divided into two separate entities because the Chechens favored sovereignty and the Ingushis sought to remain within the Russian Federation.

The Chechen declaration of independence was only symbolic when it was announced in November 1990. But after the collapse of the August 1991 coup, the Chechens seized the opportunity to implement their declaration. With Gen. Dzokhar Dudayev at the head of the Executive Committee of the Chechen People's National Congress, the government created a Chechen National Guard and established an independent customs service. Two months later, Dudayev was elected president and a parliament was formally established. The Russian Supreme Soviet denounced the elections as unlawful.

The fate of Checheniya is in limbo. Neither the Russian government nor any foreign governments recognize the sovereignty of the region. Short of military intervention, however, there is little that the Russian government can do to enforce its jurisdiction. Despite calls by some conservatives for intervention, the Russian military withdrew from Checheniya in early June so as to avoid conflict.

There have been hints that, despite his anti-Russian rhetoric, Dudayev would accept an arrangement similar to that sought by Tatarstan: if the country is recognized as sovereign, then it will enter into a confederation with Russia. However, it is far from certain that conservative forces in Russia would accept an arrangement that would turn the Russian Federation into a confederation.

Culture and Religion

The demise of the highly centralized Soviet Union will allow native cultures and religions to flourish. With the fall of "the center," knowledge of the Russian language will no longer be a prerequisite for success in politics, the military, or the arts. The Soviet military will no longer draft impressionable youth for two years and station them far from home, where in the past their parochial views were challenged. International relations will no longer be filtered through Moscow; rather, regional arrangements will proliferate. Tajikistan will be free to establish relations directly with Iran, with which it has linguistic and cultural ties. The other Central Asian states will be free to look toward Turkey and the Middle East for cultural interaction. Ukraine will look westward once again, toward Poland. The Baltic states too will be free to establish closer ties with the West, in particular with Germany and the Scandinavian countries.

Cultural Policy from Lenin to Chernenko

Lenin recognized that, for the Bolshevik party to achieve power in "imperial" Russia, a compromise that would consider the desires of the non-Russian ethnic groups was necessary. His choice of compromise was a federated state structure, one in which the ethnic and nationality groups within the empire would realize cultural autonomy and formal state powers. The rights of native language and cultural development were guaranteed by the 1922 Declaration and Treaty on the Formation of the USSR, and by the subsequent constitution of 1924.

In terms of language development, Lenin himself was an opponent of "russification" (the imposition of the Russian language and Russian values on native cultures). As a result of his influences, the union and autonomous republics and other national regions were allowed to develop their own cultures and languages through education and the press. "National communist" parties took shape in many of the republics. To emphasize this new compact, Moscow instituted a policy of "rooting" (korenizatsiya) local government and party officials in the national territories by emphasizing that they should use the native language. This policy applied to Russian officials working in non-Russian republics as well as to natives of the republics. Though the attempt to create cadres of Russians fluent in native languages failed, the development of native languages and cultures was a great success, as was the growth of literacy, particularly in the Caucasus, Central Asia, and the national regions of the RSFSR.

Russian, however, remained the de facto state language in the 1920s, a practical requirement in such a large multiethnic state. Hence compromise was reached: The nationalities retained limited cultural and linguistic rights, as well as formal political rights, but they were subject to the executive power of the Russian-speaking Communist party.

During Joseph Stalin's long reign (1928-1953), the compromise was breached. Decrees on collectivization and industrialization destroyed traditional forms of life (especially in the Ukraine and Kazakhstan); decrees on Latinization of Arabic scripts between 1928 and 1934 and on Cyrillicization of Latin scripts between 1936 and 1940 created confusion and language divisions throughout the USSR; party purges beginning in the late 1920s and continuing into the 1930s targeted "national communists" for their localism, their ties abroad, or their alleged antiparty conspiracies with other Soviet ethnic groups.

One of the most important social developments during the Stalin era was the urbanization of the Soviet Union. Between 1929 and 1959 the urban population roughly doubled as the USSR was transformed from a predominantly rural-based society and economy into a modern, industrializing, and urbanizing superpower. Thirty-two million workers left the countryside for the cities during these three decades. Many peasants were compelled to take jobs in the cities as part of Stalin's drive for industrialization; others moved there seeking a better life.

All of the above factors—combined with the mass deportations, artificial borders, and exploitative economic relationships mentioned earlier—severely strained the cultural identity of many of the smaller national groups. Stalin's successors did not worsen the situation, but neither did they improve it significantly. During the regimes of Nikita S. Khrushchev and Leonid I. Brezhnev, social and economic progress within the national republics and regions were mixed. Some progress was made in the fields of economic development, literacy, and cultural affairs, especially in the Caucasus, Central Asia, and the RSFSR.

Under Khrushchev and Brezhnev, a tacit deal was made between Moscow and the republics, especially those of the Caucasus and Central Asia. The republics were allowed to direct their own local party and administrative matters in exchange for ethnic peace. In support of this arrangement, an affirmative action program was put in place that was designed to increase the number of natives in party and government posts. The new political bosses included Sharaf Rashidov in Uzbekistan, Dinmukhamed Kunaev in Kazakhstan, Vladimir Shcherbitsky and Petr Shelest in Ukraine, Vasily Mzhavanadze in Georgia, Antanas Snieckus in Lithuania, and Turdakun Usubaliev in Kirgizia.

Moscow glossed over the many problems and pronounced in exaggerated tones that a process of "mixing" of peoples and even "uniting" of peoples was well under way. Both Khrushchev and Brezhnev declared that the nationality problem in the USSR was fully "solved." Hence, there was no need to discuss native cultures or languages. The caretaker governments of Yuri Andropov and Konstantin Chernenko followed the same line.

Cultural Policy under Gorbachev

When Mikhail Gorbachev came to power, satisfying demands for greater cultural autonomy was low on his list of priorities. His goal was economic, then later political, reform. But Gorbachev faced the dilemma that all reformers had confronted in the multinational empire: it was impossible to reform only one aspect of society without affecting other arenas. Gorbachev's economic policy of devolving decision-making authority from the central ministries to the local level and his tentative moves toward market mechanisms enhanced the power and consciousness of people in the hinterlands. His political reforms were even more influential. With the introduction of *demokratizatsia* and *glasnost,* and the concomitant decline of censorship, people were emboldened. They were free to discuss not only political and economic issues, but cultural affairs as well. As political discourse expanded, so did cultural awareness.

In April 1990 a language law backed by Gorbachev gave the union and autonomous republics the right to determine the legal status of the languages of their territories. Many of Stalin's language policies subsequently fell. For example, Turkmenistan and Azerbaijan abandoned Cyrillic script for their traditional Turkish-style Latin script.

Gorbachev did try, however, to stem the slide toward the complete autonomy of the republics over cultural matters. The April 1990 law also made Russian the official language of the USSR. Gorbachev had broken with the whitewashings of the Khrushchev and Brezhnev eras, but he was not prepared to grant the degree of autonomy that would come through the absolute sovereignty of the republics.

Reestablishment of Distant Ties

Just as the communist government had controlled discourse among Soviet citizens, so it had controlled discourse between its citizens and foreigners. The Soviet government feared that communication across the border in Central Asia, for example, could lead to a pan-Turkic or pan-Islamic movement. As a result, border crossings were tightly controlled, television and radio broadcasts were jammed, and all trade relations and cultural exchanges were planned in Moscow. When the Soviet Union collapsed, so too did the artificially stunted relations along the borders.

The Soviet Union's external borders were as haphazardly derived as its internal borders. Armenians are separated by the border with Turkey. There are Azeris and Turkmen on both sides of the Iranian border. There are Tajiks and Uzbeks on both sides of the Afghan border. The Chinese border separates Kazakh and Uigur peoples, and Buriats on both sides of the Mongolian border share a common history and language. The extent of irredentist feelings varies from national group to national group. Over time, the state borders separating some of these peoples could come into question.

Turkey and Iran were quick to restore ties with their not too distant kin. The people of Kazakhstan, Kyrgyzstan, Uzbekistan, and Turkmenistan are Moslems who speak dialects of Turkish that are understandable to Turks. The Tajiks, also Moslems, speak a dialect of Farsi that is understandable to Iranians. In early December 1991, Turkmen president Saparmurad Niyazov became the first Central

Asian leader to visit Turkey and request recognition for his county. While in Ankara, he signed agreements for cooperation in education, trade and economic development, and culture. Niyazov was followed within a month by the presidents of Uzbekistan and Kyrgyzstan, who signed similar agreements.

Iran has been competing for influence in Central Asia and the Transcaucasus state of Azerbaijan, which is also Moslem. To date, the Iranians have: provided financial aid to mosques and religious schools; begun developing oil extraction projects in Turkmenistan and Azerbaijan; agreed to use Tashkent (Uzbekistan) as a commercial air transportation hub; and begun laying the groundwork for direct telephone communications. Fearful of the expansion of Iranian influence and its Shia Islam faith, Saudi Arabia has courted and aided its fellow Sunni Moslems in Central Asia.

Enhanced crossborder contacts are not limited to Central Asia. The Ukrainians and Baltic peoples are drawn to the West by history, geography, religion, and the prospect of economic ties. In addition, Ukraine and the Baltic states enjoy the support of millions of citizens in the West who emigrated from these states or are descended from Ukrainian or Baltic ancestry.

Religion

Although the Soviet constitutions of 1924, 1936, and 1977 provided for the right to believe and the right to worship, both rights were limited by official state policy as well as by complementary constitutional provisions. Article 52 of the 1977 Constitution granted Soviets the right "not to believe" and the right to "conduct atheistic propaganda." After 1917, church and state officially were separated, but in reality the former was subjugated to the latter. The charity, missionary, and educational activities of religious organizations, in particular those of the Russian Orthodox Church, were limited severely. Church lands were nationalized. Especially during the years of civil war (1918-1921) and cultural revolution (1928-1932), religious persons and the organized church itself suffered physical persecution at the hands of the party and its fronts.

Russian Orthodox Church.   Between 1925 and World War II, the Russian Orthodox Church was forbidden by the government to select a patriarch, its spiritual leader. In 1929 the Law on Religious Associations gave legal force to many of the ad hoc Communist party actions taken in the years before. Between 1914 and 1941, the number of Russian Orthodox Church buildings decreased from an estimated 54,400 to 4,200; its priests decreased from 57,000 to 5,600; its monasteries decreased from 1,498 to 38; its seminaries decreased from 57 to 0; and its bishops decreased from 130 to 4.

During World War II, Stalin allowed a renewal and reinvigoration of the Russian Orthodox Church because he needed to inspire nationalism in the Russian people in defense of the motherland. Eighteen thousand parishes were reopened and enjoyed a revival into the late 1950s. This policy, however, extended neither to the Ukrainian and Belorussian autocephalous (independent) Orthodox Churches nor to the Ukrainian Uniate Church (allied to Rome), which was persecuted after World War II and subjected to the authority of the Moscow Russian Orthodox patriarch (who was subject to Communist party controls).

The most concerted and violent persecution of religious groups after World War II occurred between 1959 and 1964 during Nikita Khrushchev's antireligion offensive. During this period many of the parishes and monasteries reopened during the war were closed. Of the twenty thousand church buildings in existence by 1959, eleven thousand were shut by Khrushchev's campaign. Although the official antireligious program ended with Khrushchev's ouster in 1964, its effects and militant spirit continued into the Brezhnev period. By 1966 only seven thousand church buildings remained open. Another effect of Khrushchev's campaign was to split the Russian Orthodox and the Baptists (the two main targets of the campaign) into official (party-sanctioned) and nonofficial (dissident) groups.

Only in the late 1980s did official antireligion policies begin to lose their force. Liberal intellectu-

Priests of the Russian Orthodox Church celebrate Easter, April 1990.

als and party reformists, including Gorbachev, came to believe that religious and moral values had to be a part of perestroika. At his December 1989 meeting with Pope John Paul II (which resulted in negotiations for the establishment of diplomatic ties between the USSR and the Vatican), Gorbachev declared his support for "respect for the national, state, and spiritual and cultural identity of all peoples." Religious institutions in the Soviet Union were allowed to revive physically. Soviet medieval historian Dmitri S. Likachev, with the aid of Raisa Gorbachev, established a Soviet Cultural Fund for the protection and rebuilding of historic and religious monuments of the Soviet Union.

In 1988 the Russian Orthodox Church, the largest Eastern Orthodox Church in the world, celebrated the millennium of Christianity in Russia, marking the A.D. 988 conversion of Kievan Russia to the Christian faith under Grand Prince Vladimir of Kiev. Counting 96.7 million nominal believers as its own, the Russian Orthodox Church is the largest and best organized church in the former USSR. In October 1989, after thirty years of prohibition, an Orthodox seminary was allowed to resume teaching. Church schools were revived without harassment. Priests and church authorities gained access to television and the press. The bells of St. Basil's Cathe-

dral in Red Square rang in January 1990 for the first time in seventy years. And on January 7, 1990, for the first time in Soviet history, Soviet television broadcast Russian Orthodox Christmas services.

The renunciation of Marxist-Leninist ideology liberated the Russian Orthodox Church and its fellow churches from official state-sponsored persecution. Symbolically, religious holidays—including Easter Sunday and Christmas day—were made official state holidays by Yeltsin's government. Yet to be determined is how much church property will be returned to the church.

Other Religious Groups. Islam (mostly Sunni Moslem) is the second largest religious faith in the former USSR. About 20 percent of the people of the former Soviet Union practice Islam, a tie that binds former Soviet adherents to the Turkic, Arabic, and Persian cultures of the Middle East and Asia. Moslems live in the Crimea, the Tatar regions, Bashkiria, North Caucasia, Daghestan, and particularly in the republics of Azerbaijan (mostly Shi'ite Moslem), Kazakhstan, Uzbekistan, Kyrgyzstan, Turkmenistan, and Tajikistan.

Until 1928 the Moslem clergy maintained a strong hold on the courts, schools, and landholding in these regions. Twenty-six thousand mosques and forty-five thousand mullahs served Moslems at the time of the Bolshevik revolution. By 1990 only four hundred fifty mosques and some two thousand mullahs were allowed to function. But underground and unofficial congregations, including Sufi Brotherhoods (conservative Moslems), were widespread.

The Roman Catholic Church has up to 3.5 million believers in the former USSR, with 2.5 million of them concentrated in Lithuania. Crowds of Belorussian and Eastern Polish (Poles who remained in the USSR after Polish-Soviet borders were redrawn after World War II) Catholics welcomed Josef Cardinal Glemp, primate of Poland, on his trip to their homeland in September 1988.

Eastern Rite Catholics (Uniates) are concentrated in Ukraine, comprising people whose ancestors accepted the authority of the pope in the late 1500s in exchange for being allowed to practice what are essentially Eastern Orthodox doctrines and rituals. Uniates suffered some of the worst persecution and repression at the hands of the Soviet government, largely because of their Ukrainian homogeneity and allegiance to Rome. After World War II, the Uniate Church was officially disbanded in the USSR and made a part of the Russian Orthodox Church. Its standing improved as Vatican-Kremlin relations warmed, and Ukrainian Catholic parishes were once again allowed to officially register with the state. In April 1990, despite protests from Orthodox believers, the Cathedral of St. George in Lvov was transferred from Orthodox control to the control of the Ukrainian Catholic Church.

Protestants number almost four million in the former Soviet lands. Up to 850,000 Lutherans are concentrated in Latvia and Estonia and are among the German settlers of Central Asia and Siberia. The remaining Protestant believers include Baptists, Evangelicals and Pentecostals, Adventists, and Jehovah's Witnesses. These groups endured particularly harsh persecution because of their unofficial status, their missionary zeal, and their ties abroad.

Judaism occupies a unique and difficult place in society. Living mostly in the cities of European Russia and speaking Russian as a native or second language, Jews belong to both a religious and a nationality group. The Jewish Autonomous Region of the Far East, established in 1928 as a homeland for the USSR's Jewish population, borders China and has Yiddish, used in many schools, as its official language.

Russian and Slavic peoples long have experienced strained relations with the Jewish communities and individuals living among them (diaspora Jews found refuge in Eastern Europe after migrations from the West in the fifteenth and sixteenth centuries). Open anti-Semitism became a harsh reality in late imperial Russia as reactionary groups, with the tsar's approval, imposed pogroms, or repressive policies (from deportation to murder), on the Jews of Eastern Europe. Jews suffered varying levels of discrimination and persecution during Soviet rule. In recent years, open anti-Semitism has reappeared, as some extremist groups have blamed Jews for problems afflicting Russia.

In the Caucasus, the Georgian Orthodox Church and Armenian Apostolic Church have survived and prospered as national Christian churches and are the most cohesive and well-organized churches in the former Soviet Union. Faring less well have been several Russian religious sects that broke off from the Orthodox Church and are dispersed mainly within the Russian Federation: the Old Believers (numbering two million), the Molokans, and Dukhobors. Approximately fifty thousand Buddhists, mostly among the Buriat ethnic groups, are in the Soviet Far East. In 1988 Hare Krishnas were recognized as an official religious group.

Lastly, between six million and ten million confirmed atheists are in the USSR, for whom the ideologies of socialist equality and scientific atheism have become a secular religion. These atheists trace their roots to the League of the Militant Godless of the 1920s and 1930s, the Knowledge Societies of the 1950s, 1960s, and 1970s (both of which spread atheistic propaganda), and the "god-creating" movement, organized by several early Bolshevik leaders.

The Future of the Commonwealth

Strobe Talbott has described the Commonwealth of Independent States as "a misnomer wrapped in a contradiction inside a political fiction." Indeed, the member states joined the commonwealth with divergent views of its purpose. Ukraine, Moldova, and Azerbaijan saw the CIS as a divorce court—an accommodation for holding the economic and military infrastructures of the old Soviet Union together until it became practical to dissolve them. Russia and Kazakhstan, at the other extreme, saw the CIS as a federation with wide-ranging coordinating powers that would maintain the old infrastructures. The chasm between those two positions was so vast that the commonwealth could not serve the purposes of all members. As time has passed, it has become increasingly clear that the CIS, in its present form, is destined to be a transitional arrangement.

Each member state will have to weigh the factors for and against remaining in the commonwealth. Each faces a different set of centripetal forces pulling it toward, and centrifugal forces pulling it away, from the other former Soviet republics. In the very near term, even Ukraine has good reasons to remain a member. The CIS, despite its shortcomings, provides Ukraine with a forum for negotiating the allocation of Soviet conventional forces and government assets. More importantly, the addendum to the accord gives Ukraine some legal authority over the nuclear weapons still on its soil. Once those weapons are dismantled, and once the Soviet legacy has been resolved, the centrifugal forces of anti-Russian sentiment and Ukrainian nationalism will far exceed any centripetal factor.

Azerbaijan and Moldova also are likely to exercise their right to withdraw from the commonwealth. Article 10 of the accord reserved to each member state "the right to suspend the . . . agreement or its individual articles by notifying the agreement's participants a year in advance." Their withdrawal, however, would not be the end of the commonwealth, as Yeltsin himself pointed out in a June 11, 1992, interview: "It cannot be ruled out that one state or two will quit the CIS, but this is not a drama or a tragedy."

The future composition and function of a rump CIS are hard to anticipate. Additional states will almost certainly withdraw. But it is likely that at least several of the Central Asian states will remain with Russia in the commonwealth. This rump commonwealth will survive only if its remaining members reach a consensus on its purpose. Will it evolve along the lines of the United Nations—a debating forum with no real power to enforce its decisions? Or will the CIS develop permanent coordinating institutions that create meaningful economic, military, and social links between states?

On May 25 Boris Yeltsin and Nursultan Nazarbayev, the two strongest advocates of the CIS, signed a bilateral treaty that covered the very issues the CIS was supposed to coordinate. The state-to-state agreement provided for a common market, an open border for goods and services, a single security zone, and the sharing of military bases and test sites. The signatories stated their hope that other former republics would sign similar bilateral agreements. If the most basic issues of interstate relations are to be conducted on a bilateral basis, then the commonwealth has no substantive function.

The fate of the CIS as a political entity is only a part of a broader question. Given the capriciousness of borders, the geographic intermingling of peoples, and national animosities that date back centuries, what will become of the people of the former Soviet lands?

A look at the history of decolonization in the twentieth century is instructive in this regard. The legacy of the Austro-Hungarian empire's 1918 dissolution still influences events almost three-quarters of a century later; disputes between Czechs and Slovaks, Serbs and Croats, and Magyars and Romanians are all reverberations of the Austro-Hungarian crash. Similarly, the collapse of the Ottoman and British empires left behind unnatural boundaries and unresolved national disputes that had been suppressed by the imperial center. The situations created by past imperial policies and boundaries contributed to the contemporary conflicts in Lebanon, Cyprus, Kashmir, Kuwait, and elsewhere.

Just as the dissolution of those three empires resonate today, so the aftershocks of the Russian empire's breakup will likely last generations.

CHAPTER **8**

THE ECONOMY

The USSR's economic system failed miserably. Despite its having the world's largest land mass, an educated population, and tremendous deposits of natural resources, Soviet communism did not deliver the prosperity promised by generations of Soviet leaders. Every Soviet leader since Joseph Stalin attempted to improve the economy, but none of them could overcome the system's inherent inefficiencies and contradictions. During much of the 1970s and 1980s the growth rate was highly disappointing.

Mikhail Gorbachev tried to reverse this situation by implementing increasingly radical economic reforms during the late 1980s. These changes, however, failed to produce short-term gains. The Soviet people likely would have been tolerant of almost any reform that produced an obvious improvement in their standard of living. But the economy not only failed to improve, it fell into disarray. Economic indicators declined, lines at stores grew, and many food and consumer items became increasingly scarce.

By 1991 the Soviet economy was in free fall. Production dropped more than 11 percent that year. The International Monetary Fund estimated that inflation was 140 percent in 1991 and could exceed 1,000 percent in 1992. The ruble no longer was universally accepted as a medium of exchange, and enterprises resorted to barter. Perhaps the most frightening failure was the collapse of the food supply system, which left large cities like Moscow and St. Petersburg threatened by a food crisis.

Gorbachev dismantled the old system, but he failed to establish an effective replacement. His successors—Boris Yeltsin and new leaders in the former republics—faced the daunting task of transforming the broken command economy into one based on market economic institutions and principles. If they were to succeed at improving the standard of living, they had to be willing to implement broad economic reforms that Gorbachev never accepted. By fall 1992, the Yeltsin team—as well as those in Ukraine, the three Baltic states, and some other former republics—had taken important strides in that direction.

As a consequence, the West welcomed Russia and its neighbors back into the international fold and offered large-scale assistance. But, as IMF managing director Michel Camdessus said in a speech, "in the end the bold and comprehensive programs the republics design must reflect their strategy. . . . International financial assistance . . . can only be a complement to their efforts, their savings, their investment in infrastructure and in expanding the productive base of the economy."

Those efforts will be tested in the months and years ahead. Eventually, Russia and some of the other states of the former Soviet Union have the potential to become wealthy European nations. From the perspective of the economic crisis gripping those states in 1992, however, achieving this outcome appeared only as a very distant goal.

Establishing the Soviet Economy

Soviet economic problems did not originate during the regime of Mikhail Gorbachev. The system contained severe structural, managerial, and philosophical weaknesses. Some dated from tsarist times;

The backwardness of the Russian economy was largely responsible for the army's disastrous defeats from the Crimean War to World War I. Here, tsarist troops hail the February Revolution that toppled the monarchy, which they believe will end the war.

many others were introduced after the Bolshevik Revolution.

The heart of the Soviet economic dilemma, however, was the legacy of Joseph Stalin. The system that Stalin built upon the foundation of Marxist and Leninist theory was one in which the state owned all productive resources, excluding small family farm plots; central planners in Moscow controlled almost every aspect of the economy; defense and heavy industry were favored at the expense of consumer welfare; and foreign trade links were minimized to insulate the economy from outside influences.

Stalin devoted the Soviet economy to the political goals of maintaining centralized power and maximizing industrial and military strength. This course hindered economic efficiency and production and created a populace that was economically dependent on the central government.

Tsarist Economy

The Bolsheviks' economic plans in 1917 were constrained by conditions they had inherited from the tsars. Russia had the weakest economy among the European powers. Economist Alec Nove, in *An Economic History of the USSR,* calculated that Russian per capita income in 1913 was less than 25 percent of per capita income in the United Kingdom and less than 50 percent of Austria-Hungary's. During the two previous decades, per capita income had grown at a slower rate in Russia than in any other European power. Only size made Russia a great power. It had a large population to fill the army's ranks, an abundance of natural resources (including oil and gold), and a massive land base.

Tsarist policies—laced with xenophobia and conservatism—stunted industrial progress. The attempts to minimize Western influences denied Russia many benefits of the industrial revolution. Full centralization of economic power in the tsar meant that the entrepreneurial class developed slowly, which stunted innovation. And the tsars invested little in basic infrastructure—roads, bridges, railroads, and communications—that would have spurred industrial development and commerce. The humiliation of Russia's defeat by Japan in the Russo-Japanese War of 1904-1905 led to some reform. But when World War I began in 1914, the Russian economic system was on the verge of collapse.

Tsar Nicholas and his advisers failed to see the disastrous consequences of entering World War I. Given Russia's backward economy, limited infrastructure, and urban revolutionary upheaval, it was surprising that the Russian war effort lasted as long as it did. By the November 1917 revolution and Russia's withdrawal from the war, the economy was completely devastated. Key industrial regions (in the north and west) were ceded to Germany in the Brest-Litovsk Treaty. Adding to the confusion, the Bolsheviks could not control their own countryside, where White (anti-Bolshevik) and Green (peasant) militias established control. The Russians recovered some land from Germany after it was defeated by the Western allies in 1918. But as a result of the Russian civil war and the 1920 Russo-Polish War, the Bolsheviks surrendered their claims to Finland, the Baltic states, Polish territories, and Bessarabia, all among the most developed regions under its control.

War Communism and NEP

Although Marxist doctrine addressed international class harmonization, the withering away of the state, and many other economic and social theories, it provided few concrete instructions for establishing an economic system. Trusting in the imminence of a world revolution that would bring Russia assistance from the developed nations of Europe, the Bolsheviks adopted radical policies. Lenin called for nationalization of all banks and large commercial enterprises, the end of commercial secrecy, and measures to ensure rationing of resources. The Bolsheviks gained urban support by allowing workers' soviets (councils) to manage enterprises. In the countryside, Lenin allowed the peasants to seize the land.

When the world revolution failed to occur, the Bolsheviks had to address their problems without the aid of an international community of socialist states. In 1918 the civil war and an urban food crisis forced Lenin and his colleagues to adopt a new, more draconian policy—War Communism. Lenin ordered requisitions of peasant grain to prevent hoarding, free trade was outlawed, and managers replaced workers' control at enterprises. To pay for accelerated wages and large government deficits, the Bolsheviks printed more and more money, and the ruble lost its value. At the height of War Communism, severe penalties were applied to enforce efficiency in the work place. *(War Communism, p. 36)*

War Communism was largely unsuccessful—inflation increased, grain production stagnated, and the nation's infrastructure continued to collapse. In early 1921 the government was shaken when sailors at the Kronstadt naval base, who had supported Lenin in 1917, rose in revolt—only this time against the Bolsheviks. The revolt was crushed, but Lenin reacted by replacing forced requisitions of grain with a progressive tax—the first step in Lenin's New Economic Policy (NEP). Under NEP, the center retained control of the "commanding heights" (heavy industry, banking, foreign trade, wholesale commerce, and transportation), but free enterprise and competition were reintroduced into the agricultural, small business, and retail sectors. The Soviets also showed greater interest in international trade. Lenin declared that Soviet representatives to the post-World War I Genoa Conference in 1923 would go not as communists, but as merchants. *(New Economic Policy, p. 41)*

Analysts draw parallels between NEP and the policies that Gorbachev tried to implement. Private and cooperative ownership were permitted in agriculture and industry. The government strove to construct a healthy financial system to replace widespread use of barter. NEP's stress on foreign contacts also paralleled Gorbachev's theme of international economic interdependence.

Although NEP seemed to improve the economy, it also contradicted Marxist dogma. Stalin, who emerged after Lenin's death in 1924 as the most powerful Soviet leader, used NEP's successes to outmaneuver his opponents on the left who had opposed NEP. In 1928, however, citing the need to combat both external and internal enemies, Stalin brought NEP to its conclusion and attacked those on the right who continued to support it.

Stalin's Economic Priorities

On February 4, 1931, Stalin stated:

One feature of the history of old Russia was the continual beating she suffered because of her backwardness. She was beaten by the Mongol Khans. She was beaten by the Turkish beys. She was beaten by the Swedish feudal lords. She was beaten by the Polish and Lithuanian gentry. She was beaten by the British and French capitalists. She was beaten by the Japanese barons. All beat her—because of her backwardness. . . . They beat her because to do so was profitable and could be done with impunity. . . . Such is the law of the exploiters—to beat the backward and the weak. . . . That is why we must no longer lag behind. . . . We are fifty or a hundred years behind the advanced countries. We must make good this distance in ten years. Either we do it, or we shall be crushed.

Stalin's program was clear: the Soviet Union would rapidly industrialize itself at all costs. The urgency of building "socialism in one country" justified the use of terror and forced austerity. Along with his drive to industrialization, Stalin brutally collectivized the peasantry and centralized all economic activity under his direction. *(Collectivization and Industrialization, pp. 47-49)*

The first changes occurred in the countryside, where entrepreneurial peasants were profiting from private trade. Between 1926 and 1930 this trade was virtually wiped out. In 1929 Stalin called for full collectivization and a class war against the *kulaks* (better-off peasants). Severe requisitioning of grain by Soviet authorities and peasant resistance to collectivization (many peasants destroyed their livestock rather than turn it over to the authorities) led to a famine that killed millions of people.

According to Stalin, because the Soviet Union faced a future conflict with capitalist nations, heavy industry and defense production had to be given primacy over consumer-oriented manufacturing. This industrial allocation helped the Soviet Union to survive World War II, but historians have criticized Stalin for the massive human and economic cost of his forced industrialization. John Scott, an American who traveled and worked in Russia in the 1930s, observed in his book, *Behind the Urals,* "ten million tons of steel will make a great many tanks whose military effectiveness bears no relation to the price paid for the steel."

Stalin intended to ensure total central control of the economy by developing comprehensive plans for economic activities. The First Five-Year Plan (FYP) was adopted in 1928. Although the plan was not achieved, it was declared fulfilled at the end of 1932. The Thirteenth FYP would have determined economic policy for 1990-1995, but it was never implemented.

Stalinist Economic Legacy

Under Stalin, numerous inefficiencies became deeply ingrained in the Soviet system. These inefficiencies continued to act as a drag on the Soviet economy during the regimes of Stalin's successors.

The Stalinist approach placed planners and factory managers at odds. Planners tried to promote the efficient use of resources by imposing ambitious production quotas, while factory managers lobbied to keep quotas as low as possible. Planners demanded that managers meet a confusing array of guidelines for everything from numbers of employees to the use of excess scrap metal. Managers frustrated planners by finding the simplest, and sometimes most inefficient, ways to meet quotas. Told to make two tons of nails, a manager could technically fulfill a quota by making twenty nails weighing a tenth of a ton each. Moreover, because managers were judged according to amount of production, they had little incentive to pay attention to the cost of the inputs or the effect their operations had on the environment.

Planning also induced managers to hoard labor and materials so quotas could be met even when planners failed to provide necessary inputs. Because quotas were automatically "ratcheted" up slightly above levels achieved the year before, managers often hid the true productivity of their enterprise and depressed production during the early part of a quota period. This led to "storming"—speeding production late in the month so that the quota was barely achieved.

The planners' tendency to construct "taut" plans (pushing the system to its maximum utilization) did not allow for upkeep of plants and machinery. John Scott, in the 1930s, described an explosion that destroyed a blast furnace (the circumstances were reminiscent of the Chernobyl nuclear disaster a half century later): "For two weeks prior to the disaster everybody connected with the furnace had known that the tapping hole was in bad shape. . . . Nobody realized the dangers . . . and no one wanted to take responsibility for shutting down the furnace . . . when the country needed pig iron very badly."

The absence of private ownership inhibited worker initiative and resulted in the production of poor quality goods that plagued the Soviet consumer. Workers saw little connection between their personal welfare and their job performance. The practice of paying collective farm workers by the hour, instead of according to the volume and quality of their output, virtually ensured that their productivity would be poor. Labor productivity in industry was low for the same reason.

State ownership also contributed to a high level of corruption, which could be justified more easily because no one really loses from thievery when the state owns everything.

In contrast to capitalism, which seeks to ensure competition as the source of economic dynamism, the Soviets tried to eliminate competition. With profits guaranteed and without competitors who could sell lower-priced or higher-quality goods, producers did not have to respond to market demands. In many cases, the Soviets concentrated production of a particular product in a single location. One survey found that "of 5,884 product lines, 77 percent were supplied by just one producer." This concentration produced monopoly distortions and left the entire economy at the mercy of a breakdown in one factory.

Finally, Stalin's attempt to isolate the country from international interference had severe economic consequences. Technological innovations were not imported, thus perpetuating the Soviets' technological backwardness in many areas of industry. Because producers did not have to compete against imports, the quality of Soviet goods fell far behind international standards. The Soviets could not earn hard currency through exports of manufactured items. Soviet producers also gained no experience on how to compete for business in the international marketplace.

Attempts at Reform

In his seminal work on Soviet reforms, *Reforming the Soviet Economy,* Sovietologist Ed Hewett of the Brookings Institution notes:

In the post-Stalin era Soviet leaders have never been even close to fully satisfied with the performance of the economic system. . . . There is no year in which some change in the Soviet system is not introduced, some new experiment not begun. . . . This constant tinkering with the system has never had the desired effect. As a result, the leadership has gone for a new reform package at fairly regular intervals, taking elements from previous reforms and experiments, but possibly some new ideas also.

Hewett cites five major economic reform initiatives in the post-Stalin era. In 1957, Nikita S. Khrushchev launched his *sovnarkhoz* (economic councils) reforms, in which regional economic councils were granted greater influence vis-à-vis central authorities in economic decision making. In 1965 Prime Minister Aleksei Kosygin and First Secretary Leonid I. Brezhnev initiated the "Kosygin reforms," which sought to fine tune the control and planning system, increase initiative in the enterprises by linking bonuses more closely to performances, reorganize the pricing system, and improve consumer welfare. A third set of reforms was introduced in 1973 to "reduce the size of administrative hierarchy in industry and increase the efficiency with which industrial enterprises were managed by the center." Another wave of minor (and unsuccessful) economic reforms was implemented in 1979. Gorbachev's economic programs launched in 1985 represented the fifth attempt at reform.

None of the first four reform programs attempted to change the basic structure of the Soviet economic system. The leadership consistently declined to allow market forces—such as prices, competition, and consumer demand—to operate. Until Gorbachev, economic reform movements amounted to little more than attempts to fine tune the Stalinist system in search of greater production and efficiency. Though Gorbachev's economic reforms were much more extensive and encouraged limited free enterprise, even he did not repudiate entirely the centralized command economic system. He seemed to believe that an ideal allocation of resources could be found through central planning, rather than market mechanisms and private ownership.

Economy under Khrushchev and Brezhnev

During the 1950s and 1960s the Soviet economy inspired Third World leaders because it achieved strong growth, while central authorities retained control over resources and production. According to Alec Nove, the economy grew by almost 10 percent into the mid-1960s. However, this impressive growth was due primarily to the country's ability to exploit its natural resources. Soviet leaders consistently relied on extensive growth (adding to the resource pool through greater exploitation of natural resources and labor) rather than intensive growth (qualitatively more efficient use of resources). For example, Khrushchev opened up huge tracts of land for agricultural use under his Virgin Lands program of the 1950s. Brezhnev continued land reclamation programs and turned to Siberia's vast mineral, gas, and oil deposits as another source of unexploited natural resources.

This emphasis on extensive growth led to declining economic efficiency as the productivity of labor, capital, and land all plummeted. It also wasted resources. The number of unfinished projects increased dramatically because they were begun without full cost assessments. Throughout the economy the Soviets failed to invest adequately in infrastructure.

Despite celebrated technological feats, such as the launching of Sputnik in 1957 and the dramatic expansion of the Soviet nuclear arsenal, the Soviet economy under Khrushchev and Brezhnev fell far behind the West technologically. It also failed to catch up with Western economies in terms of GNP, per capita income, consumption, or any other major economic indicator.

Khrushchev and Brezhnev responded to economic problems by rearranging priorities instead of introducing new methods. For example, during the post-Stalin era the leadership gave consumer welfare a higher priority. Under Khrushchev this meant more investment in the chemical and fertilizers industry to increase food production. Brezhnev literally bought the relative domestic calm of the late 1960s and early 1970s through his commitment to consumer welfare. At his first party congress as party chief, in 1966, Brezhnev pledged "a fuller satisfaction of the material and cultural requirements of the Soviet people." In the years 1965 to 1972, per capita consumption rose 5 percent while per capita income was up 6.9 percent. Although these gains were substantial, at the Twenty-fifth Party Congress in 1976 Brezhnev acknowledged difficulties: "We have not learned to accelerate the development" of consumer goods.

Trade with other nations was minimal during the 1970s, but for the first time the Soviets became dependent on what little trade did occur. Because the agricultural sector continued to lag, after 1970 the country was transformed from an exporter to the world's largest net importer of grain. These costly grain imports could only be paid for with hard currency earned through the export of raw materials.

While Brezhnev allowed some further economic freedoms—for example, greater leeway for private plots—he was unprepared to institute effective reforms. Instead, as Soviet specialist Marshall Shulman noted in *Foreign Affairs* in October 1973, the Soviets "opted for a massive effort to overcome its [the Soviet economy's] shortcomings by increasing the flow of trade, advanced technology and capital from abroad." Shulman also noted that Brezhnev was willing to accept some opening to the West: "The realization of these [Brezhnev's] expectations manifestly requires an international climate of reduced tension." Consequently, the Brezhnev regime

An open pit coal mine in the Krasnoyarsk region of Siberia. Khrushchev and Brezhnev relied on the exploitation of vast natural resources to drive economic growth.

pursued détente with the West. *(Détente, p. 90)*

Soviet economic problems accelerated in the late 1970s. Labor productivity continued to fall as workers were given little incentive to improve their output. Soviet farmers, for example, produced less than one-third the amount of agricultural products produced by American farmers, despite outnumbering them five to one in 1980. The tactic of extensive growth, meanwhile, no longer could mask the inefficiency of the system. New agricultural lands could be opened only by risking further erosion of the environment. Plentiful stocks of raw materials were available, but the richest untapped deposits were in remote regions. In many cases the Soviets lacked the high-technology equipment required to extract the materials. The annual growth rate of the Soviet labor force dropped from 2 percent in 1970 to only about 1 percent in 1980.

Historian Martin Malia points out that evidence of the financial disarray that would emerge under Gorbachev could be seen in this period: "the first sign of the coming Soviet economic collapse, which went unnoticed in the West, was the increase in state subsidies to unprofitable enterprises at the end of the 1970s. ... During this period, more than 30 billion rubles of the state budget were allocated annually to support unprofitable industrial enterprises."

Perhaps most alarming was the effect of the defunct economy on Soviet society. Alcoholism in particular had increased dramatically during the Brezhnev years. Soviets drink three times as much distilled spirits as their West European peers and twice as much as East Europeans. The Soviet Union was the only country in Europe with a long-term decline in life expectancies, and the average Soviet citizen could expect a shorter life than the citizens of every other Eastern European nation. By the time the aging Brezhnev died in 1982, the Soviet leadership realized that it had to commit itself to broader economic reform. Soviet leaders, however, remained resistant to fundamental change that could threaten their hold on power or violate basic Marxist-Leninist economic principles.

Andropov and Chernenko Interregnum

Yuri Andropov (general secretary, November 1982-February 1984) repeatedly stated that his "highest priority" was reviving the economy. Since he admitted, "I do not have ready recipes" for solving the country's financial problems, he encouraged greater debate and considered nontraditional solutions. For example, he said the Soviet Union should "take account of the experiences of the fra-

The planned economy allowed Soviet leaders to channel resources into selected areas. As a result of skewed investment patterns, the USSR was a world leader in some areas and far behind in others. Here, the Soviet space shuttle sits on the launch pad.

ternal countries" (Hungary and possibly China). He even was prepared to offer capital incentives in return for more efficiency: "Shoddy work, inactivity, and irresponsibility should have an immediate and unavoidable effect on the earnings, official status, and moral prestige of workers." He also underlined the need "to extend the independence of enterprises and collective farms." Finally, Andropov is remembered most for his campaigns to reduce corruption and alcoholism.

Despite his rhetoric and support for limited experimentation, Andropov did not introduce the type of decentralizing reforms needed for an efficient economy. Most importantly, he did not try to weaken the authority of the bureaucrats who ran the economy.

Andropov's term in office can be viewed as a very modest positive step forward. He promoted reform-minded leaders such as Nikolai Ryzhkov and Mikhail Gorbachev, and he allowed a more open and realistic debate on economic issues. But Andropov was not a crusading reformer. His one-time confidant, Oleg Bogomolov, stated in 1989: "Andropov is being idealized now. If he had lived he probably would have changed things some, but he would not have touched overlying structures of society. He was careful and conservative." *(Andropov reforms, p. 100)*

As a long-time Brezhnev protégé, Konstantin Chernenko (February 1984-March 1985) favored his benefactor's conservative style. He seems to have feared a popular uprising like the one in Poland in 1980-1981 and therefore emphasized Brezhnev's policy of greater emphasis on consumer welfare. Chernenko's most important contribution may be that he did not stifle the open debates that had been initiated under Andropov and did not impede Gorbachev and other young leaders from assuming positions of authority.

Under Andropov and Chernenko the economy continued to deteriorate, especially the agricultural sector. The country suffered its sixth consecutive bad harvest in 1984, due both to poor weather and inefficient farming. Chernenko responded by calling for land reclamation—a retreat to the policy of extensive growth. *(Chernenko "Interregnum," p. 103)*

Gorbachev: Hero or Failure?

Mikhail Gorbachev's foremost policy concern was improving the economy. In April 1985, at the first Central Committee plenum after he came to power, he stated, "The development of Soviet society will be defined in decisive measure by qualitative shifts in our economy, by the transfer of it onto the rails of intensive growth." Gorbachev's efforts became progressively more radical as each successive round of reforms failed to reinvigorate the economy. Yet he declined to sponsor far-reaching reforms, such as the breakup and privatization of state-owned monopolies, complete price restructuring, and full privatization, which were vital to recharging the Soviet system.

Gorbachev's reforms had, however, undermined the stability of the Stalinist economic system. As James Noren wrote in *Soviet Economy*, "The leaders gradually and belatedly realized that the macroeconomic balance that was for the most part preserved under the old system of central planning and administrative controls was erod[ing] quite rapidly." In pursuit of reform, the security and predictability of the old system had been stripped away, but they had not been replaced by the efficiency, competition, and opportunity that a market could eventually provide. As a result, the Soviet economy was plunged into a depression in the late 1980s.

It is not clear, however, that Gorbachev could have moved forward with economic reforms more quickly than he did. Political resistance to economic reforms among party leaders, central planners, and bureaucrats throughout the system was strong. Moreover, many Soviets felt threatened by the economic upheaval that reforms were certain to bring.

It is also unlikely that quicker reforms would have spared the pain of transformation to a market economy. As the experiences of East European nations have demonstrated, moving from a command to a market economy inevitably creates unemployment, inflation, and a host of other economic woes during the period of reform.

Gorbachev never fully embraced market economic reforms. But despite his caution and his devotion to some of the principles of the old system, he must be credited with beginning to free the Soviet economy from Stalin's legacy. His leadership set the stage for the economic revolution promoted by Boris Yeltsin.

Stage One: Moderate Reforms. At first, like Yuri Andropov, Gorbachev tried to increase growth by reintroducing discipline and implementing moderate changes. Gorbachev introduced his early reforms without developing a blueprint. He wrote in *Perestroika: New Thinking for Our Country and the World,* that progress would come "step by step in the chosen direction, rounding out and perfecting the economic mechanism on the basis of acquired experience, getting rid of everything that is obsolete or has not proved itself."

Gorbachev hoped to improve productivity by increasing investment in research and development, retiring industrial equipment sooner (Soviet equipment was used three times longer than in the West), and expanding the use of computers and other technologies. Modernization in the machine building and high-technology sectors was to account for two-thirds of GNP growth. The rest was to come from what Sovietologist Herbert Levine called a "people program" to increase worker and managerial efficiency. The plan mixed threats with promises of future improvements in consumer welfare. Gorbachev also restricted alcohol sales in an attempt to overcome that traditional problem. More importantly, he reduced wage controls, allowing managers to reward productive work.

Gorbachev supplemented these reforms with minor changes to the economic mechanism. He called for movement toward cost accounting, "self-financing," and *khozrashchet* (the reduction of costs and expansion of profits in accordance with basic economic laws). A new "Law on Light Industry" allowed enterprises to retain 70 percent of their profits. Unprofitable enterprises were told that they could no longer depend on state subsidies. The Law on Private Enterprise (November 1986) legalized certain small-scale private businesses. Gorbachev also took some initial steps to decentralize foreign trade as some industries received the right to conduct trade without interference and joint ventures

Shortly after becoming general secretary, Mikhail Gorbachev attempts to spur the economy by going directly to the people—consumers as well as workers.

would now be permitted. Continued restrictions on ownership rights of these joint ventures, however, limited foreign interest through 1987.

The results of Gorbachev's first two years were disappointing, partly due to the program's own contradictions and partly due to unforeseen setbacks, including bad weather, strikes, and the nuclear accident at Chernobyl. Despite some signs of improvement (GNP increased more than 2 percent per year), most of the plan's key modernization targets went unmet. High growth targets made managers unwilling to slow production to replace equipment. Machine building, the program's centerpiece, saw zero growth. Most troubling was the scant improvement experienced by Soviet consumers, as per capita consumption rose less than 1 percent annually. Because of wage liberalization, consumers found themselves with excess cash. Shortages became common. Soviet citizens also felt the dearth of cheap alcohol as legal sales were cut by more than one-third (the resulting reduction in tax revenues also hit the Soviet budget). Workers responded with the Soviet Union's first reported strikes.

Stage Two: June 1987-Summer 1989. Consumer demands led Gorbachev to consider more radical steps. At the June 1987 Central Committee plenum, he described his new reform proposals: "the

transfer of enterprises to complete cost accounting, a radical transformation of the centralized management of the economy, fundamental changes in planning, a reform of the price formation system and of the financial and crediting mechanism, and the restructuring of foreign economic ties." Gorbachev's plan was a significant step toward decentralizing the economy. Planning was to be reduced, and new "state orders" would eventually cover only 20-25 percent of enterprise production. The supply system also would be decentralized, as wholesale trade was to account for 80 percent of sales by 1992. Wage controls were to be lifted further, with a long-range goal of 60-70 percent of the work force employed in enterprises that tied salary increases to worker performance and enterprise profits. By 1988 enterprise autonomy would be widened so that 40 percent of all enterprises were to finance their own activities without recourse to government subsidies. In December 1988 all enterprises were granted restricted access to foreign trade, although the government vacillated in this area.

Despite the changes, slow economic growth continued and key economic goals were not achieved. Unfinished capital construction increased by 8.7 percent in 1988, despite efforts to end such waste. Machinery "did not meet world technological standards" according to the 1988 Soviet year-end report. Workers became even more unhappy and labor unrest increased—the most notable example being the coal miners' strike in the Donbass region in the summer of 1988, which threatened to create a nationwide energy shortage and to cripple the transportation system. Per capita consumption increased only 1.5 percent in 1988 and persistent consumer complaints forced the leadership to again increase investment in the consumer sector. In addition, Gorbachev's plans were again hampered by unexpected disasters, the most dramatic of which was the Armenian earthquake on December 7, 1988, which killed 25,000 people, left 500,000 homeless, and required a major budgetary investment.

Perhaps most alarming, however, was the increasing chaos in the country's financial system. Enterprises used their new freedom to increase wages to keep restive laborers from striking. This led to a rapid growth in forced savings because quality goods continued to be scarce. In November 1988 Soviet authorities for the first time reported inflation (of less than 1.5 percent, although unofficial estimates put the level as high as 10 percent). The government also began to run up large budget deficits, caused in part by higher government subsidies to pay for increased wages. In November 1989 the government acknowledged a massive expansion in the internal deficit to 120 billion rubles, almost 14 percent of Soviet GNP. Hard currency debt had expanded rapidly during Gorbachev's tenure and by 1989 was approaching $60 billion. Failure to repay creditors—at first by individual enterprises, and later by the government itself—severely tarnished the Soviet credit rating.

Stage Three: Experimentation and Free Fall. Gorbachev's last two years in office saw wide-open debate on the economic future of the Soviet Union. But growing political upheaval, a frightening loss of control in the financial system, a deterioration of the Soviet Union's international economic position, increasing labor unrest, and many other factors pushed the Soviet economy deeper into chaos.

In October 1990, after much discussion and the development of several promising draft economic plans, the Soviet government adopted the "Presidential Plan," which proposed some genuine market reforms. "If its prescriptions could be carried out," said Sovietologist Gertrude Schroeder, "the Soviet economy finally would be off the 25-year treadmill of reform programs that had failed to re-form the institutions of socialist central planning." However, the plan was vague in many important areas and lacked a firm timetable for implementation. Consequently, the government continued to pursue reforms at the margins.

Gorbachev's tinkering did nothing to improve the economy or set it on the path toward long-term stability. For example, price increases were implemented in April 1991 that could have helped to control excess demand. But they were more than offset by rapid monetary growth. The government also was unable to control spending. The combined federal and local government budget deficits increased by 20 percent in 1991.

Political uncertainty may have prevented implementation of effective economic measures even if the Soviet leadership had the political will to do so. Economic chaos was exacerbated by the growth of regional assertiveness. In 1990 every republic declared its economic sovereignty. The decrees and laws of the Soviet government were routinely ignored, circumvented, or directly challenged by the republics and even by smaller jurisdictions. Republics began restricting trade with each other, causing reductions in economic output. Worst of all, large-scale violence erupted between and within republics. Fighting between Armenia and Azerbaijan over Nagorno-Karabakh and within Georgia caused economic slowdowns in all three republics.

The results were catastrophic. Production fell about 11 percent in 1991. Inflation accelerated (reaching an annualized rate of 300 percent in December) as the government implemented price increases and financed its deficits by printing money. Inflation and fear of further monetary reform caused runs on stores as consumers tried to get rid of worthless rubles. Unemployment increased and Soviet international trade fell dramatically. Finally, the government announced that reserves had dropped to just a few days' worth of imports and that it could no longer make payments on its hard currency debt, which had surpassed $60 billion.

By the time of the August 1991 coup the situation was ripe for change. As Timothy Colton noted, "The front in 1991 was that of political and economic transformation, a battle to which Gorbachev committed his government in 1985 but which could not be furthered or even managed without his relinquishing command."

The Yeltsin Transformation

The failed August 1991 coup severely diminished Gorbachev's authority and the threat of a rightist resurgence. Boris Yeltsin's leading role in opposing the coup and his stature as a popularly elected president of Russia provided him with a mandate to pursue far-reaching economic reform. During the first year following the coup, Yeltsin moved to transform Russia's centralized command economy to one based on the free market. He and his team of advisers took some of the important and painful steps required to accomplish this task.

Nevertheless, it was far from certain that Yeltsin could succeed. He inherited an economy mired in a depression and a populace exhausted by the economic upheaval created by the inefficiencies of the communist system and the failure of the Gorbachev reforms. Although several East European nations that were trying to achieve a similar transition made some progress, their experiences demonstrated the extreme pain involved in making such a transformation.

To establish quickly a market economy and enter the world economic system, the government would have to completely free prices, privatize industry, allow inefficient enterprises to go bankrupt, and reduce government debt. Inevitably these policies would lead to severe unemployment. It was unlikely that Russian workers, who relied upon state-guaranteed employment for generations, would tolerate high unemployment for long.

If the Russian government chose a more gradualist approach that avoided or delayed painful steps, it risked hyperinflation, that in turn could necessitate a reintroduction of price controls and central economic management. A piecemeal approach aimed at easing the severity of economic transformation risked stringing out indefinitely the prevailing economic stagnation and uncertainty.

During the summer of 1992, Yeltsin and his team slowed reform in response to political pressure from conservatives and industrial leaders and increasing public criticism of the continuing economic hardships. Some Western observers contended that these delays indicated that the political barriers to economic "shock therapy" were too great to allow for a rapid transformation. Virtually all observers agreed, however, that the Russian economy had not yet bottomed out. The most difficult stage of reform was still ahead.

Yeltsin's Plan

Armed with the legitimacy provided by his popular election and his leadership during the failed August coup, Boris Yeltsin advanced his economic reform strategy in the fall of 1991. He promoted a team of young economists (labeled the "thirty-somethings") who appeared to be devoted to radical reform. The team was headed by Finance Minister Yegor Gaidar, whom Yeltsin subsequently named acting prime minister in June 1992. The team members' enthusiasm for rapid reforms was based on their economic philosophy and their political calculations that public acquiescence for reform inevitably would decline as economic hardships became more severe.

Yeltsin waited until after the USSR Congress of People's Deputies passed legislation transferring most authority to the republics in September 1991 before describing his plans. On October 28, in an address before the Russian parliament, he made his first major economic policy statement. He promised to initiate a bold program that would include price liberalization, privatization, and land reform. Yeltsin also stated his intention to maintain a tough monetary and credit policy to limit the inevitable inflation. Privatization would initially focus on small enterprises and farms, but eventually it would include large enterprises. Yeltsin claimed that the reform package would produce positive results by the fall of 1992.

Yeltsin's reforms held much more promise than past reform efforts because they were aimed at overturning the old system and establishing a free market in its place. In contrast to the piecemeal approach of Gorbachev, his plan also represented a comprehensive and coordinated attempt to restructure the entire economy.

On January 2, 1992, a week after Gorbachev had resigned and the USSR had officially ceased to exist, the Yeltsin team implemented its plan to free most prices. Price liberalization was designed to increase the incentives to engage in entrepreneurship, reduce the state budget deficit by cutting the costs of subsidies, undermine black market activity, create competition, and encourage producers to bring their goods to market. After the January 2 liberalization, approximately 90 percent of prices were free of government control. The government also increased the price of those goods remaining under control—mainly energy and transport—three to five times. Prices were not fully liberalized in the key area of housing.

Yeltsin and his team also took steps to cut government spending and reduce the central government's budget deficit, which soared to 20 percent of gross domestic product (GDP) in 1991. The budget approved in early 1992 called for a deficit of only 1 percent of GDP, as state spending was to be slashed and projected tax revenues were to be increased through the introduction of a value-added tax as well as new taxes on profits and wages. Cuts in defense spending, as large as 70 percent, were expected to produce a savings windfall.

Gaidar promised not to run the printing presses to paper over Russia's internal deficits. The government also attempted to stem the growth of internal credit (which grew almost 100 percent in 1991) by increasing bank capital reserve requirements and adopting other measures to curb bank lending.

During the spring, Yeltsin moved ahead slowly on the privatization of small businesses and farms. The first-ever auction of smaller companies was conducted in Niznhi-Novgorod in early 1992. By March 15 more than 2,500 enterprises had been sold by the state property committee. Nevertheless, this number represented only a small fraction of Yeltsin's goal.

A large percentage of the private sector growth that did occur was the result of spontaneous privatization, where former ministries, managers, or even workers expropriated their enterprises with seeming impunity. These spontaneous privatizations were described by Simon Johnson and Heidi Kroll as "a mixed phenomenon, partly improving efficiency and partly constituting theft." This activity threatened to create public resentment of "insiders" who managed to get rich from their connections to the old system.

In August 1992 Yeltsin announced a sweeping plan to privatize industry and turn Russian citizens into shareholders. The method he chose was a voucher system under which each Russian would receive a voucher worth 10,000 rubles (about $60). The vouchers would be distributed beginning October 1, 1992. They could be used to purchase shares of large state enterprises, or they could be traded or sold. By using the voucher system, Yeltsin hoped not only to smooth the process of privatization, but also to give ordinary Russians a stake in the private economy that would lift public morale and widen support for reforms.

Opposition to Yeltsin's Reforms

Many Russians denounced Yeltsin for implementing reforms too abruptly. Vice President Aleksandr Rutskoy repeatedly attacked the reforms, which he claimed would lead to "anarchy." By July 1992 a poll indicated that Rutskoy, a voice of the Russian right, had surpassed Yeltsin in public approval. Yeltsin's plummeting popularity was directly attributable to economic conditions. During the first six months of 1992, industrial production fell an estimated 14 percent, while prices for most consumer goods rose an average of ten times.

Yeltsin's opponents attempted to slow economic reform at the Sixth Russian Congress of People's Deputies in April 1992. Conservatives, led by parliamentary chief Ruslan Khasbulatov and Rutskoy, pushed for a no-confidence resolution against Yeltsin. A motion to bring such a resolution to the floor on April 6 failed 447-412 with 70 abstentions. Several days later the Congress did pass a resolution calling for a moderation of reforms. After Yeltsin's entire cabinet on April 13 offered their resignations (which Yeltsin refused to accept) to protest opposition to the Yeltsin program, the deputies passed a declaration supporting the continuation of reforms. Those who advocated a slower approach to reform claimed that the Congress had supported their point of view. But Yeltsin's team emerged from the Congress with a self-proclaimed mandate to continue rapid reforms.

During the summer, however, Yeltsin seemed to back away from rapid reform as pressure for moderation grew from the Civic Alliance, a center-right political organization headed by industrialists who admitted the need for reforms but opposed the rapid pace of the Yeltsin program. The leader of the Civic Alliance, Arkady Volksy, charged that reforms—in particular tight monetary policies and severe limits on credit—had to be relaxed to prevent a total collapse of the economy. During the second quarter of 1992, Gyorgy Matyukhin, the governor of the Central Bank of Russia, had backed money growth to spur the economy, despite Gaidar's assertions that strict monetary control had to be maintained. (Ironically, Matyukhin eventually resigned in protest to parliamentary demands for an even looser money supply.) But by the beginning of summer, Gaidar himself defended a loosening of the government-imposed limit on credits to enterprises: "When prices go up 500 percent, a 15 percent increase in credits is terribly tight." In May and June Yeltsin and Gaidar responded to the threat of strikes by agreeing to allow a loosening of the money supply. They also gave more credit to enterprises unable to pay their bills, rather than allow them to go bankrupt.

In June, Yeltsin took two other steps that indicated he was protecting himself against attacks from the right. First, although he continued to seek financial help from the West, he asserted that Russia would not be strictly bound by the International Monetary Fund's conditions for aid. Second, he appointed three deputy premiers—Vladimir Shumeyko, Viktor Chernomyrdin, and Georgy Khizha—who were supported by the Civic Alliance.

Future of Reform

Yeltsin's willingness to allow a relaxation of credit, his appointments, and his more cautious approach to reform during the summer of 1992 led many Western observers to assert that momentum for rapid reforms was collapsing under the weight of public dissatisfaction and high-level opposition. Although Yeltsin retained a solid core of support among Russians who continued to favor liberal reforms, he was said to have lost the resolve to pursue radical reform under pressure from the Civic Alliance and other opponents.

This view fails to acknowledge that given the pain and dislocations inherent in radical economic reform, compromises along the way were inevitable. If Yeltsin hoped to sustain the nucleus of his economic reform program, the implementation of the reforms could not be allowed to devastate Russian society. In addition, because presidential decrees could be resisted effectively by the Russian parliament and officials charged with implementing reforms on location, Yeltsin needed not only the personal will to reform, but also a working coalition that would support reform.

In August 1992, the Yeltsin government's commitment to reform was strongly reaffirmed by its introduction of the voucher privatization plan and its resistance to an announcement by the Russian Central Bank that it would cancel the debts between Russian enterprises.

Yeltsin had vowed that his reform program would continue. He declared his intention to privatize all small shops as well as food production and supply companies, allow private ownership of land, de-monopolize most large enterprises, and make Russia a more hospitable environment for international trade and investment. Most important, the Yeltsin team intended to further liberalize prices and to make the ruble convertible (for trade in goods and services) by the end of 1992.

Another important task still ahead was the reining in of interenterprise debts estimated at more than a trillion rubles. These debts were increasing, partly because enterprises continued to ship goods to each other without sufficient funds to make payment. As Gaidar put it, "They used to send products and assume that they would be paid somehow." If Yeltsin allowed some short-term writeoff of debt, he would have to ensure that the government deficit was not perpetuated by inefficient enterprises.

Rapid growth in the private sector depended on development of an infrastructure as well as on legal guarantees to private businesses that they could operate without undo legal entanglements. The Soviet communist era had bequeathed an overburdened transport system, a nonexistent private supply network, a banking system incapable of making loans based on rational economic criteria, no legal guarantees of property rights, and no conception—legal or intellectual—of bankruptcy.

The short-term impact of the steps taken to alleviate these problems was a further slide in standards of living. Some analysts predicted production could fall more than 20 percent in 1992. Inflation was expected to run about 1,000 percent for 1992, and the liberalization of prices had wiped out the savings of most workers. The Yeltsin team knew that these blows to the average citizen could quickly lead to political upheaval. Therefore, they set their sights on halting the economic slide within one year, and hoped for growth as early as the first half of this decade.

What was clear was that Yeltsin's period of grace had come to an end. For some months his prominence and legitimacy allowed him to set reforms in motion by decree. But by the summer of 1992 the success or failure of Yeltsin's reforms depended on his ability to construct a working coalition that would back reforms. Given the strength of the opposition and the enormity of Russia's economic problems, maintaining such a coalition would be difficult.

CIS Economic Issues

Economic restructuring in Russia and the independent states was greatly complicated by the legacy of seventy years of forced economic unity. For many of the republics at least 90 percent of trade occurred with the other members of the Union. PlanEcon, a consulting firm, estimated that before 1992 nine of fifteen republics exported at least 60 percent of total production to the other republics of the Union. The economic survival of the independent states required a continuation of cooperation. But in many states political resistance to limitations on sovereignty threatened continued economic cooperation. *(Commonwealth economy, p. 150)*

Soviet policies also produced a situation in which many goods are made by single-location enterprises that hold a monopoly (over 90 percent of the former Soviet Union's production). Products produced almost entirely in a single location include concrete mixers (produced in Tuva, Russia), electric locomotives (Novocherkassk, Russia), locomotive cranes (Kirov, Russia), sewing machines (Podolsk, Russia), open-pit power shovels (Novokramatorsk, Ukraine), heavy dump trucks (Minsk, Belarus), cotton harvesters (Tashkent, Uzbekistan), aluminum foil (Kanaker, Armenia), air conditioners (Baku, Azerbaijan), and coated pipelines (Rustavi, Georgia). Many other products were produced in just two or three locations. Industries dependent on a particular monopolized product (such as the cotton industry's dependence on cotton harvesters) are vulnerable to strikes, political upheaval, high tariffs, or dramatic increases in price resulting from the conditions of monopoly. Without continued economic integration or extensive trade cooperation, the lack of diversification in the economy of the former Soviet Union could cripple whole economic sectors of individual states.

Recognizing their economic interdependence, the states of the former Soviet Union have attempted to maintain economic links. Eight of the countries signed an accord in March 1992 on free trade and customs. The states also have cooperated to maintain transportation and communication links between them and to jointly manage the USSR's debt. Even the Baltic states, which shunned membership in the CIS, tried to negotiate agreements to preserve some economic links.

Nevertheless, efforts of individual states to achieve total independence have weakened their economic ties. Major differences over economic issues quickly surfaced. In February 1992 all eleven CIS members agreed to augment interstate trade by maintaining the use of the ruble. Within several months, however, several states had taken steps to establish their own currency. By August, Estonia, Latvia, and Azerbaijan had issued new national currencies. Several other states, including Ukraine, were on a timetable to do so.

Developments in Russia—and perhaps Ukraine—undoubtedly have a large impact on the economies of their neighbors. The newly independent states protested that Russia was forcing reforms on them faster than they would like. Russia's January 2, 1992, price liberalization, for example, forced other states to similarly release prices. Without comparable domestic reforms, the authorities in Ukraine and elsewhere recognized that lower prices in their nation would attract rubles from Russia and lead to an excessive outflow of goods and services.

An important change that followed economic independence was Russia's abandonment of its role as a "cash cow" for the other states. Before the break-up of the Soviet Union, Moscow heavily subsidized trade with the other republics in an effort to maintain political stability. This was accomplished through artificial pricing—natural resources were sold to the republics at artificially low prices. If world market prices were used in all exchanges, most of the republics would have posted huge trade deficits with Russia. Estimates of the level of subsidization run as high as 7 percent of the former Soviet Union's GNP.

Post-Soviet Russia was not willing to continue broad financing of these deficits. Therefore each state had to reduce consumption of many traditional inputs from Russia. The impact was in places severe, as prices began to spiral and production slumped throughout the CIS. Russia moved toward ending significant capital flows to other republics, leaving them to finance their own development.

Russia, then, had the most to gain from a switch to world market prices, while countries that possessed few raw materials and produced an abundance of low-quality consumer products had the most to lose. The argument for Russia's moving ahead independently and rapidly to world pricing was compelling. As John Van Oudenaren of the Rand Corporation told the *New York Times*,

"There is no advantage in preserving a union in which you can only move as fast as the slowest actor."

The pace and scope of reform in each former republic was driven by local conditions. The resource-poor Baltic states, for example, needed to find new markets for their products, and therefore moved quickly to implement market reforms and liberalize their approach to trade. Some Central Asian republics, however, were able to delay key reforms because raw material resources and ready markets insulated them somewhat.

Problem Sectors

In addition to achieving fundamental reform such as lifting price controls, privatizing industry, and encouraging domestic investment and entrepreneurship, the states of the former Soviet Union had to address specific problems in key sectors of the economy. Three sectors of particular concern were agriculture, energy, and international economic relations.

Agriculture

For decades agriculture was a major stumbling block for the Soviet economy. Improving farm efficiency, however, has never been more crucial to a Moscow government than it is now for Boris Yeltsin. Importing large quantities of grain requires hard currency that would be available for other purposes, and the availability of food that is both high in quality and affordable would be an enormous boost to consumer confidence. If agricultural production does not improve, food shortages could ignite civil unrest.

An early priority of the Bolshevik regime was to reach an accommodation with the peasants that would overcome their anti-Bolshevik sentiments and ensure adequate food supplies in the cities. Although Lenin ordered forced requisitions of grain during the War Communism period (1918-1921), he sought to establish working relations with the peasantry during the New Economic Policy of the 1920s. The state promised to provide more con-

Some of the first settlers of the Virgin Lands pitch their tents in the early 1950s.

sumer goods to the villages and to use a *prodnalog* (tax in kind) instead of requisitions to acquire agricultural goods.

In the late 1920s Stalin returned to the use of requisitions and began mass collectivization of the peasantry into communal farms *(kolkhozi)*. Many poorer peasants actively supported collectivization because the program took land from the richer peasants *(kulaks)*. The policy escalated out of control, however, and peasants who resisted collectivization were labeled kulaks and deported to labor camps. Alec Nove described the short-term results: "The peasants were demoralized. Collective farms were inefficient, the horses slaughtered or starving [peasants slaughtered their animals instead of turning them over to the authorities], tractors as yet too few and poorly maintained, transport facilities inadequate, the retail distribution system utterly disorganized by an over-precipitate abolition of private trade." The establishment of collectivized agriculture was brutal, and the system failed to fulfill the Soviet Union's food needs.

Agricultural reform was a high priority for Khrushchev and Brezhnev. As Nove states, Khrushchev's Virgin Lands program "between 1953 and 1956 increased cultivated land by 35 million hectares, an

area equivalent to the total cultivated land of Canada. World history knows nothing like it." Brezhnev used river diversion and land reclamation schemes to further increase Soviet arable lands.

Despite these aggressive investment programs, growth of agricultural output fell further below domestic needs, leaving the Soviets, in the 1970s, dependent on grain imports. Soviet authorities also attempted to improve agricultural productivity by allowing more private plots and private food markets where prices were not strictly controlled. During much of the 1970s and 1980s private plots used less than 3 percent of arable land but produced about 30 percent of total agricultural output. Their success demonstrated that the most serious defect of the Soviet agricultural system was a lack of incentive to produce on state-owned farms. Collective farmers are paid on a wage basis, not for the output of their land. Consequently, they have little incentive to use state-owned land efficiently.

Under Gorbachev, the government searched for ways to improve agricultural production. Gorbachev revived a Khrushchev concept—independent brigades. These brigades consisted of ten or twelve collective farm peasants who would work a designated portion of the land on the farm. They would receive extra wages if they achieved above-plan output. Gorbachev also established an agricultural super-ministry—*Gosagroprom*. It was to coordinate the industrial, research, and economic needs of the agricultural sector.

Despite these moves and an increase in investment, agricultural output remained static at best (declines of 2.5 and 2 percent in 1987 and 1988, and growth of only 1.9 percent in 1989). Responding to these failures, Gorbachev announced in February 1990 that "all obstacles should be removed in the way of the farmer, he should be given a free hand." Toward this end, the government officially encouraged the establishment of private farms, and farmers were permitted to lease collective-farm property. In early 1990 the government also advocated inheritance of private land by the owner's children.

Gorbachev's policies, however, failed to substantially increase the productivity of Soviet farms, in part because the agricultural sector was not immune to the disarray of the entire economy. Reductions in the supply of oil and other necessary agricultural inputs, which had been provided by the state, hampered grain production. According to Soviet estimates, wheat production fell by 60 million tons in 1991.

The Yeltsin government's freeing of prices in January 1992 created more short-term problems for farmers. The prices farmers could get for many agricultural products increased as much as ten times. But the prices of machinery, spare parts, tools, construction materials, fertilizers, and fuel rose much faster. Both private and state-run farms had to go deeply in debt to stay in operation.

A major problem for both private and public farmers has been the poor state of rural infrastructure. The lack of proper storage and transportation facilities causes losses of up to 30 percent of agricultural output. In fact, a mission by the U.S. Department of Agriculture in 1991 found that the Soviet Union produced enough food to feed the population, but that the loss of up to 50 percent of some commodities showed that "distribution, more than production, is at the heart of the USSR's food problem." Reforms must encompass not only farmers and their land, but also the structures that transport, store, and market agricultural products.

Farmers also must cope with the lack of a private supply network. Until now, farmers did not worry about supply lines or marketing networks. Today's farmers either have to create their own rural infrastructure or wait for private businesses to fill the gaps.

Privatization is seen as the key to increased production, but the former Soviet states have made only modest progress toward this goal. Private farmers numbered only 100,000 in April 1992. About 80 percent of farms in Russia were still state-run collectives. According to Russian government statistics, more than half of all private farms in Russia lack electricity. Because of the scarcity of machinery, private farmers have had to band together to share tractors, trucks, and other implements. Private farming by individuals also has been hampered by the lack of comprehensive farming knowledge among collective farmers, many of whom are specialists at a single task.

The most formidable obstacle to privatization of agriculture probably continues to be rural conservatism. As the *Financial Times* pointed out,

> The principle is indeed difficult to comprehend for peasants used to being looked after by a state on land which was supposed to belong to everybody. . . . Their psychology is a preference that all should be poor together, rather than allow the more enterprising to be better off.

This mind-set pits private farmers against their neighbors in state farms who challenge their right to own land and against local authorities who see private farmers as a threat to their political power. The battle between these two ideologies will determine whether Russia's capacity to feed itself will once again be fulfilled.

Energy

Revitalizing the energy sector and energy production is central to the ultimate economic success of Russia and the CIS. The revitalization of industry requires a steady, affordable supply of energy to run machinery and transportation networks. In addition, oil and natural gas have been the former Soviet Union's most important hard currency exports.

Russia is the only major industrial nation not dependent on foreign sources of energy. It has the largest reserve of oil in the world outside the Persian Gulf. It also has more than 37 percent of the world's proven natural gas reserves, abundant coal supplies, and an effective hydroelectric program. Finally, nuclear power plants produce about 6 percent of the former Soviet Union's power, though safety considerations in the wake of the Chernobyl nuclear disaster in 1986 may curtail the role of nuclear energy.

However, what Leslie Dienes of Radio Liberty called "crash programs involving massive infusions of resources, hasty improvisation, and gigantic waste" have produced a collapse in the energy sector. As in agriculture, the Soviets failed to develop an adequate infrastructure to support resource exploitation. They also failed to develop advanced energy-related technologies and shunned foreign investment in their energy structure. Only late in Gorbachev's tenure did the Soviet Union start charging world prices for oil delivered to their East European partners.

Although domestic oil and gas prices have been increased three to five times under Yeltsin, the price remains as much as forty times below world market prices—depending on the exchange rate used. Low official prices have encouraged enterprises to waste precious energy resources. The artificially low prices also have created conditions under which an energy resource black market can flourish.

Energy production has fallen drastically since 1988 and was expected to fall 10 percent in 1992. About one-seventh of the oil wells in the former Soviet Union are not operating. The *Financial Times* points out that "formerly oil-rich states . . . may become oil importers in the first half of the 1990s." Some of the downturn has been offset by natural gas production, which continues to grow and may eventually replace oil as the country's main foreign exchange earner. While energy shortages are causing lower production throughout the economy, the worst result of energy shortfalls was the loss of hard-currency income from exports.

Russian authorities now have decided to sell as much of their production as possible at world market prices. This has meant that traditional partners—Eastern Europe, Cuba, and the other former Soviet republics—bear the brunt of Russia's need for hard currency.

Russia and the independent states have found it difficult to develop the necessary technology to promote the energy sector. Major capital investments have become necessary to replace outdated energy production equipment. Foreign investors offer the best short-term solution to the problem of developing energy resources. Though the Soviets had many skilled workers and technicians in the field, Western technology in such areas as extraction and environmental protection is superior. Western oil companies also can provide the oil industry with management skills and greater understanding of the international marketplace.

Yeltsin's team has taken some key steps to liberalize rules that govern foreign energy investment, including allowing full foreign ownership of energy resources and removing restrictions on profit repatriation. PlanEcon has reported that Russia may sign as many as 50 deals with Western oil companies in 1992.

Nevertheless, despite the potential for mutually beneficial agreements between Western oil companies and the former Soviet states, foreign investors have been cautious. Through June 1992 foreign oil companies had invested just $200 million in the Commonwealth. Only 13,000 barrels of oil per day were produced by operations in which Western companies were participating. This compares with the CIS's total production of about 9 million barrels per day.

Foreign investors have a number of concerns. One is the uncertainty of who owns the rights to energy resources that Western companies are interested in developing. Officials at every level—federal, local, and even in the enterprises—proclaim jurisdiction over energy resources. Another major concern is the uncertain tax regime. For example, in early 1992 the Russian government announced a $6 a barrel export tax. Unless Russia, Kazakhstan, and other states with oil deposits can persuade Western oil companies that they will be able to repatriate

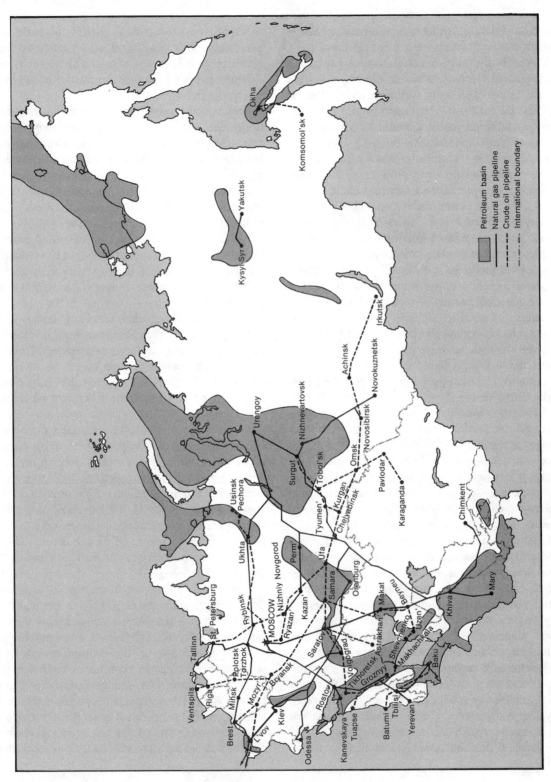

The oil and gas pipeline network of the former Soviet Union

Key:

- Petroleum basin
- Natural gas pipeline
- Crude oil pipeline
- International boundary

Ventspils, Riga, Tallinn, St Petersburg, Rybinsk, Torzhok, Polotsk, Minsk, Brest, Lvov, Kiev, Odessa, Mozyr, Bryansk, MOSCOW, Nizhniy Novgorod, Ryazan, Kazan, Perm, Ukhta, Pechora, Usinsk, Surgut, Urengoy, Nizhnevartovsk, Tobol'sk, Tyumen', Kurgan, Chelyabinsk, Omsk, Novosibirsk, Novokuznetsk, Achinsk, Irkutsk, Yakutsk, Kysyl-Syr, Komsomol'sk, Okha

Ufa, Samara, Orenburg, Saratov, Volgograd, Rostov, Kanevskaya, Tuapse, Tikhoretsk, Groznyy, Astrakhan, Makat, Beyheu, Shevchenko, Uzen, Makhachkala, Khiva, Mary, Chimkent, Karaganda, Pavlodar, Baku, Tbilisi, Yerevan, Batumi their profits and their investments will not be nationalized during some future political upheaval, investors will remain hesitant.

International Economic Relations

Before Mikhail Gorbachev came to power, deliberate economic isolationism was a trait of Soviet economic policy. The government severely restricted foreign investment, limiting foreign companies' interest in the Soviet economy.

Western policies also contributed to Soviet economic isolation. In 1974, after several years of improved trade relations between the United States and the Soviet Union, the U.S. Congress passed the Jackson-Vanik amendment. This legislation conditioned the granting of most-favored-nation (MFN) trading status on Moscow's willingness to liberalize its emigration policies. The Brezhnev government rejected this condition and the United States' attempt to use economic leverage to force political change in the Soviet Union.

Through CoCom (the Coordinating Committee on Multilateral Export Controls), Western nations jointly restricted since 1949 the transfer of high-technology goods to the Soviet Union. The primary purpose of CoCom was to prevent the Soviet Union from acquiring technology that could contribute to its industrial and military strength. In 1992 restrictions on technology transfers to the former Soviet republics were relaxed. Western governments also leveled economic sanctions against the Soviet Union in response to specific Soviet foreign policy activities, such as the invasion of Afghanistan in 1979 and the imposition of martial law in Poland in 1981.

Traditionally, trade authorities in Moscow prided themselves on maintaining balanced trade relations with their trade partners. The United States was one of the few countries with which the Soviets ran a trade deficit. This deficit was offset by a surplus vis-à-vis Western Europe. Moscow pursued trade with the West mainly when it needed food or technological imports not prohibited by CoCom. Trade with allies in Eastern Europe and other socialist states often resulted in economic losses for the Soviets. Moscow routinely subsidized exports (especially energy resources) to socialist nations in an effort to strengthen the economies of its allies and increase Soviet political leverage in those states.

Most items exported in large quantities were raw materials. In 1986 machinery, equipment, and consumer goods accounted for only $18 billion of the Soviet Union's total $97 billion in exports. The most important export was oil. This left the USSR vulnerable to oil price fluctuations. When the prices dipped, as they did in the 1980s, the Soviets experienced shortages of hard currency needed to pay for imported consumer goods and grain.

Gorbachev Program. Expanding international economic relations was an important feature of Mikhail Gorbachev's economic restructuring program. Gorbachev directed the State Committee for Foreign Economic Relations to allow enterprises to develop their own foreign trade relationships. He and his advisers hoped this measure would increase the flow of Western technology into the Soviet Union and improve the capacity of Soviet enterprises to export. Instead of enhancing the Soviet Union's export earnings, the liberalized trade rules allowed state-owned enterprises to increase rapidly the country's imports. For the first time the Soviets encountered major trade deficits (up to $16 billion in 1991), a growing foreign debt burden (more than $70 billion by fall 1992), and an inability to make payments on imports (enterprises had run up more than $5 billion in trade arrears by early 1990).

Gorbachev attempted to bring realism to the Soviet exchange rate regime. In 1989 his government devalued the exchange rate for tourists from 1 ruble per 1.6 dollars to 1 ruble per .16 dollars and announced plans for full currency reform in the early 1990s. In October 1989 the first currency auction where enterprises were able to buy hard currency at market rates was held. Nevertheless, the Soviets fell far short of establishing a fully convertible ruble.

Gorbachev also tried to enhance foreign investment by backing new laws that made joint ventures more attractive. By 1990, 1,274 joint-venture agreements had been signed, but many existed only on paper and foreign participation in the Soviet economy remained limited.

In 1991 imports fell nearly 50 percent from the previous year. The Soviets' continued exportation of raw materials produced a trade surplus, but the fall in imports caused reverberations throughout the economy, as necessary inputs were unavailable for certain industries. Soviet and Russian creditworthiness was downgraded by international credit markets. Western countries stepped in to help when the Soviets could no longer make debt payments. Meanwhile, the Soviet Union was negotiating entry into the International Monetary Fund (IMF), the International Bank for Reconstruction and Development, and other international organizations. Membership could provide technical expertise and financial support to help stabilize and restructure the economy. As the economic and financial situation deteriorated further, Western donors began to offer direct humanitarian aid—particularly Germany, which wanted to encourage the rapid removal of remaining Soviet troops from the former East Germany.

Economic Relations under Yeltsin. Yeltsin and his team focused much effort on increasing international support for Russian economic reforms and international involvement in the Russian economy. Yeltsin stated that improved economic relations were vital to Russia's reform effort, its technological progress, and its future prosperity.

The Yeltsin government worked to craft a reform program that the International Monetary Fund and Western creditors would accept. In early 1992 it adopted a premembership, "shadow program" with the IMF, which gave preliminary approval to the plan on March 31, 1992. Then on April 27, 1992, Russia and most of the Soviet successor states were admitted as full members of the IMF and World Bank. The IMF, along with the World Bank and individual nations, announced their intention to provide large loans to Russia and the other former Soviet states that would support the stabilization of their currencies and the restructuring of their economies. Loans and other aid, however, were conditioned on adoption by the former Soviet states of acceptable reform programs.

The Yeltsin government and the IMF conducted tough negotiations on Russian commitments to free market reform. Resistance to Yeltsin's reforms in the Russian parliament slowed reform and delayed conclusion of a "standby agreement" between Russia and the IMF. A standby agreement is a detailed understanding between the IMF and a recipient nation on how reforms will proceed. Such an agreement is regarded as an IMF endorsement of a country's reforms by most private investors. The IMF's planned $4 billion "standby loan" and credits from other sources, including the World Bank and the Group of Seven (G-7) industrialized nations (which are awaiting an IMF endorsement), could not go forward without a standby agreement. Through August 1992, the IMF had declined to make such an endorsement, though IMF representatives indicated they were pleased by progress in some aspects of the Russian reform program, especially a drop in the rate of inflation. The IMF did, however, release a $1.04 billion interim loan to Russia.

The states of the former Soviet Union also sought bilateral aid from the industrialized nations. Following international assistance conferences in Washington in January and Lisbon in April 1992, the G-7 nations (the United States, Britain, France, Germany, Canada, Italy, and Japan) proposed more than $24 billion in assistance, including both bilateral and multilateral aid, contingent on adoption of an IMF standby agreement.

Yeltsin and leaders of the other former Soviet republics expanded on Gorbachev's opening to foreign trade and investment. Yegor Gaidar told the *Economist* in April, "Risk capital exists [internationally], and Russia is the best place in the world for it. We can get large amounts of western investment." Loosened investment regimes adopted in the former republics began to attract the interest of foreign firms.

Most private investors, however, took a cautious approach toward Russia and the other former Soviet states. The possibility that leaders who are less hospitable to foreign investment than Yeltsin will come to power and the Russian government's slow progress toward a fully convertible ruble hindered foreign trade and investment. The Russians counted on a $6 billion currency stabilization fund—part of the

$24 billion G-7 package—to help maintain the exchange rate.

Russia's Future

On the first anniversary of the failed coup, Yeltsin said in a televised speech: "We went into the water not knowing how to swim, but we didn't drown. Now we can show the best characteristics of Russians—patience, wisdom, initiative—as you showed in August 1991." The perseverance needed to stay the course on economic reform will be much greater than that required of the Russian people during the short-lived August 1991 coup.

The Yeltsin government is faced with building a working economy on the economic ruin of the old system. Poland, Hungary, and Czechoslovakia faced the same situation and made significant progress in establishing market economies. To some degree, they are models for Russia. In 1989 Polish president Lech Walesa joked that this process of resuscitating an economy was like making fried eggs after the eggs were already scrambled. Like its East European neighbors, Russia broke with the Stalinist legacy, but the task of creating a free market in its place is daunting.

Given Russia's great economic potential there is reason to be optimistic. If fully developed with modern technology, Russia's vast supplies of oil and other natural resources could fuel growth. International assistance and privatization could rapidly stimulate business activity.

But it is uncertain if Yeltsin's reform program can survive the political opposition that has been generated by the hardships of inflation, unemployment, and economic uncertainty. The peoples of Russia and the other former Soviet states have come to expect guaranteed employment, cradle-to-grave social services, and a business environment free of the fear of bankruptcy. As economic hardships mounted, workers and managers alike frequently remarked that they expected in the end that the government will bail them out as it has in the past.

Moreover, Russians were pessimistic about reforms when they began. A January 1992 poll found that almost 50 percent of Russian citizens felt that the situation would worsen in 1992. Conservatives whose privileges under the old Soviet system have been eroded by reforms used popular discontent to their own advantage. The government, therefore, has been slow to take on the toughest economic-political problems, such as how to limit government credits to state enterprises without forcing them into bankruptcies that would leave thousands of workers unemployed.

While the substance and scope of economic reform under Yeltsin changed dramatically from the Gorbachev years, the process of moving reforms ahead did not. Yeltsin, like Gorbachev, has constantly had to balance the progress of reforms against the political survival of his government and himself. Though Yeltsin's popular election and performance during the coup gave him the political resources to advance a radical reform plan, the exhaustion and pessimism most Russians feel substantially limit the time Yeltsin has to produce positive economic results.

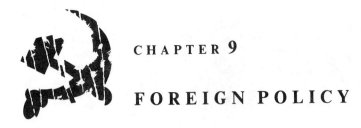

CHAPTER **9**

FOREIGN POLICY

Unlike economic reform, which did not greatly accelerate until after the breakup of the Soviet Union, Moscow's foreign policy was almost fully transformed under Mikhail Gorbachev. The growing economic and ethnic crises at home and a recognition that the existing confrontational posture abroad was counterproductive to Soviet interests led the Gorbachev government to adopt conciliatory policies aimed at eliminating military tensions and gaining Western economic assistance.

For most of its existence the Soviet Union had been inherently hostile toward the capitalist nations. The transformation of Soviet foreign policy in the late 1980s and early 1990s amounted to a gradual surrender in the decades-long cold war. The Soviets renounced Marxism-Leninism, withdrew from their Eastern European empire, cut off funding to Marxist clients in the developing world, reduced their defense expenditures, and vigorously pursued arms control.

Russian President Boris N. Yeltsin continued these policies and expanded upon them while wrestling with new problems stemming from the Soviet Union's breakup into fifteen new nations.

Soviet Foreign Policy

Almost since the October Revolution, Western observers have debated the role of ideology in Soviet foreign policy. The men who carried out the revolution were unshakable in their belief in communism. But it is unclear how much of Soviet foreign policy can be ascribed to ideology and how much has been based on cold calculations of the interests of the Soviet state.

In accordance with Marx's writings, the Bolsheviks expected that, following the revolution in Russia, other revolutions would occur throughout Europe, making traditional foreign policy unnecessary. After a world socialist revolution, the Bolsheviks believed, national boundaries would cease to have any meaning.

The Bolsheviks not only expected other revolutions, but they also depended on them. They believed that without the benefit of fraternal socialist nations in Western Europe, a single backward socialist Russia would not be able to survive. Marx wrote that the capitalist countries would see in the nascent socialist movement the seeds of their own destruction and would seek to crush it at any cost. Socialism would fight back using its inherently more powerful system of production and the loyalties it could call upon among the proletariat of the capitalist countries. The world would divide along class lines until the final victory of socialism.

So at first the Bolsheviks devoted themselves to fomenting revolution abroad and ignored most of the traditional niceties of diplomacy. In a famous episode Leon Trotsky, upon being named commissar for foreign affairs, declared that he would simply issue a few proclamations and then close down the ministry.

The expected revolutions, however, did not materialize. The Bolsheviks promoted the collapse of the tsar's army, believing that a socialist country would not need such an archaic institution. Meanwhile, during late 1917 and early 1918, German troops were advancing deep into Russian territory virtually unhindered. Instead of fighting them, the

Bolsheviks attending the Twelfth Party Congress pose in the Grand Palace of the Kremlin, 1923. Early Bolshevik foreign policy was more heavily influenced by ideology than was Stalinist policy.

Bolsheviks tried to persuade the German soldiers that serving in the army went against their class interests and that they should revolt. This failed to stop the advance and the Bolsheviks were forced to accept harsh peace terms in the Treaty of Brest-Litovsk, giving away territory containing about a quarter of the population of the Russian empire. *(Brest-Litovsk, p. 36)*

Ideology vs. State Interest

After the early 1920s, when it became obvious that a wider European socialist revolution was not imminent, Soviet leaders often subordinated ideology to pragmatic calculations of state interest when formulating foreign policy. Nevertheless, until Mikhail Gorbachev initiated his policy of "new thinking" Soviet leaders insisted that their foreign policy (like their domestic policy) was scientifically determined, and that it sprang directly from the writings of Karl Marx and Vladimir Lenin.

When Soviet leaders found Marxist-Leninist ideology to be inconvenient, they modified it to conform with their conception of the prevailing interests of the Soviet state. In 1928 Joseph Stalin discarded the notion that immediate world revolution was essential for building socialism when he adopted the doctrine of "socialism in one country." Because other revolutions were not forthcoming, Stalin proposed that the best way to advance socialism was to strengthen the Soviet Union, the world's only socialist state, against expected capitalist attacks. Following this principle, Stalin launched a massive industrialization effort, while relegating foreign relations to a secondary status.

Protecting the motherland was the justification for the 1939 Molotov-Ribbentrop Pact with Nazi Germany. The pact, which pledged nonaggression between the two powers and carved up Eastern Europe into spheres of domination, shocked many Soviet citizens and foreign communists because Hitler's National Socialist ideology was hostile to communism. The Soviets justified the pact, however, as the best way to avoid war and protect the gains of socialism. Later Stalin's supporters claimed that the two years of peace between the signing of the pact and the 1941 German invasion had allowed the Soviet Union to better prepare for the war.

"Peaceful coexistence" was Nikita Khrushchev's contribution to Soviet foreign policy doctrine. Lenin had coined the phrase, but Khrushchev gave it new meaning for the atomic age. He argued that the advent of nuclear weapons made it exceedingly dangerous to insist that armed conflict with the West was inevitable (as Stalin had done). Khrushchev said that because of the enormous destructive potential of nuclear weapons, both the socialist and capitalist states would avoid armed conflict that could result in their destruction. Competition would move instead to the economic arena, where he was confident that socialism, with its superior economic mechanism, would "catch up and surpass" capitalism.

The socialist-capitalist competition continued under Leonid I. Brezhnev, but under the conditions of détente. Beginning in 1968, the Soviet Union signed a series of treaties with the United States, and relations became warmer than at any time since the end of World War II.

Correlation of Forces

In Marxist-Leninist theory, the sum of all factors that affect political influence and dynamism—economic, political, and military strength; national confidence; ideology; alliance relationships; and so on—is known as the correlation of forces. Under Brezhnev, Moscow believed that the correlation of forces was finally beginning to turn decisively in the direction of socialism. The Soviets had achieved rough nuclear parity with the United States in the late 1960s, had shown the political will to use their new muscle (in Czechoslovakia for example), and were aggressively pursuing their interests around the globe. Many different factors are included in the correlation-of-forces model, but Brezhnev regarded the massive Soviet military build-up as the key component.

For the Soviets, détente was a codification of their equal status with the United States. They believed that the United States had been forced to the negotiating table by the growing power of the Soviet Union. The Americans could not dictate terms from a position of strength and were thus forced to seek accommodation through negotiation. According to an old axiom of tsarist policy, resorting to diplomacy is itself a demonstration of the failure of policy.

Brezhnev saw détente as a green light from the United States to proceed as he wished. The rapid growth of Soviet defense expenditures continued. Meanwhile, the Soviet Union became involved in one Third World country after another in an attempt to expand its influence beyond Europe's deadlocked borders and to further improve the correlation of forces. Under Brezhnev, the Soviet Union for the first time began committing ground troops, and the troops of its proxies, to distant conflicts around the globe. During the second half of the Brezhnev period, the Soviet Union and its proxies introduced troops into Afghanistan, Angola, Cambodia, Ethiopia, Grenada, and South Yemen.

The correlation-of-forces model assumed that other states would seek accommodation with the Soviet Union when it was clear that socialism was gaining ground globally. But this assumption proved to be incorrect. Relations with the other major powers worsened significantly during the late 1970s and early 1980s, as the United States, Western Europe, China, and Japan moved more aggressively to contain Soviet expansionism and match the growth of Soviet military power.

The Soviets had expected that the West would be forced to continue détente, despite its objection to many Soviet activities. But the United States and its allies never felt so compelled. In 1979 the U.S. Senate refused to ratify the SALT II Treaty. Reacting to the Soviet invasion of Afghanistan, the West imposed sanctions and the United States supplied arms to Afghan guerrillas fighting the Soviets. American defense spending began to increase under President Jimmy Carter and accelerated rapidly under President Ronald Reagan in the early 1980s. Relations became further strained with the declaration of martial law in Poland in 1981 and the Soviets' downing of a Korean Airlines jet in 1983. Western Europe permitted the installation of U.S.-made Pershing II intermediate-range nuclear missiles in 1983, despite heavy Soviet pressure to reject the deployment. While Sino-Soviet relations remained cool during the 1970s and 1980s, Sino-American relations improved dramatically following President Richard Nixon's trip to China in 1972 and Carter's 1979 recognition of the People's Republic of China. Meanwhile the invasion of Afghanistan had cost the Soviet Union much good will throughout the Islamic and developing worlds.

The "New Thinking"

By 1985 when Gorbachev came to power, the perceived improvement in the correlation of forces had not led to foreign policy gains. Instead, the Soviet search for absolute security and superpower status through military strength and an expansion of influence abroad had led to a high level of global tension and to the hostile opposition of most of the industrialized world. Soviet policy had created new threats and greater insecurity than before. In addition, massive expenditures on the military had impoverished other sectors of the Soviet economy. Even Soviet successes in the developing world were tarnished. Propping up marginally loyal pro-Soviet governments in strategically unimportant countries with foreign aid and military commitments had become a costly expense that was hard to justify.

Gorbachev, therefore, had inherited a foreign policy that was failing to correspond to real international conditions and the needs of his country. In response he advanced a fundamental reform of Soviet foreign policy that he labeled the "new thinking." Under the new thinking, Gorbachev and his foreign minister, Eduard Shevardnadze, led a movement to redefine national security and de-ideologize foreign policy.

Learning from the bitter lessons of the Treaty of Brest-Litovsk, the Soviets were firm believers in the value of military strength for achieving foreign policy goals. Under Brezhnev in particular, military might was seen as the road to security. The stronger the military, the more secure the country would be. Gorbachev, however, developed a much broader definition of security. He maintained that because no military means exist of repelling a nuclear attack once launched, the strongest military could not absolutely ensure a nation's security. In his 1987 book *Perestroika: New Thinking for Our Country and the World,* Gorbachev wrote that "Security can no longer be secured through military means. ... The only way to security is through political decisions and disarmament."

Foreign Minister Shevardnadze's speech to the Twenty-eighth Party Congress in July 1990 now seems prescient.

One can arm oneself to the teeth and still be afraid of attack. But it is also possible to be sure that you will not be attacked because your policy creates conditions where the country will have no enemies or opponents. ...
Clearly, if we continue the way we have done it before, ... that is to spend one fourth of our budget on military expenditures ... we will ruin the country.... We simply would need no defense because a ruined country and a poor people do not need an army.

In accordance, the Soviet Union reduced its military spending and vigorously pursued arms control initiatives with the United States. In 1987, after making significant concessions, Gorbachev signed the Intermediate Nuclear Forces (INF) treaty with the United States. This treaty provided for the elimination of all missiles with ranges between 300 and 3,400 miles. It also encouraged the Soviet Union and the United States to accelerate work on other arms control initiatives. *(INF Treaty, p. 227)*

In addition to arms control, the new thinking's redefinition of national security could be seen in Moscow's refusal to intervene militarily to prevent the collapse of Eastern Europe's communist regimes in 1989. The Soviet Union also withdrew its troops from Afghanistan during 1988 and 1989, thus freeing itself from a conflict that had cost billions of rubles and had hindered improved relations with numerous other countries.

Under Gorbachev ideological rhetoric largely disappeared from Soviet foreign policy statements. In effect, the new thinking was a decision to become a cooperative member of the international community. The Soviet Union would continue to defend itself and act in its self-interest, but the increasingly unsuccessful ideological trench warfare that had characterized Soviet foreign policy (even during the days of détente) was to be abandoned.

In a dramatic speech before the United Nations General Assembly on December 7, 1988, Mikhail Gorbachev announces unilateral troop reductions and the deideologization of Soviet foreign policy.

In his historic speech before the United Nations on December 7, 1988, Gorbachev said that the new thinking includes "deideologizing the relations between states. We are not abandoning our convictions, our philosophy, or our traditions, but neither do we have any intention to be hemmed in by our values."

Russian Foreign Policy under Yeltsin

After the Soviet Union ceased to exist, Russia claimed to be the successor state to the Soviet Union. Given Russia's size, its military strength, its central position in the new Commonwealth of Independent States, and Boris Yeltsin's intention to continue to cultivate good relations with the West, there was little objection outside the former Soviet Union to Russia's assuming this role.

Russian foreign minister Andrei Kozyrev has written that, as an independent country, "Russia will not cease to be a great power. But it will be a normal great power. Its national interests will be a priority. But these will be interests understandable to democratic countries, and Russia will be defend-ing them through interaction with partners, not through confrontation."

So far Russia has lived up to this policy declaration. It has shunned confrontation in favor of cooperation with the world community. It has pursued collective solutions to regional problems while opening itself up to trade and economic assistance from the West. Ironically, perhaps the greatest possibility is for Russia to become involved in a conflict in the short term with the other former Soviet states. The presence of significant Russian minorities in neighboring states is creating tensions as Moscow attempts to ensure the interests of ethnic Russians.

Few nations have ceased to regard Russia as a great power, even though it is now playing a much smaller role in international affairs than it was during the Soviet period. This diminishment of relevance, however, is due less to the breakup of the Soviet Union than to Russia's prostrate economic situation. The Russians understand that economic reform and revitalization demand most of their energies and nearly all their resources. If Russia succeeds in rebuilding its economy, history would suggest that Russia will reassert itself in international affairs.

Russia and Messianism

A certain amount of messianism always has been an element in Russian foreign policy. Communist internationalism is only the most recent example. Under the early tsars, Muscovy saw itself as the third Rome, moral successor to the Roman and Byzantine empires, which had been overrun by infidels. This gave Russian expansionism a moral justification and a civilizing mission.

The sense of mission in Russian foreign policy has largely been replaced with more traditional calculations of national interest, but it still exists. Sergei Stankevich, state counselor of the Russian Federation for policy issues, has argued that the Russian nature demands that foreign policy must include some sort of mission:

Categorical assertions to the effect that Russia is required to immediately renounce messianism have been heard increasingly of late. If what is meant is a renunciation of the global mentorship of the communist rulers who stinted on either other's money or other's lives ... there is no point in arguing with this proposition. But what if we should rush to the other extreme: go so far in our denial of messianism as to jettison the similar sounding, but not identical, concept of "mission." A policy that is built on interests alone is highly vulnerable, and in Russia, in my view, it would be disastrous. Aside from interests, a mission, not degenerating into messianism of course, is needed.

Stankevich's proposed mission is for Russia to operate as a bridge between the countries of East and West.

Another mission for Russia is to act as protector of the millions of Russians now scattered among the other fourteen former Soviet republics. Under Kozyrev, Russia has developed a new-found interest in the international protection of human rights. He has strongly indicated that protecting the human rights of Russians abroad is his primary foreign policy goal with respect to the other CIS countries. While he has insisted repeatedly that this would be accomplished within the appropriate legal framework, Kozyrev has hinted that, if necessary, Russia would use force to protect the rights of Russians in other states.

Although the Soviet Union made dramatic improvements in human rights under Gorbachev, he never dropped his assertion that human rights were an internal matter and no one else's business. Kozyrev, however, has advanced the principle enshrined in numerous international documents that a state's human rights violations are a legitimate concern of other countries and international organizations. He supports strengthening the Conference on Security and Cooperation in Europe as an agent of human rights enforcement, and he has called for its more active involvement in the former Soviet republics. Kozyrev has stated: "The creation of a civilized society in the Russian Federation is impossible without full protection of human rights. With this in view, we try to use international mechanisms and promote, to a certain extent, interference into our internal affairs."

Russia as a Great Power

Russia has been a major force in international affairs for a thousand years. Stripped of the outlying regions of its vast empire, Russia may no longer be a superpower, but it can claim great power status. Russia still possesses the 150 million people of the Russian Federation, a tremendous industrial base, vast natural resources, and a large share of Soviet military power.

Many scholars are now reexamining the behavior of tsarist Russia, seeking clues on what to expect from the new Russian state. To a certain extent, Russia's geography, neighbors, and national character will determine its interests and goals. But the experiences of the Soviet period also will profoundly affect Russian foreign policy.

While the new Russian government will certainly make many mistakes and false starts, it is unlikely to repeat the more egregious errors made by previous regimes. For example, the Romanov Dynasty and the 1917 Provisional Government of Alexander Kerensky were both directly brought down by forcing the country to fight a massive foreign war for which it was completely unprepared and unwilling. The communists directed tremendous resources into a military buildup and bloody foreign involvements (primarily Afghanistan) that ultimately became a burden the country could not sustain. These lessons will not be easily forgotten, although they are tempered by the bitter memories of an unprepared Russia, forced to suffer through three years of German occupation during World War II.

The international environment is profoundly different and less hostile today than that faced by Tsar Nicholas II or the early communist regime. The Bolsheviks were inherently hostile and suspicious of the other major powers and would have been so regardless of the behavior of the other countries. But this should not obscure the reality that the United States, Great Britain, France, and others were displeased with this new regime that had taken their Russian ally out of World War I, and that they sent troops to fight with the Whites in the Russian civil war.

Today, nearly every major country has given its verbal, and in many cases material, support to the Yeltsin government. Tensions have all but disappeared and billions of dollars in aid are pouring into the CIS. While a certain Russian suspicion of the outside world is inherent, this outpouring of good will likely will have an impact on future Russian calculations regarding their role in the world.

Domestic Context of Foreign Policy

The serious domestic problems faced by Gorbachev were an important factor in the development of the new thinking. Ballooning internal problems had become so severe that the leadership could no longer muster the necessary resources to continue the old style of foreign policy. The domestic crisis has worsened dramatically under Yeltsin, eliminating for the time being the option of pursuing an active foreign policy. The resources simply are not available. Even disregarding such costly undertakings as military expansion or foreign aid, the Soviet Union has struggled to pay its share of the expenses of the Madrid stage of the Middle East process, about a million dollars.

Foreign policy is now being used primarily as a tool to develop a supportive international environment for Russian domestic policy. As stated by Yeltsin, Russian foreign policy has two main tasks: "to secure Russia's entry into the civilized [world] community" and "to enlist maximum support for efforts toward Russia's transformation."

This is a fundamental change from the traditional tsarist and Soviet approach of harnessing domestic policy for foreign policy ends. A powerful military, extracted from the poor Russian peasantry with tremendous suffering, was the tsars' primary tool in promoting Russian interests abroad. In the early 1930s Stalin drove the country in a massive industrialization drive at a cost that can be counted in the millions of lives. The primary purpose was to modernize and expand the military, preparing the country for the expected conflict with a resurgent Germany. Since that time, the economy has been top heavy with heavy industry and arms production and lacking in light industry and production of consumer goods.

Under Yeltsin, efforts to preserve Russia's status in the world and to maintain its political and military influence abroad as a superpower have been largely set aside as the country struggles on the brink of collapse. He has focused efforts in foreign policy on proving that Russia is a good candidate for aid and investment and creating a peaceful and cooperative international environment for Russia's reform program.

Multiple Tracks of Russian Foreign Policy

The new Russian government is pursuing two sets of relationships simultaneously: those with the West and those with the CIS countries. Close to home, good relations and relative stability among the CIS countries are absolutely critical for the Russian reforms to succeed. Kozyrev has stated that this is his foremost foreign policy concern. If relations with Ukraine or Kazakhstan sour or lead to conflict, Yeltsin's reform program is doomed and good relations with the West will do little to ease the blow.

Fighting among the other states of the former Soviet Union, such as Armenia and Azerbaijan, also creates problems for Russia. Agreements between CIS nations become more difficult to achieve, the conflicts produce refugees, and economic disruptions caused by the fighting hamper economic recovery for the CIS as a whole because of the tight economic integration between the new states.

Despite Kozyrev's emphasis on relations with Russia's neighbors, he has had greater success in dealing with the West. He has declared that

Russia must join the club of the most dynamically developing democratic states in order to occupy among them the fitting place that history and geography have ordained we should hold. We have the United States (via the Bering Strait), Japan, and Western Europe as neighbors. We have simply no insurmountable disagreements or conflicts of interests with this category of countries; indeed, we have every possibility of having friendly relations and in the long term even alliance relations with them.

The strong Western orientation of Kozyrev's policies has produced closer ties and pledges of aid from the former enemies of the Soviet Union. But this orientation has been criticized by more conservative Russians. Stankevich has characterized Kozyrev's efforts as "hastily pulling onto the broad Russian shoulders the Atlantic dinner jacket and bow tie."

In geography and national identity, Russia is a country that straddles both East and West. Kozyrev's search for close ties with the West is understandable. Only the West can supply the aid, commercial links, and investment that Russia needs. But Russian ties with the West have always been marked by a degree of hesitation and suspicion. Despite the current close coordination, such sentiments are being voiced in Russia in criticism of Kozyrev's Western slant.

Relations with Europe

At the end of World War II, when Soviet troops were moving westward across Europe, Stalin drove them onward as rapidly as possible, often sustaining losses far greater than necessary, to cover as much territory as possible before the Americans arrived. Once the land was occupied, the actual consolidation of communist power was a fairly slow process in most of Eastern Europe, lasting several years. The

complete overturning of society, including massive collectivization and nationalization with indiscriminant use of terror, did not begin in earnest until 1948.

In that year, fearing the spread of Josep Broz Tito's independent style of communism from Yugoslavia to the rest of Eastern Europe, and feeling American pressure from the Truman Doctrine and Marshall Plan, Stalin speeded up the pace of change. Eastern Europe was rapidly rebuilt on the Soviet model. Massive purges of suspected Titoists were carried out, much like the Soviet show trials of the thirties. During the years from 1948 to the Twentieth Party Congress in 1956 the leaders of Eastern Europe came to base their rule almost entirely on Soviet support. From that time forward, the leaders of Eastern Europe struggled unsuccessfully for popular support. Their failure was evidenced by the rapid tumbling of one regime after another in 1989 when Soviet support was withdrawn.

The steady consolidation of communist power led to increasing apprehension in the West. On April 4, 1949, the North Atlantic Treaty was signed by twelve countries, including the United States, Great Britain, and France. This was seen by Moscow as a clear threat to its empire. In 1954 West Germany was admitted as a full member of NATO. In retaliation for the rearming of West Germany, Moscow and its East European allies signed the Warsaw Pact the following year.

De-Stalinization

Beginning with Khrushchev's famous Secret Speech condemning Stalin before the Twentieth Congress of the Soviet Communist Party in 1956, there was a steady relaxation of political control throughout the Soviet Union and Eastern Europe. Tight limits on conformity were relaxed. Tito was welcomed back into the communist fold, undermining the leaders of Eastern Europe who had made careers out of following Stalin and purging alleged Titoists. In Poland and Hungary, Stalinist leaders were deposed for more moderate nationalist communists with Soviet approval. In Poland, Wladislaw

Gomulka oversaw de-Stalinization while maintaining the party's authority—although just barely. In Hungary, relaxation triggered more demands, to the point that on November 1, 1956, the new Nagy government announced Hungary's withdrawal from the Warsaw Pact and the creation of a multiparty system. The result was a swift and bloody invasion by Soviet troops a few days later. Such measures were not used again until the 1968 Prague Spring.

In the case of Czechoslovakia, in the late 1960s a liberal communist regime had agreed to democratization and an open press, seriously threatening the Communist party monopoly of power. Once again, the Soviets felt compelled to invade. The invasion was justified after the fact by the Brezhnev Doctrine, published in Pravda on September 25, 1968. The Brezhnev Doctrine explained that relations among socialist states were different from those among capitalist states. Whenever socialism was threatened in any one country, the socialist bloc as a whole had an obligation to intervene to protect it. (Invasion of Czechoslovakia, p. 88)

The New Thinking in Eastern Europe

By the 1980s Moscow was faced with the breakdown of communist control in many parts of Eastern Europe. Protests were seen in every country except Bulgaria. Poland in particular seemed on the verge of a collapse. Under the Brezhnev Doctrine, the Soviets would have intervened to support their satellites. However, several factors caused the Soviet leadership to reject this approach. A Soviet military intervention would have been the death knell for the improvement of relations with Western Europe and the United States that Gorbachev sought and would have put unbearable strains on an already restless Soviet society. The old approach to Eastern Europe was also interfering with Gorbachev's program of perestroika. To achieve his goals, Gorbachev required a completely new approach to the region.

At the end of Gorbachev's 1988 visit to Yugoslavia, a joint communiqué was issued clearly rejecting the Brezhnev Doctrine and affirming the principles of "mutual respect for independence, sovereignty, and territorial integrity, equality and impermissibil-

ity of interference in internal matters under any pretext whatsoever." Soviet foreign ministry spokesman Gennady Gerasimov quipped that the "Sinatra Doctrine" was in force in Eastern Europe. Those countries were free to "do it their way."

Despite all of these declarations, most Western observers believed that if communist regimes were threatened in Eastern Europe, Gorbachev would still take some sort of steps, be they military, economic, or diplomatic, to keep communists in power and the Warsaw Pact intact. Only when the Solidarity government headed by Prime Minister Tadeusz Mazowiecki came to power in Poland in August 1989 did it become evident how serious Gorbachev was.

The changes that occurred in Eastern Europe in 1989 followed two very different paths, although they headed toward the same results. Hungary and Poland had struggled with reforms for years. Consequently, both countries became early supporters of Gorbachev and perestroika. In Bulgaria, Czechoslovakia, East Germany, and Romania, however, the hardline leaders did whatever was necessary to maintain their power as long as possible, giving in to demands for change only after hundreds of thousands had taken to the streets to demand it. All six countries, however, experienced revolutions that fundamentally changed the old order.

With the collapse of the Eastern European satellites, Soviet relations with Western Europe shifted markedly. Fears of a Soviet invasion disappeared. Europe, formerly divided into two armed camps—NATO and the Warsaw Pact—became unified as the former satellites scrambled to develop economic and political relations with Western Europe. A number of the countries of Eastern Europe and the CIS countries have even expressed their interest in membership in the European Community and NATO.

Germany. The most dramatic events of 1989 took place in East Germany. Erick Honecker, the Communist leader of the German Democratic Republic (GDR), had long rejected the idea that perestroika was applicable to East Germany. He said it was a solution to Soviet problems, not German ones.

Austrian foreign minister Alois Mock and Hungarian foreign minister Gyula Horn cut the barbed wire on the Austrian-Hungarian border, July 27, 1989.

The revolutionary course in East Germany was catalyzed by Hungary's announcement that it was tearing down its border fences with Austria as part of its liberalization process. During the summer of 1989, thousands of East Germans traveled to Hungary and flooded across the open border to Austria, and from there to West Germany, where they were automatically given West German citizenship, a luxury not enjoyed by other refugees. In response, travel to Hungary was restricted, causing thousands to flee to the West German embassy in Prague, because Czechoslovakia was the only other country to which East Germans could freely travel without a visa. Travel to Czechoslovakia was soon cut off as well.

This move caused East Germany to explode. Thousands began marching for democracy in Leipzig in weekly demonstrations that became steadily larger. The Leipzig police refused to fire on the demonstrators, despite orders from East Berlin to use any means necessary to stop them. The central government was unprepared to cope with the hundreds of thousands of people in the streets and on October 18, 1989, Honecker resigned and was replaced by Egon Krenz, the former chief of security.

Krenz promised to follow a more moderate path. He traveled to Moscow and proclaimed himself a disciple of perestroika on his return. On November 9, 1989, he opened the Berlin Wall. Extensive economic and political changes were promised, but the protests continued. Within a month, Krenz and his whole government had been forced to resign. Hans Modrow, a moderate Communist leader from Dresden, formed an interim government in coalition with several opposition groups to prepare for elections.

As in Hungary, left-wing parties were defeated at the polls. The Christian Democratic Union (the party of conservative West German chancellor Helmut Kohl) gained the most seats in the parliament and began moving quickly toward unification.

The first step in unification was a monetary union that replaced the virtually worthless East German currency (ostmark) with the West German deutschemark on July 2, 1990. The so-called four plus two conference, composed of the four victors of World War II—Britain, France, the Soviet Union, and the United States—plus the two German states, hammered out the formal political conditions of unification. This culminated in the powers agreeing on October 1, 1991, to give up their status as occupiers of the divided Germany. Formal unification took place two days later.

By far, Germany has been the most generous in providing aid to the Soviet Union and now Russia. In unification, Germany has gained the most from the Soviet retreat from Europe. Yet many Russians still nervously recall the bitter three-year German occupation of their country during World War II and view unification with tremendous misgivings. Under a treaty signed days after unification, former Soviet troops are being pulled out of eastern Germany in a withdrawal that will be completed by the end of 1994. To ease the withdrawal and alleviate Russian fears, Germany has provided more than 75 billion deutschemarks of aid. Much of it will directly offset the cost of withdrawing Russian troops from Eastern Germany, including German construction of tens of thousands of apartments in Russia for the returning troops.

Helsinki Conference

More than any other organization, the Conference on Security and Cooperation in Europe (CSCE), known as the Helsinki Conference, has become the vehicle for promoting a unified Europe and working to resolve European security problems. The Helsinki Final Act, signed by the heads of state of thirty-five countries (including the United States and Canada) on August 1, 1975, was the political settlement of World War II. It recognized all established borders in Europe. It also pledged the signatories to act in accordance with a number of international human rights principles.

All of the countries from the former Yugoslavia and the former Soviet Union have joined the Helsinki Conference, expanding its membership to fifty-two. The conference has taken an active role in seeking to resolve the Yugoslav crisis. Because the conference is the only organization that includes all European countries, a number of members have suggested expanding its responsibilities beyond the realm of human rights, possibly to include security and peacekeeping.

An agreement concluded at the July 1992 CSCE summit in Helsinki gives the CSCE the authority to

initiate peacekeeping operations and call on members to contribute resources to such operations. The Helsinki Conference's effectiveness, however, is limited by procedural rules that allow any member to veto a CSCE decision (except for measures related to human rights).

IMF and Financial Assistance

Since 1990, the nations of Western Europe have provided financial aid to the Soviet Union and the other CIS countries. The West European states have taken the attitude that the continuation of the reforms, particularly in Russia, is in their vital national interests. The cost of aid is justified as being a bargain compared with the cost of rearming against the hostile and nationalistic Russia that might arise from the ashes of a failed effort at reform.

At the end of World War II, the victors held a conference in Bretton-Woods, New Hampshire, to discuss the financial and monetary arrangements that would shape the post-war world. Two institutions, the International Monetary Fund (IMF) and the World Bank were established at the conference to provide, respectively, short-term and long-term financial support for member countries. Today, the IMF provides short-term balance-of-payments assistance to countries around the globe while advising them on economic recovery and enforcing on them its economic formula of fiscal austerity, tight monetary policy, and currency devaluation to promote exports and curb imports.

Although the Soviet Union participated in the Bretton-Woods Conference, it refused to join the institutions. However, the Soviets have expressed keen interest in them during the past several years. In April 1992, the IMF granted Russia and most of the other CIS countries membership in the organization. Financial assistance was to be contingent on final IMF approval of their economic recovery plans. At the same time the Group of Seven industrialized countries offered a package of aid including $18 billion in balance of payments support for 1992 and a $6 billion ruble stabilization fund to ease the transition to a convertible currency. Disbursement of the aid was to be carried out by the IMF and would depend on continued success in adhering to the rigorous IMF austerity program. Successful adherence to the IMF program was critical because it would bolster confidence in the republics' economies and spur private investment and financing.

The United Nations

Under Gorbachev, the Soviet role at the United Nations changed dramatically. When the UN Security Council was first established after World War II, the Soviets had insisted on the right to veto any security action that it might authorize. During the cold war, the power to veto, exercised by the five permanent members of the council, severely limited its role in international security affairs. Most areas where concrete actions could be taken to prevent a conflict were points of superpower contention and thus not resolvable by the council. The Korean War was a unique exception. During debate on the North Korean attack on South Korea, the Soviet delegation was absent in a gesture of protest. This permitted the Security Council to pass a resolution authorizing force to defend South Korea.

The council did not authorize force again until 1990 when it asked UN members to use force to compel Iraq to leave Kuwait. The resolutions that punished Iraq with economic sanctions and authorized the use of force to push Iraq out of Kuwait could never have passed a few years earlier, when Iraq had been a Soviet client state. However, by 1990, the Soviets had deemphasized efforts to expand their influence in the Middle East, and were instead focusing on promoting their nation as a good member of the international community and good candidate for aid and investment. The Soviet UN representative therefore voted for the resolutions targeted against Iraq.

After the collapse of the Soviet Union, Russia slipped quietly into the Soviet seat on the Security Council without any challenge from the other members. For many years, there had been pressure to revamp the council, either to admit as a permanent member Japan, Germany, or one of the large Third World powers such as Brazil, India, or Nigeria. Opening the discussion of the Soviet seat would

have quickly led to issues that the other permanent members of the council preferred to avoid.

The new spirit of cooperation at the UN has given it an active role in solving a number of conflicts around the world. United Nations peacekeeping troops have been sent to Croatia and Bosnia-Herzegovina in response to the bloodshed there. The UN also has undertaken operations to administer Cambodia and prepare for elections in that war-torn country, its largest effort ever. This role would not have been possible without the new Russian cooperation.

Russia likely will continue to promote collective action by the council. Because Russia has a veto, it can do much to shape council policy. The United Nations, therefore, offers Russia a low-cost way to advance its interests and exert diplomatic influence.

The Islamic World

Relations with the Islamic world have been important to both Russia and the Soviet Union. In the nineteenth century, competition between Russia and British-dominated India for control of the broad stretches of Asia that separated them was referred to as "the Great Game." During this period, the area known as Turkestan was annexed by the tsars and later became the five republics of Soviet Central Asia.

Later, the long southern border of the Soviet Union, which was contiguous to many important Islamic states, guaranteed that Soviet foreign policy would be active in the region. Despite its intense interest in Islamic areas that bordered on the Soviet Union, such as Iran, Turkey, and Afghanistan, the Soviet Union did not play a large role in Arab regions farther to the south until the 1950s.

Relations with Arab Nations

In 1955 Egypt became the first Soviet client state in the Middle East and the first Arab state to purchase Soviet-made arms. (In 1973, Egypt became the first Arab state to order all Soviet advisers out of the country and break its ties with Moscow.) During the Brezhnev period, Moscow developed a collection of clients in the region, including Syria,

Libya, Yemen, Iraq, and the Palestine Liberation Organization (PLO). These were the key "rejectionist states," who were unwilling to compromise with their enemy, Israel.

The Soviet Union's Arab clients depended on Moscow to provide arms and financial aid and to act as a counterweight to the United States, which backed Israel. Following the 1967 Six-day War and the 1973 Arab-Israeli War, the Soviet Union replenished the Arab states' depleted arsenals. Nevertheless, the Soviet Union always remained an outsider to the region, unlike the United States which managed to make itself a central figure in the continuing peace process. Communism never fully succeeded in establishing itself anywhere in the Middle East, primarily because it did not appeal to Arab nationalists, who, although secular in their orientation, did not accept its atheism.

Under Gorbachev, the Soviets sought to broaden their ties to the moderate Arab states and Israel instead of relying entirely for influence on their hardline client states. This was greatly facilitated by the Soviet withdrawal from Afghanistan. Few Arab states were comfortable maintaining close ties with a government that had occupation troops in another Islamic state.

During the 1990s the rejectionist states have struggled to survive, as Moscow has discontinued most aid. They have been forced to adapt to a Middle East dominated by a single outside superpower—the United States. Syria, the key Soviet ally after the loss of Egypt, has cautiously moved to improve its ties with the United States while maintaining its adversary posture toward Israel. Syrian troops fought with the U.S.-led coalition against Iraq in the 1991 Persian Gulf War. Libya's Moammar Khaddafi has found himself increasingly isolated by U.S. hostility. South Yemen, bordering on economic collapse, chose to unite with moderate North Yemen and give up its radical socialist ideology. The PLO, once strongly supported by the Soviet Union, has found itself in the world after the Persian Gulf War with very few friends or resources to draw upon. As a result, the Palestinians, like the Syrians, have participated in the ongoing peace talks with Israel with few cards to play.

Relations with Israel

Although the Soviets were supporters of Israel at the time of its founding, relations soured when the Soviets sought influence among the Arabs. In 1967 the Soviets severed diplomatic relations with Israel in response to the Six-day War. This move hindered Moscow's efforts to be involved in the Middle East peace process during the 1970s and 1980s. Soviet-Israeli relations continued to be extremely hostile until the advancement of the new thinking. Gorbachev made numerous good will gestures and steadily expanded contacts with the Jewish state, establishing consular relations in 1987.

Gorbachev also removed Jewish emigration as a point of contention by eliminating nearly all restrictions to departure. Since the beginning of 1990, nearly 400,000 Jews have left the Soviet Union. Israel's welcome of all Soviet Jewish immigrants combined with restrictions on their immigration to the United States has led to a flood of immigrants, overwhelming Israel's ability to absorb them.

Establishment of full diplomatic relations was, however, long delayed by Soviet insistence that Israel first agree to take part in an international peace conference, a proposal that had been on the table for decades. Moscow saw such a conference as a way to gain a role in the Middle East peace process. Israel was reluctant to take part in an international conference in which it would be outnumbered by hostile Soviet and Arab delegations and insisted that full diplomatic relations with the Soviets must precede any conference.

The dramatic changes in the political landscape as a result of the failed August coup and the Persian Gulf War made a peace conference politically feasible. Moscow restored relations with Israel on October 17, 1991, simultaneously with the announcement of the Madrid Peace Conference between the Arabs and the Israelis.

Formally, the conference and subsequent rounds of negotiations were jointly hosted by the United States and the Soviet Union. However, it became evident early on that the dominant role would be played by the American partner. Russia has continued the Soviet role as a sponsor of the peace negotiations, but its participation has been relatively limited and pro forma.

Persian Gulf War

The Soviet Union's response to the Iraqi invasion of Kuwait in August 1990 was a testament to how much its foreign policy had changed. Iraq was a nominal client state of Moscow, though the two governments were not extremely close, in part because the Soviets maintained closer relations with Syria, an Iraqi rival. Nevertheless, the Soviet Union was Iraq's major arms supplier and Soviet advisers were stationed in the country.

Soviet leaders were outwardly angered by Iraqi leader Saddam Hussein's attack on Kuwait. The Soviets appeared to have been manipulated and misled about Saddam's intentions. The Soviet government responded by supporting the U.S.-led coalition that was assembled to oppose Iraq and liberate Kuwait. Moscow immediately suspended arms shipments to Iraq and demanded its unconditional withdrawal from Kuwait.

In the past, Moscow would never have supported United Nations-sponsored sanctions against a client state. On August 6, however, the Soviet Union joined in the Security Council vote that established a trade embargo against Iraq. In November the Soviets voted with the majority of council members to authorize the use of force against Iraq to drive it from Kuwait.

Gorbachev, however, chose not to send Soviet troops to the Gulf. The trauma of the Afghanistan war remained fresh in the minds of the Soviet public. Another deployment in a foreign war zone was not likely to be popular. In addition, the use of Soviet troops against Iraq, a recent Soviet client, would have angered many Soviet conservatives and military leaders. Because the Soviet Union's conduct in supporting the coalition's effort was seen as extraordinary compared with its past obstructionist behavior, Moscow would have derived little additional international benefit from sending troops.

While supporting the coalition, the Soviet Union launched peace initiatives designed to strengthen its international image, demonstrate that the Soviet Union still had an independent foreign policy, and placate Soviet conservatives. Gorbachev, however, did not want to be perceived as tilting toward Iraq, for fear of alienating the West (which was much more important to Soviet long-term interests than Iraq) or squandering the good will that had been built up among moderate Arab nations by Soviet backing of UN resolutions against Iraq. Saudi Arabia and the smaller Persian Gulf states had announced November 29, 1990, that they would offer Moscow as much as $4 billion in financial aid and loans.

The Soviet Union became the focus of last-minute diplomatic efforts to avoid a ground war. The Iraqis sought Soviet mediation to construct a proposal that would allow them a face-saving retreat out of Kuwait. In cooperation with Baghdad, Moscow developed such a proposal, but the Bush administration rejected it, declaring that the plan contained too many unacceptable conditions. The coalition launched its ground war on February 24, driving Iraqi forces from Kuwait in just four days. Although the Soviets had supported the coalition, Iraq's quick defeat was alarming to Moscow. The Iraqis' Soviet-made equipment had performed poorly in combat against Western weapons, calling into question the quality of the Soviets' own arsenal.

Afghanistan

Afghanistan was demarcated in the early twentieth century as a buffer state between the British colonies in South India and the Russian Empire. It was inhabited by a mosaic of different peoples and had little national integration. Although the country was ruled by a king, most areas within Afghanistan retained their local systems of self-government and their hostility to invaders, built up over centuries.

In 1973 King Zaher Shah was removed in a military coup and Prime Minister Mohammed Daoud took power as president. Pro-Soviet officers, disappointed with Daoud, staged another coup in April 1978, killing him. Power was turned over to a Marxist-Leninist party that embarked on a radical agenda, relying heavily on Soviet backing and driving much of the population into revolt. By the end of

Some of the last Soviet troops to leave Afghanistan wave from atop their tanks on the Salang Highway, February 2, 1989.

1979 Islamic fundamentalist guerrillas had pushed the regime to the verge of collapse. Moscow feared the establishment of a second fundamentalist regime on its southern border (the Islamic Republic of Iran had been established the year before) and was concerned about the destabilizing effect this would have on the large Muslim population in the Soviet Central Asian republics bordering Afghanistan.

On December 24, 1979, the Soviets began airlifting troops and supplies into Afghanistan, ultimately committing more than 100,000 troops. While most cities and towns were quickly captured, guerrillas calling themselves mujahideen (holy warriors) followed the centuries-old pattern of resisting invaders from the mountainous Afghan terrain. Despite the tremendous technological advantage of Soviet forces, the guerrillas proved impossible to dislodge.

To Soviet surprise, reaction from the West and the Third World was swift and harsh. The invasion was condemned by the UN General Assembly on January 14, 1980, by a vote of 104 to 18. Fifty-six countries boycotted the 1980 Moscow Olympics. Years of Soviet efforts to develop relations with the Islamic world collapsed under fierce Islamic criticism of the invasion. Fearing a Soviet threat to Persian Gulf oil supplies, American relations with the Soviet Union worsened and the United States began to supply the mujahideen with substantial military and economic aid.

Throughout the 1980s the Soviets became further bogged down in Afghanistan, unable to secure a decisive victory in the increasingly costly war. Tens of thousands of returning Soviet soldiers, many disabled in the war, became a dissonant element in Soviet society. Like the American soldiers who returned from Vietnam, many were unsure of why they had been sent to fight in the first place.

In 1986 Gorbachev hinted that he would be willing to withdraw Soviet forces, making his famous reference to the Afghan war as a "bleeding wound." After years of negotiations, accords were signed in April 1988 under which the last Soviet soldiers were to be withdrawn on January 15, 1989.

Despite expectations that it would fall quickly without Soviet troops, the weakened regime managed to hold most of the major cities in the country for several years. Soviet military assistance to the Afghan government continued until the end of 1991, when it was stopped concurrent with the end of American aid to the guerrillas. A collection of guerrilla groups finally overran Kabul in April 1992. After overthrowing the government, these groups soon began fighting among themselves for power. A shaky coalition government was established pending elections and arrangements were being drawn up with the United Nations for the return of the estimated six million Afghan refugees in Pakistan and Iran.

During the cold war of the early 1980s Afghanistan was a symbol of Soviet aggression and American determination to "contain" what was seen as a move for the strategic Persian Gulf. Now, however, both sides have lost interest in the continuing internecine fighting in Afghanistan. Unfortunately, as with many other former fronts in the cold war, over a decade of fighting has left Afghanistan among the most impoverished of countries.

Central Asia

Since the collapse of the Soviet Union, the five Central Asian republics (Kazakhstan, Uzbekistan, Kyrgyzstan, Tajikistan, and Turkmenistan) have become the objects of a competition for influence between Turkey and Iran. Moreover, having long been accustomed to being ignored by the outside world, these republics are relishing their arrival on the international scene and the attention they are receiving. Fears that they would fall under the influence of religious fundamentalists have led to Western diplomatic efforts to reach out to them. All were admitted to the United Nations and the CSCE in early 1992.

Turkey and Iran have made strong diplomatic efforts to present themselves as the two basic models for development in Central Asia. Turkey represents the path toward secular democracy with a market economy and a western orientation. Since

the establishment of the Turkish Republic by Kemal Ataturk after World War I, Turkey has been a strictly secular state. In recent years, it has made no secret of its desire to be a part of Europe and a member of the European Community. The strong export-driven Turkish economy is one of the IMF's success stories, having suffered through years of IMF-prescribed austerity measures.

Kazakh, Kyrgyz, Uzbek, and Turkmen are Turkic languages, so speakers of these tongues have a natural affinity for Turkey and there is a great deal of support for the Turkish model, encouraged by Western and Turkish diplomacy. After a visit to Turkey in December 1991, Kyrgyz president Askar Akayev spoke glowingly of the Turkish model for Central Asia. Kazakh president Nursultan Nazarbaev has stated, "We want to implement a free-market economy. For this, our only model is Turkey." Even conservative former communist leaders such as Islam Karimov of Uzbekistan and Saparmurad Niyazov of Turkmenistan find Turkey an attractive model, when compared with the Islamic fundamentalism of Iran. Turkey sees Central Asia as an opportunity to develop an area that is a natural sphere of cultural and political influence and, in addition, create a large market for Turkish consumer goods. Turkey is investing millions of dollars in a satellite project to bring Turkish news, entertainment, and cultural programming to Central Asia and Azerbaijan.

Iranian foreign minister Ali Akbar Velayati has actively courted the Central Asians, particularly Tajikistan, which has strong cultural and linguistic ties with Iran. The two states have signed an agreement for Iran to help develop Tajikistan's petroleum industry. While Tajikistan is undergoing something of a religious revival, not surprising after seventy-five years of communism, there is little evidence that Iran's religious fundamentalism and anti-Western stance has found fertile ground there.

It is unrealistic to expect that further ties will not develop between Iran and the Central Asians. Nevertheless, leaders of these countries all understand that there is a limit to what Iran can offer them. Significant economic aid and investment will have to come from the West. A major shift into the

Iranian sphere would leave them largely isolated, like Iran itself.

Conflict in Nagorno-Karabakh

With the demise of the Soviet Union, the internal dispute between Armenia and Azerbaijan over the Nagorno-Karabakh Autonomous Oblast became an international issue. Previously, Moscow had discouraged outside efforts to resolve the conflict. Since independence, the CSCE, France, Turkey, Iran, and Russia itself have all been involved in seeking a resolution of the conflict.

Russian foreign minister Kozyrev has expressed interest in further involvement by CSCE, possibly including the use of peacekeeping troops. France has proposed a cease-fire, followed by demilitarization of the region, to facilitate humanitarian relief for the population of Nagorno-Karabakh.

Iran and Turkey have both sought to play a mediating role to expand their influence in Azerbaijan. Meeting with Armenian and Azerbaijani officials in mid-February 1992, Iranian diplomats negotiated a three-day cease-fire beginning on February 27. However, it failed within hours due to a renewed Azerbaijani offensive.

Because of its close historic ties and geographic proximity to Azerbaijan, Turkey is moving dangerously closer to giving up its neutrality and assuming an active role. Turkey was the first country to recognize Azerbaijan and has supplied it with large amounts of aid. Turkish prime minister Suleyman Demirel is under pressure from domestic public opinion to take a more active role, or even intervene militarily. Such a move could, however, be extremely costly for Turkey. Western sympathies already lean toward Armenia. Active intervention could place Turkey directly in conflict with its NATO allies. However, if the conflict expands, a passive or neutral role may cost Turkey dearly in its competition for influence in Azerbaijan and Central Asia.

Relations with East Asia

During the 1980s the Pacific rim was the world's most economically dynamic region. Japan solidified its standing as the second largest economy and invested billions of dollars overseas. China, though still under the governance of an often repressive communist regime, experienced impressive economic growth as it adopted far-reaching economic reforms. South Korea, Taiwan, Singapore, and Hong Kong became known as the four dragons, because of their extremely rapid economic growth and development.

The Soviet Union, however, was almost completely locked out of the potential economic benefits of good relations with the growing economies of East Asia. Soviet support for Communist allies Vietnam and North Korea, its downing of a Korean airliner in 1983, its continuing military threat to the region, and its unwillingness to compromise on territorial disputes with Japan and China had undermined relations with the nations of East Asia. Gorbachev sought to reach out to these countries by reducing military tensions, reining in communist allies, for example discouraging Vietnam's interference in Cambodia, and expanding diplomatic contacts.

These efforts succeeded in improving relations with the nations of East Asia, though many points of contention remained for Boris Yeltsin to resolve. Yeltsin had sought aid and investment from the East Asian nations, while deemphasizing relations with North Korea and Vietnam.

China

When the People's Republic of China was proclaimed on October 3, 1949, it was the beginning of the end of absolute Soviet domination of the Socialist bloc even though Chinese communist leader Mao Zedong was obedient to Stalin's political line. Sino-Soviet relations continued on a steady footing until Khrushchev began his opening to the West in 1955. Mao resented Khrushchev's attempt to improve relations with the United States and feared any improvement would come at China's expense. Mao began to warn of the dangers of cooperating with the capitalist world. The Soviets denied their disagreements with the Chinese for as long as possible to present the West with a unified Socialist bloc.

The split, however, came into the open in 1960 with the increasingly public Chinese attacks on Soviet "revisionism."

While on the surface the split was couched in terms of an ideological dispute, in reality it ran much deeper. Fundamental differences in the histories, cultures, levels of economic development, geographies, and goals of the two communist giants made them unnatural allies, linked only by a common ideology and a common enemy. As the two great competing Asian land powers, it was improbable that their close relationship could continue. Thus they were never able to reconstruct the alliance, even after Khrushchev had departed and the ideological disputes had long become irrelevant. In the years following Khrushchev's ouster, Sino-Soviet relations worsened as a result of competition for influence in Hanoi during the Vietnam War, the Chinese Cultural Revolution, launched in August 1966, and the Soviet military buildup along the Sino-Soviet border.

The cultural revolution was accompanied by escalating propaganda exchanges and the disintegration of meaningful cultural and diplomatic relations between the two nations. Khrushchev's successors were faced with an "ally" who refused to cooperate with them in the Socialist bloc and the Third World and who brushed aside all attempts to improve relations. In addition, since 1963, Beijing had openly denounced nineteenth-century border treaties between Russia and China as being "unequal." Mao claimed that nearly a million square miles of Soviet territory rightfully belonged to China. Finally, China's emergence as a nuclear power a year earlier added a new dimension to the Chinese threat.

Consequently, the Soviets began to increase substantially their military strength along the Chinese border. In January 1966 the Soviet Union signed a treaty of friendship, cooperation, and mutual aid with Mongolia, which led within a year to the deployment there of a hundred thousand Soviet troops. Beginning in January 1967, a number of confrontations took place between Soviet and Chinese troops patrolling in disputed border areas. These incidents intensified following the Soviet invasion of Czechoslovakia. Beginning in the spring of 1969, the Sino-Soviet border exploded into sporadic armed conflicts which continued for months, ending only when China backed down after Soviet hints of an attack against Chinese nuclear facilities. The decade came to an end with China regarding the Soviet Union as its greatest enemy and painfully aware of its diplomatic isolation and vulnerability to a Soviet nuclear attack.

Triangular Diplomacy

In the Chinese Civil War, the United States had sided with the Kuomintang against the Communists. When the Nationalists were forced to flee to Taiwan, a wave of recriminations swept Washington, with all sides trying to fix blame for the "loss" of China. Out of the resulting sense of obligation, military guarantees were given to Taiwan, and official recognition was withheld from the People's Republic of China.

China's emergence from the Cultural Revolution, its experience of vulnerability during the Sino-Soviet border crisis of 1969, the beginning of U.S. troop withdrawals from Vietnam, and the continuing Soviet military buildup on the Chinese border created the conditions under which a Sino-American détente could begin. China needed to seek accommodation with its less threatening enemy—the United States—to enhance its security against the Soviet Union.

The thaw in U.S.-Chinese relations took a dramatic step on July 15, 1971, when President Nixon announced that he would visit Beijing in early 1972 "to seek the normalization of relations between the two countries." The initial Soviet reaction was restrained, but Kremlin leaders privately began to display renewed interest in pursuing détente with the West. Meanwhile, U.S.-Chinese relations continued to develop steadily. President Carter recognized the People's Republic of China on December 15, 1978, and full diplomatic relations were established two weeks later. Moscow warned against using the continuing Chinese-American détente against the Soviet Union. Washington insisted that the establishment of relations with Beijing would not affect U.S.-Soviet relations. The Chinese, however, did not hesitate to call for U.S.-Chinese-Japanese cooperation against the Soviet Union. Although a formal anti-Soviet Asian alliance was not forthcoming, Soviet interests in Asia were opposed during the 1980s by three powerful nations with a shared interest in containing the Soviet Union.

Sino-Soviet Rapprochement. In 1988 Gorbachev indicated his desire to seek a rapprochement with China through a summit meeting with Deng Xiaoping. Beijing reminded the Soviets that no summit could be held until they met three longstanding Chinese conditions for improved relations: withdrawal of Soviet forces from Afghanistan, an end to Soviet support of Vietnam's occupation of Cambodia, and a reversal of the Soviet arms buildup along the Chinese border.

To the surprise of Western analysts, all three conditions were addressed in 1989, clearing the way for a summit and improving Moscow's standing in the region in general. The last Soviet troops left Afghanistan in February 1989. As part of the unilateral troop cuts announced by Gorbachev at the United Nations in December 1988, the bulk of Soviet troops were removed from Mongolia. The last Vietnamese troops (presumably under heavy Soviet pressure) left Cambodia in September 1989, although there are continuing allegations that thousands remained behind, wearing Cambodian uniforms.

On May 15, 1989, Gorbachev became the first Soviet leader to meet with his Chinese counterpart since Khrushchev held a summit with Mao in 1959. The trip marked the formal normalization of Sino-Soviet relations after a thirty-year rift. Nevertheless, serious problems remained in the relationship, and the trip highlighted the new ideological division running through Sino-Soviet relations.

Gorbachev's domestic reforms had sent shock waves across China. Chinese students, who had taken over Tiananmen Square to protest for democracy in the weeks before Gorbachev's trip to China, had been galvanized by events in the Soviet Union and they invoked Gorbachev's name as a symbol of hope. Although the protests coincided with Gorbachev's trip largely by accident, his presence was fully exploited by the demonstrators. While Gorbachev was in Beijing, the crowds swelled at one point to more than a million people, and the Chinese government was greatly embarrassed by the massive outpouring of support for Gorbachev's reforms. On May 20, a few days after Gorbachev had left, the protests were violently crushed with tanks, and thousands were killed or imprisoned.

During the 1980s and 1990s China's foreign policy primarily sought to create a stable international environment that would allow China to pursue its internal development as it saw fit. China walks a fine line in seeking to reform its economy while maintaining tight political controls. Perestroika rocked the stability Chinese leaders were trying to retain, by presenting a model for simultaneous political and economic reform, creating tremendous pressure for change.

Relations with China under Yeltsin. The Chinese leadership welcomed the August 1991 Moscow coup as a sign that the Soviet Union had decided to abandon its reckless course and rejoin the socialist camp. The coup's subsequent collapse was no doubt a great disappointment for the Chinese leadership. It was virtually ignored by the Chinese press, which also has given scant attention to other events related to political reform. To the extent that the reforms are addressed at all in the Chinese press, they are criticized as moves away from socialism and blamed for the chaos sweeping the CIS.

Should Russia succeed in making the transition to a stable democracy with a market economy, it would present China with a model for reform that might be very influential in the near future when the country undergoes a generational change of the top leadership. On the other hand, continued political instability could spread into China or send refugees south fleeing civil conflicts. This is particularly a concern in Xinjiang province, which borders Soviet Central Asia and includes many of the same ethnic groups.

Despite their fundamentally opposed approaches to domestic reform, both China and Russia appreciate that continued good relations are critical if they are to avoid returning to the confrontational days of the Brezhnev era. Russian foreign minister Kozyrev traveled to Beijing in March 1992 with a number of proposals for improved Russian-Chinese relations. The two nations may further scale back armed forces designated to defend against the other, and Kozyrev proposed eliminating tactical nuclear weapons along the Sino-Russian border.

The Yeltsin government also has offered to expand military sales and military cooperation with China. During Kozyrev's visit, the two nations agreed to accelerate a pending sale of twenty-four Soviet Su-27 aircraft to China.

Japan

Of all the major industrial powers, Japan was the most reluctant to expand its relations with the Soviet Union under Gorbachev, and it is the most hesitant to provide assistance to Yeltsin's Russia. A deep distrust exists between the two countries, which are the only World War II combatants that have not signed a peace treaty formalizing the end of the war. Better relations with Tokyo are an essential precondition for Russian participation in the East Asian economy and for significant Japanese participation in the Western program of assistance to Russia.

Before relations can be improved, Russia must find a solution to the dispute over four Russian-occupied islands at the southern end of the Kuril chain, known in Japan as the Northern Territories. These four islands were seized by the Soviet Union in the closing days of World War II. They are strategically important because they straddle the entrance to the Sea of Okhotsk, where Russian submarines often hide. They are economically valuable because they are surrounded by a fertile fishing area. The closest of the Russian-held islands is less than a mile from the Japanese coast.

Since 1945 Japan has insisted uncompromisingly on the return of all four islands and has refused to sign a treaty ending the war until the issue is resolved. Gorbachev moderated the previous Soviet hard line on the issue, at least recognizing that grounds existed for discussion. But he was not prepared to hand back the islands. In the spring of 1991 Gorbachev became the first Soviet leader to visit Japan, but the trip produced few results because of deadlock over the Northern Territories issue.

Yeltsin has indicated his desire to see the issue resolved. However, under pressure from Russian conservatives and nationalists, he canceled a trip to Japan scheduled for mid-September 1992 at which the issue of the Northern Territories was to be discussed. Both Russian and Japanese officials acknowledged that Yeltsin canceled the trip because of domestic political concerns. His conservative opponents had denounced the idea of giving up the islands, saying that yielding Russian lands would damage national pride and set a precedent that could induce other nations to press territorial claims against Russia. Opinion polls indicated that up to 60 percent of Russians favored holding on to the islands.

Nationalist sentiments may continue to determine Russian policy toward Japan. But given Japan's power in the Far East and its conditioning of aid to Russia on a settlement, Moscow has much incentive to make concessions that could lead to a compromise. Various proposals have been floated in which two islands would be given back immediately and the others returned after some transition period. Domestic politics in Russia, however, complicate efforts to reach a compromise.

Even if the Northern Territories dispute is resolved, a Russian rapprochement with Japan may be limited. Beyond a relaxation of military tensions, Russia has relatively little to offer Japan. The opportunity to invest in Siberia and the Russian Far East is provocative, but it would be extremely difficult and costly, in comparison with Japan's other investment opportunities in the more hospitable countries of East Asia. Moreover, Japan's military alliance with the United States is the cornerstone of prosperity in East Asia. America is also Japan's closest trading partner. Japan is unlikely to do anything that would put this alliance at risk.

Former Client States in the Developing World

From the 1950s through the mid-1980s, the Soviet Union constructed a network of client states that reached throughout much of the developing world. The Soviet leadership touted the existence of these regimes as evidence that the world socialist revolution was making progress. With the rise of the new thinking, however, these client states, to which Moscow provided billions of dollars of support, began to be regarded not as an asset but as a burden.

Most of these pro-Soviet regimes were communist—or at least had adorned themselves with Leninist rhetoric for the benefit of their Soviet patron. However, nearly all were extremely backward, had dubious strategic value, and survived only with the benefit of huge subsidies and sometimes military involvement by Moscow. As the Soviet economy began to falter in the 1980s, it became increasingly difficult to justify the expense of propping up clients in Asia, Africa, and Latin America. Perhaps more importantly, Soviet adventures in the Third World were a hindrance to improved relations with the United States, Western Europe, China, and Japan.

Consequently, Gorbachev began the process of disentangling the Soviet Union from Third World allies and military engagements. Under Yeltsin, that process largely has been completed. Economic and military support for traditional Soviet clients have been sharply cut or eliminated. Russia's withdrawal from the Third World has left former allies to manage as best they can. Some, like Afghanistan and Ethiopia, have collapsed without Soviet military support. Others, such as Mongolia, Mozambique, Vietnam, and Nicaragua have discarded or moderated their socialist ideology and sought better relations and aid from the West. Finally, Cuba and North Korea have chosen to circle their wagons and reject any compromise with the forces of capitalism.

Cuba

Soviet involvement in Latin America began with the Cuban revolution in 1959. After that, the Soviets sought to expand their influence through military aid and Cuban support for guerrilla movements in the hemisphere. Beyond helping to spread Soviet influence, the Cuban revolution was a reaffirmation of the success and dynamism of Marxism-Leninism as an ideology. It also provided a forward base for gathering intelligence. Soviet efforts to use Cuba as

a missile base led to the Cuban missile crisis in 1962. *(Cuban Missile Crisis, p. 75)*

Fidel Castro's willingness to send combat troops overseas to support socialist regimes made him an important Soviet ally. During the 1970s, Soviet aid to Cuba annually was between four and six billion dollars, about 20-30 percent of the entire Cuban GNP.

Beginning in 1985, Cuba and the Soviet Union followed increasingly divergent paths. Gorbachev sought a reversal of the aggressive Third World interventionism of the 1970s and saw Castro as the principal culprit behind much of it. Castro criticized perestroika as a break with socialism, while tightening his hold on power and cracking down on dissent.

Since shortly after the revolution, the United States maintained a total economic boycott on Cuba, resulting in Cuba's depending on the Soviet Union and Eastern Europe for 85 percent of its trade. Before Gorbachev, the Soviets also had given Cuba billions of dollars each year in aid and subsidized imports, especially petroleum products. As Moscow's financial crisis and differences with Havana grew and U.S.-Soviet relations warmed during the late 1980s, Gorbachev began decreasing Cuban aid. By 1992 aid had been cut off completely.

The collapse of the Eastern bloc has devastated the Cuban economy. Shortages of energy, food, and other goods have become chronic and severe. The scarcity of fuel has hampered transportation and reduced electricity production. On September 5, 1992, Castro announced that construction of a Russian-built nuclear power plant near the city of Cienfuegos would cease, because Russia insisted on being paid in hard currency for work done on the plant. The suspension of the project, which was supposedly 70 percent complete, was a heavy blow to Cuba, as the plant could help to relieve Cuba's severe energy problems. Although some trade will continue between Russia and Cuba, Moscow has indicated that it will no longer subsidize trade or accept barter arrangements.

Nevertheless, Russia has not entirely severed its involvement in Cuba. Although Yeltsin has pledged

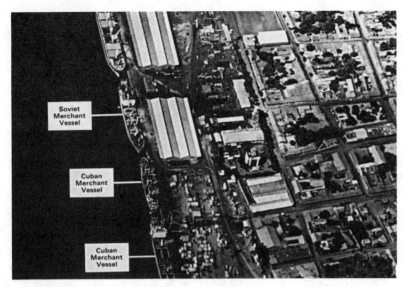

Soviet and Cuban merchant ships docked in the Nicaraguan port of Corinto. The United States closely monitors the fraternal assistance rendered by the USSR and Cuba to the Sandinista government.

to withdraw the approximately twenty-eight hundred Russian troops in Cuba, only a handful of them had been withdrawn as of late spring 1992. Their departure has been slowed by shortages of barracks space in Russia. The Russians also have chosen to maintain their large electronic listening facilities in Cuba, which still monitor American communications and military movements.

Despite the loss of ideological and financial support from the Eastern bloc, Castro cannot be counted out. As the only leader in Latin America who has completely rejected the all-powerful "norteamericanos," he has proven to be a natural survivor.

Nicaragua

Unlike Cuba under Castro, the communist Sandinista government of Nicaragua had little staying power without its Soviet prop. The Sandinistas, who came to power through a revolution against the dictator Anastasio Somoza in 1979, quickly became Castro's closest ally in the hemisphere. Along with extensive aid from the Soviet Union and Eastern Europe, Cuban military backing helped Nicaragua to build the strongest army in Central America. But Nicaragua soon became involved in a protracted

civil war with the contras, an American-backed guerrilla army operating out of Costa Rica and Honduras.

For ten years the contra war, along with an American economic blockade, ravaged the country. At the end of 1989 inflation reached 1,700 percent, with at least 25 percent unemployment. In 1990 Sandinista president Daniel Ortega agreed to hold open elections as a means of getting the United States to cut off aid to the contras. Gorbachev likely played a role in convincing the Sandinistas to hold free elections. The war in Nicaragua had long been a sore point in Soviet-American relations.

In a major upset, Violeta Barrios de Chamorro of the United Nicaraguan Opposition defeated Ortega for the presidency on February 25, 1990, by a vote of 55 percent to 40 percent. Contrary to the demands of the more conservative members of her coalition, Chamorro retained Humberto Ortega (the brother of Daniel Ortega) as the head of the army, and she made other efforts to reach out to the Sandinistas, still the largest single party in Nicaragua.

Nevertheless, national reconciliation in Nicaragua has been slow in coming. Despite the end of the war, tensions remain high. Some groups of contras have sought to reignite the war, claiming that Chamorro has sold out to the Sandinistas in attempting to placate their demands. Because of divisions in her government and her country, Chamorro has been unable to fully pursue economic and political reform.

Angola

During the 1970s, the Soviets were indirectly involved on much of the African continent through their Cuban ally. Cuba provided troops, military advisers, and technical personnel to seventeen African governments and three insurgencies. The Soviet Union paid the bills and provided material support.

After the collapse of Portugal's African empire in 1975, Angola became the Soviet Union's staunchest African ally. Cuba provided tens of thousands of troops to defend the ruling MPLA (Popular Movement for the Liberation of Angola) against American-supplied UNITA (Union for the Total Independence of Angola) forces. Reflecting the stalemated situation and the declining Soviet interest in continuing the conflict, a U.S.-mediated agreement among the combatants was reached in December 1988. This agreement led to a complete Cuban withdrawal and a commitment to hold elections in September 1992.

In March 1992 Foreign Minister Kozyrev began his first African diplomatic tour with a visit to Luanda, stressing Russia's interest in continuing ties with Angola during the process of rebuilding the country. He hinted at Russian interest in military cooperation, part of Russia's larger effort to find new markets for its arms industry.

Vietnam, Laos, and Cambodia

Since the cutoff of Soviet aid in 1991, Vietnam has been seeking to recast its image, opening its doors to investment and trade and mending relations with the West and its capitalist neighbors. Vietnam has withdrawn its troops from Cambodia, leaving the regime it installed in 1978 to a massive UN-organized effort at national reconciliation after years of civil war, stretching back to the late 1960s.

Hanoi also has sought foreign investment and normalized ties with the United States, including an end to the U.S. economic boycott and ban on aid from all international organizations of which the United States is a member. The Russians claim they are owed 10 billion rubles by Vietnam and 800 million by Cambodia. Russia is pulling back from its huge naval base in Cam Ranh Bay, Vietnam, but, as in Cuba, will probably retain its intelligence-gathering presence at the facility.

Laos, one of the poorest countries in the world, is also struggling to survive the end to years of Soviet largesse. From 1985 to 1990, Laos received $410 million in military and economic aid. Now it is opening its doors to Western investment, recently enacting one of the most liberal laws on foreign investment in Southeast Asia.

North Korea

With the loss of most of its socialist allies, North Korea is now perhaps the most isolated society on earth. The loss of Soviet aid and cheap oil has devastated the North Korean economy, but few steps have been taken to seek accommodation with the outside world. Some foreign investment has been encouraged, but under very strict controls.

Negotiations have been under way with South Korea for several years, but military tensions remain high. Western experts believe that North Korea is secretly engaging in a crash effort to develop a nuclear capability and may now be within several years of possessing a bomb. Kim Il Sung, age eighty, has led North Korea since the end of World War II. It remains to be seen whether the closed society he created will survive him. With the economy near collapse, pressures for a rapprochement with the booming South—where per capita income is more than five times greater—may become overwhelming during the political transition that will follow Kim's death.

Foreign Minister Kozyrev's tour of East Asia in March 1992 demonstrated the new direction of Russian foreign policy toward Korea. He stopped at Seoul, the capital of South Korea, which has given Russia a large package of credits and has expressed interest in investing heavily in Russia, but he bypassed North Korea entirely.

CHAPTER **10**

RELATIONS WITH
THE UNITED STATES

In his historic speech to the U.S. Congress on June 17, 1992, Boris Yeltsin declared: "Acting on the will of the people of Russia, I am inviting you, and through you the people of the United States, to join us in partnership in the name of a worldwide triumph of democracy, in the name of liberty and justice in the twenty-first century."

Yeltsin's words reflected the remarkable transformation of relations between the former cold war antagonists. After World War II the United States and the Soviet Union had developed a hostile rivalry based on their conflicting geopolitical goals, their competing ideologies, and their reciprocal military threat. American post-World War II policy aimed at containing Soviet expansionism, building alliance systems to oppose Soviet military power, and isolating the Soviet Union diplomatically. The Soviets sought to solidify their domination of Eastern Europe, develop new anti-Western allies around the world, and ensure their own security through military might.

In the late 1980s the superpower relationship began to change. In an effort to repair his country's ailing economy, Soviet leader Mikhail S. Gorbachev de-emphasized the USSR's quest for international influence and sought to divert funds from military production to the civilian economy. Competition with the United States was subordinated to a new superpower cooperation that would allow the Soviets to focus on their enormous domestic problems.

After the breakup of the Soviet Union in late 1991, Yeltsin attempted to move Russia still further from the cooperation of the Gorbachev era to the

partnership he espoused in his speech to Congress. His government and the governments of many other former Soviet states made significant compromises to the United States in arms control and other areas, while asking for American aid in rebuilding their economies on free market principles.

The political, social, and economic conditions in the former Soviet Union changed with such speed that U.S. policy had difficulty keeping up. The key cold war issues of the arms race, the European military balance, and competition for influence in the developing world were largely replaced by the questions of how the United States could best aid the domestic transformations of the former Soviet states and how to achieve stability in a vast multiethnic empire where weapons of mass destruction were plentiful.

Comparisons have been drawn between the former Soviet Union in 1992 and Germany and Japan in 1945. The United States helped its devastated World War II enemies to rebuild their societies and economies. The result was a profound transformation of the defeated nations into thriving democracies and important American political allies and economic partners. Many U.S. policy makers argued that the United States needed to take the same approach with the former Soviet Union.

In a speech at Princeton University on December 12, 1991, Secretary of State James A. Baker III described the importance of helping the former Soviet republics to establish democratic governments and free markets:

Boris Yeltsin concludes his historic speech to a joint session of the U.S. Congress, June 17, 1992.

If during the Cold War we faced each other as two scorpions in a bottle, now the Western nations and the former Soviet republics stand as awkward climbers on a steep mountain. Held together by a common rope, a fall toward fascism or anarchy in the former Soviet Union will pull the West down, too. Yet equally as important, a strong and steady pull by the West now can help them to gain their footing so that they, too, can climb above to enduring democracy and freedom.

The U.S. debt problem and weak economy, as well as fears that the reform movement in Russia and elsewhere might be reversed, at least for the time being prevented the adoption of a massive aid package on the scope of the Marshall Plan, which helped to rebuild Europe after World War II. But the United States continued to see the outcome of the revolution in the former Soviet Union as the key to stability in Europe and much of Asia and as central to U.S. security. For their part, Russia and the other republics knew that the United States was the most important source of outside aid and political support. Therefore, both parties had much incentive to make partnership a reality.

Historic Adversaries

Throughout most of Soviet history, the United States was an adversary. American forces were among the Allied contingent sent to Russia following the Bolshevik withdrawal from World War I in 1918. The Allies sought to protect war supplies sent to Russia before it had concluded its separate peace with Germany and to support White armies that were fighting to overthrow the new Bolshevik regime. By 1920 the Bolsheviks had gained the upper hand in the civil war, and most Allied troops had been withdrawn from Russia. The Red Army defeated the remnants of the White forces by 1921. *(Foreign Intervention, p. 38)*

After the civil war, the Bolsheviks attempted to gain recognition and loans for reconstruction from the United States and other major powers. The United States, however, refused to recognize the Bolshevik government or lend it money, although Washington did aid Russian famine victims through the American Relief Administration. In March 1921 the United States also excluded the Bolsheviks from participating in an international naval conference held in Washington. The Bolsheviks were resented in the United States for their revolutionary propaganda, their withdrawal from World War I, and their refusal to pay tsarist debts.

During 1924 most European countries, believing that the Bolsheviks had consolidated their power, recognized the Bolshevik government. The United States, however, refrained from doing so until November 16, 1933. The decision to establish formal ties with the Soviet Union was motivated primarily by Adolf Hitler's rise to power in Germany and the Japanese occupation of Manchuria in 1931-1932. In return for recognition, Moscow promised to stop disseminating propaganda aimed at overthrowing the U.S. government and to protect the rights of U.S. citizens in the Soviet Union. These promises were not kept, however, and U.S.-Soviet political relations remained cool and distant.

The U.S. entry into World War II following Japan's attack on Pearl Harbor, Hawaii, December 7, 1941, transformed the United States and the Soviet Union into active wartime allies. During the war the United States shipped billions of dollars of supplies to the USSR to sustain the Soviet war effort against Nazi Germany. Nevertheless, even during the war, the Soviet Union and the United States were uneasy partners, linked only by a common enemy.

In the closing stages of World War II, President Franklin D. Roosevelt believed that an oligarchy was forming between the great powers that would create a stable postwar order. The wartime partnership between the Soviet Union and the United States, however, quickly broke down when the Axis powers were defeated. Soviet domination of Eastern Europe, disagreements over the future of Germany, and other issues combined to create a cold war between East and West. *(Cold war, p. 59)*

During the cold war, world affairs became increasingly bipolar, as the United States and the Soviet Union competed for the friendship of peoples around the world. The United States and the nations of Western Europe created the North Atlantic Treaty Organization (NATO) as a response to the military threat from the Soviet Union. The Soviets countered by establishing their own alliance system—the Warsaw Pact—with the nations of Eastern Europe.

During the tenure of Nikita S. Khrushchev, the Soviet Union solidified its claims to being a superpower. But this status was primarily one-dimensional because it depended largely on military power. The USSR remained a limited player in the international economy. Moscow viewed America as the principal obstacle to its international ambitions and sought to compete with the United States in areas outside the military realm. The Soviets saw U.S. efforts to "contain" them and deal with them "from a position of strength" as direct challenges to their superpower status and concomitant right to exercise influence internationally.

The United States, besides being the Soviets' foremost adversary, was the yardstick by which the Soviets measured their own success. Soviet leaders wanted the United States to consider the USSR as its equal. Premier Khrushchev noted in his memoirs how opposition to the United States was coupled with admiration: "America occupied a special place

in our thinking about the world. And why shouldn't it? It was our strongest opponent among the capitalist countries, the leader that called the tune of anti-Sovietism for the rest."

As Sovietologist Dimitri Simes has explained, throughout the 1960s and 1970s there was "fear and competitive impulse" in the U.S. and Soviet images of each other. "But in the American case they were mixed with contempt; in the Russian, with jealousy and respect." The Soviets expected the United States to treat U.S.-Soviet relations as the most important aspect of world relations.

The wily, gregarious Khrushchev vacillated in his policy toward the Americans. The Soviet military was upgraded under his guidance, with emphasis on nuclear forces. Yet Khrushchev advanced the concept of peaceful coexistence with the West, and this idea became a cornerstone of Soviet foreign policy even after his removal from power in 1964.

Peaceful coexistence did not end superpower confrontation, however. Soviet attempts to gain a military advantage by deploying nuclear missiles in Cuba led to the Cuban missile crisis in 1962, during which President John F. Kennedy estimated the chances of nuclear war between the superpowers as "one in three." Yet peaceful coexistence was a recognition that because of the destructive power of nuclear weapons, war had to be avoided. *(Cuban missile crisis, p. 75)*

During Leonid I. Brezhnev's tenure as top Soviet leader, the Soviets reached nuclear parity with the United States. The cold war was moderated in the 1970s by the efforts of U.S. and Soviet leaders to pursue a détente—a relaxation of tensions. *(Détente, p. 90)*

Although the superpowers cooperated on many issues during the era of détente, including arms control, they remained competitors. The fundamental adversary relationship had not changed. The Soviets continued their military buildup, and in the name of advancing the international socialist revolution they continued their aggressive support of Marxist governments and guerrilla groups. Yet a group's hostility toward the West and willingness to permit Soviet influence in its affairs had more to do with Moscow's decision to extend economic and

The Cold War, McCarthy, and the "Red Scare" Pervade the

Soon after World War II, rising tensions between the United States and the Soviet Union, coupled with the disclosure that a communist spy ring had been operating in Canada, prompted a wave of concern over communist espionage and subversion within the United States that became known as the "red scare."

Few movements in U.S. history have so pervaded the fabric of national life as the anticommunist movement of the late 1940s and early 1950s. Not only did states have their own anticommunist statutes and legislatures their own un-American activities committees, but loyalty oaths and investigations became commonplace both in public and private employment. Some veterans organizations became involved in the movement to expose and eliminate alleged communist influence in American life.

There were widespread efforts to weed out communists and communist sympathizers in the legal profession, on college and university faculties, in the mass communications field (especially motion pictures and radio), and in many other industries not directly involved in the nation's security.

Fear of communist infiltration of the federal government first focused on the State Department. The revelations in the *Amerasia* case, involving the discovery of secret U.S. records in that allegedly procommunist magazine's files, began a series of congressional investigations of communist subversion that continued for years. The *Amerasia* case also figured in President Truman's initiation of a comprehensive loyalty program for all government employees in 1947.

That same year, Congress reached out beyond the government in its anticommunist crusade. It moved against communist labor leaders by attaching a noncommunist affidavit requirement to the Taft-Hartley Act, and the House Un-American Activities Committee (HUAC) undertook a controversial probe of the motion picture industry. Ronald Reagan, then the newly elected president of the Screen Actors Guild, testified as a friendly witness before HUAC in October 1947. He supported the blacklist that Hollywood producers created to deny work to actors and writers suspected of having communist ties.

But it was the committee's investigation in 1948 of State Department official Alger Hiss, and Hiss's subsequent conviction for perjury, that established internal communism as a leading political issue and the committee as an important political force. The case against Hiss was based on testimony by Whittaker Chambers and Elizabeth Bentley, members of the American Communist party, who alleged that at least seventy-five government officials had been involved in spying during the 1930s. The charges against Hiss, which at one point appeared flimsy to other committee members, were vigorously developed by Richard Nixon, then a young member of the committee. Truman called the investigation a "red herring."

Between 1950 and 1954 Congress enacted a wide variety of restrictive legislation. High priests of the anticommunist movement were congressional investigators—members of HUAC, the Senate Internal Security Subcommittee, and, briefly, the Senate Permanent Investigations Subcommittee headed by Joseph R. McCarthy, R-Wis. Viewed as heroes by their supporters, as witch-hunters and character assassins by opponents, these men were largely responsible for the Internal Security Act of 1950, the Communist Control Act (CCA) of 1954, and other antisubversive laws.

With the return of Congress to Republican control in 1953, McCarthy assumed chairmanship of the Senate Permanent Investigations Subcommittee, and under him that group became a headline forum for anticommunist charges.

On June 19, 1953, Julius and Ethel Rosenberg, a married couple convicted of conspiracy to commit espionage by passing atomic information to the Soviets, died in the electric chair. The Rosenbergs were the first civilians to be executed for spying, and their case aroused considerable controversy.

Before the 1954 midterm elections, Republicans and Democrats traded charges with abandon. McCarthy accused the Democrats of "twenty years of treason," and the Democrats, hoping to embar-

Fabric of American Life

Rep. Richard Nixon, R-Calif. (left), and Chairman John McDowell, R-Pa. (center), of the House Un-American Activities Committee question Dr. Edward U. Condon (right) in March 1948. Condon, director of the National Bureau of Standards and a noted atomic scientist, was suspected by the committee of disloyalty to the United States. He was accused of associating with "alleged Soviet espionage agents" and with being "one of the weakest links in our atomic security." Though never substantiated, the committee's charges dogged Condon for years.

rass the Eisenhower administration, countered with legislation to outlaw the Communist party. The result was the Communist Control Act, the most controversial of the antisubversive legislation enacted in 1954. The CCA was a patchwork law of doubtful impact.

Anticommunist fervor reached its peak in 1954, but the movement began to wane after the Senate censured McCarthy by a 67 to 22 vote on December 2 of that year for acting contrary to Senate traditions during his investigations of alleged communist activity. In ensuing years the courts and Congress curbed some of the most extreme anticommunist laws and regulations. Some others never were enforced com-

pletely or were repealed quietly. The demise in January 1975 of HUAC, renamed the Internal Security Committee in 1969, ended thirty years of controversy over its pursuit of subversives.

A new measure of anticommunist sentiment developed in the early 1960s. The Supreme Court in 1961 upheld an order requiring the Communist party to register under the Internal Security Act. Congress tightened antisubversion acts and tried to curb the flow of communist propaganda into the United States. New anticommunist organizations, notably the John Birch Society, also emerged—to the accompaniment of widespread criticism and with marked lack of political success.

military aid than the group's ideological commitment to Marxism-Leninism. Similarly the United States backed some anticommunist governments and groups that were not committed to democratic principles. The two superpowers thus engaged in a traditional great-power contest for geopolitical influence around the world that only partially was motivated by their ideological differences.

Many conservatives in the United States criticized détente for providing benefits to the Soviets while bringing the West little more than a false sense of security.

Gradually during the second half of the 1970s enthusiasm for détente waned in the United States. The Soviets were perceived as using every possible loophole in the arms control treaties concluded under détente to continue their military buildup. Moscow stepped up military aid to the anti-Western governments of Angola, Ethiopia, and Afghanistan and supported the Vietnamese invasion of Cambodia in late 1978. In addition, the Kremlin resisted Western attempts to force it to improve its domestic human rights record, particularly in the area of emigration. Finally, the Soviet invasion of Afghanistan in December 1979 destroyed what was left of détente.

Thus as the 1980s began the U.S.-Soviet relationship had returned to its "normal" state of acrimony and suspicion. President Ronald Reagan denounced the Soviet Union and accelerated a military buildup begun under Jimmy Carter. Reagan said in his first presidential news conference in January 1981 that "so far, détente's been a one-way street the Soviet Union has used to pursue its own aims." He also claimed that the Soviets reserve the "right to commit any crime, to lie, to cheat." In 1983 he called the USSR "an evil empire" and "the focus of evil in the modern world."

Reagan's harsh rhetoric came amid intensified nuclear arms competition, stagnating arms control talks, continuing conflict between superpower clients in the Third World, and similarly harsh rhetoric from Soviet leaders.

During the early 1980s the state of arms control negotiations became a measuring stick of the superpower relationship. In late 1983, after West European countries began accepting the deployment of NATO intermediate-range nuclear missiles and ground-launched cruise missiles (GLCMs), the Soviets broke off all major arms control negotiations. Talks did not resume until after Gorbachev had become Soviet general secretary in March 1985. Superpower relations had been further strained by Reagan's 1983 proposal to build a space-based antiballistic missile defense—the Strategic Defense Initiative (SDI). SDI was seen by the Soviets as an attack against their two weakest areas: their economy and their technological capabilities.

Under Gorbachev, U.S.-Soviet relations continued to be based on competition. The new Soviet leader, however, brought a new pragmatism to negotiations and appeared to conduct business with the United States with an eye toward supporting Soviet domestic needs. He also provided a challenge to the U.S. leaders in the area of public relations, as he skillfully lobbied to improve the international image of the Soviet Union.

In 1987, with the conclusion of the Intermediate-range Nuclear Forces (INF) treaty eliminating all intermediate-range nuclear missiles from Europe, superpower relations began to change fundamentally. The Soviets had made several major concessions in agreeing to the treaty, the terms of which were close to a proposal made by Reagan in 1981. Meanwhile, the Reagan administration had ceased its harsh anti-Soviet rhetoric and was exploring new areas for superpower cooperation.

Soviet actions in 1989, including withdrawal of forces from Afghanistan and consent to the establishment of democratically elected governments in Eastern Europe, persuaded most U.S. policy makers that the Soviet Union had changed dramatically. Moreover, Soviet society was being transformed. As Marxist-Leninist ideology lost its luster, non-Russian minorities clamored for greater autonomy, the Communist party leadership introduced democratic processes, and Soviet society increasingly became subject to the rule of law. In response to these changes, the United States began trying to support the domestic transformation of the Soviet Union. By the time of the failed August 1991 coup that precipitated the Soviet breakup, superpower relations had already entered a new stage where cooperation had replaced competition.

Arms Control

Throughout the 1960s, 1970s, and 1980s arms control was the central element of negotiations between the United States and the Soviet Union. Both sides stated their desire to conclude agreements that would reduce or otherwise restrict the construction and deployment of nuclear weapons. Some agreements were achieved to limit the size of the superpower arsenals, but mutual fear and distrust continued to fuel an expensive and dangerous arms race.

Beginning in the late 1980s, the fundamental change in Soviet foreign policy under Mikhail Gorbachev created conditions which led to arms control agreements that significantly reduced the nuclear arsenals of the superpowers. With the breakup in 1991, the dynamics of arms control changed as the United States was faced with four new countries—Russia, Ukraine, Belarus, and Kazakhstan—with nuclear weapons on their soil. Arms control initiatives came to depend not just only on relations between Washington and Moscow, but also among the nuclear weapons states of the former Soviet Union.

Test Ban

The difficulties in reaching a strategic arms agreement were evident in the long and arduous negotiations to limit nuclear weapons testing—the first major arms control goal pursued by the superpowers. The Soviets opposed on-site inspection measures demanded by the United States. In addition, a ban on testing was viewed by some U.S. officials as a backdoor approach to total nuclear disarmament. Henry A. Kissinger, then a Harvard professor and later secretary of state, took note of this connection in an article in the October 1958 *Foreign Affairs*. "If a cessation of nuclear testing is a 'first step' to anything," he wrote, "it is to an increased campaign to outlaw nuclear weapons altogether."

Despite overtures from Soviet premier Khrushchev, President John F. Kennedy ordered a build-up of intercontinental ballistic missiles (ICBMs) soon after taking office in 1961. The buildup was intended to counter what many U.S. defense analysts perceived as a "missile gap" that favored the Soviet Union. In actuality, a gap in missile capabilities did exist, but it favored the United States. Not until after the Cuban missile crisis of October 1962 did the two sides undertake serious negotiations on a nuclear testing agreement. A limited treaty ending experimental nuclear weapons tests in the atmosphere, outer space, and under water was signed by the United States, the Soviet Union, and Great Britain in August 1963. More than 110 other countries subsequently signed the test ban treaty.

Although the test ban treaty was a positive step, it did not signal a new era of arms control. Both sides proceeded to conduct their testing underground. The United States conducted more nuclear tests (469) in the ten years after the test ban than it had in the previous eighteen years (424).

Arms Buildup

The American strategic buildup, which began two years before the treaty was signed, continued for the rest of the decade. The number of ICBMs was substantially increased, submarine-launched Polaris missiles were developed and deployed, supersonic fighter-bombers were ordered, and, by 1965, contracts had been given to the Boeing Company for work on multiple independently targeted reentry vehicle (MIRV) technology that would allow a single missile to carry several warheads.

Meanwhile the Soviet Union was pursuing its own nuclear weapons buildup. During the early 1960s its arsenal was inferior to the U.S. nuclear arsenal, but it was large enough to provide a credible deterrent to an attack. By the late 1960s the Soviets had achieved rough nuclear parity with the United States. The Soviet buildup focused on ICBMs and antiballistic missile (ABM) systems. In 1966, for example, the Soviet Union had about one-third as many ICBMs (250) as the United States. Two years later, according to U.S. estimates, the Soviets had 900.

A number of factors hindered arms control efforts during the 1960s, including the growing American involvement in Vietnam, the Soviet invasion of Czechoslovakia in August 1968, and the strategic buildups under way in both superpowers. Nevertheless, two important multilateral agreements on nuclear weapons were signed in the late 1960s: a 1967 treaty banning the orbiting of devices equipped with nuclear weapons and the 1968 Nuclear Non-Proliferation Treaty (NPT). The NPT established international safeguards to prevent the spread of nuclear weapons to nations not already possessing them.

SALT I

In June 1969 President Richard M. Nixon urged talks with the Soviet Union on limiting strategic nuclear weapons. The talks eventually began November 17, 1969, in Helsinki, Finland. After U.S. and Soviet negotiators worked arduously to prepare the documents, Nixon and Leonid Brezhnev signed the strategic arms limitation (SALT) accords on May 26, 1972.

The SALT accords included both a treaty limiting ABM deployments and an executive agreement designed to limit offensive weapons and missile-carrying submarines. Under the ABM treaty, both the United States and the Soviet Union were limited to one ABM site for the defense of their capital cities and one additional site each for the defense of an ICBM installation. (In 1973 Congress prohibited the Defense Department from beginning work on the ABM site to defend Washington.)

The five-year interim agreement limiting offensive missile launchers—land-based silos and submarine missile tubes—left the United States with 1,710 launchers, of which 1,054 were ICBMs and the remaining 656 were SLBMs (submarine-launched ballistic missiles). The White House estimated the total Soviet strategic missile launcher strength to be 2,358—1,618 ICBM launchers and 740 SLBM launchers. Besides the numerical edge, the Soviets also had the advantage in throw-weight, estimated at several times that of U.S. capacity. (Throw-weight is the measure of a missile's lift potential and ultimately the number and size of warheads a missile can carry.)

The United States, however, had a numerical advantage in warheads, as well as superiority in strategic bombers—460 at the time, compared with a Soviet total of 140—and aircraft that could strike the Soviet Union on one-way missions from European airfields.

When Brezhnev came to the United States to meet with President Nixon in June 1973, the talks were marked by their jovial tenor, not by their substance. The leaders signed several relatively minor agreements and a vague declaration that they hoped would guide U.S. and Soviet arms negotiators. The details of a permanent strategic arms limitation treaty to replace the earlier interim agreement were left for negotiators to work out.

Only a month before he would resign from the presidency, Nixon went to Moscow amid considerable domestic criticism seeking a breakthrough in permanent limits on offensive nuclear weapons. Instead of broadening and extending the five-year-old SALT treaty, however, Nixon and Brezhnev were able to sign only a treaty placing more limits on underground nuclear tests and a protocol restricting each nation to just one ABM site. The leaders agreed to seek a new interim SALT accord that would last through 1985.

After Nixon resigned in August 1974, President Gerald R. Ford went to Vladivostok in the Soviet Far East to meet with Brezhnev. No major agreements were expected from the summit, but Ford and Brezhnev surprised officials and the public by announcing a tentative agreement on limiting strategic offensive nuclear weapons and delivery vehicles. The Ford-Brezhnev talks jump-started the stalled SALT negotiations.

SALT II

Détente already had begun faltering before Jimmy Carter became president. Continued concern in the United States over the growth of Soviet and Warsaw Pact military capabilities prompted calls for more spending on defense. Under Carter, the United States gradually increased defense spending while pursuing a broad arms control accord with the Soviets.

Soviet leader Leonid Brezhnev and President Richard Nixon share a lighter moment aboard the presidential yacht Sequoia *in June 1973.*

At the SALT talks in Geneva in May 1977, negotiators developed an arms control blueprint to supersede the disputed Vladivostok agreement. The blueprint included a treaty placing ceilings on ballistic missiles until 1985 and a statement of general principles regarding the follow-up negotiations.

The proposal, however, drew criticism from members of the U.S. Senate who claimed that the Carter administration had conceded too much. Opponents faulted the administration for failing to sufficiently restrict the Soviets' Backfire bomber and argued that no limits should be placed on U.S. cruise missiles (small missiles launched from ships, planes, or ground sites that travel at low altitudes at subsonic speeds toward their targets). They pointed to the importance that the United States' allies attached to the cruise missile for West European defense. The NATO allies themselves had voiced fears that the United States had made too many concessions in the arms talks. Critics also contended that the limits on Soviet land-based missiles were too high, and they questioned whether key features of the agreement could be verified.

The administration countered by saying the agreements contained significant Soviet concessions and were better than the Vladivostok accord. It argued that the Backfire's effectiveness had been exaggerated and that the proposed limits on U.S. bombers with cruise missiles were not unduly restrictive.

Despite months of criticism, SALT negotiations continued through 1978. In May 1979 the two governments announced that a treaty would be ready to sign at the upcoming Vienna summit June 15-18. The treaty set basic numerical limits on intercontinental missiles and bombers through 1985:

- Of 2,250 weapons allowed each country (after 1982), no more than 1,320 could be missiles with multiple warheads (MIRVs) or bombers carrying long-range cruise missiles.
- Of those 1,320, no more than 1,200 could be missiles.

- Of those 1,200, no more than 820 could be land-based missiles (ICBMs).

Additional restrictions on mobile land-based missiles and cruise missiles launched from land or ships would run only until 1982.

Once home, Carter ran into significant trouble in trying to get SALT II ratified. A Soviet combat brigade was discovered in Cuba in 1979, and debates over its significance became daily events in Congress. Finally, in November 1979, the Senate Foreign Relations Committee voted to send the treaty to the full Senate. But after the Soviet Union invaded Afghanistan in December 1979, Carter, knowing the treaty had no chance of passing, asked the Senate to delay its consideration indefinitely. He pledged, however, to observe the unratified treaty as long as the Soviets observed it.

Reagan Takes Office

President Reagan came into office in 1981 stating that the United States was strategically inferior to the Soviet Union and that the imbalance needed to be redressed. The administration declared that unless the Soviet Union made some unilateral cuts in its nuclear forces, the United States would need to modernize its own forces before it would be ready to negotiate toward mutual reductions. The Soviet Union maintained that the nuclear arsenals of the two superpowers were roughly equal in strength.

Despite the administration's belief that it was not a propitious time for arms control, three important constituencies—the NATO allies, Congress, and the American public—wanted the United States to continue to seek arms control agreements. Each constituency possessed leverage that disposed the Reagan administration to negotiate. West European governments could decide not to abide by a 1979 NATO decision to deploy American Pershing II intermediate-range missiles and ground-launched cruise missiles (GLCMs) on their territory; Congress could limit funding for the administration's nuclear weapons modernization program; and many Americans might vote for the Democratic ticket in 1984.

INF Negotiations

The INF negotiations were prompted by the Soviet deployment, during the late 1970s, of medium-range SS-20 missiles targeted on Western Europe. Helmut Schmidt, then chancellor of West Germany, sounded the alarm for American action. He feared the European allies were becoming "decoupled" from the U.S. nuclear deterrent and that the large Soviet advantage in intermediate-range nuclear weapons would leave the NATO allies vulnerable to an attack or to political blackmail. If the allies could not counter the Soviet missiles with comparable weapons deployed on European soil, the Kremlin might think it could strike, or credibly threaten to strike, Western Europe, without fearing retaliation from the U.S. strategic arsenal. In December 1979, during the Carter presidency, NATO decided to adopt a "dual-track" approach. This meant preparing to deploy new intermediate-range nuclear weapons in Europe while simultaneously trying to negotiate with the Soviets to reduce such forces.

In November 1981 Reagan announced the "zero-option" proposal. Reagan offered to cancel the deployment of U.S. Pershing IIs and GLCMs in Europe if the Soviets would dismantle their SS-20s and their older intermediate-range SS-4 and SS-5 missiles. From the Soviet perspective, there were two major problems with this proposal. First, it did not take into account the French and British nuclear missiles targeted on the USSR. Second, the Soviets would be trading operational weapons for U.S. systems that were not yet deployed.

In the summer of 1983, Soviet leader Yuri Andropov indicated some flexibility on INF, but on September 1 a Soviet pilot shot down a commercial Korean airliner that had strayed into Soviet airspace. All 269 people aboard were killed. The incident exacerbated U.S.-Soviet relations and undermined any chance for progress in arms control negotiations. On November 23, 1983, after the West German Bundestag voted to accept the deployment of Pershing IIs on its soil, the Soviet INF negotiators walked out of Geneva without setting a date for the resumption of talks.

START Talks

After more than ten years of the SALT process, the Reagan administration decided to rename the main forum for arms control negotiations with the Soviet Union. To emphasize the new approach geared to "reductions" instead of "limitations," Reagan's team came up with the name Strategic Arms Reduction Talks, with the appealing acronym START.

In the START negotiations of 1981-1983, U.S. proposals primarily were designed to limit land-based ballistic missiles and throw-weight. Administration arms control advisers warned that Soviet "heavy" SS-19s and SS-18s, loaded with six and ten warheads, respectively, created a "window of vulnerability" in the U.S. nuclear deterrent. They maintained that the speed, accuracy, and potency of these missiles made them first-strike weapons capable of knocking out vulnerable U.S. land-based missiles. Some conservative U.S. analysts advanced a grim scenario wherein the Soviets would destroy a high percentage of the U.S. ICBM force in a first strike and then blackmail the American president into capitulation by threatening U.S. cities with a second strike if the president chose to retaliate with crippled forces. If the Soviets perceived the United States to be vulnerable, they might pursue their foreign policy goals more aggressively, resulting in superpower confrontations in which the United States might have to back down.

Many experts disputed that a "window of vulnerability" existed, including the Commission on Strategic Forces, established by Reagan in January 1983 and headed by retired lieutenant general Brent Scowcroft. The commission was charged with developing a basing plan for the new MX missile. In April the Scowcroft commission presented its report questioning the "window of vulnerability." The report argued that the U.S. strategic triad of land-based, sea-based, and air-launched nuclear weapons was not, for the immediate future, vulnerable to a disarming Soviet first strike.

Nevertheless, the Reagan administration remained committed to strengthening U.S. defenses and maintaining a hardline approach toward arms negotiations with the Soviets. The USSR dismissed the U.S. START position as biased against ICBMs, which carried approximately 70 percent of Soviet strategic nuclear warheads compared with only about 20 percent of American strategic warheads. At the end of the year, when the United States began deploying the Euro-missiles, Soviet START negotiators joined the Soviet INF negotiators in leaving the bargaining tables, saying that the strategic balance had been altered and would require a new assessment.

Debate on Reagan's SDI

On March 23, 1983, Reagan gave a speech challenging the scientific community to develop the technology for a space-based antiballistic missile defense that would one day make nuclear weapons "impotent and obsolete." During the first half of his second term, the issues surrounding arms control were dominated by the debate over the Strategic Defense Initiative, commonly referred to as "Star Wars."

The initiative sparked tremendous controversy. Supporters argued that SDI might eventually free the world from living under the "terror" of mutual assured destruction (MAD), the doctrine that both superpowers are deterred from starting a nuclear war by the threat of a devastating nuclear retaliatory strike.

Advocates of SDI also said strategic defense would be a stabilizing factor because it could enhance deterrence. They suggested that an ABM system protecting U.S. ICBM silos would so complicate calculations in Soviet strategic planning that a disarming first strike would be nearly impossible. The Soviets, SDI proponents contended, would never rationally launch a first strike knowing that relatively few ballistic missiles would penetrate the American defense. Supporters also argued that the United States needed a defensive system to protect itself from hostile Third World leaders who might one day gain access to nuclear weapons.

Critics argued that SDI's development would escalate the arms race because the Soviet Union would upgrade its offensive forces to maintain its ability to penetrate the American defense. They suggested SDI research could undermine the ABM treaty, and Soviet countermeasures might draw both sides into an arms race in both offensive and defensive weapons that would be even more dangerous and expensive than the existing one.

Opponents also questioned SDI's price and efficacy. It was projected to cost hundreds of billions of dollars in research and development, and many scientists believed that such a defensive system would never function effectively. In September 1985 the Office of Technology Assessment, a nonpartisan agency of Congress, said that a ballistic missile defense able to ensure the survival of the U.S. population did not appear to be technologically feasible unless the Soviet Union agreed to significant limits on its nuclear weapons. The study suggested that a U.S. effort to develop SDI would probably provoke the Soviet Union to increase its offensive forces.

Space-based antiballistic missile defense was challenged on the grounds that it could never be tested under realistic circumstances and that, even if it worked, it would not defend the United States against cruise missiles and bombers. Furthermore, some argued, a defensive system itself would not be survivable in space, if attacked by offensive space weapons.

Soviet leaders, who feared SDI was the beginning of a technology race that the Soviet Union could not win or afford, adamantly protested its proposed development. The Soviets called it part of a U.S. first-strike strategy that would negate the Soviet Union's ability to maintain a credible nuclear deterrent. They claimed that American strategic planners might expect that, after wiping out a high percentage of Soviet nuclear weapons, the American defense could repel the remainder of the depleted Soviet strategic forces. Moscow vowed to take countermeasures if the United States proceeded with SDI development.

Reagan steadfastly supported SDI and declared that the research and development program would be nonnegotiable. During Reagan's second term, hope for arms control between the superpowers appeared to rest on the resolution of the SDI issue.

Resumption of Talks

No formal arms control negotiations between the United States and the Soviet Union took place in 1984, but in January 1985 U.S. secretary of state George P. Shultz and Soviet foreign minister Andrei Gromyko met in Geneva to discuss possibilities for resuming talks. Following the meeting they announced that their respective countries would begin negotiations in Geneva on three types of weapons: intercontinental or "strategic" weapons; intermediate-range nuclear forces in Europe; and space weapons.

The March 12 opening of the Geneva talks coincided with a change at the top in the Kremlin. On March 10 Soviet leader Konstantin U. Chernenko died; Gorbachev was named general secretary the next day. On March 13 Reagan reversed his longstanding opposition to a get-acquainted summit meeting and offered to meet with Gorbachev. The two countries on July 3 formally announced a Reagan-Gorbachev meeting to be held in November.

There were two main reasons for the Soviet decision to return to the bargaining table. First, Moscow wanted to prevent, or at least slow down, the development of SDI. Second, by walking out of the arms control talks, the Soviets had made a costly public relations mistake in the contest for Western European public opinion. The Soviet Union not only failed to prevent the deployment of new American missiles in Western Europe, but it also appeared the more intransigent of the two superpowers when it came to pursuing arms control.

The November 1985 summit in Geneva was heralded for reducing the high tension in superpower relations, but the meeting produced no surprise announcement of arms agreements. In a joint communiqué released November 21, Reagan and Gorbachev called their discussions "frank and useful," while acknowledging that "serious differences remain on a number of critical issues."

On arms control issues, the communiqué called for "early progress" on weapons reduction. Two areas were singled out: agreement on a 50 percent reduction in nuclear weapons of the two sides and a separate agreement on intermediate-range missiles in Europe.

The communiqué made no reference to Moscow's demands that an agreement to ban SDI and other space weapons accompany limits on intercontinental and intermediate-range nuclear missiles in Europe. But in a postsummit news conference Gorbachev seemed to reaffirm the Soviet position that SDI limits would have to be part of any arms deal.

Reagan made it clear following the summit that the United States would continue to abide by the unratified SALT II treaty after it expired December 31, 1985, if the Soviets did the same. In a December 23 report to Congress, he officially confirmed U.S. intentions to continue complying with SALT II. But at the same time he accused the USSR of new arms control violations.

On May 27, 1986, however, Reagan announced that the United States no longer would observe the SALT II agreement, thus ending the six-year policy of informal SALT II compliance. Reagan said he was taking the step because the Soviets repeatedly had violated the terms of the treaty. The United States formally exceeded the numerical weapons limits in the treaty on November 28, 1986, when it put into service the 131st B-52 bomber equipped to carry long-range cruise missiles.

Reykjavik Summit

Arms control negotiations made little progress during the spring and summer of 1986. In the hope of advancing the arms talks and setting the agenda for a full summit to be held soon in the United States, Reagan and Gorbachev agreed to meet in Reykjavik, Iceland, October 11-12. At this "minisummit," Reagan and Gorbachev discussed making sweeping reductions in their countries' nuclear arsenals. In addition to making progress on an INF agreement, the two apparently agreed on major elements of a START agreement, which included ceilings for each side of 1,600 "strategic delivery vehicles"—ICBMs, submarine-launched ballistic missiles, and long-range bombers; 6,000 warheads carried by those missiles and bombers; and 154

"heavy" ICBMs, carrying a total of no more than 1,540 warheads.

The talks broke down, however, over Gorbachev's demand for a ten-year moratorium on field tests (all research done outside a laboratory) of SDI components. Reagan adamantly refused to agree to limit SDI efforts, even in return for major cuts in Soviet weapons levels. Gorbachev, in an October 14 televised address in Moscow, said that he favored "reduction and then complete elimination of nuclear weapons" but that SDI amounted to a "new stage of the arms race." Nevertheless, Gorbachev indicated that Soviet concessions made in Iceland would remain on the table.

INF Treaty

During 1987 U.S.-Soviet arms control efforts focused on intermediate-range nuclear forces in Europe. Several Soviet concessions made conclusion of a treaty regarding these weapons possible. First, Moscow decoupled progress on an INF treaty from progress on limiting SDI. Second, the Soviets became more accepting of extremely intrusive verification procedures demanded by the United States. Finally, the Soviets agreed to terms that were close to Reagan's zero-option plan first proposed in November 1981. At that time, the plan was quickly rejected by the Soviets and widely dismissed as unrealistic by most defense analysts.

On December 8, 1987, Gorbachev and Reagan signed the INF treaty at a summit in Washington. It required the destruction within three years of all missiles with ranges of between 500 and 5,500 kilometers (roughly 300 to 3,400 miles), together with their associated launchers and support facilities. A total of 859 U.S. missiles and 1,836 Soviet missiles were to be destroyed.

In terms of the number of nuclear warheads that would be removed from service, the ratio was lopsided in the United States' favor, since a large proportion of the scrapped Soviet weapons were triple-warhead SS-20s. All of the U.S. missiles were single-warhead Pershing II and GLCMs.

To verify compliance, the pact established an unprecedented system for each country's inspectors to visit, on very short notice, facilities in the other country where the banned missiles had been deployed, stored, or serviced.

The U.S. Senate approved the treaty on May 27, 1988, by a 93-5 vote. The documents of ratification for the treaty were exchanged by Reagan and Gorbachev at a summit in Moscow May 29-June 2. Actual destruction of INF missiles began on August 1.

The U.S.-Soviet arms agreement was the first to be ratified since 1972. It also was the first to mandate the destruction of a whole class of nuclear weapons. The successful INF negotiations revolutionized the arms control climate. Extensive arms control agreements covering other types of weapons appeared to be possible.

Moscow Summit

With the INF treaty completed, U.S. and Soviet leaders devoted more attention to making progress in START negotiations. At the 1988 Moscow summit, Gorbachev and Reagan agreed to order their negotiators to resume work on a treaty cutting arsenals of long-range nuclear weapons by 30 to 50 percent. But SDI remained the greatest obstacle. As in previous summits, Reagan and Gorbachev effectively agreed to disagree on the testing of SDI, thereby postponing tough decisions.

In lieu of a START pact, Secretary of State Shultz and Soviet foreign minister Shevardnadze signed two minor arms accords May 31:

- An agreement requiring each country to give the other at least twenty-four hours' advance notice of the test launching of any land-based or sea-based ICBM.
- An agreed-upon experiment for measuring underground nuclear tests in each country.

The purpose was to determine verification requirements for an unratified 1974 treaty establishing a limit of 150 kilotons on underground tests. The two sides also pledged to work on new agreements that would allow ratification of that treaty and a companion 1976 treaty establishing limits on peaceful nuclear explosions.

Gorbachev Troop Cuts

Six months after the Moscow summit, on December 7, 1988, Gorbachev delivered a historic address to the UN General Assembly. In the speech he broke dramatically with traditional Soviet rhetoric, criticizing the role of military force and ideological struggle in world affairs. He announced Soviet plans to cut five hundred thousand of the country's nearly five million troops by 1991. Gorbachev also called for "consistent movement" toward a START agreement, "while preserving the ABM treaty."

Gorbachev's troop cut proposal prompted cautious optimism from Western officials. They noted that it seemed to meet NATO's insistence that any Soviet troop cut be tailored to hit in particular those Soviet forces in Eastern Europe that Western allies long had claimed were poised to mount a blitzkrieg against West Germany.

Although Gorbachev presented his arms cuts as unilateral, he subsequently told reporters that he hoped the United States and its European allies "will also take some steps."

On March 6, 1989, the Conventional Forces in Europe (CFE) talks opened in Vienna. These negotiations replaced the Mutual and Balanced Force Reduction talks and included representatives of all NATO and Warsaw Pact countries. The CFE talks sought to reduce the alliances' inventories of conventional weapons such as tanks, aircraft, and artillery pieces, as well as the number of military personnel deployed in Europe. In late May President George Bush outlined a comprehensive approach to limiting conventional forces at a NATO summit in Brussels. The central feature of his plan proposed that the United States and Soviet Union reduce their troop strength in Europe to 275,000 troops each. At the NATO summit, Western leaders also agreed to link progress in the CFE talks to negotiations on reducing short-range nuclear weapons in Europe.

Malta and Washington Summits

Bush and Gorbachev held a shipboard summit off the Mediterranean island of Malta, December 2-3, 1989. The astonishing events in Eastern Eu-

Mikhail Gorbachev and George Bush greet bystanders between negotiating sessions in Washington, D.C., June 1990.

rope tended to upstage the Malta summit. The entire leadership of the East German Communist party resigned on December 3 as Bush and Gorbachev were winding up their talks. The next day, mass protests in Czechoslovakia forced concessions from that country's teetering Communist leadership.

Bush and Gorbachev agreed to speed up negotiations on arms control and economic issues—in effect keeping superpower relations on a par with the pace of political change in Eastern Europe. Bush and Gorbachev said they hoped a START treaty could be signed during 1990. The two sides also stated their intention to hasten their work on multilateral treaties limiting conventional forces in Europe and banning the use and possession of chemical and biological weapons.

Despite U.S. and Soviet efforts, a START treaty was not ready to sign by the time Gorbachev came to Washington at the beginning of June 1990. The two leaders settled for signing statements outlining the major areas of agreement in the START treaty and setting goals for further reductions.

Bush and Gorbachev also signed a chemical weapons treaty at the Washington summit. It committed both sides to halt production of chemical weapons as soon as the pact was ratified. It mandated that both powers would begin destroying their stocks of chemical weapons in 1992 so that by the year 2000 their arsenals would be half their present size. Two years later their chemical weapons stocks were to be just 20 percent of their existing levels.

CFE Treaty

On November 19, 1990, the Conventional Armed Forces in Europe (CFE) Treaty was signed by the United States, the Soviet Union, and the twenty other European nations that made up NATO and the Warsaw Pact. The treaty, produced by months of intricate negotiations, committed the signatories to reduce the number of tanks, artillery pieces, helicopters, and aircraft deployed between the Atlantic Ocean and the Ural Mountains. These cuts were aimed at reducing the offensive potential of the armies of the two alliance systems. Events in the Soviet Union and Eastern Europe, however, largely superseded the treaty.

Long before the U.S. Senate ratified the treaty in November 1991, the Soviet Union had made massive unilateral cuts in its armed forces deployed in Europe, and on July 1, 1991, the Warsaw Pact was officially dismantled. In the months after the dissolution of the USSR, most of the former republics moved to establish their own militaries. President Yeltsin committed Russia to continue the pullout of forces from Germany, and he announced that Russia's military would be reduced to between 1.0 million and 1.5 million troops by 1995. This compared with a Soviet army that in 1990 still contained 4 million troops. Under budgetary pressure, the United States might also reduce the number of forces in Europe beyond the CFE limits. Nevertheless, the U.S. Senate ratified the treaty and the Bush administration urged states of the former Soviet Union to ratify it as a way of formally codifying limitations on military equipment in Europe.

The former Soviet states that have territory west of the Urals agreed in May 1992 on a formula for allocating the cuts in military equipment required by the CFE treaty. Russia was to receive between one-half and two-thirds of the equipment allowed under the treaty, with Ukraine getting the next biggest share. As of August 1992, the individual states had not ratified the treaty.

START Treaty

Just weeks before the failed August 1991 coup, presidents Bush and Gorbachev signed the Strategic Arms Reduction Treaty (START) in Moscow on July 31. The treaty went beyond the SALT agreements of the 1970s by mandating actual reductions in the strategic nuclear forces of the two powers. Within seven years of ratification, the START treaty was to reduce the number of Soviet ballistic missile warheads by about 50 percent and the number of U.S. warheads by about 35 percent. This formula would leave the United States with about eighty-five hundred strategic nuclear warheads and the (now former) Soviet Union with sixty-five hundred.

After the failed coup, however, President Bush sought to quickly advance arms control beyond the START limits. On September 27 he announced sweeping unilateral arms reduction measures, including the removal of short-range nuclear weapons from naval vessels and bases in Europe and Asia and the end of the practice of keeping part of the U.S. strategic bomber force on constant alert. Gorbachev responded October 5, by announcing his intention to reduce Soviet strategic warhead levels below the START limits and eliminate all Soviet tactical nuclear warheads.

The end of the Soviet Union and Gorbachev's resignation on December 25, 1991, complicated the ratification and implementation of the START treaty. New arrangements had to be worked out between the United States and newly independent republics. In the meantime, the Bush and Yeltsin administrations attempted to advance strategic arms control beyond the START agreement. Fearing that Yeltsin's hold on power was not completely secure in the unpredictable Russian political climate, Bush sought to quickly conclude arms reduction agreements favorable to the United States in case a less friendly regime came to power.

American negotiators proposed reducing each side's nuclear arsenal to 4,700 warheads and banning multiple-warhead land-based missiles (which were the backbone of the Russian strategic nuclear force). Yeltsin proposed instead to reduce the arsenals to as few as 2,000 to 2,500 warheads. This proposal was designed to force the United States to make cuts in submarine-launched missiles, where it held a significant advantage.

At the June 1992 summit in Washington between Yeltsin and Bush, the two leaders announced an unexpected agreement to cut their arsenals to roughly half the levels envisioned by the START treaty. The Joint Understanding on Nuclear Arms Reductions would reduce current levels of strategic nuclear warheads by two-thirds over the following seven to ten years. Under the agreement the United States would be left with about 3,500 warheads and Russia would be left with about 3,000. The agreement represented a compromise between the Russian and American positions. While it would force the Russians to eliminate all of their land-based multiple-warhead missiles, it also would force the United States to cut its submarine-launched missile arsenal in half.

Despite this new agreement, the two sides stated their intention to ratify the START treaty. They planned to convert the Joint Understanding into a treaty that would also be subject to ratification by the U.S. Senate and Russian parliament.

Non-Russian Nuclear States

Although the disintegration of the Soviet Union clearly weakened the direct military threat to the United States, it created new arms control challenges for Washington and the newly independent states. The Soviet Union possessed a staggering 27,000 nuclear warheads. Most of these were deployed or stored in Russia. However, a substantial portion (about 25 percent) were kept in three other republics—Ukraine, Belarus, and Kazakhstan. In effect, the breakup of the Soviet Union had yielded four new nuclear powers where previously there had been only one.

The three smaller states indicated that they did not want to keep their nuclear weapons. In part, this attitude stemmed from the severe environmental damage in Ukraine and Belarus caused by the 1986 Chernobyl nuclear power plant accident and by decades of Soviet nuclear testing in Kazakhstan. The leaders of the three states, however, sought to use their possession of nuclear weapons as leverage in their relations with Russia and the United States.

In December 1991, when the CIS was created, the non-Russian nuclear states agreed to transfer the tactical nuclear weapons (those having a short range and designed for use on a battlefield) on their territory to the Russian republic, on the condition that all of them would be dismantled. In November the U.S. Congress—concerned about the possibility that some of these weapons could be sold, transferred, stolen, or misplaced—authorized the Defense Department to use $400 million of previously appropriated funds to help the former Soviet republics secure and destroy these weapons. By May 1992, despite a dispute between Ukraine and Russia over monitoring of the dismantlement process, all tactical nuclear weapons from the three nations had been moved safely to Russia, where they were being destroyed.

Dealing with strategic nuclear weapons proved more difficult. The three non-Russian states possessed some older missiles scheduled to be dismantled under the terms of the START treaty, but they also possessed some newer missiles. As with tactical weapons, the Bush administration promoted the destruction or transfer to Russia of all strategic weapons in the non-Russian states. Both Ukraine and Kazakhstan sought financial aid and security guarantees from the United States in exchange for doing so. The United States did extend some financial aid to the three states and expanded contacts, but it declined to offer security guarantees.

In May 1992 a protocol to START was signed in which all four nuclear nations of the former Soviet Union were named successor states of the USSR with regard to the START treaty. This protocol left the four to decide among themselves how to meet the START limits. The leaders of Ukraine, Belarus, and Kazakhstan promised to render their nations nuclear free by the end of the START treaty's seven-year implementation period. They also committed to signing the Nuclear Non-Proliferation Treaty as non-nuclear states.

Therefore, Russia was expected to be the only nuclear power to emerge from the former USSR. Significantly, it had retained authority over the nuclear command and control system of the Soviet military. Consequently, it could launch strategic nuclear weapons on the territory of the non-Russian states. Like strategic nuclear weapons within Russia, these weapons could not be fired unless the president and defense minister of Russia transmit codes that enable the weapons. The leaders of Ukraine, Belarus, and Kazakhstan were not part of the command and control system, but President Yeltsin promised to consult with them before launching nuclear weapons.

Economic Relations

Before the breakup of the Soviet Union, U.S. policy toward economic relations with the Soviets centered on the issue of how to balance the interests of American businesses and farmers who wanted to sell to the Soviet market against the U.S. goal of limiting Soviet economic and military strength. In part because U.S.-Soviet economic ties were not crucial to the American economy and defending against the Soviet military threat was a major concern, commercial interests were almost always subordinated to national security interests. As a result, trade and other forms of economic cooperation were severely restricted by the U.S. government.

With the fall of communism, however, the U.S. approach to economic relations with the former Soviet Union has reversed. Greater economic cooperation with Russia and the other states is seen as enhancing the prospects for the success of democracy and free market principles. Consequently, the United States has lifted many restrictions against commerce with the former Soviet Union and is actively encouraging greater involvement by U.S. companies.

History of U.S.-Soviet Economic Ties

After the North Atlantic treaty was signed in 1949, the United States and its allies set up a coordinating committee (CoCom) to seek common policies on exports to communist nations. From the outset the allies agreed to bar shipments of arms to the East bloc, but they differed on what other items should be included in CoCom's list of embargoed goods. The United States consistently argued for a more extensive listing than did the Europeans.

Restrictions on trade with communist countries were relaxed somewhat with the passage of the Export Administration Act of 1969 (PL 91-184). The act, which replaced the expiring Export Control Act of 1949, contained a provision enabling U.S. companies to sell items to communist nations if the items were freely available from other areas or countries, such as Western Europe and Japan. Supporters of eased restrictions argued that cold war hostilities had quieted and that the main effect of the controls in the old act was to deny U.S. exporters access to a growing East European market.

Despite this relaxation, trade between the United States and the Soviet Union remained small. The Soviet Union failed to manufacture many goods of a sufficiently high quality to market in the West. In addition, the inconvertibility of the ruble and the enormous obstacles to foreign businesses operating or investing in the Soviet Union limited trade and commercial ties.

Trade under Détente. At the 1972 Moscow summit, Nixon and Brezhnev agreed to improve and expand economic relations. The statement on basic principles released at the end of the summit noted that both sides viewed commercial ties "as an important and necessary element in the strengthening of their bilateral relations." The two countries established the Joint United States-USSR Commercial Commission on May 26, 1972. They announced July 8, 1972, that the United States had advanced to Moscow a $500 million line of credit in return for a Soviet pledge to buy $750 million worth of U.S. grain over a three-year period. On July 5 the Soviets had contracted to buy more than 8.5 million tons of U.S. grain. Large U.S. grain sales became important to both American farmers and the Soviet government. They have been one of the most conspicuous features of the U.S.-Soviet economic relationship since 1972.

A major stumbling block to broader economic relations between the superpowers was settlement of the Soviet Union's World War II Lend-Lease debts to the United States. The Nixon administration insisted on settlement as part of any broad trade agreement. Negotiations culminated October 18, 1972, with the signing of a three-year trade pact and an agreement on repayment of the Lend-Lease debts.

Before the trade agreement could be implemented, Congress needed to approve most-favored-nation (MFN) status for Soviet products. MFN status meant that Soviet products would be subject to the same U.S. tariffs and rules that govern the products of other nations. If Congress refused to grant MFN status, the pact could not be implemented and the Soviet Union would not have to repay its $722 million in Lend-Lease debt.

Grain is loaded for shipment to the Soviet Union in Newport News, Virginia, April 1973. U.S. farm interests grew dependent on massive Soviet grain purchases in the mid-1970s, which complicated the U.S. government's subsequent efforts to use the grain trade as a political tool.

President Nixon followed up his commitment made to Kremlin leaders at the Moscow summit by submitting to Congress April 10, 1973, a bill empowering the president to extend MFN status to the Soviet Union.

Anti-Soviet sentiment in Congress, however, had increased as a result of the Kremlin's backing of the Arab states in the 1973 Middle East war and its restrictions on Jewish emigration from the Soviet Union. By the end of March 1973, 76 senators and 273 representatives joined in sponsoring an amendment aimed at rejecting MFN treatment and the extension of credits, credit guarantees, or investment credits to any nonmarket-economy country denying or taxing emigration. The amendment initiative was led in the Senate by Henry M. Jackson, D-Wash., and in the House by Charles A. Vanik, D-Ohio. Over administration opposition, the House December 11 passed the trade bill containing the restrictive Vanik amendment. The Nixon administration protested that emigration from the Soviet Union by Jews and others would be facilitated not by confrontation but by an overall improvement in East-West relations.

The Senate did not act on the trade bill until late in 1974. Throughout the year, the Soviets asserted that emigration was an internal matter unrelated to U.S.-Soviet affairs. Congress passed the bill—the Trade Act of 1974—December 20. Soviet reaction came quickly. Secretary of State Henry Kissinger announced January 14, 1975, that the Kremlin had informed the White House it rejected the terms for trade contained in the Jackson-Vanik amendment and accordingly would not put into force the 1972 trade agreement. Trade continued between the two nations, but at a lower level than the trade pact likely would have produced.

U.S. Economic Sanctions. Commercial relations between the United States and the Soviet Union were damaged severely by the Soviet invasion of Afghanistan in December 1979 and the subsequent economic sanctions the Carter administration imposed on the USSR. Among other measures, Carter prohibited sales of grain to the USSR and expanded controls on items incorporating high technology.

By the spring of 1981 U.S. farmers had become increasingly vocal in their opposition to the embargo. In part to placate farmers and in part to fulfill a campaign pledge, President Reagan lifted Carter's embargo on grain sales to the Soviet Union on April 24, 1981. During the 1980s the superpowers signed several grain sale agreements, including a five-year purchasing arrangement in 1983.

Although Reagan lifted the grain embargo, he called for stricter controls on sales of high technology items to the Soviet Union. After the Polish government imposed martial law in December 1981, Reagan announced new economic sanctions against Moscow. He suspended all validated export licenses for the Soviet Union and broadened the list of goods requiring licenses to equipment or technology needed for the transmission or refining of oil and natural gas. A principal goal of the sanctions was to prevent the Soviets from using U.S. technology to build a natural gas pipeline linking the vast natural gas reserves east of the Ural Mountains with markets in Western Europe. Reagan argued that the pipeline would make Western Europe overly dependent on the Soviet Union for energy supplies and would provide billions of dollars in hard currency to prop up the ailing Soviet economy.

The president raised the international stakes June 22, 1982, by also prohibiting foreign subsidiaries of U.S. firms from selling pipeline equipment and technology to the Soviets and prohibiting foreign companies from selling the Soviets those products under U.S. licenses. This move brought an angry reaction from Western European governments, which claimed that Reagan was attempting to use U.S. law to force non-American companies to break valid contracts. Great Britain, France, and Italy defied the ban and ordered their companies to fulfill their contractual obligations to the Soviet Union. In November Reagan relented and lifted the sanctions related to the pipeline.

East-West tension over Afghanistan, Poland, and the conflicts in Central America and the Middle East created a slump beginning in 1980 in U.S.-Soviet trade, which had peaked in 1979 when American nonfarm exports to the USSR totaled $749 million. A year later exports had fallen to just $363 million.

Economic Ties under Gorbachev. After Mikhail Gorbachev came to power, U.S.-Soviet trade grew, but it remained minuscule in comparison with U.S. trade with other industrialized nations. Soviet exports to the United States grew from about $600 million in 1986 to about $700 million in 1989. Imports from the United States jumped from

$1.2 billion to $4.3 billion in that same time period.

Under Gorbachev, the Soviets sought to use hard currency to purchase high technology and machine tools to modernize Soviet industry. But the bulk of imports from the United States were grain shipments needed to make up for the failure of Soviet agriculture. The Soviets purchased $3.3 billion worth of U.S. grain in 1989. The bulk of Soviet exports to the United States consisted of petroleum products, minerals, and chemicals, along with some vodka, caviar, and furs.

At the Malta summit Bush proposed a trade agreement, contingent on the Soviet Union's codifying its new emigration policy in law. The agreement, which would give the Soviet Union MFN status, was signed when Gorbachev came to Washington at the beginning of June 1990. After leaving Washington, Gorbachev traveled to Minneapolis and San Francisco, where he urged American businesses to become involved in Soviet projects.

The Future of U.S.-Russian Economic Ties

The efforts of the Yeltsin government to turn Russia into a free-market democracy enhance the prospects that U.S.-Russian economic relations will expand greatly. Both governments have acted to facilitate mutual trade and investment.

Several agreements aimed at improving economic relations were signed by Bush and Yeltsin at the June 1992 summit in Washington. The leaders concluded a bilateral investment treaty and a taxation treaty that encourage investment by creating procedures for repatriating profits in hard currency, settling disputes, and establishing tax arrangements that preclude taxation by both nations of the same profits. Bush and Yeltsin also finalized the trade agreement originally signed by Bush and Gorbachev in 1990. The U.S. Senate had ratified the agreement in November 1991, and the Russian parliament ratified the pact just before Yeltsin came to Washington. Under the pact, Russian and American products enjoy MFN status in the other nation. A side letter to the agreement established procedures for Russia's repayment of its World War II Lend-Lease debt.

The United States has attempted to make doing business in the former Soviet Union easier for U.S. firms. Trade restrictions, including the majority of those involving high-technology exports to the former Soviet Union, have been lifted. The Overseas Private Investment Corporation (OPIC) has been authorized to offer political risk insurance to American firms doing business in the former Soviet Union. In addition, the United States has expanded agricultural commodity credit and Export-Import Bank credit guarantee programs targeted at Russia and the independent states.

Although some American businesses, especially energy companies, have moved toward investing in Russia and the other former Soviet states, most American corporations have taken a cautious approach. The cost of doing business in Russia is high, and the possibility that the Yeltsin government will fall or be forced to slow reform makes long-term investments in Russia risky.

Many companies have discovered that the former Soviet Union still is a difficult place to do business. The goals of American and other foreign firms often differ significantly from those of their Russian partners. The Russians would benefit most from help in establishing manufacturing that produces goods that can be exported. Foreign companies are attracted mainly by the untapped Russian market, rather than by the chance to set up production in Russia or elsewhere in the former Soviet Union. Goods intended for the international market can be manufactured more easily, at a lower cost, and with better quality in the newly industrializing countries (for example, Thailand, South Korea, Singapore, Taiwan, Mexico, and Brazil).

Despite the conclusion of the U.S.-Russian trade agreement, Russia is not close to becoming a major American trading partner. The Russian economy still produces little that Americans seek to buy. Vodka and some raw materials will be cheaper under the trade agreement, but it is unlikely that Russian manufactured goods will soon find much of a market in the United States. In addition, the ruble must become fully convertible before trade can flourish.

Nevertheless, as long as the United States perceives that it has a security and political interest in improving trade and economic cooperation with the former Soviet Union, commercial relations will continue to expand. Russia's vast reserves of oil and other natural resources may allow it to develop a strong trading relationship with the United States, even before it develops an export manufacturing potential.

After the Cold War

During the failed August 1991 coup in the Soviet Union the United States and the rest of the world held its breath. Alerted by the weakening of Gorbachev's hold on power during the previous year, many analysts had warned that some type of rebellion by reactionary forces in the military or the Communist party could reverse the process of reform and reinvigorate the cold war. The announcement by the coup plotters that Gorbachev was "ill" and that they had assumed power seemed to confirm the worst fears of many Americans. The quick failure of the coup, however, demonstrated that support for communism had passed. The Soviet Union rapidly splintered into fifteen independent nations, and Boris Yeltsin advanced his radical reform program in Russia.

The United States had grown comfortable with Gorbachev. Although he professed to being a communist, his genuine efforts to improve relations with the West, advance arms control, and open up Soviet society had persuaded many American policy makers that U.S. goals could best be achieved if he remained in power. Critics have charged that until the coup Bush and his advisers continued to embrace Gorbachev as the preferred negotiating partner, even though Yeltsin had emerged in 1990 as the leader most likely to advance democracy. Gorbachev had exploited his domestic weakness as a bargaining point, saying that the United States needed to support him to avoid having to deal with someone less conciliatory. Yeltsin's election in May 1990 as president of the largest republic in the USSR, however, signaled that Soviet liberals dedicated to radical reform might be more likely than conservatives to replace Gorbachev if he lost power.

Yeltsin's courageous stand during the coup, and his displays of strength relative to Gorbachev afterward, caused the United States to reorient its policy toward Yeltsin. The Russian leader's accommodating attitude made this reorientation easy. Through flexibility on arms control, an apparent commitment to economic reform, cooperation in resolving a multitude of contentious cold war issues, and his engaging performance at the June 1992 Washington summit, Yeltsin won the admiration of most American policy makers and citizens. All but the hardest-line cold warriors in the United States came to believe that Yeltsin was sincere in his pursuit of a reformed Russia and a highly cooperative American-Russian relationship. A consensus developed that Yeltsin, the best hope for engineering a transformation of Russia into a nonthreatening and fully democratic nation, must be supported. Virtually every American policy maker believed that there was no preferable alternative to Yeltsin.

Aid to the Former Soviet Union

To accomplish the goal of helping democracy to survive in the former Soviet Union, the United States cooperated with other leading nations, especially Germany, to provide financial aid to Russia and the other former Soviet states. On April 1, 1992, President Bush and Chancellor Helmut Kohl of Germany announced that the Group of Seven (G-7) industrialized nations had agreed to provide the former Soviet Union with $24 billion in financial assistance, conditioned on the progress of its states in reforming their economies. The package was to include $11 billion in bilateral assistance from the individual G-7 nations and a $6 billion ruble stabilization fund. Aid would be delivered in the form of export credits, loans from international financial institutions, education and training assistance, help in establishing political and financial structures, and wide-ranging technical assistance.

There was no guarantee that the investment would pay off. No matter how much aid and support the United States and the Western allies provide, they cannot ensure that democracy will survive in Russia. Its future will be determined by what happens within the country. But aid might provide a big enough cushion to prevent a disastrous social upheaval generated by economic hardships.

The package was seen as an important vote of confidence for Yeltsin from the international community. Faced with domestic opposition to his reforms, Yeltsin could cite this international endorsement of his approach. He also could counter conservatives who criticized his pro-Western stance, by pointing to the tangible benefits of aid that resulted from his policies.

Despite dissatisfaction with foreign aid and public perceptions that he was spending too much time on foreign affairs, President Bush supported U.S. participation in the aid program. The United States also has favored a major restructuring of the former Soviet Union's $70 billion foreign debt. In a June 17, 1992, joint news conference with Boris Yeltsin during their Washington summit, Bush justified U.S. support for Russia with these words: "Success for Russian democracy will enhance the security of every American. Think for just a moment about what that means—not for presidents, nor for heads of state or historians, but for parents and their children. It means a future free from fear." Proponents of providing financial aid to the Soviet Union have supported the president's position by saying that no investment in American national security could be more valuable than helping Russian economic and political reforms succeed.

Russia vs. Other Republics

Many foreign policy analysts criticized the Bush administration for focusing too much attention on Russia and adjusting slowly to the disintegration of the Soviet Union. Before the breakup, President Bush expressed a preference for the Soviet Union's remaining unified. Contributing to his position were a desire to preserve the continuity of an improving U.S.-Soviet relationship, a concern for the arms control agreements that had been previously concluded with the Soviet Union, and a fear that the splintering of the Soviet Union would result in ethnic warfare that would destabilize parts of Asia, Europe, and the Middle East.

President George Bush and President Nursultan Nazarbayev of Kazakhstan sign a range of agreements on the White House lawn, May 19, 1992.

Although the United States recognized all the former Soviet republics as independent states, it was slow to deploy ambassadors or set up embassies in some of the new states. American diplomatic recognition was important to the new republics because it bolstered their legitimacy and was a critical prerequisite to significant foreign investment. United States policy on recognizing the various former Soviet republics was to seek assurances of their commitment to the principles of democracy and human rights—particularly protection of minority rights—and transition to a market economy.

Because of their possession of nuclear weapons and their size and prominence in the CIS, Ukraine and Kazakhstan have received special American attention. Both President Leonid Kravchuk of Ukraine and President Nursultan Nazarbayev of

Kazakhstan visited Washington in mid-1992 to meet with President Bush and discuss arms control issues. The two leaders made strong impressions as responsible leaders who wished to expand relations with the United States.

The United States has a large interest in the maintenance of good relations between Ukraine and Russia. Although the United States has had little to say about the disputes between these two nations over the Black Sea Fleet and the status of the Crimea, it is conceivable that at some time in the future the United States might play the role of mediator.

Because the survival of Yeltsin and his reforms has been the primary goal of U.S. policy toward the former Soviet Union, the United States has been patient with Russian activities in other former Soviet republics. For example, the United States avoided demanding that Russia immediately withdraw its troops from the Baltic states, despite strong pressure from Americans of Baltic descent to make such demands. American criticism of the activities of the Russian military in Moldova also was muted. Implicit in the U.S. approach to relations with the former Soviet Union was a belief that Yeltsin, like Gorbachev, was vulnerable to attacks from the right. Since Yeltsin's continuing hold on power has been seen as central to the continuation of Russia's relatively benign foreign policy, short-term goals, such as the removal of Russian troops from the Baltics, have been subordinated to the goal of bolstering Yeltsin. Some observers in the United States, including high-ranking administration officials, reasoned that the Baltic states and other non-Russian republics would most likely be able to achieve a complete and secure independence if Yeltsin's reforms were allowed to proceed.

Prospects for Cooperation

If democracy survives in Russia, the prospects for expanding U.S.-Russian cooperation are excellent. Although the Soviet Union was a longstanding enemy, the two superpowers avoided a direct military conflict throughout the cold war. Most Russians and Americans do not hold strong enmities for the people of the other nation. To many Americans, ordinary Russians were among the foremost victims of the failed communist experiment.

The current era of friendly relations between Russia and the United States has not existed long enough to completely dispel decades of suspicion, competition, and hostility. Moreover, even if arms control efforts achieve large cuts, both sides will continue to have thousands of nuclear warheads that can reach the territory of the other. In time, the two countries may come to regard each other's nuclear arsenals with as little concern as the French, British, and Americans view each other's nuclear weapons. But twentieth century history will perpetuate some level of distrust.

Yet the perceptions driving U.S.-Russian relations have changed fundamentally. Soviet and Russian events have resulted in irreversible alterations in the international landscape that even the most reactionary Russian leader would be unable to change. For example, the credibility of a conventional Russian invasion of Western Europe is beyond restoration. In addition, regardless of who runs Russia, its domestic problems preclude a return to large-scale foreign adventurism in the near term.

The new U.S.-Russian relationship has produced cooperation and agreements that are startling against the backdrop of forty-five years of cold war. Russia offered for sale and the United States agreed to purchase nuclear fuel. The United States has begun work on a plan to help Russia develop a commercial banking system from scratch. The two nations have set in motion plans for greater military cooperation, including exchanges of officers and an expanded dialogue between senior officials on security issues. Secretary of State Dick Cheney has said that joint U.S.-Russian military planning and maneuvers should be considered. Yeltsin has opened his nation and its files to U.S. investigators seeking information about missing American soldiers from World War II, the Korean War, and the Vietnam War.

Regardless of Yeltsin's fate, the two superpowers will continue cooperating at some level, because it is in their mutual interest to do so. Both sides seek to facilitate the reduction of their defense and military aid budgets by concluding arms control treaties and avoiding military competition. The dangers presented by nuclear and chemical weapons proliferation and terrorism threaten the security of both nations and create opportunities for mutual action. Although Russia needs expanded trade relations more than the United States does, American businesses will benefit from commercial opportunities in Russia. The complications created by the emergence of a united Germany and the ethnic rivalries in Eastern Europe and the former Soviet Union also increase the common interest of the United States and Russia in preserving stability.

PART III

COUNTRY PROFILES

---

11. THE BALTIC STATES

12. THE CENTRAL ASIAN STATES

13. THE TRANSCAUCASIAN STATES

14. THE WESTERN STATES

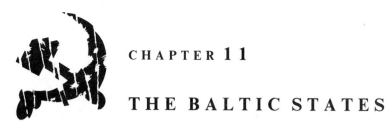

CHAPTER **11**

THE BALTIC STATES

Estonia

The northernmost of the three Baltic republics, Estonia was recognized as an independent state by the Soviet government on September 6, 1991. Estonia's resilient nationalism and desire for self-determination survived half a century of intense russification by the Soviet government. Together with the other Baltic republics of Latvia and Lithuania it refused to join the Commonwealth of Independent States.

Estonia is linked linguistically with Finland, its neighbor fifty miles to the north across the Gulf of Finland. The national language belongs, with Finnish and Hungarian, to the Finno-Ugric group.

Estonia's land, left swampy and low by glaciation, set a distinctive physical pattern of isolated farmsteads from earliest times. Thus, unlike the Russians, Estonians generally favored individual efforts in agriculture. Joseph Stalin's massive drive to collectivize farms met with aggressive resistance and resulted in the forced deportation of many Estonians and their replacement by Russians.

Ethnic Russians make up more than 30 percent of the state's population of 1.6 million. Estonians account for 61.5 percent, down from 88.2 percent in 1934. Ethnic Russians generally opposed Estonia's drive for independence.

At 17,413 square miles, Estonia is the third smallest of the former Soviet republics and the smallest of the three Baltic lands. Estonian territory includes some fifteen hundred lakes and eight hundred islands. A large portion of Lake Peipus, Europe's third largest, is situated in Estonia on its

eastern border with Russia. Latvia is to the south and the Baltic Sea and Gulf of Riga to the west. These waters strongly influence the climate, which is moderate.

Estonia has one of the most advanced economic infrastructures and well-trained work forces of the former Soviet republics. Under Mikhail Gorbachev's policies, Estonia became a testing ground for economic liberalization, and more than fifty self-financing cooperative ventures were begun. But years of forced development have also left extensive environmental damage.

History. Baltic tribes that had long inhabited present-day northern Estonia came under the domination of Danish invaders in the early thirteenth century. The Danes founded Reval, the current site of Tallinn, the capital, in 1219. By 1224 the southern portion of the country, after twenty-five years of fighting, had been brought under a semblance of control by the German crusaders, the Knights of the Sword. In 1346 the Danes sold their Estonian holdings to the German Teutonic Knights. Under German influence, the region became a trading center, with several Estonian cities joining the Hanseatic League. In the sixteenth century the Germans also brought the Reformation to Estonia, establishing Lutheranism as the dominant religion.

In the midseventeenth century Estonian nobles and the merchant-dominated towns sought and received the protection of Sweden. But this arrangement ended in 1721 when Russia, under Peter the Great, defeated Sweden and established control over Estonia. The conquest gave the tsar his window to the Baltic and allowed him to create a northern fleet, headquartered at Reval.

The abolition of serfdom in Estonia in 1817 did little to improve the lot of Estonian peasants, and uprisings among them were common. Their resistance provoked an angry Moscow to intensify, in 1881, its efforts to russify the region.

Estonians took advantage of the chaos of the Bolshevik revolution to declare their independence on February 24, 1918. The Estonian declaration was recognized by many of the major world powers. Estonian nobles sought Germany's protection and German troops subsequently occupied the country. Under the terms of the 1918 Brest-Litovsk Treaty, the new Soviet government renounced its sovereign rights to Estonia. But within months after Germany's World War I defeat and its withdrawal from Estonia, the Bolsheviks invaded. They were repulsed by an improvised Estonian army assisted by Finnish volunteers and a British fleet.

The constituent assembly in Tallinn again reaffirmed the country's independence, but the Soviets continued to attack because anti-Bolshevik "White" forces were using Estonia as a sanctuary and staging area for their forays into Russia during the Civil War period. The Soviets and Estonians finally made peace in early 1920, when Moscow recognized Estonia's independence.

The Bolsheviks secretly encouraged ethnic Russians in Estonia to stage a coup against the government, which in late 1923 had declared the Communist party illegal. The uprising occurred in early 1924, aided by arms clandestinely supplied by Moscow. The coup was rapidly suppressed and provoked a wave of anticommunist, anti-Soviet feeling that virtually eliminated their influences in Estonia.

In 1939 Germany and Russia struck a secret bargain that doomed the freedom of Estonia and the other Baltic states. Under the Molotov-Ribbentrop nonaggression pact, the Soviet Union pledged not to intervene in Germany's plans to conquer Poland. In return the Germans recognized a Soviet sphere of influence that included the Baltic states. Moscow forcibly occupied Estonia in 1940 and installed a local communist government that endorsed Estonia's annexation to the USSR. This annexation was never recognized by the United States.

Invading Nazi armies overran the country in 1941 but the Red Army retook it in 1943. In 1940 and after World War II, Stalin's government imprisoned, executed, or deported thousands of Estonia's citizens and replaced them with loyal Russians. All the capitalist institutions of the once-free republic were subjected to intense communization. Under Stalin's successors, Estonia became an electronics manufacturing center, and its rich deposits of oil shale and peat were aggressively exploited.

Government and Politics. The Estonian Communist party had, even before the failed August 1991 coup, declared itself independent of the Communist party of the Soviet Union. After the coup its power waned considerably. The Popular Front of Estonia, a broad-based coalition of parties espousing independence, nationalism, and environmental protection, played a unifying role in the republic's drive for independence. With independence achieved, however, many of the coalition parties began vying for a share of power, including two parties founded in 1988 to represent the interests of Estonia's Russian population.

The Supreme Council is the highest legislative body and its members were chosen in free elections in March 1990. It selects a chairman who is empowered to name a prime minister. The prime minister's choices for ministerial posts are subject to approval by the chairman.

The chairman, Arnold Ruutel, a moderate nationalist who has served in the post since 1983, chose Edgar Savisaar as prime minister after the 1990 elections. Savisaar, a strong advocate of a market economy, resigned in January 1992 in protest over the council's refusal to grant him special authority to deal with Estonia's worsening economic conditions. He was replaced by Tiit Vahi, who had served as transportation minister. Elections for a new Estonian Congress were scheduled for the fall of 1992.

Current Issues. Before the newly found independence, ethnic Russians enjoyed a privileged position in Estonia. Now it is unclear if they will even be granted citizenship. Many Estonian nationalists desire to establish total cultural and political control of their country by excluding the ethnic Russian minority and promoting the Estonian language. Most Russians in Estonia are similarly determined to protect their economic status and position, though some have chosen to return to Russia.

Estonian was declared the official language of the state in early 1989. On February 26, 1992, the Estonian parliament granted automatic citizenship only to individuals who were citizens in 1940 and their descendants. Those who did not qualify could earn citizenship by living in Estonia for two years and passing an Estonian language proficiency test. Applicants who met these criteria would receive citizenship after another one-year waiting period. Although some Estonian officials suggested that the language requirement would not be implemented, several Estonian Russian groups organized strikes to protest the law, and the issue remained highly charged.

The collapse of the Soviet Union and its intricate web of economic interconnections has created severe short-term difficulties for Estonia, which is dependent on Russia and other Commonwealth states for many of its raw materials and most of its sophisticated manufactured goods. Estonia's oil shale and peat deposits provide it with adequate fuel supplies, but it has had difficulty finding markets for its products. Estonians, once the highest paid of all Soviet citizens, have had to adjust to a lower standard of living.

The government has actively promoted privatization and a market economy, but the initial stages of the reform program have been painful, with most prices doubling or tripling while incomes stagnate. An aggressive drive to encourage foreign investment appeared to be enjoying some success by mid-1992. Estonia and the other Baltic states have also applied for membership in the European Community. Though membership is not imminent, Estonia has declared its intention to seek closer political and economic links with Europe.

The three Baltic republics have been discussing the timing and nature of political and military integration for several years, but national differences have made agreement difficult. All three, however, have agitated for the removal of Russian troops. Estonia is considered to be the most hesitant to commit to closer integration, but economic necessity and a common Baltic distrust of Russia could lead to a Baltic alliance.

Latvia

Latvia occupies the central position of the three Baltic states in terms of geographic size (25,200 square miles), location, and population. Like Lithuania and Estonia, it is dependent on Russia for raw materials and as the market for its manufactures. It also must deal with the corrosive legacy of a half-century of Soviet rule, with the damage done to its environment by Moscow's quota-obsessed command economy, and with the continued presence of a large ethnic Russian minority that fears for its future in the new, Latvian-ruled nation.

Traditionally known as the "workshop of the Baltic," predominantly Lutheran Latvia has been a commercial center since its domination by the Germanic Hanseatic merchants six centuries ago. Riga, its ice-free port and capital, is a vital commercial center and point of transit for goods and raw materials entering and leaving the former Soviet Union. Even after Latvia became independent in 1991, a large share of Russia's grain imports and oil exports continued to pass through Riga's docks. The geography of Latvia is characterized by flat, swampy plains and forests. The state is poor in natural resources, though it does export some timber.

Before the breakup of the Soviet Union, Latvian factories produced half its motorcycles, a fifth of its radios, most of its telephone switching equipment, and many of its electric buses and trolley cars. This well-developed industrial sector brought Latvians one of the highest standards of living in the former Soviet Union. The economic difficulties of Russia and Latvia's other business partners, however, have left many Latvians out of work. Ethnic Latvians, for whom independence was the realization of a dream, now face the harsh reality of reconstructing a devastated economy.

The Baltic states

In 1935, 77 percent of the population was Latvian, and only a third of them lived in cities and towns. By 1989, after nearly fifty years of Soviet rule, 34 percent of Latvia's 2.7 million people were Russian and 52 percent were Latvian, the largest proportion of Russians in any of the former republics except Russia itself. Now nearly 75 percent of Latvia's citizens live in urban areas.

History. Isolated tribes that spoke the tongue from which modern Latvian derives inhabited the region that is now Latvia from around 1000 B.C. By the early thirteenth century A.D., the Germanic Knights of the Teutonic Order had established effective control over most of the region, taking large landholdings for themselves and relegating the native Latvians to serfdom.

What is now Latvia was then two states, Livonia in the north and Courland in the south. By the late fifteenth century, after fighting debilitating wars with Poland and Russia, the Latvian states came under the rule of Warsaw. But Sweden gained control of Livonia in 1629 and ruled it for nearly a century. The Reformation and Lutheranism swept Latvia in the sixteenth century, finding a receptive group in the Germans who dominated the region's commercial life and who ruled as landed gentry in the rural areas.

In the eighteenth century Russian forces under Peter the Great defeated Sweden and asserted control over Latvian territory. Under the Peace of Nystadt, signed in 1721, Russia was given possession of Livonia, including the city of Riga. The ice-free port gave Russia access to the Baltic Sea, improving both its trade and military position. By 1795 Russia had replaced Poland as the ruler of Courland and was in control of all of present-day Latvia.

This first period of Russian control over Latvia was to endure until the Russian Revolution. After the tsar's fall in March 1917, Latvia requested independence. But in September it was occupied by the German army. Under the 1918 Treaty of Brest-Litovsk, the Bolsheviks ceded Latvia to Germany. That November, when Germany was defeated by the Western allies and the Bolsheviks abrogated Brest-Litovsk, Latvia declared its independence. In 1919, however, the Red Army occupied Riga until it was expelled by a German force. Finally, in late 1919, the Latvians, backed up by British and French warships, defeated the Germans. The new nation was devastated by the fighting, but it had achieved self-rule. On August 11, 1920, Moscow renounced any claims to Latvia in a peace treaty signed in Riga.

After the war, extensive land reform broadened the base of agricultural ownership with a commensurate resurgence in prosperity. The Latvian state focused on developing economic and political ties with Western Europe in this period, a return to its historical roots. Domestic politics suffered from a chronic instability and a series of short-lived coalition governments. In 1934, however, Prime Minister Karlis Ulmanis suspended parliament, assumed the additional office of president, and ruled as a strong executive until World War II.

Latvia had adopted a posture of neutrality before the conflict began, signing nonaggression pacts with both Nazi Germany and the Soviet Union. But the infamous secret agreement contained in the Molotov-Ribbentrop Pact of 1939 placed Latvia in Moscow's sphere of influence. Germany invaded Poland in September 1939, and by mid-1940 Soviet troops had completely occupied Latvia. Within weeks, cowed and compliant parliaments in the three Baltic states had elected communist majorities who then petitioned Moscow to join the Soviet Union.

In 1941 German forces invaded Latvia during its offensive against the Soviet Union. Latvia was retaken by Soviet troops in 1944. Again the Latvian nation and its economy lay in ruin. Moreover, Stalin launched a brutal campaign in Latvia and the other Baltic republics to weed out and destroy any semblance of nationalist opposition. Thousands of Latvians were accused of collaboration with the Germans and either executed or deported to Siberia, their place in the communist order being taken by ethnic Russians. The economy was speedily communized and integrated into the central Soviet system.

Government and Politics. During 1989 and 1990, Latvia cautiously followed Lithuania's lead in pushing for independence from the Soviet Union. The Latvians declared in May 1990 that they were moving toward full sovereignty, but that their declaration of independence would not take effect for five years. On August 21, 1991, shortly after the aborted coup in Moscow, Latvia declared its full independence. The United States recognized Latvia on September 2, and Soviet recognition followed on September 6. Like the other Baltic states and Georgia, Latvia chose not to join the Commonwealth of Independent States.

After the coup, the Latvian Communist party was abolished and much of its property seized. Many of its members who supported Latvian independence subsequently joined the Latvian Democratic Workers' party, which has little influence over political affairs.

A number of parties and coalitions of parties have formed and re-formed as Latvia has attempted to establish a multiparty democracy. Many of these parties have been or remain affiliated with the Latvian Popular Front, a broad coalition united behind the goal of achieving full independence. Several political organizations represent the interests of the large ethnic Russian minority, which has grown increasingly concerned about Latvian nationalism.

Since independence, Prime Minister Ivars Godmanis's government has undertaken the difficult transition to a market-based economy, freeing many prices and overseeing the start of a return to privatized agriculture. The issue of returning property seized by the Soviets or compensating its original owners has proved intractable, however, and the new Russian government has been unable to agree with the Latvians about which formerly Soviet-owned plants and enterprises will revert to local ownership.

The nation is ruled by a parliament called the Supreme Council, the chairman of which is the head of state. The current Supreme Council was elected in early 1990 in free elections. Anatolijs Gorbunovs, a pragmatic former communist, has served as chairman since 1988. New elections were to be held in late 1992 or early 1993.

Current Issues. Latvia's government must contend with the same three major issues that confront its Baltic neighbors: revitalizing the economy, cleaning up the environment, and resolving the status of the Russian minority.

Latvia has suffered from many of the same economic troubles as most other former Soviet republics. Unemployment has risen sharply, the populace has had to adjust to the collapse of the Soviet welfare system, and the government has not been able to control inflation. There have been frequent interruptions in the deliveries of raw materials from Russia, and the decline in Russia's buying power has reduced the demand for Latvian goods. Latvia's economic troubles were intensified in 1992 by a drought that reduced agricultural production and by a series of forest fires that destroyed hundreds of thousands of exportable trees.

The Soviet industrialization drive left Latvia with extensive chemical, petrochemical, and electrical industries, but over the last few years the aging plants have created pressing environmental problems that are likely to persist because of a chronic lack of funds. There is also concern that the plants must soon undergo extensive modernization to stay competitive in world markets.

The former Soviet navy maintained two major bases on the Gulf of Riga for the Baltic Fleet. The world learned in mid-1992 that Soviet naval commanders had long followed the practice of dumping toxic nuclear waste and unexploded bombs just off the Baltic coastline—one document said the practice had begun at the end of World War II and ended just before the public learned of it. Seepage of the waste from deteriorating casings could result in severe environmental degradation of the Baltic Sea, but Latvia and Estonia lacked the money to begin a salvage campaign.

The Russians have failed to comply with Latvian demands that all formerly Soviet military forces stationed in the country be withdrawn, and the continued presence of a professional cadre of officers and noncommissioned officers has produced several confrontations between the regular troops and Latvian defense forces. Moscow has claimed it is moving as fast as it can, given the need to withdraw troops from elsewhere in Eastern Europe and the severe housing shortage for troops in Russia. The Russian regulars, Latvians allege, have begun selling arms and materiel and have clandestinely supported ethnic Russian antigovernment activities. As such, they comprise a "continued threat to Latvian independence," according to government officials. Latvia's plans to establish a defense force and border guard have been severely hampered by a lack of funds.

The Latvian language has become a rallying point for Latvian nationalism and a mechanism to assert cultural dominance. Under the terms of a draft law adopted by the Supreme Council in October 1991, citizenship would be granted only to those residents who were Latvian citizens in 1940 or their direct descendants. Those who do not meet these criteria (mostly ethnic Russians) would have to have lived in Latvia for sixteen years and be fluent in the language before they could receive citizenship. As of October 1992, a definitive citizenship law had not been enacted.

Lithuania

The Baltic republic situated nearest to the West, Lithuania is also the largest in area and in population. The Lithuanians took the lead in agitating for severance from the Soviet Union during the rule of Mikhail Gorbachev. Lithuania's 1990 declaration of independence provoked the Soviets into stern economic and military reprisals, actions that stiffened Lithuanian resolve. The failed Moscow coup of August 1991 finally created conditions under which Lithuania and the other two Baltic states could establish their complete independence.

Unlike Estonia and Latvia, which both have high percentages of ethnic Russians, Lithuanians account for more than 80 percent of the 3.7 million people in the country, some 2.9 million people, according to the 1989 Soviet census. Russians are the second largest group at 9.4 percent and Poles form about 7 percent. Despite the country's forced industrialization at the hands of the Stalin regime in the post-World War II years, Russians did not emigrate there in the great numbers in which they flowed into the other Baltic lands; they constituted some 2.5 percent of the population in 1937.

The Baltic Sea, Poland, and Kaliningrad (an isolated portion of the Russian Federation) lie to Lithuania's west and southwest. Latvia is to its north, and Belarus borders it on the east and southeast. Vilnius, the capital, is in the southeast near the border with Belarus. Klaipeda, an ice-free port on the Baltic, is an important point of entry for goods entering and exiting the former Soviet Union. As of mid-1992, it was still the site of a major Russian naval base.

Once predominantly agricultural, Lithuania became a major manufacturing center under Joseph

Stalin's industrialization drive. Before the collapse of the Soviet Union it produced more than two-thirds of that country's electric motors as well as many of its consumer electronics, computers, and industrial robots. It also produces nearly 70 percent of the world's amber.

History. Around the fifth century, the pagan tribes of the region that is now Lithuania formed a loose confederation. But it was not until the early thirteenth century, under the threat of invasion from the German Teutonic Knights, that the groups coalesced into an effective political union. Its leader Mendog was baptized in 1251 and two years later was named king by the pope. His conversion seemed motivated by strategic concerns more than spiritual ones, however, and he repudiated Christianity in 1263.

By the early fourteenth century Lithuanian rulers had extended their dominion as far south as Kiev and as far west as Poland, establishing, during the reign of Gedimen (1316-1339), Vilnius as the capital of the empire. By the end of that century, the Lithuanian Empire stretched south to the Black Sea. A dynastic union with Poland took place in 1385, and the Lithuanians soon adopted the Roman Catholicism of the Poles.

The Polish influence in Lithuania became pervasive over time, creating a gentry culture that subjected the peasant population to the domination of wealthy nobles. The Polish language was spoken by all but the lowest classes. The cooperation between wealthy landowners and leaders of independent towns gradually weakened the power of the Lithuanian princes, until the nation became an impotent constitutional monarchy.

In 1795 the dual Lithuanian-Polish state was divided between Russia and Prussia with most of ethnic Lithuania falling to Moscow. When Lithuanian nobles rose in revolt in 1830, Moscow's reprisal was swift and ruthless. Russian was made the official language, Catholic monasteries and churches were closed, and Russians were sent to Lithuania to run the government. Lithuania all but disappeared during this campaign of russification. After another revolution in 1863, use of the Lithuanian language was banned, practitioners of Catholicism were deported, and Russian control of the government and social institutions intensified.

In 1915 during World War I, German forces occupied the country and stayed for three years. After Germany's defeat by the Western powers in 1918, an independent Lithuania was proclaimed. But Bolshevik and Polish armies soon were fighting over Lithuanian territory, while Lithuanian independence forces attempted to repel both foreign armies. The Lithuanians prevailed, but Poland, which had captured Vilnius, held on to the capital city until the beginning of World War II. That occupation has clouded Lithuania's relationship with Poland ever since.

The secret protocol to the Molotov-Ribbentrop Pact of 1939 assigned Lithuania and the other Baltic states to the Soviet sphere of influence. Soviet forces invaded Lithuania in 1940 and quickly annexed the country. Historians estimate that as many as a million people in Lithuania were resettled or deported and thousands were executed during Stalin's rush to sovietize the nation and its institutions. When German forces drove the Red Army out in 1941, they were welcomed as heroes and saviors by many Lithuanians, who began a revolution to reclaim their independence the day after the Germans first attacked the Soviet Union. Adolf Hitler's emissaries proved the equals of the Soviets in brutalization, however, and the Lithuanian population, particularly those who were Jewish, suffered enormously. In reaction to the German occupation, a guerrilla movement formed; it continued to fight the Soviets until the mid-1950s.

The land and its people were devastated by 1944 when Soviet forces drove the Nazis out. But in an all-too-familiar pattern, Stalin continued the ruthless practices of sovietization that had characterized the prewar period of Soviet occupation. Rapid industrialization soon had turned the war-torn land into a manufacturing center with a sophisticated infrastructure. Stalin's heirs continued to develop the Baltic region while repressing any manifestation of resurgent nationalism.

Under Mikhail Gorbachev's policies of perestroika and glasnost Lithuanian nationalism expanded and focused on the goal of independence. In 1989 the local Communist party declared its independence from Moscow and allied itself with the popular front movement Sajudis. On March 11, 1990, Lithuania unilaterally declared itself independent from the USSR, prompting a struggle of wills with Moscow. Several days later the USSR Supreme Soviet passed a law that allowed union republics to secede, but only after a six-year transition period and with possible loss of territory and financial reparations. Gorbachev demanded that Lithuania rescind its declaration of independence before any secession negotiations could take place, and he placed economic sanctions on Lithuania to coerce a settlement. Despite this demand, Moscow held informal negotiations with Lithuanian representatives in May. Tensions eased slightly, but Lithuania continued to demand independence and Gorbachev, fearing that caving in to Lithuanian demands would encourage nationalist movements throughout the Soviet Union, maintained a hard line.

In January 1991, with the world's attention riveted on the crisis in the Persian Gulf, Soviet forces in Lithuania moved to establish their control over the republic. On January 13 Soviet troops killed fifteen protesters in Vilnius as they seized the local television station. Gorbachev claimed that the troops had acted on the orders of a local military commander. Boris Yeltsin, at that time president of the Russian Federation, reacted to the incident by signing mutual security pacts with the three Baltic republics and calling on the Soviet government to recognize Baltic sovereignty.

Soon after the aborted August 1991 coup it became clear that the political establishment in Moscow, dominated by Yeltsin, would not attempt to hold the Baltic states in the union. All three were recognized as independent by the Soviet government in early September.

Government and Politics.   Lithuania, in December 1989, became one of the first states of the old Soviet system to do away with the Communist party's monopoly of power; in the days following the August 1991 coup, the party was banned completely. In the pattern of the other Baltic states,

Lithuania experienced the formation of a wide variety of political groups whose agendas ranged from nationalism to environmentalism. Contentious disputes over domestic issues have emerged from the unity displayed by disparate groups before independence.

The umbrella group Sajudis, or Lithuanian Reform Movement, which formed in 1988 to pursue independence, incorporates a number of these parties and is dominant in the Supreme Council or parliament. New elections to the Supreme Council were not scheduled to occur until 1994 or 1995.

The government of Vytautas Landsbergis, chairman of the Supreme Council, faced a herculean task of remaking a nation both politically and economically, a process complicated by residual anti-Soviet resentment over decades of Communist party rule. Landsbergis, a former music professor and the first chairman of Sajudis, became well known in the West during the struggle for independence.

Current Issues.   Despite an attempt to reorient Lithuania toward the West, a campaign aided by the Lithuanian population in the United States and Canada, Lithuania remains economically tied to Russia, its largest trading partner and the supplier of most of its raw materials and energy. The Lithuanian government has attempted to pursue genuine economic reform. The collapse of the Russian economy and periodic energy shortages, however, have contributed to a sharp decline in Lithuania's economy. Inflation in mid-1992 was estimated to be running at 1,000 percent annually, unemployment was up sharply since independence, and the gross domestic product had fallen about 30 percent since 1990. Hard-liners and reformers have argued over the pace of political and monetary reform and the privatization of former state-owned lands and plants.

Lithuania has the advantage of a strong agricultural sector; it is self-sufficient in most foodstuffs. Much of its electrical power comes from two Chernobyl-style nuclear reactors on its territory; their safety and reliability have been pressing concerns. While the government has actively pursued economic and political involvement with the West, the lack of a stable economy and a fully convertible currency has deterred foreign investment, a crucial element in the republic's economic program.

The continued presence of Soviet troops on Lithuanian territory, and Russia's reluctance to remove them because of the scarcity of jobs and housing at home, has become a major problem for the Vilnius government. The troops, increasingly left on their own by a disintegrating central command, have been caught selling weapons and stealing industrial materials, ostensibly to support themselves and their families. Lithuanians regard the presence of the Russian troops as a grave national security threat and have agitated for their removal. In September 1992 Boris Yeltsin signed an agreement with the Lithuanian government pledging to withdraw the troops within a year.

Lithuania has sought an alliance with the other Baltic states, but the effort has stalled amid disagreements over the pace and the nature of the cooperative effort. For example, each of the three is creating its own new currency, which requires settling complex questions of convertibility and exchange rates.

Although the dominant size of the ethnic Lithuanian population has prevented the severe ethnic troubles experienced by Latvia and Estonia, the minority Russian community has opposed efforts to implement a stringent citizenship law that makes Lithuanian the official state language and requires fluency in it from would-be citizens. Some Russians have returned to Russia, though most have stayed. Lithuania's ethnic Poles have been accused of supporting the failed coup in Moscow. Largely as a result, the parliament dissolved the local governments in two Polish regions of the country in late 1991, bringing protests from the Polish government.

CHAPTER 12

THE CENTRAL ASIAN STATES

Kazakhstan

Kazakhstan has functioned as a strategic bridge between Russia and Asia and a transition zone where Slavic Russians and the Asian nationalities mix, not often easily. It is the only state of the former Soviet Union where the local nationality group makes up less than half of the population. Kazakhs and Russians each make up slightly less than 40 percent of the population. This mix has explosive potential, but through mid-1992 the leadership of the republic had maintained stability through a careful strategy of accommodating the interests of both major ethnic groups.

Kazakhstan is the second largest state of the former Soviet Union, ranking behind only Russia. It is six times larger than Ukraine, the third largest state. Its land area of nearly 1,060,000 square miles covers 12 percent of the former USSR. Only eight nations in the world have a larger land area.

The republic was long considered by Moscow as a vast, inhospitable buffer to China, with which it has an 800-mile eastern border. To the north and west of Kazakhstan is the Russian Federation. To its south lie Uzbekistan and Kyrgyzstan.

With its arid climate and steppe-desert terrain, Kazakhstan seemed to tsarist Russia to be fit only for the primitive nomadic life of scattered herders. The discovery of enormous oil and mineral deposits altered that perception. The Soviets rapidly exploited these resources and created a sizable industrial base.

Kazakhstan is home to some one hundred different national groups and a total population of 16.5 million. In the 1939 census the population was 62 percent Kazakh, 19.7 percent Russian, and 13.2 percent Ukrainian. By the 1989 census, largely as a result of Russian resettlement in the burgeoning industrial region, these proportions had changed dramatically: 39.7 percent were Kazakh, 37.8 percent were Russian, 5.8 percent were German, and 5.4 percent were Ukrainian. Demographers consider the republic the least homogeneous of the former Soviet republics.

Because of Kazakhstan's vast stretches of uninhabited land, the Soviets conducted nuclear tests at Semipalatinsk, causing substantial environmental damage. Small but insistent political groups in Kazakhstan have focused on stopping further environmental degradation. During 1992 Kazakhstan cooperated with Russia and the United States to move all tactical nuclear weapons from its territory to Russia where they were stored and eventually will be destroyed. However, Soviet nuclear weapons and long-range ballistic missiles that were deployed on Kazakhstan's territory remain and have been an important element in Kazakhstan's relationship with Russia and the United States.

History. The first authenticated reference to the Kazakhs is from a Persian explorer, circa 1020. A branch of the Kyrgyz people and of Turkish origin, they later came under the rule of Genghis Khan and eventually became part of the Golden Horde. Islam was established in the area in the sixteenth century. However, the fragmented, nomadic social structure in what is now Kazakhstan hindered the strict observance and organization of the faith. While Islam is the predominant religion, it has not had within Kazakhstan the influence politically and socially that it enjoys in the other Moslem republics. Most Kazakh Moslems are of the Sunni sect.

Probably owing to a patriarchal division by a khan for the benefit of his three sons and heirs, the Kazakhs have long been divided into three large "hordes," the great, the little, and the middle, each occupying separate regions. Each horde is subdivided into races, then tribes, then sections, branches, and finally into small five to fifteen family units called "auls." These divisions still have a powerful influence on Kazakh society.

By the nineteenth century, Moscow had consolidated its control over Kazakhstan, and large numbers of settlers from Russia moved into the area. Russian migration eastward over the Ural Mountains and into Kazakhstan's northern black earth region soon resulted in the establishment of agricultural settlements, disrupting the traditional nomadic life of the Kazakhs. Later this movement continued toward Kazakhstan's southeastern portion, in the Lake Balkhash region, where farming by irrigation was established.

In 1917, following the overthrow of the tsar, Kazakhstan declared its independence, but by 1920 the Bolsheviks had reestablished control. In 1936 Kazakhstan was designated as a union republic. Rich in agricultural potential, Kazakhstan was a prime target of Joseph Stalin's drive to collectivize agriculture. Resistance to this program among Kazakhs was widespread. By the conclusion of the collectivization campaign, as many as 1.5 million Kazakhs had perished along with virtually all their livestock.

Kazakhstan suffered further under Nikita Khrushchev's ambitious "Virgin Lands" campaign. This program attempted to solve the Soviet Union's chronic agricultural production problems by greatly increasing the amount of acreage under cultivation. A large share of the available virgin lands was in Kazakhstan. The campaign has also been regarded by some historians as an attempt to russify the area. This crash program had some successes, but its lingering legacy in Kazakhstan is one of severe environmental degradation.

Mikhail Gorbachev's efforts to weed out corruption and inefficiency among long-entrenched communist organizations in the various republics led to anti-Russian unrest in Kazakhstan in December 1986. Major riots erupted in the capital, Alma-Ata, when Gorbachev accused the veteran Kazakh Communist party leader Dinmukhamed Kunaev of corruption and replaced him with an ethnic Russian loyalist. Three years later, in 1989, with nationalist sentiments steadily on the rise and anti-Russian feelings commensurately increasing, Gorbachev appointed a Kazakh, Nursultan Nazarbayev, to the post.

Government and Politics. Kazakhstan is ruled by the Socialist party of Kazakhstan, the former Communist party, which holds a 70 percent majority in the unicameral legislative body, the Supreme Council (formerly the Supreme Soviet). Dozens of other parties have been formed, including parties representing Kazakh nationalists, ethnic Russians, and environmentalists.

In August 1990 the 510-member Supreme Council elected Nazarbayev as president. He was again elected president, this time by popular vote, in a December 1991 election in which he ran unopposed. He enjoys strong support among both the Russian and Kazakh communities and is regarded as an opponent of extremism. He has actively promoted a secular regime oriented to the West. Following the August 1991 coup attempt in Moscow, Nazarbayev resigned from the Communist party, but he has pushed for preservation of the party under the new name with substantive reforms. Old-line local party leaders actively opposed this "abandonment of communism" by the new party but have not mounted a serious political threat to Nazarbayev's rule. He has kept intact the administrative bureaucracy left over from the Soviet period.

Nazarbayev has coopted several popular political initiatives as his own, particularly in the area of the environment. After the Moscow coup failed, he closed the Semipalatinsk nuclear test site. While governing with an authoritarian hand, through 1992 he had allowed a greater degree of press and political freedom than the other leaders of Central Asian states. Islam has had a resurgence in the republic, where religious freedom is officially upheld. Nevertheless Islam remains weaker in Kazakhstan than in other areas of Central Asia.

Current Issues. Prospects for Kazakhstan's future will depend greatly on how successfully it addresses the complicated ethnic issues facing the country. The sizable Russian minority concentrated in the cities and in the north fears growing Kazakh nationalism. The recently empowered Kazakh majority seeks to extend its power. In 1989 Kazakh was declared the official language. This declaration was affirmed in the proposed draft constitution unveiled in June 1992, although the document also acknowledges the importance of Russian.

Closely linked to the ethnic issue are Kazakhstan's relations with Russia. In mid-1991 Russian president Boris Yeltsin called for a review of Russia's borders with adjacent republics seeking to secede from the Soviet Union. Yeltsin's statement caused fears among Kazakhs that Moscow intended to annex the black earth region of rich farmland that lies near the northern frontier. Russian and Kazakh officials met to reassert the rights of ethnic minorities to government protection and the inviolability of the borders.

Nazarbayev has attempted to maintain a close working relationship with Moscow, while at the same time appeasing Kazakh nationalists. His government has advocated policy coordination among the countries of the commonwealth and has concluded economic cooperation agreements with a majority of the new republics, including Russia. The tight integration of industry in Kazakhstan with industry in Siberia has forced the Nazarbayev regime to follow Russia's economic lead.

Kazakh citizens enjoy the highest standard of living among the Central Asian republics. Kazakhstan has the advantage of large reserves of exportable natural resources, including oil, gold, natural gas, copper, zinc, titanium, magnesium, uranium, and chromium. It has actively sought Western, Middle Eastern, and Asian joint-venture partners to exploit these riches. The government has initiated a program of privatization that would redistribute

ownership of retail establishments, dwellings, and some industry. There is also official support for a gradual transition to private farming and ownership of livestock.

In May 1992 the Nazarbayev government signed a joint venture agreement with the U.S. oil company Chevron to develop the Tengiz oil field, one of the largest untapped deposits of oil in the world. The agreement has been viewed as a test of Kazakhstan's willingness to permit full foreign involvement in its economy. In June of that year, Kazakhstan formed a consortium with Oman to construct a pipeline that would transport Kazakh oil to foreign markets. The government's rush to find foreign business partners, particularly in oil and mineral extraction, could produce a xenophobic reaction from nationalists who object to the relinquishment of national proprietary rights over critical resources.

Kazakhstan's grain harvest ranks third among the former republics and its crop area amounted to some 17 percent of the old Soviet Union's total. Fruit, tobacco, and cotton also are produced. Livestock, particularly sheep, help make it a meat and wool exporter. An overreliance on agricultural chemicals, however, has resulted in dire environmental problems, which contribute to serious public health risks in certain areas. Like Uzbekistan, Kazakhstan must contend with the shrinking Aral Sea and windblown salt from the dry areas of its seabed. Radioactive wastes from decades of nuclear testing further complicate the task of environmental restoration. Some public health experts blame these environmental problems for Kazakhstan's abnormally high rate of birth defects.

With Russia to its north, China to its east, and other volatile Central Asian republics to its south, Kazakhstan's national security is precarious. It was one of four nuclear powers to emerge from the Soviet Union. Antinuclear sentiment and the complications created by a nuclear arsenal led Nazarbayev to declare his intention to eventually remove all Soviet nuclear weapons from Kazakh territory. By mid-1992 all tactical nuclear weapons had been transported to Russia for storage and eventual destruction. The Kazakh government also committed to ratifying the Strategic Arms Reduc-

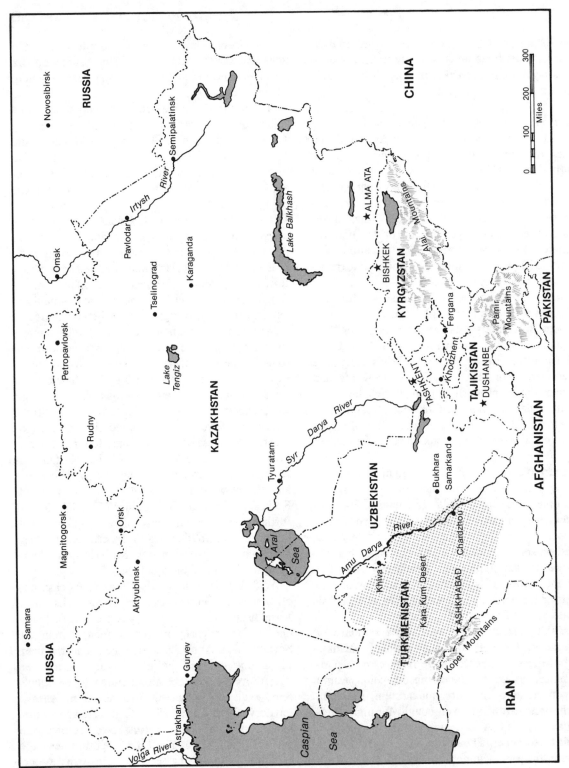

Central Asian states

tion Talks Agreement (START) with the United States. It has moved slowly, however, toward relinquishing Soviet strategic nuclear weapons. During Nazarbayev's visit to the United States in May 1992, he attempted to secure security guarantees from President George Bush in return for relinquishing the strategic weapons. The Bush administration declined to extend such guarantees to any former Soviet republic.

Kazakhstan shares a border with China's Xinjiang Province, which has a long and turbulent history of rebellion against the central government, be it mandarin or communist controlled. The province also contains about a million ethnic Kazakhs. Beijing is reportedly alarmed at the ripple effect of Kazakh independence and the fact that Moslem guerrillas are using the new republic as a sanctuary while increasing their anti-Chinese activities. As Beijing grows more concerned about the incipient rebellion, it may pressure Kazakhstan to secure the border or to allow a Chinese incursion to eliminate the sanctuary. Either move would be perceived by Kazakh Moslems as hostile and could further exacerbate ethnic and border tensions. Despite these potential strains, Nazarbayev has aimed to make his nation an economic link between Russia and China.

Kyrgyzstan

Kyrgyzstan is among the poorest nations of the Commonwealth of Independent States. In recent years it has struggled to free itself from economic dependence on Moscow and has enacted a series of economic and political reforms that represent a sharp break with its command-economy past.

Kyrgyzstan bore the brunt of Joseph Stalin's efforts to russify Central Asia in the late 1920s and early 1930s. The dictator's repressive program resettled substantial portions of the native population. Russians assumed control of the government and the economy. The resulting ethnic ill-will lingers to this day. Russians reportedly are leaving Kyrgyzstan in significant numbers, fearing persecution by the Kyrgyz majority.

Tensions between the Kyrgyz and a large Uzbek minority led to a serious armed conflict in mid-1990

in which 250 people were reportedly killed. The incident contributed to mass demonstrations against Communist rule, the removal of Kyrgyzstan's hardline leader, and the installation of Askar Akayev, a reform-minded president with apparently widespread support.

The Kyrgyz, according to the 1939 Soviet census, comprised more than two-thirds of the republic's population. But in the 1989 census they formed just 53 percent of the population of 4.3 million. Russians made up 21.5 percent and Uzbeks, 12.9 percent. There are also sizable populations of Ukrainians (2.5 percent) and Germans (2.4 percent), the result of early Soviet resettlement efforts. The capital, Bishkek (formerly Frunze), is largely populated by Russians and other ethnic Slavs, while the Kyrgyz predominate in rural areas.

Kyrgyzstan borders Kazakhstan to the north, with China as its eastern frontier. Tajikistan lies to its south and Uzbekistan to its west. Kyrgyzstan is extremely mountainous, with half of its 77,415 square miles lying above the ten-thousand-foot level. Only 7 percent of the land is arable, and much of the rest is devoted to raising livestock.

Most of the Kyrgyz are Sunni Moslems with Turko-Mongolian origins. Their culture, language, and historic heritage have much in common with modern Turkey—a common bond that may help to shape the new republic's future development. Turkey, more than any other country, has offered assistance and recognition to the Kyrgyz government.

History. The Kyrgyz are first mentioned in history by a report an emissary sent to the Eastern Roman emperor Justin II in 569. They came to the region from the north, their origins likely being around the Yenisey River in Siberia. The Mongol invasions of the thirteenth century apparently forced more of the Kyrgyz south into the mountain strongholds of their present homeland. In the seventeenth century Russians and others began another series of invasions, followed by the Manchus in the mid-eighteenth century. The Russians pushing down from the north established a settlement on the Issyk-Kul Lake's southeastern end and had, by 1876 after a series of punitive incursions, brought the region into their empire as the easternmost edge of Russian Turkmenistan, a mountain wall against China.

Settlers from tsarist Russia displaced native Kyrgyz from traditional grazing areas. The Russian presence led to periodic Kyrgyz rebellions and harsh reactions from the authorities. The victorious Bolsheviks made the region part of their Turkestan Autonomous Republic formed in 1918. It became the Kara-Kyrgyz Autonomous Province in 1924 when Moscow decided to partition the region according to ethnic groupings. In 1926 it became the Kyrgyz Autonomous Republic and then, in 1936, a union republic.

Under early Bolshevik rule the Kyrgyz enjoyed a cultural and political rebirth. Stalin's ascendance reversed these developments. Native leaders were replaced by Russian loyalists and russification began on an enormous scale with the aim of making Kyrgyzstan a dependable source of cheap raw materials. The highest ranking Kyrgyz Communists, among them three successive first secretaries, were executed. The party's ranks of native Kyrgyz were systematically depleted and replaced by Russians. Until 1991 Russians controlled the ruling Communist party.

Government and Politics. In March 1990 the unicameral Kyrgyzstan Supreme Soviet, consisting of 350 members, was elected with an overwhelming Communist party majority. The ethnic-based demonstrations three months later against hard-line Communist rule and the harsh political reprisal that followed led the Supreme Soviet to vote long-time party boss Absamat Masaliyev out of office in October 1990. The Supreme Soviet replaced him with reform-minded Askar Akayev, a physicist and former head of the Kyrgyz Academy of Sciences. A year later, Akayev, the only candidate nominated, won 95 percent of the vote in the republic's first popular presidential election. He enjoys strong support among both Kyrgyz and Russians.

The Kyrgyzstan party, a large umbrella group of many factions, is the dominant political party. The Kyrgyz National Revival party, or Asaba (Banner), broke away from the larger party and was legally registered in 1991. After the failed August 1991 coup in Moscow, Akayev banned the Kyrgyz Communist party and seized its property.

Akayev has advocated a gradual move toward democratization and has sought to establish freedom of the press. He has opposed direct Supreme Soviet elections because of their destabilizing effect, given persistent ethnic tensions. He has moved to reassure Moslem clerics on freedom of religion and promised to respect the ethnic rights of all citizens in the republic. Islamic fundamentalism has failed to make significant gains in Kyrgyzstan.

Kyrgyzstan was the last of the republics to approve a declaration of state sovereignty because of Masaliyev's determined opposition to any change in the Soviet status quo. Since his ouster and following the August 1991 coup attempt in Moscow, Akayev has been exceedingly energetic in his support of Russian president Boris Yeltsin. During the coup Akayev sent his representatives to other republics to encourage their opposition to the junta. He has supported Yeltsin's reform principles.

Current Issues. Kyrgyzstan's underdeveloped economy is heavily dependent on Russia. Some 70 percent or more of its trade is with Russia, and good relations between the two are essential for the smaller state's future. Adopting Yeltsin's economic reforms, Akayev partially liberalized prices in January 1992 while keeping prices for basic foodstuffs controlled. He then raised salaries of many public employees. Akayev also has moved toward significant land reform. Of all the Central Asian states, Kyrgyzstan has progressed the furthest along the road to economic and political restructuring.

Kyrgyzstan has large reserves of mercury, antimony, and uranium, with which it can earn hard currency. But its industrial base is less developed than that of most of the other republics and it has a weak infrastructure, partly as a result of its terrain and partly because of the constant threat of earthquakes.

Kyrgyzstan has been energetic in attempting to lure sorely needed foreign capital. The new government has aimed at diversifying its economy with light manufacturing enterprises. Trade regulations have been modified and tax and custom barriers simplified to attract more foreign involvement in the economy. Kyrgyzstan also has enacted new rules to protect foreign investment.

Reacting to Kyrgyzstan's commitment to democracy and human rights, the United States offered to establish relations with it on December 25, 1991. The only other Central Asian republic accorded this treatment was Kazakhstan. The U.S. government has provided humanitarian and technical aid to Kyrgyzstan, perhaps hoping that a successful economic and political reform effort there can serve as a model for the region.

The long years of Russian control resulted in a poorly educated, impoverished Kyrgyz majority that is both needful of Russian expertise and deeply resentful of its continued dependency. The newly empowered majority's violent reactions to other ethnic groups over land, water, and economic issues reflect a turbulent history of exploitation by outsiders. Akayev has attempted to control ethnic tensions by advancing his broad, secular reform program and appointing officials from all major ethnic groups. The task before the Kyrgyz people is to resolve these ethnic differences and focus on reconstructing their country on a new economic and political model.

Tajikistan

Tajikistan has been the most volatile of the Central Asian states since the crumbling of the Soviet Union. In September 1992 Tajikistan's longtime ruler, Rakhmon Nabiyev, was ousted from power by opposition militia forces. But Nabiyev loyalists have fought back, escalating the conflict into civil war.

Tajikistan's terrain consists of mountains and plateaus of the formidable Pamir and Alai ranges, the aptly named "Rooftop of the World." Even the lowest valleys in the Pamir massif are more than 10,000 feet above sea level. Tajikistan's arid climate is also severe. In a recent nine-year period, a mere 2.3 inches of precipitation was measured. Outside the capital of Dushanbe, most buildings are of simple one-story construction because of the continuing threat of earthquakes.

The difficult terrain and harsh weather have con-

tributed to making Tajikistan, by many measures, the poorest and most underdeveloped of the former Soviet republics. Its public works infrastructure barely meets minimum requirements for transportation and communication. Huge hydroelectric projects designed to make use of the republic's large, turbulent rivers have not yet been completed, and electrical shortages are chronic, placing stringent limits on industrial development. Tajikistan's dubious superlatives among the states of the former Soviet Union include: the highest infant mortality rate, the lowest literacy rate, the lowest per capita income, and the largest proportion of rural population.

At 55,809 square miles, Tajikistan is the smallest of the Central Asian republics. It is bordered on the north by Uzbekistan (which also forms its western frontier) and Kyrgyzstan, on the east by China, and on the south by Afghanistan. The republic's largest national group is the Tajiks, who comprise 62.3 percent of the total population of 5.1 million. Uzbeks make up nearly 24 percent and Russians, 7.4 percent. The Gorno-Badakhshan Autonomous Region, entirely within Tajikistan's borders, lies in the Pamir range and borders China and Afghanistan. Its population is overwhelmingly Tajik.

Until the introduction of cotton production by Soviet central planners, the chief occupation in Tajikistan was stock raising, mostly of sheep. Northern Tajikistan contains coal and oil deposits, and the republic is a major producer of uranium.

Nearly 85 percent of the Tajiks are Sunni Moslems. Early observers noted that most of the Islamic population did not adhere to disciplined worship practices, possibly because of the seminomadic existence of many of its people and scattered settlement patterns. In recent years, however, fundamentalist Moslems have made strong gains among the Tajik believers.

History. Persians, forerunners of today's Iranians, settled in the region that is now Tajikistan in the sixth century B.C. Their descendants, the Tajiks, still speak a dialect similar to Farsi, the language of Iran. For many centuries the Tajiks, isolated by mountain barriers, managed to escape the ravages of invasion. During the seventh century, however, Arabs invaded from the south and eventually established Islam as the religion of the region. Six hundred years later the Mongols swept through, followed by Uzbeks in the fifteenth century. Afghans and the khans of Bukhara from their stronghold south of the Aral Sea continued incursions through the eighteenth century. In the nineteenth century Russia established control over the area, making Tajikistan part of its Turkestan Province.

In 1924 the Soviets created the Tajik Autonomous Republic within a newly founded Uzbek Soviet Socialist Republic. In 1929 the Tajiks gained full union republic status. As in other areas of Central Asia, Joseph Stalin collectivized Tajikistan's agriculture despite strong resistance. During and after World War II, Stalin forcibly exiled large numbers of Volga Germans from the Volga-German Autonomous Republic and Tatars from the Crimea and the northern Caucasus to Tajikistan. Few ethnic Germans remain there today, but Tatars constitute 1.4 percent of the population.

Government and Politics. During the 1991 Moscow coup attempt, governments of most of the republics tried to distance themselves from the Communist party. Tajikistan's highly conservative government did not, announcing support for the cabalists. When the coup plotters failed, the Tajik communists were forced from power by anticommunist groups. After three months of political instability, however, the communists again took control of the government. Tajikistan became the only new republic where the old rulers had lost and then reclaimed their power. The Communist party underwent a name change following the coup attempt, calling itself the Socialist party of Tajikistan. By December of that year it had reverted to the old nomenclature. Until his ouster in August 1992, Rakhmon N. Nabiyev, the first secretary of the Tajik party's Central Committee, had been the republic's boss for most of the previous two decades. In the late fall of 1991 Nabiyev won a popular election for president, tallying nearly 60 percent of the total vote in defeating the candidate of the Democratic Opposition Bloc, a coalition of Islamic

and secular parties. Participation of the religious parties was permitted after the lifting of the ban on their participation just before the November election. Nabiyev's victory brought charges of vote fraud and massive protest demonstrations in Dushanbe, the capital. By mid-1992 protests had paralyzed the country's cities, and Nabiyev suspended civil liberties. The parliament endorsed his demand for direct presidential rule for a six-month period.

The opposition parties had been gaining in strength and numbers since September 1989 when the "Rastokhez" Popular Front was formed by a number of leading writers and intellectuals. Following demonstrations in February 1990 protesting alleged favoritism to refugee Armenians, a stringent government crackdown led to a suspension of opposition parties from elections to the Supreme Soviet. As a result, 94 percent of the deputies elected were communists. The Rastokhez Popular Front joined three other parties in a coalition that named a single candidate to contest the 1991 presidential election. Moderate elements controlled the opposition parties, but fundamentalist Moslems whose avowed goal is to form an Islamic state have gained in strength. Nabiyev's supporters frequently appealed to fears of fundamentalist Islamic rule to rally wavering Tajiks.

On September 7, 1992, after months of unrest, opposition forces cornered Nabiyev at the Dushanbe airport and forced him to resign. The Tajik Supreme Soviet had earlier delivered a vote of no confidence against Nabiyev.

Current Issues. The civil war in Tajikistan has been complicated by the presence of approximately 10,000 Russian troops charged with protecting ethnic Russians. Many were caught in the crossfire. The Russians fought pitched battles with Tajik rebels who raided Russian posts and stole arms, including tanks. In one incident thirty-five Russian soldiers were taken hostage. The Russian troops' participation exacerbated the anti-Russian sentiments of many Tajiks, and ethnic Russians began to flee the country.

In response to the fighting, Uzbekistan's president, Islam Karimov, closed the border with Tajikistan, preventing refugees from entering his country. He also cracked down on the Uzbek opposition to prevent Islamic-based demonstrations from erupting in Uzbekistan. Even before the civil war, Tajikistan's relations with its sister Central Asian republics, particularly Uzbekistan, were tenuous because of historical ethnic hostilities and border disputes.

By the end of September 1992, Akbarsho Iskandarov, the acting president of Tajikistan, had not been able to convene a meeting of the Supreme Soviet. With few political controls on the combatants, there appeared little chance that the war could be resolved quickly. The conflict was rooted in long-standing tribal animosities and territorial disputes that were unlikely to be easily extinguished. Tajiks from the southern region of Kulyab formed the core of Nabiyev's support. Some ethnic Tajiks from Afghanistan crossed the border to fight on the side of the anti-Nabiyev forces.

The ongoing political turmoil has left pressing economic issues essentially unaddressed. To shore up his tenuous position, Nabiyev indulged in traditional pork-barrel politics, increasing wages and pensions, lowering the prices of food staples and vodka, and using funds budgeted for security purposes to cover the deficit. Russian president Boris Yeltsin promised 400 million rubles in aid and the Canadian government agreed to sell up to one million tons of wheat to Nabiyev's government in 1992.

The country lacks sufficient funds or expertise to begin diversifying its economy or to complete several massive public works projects that would supply much needed electric power and irrigation. The civil war appeared to end the possibility of significant foreign investment in the near future.

Turkmenistan

Turkmenistan, the southernmost Central Asian republic, combines economic backwardness with social stagnation. Politics are characterized by centuries-old tribal rivalries exercised within the communist bureaucratic structures that have survived despite calls for change within Turkmenistan and the movement toward reform in other parts of the former Soviet Union.

The vast majority of Turkmen are Sunni Moslems who speak various dialects of the Turkic language. Most reside outside the republic's cities and some live the nomadic life of their ancestors, although the collectivization of agriculture has made this life rare.

The Kara Kum Desert, one of Central Asia's largest, covers much of Turkmenistan's 190,000 square miles. The Kopet-Dag range, a rugged mountain chain as long as the Alps, forms the desert's southern edge and borders Iran's northern frontier.

Turkmenistan's western border is the Caspian Sea. To the north and east are Kazakhstan and Uzbekistan; to the south and southeast are Iran and Afghanistan. The republic's population of 3.53 million, according to the 1989 Soviet census, is 72 percent Turkmen. Russians and Uzbeks each comprise about 9 percent of the remainder. The capital, Ashkhabad, is set in an oasis of the Kara Kum near the Kopet-Dag mountains. It was the southernmost major city in the Soviet Union and lies only twenty-five miles from Iran.

During the Soviet era, Russia bought Turkmenistan's cotton, oil, natural gas, and other raw materials at artificially low prices. In return it received food and finished goods at similarly subsidized prices. This arrangement retarded Turkmenistan's industrial development. Though it lacks a solid industrial base, Turkmenistan does have significant quantities of oil and natural gas that can be sold for hard currency. Given these resources and Turkmenistan's small population, the nation is in a better economic position than most of its Central Asian neighbors.

Because Soviet planners viewed Turkmenistan for five decades primarily as a cotton-growing region, the new state's food production is underdeveloped and large quantities must be imported. Turkmenistan accounted for nearly 16 percent of all Soviet cotton production before the dissolution, and it now faces a difficult road in diversifying its agricultural base. As in Uzbekistan, the environmental damage done by the demanding mix of forced irrigation and chemically dependent agriculture remains a gnawing problem. Only 2 percent of Turkmenistan's land is considered arable.

History. Turkmen tribes have long wandered the region that encompasses present-day Iran, Afghanistan, and Turkmenistan. Arab explorers first mentioned one of the tribes, the Salors, in the seventh century. Arab writers of the tenth century observed that the tribes were much feared by their neighbors because of their warlike nature. Even up to the Russian conquest in the late eighteenth century, the kidnapping and ransoming of Russians and Persians was a major enterprise of the Turkmen.

Although populated by fiercely independent tribes, the country has been dominated by a succession of foreign conquerors. In the seventh and eighth centuries, Arabs conquered the region and introduced Islam, which flourished. Other Turkic tribes invaded the area beginning in the tenth century. These tribes gave way to the Mongols in the thirteenth century. During the eighteenth century, Russia extended its empire to the Caspian Sea, establishing a textile mill at Astrakhan. By the late nineteenth century, the tsarist government had gained control over the entire region. The subsequent migration of large numbers of Russian farmers into the area and the resulting loss of grazing land provoked the increasing hostility of the nomadic Turkmen.

In the tumultuous aftermath of the Bolshevik Revolution, Turkmen nationalists, with the active assistance of the White Army and British agents, established a provisional independent government. It endured until 1920, when the triumphant Red Army reestablished control over the region. The Turkmenistan Soviet Socialist Republic entered the Soviet Union in 1925.

The Turkmen violently resisted Stalin's forced collectivization of agriculture (1928-1932), which threatened their traditional nomadic way of life. The government responded with mass arrests, deportations, and executions. The republic's own Communist party hierarchy, including the entire membership of the Turkmenistan Politburo, was decimated. Massive collective farms and irrigation schemes, along with the expansion of mining and manufacturing activities, eventually changed the nomadic Turkmen into a sedentary people.

Government and Politics. Six months after the August 1991 coup attempt in Moscow, the Turkmen Communist party became the Democratic Party of Turkmenistan. However, the name change was cosmetic. No opposition is permitted and the government is under the control of former party personnel and their entrenched bureaucratic machinery. Saparmurad Niyazov, the former first secretary of the Communist party, was named president by the Communist-dominated Turkmenistan Supreme Soviet in late 1990.

Niyazov has made extensive use of political repression to prevent the rise of any organized opposition. Opposition parties and demonstrations have been banned and the government prevented representatives of the small Agzybirlik (Unity) popular front from registering to run in the January 1990 elections to the Supreme Soviet. Prominent critics and activists were detained after the August 1991 coup attempt for criticizing Niyazov's much-delayed denunciation of the failed overthrow. Censorship is widespread, and the populace has a low level of political awareness.

Though Niyazov is a Turkmen, he was educated in Moscow, is married to a Russian, and has chosen to retain in office many Russian bureaucrats. As a result, he has been denounced by some Turkmen nationalists as an outsider.

Current Issues. Although prices for many goods were decontrolled in January 1992, Turkmenistan's economic situation forced it to maintain its historical trade links with Russia. Under the terms of a 1992 treaty on trade and economic cooperation, Russia was to import Turkmen natural gas and farm products and export to Turkmenistan cars, tractors, finished metals, and textiles. Ashkhabad's relations with its Central Asian neighbors and the other Commonwealth states remained similarly dependent, the legacy of the failed command economy. Turkmenistan has had a long and contentious dispute with neighboring Uzbekistan over irrigation water from the Amu Darya, which serves as part of the border between the two.

Niyazov has attempted to expand foreign contacts as a way of decreasing his nation's economic dependence on Russia and broadening the possibilities for investment. Iran and Turkey have made overtures to Turkmenistan, which has responded to both by signing various agreements on economic and cultural cooperation. Though Turkmenistan has friendly relations with Iran and is cooperating with its southern neighbor in the development of oil and gas reserves, the Turkmen people have not embraced Islamic fundamentalism. Turkmenistan has increased commerce with Afghanistan and, in an effort to broaden its economic reach, established commercial relations with Japan, China, and Europe. Turkmenistan's leaders voted to form a defense ministry in early 1992 but have accepted (with some discomfort) the continued presence of Commonwealth armed forces on their soil. Given the state's dire economic condition, the creation of a Turkmen military appears likely to be deferred for some time to come.

One result of the government's tight control of society was the lack of serious ethnic and nationalist upheavals that traumatized many of the other former Soviet republics. However, Russians and Kazakhs have experienced discrimination and are leaving the nation in large numbers.

The Communist party, by another name, remains in firm political control, and the people it rules so far have shown little appetite for either political or economic reform. This quiescence could end, however, if exposure to free market economies raises economic expectations or if the Turkmen people perceive that wealth generated by the sale of natural resources is not being distributed equitably.

Uzbekistan

Uzbekistan is the most populous of the five Central Asian states and the only one that shares a border with the other four. Comprising nearly 175,000 square miles—larger in size than California—Uzbekistan is an ancient center of oasis cultivation whose largely desert terrain is dependent on irrigation from waterways that rise in mountains on its periphery. Inexorable geological alterations have led to increasing desiccation and desert encroachment in many areas of this Central Asian nation.

These elements and an overreliance on single-crop farming pose increasing threats to Uzbekistan's environment and agriculturally based economy.

Uzbekistan is bordered on the north and west by Kazakhstan, on the south by Turkmenistan and Afghanistan, and to the east by Tajikistan and Kyrgyzstan. It is a predominantly Moslem state lying at the epicenter of the region's estimated 60 million Moslems. According to the 1989 Soviet census, Uzbekistan has a population of 19.9 million, of whom 14.1 million (or 71 percent) are Uzbek. Also living in Uzbekistan are 1.65 million Russians, 934,000 Tajiks, and 808,000 Kazakhs. Uzbekistan is the third most populous of the former Soviet republics, behind Russia and Ukraine. Contained within its borders is the Karakalpak Autonomous Republic.

Uzbekistan is the world's third largest producer of cotton and the major source of the crop for the former Soviet Union. Because cotton is demanding of irrigation, herbicides, and pesticides, it leaves soils depleted of vital nutrients and unproductive for other crops. Nearly 75 percent of the nation's arable land is used to grow cotton. About 3.7 million hectares of cultivated land in Uzbekistan depend on irrigation networks, which stretch nearly 93,000 miles in length.

Under the aegis of Moscow's quota-driven central planners, cotton monoculture came to dominate other agricultural and industrial endeavors in the republic. This reliance on cotton precluded the cultivation of significant food crops, forcing Uzbek leaders to import grain and other foodstuffs. Cotton production also has left the environment severely degraded. The Aral Sea, which lies between Uzbekistan and Kazakhstan, is the most notable environmental disaster. Its surface area has shrunk some 40 percent, and it is increasingly threatened by contaminated surface runoff.

A third of Uzbekistan's population now lives in poverty, and this segment seems likely to grow. Industry, given the long dependence on cotton, is largely undeveloped. Uzbekistan does account for a third of the gold mined in the former Soviet Union, but the mining processes have been environmentally harmful.

History. Uzbekistan derives its name from Uzbek Khan, a fourteenth century leader of the Turkic tribes within the Mongol Empire known as the Golden Horde. He introduced Islam to the region. Early in the sixteenth century, the Uzbeks extended their dominance over most of what was then called Turkestan and which subsequently became the five Soviet Central Asian republics.

Contacts between the Uzbek khanates and tsarist representatives first occurred in the mid-1530s during the reign of Tsar Ivan IV and primarily revolved around trade. The Russians began incursions into the region in the 1840s, establishing a fortification on the Aral Sea in 1847. By 1864 Russian forces controlled Tashkent, the present-day capital of Uzbekistan. Within a decade, the invaders effectively ruled the area they called Turkestan Province. Moscow's control and exploitation of the region led to the end of traditional Uzbek nomadic society. In its place came railroads, towns, cotton-based agriculture, and a Russian entrepreneurial class, the beginnings of the colonial-style society that came to characterize Uzbek-Russian relations during the long period of Soviet rule.

In 1916, with tsarist Russia experiencing the rigors of World War I, Moscow began imposing stringent restrictions upon an already distrustful and angry Moslem populace in Uzbekistan. As a direct consequence, a general revolt erupted and sporadically flared until the Red Army defeated the Moslem guerrilla fighters (known as the Basmachi) in 1923.

During the mid-1920s the Bolsheviks attempted to consolidate their political and administrative power in outlying regions. Under Lenin's relatively pragmatic sway, the new republics were allowed to develop their own cultures and languages through schools and the press. As a result of this implicit encouragement, "national communist" movements arose with native leaders occupying positions of local power.

Joseph Stalin, however, brutally suppressed these movements, replacing the leaders with his own loyalists. In 1936 the Uzbek Soviet Socialist Republic, now firmly under the Communist party's thumb, was established in the political form that endured until 1991.

Government and Politics. The state is ruled by the People's Democratic party of Uzbekistan, which was, until it renamed itself on September 14, 1991, the Communist party. In early 1990 a unicameral Supreme Soviet, which consists of 360 deputies, was chosen in tightly controlled elections. The Communists retained complete control of the legislative body and named Islam Karimov, the Communist party leader, to the newly created post of president. The president chose a cabinet of ministers shortly thereafter to administer the government. A declaration of independence was announced on August 31, 1991, by the Supreme Soviet, which also announced that the republic would henceforth control its own socioeconomic and foreign policies and assume control over all industries within its borders. Along with the other Central Asian republics, Uzbekistan joined the Commonwealth of Independent states on December 21, 1991.

Uzbekistan held a direct presidential election in December 1991. An opposition candidate was permitted to run for the first time, albeit against an entrenched political machine with overwhelming legal and extralegal advantages, including the wide use of patronage. Karimov was elected president by an 86 percent to 14 percent margin. A referendum on independence was conducted concurrently and unsurprisingly won 98.2 percent of the vote.

Karimov is considered a "national communist." He resigned from the central Communist party Politburo after the aborted August 1991 Soviet coup. Concurrently, in Uzbekistan, he confiscated party property, banned party organizations in and out of the government, and engineered the cosmetic change in the Communist party's name. Whatever its label, the party and many of its institutions remain in place. Nevertheless, it must contend with closer public scrutiny and a growing opposition.

Although Karimov has identified himself with Uzbek nationalism, he also has retained strong support among the local Russian population. Russians regard him as the leader most likely to maintain order and protect their interests.

Fear of the uncertain future has contributed to the public's lingering reliance on the former Communists and their administrative structure. They provide, after all, the only government most Uzbeks have ever known. But support for the Communists is not deep, and mass demonstrations against them have forced Karimov to promise reforms and concessions, including the registration of all political parties.

In the presidential election, the chosen opposition party was the Erk (Freedom) Party whose small political base was primarily composed of urban intellectuals. Erk chairman Muhammed Salih, a poet, ran as the party's presidential candidate on an anti-Communist platform that pledged adherence to human rights. The Birlik Popular Front (Unity) Movement, which was not allowed to register for the election, is the largest opposition group. It has a nationalist platform and a broader, more radical social base that includes social democrats and environmentalists. It appeared to represent a greater threat to the entrenched powers and has been the target of repression. The Islamic Rebirth party, also not permitted to register or field a candidate, holds the potential of becoming the predominant political force in Uzbekistan. It is considered to be increasingly influential, not only in Uzbekistan, but also throughout Central Asia. Karimov is under growing pressure to recognize it as a legal party.

Current Issues.   Nationalist sentiments, abetted by strong Islamic beliefs, were never completely suppressed in Uzbekistan during the period of Soviet rule. The chasms between the remnants of communism's materialism and the religious orthodoxies of the Sunni Moslems in the nation seem likely to widen. Moslem states such as Iran and Saudi Arabia offer tantalizing examples of semi-theocracies in practice and could be adopted by Uzbekistan as models.

The turmoil generated by the disintegration of the Soviet Union has, in Uzbekistan and elsewhere, fanned the flames of nationalist discontent and age-old ethnic antipathies. Relations among Uzbeks, Tajiks, and Kazakhs, always uneasy, have entered a new era of tension and confrontation.

Most of the politically unstable Fergana Valley lies within eastern Uzbekistan. This valley, which also stretches into Kyrgyzstan and Tajikistan, is a hotbed of opposition to the government. Because it is the intersection where many of the region's ethnic groups meet, the Fergana also has been the site of ethnic clashes. In mid-1990 about two hundred fifty people were killed in fighting between Uzbeks and Kyrgyz and Soviet troops.

Growing nationalism and a resurgence of Islam have prompted fears among Uzbekistan's large ethnic Russian population. Some Russians have left Uzbekistan, eroding what amounts to the new nation's pool of technicians and managers. A general exodus of educated Russians would leave large gaps in the Uzbek labor force and further exacerbate its economic problems.

Recognizing their economic dependence on Russia and other members of the former Soviet Union, Uzbekistan's leaders have sought to conclude commerce and trade treaties with these states. The treaties are intended to establish trade links replacing the web of economic interrelationships and dependencies developed during the Soviet era. Uzbekistan also has proposed a regional union of the five Central Asian republics but has been rebuffed, largely because of fears that it would dominate such a group.

Uzbekistan's environmental problems appear intractable and may act as a drag on economic growth. The overzealous application of dangerous agricultural chemicals has affected the health of the land, the water sources, and the rural populations. Most experts doubt the shrinking of the Aral Sea can be reversed any time in the near future. Reducing Uzbekistan's cotton production would conserve water, decrease the use of pesticides, and open up acres for food production, but such a course would be painful in the short run as established revenues from cotton sales are lost. The Birlik opposition party owes its rise in great measure to growing public anger over continuing environmental degradation.

Because of Uzbekistan's size and location the choices it makes heavily influence the rest of the region. During the first half of 1992 its government chose to preserve the status quo while implementing minor political and economic reforms aimed at mollifying the populace. As economic and environmental pressures mount, however, nationalism, Islamic fundamentalism, and ethnic tensions could threaten the status quo.

CHAPTER 13

THE TRANSCAUCASIAN STATES

Armenia

Where once the Kingdom of Armenia stretched from the Black Sea to the Caspian Sea and its southern boundaries lay well within present-day Turkey, the new Armenia is almost tiny, reduced by foreign rulers to its present dimensions. At 11,620 square miles, about the size of Belgium, it is the smallest republic of the former Soviet Union. Yet Armenia's church, culture, and language (which is of the Indo-European linguistic branch) have survived and remained sources of fierce nationalist pride.

Ethnic Russians account for less than 2 percent of Armenia's population of 3.28 million, the smallest percentage of Russians in any of the new republics. More than 93 percent of the people are Armenian (the largest proportion of any ethnic group living in its own state) with Azeris and Kurds making up most of the rest of the population. But much of the Azeri population, numbering some 56,000, has reportedly fled the republic largely as a result of Armenia's ongoing conflict with its neighbor to the east, Azerbaijan. Georgia lies to the north, Turkey and Iran to the south and west.

Economically, Armenia is closely linked to the other states of the former Soviet Union. It depends on them for much of its food and energy imports and as the purchasers of the majority of its exports. Many of its prominent industries, including machine tools and foundry equipment, require inputs from outside Armenia.

A massive earthquake in December 1988 caused extensive damage and killed an estimated 25,000 people. The quake destroyed or damaged as much as 30 percent of the republic's industrial plant and left up to 500,000 people homeless. Since 1991 Azerbaijan has maintained a rail, road, and fuel blockade against Armenia. Recent transportation disruptions in Georgia, through which Armenia receives many of its imports, further wounded the economy. A nuclear power station, closed earlier because of safety concerns, was reopened to alleviate the energy shortage.

History. Since Babylonian times, Armenia has struggled continuously for independence against the imperialist domination of its neighbors. The Persian and Turkish empires alternated control over most of the original Kingdom of Armenia with the Turks gaining predominance by the early fifteenth century. Under the rule of Mohammed II the Christian communities in the old kingdom were organized under their own ecclesiastical chiefs who were, over time, given absolute authority in civil and religious matters. The system of rule resulted in the Armenian bishop's becoming the political leader of the kingdom as well as its spiritual head.

Tsarist Russian forces first appeared in the Transcaucasian region at the end of the eighteenth century. By 1828, after a victory over the Persian Empire, Moscow took possession of present-day Armenia. A large population of Armenians lived outside Russian control in the Ottoman Empire. The Turks, who distrusted the Armenians and sought to quell growing Armenian nationalism, carried out systematic massacres of Armenians in 1895 and 1896. As many as 100,000 Armenians were killed by Turkish troops and organized mobs.

In 1915, at the beginning of World War I, the Ottoman government committed an even larger genocide against its Armenian population. Armenians had pledged their loyalty to the Ottoman Empire when it entered the war, but harsh Turkish conscription methods and the forceful seizure of Armenian property quickly roused angry Armenian reaction. The Turks responded with a systematic campaign of deportation and killing of Armenians in Turkey. More than a half million Armenians are estimated to have been killed by the Turks or died during the deportation. The 1915 genocide became the most vivid Armenian national memory, one that has unified Armenians worldwide ever since.

In April 1918, witnessing the dissolution of Tsarist Russia and taking advantage of fragmented Bolshevik power, emboldened Russian Armenian nationalists and other Transcaucasians declared their independence and established the Transcaucasian Federated Republic with its capital at Yerevan. A month later this union dissolved, as Armenia, Azerbaijan, and Georgia moved to establish their individual independence. In January 1920 the Western powers gave de facto recognition to the three Transcaucasian nations. That spring, however, the Red Army seized control of the region. By 1921 the Bolsheviks gained complete control of Russian Transcaucasia and established the Soviet Transcaucasian Republic. In 1936 Armenia became, along with Azerbaijan and Georgia, a union republic.

Under stringent Communist party rule, Armenia achieved a measure of stability and economic prosperity with industrialization and the creation of hydroelectric projects. For a time, the Bolsheviks were viewed by many Armenians as their protectors from the Turks. In the great purge of the late 1930s, the Armenian Communist party leadership was decimated after incurring the personal wrath of Lavrenty Beria, the Georgian who ran Joseph Stalin's internal security apparatus. The subsequent party reorganization resulted in a structure that was completely under Stalin's control.

In 1921 Stalin laid the foundations for today's Armenian-Azeri dispute. He created the Nakhichevan Autonomous Republic out of what had been Armenian land, transferring the 2,100-square-mile area on Armenia's southwestern border to Azerbaijan's control. Azeris constitute some 90 percent of the population of this region. At the same time Stalin created the Nagorno-Karabakh Autonomous Oblast (region) out of a mountainous portion of eastern Armenia and placed it also under Azeri control, despite its predominantly Armenian population. The dictator's politically expedient subdivision created a permanent rift between Armenians and Azeris, one that smoldered for more than half a century. In 1988 violence erupted when Armenians in Nagorno-Karabakh announced their intention to reunite with Armenia. Armenians within Nagorno-Karabakh, supported by Armenia, have fought against local Azeris and the forces of the Azeri government, which has declared its intention to hold on to the region.

Government and Politics. The Communist party in Armenia lost most of its power in the wake of the multiparty Supreme Soviet elections in May 1990. That election produced a parliament without a single party majority. The Armenian Nationalist Movement (A.N.M.) has the largest bloc (slightly more than a fifth of the seats) in the unicameral parliament.

On September 21, 1991, a month after the failed coup in Moscow, 92 percent of Armenian voters endorsed independence in a referendum. The following month Levon Ter-Petrossyan of the A.N.M., a prominent Armenian nationalist dissident during the Soviet period, was elected president.

Ter-Petrossyan won legislative approval to dramatically reconstruct Armenia's economy on market-based disciplines. Since the independence referendum, the state has distributed some 80 percent of the farmland in its possession to peasant owners and has aggressively pursued the privatization of state-owned enterprises.

Current Issues. With a homogeneous and seemingly united population, Armenia's political problems appear to lie, for the moment, outside its borders. Armenia has placed a high priority on maintaining good relations with other former Soviet republics and it has concluded economic agreements with most of them. It also is a member of the Commonwealth of Independent States. Good relations with its former Soviet brethren are essential in Armenia's efforts to overcome the devastating impact of the ongoing Azeri blockade. Instability in Georgia, through which much of its commerce flows, has complicated Armenia's ability to deal with the embargo. The Azeri conflict also has forced the government to maintain a working relationship with Turkey, despite its historic enmity toward that nation, and to establish new trade relations with Iran, primarily to ensure fuel deliveries.

The ongoing ethnic conflict with Azerbaijan dominates current Armenian politics and appears likely to remain at the forefront of Armenian concerns. An Armenian proposal to establish Nagorno-Karabakh as an independent republic within the Commonwealth of Independent States elicited little enthusiasm from any of the affected parties, as has another Armenian suggestion that international peacekeeping forces be sent to the region. The Armenian government and independent Armenian groups have sent arms and aid to Nagorno-Karabakh, and Armenia funds the region's budget.

Nationalist sentiment has remained a defining element of the Armenian political character, buttressed by the collective memory of the 1915 genocide. Because of this deep nationalism and the strong cultural reaction to any situation that could lead to the victimization of Armenians, Armenian political leaders (like Azeri leaders) have little room to compromise on the issue of Nagorno-Karabakh. Though Ter-Petrossyan is considered a nationalist who has at times incited anti-Azeri activity, there are politicians and parties in Armenia espousing even more extreme nationalism than Ter-Petrossyan and the A.N.M.

Armenia has received financial and moral support from the 3 million Armenians abroad, all of whom have been given Armenian citizenship by the new government. Many of them retain strong familial ties to their ancestral homeland and maintain organized relationships with their fellow expatriates, particularly in the United States and France.

The Nagorno-Karabakh conflict, the blockade by Azerbaijan, the 1988 earthquake, and the economic

dislocations accompanying the breakup of the Soviet Union have created enormous economic problems for Armenia. While Armenia's infrastructure is reasonably well developed, it suffered extensive damage in the 1988 earthquake. The republic's landlocked position and high degree of economic dependency make it vulnerable despite its commitment to economic reform. Since 1988 its small population of just over 3 million has had to absorb hundreds of thousands of refugees—people likely to remain indefinitely. These pressures on its domestic economic capacity and the seemingly insoluble ethnic turmoil with Azerbaijan could make an increasingly militant nationalism Armenia's dominant political force for years to come.

Azerbaijan

Since 1988 Azerbaijan has been locked in an ethnic conflict with neighboring Armenia. The two Transcaucasian states have been fighting over the Nagorno-Karabakh Autonomous Oblast, an enclave situated entirely within Azerbaijan but populated largely by Armenians. Armed conflict also has occurred over the Nakhichevan Autonomous Republic, an Azeri enclave within Armenia, which is administratively a part of Azerbaijan. The enclaves were created in the early 1920s by Joseph Stalin, who sought to dilute nationalist opposition to Soviet rule in the two republics. The Azeri-Armenian conflict has claimed more than two thousand lives and has greatly hampered economic development and restructuring in the two countries.

At 33,000 square miles, Azerbaijan is the largest of the three states of the Transcaucasia region. It is the only Moslem state of the former Soviet Union outside Central Asia. Unlike the Moslems of Central Asia, who are predominantly Sunnis, most Azeris belong to the Shi'ite branch of Islam like the Iranians. Azeris, however, speak a Turkic language.

Almost half the country is arid plain, protected by rugged mountains lying to the west and south. Armenia and Georgia form Azerbaijan's western border; Russia lies to the north and Iran to the south. Nagorno-Karabakh is in Azerbaijan's mountainous western region near the Armenian border.

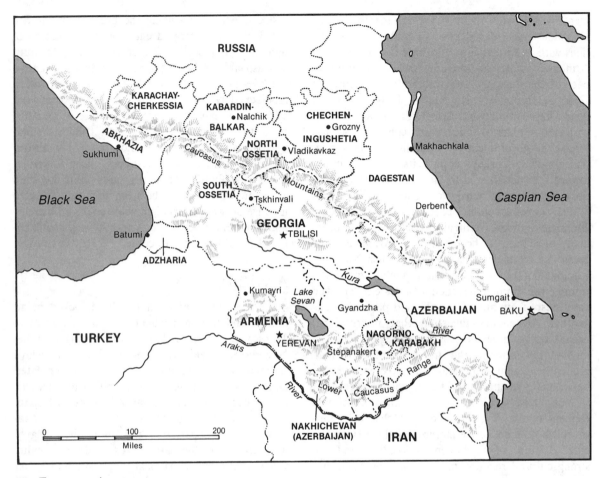

The Transcaucasian states

Azerbaijan's 7 million people are among the poorest in the former Soviet Union. The per capita gross national product averages only 70 percent of median GNP for the old Soviet Union as a whole. According to the 1989 Soviet census, 82.7 percent of the population is Azeri. Russians, who constituted nearly 8 percent of the population in 1979, were 5.6 percent of the 1989 total. Armenians also were 5.6 percent of the population in the 1989 census, but the political upheaval and violence since then have reduced their numbers substantially. As many as 300,000 fled Azerbaijan for Armenia between 1989 and 1992.

In the country's southern triangle a subtropical climate prevails and rainfall is adequate for agriculture. But throughout most of the country cultivated land must be irrigated to produce crops. Near Baku, the capital located on the Caspian Sea, are extensive oil and gas fields, making Azerbaijan the only Transcaucasian state self-sufficient in energy and one of the few former Soviet republics with the potential to export those resources. In an effort to earn the maximum amount of hard currency from energy exports, the government is aggressively courting international energy companies to attract investment and joint ventures. Because Armenia depends upon its neighbor's energy stocks, Azerbaijan's embargo of oil and gas shipments in connection with the Nagorno-Karabakh dispute has had a severe impact on the Armenian economy.

History. Bordered on the east by the Caspian Sea, Azerbaijan was an important trade route between east and west from the Middle Ages on. A land bridge near the northeastern city of Derbent was called by the Arab caravan traders who plied it "the Gateway to the East."

Though many foreign peoples laid claim to the region that is now Azerbaijan—including the Georgians, Armenians, Romans, Huns, and Mongols—Azerbaijani culture was most heavily influenced by Turks and Persians from the south. In the eleventh century, when Turkic-speaking tribes from the west began a large migration into Azerbaijan, Persians already dominated the region. The two peoples apparently coexisted harmoniously, adopting the Persian religion of Shi'ite Islam and many Turkish cultural traditions.

Persians maintained political control of the Azerbaijan region until early in the nineteenth century, but aggressive Russian attempts to challenge that rule had begun more than a century earlier during the reign of Peter the Great. His forces, after establishing a stronghold at Astrakhan on the Volga, captured the Persian outpost of Derbent in 1722 and Baku a year later. But these and other territories were restored to Persia following Peter's death in 1725.

Under Alexander I, Russia annexed Georgia, prompting a war with Persia that was fought from 1804 to 1813. The victorious Russians took possession of most of what is today Azerbaijan. Russian efforts to control the region led to another war of conquest against Persia, which brought the rest of Azerbaijan under Russian control in 1828.

In 1918, after the Bolshevik revolution, Azeris, Georgians, and Armenians united to form the Transcaucasian Federated Republic, but the "Mussavat" or Nationalist party, a right-wing Islamic faction, led Azerbaijan out of the federation soon after its establishment and formed an independent republic. In April 1920, nearly two years to the day after it was founded, the Azerbaijan republic was overrun by the Bolshevik Red Army. In 1922

Moscow grouped Azerbaijan and its Caucasian neighbors into the Soviet Transcaucasian Republic. In 1936 Azerbaijan, Armenia, and Georgia were given union republic status.

From the 1880s on Moscow actively developed Azerbaijan's nascent oil industry, concentrating the effort in the Baku region. By the turn of the century the region was the world's largest producer of oil. The Soviet government, zealously committed to rapid heavy industrialization, continued the development, firmly establishing the petroleum industry as the essential element of Azerbaijan's economy and making the republic a vital strategic asset of the Soviet state.

The importance of Azerbaijan in the Soviet economic scheme under Stalin may explain why, in the Great Purges of the late 1930s, its people suffered harsher mass repression than those in almost any other part of the country, except the dictator's home province of Georgia. Some ten thousand Azerbaijanis were summarily shot for allegedly participating in a plot to murder a Stalin loyalist; many others were deported and imprisoned. The Azerbaijan Communist party hierarchy was decimated, replaced with functionaries answerable only to Stalin.

In early 1988 the Supreme Soviet of the Nagorno-Karabakh Autonomous Region, claiming a right to self-determination, demanded its transfer to Armenia. Since that proclamation, Nagorno-Karabakh has been at the center of political events in Azerbaijan, allowing few resources or political energies to be devoted to economic reform.

Government and Politics. In response to Nagorno-Karabakh's efforts to secede from Azerbaijan, the Azeri government blockaded the region, cutting off food and fuel. In January 1990 militant Azeri nationalists rioted in the streets of Baku and attacked Armenians living there. Regular Soviet Army troops quickly intervened to ensure the interests of the Azerbaijan Communist party and secure the strategic oil fields. This move further radicalized Azeri nationalists against Soviet rule. Moscow installed Ayez Mutalibov as the new head of the Azerbaijan Communist party, and the Azeri Supreme Soviet elected him as president that May.

Supreme Soviet elections held before the vote had produced a Communist majority, with a coalition of opposition parties winning 40 seats in the 350-member chamber. The opposition charged that the parliamentary elections were fixed.

After the August 1991 coup attempt in Moscow, Mutalibov resigned as the first secretary of the Azerbaijan Communist party and oversaw the party's dissolution shortly thereafter. In September 1991 he won a presidential election in which he ran unopposed, his challengers having dropped out after faulting the election process.

Groups opposing the Communist leadership joined forces in the broad-based Azerbaijan Popular Front. In early 1992 the Popular Front mounted a campaign against Mutalibov, orchestrating massive demonstrations against the old order. In late February reports of a massacre of Azeris by Armenians in the Nagorno-Karabakh village of Khojaly enraged Azeris, many of whom blamed the Mutalibov government. On March 6 Mutalibov resigned under pressure from the opposition, who charged that he was corrupt and had taken a conciliatory position on the issue of Nagorno-Karabakh. In a resolution mediated by Russian president Boris Yeltsin and Kazakh president Nursultan Nazarbayev in the fall of 1991, Mutalibov had pledged to respect the autonomy of the region's Armenians in return for an Armenian government commitment to renounce its claim to the enclave.

In June 1992 Popular Front leader Abulfez Elchibey defeated acting president Yakub Mamedov in a presidential election that contained irregularities but was considered by outside observers to be substantially fair. Elchibey, a well-known dissident and history professor, was able to unite the opposition. He stated his desire to create a Western system of government, reform Azerbaijan's economy on the Turkish model, and defend the rights of minorities.

Azerbaijan was among the eleven republics that had signed the Commonwealth treaty in December 1991. But the Azeri parliament overwhelmingly voted in October 1992 to reject membership in the Commonwealth of Independent States. President Elchibey had opposed membership on the grounds that the nation could not join the CIS while it was fighting a war with another Commonwealth member, Armenia.

Current Issues. The success of the Elchibey government and the ability of Azerbaijan to pursue economic reform will depend on finding a solution to the fighting over Nagorno-Karabakh. Elchibey has said that Azerbaijan will never accept an independent Nagorno-Karabakh within its borders. His government has continued the battle against Armenian forces, launching an offensive in mid-1992 designed to induce Armenians in the enclave to flee to Armenia. Simultaneously, he has stated his willingness to respond to mediation efforts by international organizations. Although the armed dispute over the Nakhichevan Autonomous Republic has not been so bloody as the one raging in Nagorno-Karabakh, protecting Azeris in that region remains a concern for the Baku government.

Strong anti-Armenian sentiment in Azerbaijan limits the flexibility of any Azeri government to seek peace. In addition, atrocities have been committed on both sides, reducing public willingness to compromise. Foreign-made weapons and mercenary troops have begun appearing in Azerbaijan as rival ethnic and political factions continue to fortify themselves. In December 1991 the United States expressed its official concern about "internal arms races," singling out Azerbaijan.

Violence in the Balkans has jeopardized Azerbaijan's relationship with Russia. Moscow has complained that the Azeri government has not done enough to ensure the safety of ethnic Russians. The growing tide of Azeri nationalism led to Baku's unwillingness to accept a share of the former Soviet Union's large foreign debt and to claim that it is instead owed money. In late 1991, however, Russia and Azerbaijan concluded a trade and economic agreement that preserves Russia's status as Azerbaijan's largest trading partner. Elchibey has stated his intention to improve relations with Russia.

Though Azerbaijan is predominantly secular and lacks a strong tradition of fundamentalism, the Islamic fundamentalist movement within the country has gained strength. Some fears have been voiced in the West about the possibility that Iran's Shi'ite-dominated government will attempt to export its brand of theocracy to Azerbaijan. Yet Iran has approached Azerbaijan cautiously, because it wants to avoid arousing nationalism among the large Azeri population in northern Iran. Moreover, Turkey's influence with the Azeris reduces the chances that Iran could come to dominate Azerbaijan culturally, religiously, or politically. Diplomatic initiatives by Turkey have led to several trade and cooperation agreements with the Azeris, including one in which Azeri military cadets will train in Turkey.

A more troubling possibility is that Iran or Turkey, or minorities within those countries, might become directly involved in the fighting. The Turkish government has bitterly denounced Armenia for offensive actions against Azerbaijan taken during the war, but Prime Minister Suleyman Demirel has said Turkey would not use force against Armenia.

Azerbaijan's efforts to capitalize on its potential oil wealth, an endeavor that will require joint ventures with international oil companies, could be retarded by the political instability in the country. In addition, continuing internal challenges to the central government's authority and to its ability to conduct the day-to-day business of the republic will further erode the confidence of any future foreign capital interests. Meanwhile, the pressing economic concerns of the majority of Azeris remained unaddressed.

Georgia

In 1992 Georgia fell into the grip of ethnic and civil war. Three different disputes fueled violence that threatened to rip the country apart. In October one of the Soviet Union's most recognizable figures, former foreign minister Eduard Shevardnadze, an ethnic Georgian, was overwhelmingly elected president, bringing hope that solutions to Georgia's strife could be found. But it was unclear if even Shevardnadze, enjoying a strong electoral mandate and wide support from the international community, could bring peace to his country.

The fighting and chaos have imperiled the economic well-being of a nation that potentially was the envy of the other former Soviet republics. Few of them possess Georgia's advantages in climate, location, and soil.

Georgia is bordered on the west by the Black Sea, on the north by Russia, on the southeast by Azerbaijan, and on the south by Armenia and Turkey. It is a country of mountains and high plateaus (more than half the land area is above the three-thousand-foot level). The Meschian mountains run through the middle of Georgia, forming the watershed between the Black Sea and the Caspian to the east. This topographic feature has made Georgia's western lands lush and subtropical, while in eastern Georgia irrigation is often necessary for agriculture.

Georgian agriculture is, by Soviet standards, a success. Large quantities of citrus fruit, tea, wine, and vegetables are produced. As a result, food processing is one of Georgia's major industries. Georgia's warm Black Sea coast was a popular vacation spot of Russians, though the civil war has hurt the tourism business.

A number of large and turbulent rivers rising in the mountains give Georgia a great capacity for hydroelectric development. Like Armenia, Georgia is dependent on imports of oil and gas from Russia and Azerbaijan. Georgia's economy has been hurt by Azerbaijan's embargo of energy stocks to Armenia, through which most of these stocks must pass to reach Georgia.

With 5.5 million people in just 26,870 square miles, Georgia is one of the most densely populated states of the former Soviet Union. According to the 1989 Soviet census, 70.1 percent of the population were Georgians, 8.1 percent were Armenians, and 6.3 percent were Russians. Sizable numbers of Russians left Georgia during the early 1990s to escape anti-Russian sentiment and civil unrest. Georgia chose not to join the Commonwealth of Independent States.

Three former administrative subdivisions of the old Soviet Union exist within Georgia's borders: the South Ossetian Autonomous Region and the Abkhazian and Adzharian autonomous republics. South Ossetia and Abkhazia, in mid-1990, declared themselves sovereign republics, and their irregular forces have clashed frequently with armed Georgians.

Complicating these ethnic disputes has been a civil war between supporters of former president Zviad Gamsakhurdia, who was ousted in January 1992, and the opposition forces that now control the government.

History. Tribes from western Asia Minor and from the collapsing Hittite Empire began migrating into the area that is now Georgia in the twelfth century B.C., making Georgia one of the former Soviet Union's oldest areas of civilization. The Roman Empire under Pompey gained effective control of the kingdom of Georgia in 65 B.C. In the fourth century A.D. Georgia embraced Christianity.

From the fourth through the seventh centuries, the Georgian kingdom was a pawn in the conflicts between the empires of Rome, Persia, and Byzantium. By the eighth century an Arab emirate under the banner of Islam had been established. The subsequent weakening of both Islam and Byzantium brought about a renaissance of Georgia under the rule of the Bagratids, an Armenian noble family that emerged as the leading power among Georgia's scattered principalities. In the subsequent "Golden Age," beginning roughly in the tenth century, the Kingdom of United Georgia was founded. The central monarchy steadily subdued the interests of the feudal nobility and expanded its suzerainty from the Black Sea to the shores of the Caspian, and from the Caucasus to what is now Armenia. In 1185 the royal house agreed to limit its power, a victory for the feudal nobles who were supported by a rising merchant class. The Mongol invasion, begun in 1234, left Georgia's glories in ashes. A brief recovery of the kingdom's fortunes ended when the Mongol warrior Tamerlane carried out a series of devastating invasions that lasted from 1386 to 1404. A strong Georgian king, Alexander I, reigned over another renaissance but his successors divided and weakened the kingdom, leaving it unable to protect itself from the Persian and Turkish invasions to come.

Christian Georgia, from the fifteenth century on, continually sought the protection of other Christian nations against the Islamic powers that threatened it. Although Russia promised in a 1783 treaty to protect Georgia from the Persians, it refused to come to Georgia's aid when the Persians invaded in 1795 and sacked Tbilisi. In 1801 Russia began a gradual annexation of Georgia that was completed in 1867.

With the fall of the tsar in 1917 Georgia declared itself independent of the Russian Empire and promptly gained diplomatic recognition from many nations, including in 1920 the Soviet Union. It briefly aligned with its Transcaucasian neighbors, Armenia and Azerbaijan, in the Transcaucasian Federated Republic. But a Red Army invasion in early 1921 ended Georgian independence and led to its annexation into the Soviet Union. The invasion was ordered by two Georgians prominent in the Bolshevik power structure, Joseph Stalin and Grigory Ordzhonikidze.

Under Stalin's dictatorship, Georgia suffered political repression as severe as that endured by any other Soviet republic. In the great purge of 1937, a year after Georgia became a full union republic, two-thirds of the 644 delegates to the tenth Georgian Communist Party Congress were either exiled or shot, many on the direct orders of Stalin's secret police head Lavrenty Beria, also a Georgian. Other Stalin loyalists in positions of local power eliminated people they did not like or considered rivals.

Under Nikita Khrushchev and Leonid Brezhnev, Moscow's control of the local Georgia government greatly relaxed. The Georgian Communist party became notable for its free-wheeling corruption and growing independence from the central government. In the early 1970s Moscow undertook another set of purges, albeit of a less violent nature than Stalin's, to root out the corrupt party leaders and install functionaries loyal to Moscow. The head of the KGB in Georgia, Eduard Shevardnadze, was made first secretary of the Georgian Communist party in 1972. He served in this post until 1985, when he was appointed foreign minister of the Soviet Union by Mikhail Gorbachev. As Georgia party leader, Shevardnadze led an energetic anticorruption drive that resulted in the imprisonment of many party members as well as leading dissidents.

Under the more liberal conditions allowed under Mikhail Gorbachev, Georgian nationalism intensified. In April 1989 Soviet troops forcibly broke up demonstrations in Tbilisi. Georgian officials accused the Soviets of using poison gas against the demonstrators. The incident helped to solidify support for the growing liberation movement. On March 31, 1991, 90 percent of Georgian voters endorsed a referendum of independence.

Government and Politics.   Georgia's fervor for independence had been building for at least six years. An organized nationalist movement took shape beginning in 1985 and grew in strength as the Soviet Union steadily deteriorated and weakened. At the head of one of the largest factions, the Round Table/Free Georgia coalition, was Zviad Gamsakhurdia, the famous son of a revered Georgian writer. In 1978 the U.S. Congress nominated him for the Nobel Peace Prize for his efforts as a Georgian dissident. After the 1989 riots, he assumed a leading role in the formation of a new nation, one he proved incapable of filling.

In October 1990 Georgia held its first multiparty elections and elected a parliament of which Gamsakhurdia became chairman. A formal declaration of Georgian independence, following the referendum on the issue, was passed unanimously in April 1991. In May Gamsakhurdia was elected president with more than 87 percent of the vote, primarily because he was the most visible symbol of Georgian resistance to the Soviet Union. Because of Georgians' ardent nationalism and their persistent desire for national self-determination, the Georgian Communist party, long viewed as the arm of a foreign power, lost virtually all its influence.

Political deterioration began almost immediately. Opponents charged that Gamsakhurdia failed to condemn the Moscow coup by Communist party hard-liners in August 1991. His rule turned autocratic, erratic, even paranoid. Enemies and scapegoats were found everywhere, but most often among the growing ranks of his critics. He censored the press, ordered arrests, and suppressed antigovernment demonstrations in a manner reminiscent of Soviet methods.

Five months after Gamsakhurdia assumed office, liberal intellectuals formed the base of an opposition movement to his rule, which held daily mass demonstrations in Tbilisi. In late December 1991 dissidents lay siege to the Government House where Gamsakhurdia made his last stand.

In early January he was forced to seek asylum in Armenia. A coalition of anti-Gamsakhurdia dissidents led by Tenghiz Kitovani, an artist, and Dzhaba Ioseliani, the head of one of the militia groups that had organized to oppose Gamsakhurdia, formed a provisional government. Soon after, the provisional government, hoping to reap the benefits of Shevardnadze's international standing, announced that they had asked him to return from Moscow to help create a new government under the auspices of the Georgian State Council. Shevardnadze accepted and became the head of the provisional government in March.

Gamsakhurdia loyalists have persisted in armed opposition to the new provisional leadership, prompting warfare that has polarized the nation. Gamsakhurdia took up residence in the Chechen republic of southern Russia. The new leaders were unable to maintain lasting order or to establish a coherent political program. Shevardnadze's victory in the October elections, in which he won more than 90 percent of the vote, strengthened his authority. Voters defied appeals by Gamsakhurdia for a boycott of the election.

Current Issues.   Georgia's economic progress and entry into the world community have been severely retarded by its political instability and what many foreign observers see as virtual anarchy. Already "private armies" have done battle with each other over territory and control. Criminal organizations, which blossomed under the corrupt local Communist party leaders of the 1950s and 1960s, are well organized and deeply entrenched. These groups, armed well enough to challenge conventional military forces, have no vested interest in political stabilization. Reportedly the mafia-type criminal groups have stolen weapons from military installations, taken military hostages to obtain materiel, and sold equipment to the highest bidder. Armed gangs now rule the streets at night; some of their members reputedly do double duty as soldiers and policemen during the day. The State Council has limited power to control the security forces or the criminals.

One of the worst scenarios for Georgia is the possibility that its leaders, attempting to chart a precarious course between well-armed oppositions, will be unable to prevent a "Lebanonization" of the country in which armed militias contest one another and central governmental control ceases to exist. Historians note that other Georgian dynasties fell when well-armed and ambitious nobles tore apart the kingdom for their own parochial ends.

Georgia must also contend with its two separatist movements. The South Ossetians have attempted to unite with the North Ossetians, who occupy territory across the border in Russia. They desire to establish a single Ossetian autonomous republic within Russia. South Ossetia's guerrilla war against Georgian authority and efforts under Gamsakhurdia and his successors to suppress the separatist movement have led to hundreds of casualties and tens of thousands of Georgian and Ossetian refugees. Georgian forces have established a blockade of South Ossetia that has cut it off from the outside world. In July 1992 negotiations among Georgia, Russia, North Ossetia, and South Ossetia produced an agreement that sent peacekeeping troops from the four signatories to the region. The peacekeeping effort initially appeared to calm the region, though sporadic fighting between Georgians and Ossetians continued.

The conflict over Abkhazia appears similarly intractable. Abkhazians seek complete independence from Georgia and the establishment of their own state. During the early 1920s Abkhazia had been a union republic until it was included within Georgia a decade later. But ethnic Abkhazians now make up only about 18 percent of the approximately 537,000 people living in the autonomous republic, compared with almost 46 percent Georgians. The Tbilisi gov-

ernment, consequently, has not been inclined to compromise and the Abkhazian leadership has refused even to negotiate.

Under Soviet rule a political quota system was instituted, allowing Abkhazians to control the local Abkhazian parliament, despite their being in the minority. On July 23, 1992, the parliament declared Abkhazia an independent republic. Shevardnadze denounced the declaration as illegal. Georgian forces launched an offensive aimed at quelling the rebellion, but Abkhazia was supported by volunteers from the northern Caucasian regions of Russia and by Gamsakhurdia loyalists who saw an opportunity to bloody and embarrass the Georgian government. Georgian forces forcibly occupied the Abkhazian capital of Sukhumi, and hundreds have been killed in the fighting.

Russia has pursued conflicting policies toward Georgia and its nationalist struggles. President Boris Yeltsin has maintained a policy of neutrality while cooperating with Shevardnadze to construct a solution to the unrest. Conservative members of the Russian government, however, have given verbal support to the separatists. Shevardnadze has blamed Russian conservatives for supplying the Abkhazian separatists with weapons and Russian generals for allowing Caucasian volunteers from Russia to enter the fight in Abkhazia.

Violence and instability have crippled the Georgian economy. In mid-1992 Georgia was experiencing severe shortages of foodstuffs and energy stocks, with rationing of both. Important railways and roads had been cut by rebels or their users were being preyed upon by outlaw groups. According to some estimates industrial production had fallen by two-thirds between 1990 and mid-1992. About 20 percent of Georgians were unemployed and prices were increasing at a rate of 50 percent per month. Without an end to the fighting, reversal of these trends was unlikely.

CHAPTER **14**

THE WESTERN STATES

Belarus

The smallest of the three Slavic republics, Belarus was long known in the West as "White Russia." Its capital, Minsk, was chosen as the co-ordinating center of the Commonwealth of Independent States. Of all the newly independent states, none has maintained closer relations with Russia than Belarus. Yet the communists who controlled Belarus in mid-1992 were also looking westward toward Europe as the most likely catalyst of economic revival.

Belarus is situated on a broad, glacial plain, the southeastern portion of which is low and marshy and slopes southward into the great marshes of the Pripet River. Lithuania and Latvia border Belarus on the north, Russia lies to its east, and Poland and Ukraine lie to its west and south, respectively. Its lack of natural barriers has made it vulnerable to numerous foreign invasions. At just over eighty thousand square miles, Belarus comprises almost 1 percent of the land area of the old Soviet Union. Its climate is tempered by marine influences, and it does not experience temperatures so severe as those in Russia.

Belorussians are the fourth largest of the fifty-two major ethnic groups counted in the 1989 Soviet census, numbering some ten million. Eight million of them live in Belarus and form nearly 78 percent of the total population of 10.3 million. Russians make up 13.2 percent of the state's population, with Poles at 4.1 percent. Belarus is the fifth most populous of the fifteen former Soviet republics.

Belarus has experienced relatively little tension among its component ethnic groups. For decades, the Belorussians were subject to stringent russification efforts by Moscow. The result of these efforts has been to diminish national and cultural distinctions. Russian is the predominant language.

Russification also has made Belarus one of the more politically conservative of the new republics. Before the failed August 1991 coup attempt, its Communist party leaders resisted Soviet president Mikhail Gorbachev's policies of glasnost and perestroika. Although Belarus declared its independence on August 25, 1991, it was less anxious than most republics to break ties with the old union. In a referendum in March 1991, Belarus's voters chose overwhelmingly to preserve the Soviet Union. Belarus was also one of the strongest advocates of constructing the Commonwealth of Independent States.

History. Belorussians belong, with the Russians and Ukrainians, to the family of people called the East Slavs. Archaeologists say their settlements in parts of Russia date to the first millennium B.C.; they are thought to have constituted a major portion of the population of southern and central Russia from the time of the Scythians. At some point, the East Slavs divided into three distinct groups: The Great Russians or Russians, the Ukrainians, and the White Russians or Belorussians (so named apparently because of their native dress, not because of skin color).

Present-day Belarus was part of the Kievan state that flourished in the tenth century. During the centuries that followed, Kievan power was steadily reduced by wars of succession and by the absence of a single strong ruler. By the mid-thirteenth century, the Mongol invasions doomed it. But Kiev's legacy to the East Slavs remained enormous: a common language, literature, and culture; one religion; and, as historian Nicholas Riasanovsky has noted, "the concept of one common 'Russian' land."

By the midfourteenth century much of what is now Belarus was under the political control of the Kingdom of Lithuania, which had extended its dominion as far south as the Black Sea and as far west as Smolensk. Lithuanian rule did not challenge the "Russian" way of life and in fact seemed eager to embrace its cultural diversity: Russian even became the official language of the Lithuanian-Russian state.

By the latter part of the century Lithuania had forged strong dynastic links with the Kingdom of Poland and soon Poland's political and cultural influence in the region had eclipsed that of the Russians. But the Muscovy tsars continually challenged Polish rule, and under Ivan the Great part of Belarus was forcibly taken back from the Poles. Ivan's son Basil III pushed Moscow's power to the east bank of the Dneiper River, the current boundary between Belarus and Russia. During the period of dynastic confusion that is now called the "Time of Troubles" at the beginning of the seventeenth century, Poland, taking full advantage of Moscow's turmoil, retook the contested land, holding onto it until late in the eighteenth century. Then in 1772, when Poland was partitioned among Catherine the Great's Russia, Prussia, and Austria, Moscow reclaimed much of Belarus. By 1793 the Romanovs had recovered the remainder of the territory. During all these struggles, Belarus was a principal battleground. Its land, its people, its institutions, and its economy were repeatedly devastated by the competing powers.

The land's troubles continued in 1812 as Napoleon's army tore through on its march to Moscow and left scorched earth as it beat its retreat. Belarus had barely recovered by 1914 when World War I erupted. Its position close to the war zone brought further devastation. After the Russian Revolution, Soviet forces tried to form a Soviet republic in Belarus, but a German counterattack and occupation doomed this effort.

When the Germans withdrew in late 1918, Belorussians attempted to form a joint republic with Lithuania, but a newly independent Poland invaded the region, occupying western Belarus and portions of Ukraine. The Red Army pushed the Poles back almost to Warsaw and was then itself pushed back. The Treaty of Riga, signed in 1921, gave Poland sections of western Belarus that it had claimed as part of its "historic heritage," but the Soviets recovered some of this land within a few years.

Belarus was one of the four original Soviet Socialist Republics that were combined in 1922 to form the USSR. Joseph Stalin pursued his purges in Belarus with enormous zeal and determination. The purges claimed more than half the Belorussian Communist party membership.

In 1939, when Nazi Germany invaded Poland from the west, the Soviets invaded the Polish-held portion of Belarus from the east and quickly incorporated it into the existing Belorussian Soviet Republic. German armies overran Belarus in 1941 when they invaded the Soviet Union. During the next three years, until the Red Army pushed out the invaders, the land remained, as it had been for centuries, a battleground. At war's end, its industry was in ruins, but Stalin compounded its miseries with mass repression of the populace, charging many with treason and collaboration with the Germans. Whatever nationalist sentiment or political opposition that might have sprung from Belarus's anti-German guerrilla movements was effectively squelched. *(World War II map, p. 55)*

Government and Politics. The Communist party of Belarus was one of the most conservative in the old Soviet system. It consistently opposed reform at home and was an outspoken critic of Soviet president Gorbachev's reform movement. While the Belarus party for several years publicly espoused greater sovereignty for the republic, analysts feel that this policy was adopted more to distance the local communists from the steadily weakening Communist party of the Soviet Union than because of Belorussian nationalism.

After the failed August 1991 coup, the chairman of the Belarus Supreme Soviet, Nikolai Dementei, was forced to resign because of his support for the junta. Activities of the Belarus party were suspended and its property nationalized. Most Communists remained in their positions, however, and by December of 1991 they reconstituted themselves as the Party of Communists of Belarus.

Over 90 percent of the current Supreme Soviet's deputies are Communists elected in the March 1990 voting, which the party dominated. The largest opposition party is the proreform Belarus National Front, which has adopted a nationalist platform.

Stanislav Shushkevich was chosen as deputy chairman of the Supreme Soviet in 1990 and has since taken over the chairmanship. He made his political reputation as a critic of the 1986 Chernobyl nuclear disaster and its institutional causes, and he has vigorously pressed the issues of reparations and environmental restoration since assuming the leadership. As of mid-1992 Belarus did not have an elected presidency, the establishment of which has become a focus of the opposition.

Current Issues. The Communist government has attempted to maintain support by adopting cautiously nationalist and reformist positions. Its current agenda calls for the gradual implementation of a market economy and establishment of a multi-party democracy. The government has taken limited steps in land reform, but it has resisted progress in the area of industrial privatization. In early 1992 the Supreme Soviet voted to take command of all Soviet troops stationed on its territory and to eventually create a defense ministry with ninety thousand troops serving in a national army, which, officials say, would be purely defensive in nature.

Under longstanding Soviet policy, Belarus was heavily industrialized. It remains, however, severely deficient in raw materials, including energy stocks, and dependent upon relationships with other Commonwealth states for both the purchase of its products and for the supply of many others. It produced some 20 percent of the Soviet Union's potato crop and 30 percent of its flax, but the political disruption has created an economic downturn. Industrial production in 1991 fell an estimated 15 percent, with greater declines expected in 1992.

The government has worked to secure foreign assistance and investment, sending numerous trade delegations abroad and pressing passage of laws to protect foreign investors and private property. One such measure would give tax exemptions to companies with more than 30 percent foreign ownership. While its industrial and civil infrastructure is considered poor by Western standards, the Belarus population is highly educated and skilled. Its strategic position close to European markets and its lower labor costs drew the interest of several Asian manufacturing concerns. The heavy reliance on other Commonwealth states for many raw materials, including all energy stocks, worked to Belarus's detriment, however, and the domestic economy is likely to be vulnerable to disruptions in supplies for some time to come.

Most Belorussians, including government officials, see hope for their nation in an expansion of economic and political ties with Europe—especially Germany. The two nations have formed a German-Belorussian Cooperation Council to expand economic ties. Closer to home, Belarus has attempted to stay out of the economic and political disputes between Russia and Ukraine.

Belorussian society has been powerfully influenced by the aftermath of the meltdown of the Chernobyl nuclear reactor, which is situated in Ukraine near Belarus's southern border. Many experts contend that the disaster caused more damage to people and property in Belarus than in Ukraine. Belorussian officials estimate that nuclear contamination affected as many as two million of its citizens.

Antinuclear sentiment is pervasive in Belarus and the government has acted decisively to remove nuclear weapons from its territory. All short-range nuclear arms have been transported to Russia for dismantling, and the government has promised the United States it will remove all long-range missiles and bombers as well. Belarus has committed to signing the Nuclear Non-Proliferation Treaty as a nonnuclear state.

In the civilian nuclear area, Belarus has sought financial assistance in cleaning up regions contami-

The western states

nated by the Chernobyl accident. The legacy of the disaster continues to cloud Belarus's relations with the other Commonwealth states, which the government argues should help to pay for cleanup and

restoration costs. But with each nation of the former Soviet Union struggling with its own economic and environmental problems, there has been little movement on the issue. The government has demanded that Ukraine close down the Chernobyl plant entirely.

In 1990, four years after the accident, Belarus declared itself to be an ecological disaster area with a substantial portion of its population, lands, and waters poisoned by radioactivity. Chernobyl's long-term effect on the people and their environment will be a dominant factor in the republic's future.

Moldova

The Moldova Republic (formerly Moldavia) lies east of Romania across the Prut River. Moldovans share a common heritage with the Romanian people and their language is a Romanian dialect, the most eastern of the languages descended from Latin. For centuries Moldova was an integral part of Bessarabia, which Romania ruled politically and culturally. The long years of rule by imperial Russia and the Soviet Union never completely severed the ethnic, political, and economic bonds between Moldova and Romania.

Moldova is the second smallest of the former Soviet Union's republics, with a land area of roughly 13,000 square miles. Its population of 4,341,000 also makes it one of the most densely populated republics.

The land slopes gently downward from the Carpathian Mountains in the west. The favorable climate, broad treeless plains, rolling hills, and wide river valleys have made Moldova a rich agricultural area. Several large hydroelectric projects meet its domestic energy needs but it is not self-sufficient in fossil fuels and has few raw materials of any type. Its industrial base focuses primarily on small-scale manufacturing and food processing.

Ethnic Moldovans make up 64.5 percent of Moldova's population, according to the 1989 Soviet census. Ukrainians are 13.8 percent and Russians, 12.8 percent. With the dissolution of the Soviet Union and the subsequent unleashing of long-suppressed Moldovan nationalist sentiments, Russians and Ukrainians have grown increasingly fearful of living in a Moldovan-dominated state. Some particularly vocal Moldovan nationalists have called for reuniting Moldova with Romania, though neither

Romania nor Moldova has taken steps toward achieving this outcome.

A heavily industrialized narrow strip in the eastern part of the former Moldavia, between the Dniester River and Ukraine, is home to many ethnic Russians and Ukrainians. This region, reacting to Moldova's declaration of independence in August 1991, seceded from the new republic and declared itself to be the Dniester Socialist Republic. Its leaders announced that their purpose was to prevent Moldova's Russian population from becoming second-class citizens in a Moldova dominated by Romania. The Dniester Socialist Republic mounted an armed insurrection against Moldovan rule. The Fourteenth Russian Army, stationed in the region, supported the breakaway group, as did cossack mercenaries—ethnic Russians who arrived on the east bank in sizable, well-armed numbers shortly after hostilities began.

History. In pre-Christian times Moldova's rich pastures and the wooded slopes of the Carpathians were inhabited by a Thracian tribe called the Bessi (hence the name Bessarabia) and later by Slav tribes. The Roman emperor Trajan conquered the region in A.D. 106, making it a bulwark of Christian Europe against barbarian invasion. A century later the Goths invaded, followed in the succeeding centuries by Huns, Avars, and Bulgarians. Petcheneg Turks migrated to the region from the south in the tenth century, and the Mongols, under Batu, the grandson of Genghis Khan, invaded in the thirteenth, laying waste to the land and its peoples. Contacts with western Europe began late in the century with the establishment of Genoese trading posts at the mouth of the Dniester River. Also in that century the Volokh, ancestors of the modern-day Moldovans, left the Carpathians for the lowlands to the east, forming a principality there in 1359.

For the next four centuries the region was continually subjected to invasions by alternating waves of Turks and Crimean Tatars. In 1812 Russia forced the Ottoman Empire to cede Moldova (then known as Bessarabia) to it, taking control of all lands east of the Prut River, which included the strategic mouth of the Danube River. The Treaty of Adrianople, concluded in 1829 between Russia and Turkey, promised autonomy to Bessárabia under a Russian protectorate. But this promise was swept aside in 1848 when, in reaction to the revolution in France, Tsar Nicholas I sent his troops to the protectorate to suppress Romanian nationalists. In 1853 Russia's occupation of Bessarabia enraged Turkey and its allies and played a major role in the Crimean War of 1853-1856.

The fall of the Romanovs in 1917 emboldened Bessarabian nationalists who, renouncing all connections with Russia, declared the independence of their nation in 1918 and then promptly united with Romania. The Treaty of Paris, signed in 1920, formally recognized this union. Soviet leaders, however, continued to consider the region a part of imperial Russia that rightly belonged to the USSR. Bessarabia was spared the rigorous birth pangs of Communist rule under Joseph Stalin before World War II, its traditional way of life changing little in the years between the great wars.

The Molotov-Ribbentrop Pact of 1939 placed Bessarabia in the Soviet sphere of influence. In 1940 Soviet troops occupied the territory. Moscow created the Moldavian Soviet Socialist Republic, changing the frontiers to include the narrow strip of what had been Ukrainian land on the east bank of the Dniester and attaching to Ukraine the former North Bukovina area and a strip of coastal plain along the Black Sea.

The Russians held the area until driven out by the invading Germans in 1941. The years under Nazi occupation were particularly harsh for Moldavians, whose nationalist partisans' harassing tactics brought brutal reprisals from the invaders. There was no respite when Soviet forces reconquered the republic in 1944, however; Stalin ordered his secret police to root out Moldavian dissidents. The secret police struck indiscriminately at all members of nationalist groups. Hard-line party cadres loyal to Stalin assumed positions of control and Moscow encouraged a substantial migration of Russians and Ukrainians into the area. Many settled on the strip east of the Dniester, becoming the dominant ethnic groups there and forestalling integration with the Moldavian majority.

Popular front movements espousing national self-determination arose promptly in Moldavia and the three Baltic republics following their annexation by the Soviet Union during World War II. The descendants of these movements established themselves as formidable political entities as the Soviet Union began to disintegrate in the late 1980s.

Government and Politics. By mid-1990 the Communist party in Moldavia had been stripped of its constitutional legitimacy and banned. Its property was nationalized and its governing apparatus was left in disarray. In the Communists' stead have come a dizzying array of parties, most with nationalism at their core. All have full legal standing and were, in mid-1992, helping to prepare a new democratic constitution for the country.

Just prior to the August 1991 coup attempt in Moscow, the Moldavian parliament approved a declaration of sovereignty; immediately after the cabal failed, the parliament proclaimed the republic's independence. A wave of resurgent nationalism prompted the adoption of the Latin alphabet (instead of the Moscow-imposed Cyrillic) and the dropping of the name Moldavian Soviet Socialist Republic for the current title.

In December 1991 a direct popular presidential election was held. The victor (and only candidate), Mircea Snegur, has actively espoused economic reform, emphasizing privatization of most enterprises and farmland. He has been unable to make much progress on this agenda because of the secession crisis.

Current Issues. In March 1992, despite restraint by Moldova's government, violence erupted between Moldovan forces and those supporting the Dniester republic. The two sides fought pitched battles and a full-scale civil war appeared imminent. The situation on the east bank was exacerbated by the actions of the Fourteenth Army commander, Lt. Gen. Gennady Yakovlev, who, in January 1992, announced that he had accepted the post of Dniester defense minister and would bring the army under the control of the secessionists. His troops apparently stood aside and allowed civilians to steal weapons and vehicles from army stores on the east bank. The dreaded cossacks began to appear in the area at this time, responding to the urging—and generous offers of pay—of the Dniester republic's government.

The actions and rhetoric of high-ranking members of the Russian government in the resultant crisis have fueled Moldovan fears that hard-line Russians are promoting the secession movement. Russian vice president Aleksandr Rutskoy, in the midst of the 1992 crisis, announced his support for an independent Dniester republic and said the cossacks were "right to go to Moldova, to defend their Russian brothers." Moldovan leaders have charged Russian government organizations with financing the mercenaries.

In mid-April 1992 the foreign ministers of Moldova, Romania, Russia, and Ukraine announced a cease-fire agreement, but numerous breaches soon occurred. Direct talks between officials of Moldova and Dniester stalemated and the armed conflict resumed. Then in July Russian president Boris Yeltsin and Snegur signed an agreement creating a peacekeeping force of troops from Russia, Moldova, and the Dniester republic. The deployment initially stopped most of the fighting, though tensions remained high.

The Moldovan government also faced the problem of a secessionist movement by the Turkic-speaking Gagauzi population concentrated in the southwest. The Gagauzi, making up just 3.5 percent of Moldova's population, declared their independence shortly after the failed August coup in Moscow.

Economic progress and foreign investment were unlikely to make advances in Moldova until it resolved the conflict. Moldova was in a particularly vulnerable spot economically because of its dependence on trade with Russia and Ukraine, and the location of much of its industry in the disputed area east of the Dniester. As a result, Moldova was actively pursuing economic contacts with Romania and other European nations.

Russia

Describing the Russian Empire has long been an exercise in superlatives. At the time of its greatest expanse the empire reached from Alaska to the frontiers of Germany and occupied nearly a fifth of the earth's land area. Ninety percent of the Soviet Union's 290 million people lived on just one-third of this vast land, a testimony to the climatic harshness and difficult living conditions that prevail over much of it.

With the breakup of the Soviet Union, the Russian Federation and the fourteen other union republics have become independent nations. The Russian Federation, however, remains enormous. Covering 6.6 million square miles, it is still easily the largest country in the world—1.7 times bigger than Canada, the second largest country. Russia contains more than 11 percent of the world's land, and with 147 million people it is sixth in population behind China, India, the United States, Indonesia, and Brazil.

The geography of Russia has been likened to a vast amphitheater opening north to the Arctic. Its frontiers of formidable mountains on the south protect a huge bowl of land that slopes downward south to north. Two-thirds of its borders are maritime, but the huge land mass limits the seas' moderating effect on the weather. Within this immense landscape, the climate ranges from arctic to tropical, with most of the population inhabiting the continental climate zone.

Large mature river systems running generally on north-south axes—including the Volga, Ob, Yenisey, and Lena—formed the conduits of exploration, settlement, trade, and development. Today they are Russia's lifelines of commerce.

Great distances and harsh climates retarded Russia's development into the world power it is today. Although the country was inordinately rich in many vital natural resources, tsarist governments failed to achieve its full potential. Only after the ruthless Stalinist drive to industrialization would most of these resources be exploited and integrated into the nation's economic structure. From a backward agricultural country, Russia became an industrial giant in less than thirty years, despite the devastation of two world wars and the loss of millions of its citizens.

Siberia alone has oil reserves that are second only to those of Saudi Arabia, half of the world's known natural gas and coal reserves, and 20 percent of the world's gold. Russia's powerful rivers provide plentiful hydroelectric power. Huge belts of forest stretching east and west provide timber for export. However, only a quarter of Russia's land is suitable for agricultural cultivation. Much of it is concentrated in regions subject to severe climatological change and drought—conditions that have contributed to frequent poor harvests and food shortages.

Russia's size, natural resource wealth, and nuclear arsenal preserve its status as one of the world's most important countries. Its strategic location makes it the only nation that can claim to be both a European and an Asian power. It also has assumed the Soviet Union's seat and veto power in the UN Security Council. Thus, despite Russia's enormous internal problems and its loss of empire, it will continue to play a key role in world affairs.

Russia as the Center. Long before the decline and fall of Kievan Rus, Moscow and the Great Russians were gaining in power and prestige. Unlike the other branches of the Eastern Slavs, the Ukrainians and Belorussians, the Russians resisted foreign influences and remained a closed society—isolationist and hostile to the peoples and cultures on their frontiers. Later, when foreign influences and ideas began to infiltrate the Russian mindset, roughly from Peter the Great's reign on, they elicited distrust among certain intellectuals and acceptance among others, thus polarizing the issue into two camps—Slavophiles and Westerners.

As political power was increasingly seized by the tsars (literally "Caesars") of Moscow, their imperial ambitions grew. These early manifestations of empire looked mainly to Europe to the west and the Scandinavian and Baltic powers to the north as likely fields of conquest or influence. Later, the tsars would look south and confront Persia and Turkey. The eastern reaches, site of the great steppes, the home of the terrifying Mongol hordes and, beyond, the intransigent Chinese emperors, were perceived as a region of hostility. Imperialist notions about the East did not reach full flower in Russia until the nineteenth century, when the empire was stretched to the Pacific and beyond.

It was not until the early nineteenth century during the reign of Nicholas I that russification, the systematic imposition of Russian institutions and culture on other races, became a state policy, one that has continued, in various forms, to the present day. Nicholas, alarmed at the 1830 revolution in France and nationalist unrest in Poland, Ukraine, and Belarus, intensified efforts to centralize and standardize on a Russian model his government's rule over diverse domains.

These efforts followed a familiar pattern. Moscow dictated strict limitations on the use of the native tongue and established Russian as the first language; it installed the Russian legal code and substituted Russian government institutions for those of the locality; it favored the Russian Orthodox Church and treated other religions harshly; and it suppressed anti-Russian dissidents or others perceived as being hostile to Russian interests. Nationalists and rebellious nobles were among the first targets, but Jews were soon included and suffered some of the worst persecutions. Later, Moslems and a host of non-Russian ethnic minorities who chose to resist integration were persecuted.

The intensity of russification waxed and waned from tsar to tsar, but the process remained a bulwark of government policy. Frequently when russification was resisted forcibly the central government would either press it brutally or temporarily abandon it, depending on other tsarist priorities. As historian Nicholas Riasanovsky notes: "Russification represented in part a reaction against the growing national sentiments of different peoples of the empire with their implicit threats to the unity of the state and in part a response to the rising nationalism of the Great Russians themselves." To further Moscow's control over the periphery, the government encouraged the migration of ethnic Russians into new areas of the empire.

From the birth of the Soviet Communist party, its top leadership was almost entirely Russian. Two notable exceptions were Joseph Stalin from Georgia and Leon Trotsky from Ukraine. Though many members of ethnic minorities joined, Slavs and Russians dominated the party. Ironically, Stalin the outsider Georgian proved to be the most implacable foe of the ethnic minorities—imprisoning, executing, and exiling millions on several pretexts ranging from treason to their espousing of "nationalist forms of communism." Stalin stoked the fires of Russian nationalism when it served his purpose, first in the 1920s to consolidate Soviet power and to rebuild the country, then later during World War II to enhance patriotic fervor and sacrifice. The Great Russians, the other citizens of the Soviet Union were told, were "the binding cement of the nation" and "the most outstanding" of all the national groups in the nation. Russian control of the Communist party meant Russian control of the country. In areas outside the Russian republic where enterprises vital to the nation were located, the Russian population was certain to be proportionately higher. Many of the capitals of the former Soviet republics are heavily Russian in population *(see Table 7-1, p. 157);* the oil regions of Siberia and Azerbaijan have large Russian populations as does eastern Ukraine, site of a major industrial region.

The nation's economic activity centered around the seat of governmental power in a form of intranational mercantilism, with the periphery feeding raw materials (and tax revenues) to the center and receiving finished materials and central government services in return. Moscow is at the heart of an enormous industrial area that once supplied, on its own terms and conditions, a large majority of the former Soviet Union's manufactured wares to the union republics.

Power in Russia flowed from the center outward. In both a symbolic and a real sense, Moscow became the center of the Soviet Union's main operating universes: the political, the economic, and the cultural. Power over all three was concentrated in Moscow and carefully controlled, first by the tsars and then by their successors, the leaders of the Communist party.

The fourteen non-Russian union republics and the twenty Autonomous Soviet Socialist Republics (ASSRs) and Autonomous Oblasts (AOs) within Russia were established by Moscow to recognize the predominance of a nationality within a given area. But as creations of the center, these governmental forms had little in the way of political or economic

autonomy, despite the grandiose promises of the Soviet constitution. In most cases the autonomy involved only the use of local language and customs and the administration of routine local government functions. The Russian state ruled by the Russian-dominated Communist party directed most important facets of life.

Ethnic Division in Russia. The Russian Empire's relentless expansion began in the midsixteenth century with the defeat of the Tatars of Kazan. At its peak, some 169 different ethnic groups, far more than in any other country, lived under the Soviet flag. These groups spoke a host of tongues, many mutually incomprehensible, and they brought their own histories and ancient animosities toward one another (and toward Russia) into the empire. Under the Soviet system, these disparate peoples were held together in the Soviet Union by a powerful tandem of political power and shared Communist ideology.

While in theory these non-Russian peoples were equals with full rights to self-determination, in practice the exact opposite was true. To many of them, Soviet repression and control meant Russian repression and Russian control. As the Soviet Union and Communist party dissolved and their coercive power disappeared, the long pent-up aspirations, frustrations, and emotions among the non-Russians, many living in ethnically based enclaves, surfaced. In two cases, the governments of Checheniya and Tatarstan, both located within Russia and having non-Russian population majorities, declared their independence from Moscow. The other autonomous units within Russia's borders have militated in varying degrees for greater economic sovereignty, control over their own natural resources, and a decentralization of power that gives non-Russians more authority.

Similar activities have taken place in many of the other administrative subdivisions of the old Soviet system, some ethnically based and some not. In one case, a city—Vorkuta—attempted to withdraw from the Komi Republic. In another, a district declared itself an independent country.

This drive for greater autonomy is complicated by the fact that in many of these areas ethnic

Russians are in the majority. Anti-Russian animosities and activities have grown there in frequency and intensity as the historic mechanisms of control have withered away. The protection of both the 25 million ethnic Russians living in the newly independent republics outside Russia's borders and of the large number living in the ethnically based regions within Russia has become a source of continued tension between Moscow and these other governments.

In addition, non-Russian citizens live throughout Russia, not just in their home enclaves. Many ethnic groups have been the targets of angry and frustrated Russians. In one city, Yaroslavl, there were reports of violence against Tatars, Gypsies, and others, apparently brought about by worsening economic conditions and subsequent scapegoating of minority groups by Russians. Jewish citizens also have been reported to have suffered personal attacks.

A number of the autonomous republics have threatened to cut off their raw material exports to Russia and have seized Soviet property within their borders to assert their new sovereignty. Hard-line Russian politicians have condemned such "anti-Russian acts." Should economic conditions within Russia continue to worsen, the frequency of violent ethnic confrontations seems sure to increase.

During the long reign of Joseph Stalin, the seeds for continuing ethnic unrest were sown in a number of locations. Some of them have ripened with the Soviet Union's demise, and they appear intractable. In one example, Stalin's tactic of moving entire ethnic populations away from their homelands, then giving their lands and holdings to others supposedly more loyal (and often Russian), has come full circle. Now those deportees are demanding their property back, even though others have been living on it for decades. In the case of the Ingush, who were deported in 1944, their ancestral land is occupied by Ossetians, who refuse to give it back. The 1991 Law on Rehabilitation of Victims of Political Repression passed by the Russian parliament contains no provisions to help such deportees, however, and both sides are poised for an armed confrontation.

The splinterings and fragmentations of these ethnically based regions, several of which have strategic economic importance to the Russian Federation, create a real danger of dissolution and "balkanization" for the Russian government. President Boris Yeltsin has attempted to hold the federation together while allowing ethnic groups much greater autonomy. But many Russian leaders tend, even now, to deal with the peripheral peoples from the outdated vantage point of their former masters, further complicating the possibility of maintaining a peaceful multiethnic state.

Russia with its tangled web of ethnic interrelationships may, in the end, prove ungovernable in the current design. Some analysts have proposed that the government would be wise to preside over a controlled disintegration of Russia's legendary empire into a looser confederation of its former parts. Such a confederation might peacefully preserve normal political, economic, and cultural ties and maintain a common monetary system, military, and foreign policy. But few Russian leaders appear willing to support this concept as a solution to the country's daunting ethnic problems.

Government and Politics. Mikhail Gorbachev's twin initiatives of glasnost and perestroika set in motion the chain of events that would bring about the end of the Soviet Union and the coercive bonding power of the Communist party. The policy of glasnost, which Gorbachev intended to encourage criticism of the Communist system within that system's strictures, the better to build consensus for the system's goals and objectives, instead built up pressure for change. It soon opened floodgates of long-repressed (and suppressed) ethnic and political animosities and economic expectations that proved impossible to control.

Gorbachev's efforts to manage reform were erratic and inconsistent, further exposing the fundamental weaknesses of the Soviet political and economic systems. His vacillation in the application of state control—repression followed by an easing—emboldened new democratic groups to challenge Communist party hegemony.

Boris Yeltsin was a Communist party functionary for nearly thirty years, rising to the Politburo level under the aegis of Gorbachev. But after achieving this lofty Communist position he began to espouse reform of the party and especially its leadership. As a result, he was forced to resign from the Politburo in late 1987 when the party hierarchy found his criticisms of their elitism and privileges hitting too close to home.

Yeltsin continued his campaign for a faster pace of reform and soon became a hero to many Russians. The party attempted to keep him from running in 1990 for the Russian Republic Congress of People's Deputies, but his name was put on the ballot in more than fifty different constituencies. He was elected easily to a Moscow seat with 89 percent of the vote, and he captured the world's notice when Moscow's citizens, defying the authorities, staged mass demonstrations in his behalf. The Communists subsequently tried and failed to keep him from being elected to the Congress's Supreme Soviet. Later in 1990 he resigned from the Communist party and in 1991 became the first democratically elected president of the Russian republic.

Since the failed August 1991 coup attempt, Yeltsin has dominated Russian politics. Critics have charged that he remains an opportunistic party hack at heart, authoritarian and undemocratic, egotistical and erratic, a cynical exploiter of the trends that have convulsed his nation since Gorbachev's policies opened a Pandora's box of anti-Soviet horrors. In this view, his adherence to reform is self-serving and politically expedient. To other observers, he is a visionary reformer who perceived the need for sweeping political and economic changes long before glasnost and perestroika revealed them, and took a courageous stand, risking his career, even his life, to ensure that the Russian state would be set on a new course.

It is likely that there is truth in both positions. Yeltsin has displayed an increasing tendency to issue decrees rather than to seek consensus with the legislative branch. He has appointed loyalists to sensitive government posts, including those who have been chosen to oversee his economic reforms and privatization efforts on local levels, the so-called Heads of Local Administration and President's Representatives. Government policy and administration are becoming the province of an ever-more-powerful

executive with an electoral mandate, a development that has roused fears in some quarters of a return to authoritarian government. That Yeltsin is a "good tsar," this argument runs, is no guarantee that his successor will be the same.

Russia's government, like many of the country's institutions, is in a state of flux. Gorbachev began in the late 1980s to transfer power away from the Communist party and to the national legislature. The result has been that the basic system of Soviets continues to exist at virtually every government level but is no longer dominated by Communists or any single political entity. Under the Communists, the Soviets evolved into a unique form of government with both legislative and executive functions at every level of human activity, from workplace to neighborhood. But the Communists employed the system largely as a means of localized control and implementation of centrally dictated policies, not as a grass-roots governmental institution that reflected and acted upon parochial concerns.

The system of soviets as legislatures left a poor legacy of citizen participation in government. Many people perceived the councils as just another manifestation of the Communist party's omnipresence and eternal efforts to control their lives. After seven decades of living under such a system, however, few Russians know any other. As numerous analysts have noted, even if the daily existence of Russians within the Communist-dominated Soviet system was dull and oppressive, it had the virtue of being a predictable, self-contained system that provided cradle-to-grave security. Its death left a structural void that nothing has yet replaced. Jobs, incomes, pensions, state-subsidized rents and foodstuffs, medical care—all givens under the old governmental system—are in jeopardy in the public's mind.

The demise of the Communist party in Russia has not, however, been complete. In a state where the government controlled everything and the Communist party controlled the government, party functionaries were installed at controlling levels of government and business. Under new names but with old allegiances and far-flung bureaucratic connections, many remain in charge, resisting efforts to remove them. These efforts have been hampered by the lack of capable replacements for the Communist management class and by the Yeltsin government's inability to mount a sustained effort to root them out.

In an alarmingly high number of instances, the apparatchiks and nomenklaturas, opposed to any and all economic reforms, have systematically sabotaged privatization efforts. These holdovers from the regime, while enriching themselves at the expense of reform, have won considerable support from the conservative Russian populations outside the major urban centers, a group of people whose pressing daily concerns—food, a place to live, a job—have been seen to by the local Communist party representatives all their lives. While the Yeltsin government would like to remove them from power, it finds doing so difficult, in part because many were duly elected to their posts in the 1990 Gorbachev transition of power from party to legislature. At that time, in many parts of rural Russia, the Communists were the only cohesive and organized political group. They therefore dominated the election process and reconstituted themselves as the majority in the newly elected councils and congresses.

The seemingly overnight rupture of the Soviet structures into a still-evolving political and economic system has created uncertainties among most Russians. Yeltsin's leadership in this new "time of troubles," in tandem with the emergence of the new experience of free political expression, has given rise to organized opposition that spans the spectrum of Russian political consciousness. Even the "Kadets," who briefly jousted with Lenin's victorious Bolsheviks, have resurfaced. They are joined by monarchists, by anarcho-syndicalists, by the Socialist party, the Peasants' party, the Russian People's party, the Free Democratic party, the Green Environmentalists, the Russian Social Democratic party, the Liberal-Democratic party, the Russian Christian Democratic party, and others. They have grouped into alliances that shift and recoalesce with each policy pronouncement or decree made by Yeltsin.

Opposition to Yeltsin comes primarily from former Communists, industrialists, and Russian nationalists. Continuing inflation, unemployment, and uncertainty about the future has broadened the popular base of the Communist groups, none of which use the adjective in their titles. They have focused their appeal to the public on a retreat to the command economy. The industrialists generally want reform to continue, but at a much slower pace. Led by Arkady Volsky, the president of the Russian Union of Industrialists and Entrepreneurs, this group's core consists of managers of state enterprises. Together with allies in organized labor, they have compelled acting prime minister Yegor Gaidar and his team of economists to pursue less austere policies toward industrial credits and subsidies.

Most nationalists oppose fragmentation of the Soviet empire and support the supremacy of Russians in Russia and the protection of ethnic Russians living in the new republics. Their position on self-determination for the autonomous republics within Russia is equally rigorous. In some extreme cases, nationalists have proposed armed intervention to maintain Russia as a sovereign empire with all its parts in place. Their thèmes, like the Communists', have struck responsive chords among many Russians, who, proud of their imperial heritage, do not want to see their country disintegrate.

At times, some extremist nationalist spokesmen have resorted to ugly xenophobia and demagoguery to advance their political fortunes. One, Vladimir Zhirinovsky, a self-styled fascist whose organization, the misnamed Liberal Democratic party, reportedly received financial aid from the secret police, ran third to Yeltsin in the 1991 presidential election despite his making campaign assertions that bordered on the fanatic. The nationalism theme is a consistently enticing one, however, and even Yeltsin has felt compelled to take hard-line stances on a number of issues (most recently the return of the Kuril Islands to Japan) to maintain his nationalist credentials.

Several powerful leaders of the government, including Vice President Aleksandr Rutskoy, have sought the support of both nationalist and communist factions, as well as the military. There have been veiled threats from some high-ranking officers that their forces might have to intervene to "rescue" the nation, but the high command has assured the

Yeltsin government that it will not participate in a coup attempt. Further economic deterioration or opposition to Yeltsin's defense cutbacks could change that neutral stance.

Rutskoy has been a vocal and persistent critic of the Yeltsin government, primarily over the free-market reform issue and the dismantling of the nation's military-industrial complex. To broaden his political base, he has militantly supported armed intervention to protect ethnic Russians living in the new republics and called for a restoration of Russia's "historic" borders and a constitutional amendment ensuring the principle of a "unified and indivisible Russia."

Current Issues. Russia's vast physical size is matched by the scope of the problems it faces in remaking itself after the demise of the Soviet Union. Among the major issues that Yeltsin must address:

- Seven decades of a command economy dictated and controlled by the central government have left Russia poorly prepared for the transition it is attempting to make to a consumer-driven free-market economy able to compete in international markets. Largely because of the disruptions caused by this transition, Russia is mired in a depression. Unless the government moves forward with painful free market reforms, the economy is unlikely to improve significantly. But necessary steps, such as allowing enterprises to go bankrupt and limiting deficit spending, are likely to create greater unemployment and economic distress in the short run. It is therefore uncertain that public support can be maintained for free-market reform.
- Russia's long years of being the central component of a superpower that was able to wield profound influence over world affairs have come to an end. The accompanying loss of prestige has hurt the Russians' morale and opened the possibility that reactionary political forces could exploit the people's nostalgia for empire.
- Russia must forge new relationships with the other former republics of the Soviet Union with an eye

toward salvaging economic cooperation. For most of these new states, Russia is their largest customer and their major supplier of finished goods. The fragmentation of what was once a unitary economic entity has enormous ramifications for all these states. Many are completely dependent on Russia for raw materials and energy stocks and the ongoing disruptions in supply because of Russia's economic and labor troubles have trickled down to them. To varying degrees the issue of the 25 million ethnic Russians living in the fourteen former republics colors Russia's relationship with each of them. Many of the now-expatriates, fearing for their economic and political futures in the nationalism-driven republics, would like to return to the motherland, which has no jobs or homes to offer them. The Moscow hard-liners, seizing on this emotional issue, have pressed for armed intervention in a number of cases.

- The legacy of being a superpower—Russia's massive arsenal of conventional and nuclear weapons—worries its neighbors and the world. Russia's restless and impoverished military forces, uncertain about who commands them, threaten to become mercenaries, arms dealers, or a reactionary political force.
- The Soviet Union's long emphasis on extensive economic growth and resource exploitation, its inability to ensure the safety of its nuclear weapons plants and atomic test sites, and the Soviet government's unaccountability to a free press and people created conditions that have led to massive environmental problems for Russia. The Russian government can afford to commit few of its scarce resources to environmental cleanup. Meanwhile, public health and safety are jeopardized in many regions.
- The Communists' police-state coercion to control a myriad of contentious voices and interests is gone. But central control has been replaced by chaos and government impotence in many areas. Age-old ethnic resentments and political rivalries, kept in check by the totalitarian state, are now being settled violently as government power declines. Non-Slavic citizens of Russia fear a resurgence of its imperialism as they seek greater self-deter-

mination for their ethnically based homelands.

- The diminishment of central authority also has increased the level of crime in Russia. Criminal organizations have become bolder, often controlling illegal activities in whole towns or sections of cities and extorting protection money from individuals who open businesses. Petty crime, driven by worsening economic conditions, is also up.

- Hovering behind the wellspring of troubles is a discredited Communist party structure erected over seven decades. Its members are still prominent within Russia's governments and businesses and constitute an elite with many personal connections. To a growing number of Russians frightened about the monumental changes taking place in every facet of their daily lives and angry about the failures and policies of the reformist-oriented Yeltsin government, the Communists are a part of the "good old days" when their basic needs were met, life was predictable, and the future was a matter for the state to worry about.

The economy, however, is at the core of most of the Russian government's troubles. If the economy could be turned around, the reactionaries would have less ammunition to use against the government, the loss of empire would not be such a blow to national pride, more funds would be available for environmental cleanup, and the scarcity of economic resources would diminish as a source of crime and ethnic tension.

Even before the Soviet Union officially collapsed, its intricate and interdependent economic structure had been revealed as cumbersome and inefficient, unfettered as it was by the basic law of supply and demand. Directed by quota-minded bureaucrats, field managers met quotas by a host of shrewd and adroit maneuvers that consistently substituted quantity for quality. Quotas were met, but not market needs. State subsidies insulated inefficient and unnecessary enterprises from failure. Rigid price and wage controls and make-work employment insulated the Soviet citizen from economic risk. Even the ruble's value was a matter of state determination, its fixed rate bearing almost no relation to its true (and far lower) value.

The Soviet command economy overemphasized massive industrial complexes that have proved difficult to redirect toward manufacturing products that other nations will buy. The military-industrial complex alone maintained more than 1,100 plants, most on Russian soil, that employed some 7.4 million people and accounted for nearly a quarter of the gross national product.

The Yeltsin government's economic reform program has tackled these and other economic problems with draconian measures in the market area, steadily allowing more and more products to be traded at market levels. The resultant price increases have put many consumer goods far beyond the budgets of the average Russian. Wages have been freed too, but they have yet to catch up with prices. Privatization efforts have been complicated by a public unaccustomed to the principles of entrepreneurship and by ex-Communists who have sometimes subverted the process. Perhaps most threatening is the scarcity of necessities such as food and medicine because of the inefficient distribution system, hoarding, profiteering, and the lack of a genuine free market. The shortages have prompted the international community to send goods and financial assistance to Russia to both alleviate human needs and buy time for the Yeltsin economic reform package to be fully implemented.

Conservatives and nationalists have used the instability of the political situation and the uncertainty surrounding the draconian economic reforms to attack Yeltsin's government on a number of fronts. His agreement with the United States to sharply cut back the number of nuclear weapons was denounced as a deliberate weakening of the Russian state. Yeltsin's pragmatic attempts to maintain normal trade relations with the former republics have brought charges against his "willingness" to watch the proud Russian empire give in to its former vassal states. Rivals also denounced the pain of economic reform as unnecessary, saying the nation would be better off taking a more gradual approach to reform or returning to the command economy.

Yeltsin's personal legitimacy and his strong (though diminishing) base of support, so far, have kept conservatives from mounting a direct challenge to his leadership. But his popularity and authority could evaporate rapidly if the basic economic needs of the people remain unsatisfied. Many analysts fear that the resulting discontent and instability could herald a return to authoritarian government and the tragic death of Russian democracy.

Ukraine

On August 24, 1991, after the Moscow coup failed, the Ukrainian Supreme Soviet declared the country's independence. Three months later, the Ukrainian people supported independence with an overwhelming 90 percent majority vote in a referendum held on December 1. Ukraine participated in the creation of the Commonwealth of Independent States (CIS) that December, but Ukrainian leaders repeatedly stated that they regarded the CIS as a mechanism for achieving an amicable separation of the states of the Soviet Union, not as the basis for some type of reconstituted federation. This determination by Ukraine to seek full sovereignty, despite its close historic ties with Russia, was motivated by its recognition that independence held great economic potential and by its people's strong desires to leave behind a long history of foreign domination and preserve the Ukrainian language and church.

At 235,443 square miles, Ukraine is larger than any European country. Of the states of the former Soviet Union only Russia and Kazakhstan are bigger. Ukraine's 51.4 million people (as counted in the 1989 census) make it easily the second most populous nation of the former Soviet Union, with approximately 18 percent of the total. Its population is about 73 percent Ukrainian and 22 percent Russian. Tensions exist between those two largest ethnic groups, centered on concerns over language, postindependence economic policies, and the future of the large Russian population in the Crimea area. But as of mid-1992 these disagreements had not turned violent. Indeed, to achieve the 90 percent majority in the December 1991 referendum on independence, a majority of the Russian population had to vote for independence. There also were lingering

questions about the eventual fate of the Crimean Tatars, who were exiled by Joseph Stalin for alleged treason to scattered locations in Soviet Central Asia during World War II. They have sought, so far in vain, to return to their homes in Ukraine.

Ukraine shares a border on the west with Poland, Czechoslovakia, Hungary, Romania, and Moldova. The Black Sea and the Crimean Peninsula lie to its south, Belarus to its north, and Russia to its north and east. Ukraine's terrain is divided into three distinct areas: a marshy forest land bordering Belarus in the north; a region immediately south of that of wooded steppe with scattered forests of oak and beech; and lastly the treeless steppe zone of black earth, its agricultural heartland.

Near the border with Russia lies the Donetsk Basin, which contains huge reserves of coal and an extensive concentration of heavy industry. Ukraine has a third of the former Soviet Union's heavy industry and two-thirds of its coal. Nearly all the railroad locomotives built in the old Soviet Union were made in Ukraine. It once produced nearly half the Soviet Union's iron ore and 40 percent of its pig iron and steel. Almost a third of the world's manganese comes from Ukraine. That portion of the Soviet military-industrial complex that dealt with its most sensitive and sophisticated technology was headquartered in Ukraine and some 40 percent of the Soviets' nuclear weapons were made there.

With the collapse of the Soviet Union, Ukraine inherited a large nuclear arsenal. About 180 long-range nuclear missiles are located on its territory and the nuclear-capable Black Sea Fleet is based there also. Yet as a consequence of the 1986 disaster at the Chernobyl nuclear power plant, located about eighty miles north of Kiev, most Ukrainians are ardently opposed to nuclear technology. Ukrainian leaders have vowed to make their country a nuclear-free zone.

So long as there has been a Russian empire, Ukraine has been its breadbasket. Before the Soviet Union broke up, Ukraine's farms produced more than half of its corn and sugar, a third of its cooking oil, and a quarter of its butter and canned food.

To the non-Slavic peoples of the former Soviet Union, there was little difference between the

Ukrainians and the Russians. Indeed, both cooperated closely in the building of the modern Soviet state and the apparatus of the Communist party. Ukrainians were often regarded by the Russians as automatic supporters. One of Stalin's principal allies in the consolidation of Bolshevik power and the massive drive to collectivize the nation's agriculture and economy was Lazar Kaganovich, a Ukrainian. His actions for Stalin contributed to the great famine of 1932-1934 in which more than a million Ukrainians alone were believed to have died. Ukrainians frequently participated in russification campaigns carried out by the Communists. Like the ethnic Russians, ethnic Ukrainians settled in republics throughout the former Soviet Union and now find themselves minorities in newly independent nations.

The Ukrainian language and culture derive more from the country's long connections with Eastern Europe than from its ties with Russia. The strongest nationalist sentiments have historically been centered in the western part of the country, where fewer ethnic Russians live. The first mass demonstrations against the Soviet Union and for independence took place in the western region of Galicia. The area also is a strong supporter of the Uniate Church, which retains the Orthodox ritual but accepts Roman Catholic theology and leadership. The eastern and southern portions of the country have strong concentrations of Russians with concomitantly lower levels of feeling about the language and culture. But during the recent struggle for independence, nationalism exhibited strength throughout Ukraine.

History.   Eons ago, the land that is now Ukraine lay under a vast sea. From mankind's earliest forays into the region, it has been prized for the legacy of that geological epoch: the fertility of its black earth and the richness of its mineral deposits. Conquerors who swept through other parts of what would come to be known as Russia put down roots in Ukraine—even those transitory terrors, the Mongols, whose descendants would later become known as the Crimean Tatars. Ukraine's great artery, the Dnieper River, from ancient times was the link between the cultures of the Baltic, the Mediterranean, and the Black Sea.

Inhabited since paleolithic times, Ukraine has been a crossroads for ancient civilizations, the result of which has been an enormously rich variety of cultural intermixing; the Scythians and Sarmatians, the Classic Greeks, the traders from the Orient, and the nomads from Central Asia's steppes all left their mark on a land that agriculturally is one of the richest on earth. Its production of corn, from the third century B.C., was a mainstay of the great Mediterranean civilizations. Kiev, the capital, revered by Ukrainians as "the Mother of Cities," has been inhabited since the dawn of history and was the center of the first great Eastern Slavic empire, Kievan Rus.

Kievan Rus took shape at about the end of the ninth century A.D. with the occupation of Kiev by Oleg the Wise, a Varangian prince from Novgorod in the north. Kiev was by this time a vital commercial center and the newcomers wisely left alone much of what they found, adopting the local language and customs. Located on the Dnieper, Kiev was on the major trade route for the northern peoples of the Baltic with the Byzantine Empire. Under Oleg and his successors, the princes of Kiev, the East Slavic tribes were brought into a union.

In 988, under Prince Vladimir, Byzantine Christianity was adopted as the state religion, making Kievan Russia the dividing line between the religions of the east and west. Under Vladimir's successors, Kievan culture reached its zenith with great advances made in the areas of law, art and architecture, and education. In an effort to head off destructive dynastic disputes in his prosperous empire, Yaroslav the Wise before his death in 1054 assigned to each of his five sons a separate princedom, with the altruistic presumption that they would act together to preserve the Kievan federation. However, by the end of the eleventh century, the beginning of what is called the Appanage period, the system began to founder and civil wars left the country weak and disunited. Conflicts with aggressive European states had increased as well. The Teutonic Knights, the Poles, and the Swedes all campaigned against the weakened Kievan state. Nevertheless,

Kievan Russia endured as an increasingly fragmented and weak federation for almost two centuries until the Mongol invasion of 1236.

By 1242 the Mongols controlled all of Russia and had reduced Kiev to ashes. Moscow was established as the new capital. But before this devastating period, likely in response to the disruptive fragmentation of the Appanage period, the historic division of the East Slavs into three distinct groupings—the Russians, the Ukrainians, and the Belorussians—had begun in a series of migrations away from the scenes of conflict. This mass movement left large portions of southern Kievan Russia virtually deserted. The Ukrainians moved west and north to areas where the newly powerful Lithuanian and Polish states offered protection and stability.

The deserted portions of Old Kiev became known as Ukraine, literally "borderlands." These areas were home to a hardy band of freemen known as Cossacks, or "frontiersmen," who had military successes against the Mongols and brought security to the region. The Ukrainian Cossacks were to become a feared force fighting against Polish control of Ukraine in the seventeenth century. Later they would fight for Poland against Russia, for Russia against its enemies, and with Sweden against Russia. But their success against the Poles in the great revolt of 1648, led by Bogdan Khmelnetsky, made them an important element with which would-be conquerors of Ukraine would have to reckon.

By the middle of the seventeenth century, with the Romanov Dynasty firmly established in Moscow, civil war in Ukraine had become endemic as tsarist Russia and Poland attempted to extend their sovereignty there. In the Treaty of Andrusovo in 1667, Russia and Poland agreed to divide the country, with Russia taking control of lands east of the Dnieper and Poland the western lands. Cossack rebellions continued against both, however.

Under the rule of Peter the Great, Russia attempted to extend its control in Ukraine, but it was not until the end of the eighteenth century under Catherine the Great—after the third and final partition of Poland by the Russian, Prussian, and Austrian empires—that Moscow could formally claim the territory as its own. Catherine's alliance with the

gentry in the region brought an expansion of the serfdom already existing there. Since Peter the Great's drive to modernize Russia, Ukraine's economic potential had drawn Russian interest. During Catherine's reign this potential was increasingly developed.

Concerned with growing Russian power, the Hapsburgs of Austria encouraged the growth of Ukrainian nationalism in western Ukraine as a counter to the Pan-Slavic movement that was growing in influence in the Russian Empire. The Ukrainian movement soon spread to the eastern portions of the region. Its primary contentions were that Ukraine was separate and distinct from Muscovy Russia, that Ukraine was the direct descendant of Kievan Rus, and that Ukraine should be a separate nation.

Subsequent tsars would try to russify the Ukrainians. However, the nationalism issue seemed to be much more resonant than separatism, even with increasing tsarist suppression efforts. Revolts of serfs occurred frequently in the years before Alexander II's 1861 order to free them, but fundamental human questions of equity lay at their root, not the questions raised by the nationalists. Ukraine did not become a hotbed of rebellion during the Revolution of 1905, and most Ukrainians remained loyal to Russia during World War I.

Before the final German defeat, Ukrainian nationalists had succeeded in winning recognition from Berlin of a separate republic, and it was duly proclaimed in 1917 in the wake of the Bolshevik Revolution. The Treaty of Brest-Litovsk between the Germans and the Bolsheviks gave Ukraine its independence, but by 1919 the fledgling government, the Rada, had collapsed and Ukraine was divided again between Poland and the Soviet Union, with the former taking control of the western portions. Eastern Ukraine became a land of anarchy during the Russian Civil War, with the Red and White Armies, Ukrainian nationalist forces, and Polish regulars all doing battle. Kiev changed hands many times before the Bolsheviks triumphed, establishing Communist rule in the east and declaring Ukraine a Soviet Socialist Republic in 1921. Ukraine's current borders would not be established until 1939, however.

The interregnum between the two great wars saw the Soviet-controlled portion of Ukraine undergo a metamorphosis. Under Lenin's policies, local Communists were put in charge and they exercised a wide-ranging autonomy in civil, cultural, and economic matters. Under Stalin, however, this policy was replaced by harsh rule from Moscow. As part of Stalin's drive to collectivize agriculture in the republic during the early 1930s, the government created a famine that cost the lives of millions of Ukrainians and destroyed Ukraine's traditional way of life. The Ukrainian industrial sector was rapidly developed and became an increasingly important part of the Soviet economy. To ensure his hold over Ukraine, Stalin, in the late 1930s, decimated the Ukrainian Communist party membership, executing, imprisoning, or exiling nearly 250,000 people and replacing them with his chosen cadre. One of them was Nikita Khrushchev, who became first secretary of the Ukrainian Communist party in 1938 and would play an important role in the Soviet annexation of eastern Poland in the coming years.

Under the Molotov-Ribbentrop Pact of 1939, the portion of Ukraine claimed by Poland was placed under the Soviet sphere of influence. Red Army troops occupied the area soon after the secret agreement was signed. The wave of terror during the Stalin era had made Soviet rule in Ukraine so unpopular that the German troops who invaded and occupied it in 1941 were cheered as saviors when they first arrived. The retreating Red Army left the republic in ruins with a deliberate scorched-earth campaign, forcing the Ukrainians to fend for themselves with the Germans, whose occupation techniques proved as repressive as Stalin's. As a consequence of Nazi brutality, a resistance movement with right-wing leanings arose and mounted a vigorous guerrilla war against the Nazis and later against the returning Soviet forces; the resistance was not effectively eliminated until the 1950s.

After the war, when Stalin took his revenge against those peoples he suspected of collaboration and treason, Ukraine felt the full brunt of his wrath. The Crimean Tatars, for example, were forcibly deported to Central Asia and other locales and have yet to return to their homeland. Through a mass purging in Ukraine, Stalin further consolidated his absolute power and eliminated real and imagined sources of opposition.

The postwar period saw an economically restored Ukraine become a vital pillar of the Soviet state, second only in economic and political importance to Russia itself. Moscow's russification efforts continued under Khrushchev and Leonid Brezhnev with much success, but the seeds of Ukrainian nationalism remained alive.

Government and Politics.   Since 1988, with the formation of Rukh (literally "movement"), the Ukrainian political scene has been focused on the issue of separation from the Soviet Union. The various political factions continue to debate the nature of this independence from a variety of vantage points, but all major political groups support unquestioned Ukrainian sovereignty. Even long-entrenched Communist apparatchiks, while sometimes attempting to slow the pace of change, have gone along with the irrepressible national desire for Ukraine to finally stand alone as a nation.

Elections to the Supreme Soviet in March 1990 matched Communist candidates against those of a democratic opposition led by Rukh. The Communists won two-thirds of the seats, with much of their support coming from traditional Russian areas. By the summer of 1990 the parliament declared Ukraine sovereign but not independent.

Leonid Kravchuk, a high-ranking Communist party official, was chosen as chairman. After the attempted August 1991 coup, Kravchuk equivocated and urged business as usual. Only when it became apparent that the cabal had failed did he condemn it. Critics charged that after the coup he should have purged his government of old-line Communists. They also accused him of obstructing reform, particularly in the economic area. Kravchuk and the Communists, however, underwent a major transformation, embracing reform and Ukrainian nationalism. Days after the coup failed, the Communist-controlled Supreme Soviet declared Ukraine independent, a move that many observers regarded as the effective end of the Soviet Union. Much of the program advocated by the minority opposition was adopted by the Supreme Soviet, and the Communist party was dissolved.

Kravchuk, once the loyal party ideologue, became a fierce defender of his country's statehood. This course of action placed him in direct conflict with Russia over a number of potentially explosive issues, and he has refused to yield on the vast majority of them. In a telling example of his conversion to nationalism, he is said to insist upon speaking Ukrainian when dealing with Russian officials, this despite the fact that he is fluent in their language. On December 1, 1991, the same day that the national referendum on independence was passed by an overwhelming majority of both Ukrainians and ethnic Russians, Kravchuk was elected president by popular vote. He won 61 percent while Rukh's candidate, Vyacheslav Chornovil, won just 23 percent. Despite sometimes sharp disagreements between the two factions, they have succeeded so far in maintaining a singularly constant focus on the issue of establishing an independent Ukrainian state.

Current Issues. During Ukraine's first year of independence the most important issues facing the country concerned its relations with Russia and with the Commonwealth of Independent States. Given its integral importance to the former Soviet Union, Ukraine's determined opposition in late 1991 doomed the formation of a new version of the Soviet Union. Kravchuk's tepid support of the Commonwealth of Independent States reflects a majority view among Ukrainians that this new union is a temporary and transitional measure. Kravchuk has several times threatened to withdraw from the CIS over Russia's alleged reluctance to meet its commitments to the commonwealth.

Ukraine has asserted its independence in a number of ways. It has forged new political and economic unions with nations outside the CIS; it has moved to create its own currency; it has fought to retain industries it considers its own; it negotiated an agreement with Russia that provides for Ukrainian control of part of the 300-ship Black Sea Fleet; and it has established its own military, equipped with some of the most advanced weaponry and technology in the Soviet arsenal.

These and other actions have put the Kravchuk government at odds with Russia's new leaders. After approaching several flashpoints, Kravchuk and Boris Yeltsin solved some of these problems (such as the division of the Black Sea Fleet) and agreed to disagree on others.

Russian moves to encourage unrest in the heavily Russian enclave of Crimea (which the Soviet Union ceded to Ukraine in 1954) have succeeded, with the local parliament declaring Crimea independent of Ukraine in mid-1992 and Russia's parliament voiding the 1954 transfer soon after. The issue seems certain to remain contentious for a long time. Ukraine also has been concerned with an armed uprising of ethnic Russians in neighboring Moldova (where many Ukrainians also live), which hard-line Russian officials appear to be supporting.

The continued operation of the Chernobyl nuclear plant has been a source of tension with Belarus to the north, large portions of which were contaminated after the 1986 meltdown. The accident left both new nations with enormous environmental problems and an aversion to nuclear technology. It also contributed to Kravchuk's commitment to make Ukraine a nuclear-free state. Many short-range tactical nuclear weapons had been removed from Ukraine to Russia during early 1992. But in March, Ukraine temporarily halted the transfer because of concerns that the dismantlement process was not being properly monitored in Russia. Yeltsin and Kravchuk resolved this question in April, and all tactical nuclear weapons were removed from Ukraine by May.

That month Ukraine also signed a protocol to the START treaty with the United States that made it a successor to the Soviet Union along with Russia, Belarus, and Kazakhstan. The four states were to decide among themselves how to implement the START reductions in long-range strategic nuclear weapons. Despite Kravchuk's commitment to remove all nuclear weapons from Ukraine, he has attempted to use Ukraine's strategic nuclear arsenal as a bargaining chip with Russia. He also sought security guarantees from the United States. Washington declined to extend such guarantees, while emphasizing concern for Ukraine's security and the importance it places on Ukraine.

Ukraine's economic future will be affected greatly by how economic relations with Russia and the other former Soviet states are managed. The effect of Ukraine's independence roughly equals what would happen if the Midwest's industrial and agricultural states chose to leave the United States and become a separate nation.

While acknowledging the importance of the Ukrainian-Russian economic relationship, Kiev wants to find new markets for its products and new suppliers for its industries. Foreign investors, including a sizable number from the Ukrainian diaspora in the United States and Canada, have been put off by the slow pace of economic reform, a pace the Ukrainians say is forced upon them by what is happening to the Russian economy, to which they remain dependent. Russian actions to free prices meant Ukraine, still dependent on the ruble, had to do the same or watch many of its consumer goods disap-

pear over the border. A makeshift coupon system worked for a time as a parallel currency to the ruble while Kiev worked to create its own new currency.

Incoming prime minister Leonid Kuchma said in October 1992 after surveying the state of the Ukrainian economy: "I cannot promise you an easy life. The situation will inevitably get worse. All I will promise is that the prime minister and his team soon to be chosen will work conscientiously." According to Ukrainian government figures, consumer inflation stood at more than 1,000 percent.

Despite its severe economic problems and declining living standards, Ukraine appears committed to a more democratic and open society oriented toward the West. Public support for continuing in this direction is overwhelming and those who would reinstall the Soviet past constitute a small minority. The establishment of a strong democratic state in what was once the Communist heartland would contribute greatly to the entire region's prosperity and stability.

APPENDIX

BIOGRAPHIES

Biographies of Mikhail Gorbachev and Boris Yeltsin are given below. Following these biographies are forty-four shorter biographical sketches of other current leaders. Finally, eighteen important figures in Soviet history are profiled.

Mikhail S. Gorbachev (1931-   )

On March 11, 1985, only four hours after the announcement of Konstantin U. Chernenko's death, Mikhail Sergeevich Gorbachev, age fifty-four, became the youn-

gest general secretary in the Soviet Union's history. He also became the first top Soviet leader from the generation that rose through the party ranks after Stalin's death. Gorbachev's accession to the leadership of the Communist Party of the Soviet Union (CPSU) marked the end of an era in Soviet politics dominated by aging leaders and bureaucratic inertia

and the beginning of a period of change unprecedented in Soviet history, a period in which the truths that had been accepted since the revolution were discarded one by one.

Gorbachev was born March 2, 1931, in the village of Privolnoye in the southern wheat-growing area of Stavropol in the Russian republic. His parents were peasants of modest means. Gorbachev has one brother, Aleksandr, seventeen years his junior. Their maternal grandfather was a committed Communist who headed a collective farm. As a teenager, Gorbachev did well in school and operated a combine during the summer. Compared with other Russian families, the Gorbachevs suffered little from collectivization and World War II, although the Stavropol area was occupied by German forces for about six months.

Gorbachev entered the prestigious Moscow State University in 1950 at the age of nineteen. At twenty-one he became a member of the Communist party and three years later, in 1955, graduated with a degree in law. While in college, Gorbachev met his wife, Raisa. She became the subject of much attention in the Western press during her husband's tenure in office because of her stylishness and public visibility compared with that of preceding Soviet leaders' wives. She studied philosophy at Moscow State and has lectured on that subject. The couple has a daughter, Irina, and a young granddaughter, Oksana. Irina and her husband are physicians.

Public Career. After graduating from Moscow State, Gorbachev returned to Stavropol, where he gained recognition as a leader in the Komsomol (Communist Youth League). He began full-time party work in 1962. He received a degree from the Stavropol Agricultural Institute in 1967. Under the tutelage of Fëdor Kulakov, first secretary of Stavropol *krai* (territory), he rose quickly through the local party ranks. In 1970, at the relatively young age of thirty-nine, he assumed his mentor's post after Kulakov had been promoted to a position in Moscow. Gorbachev's selection to full membership on the CPSU Central Committee in 1971 was attributed by some to party ideologue Mikhail Suslov, who had strong ties to Stavropol.

In 1978 Kulakov died, and Gorbachev, then forty-seven, was called from Stavropol to take his place as the Central Committee secretary responsible for agriculture. Although a series of bad harvests followed, Gorbachev's career did not falter. He became a candidate member of the Politburo in 1979 and a full member in 1980. From 1979 until 1984 he chaired the Legislative Proposals Commission of the Council of the Union of the USSR Supreme Soviet.

Gorbachev continued his rise during the succession battles that followed Brezhnev's death in 1982. Under Yuri V. Andropov he was given oversight responsibility for the whole economy and lower-level party appointments. He developed a close working relationship with the ailing Andropov during the general secretary's confinement to a hospital apartment in late 1983 and early 1984.

After nominating Chernenko as party leader following Andropov's death, Gorbachev became de facto second secretary, although some tasks were shared with his rival, Grigory Romanov, the former Leningrad party first secretary who had been brought to the Secretariat by Andropov to supervise military industry. Gorbachev oversaw all aspects of the economy except for military-related industries and served as chairman of the Foreign Affairs Commission from early 1984 until July 1985. He shared supervision of state administrative organs with Romanov. After Chernenko's health began to fail, Gorbachev and Romanov alternated chairing Politburo meetings. Gorbachev's stature as a spokesman for Soviet interests abroad grew after he and his wife made a highly publicized trip to Great Britain in December 1984.

Despite Gorbachev's status as second in command, his rise was not guaranteed upon Chernenko's death. He was challenged by Romanov and Viktor Grishin, the conservative seventy-year-old Moscow party secretary. Gorbachev, however, overcame these challenges and was chosen general secretary.

On October 1, 1988, Gorbachev replaced Andrei Gromyko as chairman of the Presidium of the Supreme Soviet (president), thus combining the roles of head of the party and head of state. The Congress of People's Deputies (CPD) elected him to the revamped presidential office of chairman of the Supreme Soviet on May 25, 1989. He gave up this office in March 1990, when the CPD elected him to the new executive presidency for a five-year term. Gorbachev also was reelected general secretary of the Communist party at the Twenty-eighth Party Congress in July 1990.

Analysis. During his first year in office, Gorbachev gave little indication of being a radical reformer. Indeed, most Western observers expected him to be something of a younger and more telegenic Andropov, intent on jump-starting the economy by battling corruption and strengthening discipline at work. Like previous Soviet leaders, Gorbachev spoke of using resources more efficiently, battling alcoholism, introducing new technologies, and "perfecting the economic mechanism." He realized only gradually that political and societal stagnation were at the root of the country's economic problems and that more fundamental changes were necessary. His reforms became increasingly radical: relaxed censorship and more open societal debate; multicandidate elections; and finally renunciation of the party's monopoly on power.

As a result of Gorbachev's "new thinking" in foreign policy, he achieved great popularity in the West, particularly in Germany. He consistently ranked higher than Western leaders in Western polls measuring popularity. However, his popularity abroad was significantly greater than that at home. Whereas Westerners focused on the dramatically reduced Soviet military threat, the fall of Communist regimes in Eastern Europe, and the improvement of human rights in the Soviet Union, Soviet citizens were more concerned with the steadily declining economy. Thus, even as Gorbachev's reputation soared in the West, his political support at home weakened.

Gorbachev repeatedly displayed keen political instincts, deftly maneuvering between conservatives opposed to his increasingly radical reforms and liberals who protested that the reforms were being implemented too slowly. Besieged from the left as well as the right, Gorbachev also had to confront the increasingly restive republics. Many leaders of the republic governments, who were freely elected and as such carried greater moral and political authority and popular support, openly defied Moscow. Gorbachev's attempt to pacify the republics with a new, more liberal union treaty was the final straw for conservatives and precipitated the August 1991 coup. The coup, though unsuccessful, buried Gorbachev's chances of saving the union. He resigned as general secretary and president on Christmas Day, 1991. Gorbachev had begun a reform juggernaut that accelerated beyond his control. He was overtaken by the forces he himself had unleashed.

On January 14, 1992, Gorbachev became chairman of the International Foundation for Social, Economic, and Political Research, a nonprofit think tank founded by a former aide, Aleksandr N. Yakovlev.

Boris Yeltsin (1931-   )

Boris Nikolayevich Yeltsin became the first democratically elected leader in Russia's one-thousand-year history in May 1990 after a nearly thirty-year career as a Communist party functionary.

Yeltsin was born February 1, 1931, in Sverdlovsk (now Yekaterinburg) in the Ural Mountains of European Russia. In his 1990 autobiography, *Against the Grain,* Yeltsin described himself as "a little bit of a hooligan" in his youth. At age eleven he and two friends stole two hand grenades from a military warehouse; Yeltsin lost  two fingers on his left hand when one of them exploded.

Yeltsin graduated from the Urals M. Kirov Polytechnic Institute in 1955 with a degree in construction engineering. From 1955 to 1968 he directed building projects in and around Sverdlovsk. Inspired by Nikita Khrushchev's de-Stalinization program, Yeltsin joined the party in

1961, at age thirty. In 1968 he went to work full time for the party organization in Sverdlovsk, mostly in construction-related positions. Yeltsin was appointed first secretary of the Sverdlovsk District Central Committee in 1976 and quickly earned a reputation as a charismatic and energetic leader who effectively fought against corruption.

Public Career. Yeltsin remained in the Sverdlovsk position until July 1985 when Mikhail Gorbachev summoned him to Moscow to become head of the Central Committee Construction Department. Only five months later Gorbachev appointed him first secretary of the Moscow City Party Committee, where he replaced the aging conservative, Viktor Grishin. Three months after that, in March 1986, Yeltsin became a candidate member of the Politburo.

Shortly after entering the Politburo, Yeltsin began a campaign against party privileges and elitism. From his position as Moscow party boss he fired dozens of corrupt officials, encouraged public debate, and made an effort to make contact with the citizenry by riding public transportation and stopping to hear the complaints of people on the streets. Often characterized as a loose cannon, Yeltsin was pugnacious, temperamental, and prone to public outbursts.

Yeltsin's increasingly vitriolic outbursts made him popular with Muscovites but alienated many in the party. At the Twenty-seventh Party Congress in February 1986 he denounced the "zone beyond criticism" surrounding the party elite. At the October 1987 Central Committee plenum he criticized the Politburo, the Secretariat, and conservative Politburo member Yegor Ligachev and charged that Gorbachev was developing a cult of personality. This last tirade cost him his job and his party position.

He remained a persistent critic of both the party apparatus and the slow pace of Gorbachev's reform effort. His popularity among the Soviet people soared as a result. Yeltsin was not selected by the party to run on its slate in the 1989 elections to the Congress of People's Deputies, but he was nominated for the Congress in at least fifty constituencies. He chose to run for Moscow's national-territorial seat. In a dramatic moment during the election campaign in March 1989, Moscow city officials blocked a rally for Yeltsin, only to have nine thousand Muscovites spontaneously demonstrate in his behalf.

Yeltsin was elected to the Congress of People's Deputies with 89 percent of the votes cast. In another move to keep Yeltsin out of the policy-making arena, the party leadership worked to prevent the Congress from electing him to the Supreme Soviet. This drew protests from the liberal deputies and the public, and Yeltsin subsequently gained a seat in the higher body when an elected deputy stepped down to give him his place.

Yeltsin was one of the cofounders of the Interregional Group, the opposition bloc in parliament of more than two hundred deputies. He also became a member of the coordinating council of the Democratic Platform, the reform wing of the Communist party that advocated radical changes in the party's platform.

Yeltsin was elected president of the Russian Soviet Federated Socialist Republic (RSFSR) in May 1990 after several overt attempts by Gorbachev to influence the election in favor of his own hand-picked candidate. Then, at the Twenty-eighth Party Congress in July he announced that party membership was incompatible with his position as president and he dramatically resigned from the Communist party. Nevertheless, he continued to press Gorbachev to quicken the pace of reform, and his stature among the Russian people rose to rival that of Gorbachev.

In the latter half of 1990 and into 1991 Yeltsin agitated for the economic sovereignty of Russia. He proclaimed the primacy of Russian law over Soviet law and added his support to a revolt of republic leaders against Muscovite authority. By the summer of 1991 the Yeltsin-led revolt forced Gorbachev to renegotiate the union treaty, which was the last straw for the conservatives who orchestrated the August coup in which Gorbachev was held captive for two-and-a-half days. Yeltsin's bold defiance of the coup plotters and his demands for Gorbachev's release shattered the political will and might of conservatives and led to the dissolution of the Soviet Union four months later.

Analysis. The career of Boris Yeltsin exemplified the unpredictability of Soviet domestic politics under Mikhail S. Gorbachev. A proreform politician whose rise through the ranks had been meteoric, his fall from official grace was equally swift. Under Stalin's regime a maverick such as Yeltsin would have been shot; under Khrushchev he would have been jailed; and under Brezhnev he would have been sent to an insane asylum. Because of the transformations that Gorbachev engineered in Soviet politics, Yeltsin was able to arise again and challenge his one-time patron.

Yeltsin's appeal was formidable among common Soviet citizens and the liberal intelligentsia. His populist approach to politics and down-to-earth persona allowed the average citizen to identify with him. Gorbachev was ill-equipped to compete with Yeltsin on the political playing field that he himself had helped to create.

Yeltsin realized that to maintain his wide popular appeal he would have to produce quick, tangible results. He implemented a comprehensive and coordinated restructuring of the economy that encompassed price liberalization, privatization, and land reform. To gain IMF backing and rein in spiraling inflation he followed tight monetary and fiscal policies. His radical reform program received tempered endorsement from the IMF and other Western observers but it created painful dislocations throughout

Russian society. The jury is still out on the long-term prognosis for Yeltsin and his reforms.

Other Notable Leaders

Yuri Afanaseyev (1934-   )

A dissident historian, Afanaseyev was a leader of the opposition Interregional Group in the USSR Supreme Soviet and is now a deputy in the Russian parliament. He was a founder of the Democratic Russia movement, which brought Yeltsin to the presidency. He resigned from the movement in January 1992, claiming that it had become a tool of the executive. He has worked for a comprehensive review of Soviet history and has fought for the rehabilitation of Stalin's victims.

Abel Aganbegyan (1932-   )

An Armenian economist who helped to develop Gorbachev's program of gradual economic reforms, Aganbegyan has seen his influence wane under Yeltsin as more radical reforms have gained attention. Nevertheless, he is still a frequent commentator in the Russian press. From 1967 to 1985 he worked in virtual academic exile at the Novosibirsk State University in Siberia. The ideas of Aganbegyan and other economists at Novosibirsk caught the attention of Gorbachev and formed much of the intellectual basis for his economic program.

Askar Akayev (1944-   )

In October 1991 Akayev was elected president of Kyrgyzstan, promising democracy and a market economy. Along with Yeltsin he is considered one of the most democratic of the post-Soviet presidents. Akayev was trained as a physicist at the Leningrad Institute of Precision Mechanics and Optics. He held seats in the Soviet Congress of People's Deputies and the Supreme Soviet. In 1989 he was elected president of the Kyrgyz Academy of Sciences. Because of Akayev's strong commitment to pluralism and democracy, Kyrgyzstan was among the first republics to gain U.S. recognition.

Nina Andreyeva (1938-   )

A chemistry teacher from St. Petersburg, Andreyeva had a lengthy letter published in *Sovetskaya Rossia* (Soviet Russia) that gained national attention in March 1988. In the letter, she attacked Gorbachev's reform program as a complete rejection of socialism. She called for a return to discipline and central planning, which she complained had been weakening since Stalin died in 1953. Her letter became a rallying point for Russian nationalists. She has become an outspoken member of the extremist Russian nationalist group Pamyat (Memory).

Georgy Arbatov (1923-   )

The head of the Institute for the Study of the USA and Canada since 1967, Arbatov has been a top adviser to Kremlin officials on East-West relations. He participated in numerous superpower summits and has published articles in the Western press. He has criticized the Gaidar government for relying too heavily on economic assistance from the International Monetary Fund and the West. He also has emphasized the need for Russia to focus its foreign policy on improving relations with the other CIS states.

Oleg Bogomolov (1918-   )

The director of the Institute of World Economic and Political Research, Bogomolov is a member of Yeltsin's Presidential Consultative Council. Under Bogomolov, the institute has studied foreign economic reform experiences and their applicability to Russia. He was influential in shaping Gorbachev's economic reform program.

Gennady Burbulis (1945-   )

In April 1992 Burbulis resigned as Russian first deputy prime minister, but he remains one of Yeltsin's closest political allies. He has retained his position as a state secretary. An advocate of radical political and economic reform, Burbulis was a leading member of the Interregional Group in the USSR Congress of People's Deputies. Before entering politics, Burbulis was a professor of Marxism-Leninism at the Sverdlovsk Institute of the USSR Ministry of Nonferrous Metallurgy. Burbulis explained his resignation as first deputy prime minister by saying that he wished to avoid being answerable to the conservative Russian Congress of People's Deputies.

Anatoly Chubais (1954-   )

The Russian minister of privatization, Chubais is a key member of Gaidar's team of young economists. He was Russian deputy minister of finance, but since late 1991 he has been in charge of the privatization effort. He has announced plans to privatize vast sectors of the Russian economy by 1994.

Ivan Drakh (1936-   )

The chairman of Rukh, the Ukrainian popular front, Drakh is a central figure in Ukrainian politics. He gained a national reputation as a poet and dissident before becoming head of the Democratic party, one of the main parties in the Ukrainian parliament. Despite his long-standing prominence as an advocate of Ukrainian democracy and independence, Drakh has a reputation for pragmatism. At Rukh's third congress in February 1992, Drakh reportedly called for support of President Leonid Kravchuk, despite Kravchuk's Communist past. "Kravchuk an autocrat?" Drakh is reported to have asked. "May God make Kravchuk enough of an autocrat to keep Ukraine together."

Dzokhar Dudayev (1944-   )

A retired air force general, Dudayev seized control of the Chechen-Ingush Autonomous Republic on September 6, 1991, claiming that the Communists who ruled the republic had declined to oppose the August coup in Moscow. Dudayev has established a strong-arm dictatorial regime, threatening to use his large volunteer army to defend against any effort by the Russians to reassert their control in Grozny, the Chechen capital.

Andrei Dunayev (1939-   )

Before the August 1991 attempted coup, Dunayev was Russia's deputy minister of internal affairs. During the coup he led students of the Militia School into Moscow to defend Yeltsin and the Russian White House. For this action, Yeltsin promoted him to minister of internal affairs.

Abulfez Elchibey (1938-   )

Head of the Azerbaijani Popular Front, Elchibey was elected president of Azerbaijan with 59 percent of the vote on June 7, 1992. A specialist in oriental history, Elchibey studied Arabic philology at Baku State University. In 1975 he was imprisoned on charges of slandering the Soviet system. After his release in 1977 he worked at the Institute of Manuscripts of the Azerbaijani Academy of Sciences. He is the author of more than fifty books on oriental philosophy, history, literature, and culture. He was elected head of the Azerbaijani Popular Front when it was founded in 1989. Elchibey has said Azerbaijan will never give up control of Nagorno-Karabakh, an Armenian enclave within Azerbaijan that has been the site of fierce fighting between Azeris and ethnic Armenians seeking independence.

Yegor Gaidar (1956-   )

The acting Russian prime minister, Gaidar is the leader of a circle of young academics that is conceiving and managing Yeltsin's economic reform program. Gaidar's political fortunes are tied to the reforms, and he will rise or fall with them. He studied economics at Moscow State University, receiving his doctorate in 1988. He was political economy editor for *Kommunist* from 1987 to 1990, then became a member of the editorial board of *Pravda* in 1990. He then served as deputy prime minister of Russia but was demoted to finance minister in February 1992. In an indication of Yeltsin's determination to push forward with economic reform, he appointed Gaidar acting prime minister in June 1992. To qualify for International Monetary Fund loans, Gaidar has agreed to implement austerity measures. His efforts to restrict credits to failing enterprises have brought him into daily conflict with conservatives. His critics also have complained that he is too young to be entrusted with the Russian economy and that he lacks management experience outside of an academic environment.

Zviad Gamsakhurdia (1939-   )

The former president of Georgia, Gamsakhurdia was ousted by opposition forces in January 1992. He became a well-known dissident during the 1970s and 1980s, spending part of that period in prison. The U.S. Congress even supported him for the Nobel Peace Prize in 1978. When free elections were held in Georgia in 1990, Gamsakhurdia was chosen president by an overwhelming majority. But within months the enigmatic leader transformed himself from dissident to dictator. He suppressed dissent and forbade challenges to his rule. In December 1991 opposition gunmen took to the streets of Tbilisi, forcing Gamsakhurdia to barricade himself in a bunker in the Government House. After two weeks he fled to Armenia and was eventually given asylum in the Chechen city of Grozny by Dzokhar Dudayev. Militia forces loyal to Gamsakhurdia have continued to fight since his overthrow, staging raids and occasionally waging pitched battles against troops of the new government.

Anatolijs Gorbunovs (1942-   )

A former Communist party official, Gorbunovs has been the chairman of the Latvian Supreme Council since October 1988. He attended Riga Technical University, where he was trained as a civil engineer. Despite his many years in the Communist party apparatus, Gorbunovs is considered a moderate.

Pavel Grachev (1948-   )

In May 1992 President Yeltsin established a Russian Ministry of Defense separate from the CIS command structure and appointed Grachev as its head. During the August 1991 coup, Grachev, then commander of the USSR Airborne Forces, had thrown his support to Yeltsin. Despite his opposition to the coup, Grachev is one of a group of conservative *Afghantsi* (veterans of Afghanistan) who have risen to prominence in the Russian defense establishment and seem willing to use the military to promote their own political agenda. He has urged that ethnic Russians outside Russia should be protected, and he has spoken against market reforms.

Boris Gromov (1943-   )

As deputy minister of defense of Russia, Gromov is one of a clique of conservative *Afghantsi* (Afghanistan veterans) who occupy key positions in the Russian military. He served as first deputy minister for internal affairs under Boris Pugo, a plotter of the August 1991 coup who killed himself after the putsch unraveled. Gromov is a charismatic and popular figure who could play a leading role in any effort by the military to involve itself in politics. He was the last commander of Soviet troops in Afghanistan. The Soviet media praised him for his determination to make the withdrawal dignified and professional, despite the humiliating circumstances.

Islam Karimov (1938-   )

The president of Uzbekistan, Karimov has developed an authoritarian style of rule but has favored the Turkish model of secular development and market democracy. Karimov is a former Communist who oversaw the cosmetic restructuring of the Communist party in Uzbekistan after the failed August 1991 coup in Moscow. He was elected by the Uzbek Supreme Soviet to the newly created post of president in March 1990. He was confirmed in this post by a December 1991 popular election in which he received 86 percent of the vote, partly attributable to the substantial institutional advantages he held over his opponent. Karimov has called for creation of a Central Asian union to cope with common economic problems.

Ruslan Khasbulatov (1942-   )

The chairman of the Russian Supreme Soviet, Khasbulatov has criticized Yegor Gaidar and called for the entire government to resign. An ethnic Chechen, Khasbulatov has a doctorate in economics and has taught at the Plekhanov Institute and the Moscow Institute of National Economics. He was a strong Yeltsin supporter at the first RSFSR Congress of People's Deputies. Since being elected head of the Russian Supreme Soviet, he has attempted to advance the power of the legislative branch at the expense of Yeltsin's executive branch.

Andrei Kozyrev (1941-   )

The Russian foreign minister since October 1991, Kozyrev has promoted close ties with the West in his efforts to remake Russia into a "normal great power." Under Kozyrev, Russia has worked to strengthen the United Nations and other multilateral organizations. Because of his Western orientation, Kozyrev has been the target of nationalists and conservatives who have accused him of conceding too much in negotiations with the West. Kozyrev is a 1974 graduate of the Moscow Institute of International Relations and has written a number of books on disarmament.

Leonid Kravchuk (1934-   )

On December 1, 1991, Kravchuk became the first popularly elected president of Ukraine. Previously, he had been chairman of the Ukrainian Supreme Soviet and had a long career as a Communist party functionary. He studied political economy at Kiev University. As Ukraine radicalized in the months before its formal independence, Kravchuk recast himself from a career Communist into a Ukrainian nationalist. He initially reacted with caution to the August 1991 Moscow coup, but later he roundly condemned the plotters and resigned his party membership. Since the coup, he has aggressively defended Ukraine against any perceived Russian slight, while cooperating with Yeltsin to defuse potential issues of conflict, including the dispensation of the Black Sea Fleet and the status of the Crimean Peninsula. Kravchuk has contended that the Commonwealth of Independent States is merely a mechanism by which the former states of the Soviet Union will achieve an amicable separation. He has moved Ukraine inexorably toward complete independence from Moscow.

Vytautas Landsbergis (1932-   )

A pianist and musical theoretician before entering politics, Landsbergis has been chairman of the Lithuanian Supreme Council since March 1990. He graduated from the Lithuanian Conservatory, where he taught from 1975 to 1990. He was head of Sajudis, the Lithuanian popular front, which led the push for independence from the Soviet Union. Unlike many current leaders in the former Soviet republics, he was never a member of the Communist party. With Lithuanian independence achieved and the Sajudis coalition splintered into rival factions and parties, Landsbergis's popularity has weakened. His effort to establish a strong presidency was rejected in a popular referendum in May 1992.

Vladimir Lukin (1933-   )

At the beginning of March 1992, Lukin began his service as the first Russian ambassador to the United States since 1917. Before his appointment, he was chairman of the Committee on Foreign Relations of the Russian Supreme Soviet. Prior to becoming involved in politics in the mid 1980s, he spent nineteen years as an academic at the Institute of the USA and Canada, specializing in Sino-American relations. Lukin was an early supporter of Yeltsin during the August 1991 coup.

Ayez Mutalibov (1939-   )

In March 1992 Mutalibov resigned as president of Azerbaijan because of popular discontent with his handling of the dispute over Nagorno-Karabakh. He had been appointed head of the Azerbaijani Communist party by Moscow in January 1990. He resigned from the party after the August 1991 coup and in September 1991 was popularly elected to the presidency in an election that opponents denounced as fraudulent.

Rakhmon Nabiyev (1931-   )

In September 1992, after months of fighting between rival clans, Nabiyev was forcibly deposed as leader of Tajikistan. As the head of the Communist party in Tajikistan he had dominated the republic since the Brezhnev era. In November 1991 he was elected president in a popular election that the opposition charged was rigged. Popular unrest ensued under the guidance of a broad-based opposition coalition. Nabiyev's attempts to suppress the opposition failed. Since his ouster, groups loyal to Nabiyev have continued to fight opposition forces.

Nursultan Nazarbayev (1940-   )

The president of Kazakhstan, Nazarbayev is the most prominent Central Asian political figure. Previously head of the Kazakh Council of Ministers and then the Kazakh Communist party, he was selected as president by the Kazakhstan Supreme Soviet in April 1990. He was confirmed in this post in uncontested elections in December 1991. While his exercise of power can be authoritarian, Nazarbayev is considered more tolerant of pluralism than most other Central Asian leaders. A native of Alma-Ata, he has attempted to address pragmatically the concerns of the Kazakh and Russian populations in his nation, each of which makes up slightly less than 40 percent of the entire population.

Andrei Nechayev (1952-   )

As Russian minister of the economy, Nechayev is a member of the Gaidar team of young academics leading the economic reform program. Previously he had served as first deputy minister of economics and finance of the Russian Federation. He has a degree in economics from Moscow State University.

Saparmurad Niyazov (1940-   )

The head of the Democratic party of Turkmenistan (formerly the Communist party), Niyazov was elected president of Turkmenistan in October 1990 by that republic's Supreme Soviet. Niyazov was slow to criticize the August 1991 coup in Moscow. He has maintained stability in Turkmenistan through repression and an intolerance of political dissent. Although Niyazov has implemented a few economic reforms and sought foreign trade contacts, economic restructuring has proceeded slowly. He has retained Communist party structures and many Russian bureaucrats from the old order.

Gavriil Popov (1937-   )

An influential advocate of reform, Popov resigned as mayor of Moscow in early 1992, claiming that the city had become impossible to govern. During the late 1980s Popov became prominent as a radical economist and chief editor of *Voprosy Ekonomiki* (Questions of Economics). He was an outspoken member of the USSR Congress of People's Deputies and a leader in the opposition Interregional Group. Popov was one of about fifty delegates to the Twenty-eighth Communist Party Congress who followed Yeltsin in resigning from the party.

Aleksandr Rutskoy (1948-   )

The vice president of Russia, Rutskoy has been Yeltsin's most vocal conservative critic and could be a beneficiary of any effort to topple Yeltsin from the right. A highly decorated veteran of Afghanistan, he is a strong proponent of the military and defense industrial sector and frequently attacks Gaidar's reforms as leading the country toward disaster. Rutskoy has positioned himself as a patriot, calling for the revival of a strong central authority, the reestablishment of Russia's historic borders, and the protection of ethnic Russians living outside Russia. He is chairman of the People's Party of Free Russia. He was shot down twice over Afghanistan and spent several months as a prisoner of war in Pakistan.

Arnold Ruutel (1928-   )

A former Communist, Ruutel has been chairman of the Estonian Supreme Council since 1983. Despite his connections to the old order, his support for Estonian nationalist causes has enabled him to maintain his popularity.

Sergei Shakhrai (1954-   )

A member of the Presidential Advisory Council, Shakhrai is a close adviser to Yeltsin, primarily on legal matters. He had been chairman of the Committee on

Legislation of the Russian Supreme Soviet for two years before his resignation in October 1991. In March 1992 he also resigned as deputy prime minister. He had been heavily criticized by Speaker of the Russian parliament Khasbulatov, and conservatives had called for his resignation because of his reformist views. Like Kozyrev and several other liberals close to Yeltsin, Shakhrai has issued warnings of a possible coup from the right.

Yevgeny Shaposhnikov (1942-   )

The former head of the USSR Air Force, Shaposhnikov was appointed to replace coup plotter Dmitry Yazov as USSR defense minister after the August 1991 putsch. In December 1991 he was appointed commander of the armed forces of the CIS. He is a career air force officer who is considered a moderate. He has supported efforts to depoliticize the armed forces and bring them further under civilian control.

Stanislav Shatalin (1934-   )

A radical economist, Shatalin under Gorbachev was a member of the Presidential Council. In 1990 his "Five Hundred Day Plan" was the first proposal for completely overhauling the Soviet economy to be considered. However, Gorbachev was reluctant to implement the plan and later rejected it. Shatalin subsequently lost his influence in the government's economic reform plans.

Eduard Shevardnadze (1928-   )

In October 1992 Shevardnadze was overwhelmingly elected president of the troubled nation of Georgia. Shevardnadze rocketed to international prominence in 1985 when Gorbachev appointed him to replace Andrei Gromyko as USSR foreign minister. He advanced policies aimed at developing constructive relations with the West. He has been credited with helping to bring about the INF Treaty, the Soviet withdrawal from Afghanistan, and Soviet acquiescence to the reunification of Germany. Shevardnadze dramatically resigned as foreign minister in December 1990, warning that a right-wing coup was imminent.

Previously, Shevardnadze had served as party head in his native Georgia from 1972 to 1985. During that period he developed a reputation as a reformer who clamped down hard on corruption. In January 1992, after Zviad Gamsakhurdia was ousted from the Georgian presidency, Shevardnadze was invited to return to Georgia to head the provisional state council. He returned in March, finding himself presiding over a country consumed by an escalating civil war and two separatist movements.

Stanislav Shushkevich (1934-   )

A native of Minsk and son of a well-known Belorussian poet, Shushkevich was selected chairman of the Supreme Soviet of Belarus in September 1991. Unlike many leaders of former Soviet states, he has declined to arrange a popular presidential election. A former nuclear physicist, he became active in politics only in the late 1980s after the Chernobyl disaster. Though he came to office as a member of the opposition, he has adopted a cautious, conservative political line that emphasizes gradual reforms and good relations with Russia. Until December 1991 he was among the strongest supporters of Gorbachev's proposed union treaty.

Ivan Silaev (1930-   )

The prime minister of Russia from June 1990 until the failed August 1991 coup, Silaev resigned his office in the wake of the putsch. He was given responsibility for coordinating economic reform plans with the other republics. However, his role in the government has gradually decreased because of his association with the old guard. In December 1991 he was appointed Russian representative to the European Community.

Mircea Snegur (1940-   )

The president of Moldova, Snegur has attempted to develop a solution to ethnic fighting between Moldovans and Russian separatists in the Trans-Dniester region. A native of Cishinau (formerly Kishinev), he graduated from the Kishinev Agricultural Institute and received his candidate's degree from there in agricultural science in 1972. He worked his way through the party apparatus to become secretary of the Moldavian Communist party in 1985. In September 1990 the parliament elected him president, and he later left the party. Running unopposed, he was confirmed as president in popular elections on December 7, 1991. He has resisted plans pushed by some Moldovan nationalists for a quick unification with Romania.

Anatoly Sobchak (1938-   )

A lawyer by profession, Sobchak was elected chairman of the Leningrad city soviet in May 1990, after a group of reformists came to power there. He was among the leaders of the opposition Interregional Group in the USSR Supreme Soviet. A radical reformer, he joined a group of about fifty delegates to the Twenty-eighth Communist Party Congress who followed Yeltsin in resigning from the party.

Levon Ter-Petrossyan (1945-)

The candidate of the Armenian National Movement, Ter-Petrossyan was elected president of Armenia in October 1991. He is the former chairman of the Armenian Supreme Soviet and a leader of the Karabakh Committee (the nucleus of the Armenian independence movement). During the Soviet period, he served time in prison for promoting Armenian nationalism. Educated in Yerevan and Leningrad, he holds a doctorate in philology and is widely published in his field.

Dmitry Volkogonov (1928-)

A key military adviser to Yeltsin, Volkogonov is head of the Russian Defense Commission, which is charged with establishing the Russian Ministry of Defense. He is considered a radical reformer who seeks steep reductions in the size of the Russian armed forces. He has written an extensive biography of Stalin and has served as director of the army's Institute of Military History. Volkogonov is also chairman of the Parliamentary Committee for Transferring and Receiving the Archives of the CPSU and USSR KGB.

Arkady Volsky (1932-)

A powerful figure in Russian politics, Volsky is the backbone of the industrialists' lobby, which has fought Gaidar's efforts to cut credits to weak enterprises. He is head of the Russian Industrialists' and Entrepreneurs' Union. He served as an economic adviser to Chernenko, Andropov, and Gorbachev. Volsky has become the chief spokesman of those who support Yeltsin but oppose Gaidar and want to slow economic reform. He is considered a strong candidate to become prime minister if the Gaidar government is forced out.

Tatyana Zaslavskaya (1927-)

Since 1988 sociologist Zaslavskaya has been director of the Center for the Study of Public Opinion. Her academic work at the Institute of Economics and Industrial Organization in Novosibirsk along with that of Abel Aganbegyan laid down early foundations for Gorbachev's program of perestroika.

Vladimir Zhirinovsky (1946-)

A leader of the conservative movement Nashi (Ours), Zhirinovsky does not mince words in espousing his chauvinistic brand of Russian nationalism. He also is active in the Russian nationalist group Pamyat (Memory). He has called for decentralization and widespread privatization of the economy. But he seeks a strong central government that can reassert Russian control over all former Soviet territory. He came in third when Yeltsin was elected president in 1991, garnering more than six million votes. If an authoritarian nationalist regime succeeds Yeltsin, Zhirinovsky could well be a key figure. He supported the failed August 1991 coup.

Past Soviet Leaders

Yuri V. Andropov (1914-1984)

Two days after the death of Leonid I. Brezhnev on November 10, 1982, Yuri Vladimirovich Andropov was named to succeed him as general secretary of the Communist party. On June  16, 1983, Andropov became chairman of the Presidium of the Supreme Soviet (president), thus continuing a practice begun by Brezhnev of combining the role of head of state with that of party chief. An ailing sixty-eight-year-old when he took over, Andropov died February 10, 1984. Three days later the Central Committee chose Konstantin U. Chernenko as his successor.

Andropov was born the son of a railroad worker on June 15, 1914, in Nagutskaya, now in Stavropol territory. Andropov never received a college degree, although he attended Petrozavodsk University. Between 1930 and 1932 he worked as a telegraph operator, an apprentice film mechanic, and a Volga boatman. Andropov began work in the Komsomol (Communist Youth League) in 1936. In 1938 he was promoted to regional first secretary of the Komsomol and the following year became a member of the Communist party.

Public Career. When Germany invaded the Soviet Union in 1941, Andropov was active in party politics in Karelia, near the Soviet border with Finland. For the next decade he worked alongside Otto Kuusinen, the top party leader in the Karelian autonomous republic.

With the backing of Kuusinen, Andropov was transferred to Moscow in 1951 to work for the Central Committee. In 1953, after Soviet leader Joseph Stalin died, Andropov suffered an apparent career setback when he was posted to the Soviet embassy in Budapest. The switch from inner party politics to diplomacy, however, did not stymie his career. In 1954 he was promoted from counselor to ambassador to Hungary, a post he held until 1957.

Andropov played a leading role in suppressing the 1956 Hungarian revolt.

Between 1957 and 1967 he was back in Moscow serving as chief of the party's Department for Liaison with Communist and Workers' Parties of Socialist Countries, where he emphasized the importance of Soviet aid to socialist countries. During this period Andropov gathered around him a group of young, progressive advisers including Oleg Bogomolov, Aleksandr Bovin, and Fëdor Burlatsky, who later would become important reform intellectuals under Mikhail S. Gorbachev.

Andropov was made a candidate member of the Politburo in 1967, when he became chairman of the USSR Committee for State Security (KGB). He was promoted to full member of the Politburo in 1973 and thus became the first KGB head to have a vote on the Politburo since Lavrenty Beria was purged in 1953.

As head of the KGB, Andropov worked to destroy the dissident movement in the Soviet Union. Many prominent Soviet writers, scientists, and others agitating for greater liberalization were imprisoned or sent into exile under his authority.

In May 1982 Andropov resigned as KGB head and transferred to the Central Committee Secretariat, a better position from which to succeed Brezhnev. By that time he had already gained some important allies, including Foreign Minister Andrei Gromyko and Defense Minister Dmitry Ustinov, who would side with him in the struggle to succeed Brezhnev.

Analysis. Although Andropov's administration lasted only fifteen months, it brought significant changes to Soviet politics and society. During the last decade of Brezhnev's reign, few changes were made in the composition of the party leadership. But the complacency of the old guard was shaken by Andropov. He advanced Gorbachev and other younger leaders intent on instituting reforms, and he campaigned against corruption in the bureaucracy. Were it not for Andropov's domestic initiatives, many experts believe that Gorbachev would not have been able to consolidate his power so quickly. Consequently, Gorbachev and his reform program often have been seen as the legacy of Andropov.

Nevertheless, Andropov was not a radical reformer. Instead, he was an intelligent and loyal party leader who recognized his country's problems and tried to address them within the limits of the established system. Had he lived longer, he would not have pushed the reform process as far or as fast as Gorbachev.

Lavrenty Beria (1899-1953)

Lavrenty Pavlovich Beria, head of the secret police from 1938 to 1953, played an important role in maintaining the personal power of Joseph Stalin. The fear Beria engendered among his colleagues, however, led to his own arrest and execution after Stalin's death.

Beria was born on March 29, 1899, in Merkheuli, Georgia. His Georgian heritage endeared him to Stalin, another son of that republic. Beria was born into a peasant family and obtained a technical education in a Baku college. He joined the Bolshevik party in 1917 and began his career as a revolutionary worker in Georgia and Azerbaijan.

Public Career. Beria began working for the Transcaucasian Cheka in 1921. Later in the decade he continued his intelligence work in the Main Political Administration (GPU). Despite reports of abuses of power by Beria, Stalin promoted him to first secretary of the Transcaucasian Committee of the Communist party in 1931, a post that allowed Beria to exercise dictatorial power over the entire Transcaucasian region.

Stalin summoned Beria to Moscow in July 1938 and appointed him deputy to Nikolai Yezhov, head of the People's Commissariat of Internal Affairs (NKVD) and overseer of the purges. Yezhov was by this time marked by Stalin for execution, and his demise followed later in the year.

Beria took command of the secret police organization in December 1938. He investigated NKVD activities and is credited with rehabilitating certain victims of the purges and upgrading prison camp conditions. Beria's ability to magnify Stalin's suspicions of his colleagues and the dictator's great reliance on the secret police enabled Beria to consolidate quickly a powerful position. He became a candidate Politburo member in 1939.

World War II enhanced Beria's position. When the Germans invaded the Soviet Union in June 1941, Stalin appointed Beria to the State Defense Committee. His duties, in addition to supervising internal security and an international spy network, included the evacuation and resettlement of Soviet industry and later the production of ammunition. For his wartime service Beria was named a marshal of the Soviet Union in 1945. He became a full Politburo member in 1946.

Upon Stalin's death in 1953, Soviet leaders engaged in a power struggle. Beria was in contention for the top spot in the Soviet hierarchy, but initially a system of collective leadership was established. Georgy Malenkov became premier, Nikita S. Khrushchev served as party leader, and Beria continued to head up the secret police from his position as minister of internal affairs. Beria and the vast secret police network that he controlled were viewed by the other Politburo members as threats not only to their political aspirations but also to their lives. Determined that no one individual again would wield Stalin's power of life and death, the collective leadership led by Khrushchev and Malenkov engineered Beria's arrest in June 1953 on charges of "criminal antiparty and antistate activities." His alleged crimes included involvement with British intelligence and promotion of nationalistic sentiments. In December Beria was tried and executed.

Analysis. Beria's career is often described as that of an "evil genius" who ingratiated himself with Stalin by eliminating those whom Stalin perceived as enemies. He also is alleged to have approached his work with enthusiasm, personally torturing and killing many prisoners. Khrushchev maintained in his autobiography that Stalin, toward the end of his life, began to fear Beria.

In spite of Beria's lifetime association with Joseph Stalin, he proposed many modifications of the system after Stalin's death. In foreign policy Beria supported good relations with Western countries. He advocated restoring ties with Yugoslavia's Josip Broz Tito and opposed russification of non-Russian regions of the Soviet Union.

Beria's execution marked a turning point in the way power was consolidated in the Soviet leadership. The leading members of the Communist party had suffered more at the hands of Stalin and the secret police apparatus during the purges than had any other group. After Beria's execution a tacit understanding developed among the Politburo members that enforced retirement would replace execution as a punishment for losing favor.

Leonid I. Brezhnev (1906-1982)

During the 1970s and early 1980s Leonid Ilich Brezhnev was the unrivaled leader of the Soviet Union. From 1977 until his death November 10, 1982, he was both

general secretary of the Communist party and chairman of the Presidium of the Supreme Soviet (president)—the first Soviet leader to hold both of these posts at the same time. Brezhnev's success as a politician was achieved through means different from earlier Soviet leaders. He did not have V. I. Lenin's visionary brilliance, Joseph Stalin's genius for terror, nor Nikita S. Khrushchev's overpowering personality. Instead he gained and held power because he worked hard and was adept at cultivating allies within the Soviet leadership, bureaucracy, and military.

Brezhnev, a Russian, was born December 19, 1906, into a steelworker's family in the Ukrainian town of Kamenskoe (known since 1936 as Dneprodzerzhinsk). In 1915 he entered a school subsidized by the local steel plant where his father worked. When he graduated six

years later, Brezhnev—who referred to himself as a "fifth-generation steelman"—went to work as a hired hand, stoker, and fitter in a metallurgical plant.

In 1923 Brezhnev enrolled in the Kursk School for Land Utilization and Reclamation. After graduating in 1927 he spent three years working as a land reclamation specialist in Stalin's collectivization program. He eventually became chief of a district land department and deputy chairman of the executive committee of a soviet, and later the first deputy chief of a regional land administration.

In 1930 Brezhnev spent a brief period at the Timiryazev Agricultural Academy in Moscow before returning to his hometown in 1931. He went to work once again as a fitter in the metallurgical plant and studied in the evenings at the F. E. Dzerzhinsky Metallurgical Institute. Brezhnev, who had been a Komsomol (Communist Youth League) member (1923-1929) and had joined the Communist party in 1931, also served as secretary of the institute's Communist party committee and chairman of the plant's trade union committee.

Following his graduation from the institute in 1935, he worked as an engineer and briefly served in the Red Army as a political instructor. In 1937-1938 he was deputy chairman of the executive committee of the Dneprodzerzhinsk City Workers' Soviet and director of the city's metallurgical technical school.

Public Career. Brezhnev went to work full time for the Communist party in 1938. Although his switch to party politics came at the time of the Stalinist purges overseen in Ukraine by Nikita Khrushchev, there is no evidence that Brezhnev took part.

Brezhnev's first position was as chief of a department of the Dnepropetrovsk regional party committee. In 1939 he became the committee's secretary for propaganda and the next year secretary for the defense industry. He remained in this post until 1941, when the German army overran the city.

During World War II Brezhnev rose from colonel to major general, serving with the political administration of the southern and Ukrainian fronts and the Carpathian Military District. He fought in the Caucasus, on the Black Sea, in the Crimea, in Ukraine, and in the liberation of Czechoslovakia.

In 1946 Brezhnev became party first secretary of Zaporozhe and, one year later, first secretary of Dnepropetrovsk, both important industrial regions in Ukraine. In 1950, after spending a few months in Moscow working in the Central Committee apparatus, he became first secretary of the Moldavian republic. He was elected a deputy of the Supreme Soviet the same year.

As part of Stalin's expansion of the top leadership in 1952, Brezhnev was named a full member of the Central Committee, one of its ten secretaries, and a candidate member of its Presidium. Following Stalin's death in March 1953, most of his 1952 additions to the Secretariat and Presidium—including Brezhnev—were dropped. Brezhnev then spent a year as first deputy chief of the Main Political Administration of the Soviet Army and Navy.

In 1954 Khrushchev, maneuvering for power after Stalin's death, staked his political future on his Virgin Lands program, which was aimed at increasing Soviet agricultural output by farming previously uncultivated lands. He chose Brezhnev to help carry out the venture. From 1954 to 1956 Brezhnev served as second secretary and later as first secretary of the party in the Central Asian republic of Kazakhstan, where many acres of virgin land were opened.

Having displayed his managerial and political skills in the agrarian program, Brezhnev returned in 1956 to Moscow to become once again a secretary of the party's Central Committee (for heavy industry and capital investment; after 1959, for defense and space exploration) and a candidate member of its Presidium. Brezhnev supported Khrushchev in his struggle with the "antiparty group" in early 1957, and Brezhnev was among the supporters Khrushchev chose that year to replace his discredited opponents on the Presidium.

In 1960 Brezhnev was named chairman of the Presidium of the Supreme Soviet (president). The ceremonial post of chief of state served Brezhnev well during his four-year tenure. He gained needed experience in the noncommunist world by traveling abroad as a spokesman for the Khrushchev regime's foreign policies.

A few months after his appointment as president, Brezhnev gave up his post as a secretary of the Central Committee. In 1963, however, Brezhnev was renamed to the Secretariat. He relinquished the chief of state post in July 1964. Then, as the unofficial second secretary, he turned his full attention to supervising daily party affairs. Three months later on October 14, 1964, Khrushchev was abruptly ousted from power. His protégé Brezhnev was one of the leaders of the mutiny. He was chosen as first secretary of the party, and Aleksei Kosygin was named head of the government. At the Twenty-third Party Congress in March 1966, Brezhnev's title reverted from "first secretary" to the Stalinist-era usage, "general secretary," and the party "Presidium" was renamed the "Politburo," symbolically concluding Khrushchev's de-Stalinization drive.

Initially, the collective leadership seemed to work. Brezhnev concerned himself with party affairs and relations within the international Communist movement, while Kosygin focused on the economy and ties with the noncommunist world. But by the early 1970s Brezhnev had eclipsed Kosygin. The party leader took over Kosygin's role as the Kremlin's spokesman in international affairs and its chief negotiator with foreign powers. By the time Kosygin resigned in 1980, his influence on economic issues had similarly declined.

In 1976 Brezhnev was named marshal of the Soviet Union, the nation's highest military rank, and his position as chairman of the USSR Defense Council—commander in chief of Soviet armed forces—was publicly acknowledged for the first time.

Brezhnev had another rival, Nikolai Podgorny, dismissed in 1977 as chairman of the Presidium of the Supreme Soviet so that he could assume the post. Also in 1977 the Soviet Union adopted a new constitution, which was drafted under Brezhnev's supervision.

Analysis. In 1964, after Khrushchev's fall from power, some Western observers thought Brezhnev would be a transition figure, but he held power for eighteen years. Brezhnev was well prepared for the role of Soviet party leader. He brought a broad range of experience to the job that none of his rivals could match. He was experienced in agriculture and industry, had been a party leader in four different republics, had had seven years of political work in the military, and had gained experience in foreign affairs during his four years as chief of state.

Brezhnev's regime emphasized a "scientific approach" to decision making, implying a weighing of alternatives, an understanding of limitations, and a reliance on data. In internal politics Brezhnev displayed resourcefulness and an understanding of when to compromise and when to stand firm. He almost always managed to be on the winning side of major policy struggles.

Brezhnev pursued some apparently contradictory policies during his tenure as Soviet leader. He advanced a détente with the West that included significant arms control agreements, but he continued to challenge Western interests with a sustained arms buildup and support for leftist revolutions in the Third World. Under his leadership the USSR launched an invasion of Afghanistan in 1979 and supported the imposition of martial law in Poland in 1981. These actions soured relations with the West and contributed to the Soviets' international isolation. Brezhnev also appeared willing to accept Western condemnation of his regime's treatment of dissidents rather than institute liberalizing reforms.

Under Mikhail S. Gorbachev, Brezhnev and his policies were severely criticized. The former Soviet leader was routinely ridiculed in the mass media and became a symbol of unimaginative, stagnant, and corrupt leadership.

Nikolai Bukharin (1888-1938)

Nikolai Ivanovich Bukharin was a gifted thinker and one of the most popular Soviet revolutionary figures. In his final testament, V. I. Lenin called Bukharin "the Party's most eminent and valuable theoretician." Bukharin, however, became a victim of the Stalinist purges. He was executed in 1938.

Born in Moscow, October 9, 1888, Bukharin was attracted to radical philosophies at a young age. In 1908 he joined the Moscow committee of the Bolshevik wing of the Russian Social Democratic Labor party. Two years later tsarist authorities broke up the Moscow organization, and Bukharin was arrested and exiled to Siberia. He subsequently escaped to Europe, where he began to write theoretical as well as political tracts. He first met Lenin in 1912 in Krakow. Bukharin was one of the few Russian revolutionaries to visit the United States. In 1916 and early 1917 he edited the Russian communist newspaper *Novy Mir* (New World) in New York City.

Public Career. After the March 1917 revolution Bukharin returned to Russia, where he was named a member of the Central Committee. He played an important role in Moscow during the Bolsheviks' seizure of power and became editor of the party newspaper *Pravda*. After the November revolution he opposed Lenin's positions on several issues, most notably on whether to continue the war with Germany. Bukharin argued for a continuation of the war, while Lenin oversaw the conclusion of the Brest-Litovsk peace treaty with Germany in 1918. Despite this disagreement, Bukharin remained influential in the party and with Lenin.

In 1919 Bukharin was elected to the Comintern (Communist International) at its formation. He joined the ruling Politburo in 1924 and enjoyed great popularity within the party. He was a strong supporter of Lenin's New Economic Policy (NEP), which allowed limited free market activity in an effort to help the nation recover from many years of revolution and war.

After Lenin's death, Bukharin sided with Stalin against the faction led by Leon Trotsky. But when Stalin began reversing NEP in the late 1920s, Bukharin and his fellow leaders of the "right opposition," Aleksei Rykov and Mikhail Tomsky, opposed Stalin. As a result of his challenge to Stalin, Bukharin was stripped of his Comintern and Politburo posts in November 1929. He submitted to "political self-criticism" and was allowed to continue party work until 1937. However, because he represented a potential source of opposition to Stalin, he fell victim to one of Stalin's many purges. In March 1938 he took the witness stand as the main defendant of the third "show trial" in Moscow. The court found the former Politburo member guilty of counterrevolutionary activities, and he was executed immediately after the trial.

Analysis. Bukharin's writings are considered his most important legacy. They include *World Economy and Imperialism* (1918), *Program of the World Revolution* (1920), *The ABC of Communism* (1921), and *Historical Materialism* (1925). The evolution of Bukharin's political views charted his development from a revolutionary advocating the rapid extension of the Russian revolution to a proponent of the gradual spread of socialism. At first Bukharin believed that world upheaval would follow the Russian revolution. He lowered his expectations after the socialist revolution failed in Germany in 1923. He argued that Soviet Russia should build socialism internally. He complemented this notion with the theory that Russia would benefit economically if the assets of the wealthy peasants could be incorporated without force into the socialist system. Stalin's proposal for building "socialism in one country" was based on Bukharin's ideas, but Stalin deviated from them in launching a forcible collectivization of agriculture in 1928.

In 1988 the USSR Supreme Soviet officially rehabilitated Bukharin as part of the ongoing reevaluation of Soviet history. Bukharin's party membership was restored, many of his works were published, and he has been treated favorably in the media.

Konstantin U. Chernenko (1911-1985)

On February 13, 1984, Konstantin Ustinovich Chernenko, a party bureaucrat and longtime associate of Leonid I. Brezhnev, succeeded Yuri V. Andropov as general secretary of the Communist party. Two months later, on April 11, he became head of state when he was elected chairman of the Presidium of the USSR Supreme Soviet (president).

Chernenko, who was seventy-two years old when he took power, perpetuated the rule of old men in the Soviet Union. Weak from emphysema when he took office, Chernenko died a little more than a year later, on March 11, 1985. His death initiated an abrupt generational transition in Kremlin leadership as his successor, fifty-four-year-old Mikhail S. Gorbachev, rejuvenated the upper reaches of the party apparatus by promoting younger leaders.

Chernenko was born into a peasant family on September 24, 1911, in Novoselovo, in the Siberian territory of Krasnoyarsk. He joined the Communist party in 1929. From 1930 to 1933 he served as a border guard, a job that was glorified when Chernenko became an important member of the Soviet leadership. He was the only major Soviet leader of his generation not to have served in World War II.

Public Career. Chernenko owed much of his party advancement to his association with Brezhnev. From 1948 to 1956 Chernenko served as chief of the Moldavian Central Committee's Propaganda and Agitation Department. For three of those years, 1950-1952, Brezhnev was first secretary of the Moldavian Central Committee. In 1956 Chernenko became chief of the Mass Agitation Work Sector of the USSR Central Committee.

When Brezhnev became chairman of the Presidium of the Supreme Soviet in 1960, Chernenko was appointed chief of the Supreme Soviet's secretariat. In 1965 he was named head of the USSR Central Committee's General Department, which coordinated the activities of the various departments and handled citizen complaints and classified documents.

Chernenko was made a secretary of the Central Committee in 1976 and also retained his responsibilities for managing the General Department. He was named a candidate member of the Politburo in 1977 and became a full member in 1978.

Analysis. Chernenko appeared to be a compromise choice for the post of general secretary. Brezhnev allies sought to slow the transfer of power to the younger generation, while Gorbachev's supporters did not yet have the power to challenge the authority of the senior members of the leadership. The selection of Chernenko gave something to both camps. His advanced age and poor health made it unlikely that he would significantly delay the advancement of the younger generation, while his loyalty to Brezhnev-era leaders ensured their positions a little longer.

As a result of the stalemate between Brezhnev-era bureaucrats wary of dramatic changes and reformist leaders, such as Gorbachev, intent on reconstructing both the Soviet economy and the Soviet image abroad, little happened during Chernenko's thirteen-month tenure. The progress of the limited political reforms begun by his more activist predecessor was slowed. He reversed one of Andropov's last decisions—to cut the bureaucracy by nearly 20 percent. Chernenko did not completely halt Andropov's domestic program of economic experimentation or his anticorruption campaign, but he lacked the health, will, and vision to spur modernization and reform. In foreign relations, Chernenko supported the status quo, although he did promote the resumption of arms control talks with the United States.

Andrei Gromyko (1909-1989)

Andrei Andreevich Gromyko, a career diplomat, was elected chairman of the Presidium of the Supreme Soviet (president) on July 2, 1985. Gromyko became the highest official representative of the Soviet Union in its relations with foreign governments, although the presidency at that time was largely an honorific position. In 1988 Mikhail S. Gorbachev took Gromyko's place as president as part of the general secretary's effort to invigorate the Soviet leadership and reinforce his own power. Gromyko died at the age of seventy-nine, exactly four years after becoming president, on July 2, 1989, from an apparent stroke.

Gromyko is best known, however, as the Soviet foreign minister whose tenure spanned three decades (1957-1985). During his twenty-eight years in this post he became the most recognizable symbol of Soviet foreign policy. Near the end of Leonid I. Brezhnev's reign and through the regimes of Yuri V. Andropov and Konstantin U. Chernenko, Gromyko was not only the leading Soviet diplomatic representative, but also one of the prime architects of Soviet foreign policy.

Gromyko, an ethnic Russian, was born in Belorussia (Belarus) on July 18, 1909, and grew up on a farm near Minsk. He devoted much of his early adulthood to study and earned a candidate of economics degree in 1936. Gromyko became a doctor of economics in 1956.

Public Career. Gromyko taught at the Moscow Institute of Economics for three years before being recruited into the foreign service in 1939. Shortly afterward he was assigned to the Soviet embassy in Washington. In 1943 Joseph Stalin made the thirty-four-year-old diplomat ambassador to the United States, a post he held until 1946. Gromyko later became permanent representative to the United Nations (1946-1949) and ambassador to the United Kingdom (1952-1953). He served twice as first deputy minister of foreign affairs (1949-1952, 1953-1957). In 1957 he was appointed foreign minister under Nikita S. Khrushchev.

In tandem with his advancement within the government, Gromyko rose steadily in the Communist party. He joined the party in 1931 while still in school. He served as a deputy to the Council of the Union of the Supreme Soviet from 1946 to 1950. In 1952 he became a candidate member of the Central Committee and was promoted to full membership in 1956. He was made a full Politburo member in 1973, and ten years later he was appointed one of three first deputy prime ministers.

Analysis. As foreign minister, Gromyko traveled to more than forty countries and met most of the major world leaders of his era. He headed the Soviet delegation to every session of the UN General Assembly from 1962 until 1984 (except the 1983 opening following the Soviet downing of a Korean airliner) and participated in every U.S.-Soviet summit until the 1985 Geneva meeting between Gorbachev and President Ronald Reagan.

Gromyko was known for his refusal to make concessions but was respected for his intelligence and knowledge of the West. He was above all a loyal and pragmatic implementer of Politburo policy. As his experience and stature grew, so did his power. His 1973 selection to the Politburo signified his growing influence as a policy maker.

Gromyko also played a key role in Soviet internal politics in the 1980s. Together with Defense Minister Dmitry Ustinov, he was instrumental in Andropov's selection as general secretary over Chernenko in 1982. He also supported Gorbachev in his bid to succeed Chernenko in 1985 and delivered an eloquent speech nominating Gorbachev for general secretary. Gromyko's replacement as foreign minister in 1985 by Eduard Shevardnadze, a Georgian party boss with no diplomatic experience, caught Soviet and U.S. diplomats by surprise. Western observers suggested that Gromyko's appointment to the presidency was a reward for both his long service to the Soviet Union and his backing of Gorbachev during the succession process. But most experts also maintained that Gromyko's promotion was a graceful way for Gorbachev to retire Gromyko, thereby strengthening his own control over international affairs.

Perhaps because of his role in helping Gorbachev assume power, Gromyko was spared the criticism heaped on many Brezhnev-era officials by Gorbachev and his allies. Upon Gromyko's death, Gorbachev spoke respectfully but offered little praise: "His entire life was connected with our history, with our achievements, with our problems, with everything that falls on the shoulders of a man who is in the thick of events for the course of decades."

Lev Kamenev (1883-1936)

Lev Borisovich Kamenev gained prominence as one of V. I. Lenin's closest associates. Born in Moscow on July 22, 1883, Kamenev was the son of Jewish parents named Rosenfeld who had taken part in the Russian revolutionary movement of the 1870s. Kamenev initially became involved with Marxist circles during his high school (gymnasium) years. His interest in revolutionary philosophy grew while he studied law at Moscow University, and in 1901 he joined the Russian Social Democratic Labor party. In 1908 he traveled to Europe and began working for *Iskra* (The Spark), the revolutionary journal founded by Lenin.

Kamenev continued his underground activity in Europe and later in Russia, staunchly upholding the Bolshevik line during the debates with the Menshevik faction of the Russian Social Democratic Labor party. Kamenev, along with Grigory Zinoviev, became one of Lenin's closest literary and political collaborators.

In 1914 Kamenev went to St. Petersburg to oversee Bolshevik activities. He was arrested in 1915 and exiled to Siberia. After his release following the March 1917 revolution, he immediately returned to St. Petersburg. There he served as a leading Bolshevik spokesman and backed the policy of supporting the Provisional Government. When Lenin arrived in St. Petersburg in April he rejected cooperation with the government and began working toward a Bolshevik-led revolt and regime. Kamenev accepted the necessity of a  further revolution but endorsed a seizure of power by a coalition government made up of all socialist parties. When the revolution actually took place in November 1917, however, Kamenev backed the Bolshevik cause. He was named a member of the first Politburo.

After Lenin's death in 1924, Kamenev joined with Zinoviev and Joseph Stalin against the leader of the "left opposition," Leon Trotsky. Kamenev and his ally, Zinoviev, reversed themselves in 1926, supporting Trotsky's ill-fated attempt to thwart Stalin's growing power. Despite later recantations of their alliance with Trotsky, both men lost their important party and government positions. Kamenev was expelled and readmitted to the Communist party three times between 1927 and 1934. In 1935 he was sentenced to five years in prison for "moral complicity" in the murder of the Leningrad party boss, Sergei Kirov. The following year, after being retried in the first "show trial" of Stalin's purge, he was sentenced to death and executed on August 24.

Aleksandr Kerensky (1881-1970)

Aleksandr Feodorovich Kerensky, a member of the Socialist Revolutionary party, headed the Russian Provisional Government on the eve of the Bolshevik Revolution in 1917 and later led an unsuccessful effort to overthrow the new communist regime.

Kerensky was born on April 22, 1881, in Simbirsk (now Ulyanovsk), in the Volga region of Russia where Lenin was born. Ironically, Kerensky's father was Lenin's high school principal. Kerensky became active in populist circles while a student in St. Petersburg. As a young socialist lawyer, he defended revolutionaries accused of political offenses. The failure of the promised reforms of the 1905 Russian revolution convinced Kerensky that the monarchy should be overthrown.

After Tsar Nicholas II was deposed in March 1917, the

Provisional Government assumed power. Kerensky was the only Social Revolutionary to accept a post in the new regime. He served as minister of justice under Prince Georgy Lvov, a liberal aristocrat who was prime minister. Later, Kerensky became minister of war. At the same time, he held a post in the Petrograd Soviet and functioned as an intermediary between the Soviet and the Provisional Government.

Kerensky replaced Lvov as prime minister in July 1917, at a time when the Bolsheviks gradually were gaining support and the mood of the people was becoming increasingly radical. Kerensky's government fell to the Bolsheviks in November 1917. He escaped from Petrograd and rallied loyal troops, but his attempts to overthrow the new regime failed. He emigrated and died in New York City at age eighty-eight on June 11, 1970.

Nikita S. Khrushchev (1894-1971)

Nikita Sergeevich Khrushchev, one of Joseph Stalin's most loyal subordinates, won the struggle for power after Stalin's death. As party leader and premier, however,  Khrushchev initiated a campaign of de-Stalinization that denounced the late dictator's bloody methods and accumulation of power. Khrushchev's nine-year reign was marked by power struggles and contradictory policies in both domestic and foreign policy. He was ousted by his colleagues in 1964.

Born April 17, 1894, in the Kursk province of Russia near the Ukrainian border, Khrushchev came from a simple worker's background. Unlike many Communist leaders who joined the party as students in their late teens, Khrushchev did not join the Bolsheviks until 1918, when he was twenty-four. He spent the next three years fighting in the civil war. His first wife and two children perished during the famines of the 1920s. He subsequently married Nina Petrovna, who captured the interest of the American people when she accompanied him on a visit to the United States in 1959. The couple had three children.

After the civil war Khrushchev attended an adult technical school and engaged in party work in Ukraine. He met Joseph Stalin in 1926 while serving as a delegate to a party congress. Transferred to Moscow in 1929, Khrushchev enrolled in the prestigious Industrial Academy where Nadezhda Alliluyeva, Stalin's second wife, was his classmate.

Public Career. Khrushchev's career gained momentum in the 1930s. An able and energetic administrator, he played a central role in the Moscow subway construction project. He was named to the party Central Committee in 1934 and became a candidate member of the Politburo and first secretary of the Ukrainian Communist party in 1938. The following year he was promoted to full Politburo status.

Khrushchev's exact role in the Stalinist purges is not known, but his participation probably was substantial. He supported Stalin against the protests of those in the party who were horrified by the executions and in doing so probably escaped being purged himself.

Before World War II, Khrushchev played an important role in the Soviet annexation of eastern Poland. After the outbreak of German-Soviet hostilities in 1941, he oversaw the war effort at various field commands. One of his duties was recommending military officers for promotion. These protégés later were instrumental in helping Khrushchev consolidate his own power. In 1944 Stalin sent Khrushchev back to Ukraine to head the party. There he oversaw the republic's recovery from the devastation of the war and suppressed opposition to Soviet rule.

In December 1949 Khrushchev returned to Moscow to serve as a Central Committee secretary. After Stalin's death in 1953, Georgy Malenkov emerged as head of the government and party secretary, but Malenkov gave up his party post to Khrushchev who used the opportunity to augment his power base. Khrushchev initially upheld the Stalinist line and sided with those in the leadership who opposed Malenkov's bid for power and his more moderate course in domestic and foreign policy. Khrushchev also proposed a series of domestic reforms, including his Virgin Lands program to cultivate barren regions in Siberia and Central Asia. In 1955 Khrushchev orchestrated the demotion of Malenkov, thus securing his position as first among equals in the collective leadership. Later Khrushchev would adopt some of the policies Malenkov had endorsed, including a less hostile stance toward the West.

Khrushchev's "Secret Speech" to the delegates to the Twentieth Party Congress in February 1956 was a watershed for Soviet internal and foreign policies. In the speech Khrushchev revealed the extent of Stalin's tyranny and promised to rehabilitate the late dictator's victims. Earlier during the congress, he also proposed a policy of peaceful coexistence with the West, reversing the traditional Soviet claim that war between the capitalist and communist camps was inevitable.

This first public denunciation of Stalin shocked the communist community. East European leaders were particularly unnerved because their governments were built on Stalinist principles. Domestic upheavals occurred in Poland and Hungary. The Soviets invaded Hungary in 1956 to put down a liberalization movement that threatened communist rule. The People's Republic of China was outraged by Khrushchev's de-Stalinization campaign, which the Chinese termed a "revisionist" act by a leader whose stature could not compare with that of Stalin or of China's own leader, Mao Zedong. Despite these setbacks, Khrushchev's attack on Stalin had the desired effect—it separated him from his rivals for power in the Soviet Union by grouping them together as "Stalin's heirs," and it portrayed Khrushchev as a reformer who refused to follow Stalin's path.

Khrushchev faced formidable opposition within the Presidium (the name for the Politburo between 1952 and 1966). In mid 1957 a group of high party officials, including Malenkov, Viacheslav Molotov, Lazar Kaganovich, and Dmitry Shepilov, conspired to oust Khrushchev. He overcame the "antiparty group," as it was dubbed, by appealing to the Central Committee for support. Khrushchev's rivals were expelled from the Central Committee in mid 1957. By 1958 when Khrushchev took over the premiership, he had placed himself at the head of all party, government, and military organs and had begun developing his own "personality cult."

Khrushchev, in his conduct of foreign affairs, vacillated between threatening gestures toward the West and attempts to thaw out the cold war. Continuing disagreements with the West over the fate of Germany led to the erection of the Berlin Wall in 1961. In the fall of 1962 Khrushchev decided to install Soviet missiles in Cuba to improve the Soviet strategic position and to silence his hard-line critics in Beijing and Moscow. Instead, President John F. Kennedy's ultimatums forced Khrushchev to back down and remove the missiles from Cuba. Less than a year later the superpowers negotiated a treaty providing for a partial ban on nuclear testing.

By 1963 Khrushchev's colleagues were becoming increasingly unhappy with his domestic reforms. Neither his Virgin Lands program nor his ambitious economic plans came close to achieving their goals. A disastrous 1963 harvest intensified Soviet economic problems. Although Khrushchev tempered his drive to boost the supply of consumer goods in 1963, conservative Soviet leaders still feared that traditional investments in arms and heavy industry could be threatened. In addition, Khrushchev's bifurcation of the party and government structures into industrial and agricultural branches in 1962 displeased many leaders. These domestic factors, combined with the erosion of Khrushchev's prestige in Eastern Europe and China and the failure of his plan to put missiles in Cuba, led to his political demise. A conspiracy of the Soviet Union's highest officials removed him from power on October 14, 1964. He was replaced by Aleksei Kosygin as premier and by Leonid I. Brezhnev as party first secretary. Khrushchev lived in seclusion after his forced retirement and died September 11, 1971.

Analysis. Khrushchev had neither the theoretical brilliance and personal prestige of V. I. Lenin nor the secret-

police machine of Stalin. Instead, he relied on a reform program and his network of contacts in the party to secure his power and bring the Soviet Union out of its Stalinist past.

Khrushchev's ambition was to build the Soviet Union so that it would "overtake and outstrip" the West in technology, living standards, and international prestige. To this end he launched a variety of ambitious programs that he hoped would accelerate economic growth and make the Soviet Union a model for emulation. Many of his plans, however, ended in failure. His agricultural reforms proved disastrous, the Soviets were humiliated in the Cuban missile crisis, and relations with China grew increasingly bitter.

Despite these setbacks, during Khrushchev's tenure the Soviet Union broadened its efforts to gain influence in the Third World, expanded its nuclear arsenal, maintained domestic stability, and accomplished some impressive scientific feats. Most important, Khrushchev repudiated the terror and violence of the Stalin period. Although abuses of power continued under Khrushchev, for most Soviet citizens, the fear that had pervaded their daily lives was eliminated.

Aleksei Kosygin (1904-1980)

Aleksei Nikolaevich Kosygin became premier when Nikita S. Khrushchev was ousted by his Politburo colleagues in October 1964. Initially he was coequal with Leonid I. Brezhnev in the collective post-Khrushchev leadership. But long before Kosygin resigned as premier sixteen years later, he had lost much of his authority to party leader Brezhnev.

Kosygin was born on February 20, 1904, in St. Petersburg. His father was a lathe operator. At the age of fifteen, Kosygin volunteered for service in the Red Army and fought in the civil war until 1921. He graduated from the Leningrad Cooperative Technical School in 1924 and was sent to Siberia to help integrate that region's cooperative movement into the national economy.

Kosygin returned home in 1929 to begin his studies at the Leningrad (later Kirov) Textile Institute. After graduating six years later as a textile engineer, he went to work first as a foreman and later as a shop superintendent at the Zhelyabov factory in Leningrad. He served as director of the Oktyabr spinning mill in Leningrad from 1937 to 1938.

Public Career. Kosygin, who previously had been a member of the Komsomol (Communist Youth League), joined the Communist party in 1927 when he was in Siberia. During the mid 1930s he was active in party affairs and served on the executive committee of the Vyborg borough party organization. Kosygin's career benefited from the Stalinist purges of the 1930s. Andrei Zhdanov, a Stalin favorite who carried out the purges in Leningrad, brought Kosygin into the depleted ranks of the party hierarchy in 1938. Kosygin went to work for the party full time as the head of the industrial transportation department of the Leningrad regional party committee. Later that year he became chairman of the executive committee of the Leningrad city soviet—in effect, the mayor of Leningrad.

In 1939 Kosygin was promoted to the Central Committee and received his first national government position, that of people's commissar for light industry. He was promoted one year later to the post of deputy chairman of the Council of People's Commissars (later renamed Council of Ministers), or deputy prime minister. He remained in that position until 1953.

In the early months of World War II Kosygin played an important role in increasing production in the Soviet defense industry. He also was in charge of the evacuation of five hundred thousand people from Leningrad in January 1942. After the war he served as USSR minister of finance until 1948 and then as minister of light industry for the remainder of the Stalin period.

He continued his climb up the party ladder as well. After being elected a candidate member of the Politburo in 1946, Kosygin was made a full member in 1948. But Kosygin's fortunes soon changed. In 1948 Zhdanov died, and the following year Stalin began another round of executions and arrests, aimed primarily at the "Leningrad gang," many of whom were Kosygin's former associates.

Kosygin survived the purge but a shadow had been cast over his career. In 1952, when Stalin expanded the Politburo (which had been renamed the Presidium) from ten to twenty-five members, Kosygin was demoted to candidate status. He was the only full member to lose his seat. He did, however, retain his government positions in the Council of Ministers and Ministry of Light Industry.

Following Stalin's death in March 1953, Kosygin lost both his candidate membership in the Presidium and his government position as a deputy prime minister. He remained minister of food and light industry (later renamed the Ministry of Industrial Consumer Goods).

Late in 1953 Kosygin became a deputy prime minister once again and within a few months resigned from the consumer goods ministry to devote more time to the USSR Council of Ministers. In 1956 he was temporarily relieved of his post as a deputy prime minister and was named deputy chairman of Gosplan (the State Planning Committee).

In June 1957 Kosygin, as a member of the Central Committee, strongly supported Khrushchev in his confrontation with the "antiparty group," which sought Khrushchev's ouster. Khrushchev won the power struggle and rewarded Kosygin by granting him both candidate membership in the party Presidium and his old post of deputy prime minister.

In 1959 Kosygin was named chairman of Gosplan, thus becoming the country's chief economic planner with responsibility for the allocation of resources, production goals, and pricing. In 1960 he was elected a full member of the party Presidium and was appointed one of two first deputy prime ministers. As a deputy prime minister, Kosygin traveled frequently in Europe, Asia, and Latin America. In July 1964 he became the sole first deputy prime minister, ranking behind only Khrushchev in the government.

On October 14, 1964, a special session of the Central Committee suddenly removed Khrushchev from power. Kosygin was named to replace him as chairman of the USSR Council of Ministers, or prime minister. Brezhnev assumed Khrushchev's position as first secretary of the Communist party.

Initially, Kosygin was responsible for government affairs, including economic matters and foreign relations with nonsocialist countries, while Brezhnev was to handle party affairs and Soviet relations within the international communist movement. The division of labor seemed to work at first. While Brezhnev was busy consolidating his power within the party, Kosygin tackled the Soviet Union's economic problems. He also traveled abroad frequently. He was visiting Hanoi in early 1965 when U.S. president Lyndon B. Johnson ordered bombing raids on North Vietnam. The raids—and the entire U.S. policy in Southeast Asia—outraged Kosygin and blocked steps toward improved U.S.-Soviet relations for several years. But in 1967, during a visit to the United Nations, Kosygin met with Johnson in Glassboro, New Jersey. Although nothing substantive was resolved, the face-to-face meeting of the two leaders relieved superpower tensions.

Kosygin was actively involved in efforts to stem the tide of liberalization in Czechoslovakia in 1968. He favored negotiating and applying economic pressure to bring the Prague government back into line. Balancing Kosygin's moderate approach was the Soviet military, which favored armed intervention. Brezhnev, who was thought to have been in the middle, playing the role of mediator between the two positions, ultimately sided with the military. The Soviet decision-making process during the Czech crisis was instructive in that it showed the growing dominance of Brezhnev over Kosygin.

By the early 1970s there was no question as to who was running the Soviet Union. Brezhnev met with foreign leaders and conducted high-level talks. Eventually he came to dominate the economic arena as well. Kosygin's failing health further accelerated his loss of authority. After he suffered a heart attack in 1976, many of his duties were taken over by Nikolai Tikhonov, an ally of Brezhnev who had been named a first deputy prime minister. Kosygin had another heart attack in 1979, and on October 23, 1980, he resigned as prime minister and gave up his seat in the Politburo.

Kosygin died December 18, 1980. His life and career were praised lavishly in the official obituary.

Analysis. Kosygin had two traits that probably accounted for much of his success in Soviet politics: he was a capable administrator and he seemed to have no aspirations to the top leadership position. He was extremely competent and posed little threat to incumbent political leaders.

These characteristics may explain, in part, Brezhnev's dominance of his one-time coequal. While Brezhnev consolidated his power, Kosygin was preoccupied with the troubled Soviet economy. He was said to have regarded revitalizing the economy as the major challenge of his career. It was a challenge he was unable to meet.

V. I. Lenin (1870-1924)

Vladimir Ilich Ulyanov was born in the Volga region of Russia on April 22, 1870. Later in life he would adopt a pseudonym, Lenin, to protect himself from tsarist police

persecution. A brilliant theoretician, capable administrator, and inspiring leader, Lenin was principally responsible for bringing the Russian Revolution of 1917 to fruition.

The Ulyanov family enjoyed relatively high social status. Vladimir Ilich's father was educational administrator for the entire region of Simbirsk (the name of the region was changed to Ulyanovsk in 1924 in honor of its most famous son). The first radical in the Ulyanov family was Vladimir's older brother, Aleksandr, who as a student took part in a populist revolutionary plot to assassinate Tsar Alexander III. He was arrested and executed when Vladimir was seventeen.

Lenin attended the University of Kazan in 1887 in the juridical program but soon was expelled for participating in a student demonstration. While temporarily out of school, he spent his time reading revolutionary literature, educating himself, and developing his political views. Increasingly drawn to Marxism instead of the populist teaching his brother had adopted, Lenin was particularly impressed by two tracts: Karl Marx's *Das Kapital* and Georgy Plekhanov's *Our Disagreements*. After several years Lenin was readmitted to the university, where he completed studies for a law degree.

In the 1890s Lenin began working for the socialist cause in St. Petersburg. He traveled abroad in 1895 to meet the exiled leaders of Russian socialism, including Plekhanov. At the end of the year Lenin returned to Russia and was arrested for his work on an underground newspaper. He was sent to Siberia, but he continued writing and maintained contact with colleagues. He married Nadezhda Krupskaya, another revolutionary, who joined him in Siberia.

Public Career. While Lenin was in Siberia, the Russian Social Democratic Labor Party (RSDLP) was formed in 1898 at an illegal congress in Minsk. After his release in 1900, Lenin emigrated to Europe and established himself as a leader among the Social Democrats. He founded a revolutionary journal *Iskra* (The Spark) with Plekhanov and other prominent revolutionaries. *Iskra*, secretly distributed throughout Russia, became the guiding force of the revolutionary movement for the next several years. Around this time, Lenin dropped his real name, Ulyanov, and began signing articles with his pseudonym.

While in Europe Lenin became increasingly concerned with the revolutionary program and tactics that the RSDLP was avowing. He set out his ideas in his pamphlet "What Is to Be Done?" published in 1902. Lenin favored a tightly knit, disciplined cadre of full-time revolutionaries who would lead the workers to overthrow the tsarist regime. To support these professionals, Lenin proposed a united and highly centralized party.

Members at the 1903 congress of the RSDLP split into two factions over the issue of revolutionary tactics. The group that won a slim majority on a vote concerning the composition of the editorial board of *Iskra*, the Bolsheviks (or "majoritarians"), rallied around Lenin's leadership and his avowal of armed insurrection. The Mensheviks (or "minoritarians") were led by Plekhanov. The Mensheviks, however, soon regained control of the journal, and Lenin resigned from the editorial board. After the party split, Lenin turned his attention toward underground activity in Russia. He returned to Russia during the revolution of 1905, but the upheaval provided no opportunities to seize power, and, after a brief stay, Lenin was forced to emigrate to Europe a second time. There he continued his efforts to advance revolution in Russia, while dealing with constant quarrels within the socialist camp.

Following the establishment of the Provisional Government in 1917, Lenin secretly returned to Russia in a sealed train provided by the German government. After a tumultuous welcome at Finland Station in Petrograd, Lenin delivered two speeches before a joint session of Bolsheviks, Mensheviks, and other revolutionaries. These speeches, known as the April Theses, called on socialists to abandon collaboration with the Provisional Government and oppose Russia's efforts in World War I. He advocated "all land to the peasants" and "all power to the soviets"; that is, the transfer of government authority to the workers' councils organized in Petrograd, Moscow, and other Russian cities. The theses shocked traditional Marxists because they repudiated the Marxist dogma of revolutionary progression, a step-by-step process that ends with the seizure of power by the workers after the collapse of a highly developed capitalist system. Instead, Lenin proposed pressing forward with the revolution despite Russia's lack of capitalist development and the relative weakness of the Bolshevik party.

The year 1917 continued in a confusing pattern of unrest and uprisings. Lenin and most of the Bolshevik leaders were forced to flee Petrograd in July. From Finland Lenin attempted to foment the revolution, while much of the work on the scene was done by Leon Trotsky, who oversaw the rapid expansion of the Bolshevik party. Lenin returned to Petrograd on October 20, just a few weeks before the Bolshevik seizure of power in November. Other Bolshevik leaders, including Lev Kamenev and Grigory Zinoviev, advocated a cautious approach to revolution until the party could be strengthened further, but Lenin urged his fellow party members to take over the government. Lenin's strategy prevailed, and the Bolsheviks overthrew the Provisional Government on November 7 and 8.

As head of the nascent government with the title "chairman of the Council of the People's Commissars," Lenin quickly consolidated the Bolsheviks' tenuous control. On the domestic front, civil war broke out between the Bolsheviks and opposition groups. In an attempt to keep industry operative, Lenin imposed "War Communism," a program that centralized the economy and abolished markets and money. In foreign policy, Lenin agreed to a peace with Germany. The March 1918 treaty at Brest-Litovsk was concluded over protests from members of his own government, including Trotsky. After the Bolsheviks had won the civil war, Lenin was forced to retreat from his harsh economic policies, and in 1921 he reinstituted a degree of free enterprise under the "New Economic Policy."

During the early 1920s Lenin began working at a slower pace. Heart disease and the effects of wounds he suffered in an assassination attempt in 1918 had weakened his health. He suffered a stroke in mid 1922, causing his health to deteriorate further. He had two more strokes before his death January 21, 1924.

Analysis. Lenin was not only an administrative and organizational genius, but he also was the party's leading theoretician. He adapted Marxist theory to conditions in early twentieth-century Russia. Like Marx, Lenin took as his goal the overthrow of capitalism and the establishment of socialism. Unlike Marx, he did not consider it necessary for capitalism to develop before a revolution took place. Another departure from Marxist theory was Lenin's reliance on a professional cadre of revolutionaries to lead the workers into action. Marx envisioned rule by the entire working class, but in Lenin's view the Russian proletariat was not ready for such a responsibility.

Lenin's idealism and desire to create a better Russia are unquestionable. After coming to power he lived a simple life and worked tirelessly until his failing health limited his activities. His belief that the Bolsheviks and Marxist philosophy held the keys to improving Russian society, however, led him to justify the use of any means (including violence and terror) to secure and consolidate power for the Bolshevik party. For example, he sanctioned the creation of a political police force (the Cheka) to control dissent and ordered grain to be forcibly requisitioned from the peasants during the civil war.

Despite Lenin's unrivaled position as Soviet leader, he was unable to engineer his own succession. Before his death, Lenin wrote a letter to party leaders advising them to remove Joseph Stalin from the post of general secretary. By the time the letter was read after Lenin's death, however, Stalin's position was secure enough for him to overcome this blow to his reputation.

Georgy Malenkov (1902-1988)

Georgy Maksimilianovich Malenkov succeeded Joseph Stalin as premier in 1953 but soon lost the title and his authority in a power struggle with Nikita S. Khrushchev.

Born in Orenburg, Russia, on January 8, 1902, Malenkov was a student during the Bolshevik revolution. He joined the Red Army in 1919 and the Communist party in 1920. After the civil war he studied at the Moscow Higher Technical School, graduating in 1925. Soon after he went to work in the Central Committee bureaucracy and became a member of Stalin's personal secretariat. Between 1930 and 1934 Malenkov was in charge of the Moscow party's organization bureau. In 1934 he became a member of the organization bureau for the entire USSR. From this position, he played a particularly bloody role in the Stalinist purges of the 1930s. In 1939 he was elected to the Central Committee and the Secretariat. During World War II he oversaw aircraft production as a member of the State Defense Committee.

Stalin promoted Malenkov to full membership on the Politburo in 1946. Malenkov also served as second secretary of the Central Committee Secretariat and deputy prime minister. Because of his close association with Stalin and his official position as the second most powerful party member, Malenkov appeared to be in line to succeed him. Malenkov's position as heir apparent was reinforced in 1952, when Stalin requested that Malenkov deliver the general report in his place at the Nineteenth Party Congress in October 1952.

Following Stalin's death in 1953, Malenkov was for a short time both party first secretary and prime minister. However, within a few months Khrushchev replaced him as first secretary. Malenkov supported East-West coexistence and greater emphasis on the production of consumer goods. He also was instrumental in rehabilitating some citizens Stalin had accused of crimes.

Malenkov was challenged for supremacy by Khrushchev, who used his power base in the party to force him to resign as prime minister in 1955. Ironically, Khrushchev subsequently adopted many of Malenkov's policies, including peaceful coexistence with the West. Malenkov's final defeat came two years later, when Khrushchev attacked him and other opponents, dubbed the "antiparty group," who had conspired to unseat him. Malenkov was accused of participation in the crimes of Stalin's regime, as well as inept leadership during World War II. He subsequently was expelled from the Central Committee and demoted to the directorship of a power plant in Kazakhstan. He died February 1, 1988, at the age of eighty-six.

Viacheslav Molotov (1890-1986)

Viacheslav Mikhailovich Molotov became a familiar global figure during World War II as Soviet foreign minister, a post he held from 1939 to 1949 and from 1953

to 1956. He represented the Soviet Union at wartime Allied conferences and was a vocal proponent of hard-line policies toward the West following the war.

Born on March 9, 1890, to shopkeeper parents named Skryabin in the Vyatka province of Russia, Molotov exhibited an early interest in bolshevism. He worked in revolutionary organizations as a student and was arrested in 1909 and sent to Siberia. In 1912, after his exile had ended, Molotov sharpened his propaganda skills in St. Petersburg, where he edited and wrote for *Pravda*. Molotov participated in the 1917 Bolshevik Revolution, although he did not play a leading role.

Molotov became a member of the Central Committee in 1921. He was an early supporter of Stalin, and as Stalin consolidated his power after Lenin's death, Molotov reaped the benefits of their association. He was appointed to full membership in the Politburo in 1925 and replaced Nikolai Bukharin as head of the Comintern in 1929. Molotov's pseudonym is derived from the Russian word for "hammer," which befitted his responsibilities as Stalin's strongman in the 1920s. He worked ruthlessly to strengthen Stalin's position against his opponents, and by the early 1930s Molotov was one of Stalin's closest associates.

Stalin replaced foreign affairs commissar Maksim Litvinov with Molotov in March 1939, a maneuver designed to facilitate negotiations with Nazi Germany. Molotov's diplomatic efforts led to the Nazi-Soviet Nonaggression Pact (sometimes referred to as the Molotov-Ribbentrop Pact) signed in August 1939. This agreement allowed the Nazis to invade Poland without fear of beginning a war with the Soviet Union. It also provided for the Soviet Union's domination of the Baltic states, eastern Poland, and Finland. As Stalin's foreign representative, Molotov undertook many other diplomatic missions during and after World War II. He attended the Tehran, Yalta, and Potsdam Allied conferences.

Molotov survived a purge of the Foreign Ministry officials in 1949. He resigned as foreign minister but retained his Politburo seat. During the next several years Stalin grew increasingly suspicious of Molotov, but the dictator died before taking action against him. Molotov became foreign minister again in 1953 after Stalin's death. Party leader Nikita S. Khrushchev engineered his removal from this post in 1956.

In 1957 Molotov was a leader of the "antiparty group," which tried to unseat Khrushchev. Khrushchev outmaneuvered his rivals and held on to power. Molotov's participation in the affair led to his demotion to the obscure post of ambassador to Mongolia. In 1961 he was named Soviet representative to the International Atomic Energy Agency, but in 1962 Molotov was expelled from the Communist party during another wave of de-Stalinization.

Molotov lived in obscurity until the Soviet Foreign Ministry announced on July 5, 1984, that he had been reinstated in the Communist party in honor of his ninety-fourth birthday March 9, 1984. Molotov died November 8, 1986.

Nikolai Podgorny (1903-1983)

Nikolai Viktorovich Podgorny had a lengthy and influential party and government career during the post-Stalin era. He served as chairman of the Presidium of the Supreme Soviet (president) from 1965 until 1977, when his rival, General Secretary Leonid I. Brezhnev, forced him into retirement and assumed the position for himself.

Born February 18, 1903, into the family of a foundry worker in the Ukrainian village of Karlovka, Podgorny had a successful career as an engineer in sugar-beet refineries before he began his rise in the Communist party, which he joined when he was twenty-seven. Podgorny's skill in engineering and administration led to his appointment in 1939 as deputy people's commissar of the food industry of the Ukrainian republic. During this time, he met Nikita S. Khrushchev, who then was chairman of the Ukrainian Communist party. Podgorny later would become a Khrushchev protégé.

After serving as head of the Moscow Technological Institute of Food Industry during World War II, Podgorny returned to his post in Ukraine. In 1946 Khrushchev appointed him permanent representative of Ukraine at the Soviet Council of Ministers.

From 1950 until 1953 he served as first secretary of the Kharkov province party committee. Between 1953 and 1957 he held a number of posts in the Ukrainian Communist party and then was appointed first secretary, a position he held until 1963. During this time, Podgorny attained national prominence. In 1954 he was selected as a deputy to the Supreme Soviet; two years later he was elected to the Central Committee after being nominated by Khrushchev; and in May 1960 he was chosen as a member of the Presidium (later renamed Politburo). Three years later, he became a Central Committee secretary.

With the ouster of Khrushchev in 1964 Podgorny was widely regarded as the third-ranking leader in the Kremlin behind First Secretary Brezhnev and Premier Aleksei Kosygin. Podgorny assumed principal responsibility for party organization and instituted major reforms.

When Anastas Mikoyan resigned as chairman of the Presidium of the Supreme Soviet in December 1965, Brezhnev nominated Podgorny to the post. In that capacity he proclaimed all laws and decrees, represented the Soviet Union on official missions abroad, and received foreign dignitaries. Although the post was largely ceremonial, Podgorny continued to hold powerful party positions.

Podgorny's ouster from the Politburo in 1977 surprised Western analysts. His age (seventy-four) and health may have been factors, but it also is possible Brezhnev wanted to consolidate his power and assume the official title of head of state himself. Observers also pointed to policy differences between the two and Podgorny's criticisms of the new constitution promoted by Brezhnev. Podgorny's political career ended March 4, 1979, when he was excluded from the newly elected Supreme Soviet. He died January 12, 1983.

Joseph Stalin (1879-1953)

Joseph Stalin, one of the most powerful and feared leaders of the twentieth century, was the undisputed dictator of the Soviet Union from the late 1920s when he consolidated his power until his death in 1953. His rule was one of the bloodiest episodes in world history as tens of millions of Soviets died as a result of his policies and purges.

Born December 21, 1879, in Georgia, Stalin, unlike many revolutionary leaders, grew up in an impoverished and non-intellectual household. Georgia in the late 1890s was rife with nationalistic sentiment, a topic much discussed at the theological seminary in Tiflis, which Stalin entered in 1893 under his real name, Iosif Vissarionovich Dzhugashvili. While at the seminary Stalin became associated with Georgian nationalistic groups and began to study Marxism. His clandestine lectures on socialism resulted in his expulsion from the seminary in 1899 shortly before he was to graduate.

Stalin was drawn into propaganda and mass agitation activity for the Russian Social Democratic Labor party in Tiflis. His connection with the party led to his first arrest and deportation to Siberia in 1901. Before the 1917 revolution, Stalin's life was typical of young Russian revolutionaries of the time. Several times he was arrested and exiled to Siberia for his activities, but he always managed to return. Inspired by V. I. Lenin's writings, he had become a firm Bolshevik by 1904. Stalin gained a reputation as an efficient organizer during the revolution of 1905.

Public Career. When the Bolsheviks formed their own party in 1912, Lenin sponsored Stalin's membership on the Central Committee. Around this time he assumed the pseudonym he retained until the end of his life—Stalin, or "man of steel." Stalin was arrested once more, in 1913, and remained in Siberia until he was released after the March revolution of 1917.

Stalin gained national prominence after the Bolshevik revolution in November. He served as commissar of nationalities (1917-1923) and helped draft the Soviet constitutions of 1918 and 1923. During the civil war Stalin served in military leadership posts, as did most of the Bolshevik leaders. His conduct during the war led to bitter disputes with Leon Trotsky, the commissar of war and organizer of the Red Army.

In April 1922 Stalin emerged as general secretary of the Communist party. After Lenin's death in 1924, he and Trotsky vied for power. Although a brilliant orator and theoretician, Trotsky was defeated by the triumvirate of party leaders—Stalin, Grigory Zinoviev, and Lev Kamenev—who united against him. Stalin used anti-Trotsky propaganda to weaken his rival's support until he was able to remove Trotsky from his government positions in 1925 and expel him from the Soviet Union four years later. Stalin then turned on Zinoviev and Kamenev, who in 1926 had briefly thrown their support behind Trotsky. Until his power was secure, Stalin forged an alliance with the party's right wing, led by Nikolai Bukharin.

Stalin defeated Trotsky partly by winning support for the concept of "socialism in one country." Unlike Trotsky, who promoted world revolution as the Soviet state's first priority, Stalin, along with Bukharin, advocated building Soviet socialism in isolation before spreading the revolution abroad.

His power unchallenged, Stalin next focused his attention on the USSR's economy. Beginning in 1928 Soviet peasants were brutally collectivized and Soviet industry underwent a program of rapid industrialization. Peasants who resisted were sent to Siberia or shot. The chaos created by collectivization led to famines that killed millions of Soviets.

As the industrialization campaign reached its peak in the mid 1930s, Stalin began a ruthless process of eliminating his perceived enemies. During the "Great Purge," most of the old Bolshevik leaders (including Stalin's former allies Kamenev, Zinoviev, and Bukharin), as well as a large percentage of the military and political elite, were tried and executed. Countless other Soviet citizens were arrested and sent to labor camps in Siberia. Historians generally agree that Stalin was in firm control of the Soviet Union long before he launched the Great Purge, and the killing of other prominent Soviet leaders was not necessary to maintain his hold on power.

Stalin's 1939 nonaggression pact with Adolf Hitler kept the USSR out of World War II for two years, but the German dictator abrogated the pact in June 1941, launching a massive invasion of the Soviet Union. Stalin allied the USSR to Great Britain and eventually the United States to fight the Nazi threat.

Under Stalin's leadership the Soviet Union survived severe human losses and property devastation until the tide of the war turned with the Soviet victory at Stalingrad in early 1943. Stalin proved to be a shrewd bargainer during the wartime Allied conferences at Tehran, Yalta, and Potsdam as evidenced by his ability to secure Soviet dominance of Eastern Europe. The establishment of communist regimes there after the war contributed to the growing distrust and animosity between East and West.

By the end of the war, the "cult of Stalin" permeated every facet of life in the Soviet Union, making the dictator the authority in government, politics, art, learning, and science. Evidence suggests that Stalin was planning a second purge in the 1950s, but he died before it was implemented.

Stalin died of a cerebral hemorrhage on March 5, 1953.

He was survived by his daughter, Svetlana Alliluyeva, who gained renown when she defected to the West in April 1967. She went back to the Soviet Union to live in 1984, but in 1986 she defected again and returned to the United States. Stalin's first wife, Ekaterina Svanidze, died around 1905, leaving a son, Yakov, who died in World War II after being taken prisoner by the Germans. Stalin's second wife, Nadezhda Alliluyeva, reportedly was driven to suicide in November 1932. She and Stalin had wed in 1918. They had two children, Svetlana and a son, Vasily, an alleged alcoholic who, after a corrupt military career, died in 1962.

Analysis. Stalin was an organizer, a man of action, rather than a theoretician or original thinker. Before and during the Russian Revolution, Stalin had been overshadowed by theoretically brilliant leaders with gifts for oratory such as Lenin and Trotsky. After the revolution, however, with Lenin's health declining, Stalin's ruthlessness and skills as an organizer enabled him to gradually take control of the party.

Stalin viewed his industrialization and collectivization drives of the late 1920s and 1930s as necessary to transform the Soviet Union from a backward nation into a world power. At great human cost, Stalin succeeded in making the Soviet Union into an industrial giant. Had he not launched the industrialization drive, the Soviet Union might not have survived the German invasion in 1941.

Stalin's main goal, however, was not strengthening the Soviet Union, but gathering supreme power for himself. His paranoid pursuit of absolute control led him to order the arrest and execution of many of his colleagues and contributed to the creation of a repressive system that continues to haunt the Soviet Union. Since Stalin's death, no Soviet leader has been allowed to become so powerful that he could safely disregard the interests and goals of his fellow leaders.

Mikhail Suslov (1902-1982)

At the time of his death in January 1982, Mikhail Andreevich Suslov—a member of both the Politburo and Secretariat—was the Communist party's chief ideologist and one of the most powerful Kremlin leaders after Leonid I. Brezhnev.

Suslov came from a peasant background. He was born November 21, 1902, in the village of Shakhovskoe on the Volga in present-day Ulyanovsk *oblast* (province). In 1921 he joined the Communist party and went to Moscow to study. Following his graduation from a workers' school in 1924, he studied at the Plekhanov Institute of National Economy, graduating in 1928. He then attended the prestigious Economics Institute of Red Professors. From 1929 to 1931, while attending the institute, he taught at Moscow State University and the Stalin Academy of Industry.

Among his students were Nikita S. Khrushchev and Nadezhda Alliluyeva, Joseph Stalin's second wife.

Public Career. In 1931 Suslov was named to the party's Central Control Commission and to the People's Commissariat of the Workers' and Peasants' Inspection, a combined watchdog group used by Stalin to root out those suspected of having unorthodox views. In 1933-1934 he was in charge of purges in the Ural and Chernigov regions.

From there Suslov moved on to hold various regional party posts. In 1937 he was sent to the Rostov region, where he served first as department chief and later as secretary of the regional party organization. In 1939 he became first secretary of the party in Stavropol territory in the North Caucasus, a post he held until 1944. As chairman of the party's Bureau for Lithuania from 1944 to 1946, Suslov directed the purge in that republic.

From 1941 to 1945, during World War II, he also was a member of the military council on the North Caucasian Front and chief of staff of the Stavropol territory partisan forces. From 1939 to 1941 he was a member of the party's Central Auditing Commission, and in 1941 he became a full member of the Central Committee.

Suslov left his regional duties in 1946 and returned to Moscow to join the national party apparatus. From 1946 to 1952 he was a member of the Central Committee's Organization Bureau. In 1947 he became a secretary of the Central Committee in charge of the Propaganda and Agitation Department, which was concerned with domestic ideological control.

However, he soon began focusing on relations with other communist parties. He helped to establish the Cominform in 1947 and was a Soviet representative at the June 1948 Cominform meeting where Yugoslavia was expelled from the organization. Suslov became chairman of the Cominform in August 1948 and held that post until 1953. He was editor in chief of the newspaper *Pravda* in 1949-1950, a period during which he gave up his job as a Central Committee secretary.

In 1950 he became a member of the Presidium of the Supreme Soviet—his first high post in the government. He remained a member until 1954, the year he became chairman of the Supreme Soviet's Foreign Affairs Commission. In 1952 Suslov, with Stalin's backing, again became a secretary of the Central Committee and remained one until his death. In 1952, he also was made a member of the party's Presidium (renamed Politburo in 1966).

Following Stalin's death in 1953, the Presidium membership was reduced from twenty-five to ten, and Suslov was one of those dropped. However, in 1955 Khrushchev had Suslov promoted to the Presidium once again.

Following the ouster of Khrushchev in 1964—in which Suslov played a role—Suslov reportedly was considered for the position of party first secretary. However, Suslov preferred to take the role of second secretary, where he could concentrate on ideological matters and relations with other Communist countries. He remained in this position until his death in 1982.

Analysis. Suslov was considered to be a firm and unyielding Stalinist. Yet he helped Khrushchev defeat the "antiparty group" of old Bolsheviks in 1957 and aided the de-Stalinization campaign under Khrushchev. By 1964, however, the conservative Suslov thought the campaign had gone too far, and he conspired with other Soviet leaders to oust Khrushchev for "adventurism" at home and abroad. He backed Brezhnev to succeed Khrushchev and was known to have exercised considerable influence over Brezhnev's policies.

From the closing years of the Stalin era until he died January 25, 1982, Suslov was the Soviet Union's spokesman in the international communist movement. He reportedly played a key role in the Kremlin decisions to suppress the Hungarian revolt in 1956, to end the liberalization in Czechoslovakia in 1968 (although some sources indicated he argued against military intervention), and to push Polish authorities to take a harsher line against the independent trade union Solidarity in 1981.

Leon Trotsky (1879-1940)

Leon Trotsky, one of the greatest theoreticians, orators, and military strategists of early Soviet history, was instrumental in planning, executing, and defending the 1917 Russian Revolution. He later became Joseph Stalin's most bitter opponent.

Lev Davydovich Bronstein (Trotsky's given name) was born in Ukraine on October 26, 1879, to a Jewish family. He studied briefly in Odessa and then moved to Nikolaev, where his radical activities led to his arrest and imprisonment in Siberia. During his four years in jail (1898-1902), Trotsky became acquainted with Marxism. After his escape from prison in 1902, he assumed the pseudonym Trotsky, which was the name of his jail warden, and traveled to Europe, where he collaborated with V. I. Lenin on the revolutionary journal *Iskra* (The Spark). When the Russian Social Democratic Labor party split into Bolshevik and Menshevik factions in 1903, Trotsky sided with the Mensheviks and became an outspoken opponent of Lenin.

Around 1904 Trotsky developed his "theory of permanent revolution," which looked beyond a revolution in

Russia to a worldwide workers' struggle that would overthrow capitalism. For Trotsky, the class struggle was an international phenomenon. He would remain loyal to this theory throughout his life.

Public Career.   Trotsky returned to Russia in 1905 and was a leader of the St. Petersburg Soviet during the revolution of 1905. He was banished to Siberia in 1907, but he escaped to Europe, where he attempted to unify the badly fractured Social Democratic Labor party. He was expelled from France in 1916, spent a short time in the United States, and then returned to Russia in May 1917.

Back in Russia, Trotsky joined the Bolsheviks. Although a latecomer to the party, he was a guiding force behind the events leading to the Bolsheviks' seizure of power in the November revolution. While Lenin was in Finland hiding from the Provisional Government, Trotsky organized the Military Revolutionary Committee, which led the armed insurrection in Petrograd.

After the Bolshevik victory, Trotsky was entrusted with several positions in the new government, notably the commissariats for foreign and military/naval affairs. He established and organized the Red Army and engineered the Bolshevik victory in the civil war.

As Lenin approached death, Trotsky and Stalin emerged as rivals for leadership of the Communist party. After Lenin had died, Stalin denounced Trotsky's "theory of permanent revolution" as un-Leninist and gathered support for his own doctrine of "socialism in one country." Trotsky was stripped of his government positions in 1925, removed from the Politburo in 1927, and expelled from the Soviet Union in 1929. He spent the remainder of his life in exile in various countries, continuing to oppose Stalin through his writing.

During the purges of the 1930s, Trotsky was named as the main instigator of the alleged counterrevolutionary crimes against the Stalin regime. He was convicted and sentenced to death in absentia.

On August 21, 1940, Trotsky died in Mexico City from wounds inflicted the day before by an assassin reportedly sent to Mexico on Stalin's orders. Trotsky was survived by his second wife, Natasha, who left the Soviet Union with him and their two children in 1929. It is believed that Stalin arranged the deaths of the children, in 1933 and 1938. Stalin already had ordered the execution of Trotsky's first wife and their two children in the Soviet Union.

Of Trotsky's extensive works, many written after his exile from the Soviet Union, one of the best known is *The History of the Russian Revolution* (1932-1933).

Analysis.   Lenin called Leon Trotsky "personally perhaps the most capable" in the Central Committee, although he had doubts concerning Trotsky's "excessive liking for the administrative side of things." Trotsky had excellent organizational abilities and his skill for oratory was unmatched among his colleagues. However, his political fortunes were damaged by his early Menshevik loyalties and his proclivity for alienating his colleagues. Trotsky's concern for his political theories and their relation to world government put him in a vulnerable position against his chief opponent, Stalin, whose more immediate theory of socialism in one country was a powerfully persuasive tool.

Grigory Zinoviev (1883-1936)

Grigory Yevseyevich Zinoviev, one of the most prominent Bolsheviks during the Russian Revolution, was born in Ukraine to Jewish parents named Radomysl'sky in September 1883. Lacking any formal schooling, Zinoviev became involved with self-education circles, where he received his initial exposure to socialist theory. He joined the Russian Social Democratic Labor party in 1901, and that same year he fled to Europe to escape police persecution for his involvement in economic strikes. Zinoviev met V. I. Lenin in 1903 in Switzerland and supported his Bolshevik faction against the Mensheviks when the Social Democrats split later that year.

Zinoviev collaborated closely with Lenin in the years leading to the 1917 revolution. They returned together to Russia from Europe after the March 1917 revolution. Zinoviev, however, disagreed with Lenin's strategy of pursuing an exclusive Bolshevik seizure of power in Russia. In October Zinoviev and Lev Kamenev voted against the coup being organized by the party's Central Committee. After the revolution Zinoviev resigned from the party and demanded a coalition government composed of all socialist groups. He soon returned to the party, however, and was appointed to the Politburo. He also headed the powerful Petrograd Soviet. From his base in Petrograd, Zinoviev, according to Adam B. Ulam in *The Bolsheviks,* established "his little political kingdom from which he would not be dislodged by Stalin until 1925."

After Lenin's death in 1924, Zinoviev emerged as one of the top Soviet leaders along with Kamenev and Joseph Stalin. This triumvirate was challenged by the "left opposition" headed by Leon Trotsky. In the ongoing power struggle, Zinoviev and Kamenev became alarmed by Stalin's accumulation of power and belatedly joined Trotsky to oppose Stalin. The political struggle with the left opposition ultimately was won by Stalin with the help of Nikolai Bukharin and the "right opposition," which was then crushed in turn. Zinoviev's resistance to Stalin led to the loss of his leadership posts in 1926. In 1935 he was tried for "moral complicity" in the murder of Leningrad party leader Sergei Kirov and sentenced to ten years in jail.

A year later Zinoviev and fifteen others were tried in the first "show trial" of the Great Purge. He was convicted of a series of crimes related to allegedly treasonous and counterrevolutionary activities. Zinoviev was executed on August 25, 1936, immediately after the trial.

MAJOR EVENTS, 1900-1963

Following is a chronology of major events in Russian and Soviet history from the beginning of the twentieth century through 1963.

1900. August, international military expedition, including Russian troops, occupies Beijing to put down the Boxer Rebellion in China. December, first issue of the revolutionary newspaper *Iskra* is published.

1901. Socialist Revolutionary party is established. Russian workers and university students begin using street demonstrations as a means of protest.

1902. January 30, Anglo-Japanese alliance is formed. Vladimir I. Lenin publishes his pamphlet entitled "What Is to Be Done?"

1903. July 30-August 23, Menshevik and Bolshevik factions split in the Russian Social Democratic Labor party during the Second Party Congress, held in Brussels and London. (The First Party Congress was held March 13-15, 1898, in Minsk.)

1904. February 8, Japan attacks the Russian fleet at Port Arthur, beginning the Russo-Japanese War. May 27, Russian Baltic fleet is destroyed by the Japanese navy at the Battle of Tsushima Strait.

1905. January 22, "Bloody Sunday"—police fire at a peaceful demonstration of workers in St. Petersburg, killing more than a hundred. April 25-May 10, Third Russian Social Democratic Labor Party Congress is held in London. June, crew of the battleship *Potemkin* mutinies and sails to Romania. August 16, tsar's promise of an assembly elected by nobles, landed peasants, and the bourgeoisie fails to quell unrest. September 5, Treaty of Portsmouth (New Hampshire), mediated by President Theodore Roosevelt, ends the Russo-Japanese War. October 30, nationwide strikes begun earlier in the month force the tsar to issue the October Manifesto guaranteeing personal freedoms and establishing the first Duma.

1906. April 24, tsar publishes the Fundamental Laws. April 23-May 8, Fourth Russian Social Democratic Labor Party Congress is held in Stockholm. May 10, first Duma opens, but it is dissolved by the tsar July 21. November, Stolypin land reform program is launched.

1907. January 1, Russian government cancels peasant redemption payments. March 5, second Duma opens. June 16, tsar dissolves the Duma and changes the electoral laws so that the next Duma will support him. May 13-June 1, Fifth Russian Social Democratic Labor Party Congress is held in London. June-October, Second Hague Peace Conference fails to make progress toward European disarmament. (First Hague Peace Conference was held in May 1899.) August 31, Russia signs an agreement with Great Britain demarcating spheres of influence in Afghanistan, Persia, and Pakistan; the pact resolves Anglo-Russian differences and results in the Triple Entente of France, Britain, and Russia, which is opposed to the Triple Alliance of Germany, Austria-Hungary, and Italy. November 1, third Duma opens (it serves a full five-year term).

1908. November, Leon Trotsky becomes editor of the recently founded newspaper *Pravda* in Vienna.

1909. February, Duma passes a law on the inviolability of person. October 24, Russia and Italy conclude a secret agreement on the Balkans.

1910. January, Russia and Japan reject U.S. proposal for an "open door" policy in Manchuria. January 15-February 5, prominent Mensheviks and Bolsheviks meet but fail to restore party unity.

1911. September 14, assassination of Russian prime minister Peter Stolypin.

1912. October 8, first Balkan war begins. November 28, fourth Duma opens (it remains in session until March 1917).

1913. May 30, Treaty of London ends the first Balkan war. June-August, second Balkan war.

1914. June 28, Archduke Francis Ferdinand, heir to the Hapsburg throne, is assassinated in Sarajevo. July 30, tsar orders a general mobilization of Russian military capacity. August 1, Germany declares war on Russia; World War I begins. August 6, Austria-Hungary declares war against Russia. August 10, Austrians invade southern Poland, opening major fighting on the eastern front. November 1, Russia declares war against Turkey.

1915. September 5, tsar goes to the front to take

personal command of his armies fighting the Germans. September, Lenin represents Bolsheviks at First International Socialist Conference and advocates transforming the World War I into a civil war against imperialism.

1916. June, Russian forces win several battles, but the Germans and Austrians halt the Russian advance during July and August. December 30, Grigory Rasputin is assassinated.

1917. March 11, tsar dissolves the Duma and orders the suppression of demonstrations. March 12, Petrograd Soviet of Workers' and Soldiers' Deputies is established. March 15, Tsar Nicholas II abdicates; the United States is the first among the great powers to recognize the Provisional Government headed by Prince Georgy Lvov. April 16, Lenin arrives from Switzerland at Finland Station in Petrograd. April 20, *Pravda* publishes Lenin's April Theses. May 17, Trotsky reaches Petrograd from the United States. June 6-17, All-Russian Congress of Soviets meets. July 16-18, "July Days" mass demonstrations. July 20, Lvov resigns, and Aleksandr Kerensky takes over as prime minister. August 8-16, Sixth Russian Social Democratic Labor Party Congress is held in Petrograd. September 9-12, General Lavr Kornilov's counterrevolutionary plot fails. October 23, Bolshevik Central Committee advocates armed insurrection. November 7-8, Bolsheviks seize power. November 14, Kerensky's attempt to capture Petrograd fails. November 25, Constituent Assembly is elected. December 20, Cheka is established.

1918. January 8, President Woodrow Wilson issues "Fourteen Points" for a postwar settlement, which includes liberal treatment of Russia. January 19, Bolsheviks disband the Constituent Assembly. January 28, Bolshevik leaders order the organization of the Red Army. January 31, Russians adopt the Gregorian calendar. March 3, Russia signs the Treaty of Brest-Litovsk with Germany. March 6-8, Seventh Russian Social Democratic Labor Party (Bolshevik) Congress. March, Allied intervention in Russia begins. July 10, first Soviet Constitution is adopted, creating the Russian Soviet Federated Socialist Republic. July 16, tsar and his family are murdered by Bolsheviks near Ekaterinburg. August 30, Lenin is wounded in an assassination attempt by a Socialist Revolutionary. November 11, World War I ends. November 13, Bolsheviks repudiate the Treaty of Brest-Litovsk.

1919. March 2, Communist International (Comintern) is founded. March 18-23, Eighth Russian Communist Party (formerly Social Democratic Labor party, Bolshevik) Congress. June 28, Treaty of Versailles is signed. November-December, Red Army scores important victories over White armies.

1920. January, Allies lift the coastal blockade of the Soviet Union imposed in October 1919. March 29-April 5, Ninth Russian Communist Party Congress. April 25, Polish forces invade Ukraine. July 8, United States im-

poses a trade embargo against the Soviet Union.

1921. March 2-18, Kronstadt rebellion. March 8-16, Tenth Russian Communist Party Congress. March 17, Lenin initiates the New Economic Policy. March 18, Russia and Poland sign the Treaty of Riga, giving Poland control of disputed territories and establishing the so-called Curzon Line.

1922. April 3, Joseph Stalin becomes general secretary of the Communist party. April 16, Soviet Union signs the Treaty of Rapallo with Germany. March 27-April 2, Eleventh Russian Communist Party Congress. May 26, Lenin suffers the first of three paralytic strokes. December 16, Lenin suffers his second stroke, which limits his public activities. December 24, Lenin writes his "Testament," which evaluates his potential successors. December 30, the Union of Soviet Socialist Republics is declared.

1923. January 4, in a postscript to his "Testament," Lenin advocates replacing Stalin as general secretary of the Communist party. March 9, Lenin suffers his third stroke. April 17-25, Twelfth Soviet Communist Party Congress accepts Stalin's plan to reorganize the party. October 15, forty-six Communist party leaders present the Central Committee with the "Declaration of the Forty-Six," which criticizes the ruling regime.

1924. January 21, Lenin dies, causing the struggle for power between Stalin and Trotsky to intensify. January 27, Lenin's funeral. January 31, USSR Constitution is ratified. February 1, Great Britain recognizes the USSR, and within one year Italy, Norway, Austria, Sweden, Denmark, Mexico, France, and Japan also extend recognition. May 23-31, Thirteenth Soviet Communist Party Congress. November 6, Trotsky publishes *Lessons of October*, attacking Lev Kamenev and Grigory Zinoviev.

1925. May 12, revised Soviet Constitution is ratified. December 18-31, Fourteenth Soviet Communist Party Congress.

1926. October 23, Trotsky and Kamenev are removed from the Politburo.

1927. April, USSR and the Chinese Guomindang break diplomatic relations. November 12, Trotsky and Zinoviev are stripped of their party memberships. December, during the Fifteenth Soviet Communist Party Congress, Stalin and his followers score a decisive victory over the Trotskyites, dozens of whom are expelled from the party.

1928. August 27, United States, France, Germany, Great Britain, Italy, Belgium, Japan, Poland, and Czechoslovakia sign the Kellogg-Briand Peace Pact outlawing war. August 31, USSR announces its support of the pact. October 1, Stalin introduces the First Five-Year Plan.

1929. January 18, Trotsky is exiled from the USSR. November, Nikolai Bukharin, Aleksei Rykov, and Mikhail Tomsky, leaders of the "rightist" opposition, are expelled from the Politburo. December, Stalin advances the policy of eliminating the *kulaks* (wealthy peasants) as a class and launches a campaign to collectivize the peasantry.

1930. March 2, Stalin's "Dizziness with Success" article blames local party officials for abuses during the initial drive toward collectivization. June 26-July 13, Sixteenth Soviet Communist Party Congress.

1931. June, Stalin proposes a six-point program designed to spur industrialization.

1932. November 29, Soviets and French sign a nonaggression pact. December 31, Soviets declare that the First Five-Year Plan has been fulfilled early.

1933. November 16, USSR and the United States establish diplomatic relations.

1934. January 26-February 10, Seventeenth Soviet Communist Party Congress. September 18, Soviet Union joins the League of Nations. December 1, Sergei Kirov is murdered, setting off the Stalinist purges.

1935. May 2, Soviet-French mutual assistance treaty is signed. July 14, USSR and the United States sign a one-year reciprocal trade agreement.

1936. March 7, Hitler's armies occupy the Rhineland. July 18, Spanish civil war begins; Soviet Union provides financial aid to the left-wing Loyalist side, which is fighting the Italian- and German-backed Nationalists. August 19-24, first "show trial" is held; Zinoviev and Kamenev are among the sixteen defendants, all of whom are found guilty and executed. November 25, Germany and Japan sign the Anti-Comintern Pact. December 6, new Soviet Constitution is adopted.

1937. January 23-30, second show trial is held; thirteen of seventeen defendants are sentenced to death, the other four are imprisoned.

1938. March 2-13, third and final show trial is held; eighteen of twenty-one defendants, including Nikolai Bukharin, are sentenced to death, the other three are imprisoned. March 12, Germany annexes Austria. September 29-30, Great Britain and France agree to Germany's annexation of Czechoslovakia's Sudetenland at the Munich conference.

1939. March 10-21, Eighteenth Soviet Communist Party Congress. March 28, Spanish civil war ends in victory for the Nationalists. August 23, USSR and Nazi Germany sign a nonaggression pact. September 1, Germany invades Poland, triggering World War II; the Soviets subsequently invade eastern Poland. November 30, Soviet Union invades Finland. December 14, League of Nations expels the Soviet Union.

1940. March 12, Soviet-Finnish "Winter War" ends; Finland is forced to cede the Karelian Isthmus and other areas to the USSR. August 3-6, Lithuania, Latvia, and Estonia are incorporated into the Soviet Union. August 21, Trotsky is assassinated in Mexico City.

1941. April 13, USSR and Japan sign a neutrality treaty. June 22, Germany invades the Soviet Union. July 3, Stalin makes his first public statement on the German invasion. September 20, Germans capture Kiev. December, Soviets launch their first counteroffensive against the invading German forces. December 7, Japanese attack Pearl Harbor.

1942. January 1, Soviets sign the United Nations Declaration in Washington. June 11, USSR and the United States sign a lend-lease agreement providing for reciprocal defense aid. November 19, Soviets launch a successful counterattack at Stalingrad that traps nearly three hundred thousand German troops in and around the city.

1943. February 2, remnants of German Sixth Army surrender at Stalingrad. May 25, Stalin dissolves Comintern as concession to Western allies. November 28-December 1, U.S. president Franklin D. Roosevelt, British prime minister Winston Churchill, and Stalin meet in Tehran to discuss wartime strategy and postwar issues.

1944. January 11, Roosevelt denies that "secret treaties or financial commitments" were made at Tehran or other Allied negotiations. June 6, Allies land at Normandy, opening the western front. July 22, conference at Bretton Woods, New Hampshire, closes with the Soviet Union agreeing to subscribe $1.2 billion to the proposed International Bank for Reconstruction and Development. October 10-20, Churchill and Stalin meet in Moscow; they divide Europe into hypothetical spheres of influence.

1945. February 4-11, Roosevelt, Churchill, and Stalin meet at the Yalta conference in the Crimea. April 12, Roosevelt dies, Harry S. Truman becomes president. April 23, Russian forces fight their way into Berlin. April 25, Russian troops advancing from the east and American troops advancing from the west link at Torgau in Germany. May 7, German High Command surrenders at Reims. May 8, Allies proclaim victory in Europe. June 25, UN charter is approved in San Francisco. August 2, British prime minister Clement Attlee, Stalin, and Truman issue the Potsdam Declaration after their summit in Germany. August 6, United States drops an atomic bomb on Hiroshima. August 8, Soviet Union declares war on Japan. August 9, United States drops a second atomic bomb on Nagasaki. August 21, American lend-lease aid to the Soviet Union ends. September 2, Japan formally surrenders to the United States.

1946. January 10, first session of the United Nations opens. January 19, at the United Nations, Iran charges the Soviets with illegally occupying its Azerbaijan region. January 29, Secretary of State James F. Byrnes confirms the existence of a secret Roosevelt-Churchill promise at Yalta to allow the Soviets to capture and control Sakhalin Island and the Kuril Islands in exchange for Soviet entry into the war against Japan. March 5, Churchill delivers his "Iron Curtain" speech at Fulton, Missouri. May, Soviets withdraw their troops from Iran. October 27, Communists assume power in Bulgaria.

1947. March 12, Truman asks Congress for $400 million in funds to aid the governments of Greece and Turkey in their fight against Communist rebels. June 5, Secretary of State George C. Marshall outlines a plan for European economic recovery (the Marshall Plan) at Harvard University's commencement. July, George Kennan publishes his "X" article in *Foreign Affairs* outlining the strategy of containment. October 5, Cominform (the Communist Information Bureau, which succeeds the Comintern) is established. December, four-power conference on Germany in London breaks down.

1948. February 25, President Eduard Beneś of Czechoslovakia yields to a Soviet ultimatum to install a pro-Soviet cabinet and join the Communist bloc. June, Soviet Union begins the Berlin blockade. June 21, the United States and Great Britain launch a massive airlift of supplies to Berlin. June 28, Yugoslavia is expelled from the Cominform. August 3, Communist party member Arpad Szakasits becomes president of Hungary.

1949. January 25, Moscow announces the formation of a six-nation Council for Mutual Economic Assistance (CMEA) in Eastern Europe. April 4, North Atlantic Treaty is signed, establishing the North Atlantic Treaty Organization (NATO) alliance. May, Soviets lift the Berlin blockade. May 23, constitution of the Federal Republic of Germany (West Germany) is approved. September 21, Communist party leader Mao Zedong proclaims the People's Republic of China. September 23, Moscow announces a successful Soviet test of an atomic bomb. October 7, German Democratic Republic (East Germany) is established.

1950. February 14, Soviet Union and the People's Republic of China sign a treaty of alliance. June 25, North Korea invades South Korea. June 27, Truman orders U.S. forces under Gen. Douglas MacArthur to help repel the North Korean invasion. November 26, Chinese troops enter the war on the side of North Korea.

1951. July 10, Korean truce talks begin. November 23, Truman orders the withdrawal of all U.S. tariff concessions to the Soviet Union and Poland.

1952. October 5-14, Nineteenth Soviet Communist Party Congress. November 1, United States successfully tests a hydrogen bomb.

1953. January 13, arrest of nine Soviet doctors allegedly involved in the "Doctors' Plot" is disclosed. March 5, Stalin dies and is succeeded as premier and first secretary of the Communist party by Georgy Malenkov. March 14, Malenkov resigns as first secretary but retains the premiership. April 14, seven surviving doctors accused in the "Doctors' Plot" are exonerated. June 15, Soviet Union and Yugoslavia reestablish diplomatic relations. June 17, East Berlin riots. June 26, chief of secret police Lavrenty Beria is arrested. July 27, Korean War ends. August 8, Malenkov announces his proconsumer policy before the Supreme Soviet. August 12, Soviet Union explodes a hydrogen bomb. September 13, Nikita S. Khrushchev becomes first secretary of the Communist party. December 17, Beria is tried and found guilty; he is executed soon after.

1954. March, Malenkov asserts that war between imperialism and capitalism would mean "the destruction of world civilization." July 21, Vietnam is partitioned at the Geneva conference. October 23, West Germany is granted sovereignty and joins NATO.

1955. February 8, Malenkov resigns as prime minister and is replaced by Nikolai Bulganin. May 14, Warsaw Pact is established. May 15, Austrian state treaty is signed; Soviets subsequently withdraw their forces from the country. July 18-23, Geneva summit conference, attended by leaders of the United States, Britain, France, and the Soviet Union; Bulganin represents the USSR. September 9, USSR and West Germany establish diplomatic relations. September 27, Egypt announces that it will buy Soviet arms.

1956. February 14, Twentieth Soviet Communist Party Congress opens with a speech by Khrushchev in which he advocates "peaceful coexistence" with the West. February 24, Khrushchev denounces Stalin in his "Secret Speech" at the party congress, which ends the following day. April 18, Cominform is dissolved. June, Tito visits Moscow. June 4, State Department publishes text of the Secret Speech. June 28-30, strikes in Poland lead to a limited liberalization. July 26, Egypt nationalizes the Suez Canal. October 19, Soviet delegation meets with Polish leaders in Warsaw; they reach a compromise on Polish reforms. October 23, protests against communist rule in Hungary turn violent. October 29, Israel attacks Egypt in accordance with secret Israeli-French-British plan; British and French subsequently join the assault. October 30, Hungarian leader Imre Nagy calls for an end to one-party rule in Hungary and a Hungarian withdrawal from the Warsaw Pact. November 4, Soviet troops occupy Budapest and other major Hungarian cities, crushing the Hungarian revolution. November 7, under pressure from the United States, Great Britain and France agree to withdraw from the Sinai; Israel agrees to withdraw the following day.

1957. February, Andrei Gromyko becomes foreign minister succeeding Dmitry Shepilov. June, a coalition of Presidium members, including Malenkov, Viacheslav Molotov, and Lazar Kaganovich, demand Khrushchev's resignation; Khrushchev counters by convening the Central Committee, which supports him and removes the "anti-party group" from their government and party positions. August 26, Moscow announces the successful testing of an intercontinental ballistic missile. October 4, *Sputnik,* the first space satellite, is launched by the Soviet Union. October 15, Soviet Union and China sign a secret agreement pledging the Soviets to help the Chinese develop their own nuclear weapons. October, Khrushchev removes

Marshal Georgy Zhukov from the Presidium and as defense minister.

1958. March 27, Khrushchev ousts Bulganin as prime minister and assumes the post himself; Khrushchev continues as first secretary. October-November, Quemoy-Matsu crisis. October 31, Geneva test-ban conference opens. November 10, Khrushchev sparks the Berlin crisis by calling for the withdrawal of Allied troops in West Berlin.

1959. January 1, Fidel Castro comes to power in Cuba. January 27-February 5, Twenty-first Soviet Communist Party Congress. June 20, Soviets rescind their nuclear weapons development agreement with China. July 24, "Kitchen Debate" between Vice President Richard Nixon and Khrushchev takes place at a U.S. exhibition in Moscow. September 14, Soviet rocket hits the moon. September 15-27, Khrushchev visits the United States. December 1, twelve countries, including the USSR and the United States, sign a treaty making Antarctica a scientific preserve free of military activities.

1960. January, Khrushchev announces defense budget cuts. February, Anastas Mikoyan visits Cuba to establish diplomatic relations and sign an aid agreement. May 1, Soviets shoot down an American U-2 spy plane over the Soviet Union and capture its pilot, Francis Gary Powers. May 4, Aleksei Kosygin becomes a deputy prime minister. May 5, Soviets announce downing of U-2. May 7, Leonid I. Brezhnev becomes chairman of the Presidium of the Supreme Soviet. May 17, Paris summit conference, attended by President Dwight D. Eisenhower, Khrushchev, French president Charles de Gaulle, and British prime minister Harold Macmillan, breaks up after Khrushchev demands an apology for the U-2 flight. August, Soviet Union withdraws its technical experts from China. September 20-October 13, Khrushchev visits the United Nations.

1961. April 12, Soviet cosmonaut Yuri Gagarin becomes the first man in space. April 17, U.S.-supported "Bay of Pigs" invasion of Cuba is crushed by Castro. May 5, first American manned space flight (Alan Shepherd). June 3-4, Khrushchev and President John F. Kennedy meet in Vienna but remain deadlocked on key issues. August 13, East Germany seals border between East and West Berlin and begins building Berlin Wall. September 1, Soviet Union resumes nuclear weapons testing, breaking an unofficial moratorium. October 17-31, Twenty-second Soviet Communist Party Congress; Khrushchev's party program is approved. October 30, party congress votes unanimously to remove Stalin's remains from Lenin's Tomb and rebury them in a less honored spot near the Kremlin wall. December 10, Soviet Union breaks relations with Albania.

1962. February 10, USSR exchanges U-2 pilot Francis Gary Powers for Soviet spy Rudolph Abel, held by the United States. March 14, disarmament conference opens in Geneva; the conference recesses December 24. October 20-November 21, Sino-Indian border war. October 22-November 2, Cuban missile crisis, which ends when Kennedy announces Moscow's willingness to dismantle Soviet missile bases in Cuba. November, Khrushchev implements bifurcation of the agricultural and industrial branches of the Soviet party apparatus.

1963. February 12, Geneva disarmament conference resumes. June 4, Soviets announce abandonment of Seven-Year Plan. June 10, President Kennedy's American University speech. June 20, U.S.-Soviet "hot line" is established. July 21, talks in Moscow aimed at resolving Sino-Soviet ideological conflict end in failure. July 25, the United States, the Soviet Union, and Great Britain sign the Partial Nuclear Test Ban Treaty (Beijing denounces the pact). October 9, Kennedy approves the sale of wheat to the Soviet Union. November 22, Kennedy is assassinated; Lyndon B. Johnson becomes president.

CHRONOLOGY OF EVENTS, 1964-1992

Following is a chronology of events in Soviet and post-Soviet history from 1964 through 1992.

1964

January 2. USSR Peace Message. Soviet premier Nikita S. Khrushchev sends a personal message to all countries with which the USSR has relations, calling for the renunciation of war as a method of "settling diplomatic disputes." The plan calls for the United States to remove its military forces from West Germany, South Korea, and South Vietnam. American officials term the communiqué "disappointing."

January 29. U.S. Plane Downed. A U.S. training plane is shot down over East German airspace by a Soviet aircraft. Both the United States and the Soviet Union attempted to warn the plane during the event, in which three U.S. officers were killed. A similar incident occurs March 10 when an unarmed U.S. reconnaissance jet is downed over East Germany and its crew is held. Secretary of State Dean Rusk disclaims Soviet accusations of espionage. The three airmen are released March 27.

March 31-April 7. Khrushchev on China. While on a tour of Hungary, Premier Khrushchev denounces China several times for opposing his rejection of Stalinism and his policy of peaceful coexistence with the West. On April 5 he calls China's leaders "crazy."

April 20. Joint Statement on Nuclear Material. President Lyndon B. Johnson and Premier Khrushchev declare their intention to reduce production of material used in nuclear weapons. The United States will cut back enriched uranium production, and the Soviet Union will not build several reactors designed to produce plutonium.

May 1. Khrushchev's May Day Speech. Premier Khrushchev denounces the United States for flying reconnaissance missions over Cuba. He maintains the alleged missions violate the understanding reached between himself and President John F. Kennedy in October 1962.

May 9. Khrushchev in Egypt. Large crowds give Premier Khrushchev a tumultuous welcome after he arrives in Egypt for a two-week visit. He attends nationwide celebrations, which begin May 15, of the completion of the first stage of the Aswan Dam.

June 1. Consular Pact Signed. Soviet and American representatives sign a pact in Moscow that outlines procedures for the establishment and operation of consulates.

June 12. Soviet-East German Pact. Premier Khrushchev and President Walter Ulbricht of East Germany sign a twenty-year friendship treaty that "asserts the legal existence of a Communist state in Eastern Germany." The pact is denounced by the United States, Great Britain, and France June 26 as an obstacle to bringing peace to divided Germany.

June 16-July 4. Khrushchev in Scandinavia. Premier Khrushchev tours Denmark, Sweden, and Norway and meets with their heads of state. He reports to the Soviet people July 1 that the trip was an exercise in peaceful coexistence that may reap possible trade benefits.

July 13. Article on Sino-Soviet Split. Two Chinese Communist party publications release the ninth and most vituperative article in a series on the Sino-Soviet split. Entitled "On Khrushchev's Phony Communism and Its Historical Lessons for the World," the article asserts that the Soviet premier heads a "privileged stratum" in his country that is attempting to restore capitalism while the "masses" are being exploited.

September 30. Cyprus Receives Aid. The Soviet Union and Cyprus sign an economic and military aid agreement. In August Cyprus had appealed for Soviet aid following Turkish air attacks. Cypriot officials declare that the accord contains "no strings or conditions."

October 14-15. Khrushchev Ousted. Nikita S. Khrushchev is forced to resign as premier of the Soviet government and first secretary of the Soviet Communist party. He is replaced as first secretary by Leonid I. Brezhnev and as premier by Aleksei Kosygin. Soviet ambassador to the United States Anatoly Dobrynin October 16 reassures President Johnson of the continuation of good U.S.-Soviet relations based on peaceful coexistence. Also October 16, China's leaders extend "warm greetings" to the new Soviet leaders. A *Pravda* editorial October 17 hints Khrushchev's "harebrained scheming" and "hasty decisions" contributed to his ouster.

October 16. China Tests Atomic Device. China explodes its first atomic device. The Chinese issue a statement saying, "China cannot remain idle and do nothing in the face of the ever-increasing threat posed by the United States."

October 26. New Soviet Goals. The Soviet government newspaper *Izvestia* publishes an article entitled "A Commonwealth of Equals" in which the new regime outlines its goals for unity and equality in the communist movement. The Western media report October 30 that a document listing twenty-nine reasons why Khrushchev was removed had been circulated among Soviet Communist party officials. One of the main reasons cited was Khrushchev's poor handling of the Sino-Soviet rift.

November 6. Brezhnev Speech. Party head Leonid Brezhnev, in a speech during celebrations honoring the anniversary of the Bolshevik Revolution, declares that the new Soviet government will seek improved relations with capitalist nations. He urges greater unity within the communist world, more East-West trade, and "ever more democracy for Soviet people."

November 16. Bifurcation Reversed. The Central Committee officially reunites the industrial and agricultural bureaus of the party apparatus. The bureaucratic division had been engineered by Khrushchev two years before.

November 17. Shifts in Presidium. The Kremlin announces major personnel shifts in the Presidium and at the regional/district level of the party. Alexander Shelepin, thought to have had a key role in the Khrushchev ouster, and Petr Shelest are named full members of the Presidium.

1965

February 5. Kosygin Abroad. Premier Kosygin receives a cool reception in Beijing, where he stops on his way to Hanoi. On February 7 Kosygin assures a rally in Hanoi that his country will supply North Vietnam with "all necessary assistance if aggressors dare to encroach upon [its] independence and sovereignty."

February 9. Demonstrations in Moscow. Following American bombing raids on North Vietnam February 7, the U.S. embassy in Moscow is attacked by two thousand demonstrators, including many Chinese and Vietnamese students. The rioters throw rocks and bottles of ink at the embassy building, breaking many windows. The Soviet police guarding the embassy do not stop the attack, evoking protests from U.S. ambassador Foy D. Kohler. A

similar demonstration by about two thousand Soviet, Asian, African, and Latin American students takes place at the U.S. embassy March 4. The students break through police barricades and storm the compound in protest against American air strikes on North Vietnam. The police, who number six hundred, are forced to call in five hundred army troops to quell the rioting.

March 26. Moscow-Hanoi Agreement. The Soviet Communist Party Central Committee ratifies a military aid agreement between the Soviet Union and North Vietnam aimed at "repelling aggression on the part of the United States imperialism." The Soviet Union, China, and North Vietnam April 10 reject an offer made by President Johnson April 7 for unconditional talks to end the Vietnam War in conjunction with a U.S.-financed Southeast Asian economic development program. Moscow and Hanoi issue a joint communiqué April 18 threatening to send Soviet troops to Vietnam if the United States "intensifies" its aggressive military action.

May 6. U.S. Trade Study Findings. A twelve-member committee appointed by President Johnson to assess the possibility of increased trade with the Soviet Union and Eastern Europe recommends easing existing trade restrictions.

May 7. Soviet-Chinese Thrusts. At a Moscow rally celebrating the anniversary of V-E Day, Premier Kosygin, referring to the Chinese Communists, states that "some people contend that only a new world war can bring about the unity and solidarity of the ... international Communist movement." He adds: "We decisively reject such a position." On May 9 the Beijing *People's Daily* accuses Soviet leaders of "colluding with the United States aggressors and plotting to sell out the basic interests of the people of Vietnam and of all other countries, including the Soviet Union."

July 13. Disarmament Talks to Reconvene. President Johnson announces that the Soviet Union is once again willing to start disarmament talks in Geneva. The eighteen-nation UN Disarmament Committee is reconvened in Geneva July 27.

September 6. India Invades Pakistan. Indian troops invade West Pakistan, ostensibly to relieve pressure from Indian forces fighting Pakistani units on the border at Kashmir. In a September 7 Tass statement, the Soviet Union urges India and Pakistan to end the conflict and offers to mediate a peace settlement.

October 2. Soviet Economic Changes. The Supreme Soviet approves a series of domestic economic measures that centralize the administration of the economy. The moves are interpreted as an effort to revamp Khrushchev's system of regional economic councils.

December 6. Kosygin Attacks U.S. "Militarism." In a *New York Times* interview, Premier Kosygin accuses U.S. government officials of "trying to build up tensions, to create an atmosphere conducive to war." He maintains that American actions prevent the Soviet Union from reducing its military budget.

December 9. Mikoyan Steps Down. Anastas Mikoyan announces his resignation as president of the Presidium of the USSR Supreme Soviet. He is replaced by Nikolai Podgorny. Health problems are cited as the reason for Mikoyan's resignation.

1966

January 10. Declaration of Tashkent. Indian prime minister Lal Bahadur Shastri and Pakistani president Mohammed Ayub Khan sign the Declaration of Tashkent, ending the four-month border conflict between India and Pakistan. The negotiations, which began January 4, were mediated by Premier Kosygin. On January 11, while still in the capital of Uzbekistan, Prime Minister Shastri dies of a heart attack.

March 19. New Cultural Agreement. U.S. and Soviet officials sign a new agreement on cultural, scientific, educational, and technical exchanges extending to 1967.

March 22. Soviet Letter Attacks China. A letter reportedly written by the Central Committee to the Communist parties of Eastern Europe is published by the West German newspaper *Die Welt*. An English translation appears two days later in the *New York Times*. The letter states there is "every reason to assert that it is one of the goals of the policy of the Chinese leadership on the Vietnam question to originate a military conflict between the USSR and the United States . . . so that they may, as they say themselves, 'sit on the mountain and watch the fight of the tigers.'" The letter criticizes China for a wide range of transgressions, including provoking Sino-Soviet border conflicts.

March 23. China Rejects Soviet Invitation. China refuses to attend the Twenty-third Congress of the Communist Party of the Soviet Union. The Chinese announcement, referring to Moscow's anti-Chinese letter, states that "since you have gone so far, the Chinese Communist Party . . . cannot send its delegation to attend this congress of yours."

March 29-April 8. Soviet Party Congress. The Twenty-third Congress of the Communist Party of the Soviet Union convenes in Moscow, the first under the leadership of party chief Leonid Brezhnev. Brezhnev calls for international communist unity despite the Sino-Soviet split. Brezhnev also announces that the Presidium will once again be called the "Politburo," and the title of the Communist party first secretary will revert to "general secretary." Nikolai Podgorny is replaced on the Secretariat by Brezhnev's close associate Andrei Kirilenko. Premier Kosygin announces a new Five-Year Plan. He outlines goals in Soviet economic development while enumerating advances made since 1928, the date of the First Five-Year Plan under Joseph Stalin. These develop-

ments were regarded in the West as a confirmation that the Soviet leadership had halted Khrushchev's de-Stalinization campaign.

April 27. Gromyko Meets Pope Paul VI. Soviet foreign minister Andrei Gromyko confers with Pope Paul VI in the Vatican, thereby becoming the highest-ranking Soviet official to have a papal audience. Gromyko also meets with Italian government leaders.

May 7. Ceausescu on Foreign Policy. Romanian general secretary Nicolae Ceausescu, speaking on the forty-fifth anniversary of the Romanian Communist party, asserts Romania's national sovereignty and foreign policy independence. Ceausescu declares his intention of improving relations with Western European countries. General Secretary Brezhnev visits Bucharest May 10-13, reportedly in response to the speech.

May 10-18. Kosygin in Egypt. Premier Kosygin travels to Cairo to confer with Egyptian president Gamal Abdel Nasser. The leaders issue a joint communiqué assailing U.S. policy in the Middle East, and Kosygin urges Nasser to improve ties with Syria.

June 20-July 1. De Gaulle in USSR. French president Charles de Gaulle visits the Soviet Union in an attempt to improve Franco-Soviet relations and to reduce postwar tension between East and West. De Gaulle, a highly honored Western leader in the Soviet Union, is allowed to stay at the Kremlin.

July 4-6. Warsaw Pact Summit. Leaders of the Warsaw Pact countries meet in Bucharest. Two statements are issued on the content of the meeting, the first outlines a promise to send "volunteers" to North Vietnam if so requested by Hanoi. The second calls for a general European conference on security in Europe and increased cooperation among nations.

August 29. Anti-Soviet Rally. Thousands of Red Guards march past the Soviet embassy in Beijing in an all-day demonstration against "revisionism." Although the parade is well disciplined, Chinese soldiers and police guard the building against possible attack.

October 7. Johnson on Improved Relations. President Johnson discusses ways to improve U.S.-Soviet relations. During a speech at the National Editorial Writers' Conference, he suggests reducing the number of both U.S. and Soviet troops in Germany and increasing U.S. trade with Eastern Europe.

October 13. Kosygin Accuses China. Premier Kosygin, in a speech in Sverdlovsk, accuses China of blocking efforts by socialist countries to provide material assistance to North Vietnam.

November 4. Commercial Aviation Pact. Soviet and American officials sign an agreement providing direct air service between Moscow and New York.

November 21. Sino-Soviet Border Tension. The *New York Times* reports that Soviet diplomats openly discussed with American officials the growing concern of

Moscow over a nuclear-armed China. According to the *Times*, a U.S. official described recent talks between Secretary of State Rusk and Foreign Minister Gromyko as the "most direct, honest, objective, and non-ideological in several years." The official added, "Mr. Gromyko made clear that the break with China is quite fundamental and that Russia is now more interested than ever in settling other outstanding issues."

December 1-9. Kosygin in France. Premier Kosygin visits France to improve Franco-Soviet cooperation. On December 6 he tells reporters in Lyons that he sees a "community of interests" between the United States and the Soviet Union, but he adds: "The United States is bombing defenseless people in Vietnam. We don't see any indication of the way the United States is going to end the war. If it were ended, relations would improve."

December 15. Soviets Increase Defense Spending. The Soviet Union announces it will increase its defense spending in 1967 by 8.2 percent because of "aggressive" U.S. policies, especially in Vietnam. American officials indicate, however, that the increases in Soviet military spending were prompted primarily by tensions between the Soviet Union and China.

1967

January 25. Soviets, Chinese Clash in Moscow. China protests to the Kremlin that Chinese students in Moscow were attacked "without provocation" by Soviet soldiers when they sought to place a wreath at the Lenin Mausoleum. The Soviet government accuses the students of provoking the "wild scene."

January 27. Space Treaty Signed. At simultaneous ceremonies in Washington, London, and Moscow, representatives from sixty countries sign a treaty banning the orbiting of nuclear or other mass-destruction weapons. The treaty takes effect October 10, 1967, upon ratification by the United States, the Soviet Union, Great Britain, and eight other countries.

January 28. Anti-Soviet Demonstrations in China. Chinese soldiers take part in an enormous demonstration outside the Soviet embassy in Beijing. The troops wield rifles and bayonets in the third demonstration in as many days. The embassy's walls are plastered with posters reading "Shoot Brezhnev" and "Fry Kosygin." When the demonstrators return January 29, the Soviet government declares that it will take "necessary measures if the Chinese authorities fail to provide normal conditions for the activity of the Soviet representation." The demonstrations cease shortly afterward.

January 30. Kennan on U.S.-Soviet Relations. Former U.S. ambassador to the Soviet Union George F. Kennan tells the Senate Foreign Relations Committee that the irreparable disunity in the communist world presents the United States with an opportunity to take "greatly excit-

ing" steps to improve U.S.-Soviet relations.

February 4. Moscow Warns China. In a formal note, Moscow demands that China stop vilifying the Soviet Union and humiliating Soviet citizens in Beijing. The Soviet note coincides with an evacuation of most of the Soviet diplomatic staff and their dependents from China. By February 7 it is reported that the remaining diplomats are virtual prisoners within their compound because of China's refusal to guarantee their safety outside the area.

February 11. Consular Agreement Abrogated. Beijing radio reports termination of the consular agreement between the Soviet Union and China. Travel without visas to and from the two countries will no longer be permitted.

March 2. Soviets Willing on Arms. President Johnson reveals a communiqué from Premier Kosygin stating Moscow's willingness to discuss arms limitations.

March 16. U.S.-Soviet Treaty Approved. The U.S. Senate ratifies, by a vote of 66-28, a consular treaty with the Soviet Union signed in 1964. The treaty specifies the conditions under which each country may set up and operate consulates in the other.

April 11. Grechko Gains Post. Tass announces that Marshal Andrei Grechko has been appointed Soviet defense minister. Grechko succeeds Marshal Rodion Malinovsky.

May 18. Andropov to Head KGB. Yuri V. Andropov replaces V. E. Semichastny as chairman of the Soviet Committee for State Security (KGB).

May 24-30. Prelude to War. Tension increases in the Middle East as Arab armies are massed along Israel's borders. The United Arab Republic threatens to blockade Israel's shipping in the Gulf of Aqaba. At a UN Security Council emergency session, the Soviet delegate supports the Arab position on the basis of Israel's "provocative" stance.

June 5. Six-Day War. Israeli warplanes and troops attack Arab forces in the Sinai Peninsula and Jerusalem. On June 7, with its forces in control of the Gaza strip, Jerusalem, and much of the Sinai, Israel announces that it will accept a UN cease-fire if the Arabs do the same. Jordan accepts immediately; Egypt accepts June 8. Fighting between Israel and Syria, however, continues until June 10, when the two nations sign a cease-fire agreement after Israeli forces capture the Golan Heights. During the fighting, the United States pledges to remain neutral while the USSR denounces Israel as the aggressor June 6. The Soviet Union breaks diplomatic ties with Israel June 10 and pledges assistance to Arab states if Israel refuses to withdraw from conquered territory. Israel announces June 12 that it will not withdraw. By June 13 Bulgaria, Czechoslovakia, Poland, Hungary, and Yugoslavia also sever ties with Israel.

June 14. Soviet UN Resolution. The UN Security Council rejects a Soviet resolution calling for denunciation of Israel and the withdrawal of its troops behind the

1949 armistice lines. On the same date Israeli sources report that Moscow has resumed sending military aid to Egypt and Syria, presumably to replace arms lost during the conflict with Israel.

June 17. China Explodes Hydrogen Bomb. Two years and eight months after its first test of a nuclear device, China announces detonation of the country's first hydrogen bomb.

June 19. Johnson and Kosygin on the Middle East. President Johnson in a nationally televised speech sets forth five points for peace in the Middle East: recognition of the right of each country's existence, just treatment of Arab refugees, freedom of innocent maritime passage, arms limitation, and guaranteed territorial integrity for each Middle East country. Meanwhile, at the United Nations, Premier Kosygin calls for the condemnation of Israel, the withdrawal of Israeli forces from occupied Arab lands, and Israeli reparations to Syria, Jordan, and Egypt.

June 23-25. Glassboro Summit. Premier Kosygin and President Johnson meet at Glassboro State College in New Jersey to discuss the Middle East, Vietnam, arms control, and nuclear proliferation. President Johnson suggested the meeting after Kosygin had arrived in New York June 17 to address a special session of the UN General Assembly. The site was chosen because of its location halfway between New York and Washington. The meeting is the first between the two leaders. After the talks Johnson states, "No agreement is readily in sight on the Middle Eastern crisis and our well-known differences over Vietnam continue." Kosygin, at a televised news conference in New York, emphasizes that Israel must withdraw to the 1949 armistice lines before progress toward peace in the Middle East can be achieved.

September 8. Rusk on ABM. Secretary of State Rusk states that the lack of U.S.-Soviet cooperation in limiting nuclear missiles may force the United States to build an antiballistic missile (ABM) defense system.

November 3-7. Bolshevik Revolution Celebrated. The Soviet Union engages in a series of festivities marking the fiftieth anniversary of the Bolshevik Revolution. In a four-and-a-half-hour speech November 3 General Secretary Brezhnev denounces China for disrupting the unity of the world socialist community. Brezhnev also castigates continued U.S. military involvement in Vietnam.

1968

January 5. Dubcek Gains Power. As demands for reform increase in Czechoslovakia, Alexander Dubcek succeeds Antonin Novotny as first secretary of the Czechoslovak Communist party.

January 23. USS Pueblo Seized. North Korean forces board the U.S. Navy intelligence ship *Pueblo* in the Sea of Japan and take the ship and its crew of eighty-three

into a North Korean port. The Defense Department contends that the *Pueblo* was cruising in international waters, but the North Koreans claim the ship was on a spy mission in their territorial waters. The U.S. ambassador to the Soviet Union, Llewellyn E. Thompson, tries to enlist Soviet aid to win the release of the *Pueblo* but is rebuffed. The Soviet government newspaper *Izvestia* January 26 accuses President Johnson of manipulating the *Pueblo* incident to justify building up U.S. military forces in the area. Eleven months later, on December 23, the eighty-two surviving crew members are released.

March 23. East European Summit. The leaders of Warsaw Pact nations, excluding Romania, convene in Dresden to discuss the increasing liberalization in Czechoslovakia since the ouster of Czech Communist party head Antonin Novotny in January. Novotny's successor, Alexander Dubcek, is pressed to reverse the trends of democratization.

April 2-7. Kosygin in Iran. Premier Kosygin pays a state visit to Iran to promote bilateral economic cooperation.

June 4. Johnson in Glassboro. President Johnson delivers the commencement address at Glassboro State College in New Jersey, site of a June 1967 summit between himself and Premier Kosygin. The president appeals to Moscow to join in "the spirit of Glassboro" to work for world peace. Johnson focuses on the progress made in U.S.-Soviet relations. On June 12 an *Izvestia* article belittles the "rosy picture" Johnson drew of U.S.-Soviet relations, contending instead that relations are "frozen" until the United States ceases all involvement in Vietnam.

June 13. Consular Pact Ceremony. The instruments of ratification of the U.S.-Soviet consular treaty are formally exchanged in a White House ceremony. The treaty, which is to take effect in thirty days, was ratified by the Presidium of the Supreme Soviet April 26 and by the U.S. Senate March 16, 1967.

July 1. Non-Proliferation Treaty Signed. Sixty-two nations, including the United States, the Soviet Union, and Great Britain, sign a treaty on the nonproliferation of nuclear weapons in ceremonies in the various capitals. The signing follows ratification of the treaty by the United Nations in June.

July 4-10. Nasser in Moscow. United Arab Republic president Gamal Abdel Nasser visits Moscow amid speculation that he is dissatisfied with the level of Soviet military assistance to the Arab world. On July 5 General Secretary Brezhnev promises at a Kremlin luncheon that the Soviet Union will "always side with the Arab nations for the withdrawal of Israeli troops from all the Arab land occupied as a result of the June [1967] aggression."

July 15. Air Service Begins. The first flights take place on the newly inaugurated Moscow to New York commercial airline service. Implementation of the updated agreement, signed November 4, 1966, had been delayed by technical problems and uncertain U.S.-Soviet relations during the interim.

July 14-23. Czech Liberalization. The continuing liberalization in Czechoslovakia overseen by Communist party first secretary Alexander Dubcek causes increasing tension between Moscow and Prague. The Soviet Union and its hard-line East European allies—East Germany, Hungary, Bulgaria, and Poland—draft a letter following a summit in Warsaw July 14-15, which calls the Czech liberalization "completely unacceptable." A July 22 *Pravda* article demands that Communist party control be firmly reinstated, in part by reimposing censorship and suppressing "anti-socialist and right-wing" forces. The Soviet Union July 23 announces massive military maneuvers in Czechoslovakia that will continue until August 10. The move is interpreted as an attempt to intimidate Czech authorities.

July 29. Meeting in Cierna. At Prague's request, the entire Politburo of the Soviet Communist party and the Presidium of the Czech Communist party meet under tight security in Cierna, Czechoslovakia, to discuss the Czech situation.

August 3. Meeting in Bratislava. As a ratification of the recent meeting in Cierna, the East European allies of Moscow, along with Soviet and Czech leaders, meet in Bratislava, Czechoslovakia, and accept the Soviet position that Prague be allowed to continue in its liberalization experiment within limits. Immediately preceding the Bratislava meeting the Czech Foreign Ministry announces that all Soviet troops on maneuvers have left the country. Reportedly, the Czech government made a few concessions to Moscow, including the establishment of an "advisory council" to diminish critical news reporting.

August 9-11 and 15-17. Tito and Ceausescu in Prague. Yugoslav president Josip Broz Tito and Romanian president Nicolae Ceausescu make separate visits to Czechoslovakia. Both leaders endorse the attempt by Czech Communist party leader Alexander Dubcek and his supporters to follow an independent socialist course.

August 20-21. Warsaw Pact Invades Czechoslovakia. Shortly before midnight Soviet tanks and troops supported by forces of East Germany, Poland, Hungary, and Bulgaria cross the Czech border. The Warsaw Pact force gains control of most of the country by morning. Leading members of the liberalization movement are seized and taken to Moscow for consultations. During the following week, the number of Warsaw Pact troops in Czechoslovakia increases from the initial invasion force of 200,000 to 650,000. The intervention, which encounters minimal armed resistance from the Czech population, ends Czechoslovakia's period of liberalization known as the "Prague Spring." President Johnson denounces the invasion August 21 but admits that there is no "safe" action the United States can take. The UN Security Council supports a resolution condemning the occupation and call-

ing for the removal of Warsaw Pact forces. The resolution is vetoed by the Soviet Union. A secret congress of the Czech Communist party is held August 21-23, which elects a new leadership.

August 27. Changes in Czechoslovakia. The reversing of liberalization in Czechoslovakia begins with the return to Prague from Moscow of Czech president Ludvik Svoboda and first secretary Alexander Dubcek. The leaders announce an agreement with Moscow that results in several actions. A new Presidium of the Czech Communist party is elected September 1, superseding the secret congress results of August 23. On September 4 press censorship and disbanding of noncommunist organizations are implemented.

September 6. Kuznetsov in Prague. Soviet first deputy foreign minister Vasily Kuznetsov visits Prague unexpectedly to mediate differences in the implementation of the Czech-Soviet agreement on restructuring the Communist government in Prague. A translation of the agreement is published September 8 in the West by the *New York Times.*

September 26. Brezhnev Doctrine. *Pravda* advances a new, ideological argument to justify the invasion of Czechoslovakia by the Warsaw Pact nations. The newspaper says, in effect, that the world socialist community has a right to intervene when socialism comes under attack in a fraternal socialist country. It denies that this in any way violates Czechoslovakia's "real sovereignty." The article asserts that "world Socialism is indivisible, and its defense is the common cause of all Communists." The article, written by the publication's ideological specialist, also states that "each Communist party is responsible not only to its own people, but also to all the Socialist countries, to the entire Communist movement." The doctrine of "limited sovereignty" soon receives elaboration from top Soviet officials and subsequently comes to be known as the "Brezhnev Doctrine."

October 16. Kosygin in Prague. Premier Kosygin flies to Prague to sign a treaty concluded in Moscow October 3-4, authorizing the stationing of Soviet troops in Czechoslovakia and abolishing all vestiges of the liberalization program. The treaty is ratified by the Czech National Assembly October 18. Moscow continues its pressure on Czech officials October 19 by insisting that party membership be reduced by purging all liberal elements.

October 28. Demonstrations in Prague. Prague witnesses anti-Soviet demonstrations led by a youthful crowd on the fiftieth anniversary of the Republic of Czechoslovakia. Sporadic demonstrations continue into November, particularly on the anniversary of the Russian Revolution.

November 16. NATO Warns Soviets. After a three-day meeting, the North Atlantic Treaty Organization (NATO) Council of Ministers issues a sharp warning to Moscow that "any Soviet intervention . . . in Europe or in the Mediterranean would create an international crisis with grave consequences." The message is seen as a sign of the Western alliance's increased solidarity in the wake of the Soviet intervention in Czechoslovakia.

1969

January 20. U.S.-Soviet Overtures. President Richard Nixon, who was elected November 5, 1968, calls for a new "era of negotiation" in his inaugural address. On the same day the Soviet Foreign Ministry reaffirms an interest in renewing arms reduction talks that had broken down when Warsaw Pact nations intervened in Czechoslovakia in August 1968.

February 26. Nasser Interviewed. President Gamal Abdel Nasser of Egypt states in a *New York Times* interview that he welcomes Soviet ships in Egyptian ports but his government has not provided naval bases to any country, including the Soviet Union. Nasser says there are fewer than one thousand Soviet advisers in Egypt but that "I am asking for more."

March 2. Sino-Soviet Fighting. Tensions on the Sino-Soviet border erupt into armed conflict when Chinese forces ambush a Soviet company making a routine patrol of Damansky Island in the Ussuri River. During the rest of 1969 there would be more than four hundred skirmishes along the Sino-Soviet border.

April 17. Dubcek Resignation. Alexander Dubcek, the leading figure in the Czech liberalization program, resigns as Czechoslovak Communist party first secretary. His successor, Gustav Husak, states that the change in leadership is in the interest of Czech unity. Husak's appointment is welcomed by Moscow.

July 10. Gromyko Stresses Improved Relations. Soviet foreign minister Gromyko urges closer cooperation with the United States. In a speech to the Supreme Soviet he suggests an exchange of delegations from the Supreme Soviet and the U.S. Congress. Gromyko characterizes Chinese policies toward the Soviet Union, on the other hand, as worse than those "of our most rabid enemies."

September 11. Kosygin Visits China. En route to Moscow after attending the funeral of North Vietnamese leader Ho Chi Minh, who died September 3, Premier Kosygin makes a surprise visit to China. His talks with Premier Zhou Enlai reduce serious Sino-Soviet tensions caused by months of bloody border skirmishes between Soviet and Chinese troops.

September 18. Nixon on Mideast Arms. President Nixon in a speech to the UN General Assembly suggests a Middle East arms curb by the big powers. The Soviet Union rebuffs the suggestion.

October 7. Seabed Pact. The United States and the Soviet Union submit a joint draft to the UN conference of the Committee on Disarmament in Geneva. The pact bans nuclear and other destructive weapons outside a twelve-mile coastal limit as defined in the 1958 Geneva Convention on the Territorial Sea.

October 20. China-USSR Negotiations. Chinese and Soviet foreign ministers open negotiations in Beijing on Sino-Soviet border disputes.

November 17. SALT Meeting. The preliminary round of the Strategic Arms Limitation Talks (SALT) between the United States and Soviet Union opens in Helsinki. The U.S. delegation is led by Gerard Smith and the Soviet delegation is headed by Vladimir Semenov. The talks adjourn December 22.

November 24. Nuclear Non-Proliferation Treaty. Soviet president Nikolai Podgorny and President Nixon sign the nuclear nonproliferation treaty during separate ceremonies in Washington and Moscow. The treaty had been approved by the U.S. Senate March 13.

December 7. Soviet-West German Talks. The Soviet Union accepts West German chancellor Willy Brandt's offer to begin negotiations on a bilateral treaty normalizing relations between the two countries. The Soviet Union states that conditions for approval of the treaty include recognition of East Germany and the exchange of diplomats.

1970

January 13. Soviets Support U.S. Participation. The Soviet Foreign Ministry announces that it favors U.S. participation at a proposed security conference of all European nations.

February 15. Moscow Denies Planning Attack. The Soviet newspaper *Pravda* criticizes Western press predictions of a Soviet attack on China. The article follows a statement by the Soviet news agency Tass describing such predictions as "insinuations" designed to "increase tension" between the Soviet Union and China.

March 19. Soviet Troops in Egypt. Diplomatic observers report that a large number of Soviet troops and antiaircraft missiles have arrived in Cairo.

April 17. SALT Talks Resume in Vienna. Strategic Arms Limitation Talks between the United States and the Soviet Union resume in Vienna. The talks had recessed December 22, 1969.

April 21. Lenin's Centenary. The communist world celebrates the centenary of Lenin's birth.

April 29. Missions for Egypt. The Israeli government says it has evidence to confirm accusations that Soviet pilots are flying missions for the Egyptian air force. Soviet sources deny the accusations.

April 30. United States Invades Cambodia. President Nixon announces in a televised address that U.S. troops have begun an "incursion" into Cambodia designed to disrupt North Vietnamese sanctuaries in that country. The operation draws sharp criticism at home and abroad. American forces are withdrawn from Cambodia June 29.

June 1. Antiaircraft Missiles in Egypt. A *Newsweek*

magazine report alleges that the Soviets have installed twenty-two SAM-3 antiaircraft missile sites in Egypt. Other sites are under construction or planned. Foreign intelligence reports received in Washington June 24 indicate that Soviet pilots have taken over Egypt's air defenses.

June 26. Dubcek Expelled. Alexander Dubcek is expelled from the Czech Communist party. The action is regarded as further retaliation against the liberalization effort in Czechoslovakia.

July 10. Soviets Call for Joint Action. Soviet SALT negotiators reportedly propose that the United States and the Soviet Union agree to "joint retaliatory action" in response to any "provocative" acts or direct attacks by China. The proposal is not disclosed until 1973 and is denied by the Soviets at that time.

July 17. Nasser in Moscow. At the conclusion of a visit to Moscow by Egyptian president Gamal Abdel Nasser, a joint Soviet-Egyptian communiqué is issued calling for a political settlement of the Middle East crisis and accusing Israel of aggression.

August 12. West German-Soviet Treaty. Premier Kosygin and Chancellor Willy Brandt of West Germany sign a treaty in Moscow renouncing the use of force to settle disputes between their countries. The document includes recognition of the long-disputed Polish-East German border at the Oder-Neisse line.

September 25. Soviet Activity in Cuba. The Defense Department discloses the possible building of a Soviet strategic submarine base in Cuba. The suspicions of U.S. officials are aroused when heavy equipment is seen arriving from the Soviet Union. The United States warns Moscow against such a move, but construction efforts are denied in a September 30 *Pravda* commentary.

September 28. Death of Nasser. The president of Egypt, Gamal Abdel Nasser, dies in Cairo. Moscow issues a statement September 29 noting that Nasser's position on the Middle East conflict "will continue to enjoy our utmost support." Vice President Anwar Sadat becomes acting president.

September 30-October 2. Nixon in Yugoslavia. President Nixon becomes the first U.S. president to visit Yugoslavia, where he praises that country's nonaligned stance. Nixon's visit is the first stop of an eight-day, five-nation European tour.

October 8. Solzhenitsyn Wins Nobel. Soviet writer Alexander Solzhenitsyn wins the 1970 Nobel Prize for Literature. The Soviet writers' union October 9 calls the award decision "deplorable." Solzhenitsyn's works are banned in the Soviet Union.

October 25. Ceausescu Visits Washington. At the close of his two-week visit to the United States Romanian president Nicolae Ceausescu confers with President Nixon. The leaders reportedly discuss improving trade relations.

October 29. U.S.-Soviet Space Pact. Soviet and U.S. officials sign the first cooperative space effort agreement. The project involves a joint rendezvous and docking mission in space.

November 22. Sino-Soviet Trade Pact. The Soviet Union and China sign a trade agreement, the first since 1967. The agreement does not seem to be accompanied by a significant lessening of tension between the two countries.

December 15. Polish Worker Unrest. Demonstrations by Polish workers against increases in food prices lead to the resignation of Wladyslaw Gomulka as first secretary of the Polish Communist party. Edward Gierek replaces him. Polish troops are used to put down the unrest, which reportedly results in three hundred deaths.

1971

January 4. Harassment of Diplomats. Soviet diplomats protest harassment of Soviet officials at the United Nations by Americans and announce that the United States should "not expect" the Soviet government to ensure normal working conditions for U.S. diplomats in the Soviet Union. The protest is a response to an injury sustained by an employee of the Soviet mission to the United Nations during demonstrations in New York by members of the Jewish Defense League in late December 1970. In subsequent weeks numerous incidents of harassment of U.S. diplomats occur in Moscow. On July 8 a small bomb explodes outside the Soviet embassy in Washington, an incident for which the United States apologizes. The Jewish Defense League, which had announced January 10 a campaign "to follow, question, and harass" Soviet diplomats in New York, calls off its campaign January 19.

January 15. Aswan Dam Dedicated. Egyptian president Anwar Sadat and Soviet president Nikolai Podgorny dedicate the completed Aswan Dam. Construction of the dam had begun in 1960.

February 25. Nixon Doctrine. President Nixon presents his annual State of the World report to Congress. The speech is construed as a formal enunciation of the "Nixon Doctrine"; namely, that the United States will honor all treaties with its allies, but they will be responsible for supplying their own troops to combat conventional aggression or subversion. Nixon describes U.S.-Soviet relations during his administration as "mixed." He cites positive developments such as advances in SALT talks, the ratification of the seabed and nuclear nonproliferation treaties, negotiations on the Berlin question, and beginnings of joint space cooperation. Obstacles remain over Soviet behavior in the Middle East and Cuba.

March 30-April 9. Soviet Party Congress. Speaking before the Twenty-fourth Congress of the Communist Party of the Soviet Union in Moscow, General Secretary Brezhnev reaffirms a desire for improved relations with the United States. Brezhnev also states that the Soviets oppose Chinese attempts to distort Marxism-Leninism and split the world communist movement. Four new full Politburo members are named—Fëdor Kulakov, Vladimir Shcherbitsky, Dinmukhamed Kunaev, and Viktor Grishin. Kulakov, a member of the Secretariat, had been promoted directly to full Politburo status, while the other three men had been candidate members of the Politburo.

April 6. Ping-Pong Diplomacy. The Chinese government makes a move toward better relations with the United States by inviting the U.S. table tennis team for a visit to begin April 10. A week later President Nixon announces a partial relaxation of the trade embargo with China.

May 14. Brezhnev Proposes Troop Cut Talks. In a speech in Tiflis, General Secretary Brezhnev calls for talks aimed at reducing troop levels in Central Europe. American officials say they favor such talks as long as they have a reasonable chance of success. On June 4 NATO foreign ministers issue a communiqué saying they welcome such talks but are in need of "further clarification" from the Soviets about their nature.

May 20. SALT Negotiators to Discuss ABM Issue. The Soviet Union and the United States announce that representatives at the SALT talks in Vienna will begin negotiations on a pact to limit antiballistic missile (ABM) systems.

May 27. Egyptian-Soviet Treaty. Egypt and the Soviet Union sign a fifteen-year treaty of friendship and cooperation.

June 11. Brezhnev Proposes Naval Talks. General Secretary Brezhnev proposes talks aimed at limiting the naval operations of the superpowers.

July 4. Egyptian-Soviet Joint Communiqué. Egypt and the Soviet Union issue a joint communiqué declaring that the Suez Canal will be opened only after Israel withdraws all of its forces from Arab territory.

July 15. Nixon to Visit China. President Nixon accepts an invitation to visit the People's Republic of China in 1972. He emphasizes that the trip will in no way alter existing relations with any other country. A July 25 *Pravda* article warns the United States against using its contacts with Beijing to pressure the Soviet Union.

August 2. Soviets Expelled from the Sudan. Soviet officials are ordered out of the Sudan following a coup that almost topples Premier Mohammed Gaafar Nimeiry. The officials are accused of influencing the coup.

August 9. Indian-Soviet Pact. During a trip to New Delhi Soviet foreign minister Gromyko signs a twenty-year treaty of peace, friendship, and cooperation with India.

August 28. Brezhnev on China. Despite a recent escalation of verbal attacks against China in the Soviet press, General Secretary Brezhnev states that he does not blame China for the fact that the border talks are "going slowly" and promises the Soviets will "continue to display a constructive and patient approach."

September 11. Khrushchev Dies. The former head of the Soviet Union, Nikita S. Khrushchev, dies in Moscow at age seventy-seven. His death is ignored by the Soviet press except for one-sentence announcements in *Pravda* and *Izvestia* two days later.

October 12. Nixon to Visit USSR. President Nixon announces a working summit in the Soviet Union planned for May 1972.

October 27-November 2. Tito in United States. Josip Broz Tito, president of Yugoslavia, visits the United States. Nixon strongly commends the Yugoslavian nonaligned stance in the world socialist movement.

December 3. India Invades Pakistan. Fortified by Soviet military aid and a new twenty-year treaty of friendship with the Soviet Union, India invades East Pakistan in support of the Bangladesh rebels who had been defeated by Pakistan in April. Beijing radio accuses Moscow of "supporting, encouraging and approving India's aggression against Pakistan." The United States expresses opposition to an increased Soviet naval presence in the area. Hostilities end December 16 with the surrender of Pakistani troops and the creation of the independent Bangladesh nation.

1972

January 28. Gromyko on Nixon's China Trip. Soviet foreign minister Gromyko, speaking at a news conference in Tokyo, tells reporters that the Soviet Union does not object to improved Sino-U.S. relations provided they do not "affect adversely the safety and interests of the Soviet Union."

February 21. Nixon Arrives in China. President Nixon arrives in China for a historic seven-day visit. It is the first time an American head of state has ever visited China, and the trip caps two years of negotiations. At the conclusion of talks in Shanghai February 27 between President Nixon and Premier Zhou Enlai, the United States and China issue a joint communiqué that pledges both sides to work for a "normalization" of relations. *Pravda* expresses displeasure and contends that the United States is taking advantage of the Sino-Soviet rift.

April 11. U.S.-Soviet Cooperation. The United States offers to sell grain to the Soviet Union on three-year credit terms. The offer is extended by Secretary of Agriculture Earl Butz in Moscow. On the same day Soviet and U.S. officials sign an agreement extending and augmenting a fourteen-year-old cultural, educational, and scientific exchange program.

April 20-24. Kissinger in Moscow. Henry A. Kissinger, national security adviser to the president, visits Moscow to prepare for Nixon's forthcoming visit.

May 8. United States Mines Haiphong. President Nixon, faced with a worsening situation in South Vietnam, orders the mining of all North Vietnamese harbors. The move risks a direct confrontation with both China and the Soviet Union, whose ships are supplying Hanoi. No confrontation occurs, and Nixon's upcoming trip to Moscow is not jeopardized, despite indications of disagreement among Soviet leaders about whether to proceed with the summit.

May 22-30. Summit in Moscow. President Nixon travels to Moscow for a summit meeting with Soviet leaders. Among the many topics discussed are a European security conference and mutual balanced force reductions in Eastern Europe. Nixon and General Secretary Brezhnev sign the first Strategic Arms Limitation Treaty (SALT I) May 26. On the same day Brezhnev is reported to have assured Nixon that he would press Hanoi to settle the war in Vietnam. In a May 28 address on Soviet television, President Nixon says that as "great powers" the Soviet Union and the United States will "sometimes be competitors, but [we] need never be enemies." Nixon visits Kiev May 29 before flying to Iran May 30 for talks with the shah. He returns to the United States June 1 after a stop in Poland.

June 3. Quadripartite Berlin Agreement. The four countries that have responsibility for Berlin—the Soviet Union, the United States, France, and Great Britain—sign the "final protocol" of the Quadripartite Agreement on Berlin. The document, which is not a treaty, is expected to increase the frequency and efficiency of travel to and from West Berlin. The groundwork for the final protocol was laid in September 1971.

July 8. U.S.-Soviet Grain Deal. After months of negotiations, the Soviet Union and the United States agree on a three-year grain deal under which the Soviets will buy about $750 million worth of U.S. wheat, corn, and other grains. It is to date the largest commercial agreement between the two powers.

July 18. Sadat Expels Soviet Advisers. President Anwar Sadat orders all Soviet military advisers and experts out of Egypt and places all Soviet bases and equipment under Egyptian control. Sadat says in a four-hour speech July 24 that his decision was prompted by the Soviet Union's reticence in selling Egypt arms.

July 20-August 1. U.S. Trade Officials in Moscow. The U.S. government dispatches a thirty-member delegation, including Secretary of Commerce Peter G. Peterson, to Moscow to initiate discussion on U.S.-Soviet trade.

August 3. Restrictions on Jewish Emigration. The Soviet government announces an exit visa fee for Jewish citizens wishing to emigrate. According to Soviet officials, the fees are to reimburse the state for educational funds spent on its citizens. Fees range from $4,400 to $37,000, depending on the amount of education received.

September 5. Soviet-Syrian Security Cooperation. Syria and the Soviet Union agree to new security arrangements. The Soviet Union will improve naval facilities in two Syrian ports for Soviet use, and Syria will receive jet fighters and air defense missiles.

September 9. Soviets Continue Asian Buildup. Officials in Washington are quoted as saying the Soviets recently added several mechanized divisions to their troops on the Sino-Soviet border, increasing their strength in the area to nearly one-third of the Soviet army.

September 27. Jackson on Exit Fees. Sen. Henry M. Jackson, D-Wash., says he will introduce an amendment to the East-West trade relations act that would link trade concessions to the Soviet Union with "the freedom to emigrate without the payment of prohibitive taxes amounting to ransom." Administration officials maintain that "quiet diplomacy" is the best way to solve this problem.

October 2-3. Nixon-Gromyko Talks. In Washington President Nixon and Foreign Minister Gromyko discuss a wide range of topics. They sign documents implementing the SALT I arms accords concluded at the Moscow summit in May.

October 4. Jackson-Vanik Amendment. Sen. Henry M. Jackson, D-Wash., and seventy-five cosponsors introduce an amendment to the East-West trade bill, barring most-favored-nation status to nations that restrict emigration of their citizens. Rep. Charles A. Vanik, D-Ohio, introduces a similar measure in the House.

October 18. U.S.-Soviet Trade Pact Signed. Soviet and American officials sign a three-year trade relations agreement that includes a settlement of Soviet World War II lend-lease debt and a Nixon administration promise to push Congress to approve most-favored-nation status for the Soviet Union, despite congressional attempts to link trade concessions to a relaxation of Soviet restrictions on Jewish emigration. President Nixon promises to ask for credits for the Soviets from the Export-Import Bank as well. Trade between the United States and the Soviet Union in the next three years is projected to reach $1.5 billion.

November 7. Nixon Reelected. Richard Nixon easily defeats Democrat George McGovern to win another term as president.

November 21. SALT II Negotiations Begin. The second set of SALT negotiations begins in Geneva with the purpose of expanding the SALT I agreement.

December 18-30. Bombing of North Vietnam. American forces resume bombing North Vietnam above the twentieth parallel after peace negotiations in Paris are broken off. The massive air attacks against Hanoi and Haiphong cause many casualties and extensive damage. The White House announces December 30 that the bombings have been halted and that peace talks with North Vietnam will resume in Paris on January 8, 1973.

December 21-23. Fiftieth Anniversary of USSR. The

fiftieth anniversary of the founding of the Soviet state is celebrated in Moscow. General Secretary Brezhnev delivers a lengthy speech in which he condemns the U.S. bombing in Vietnam. He also accuses China of "undisguised sabotage" of Soviet peace efforts and of attempts to "split" the world communist movement.

1973

January 27. Peace Agreement Signed. The United States, North Vietnam, South Vietnam, and the Viet Cong sign a peace agreement in Paris. Although the pact calls for a cease-fire in Vietnam, it does not end the fighting in Laos or Cambodia. On January 23 President Nixon had announced the completion of the agreement.

March 11-14. Soviet-U.S. Trade Talks. Secretary of the Treasury George P. Shultz discusses U.S.-Soviet trade with General Secretary Brezhnev in Moscow. On March 15, Sen. Henry M. Jackson, D-Wash., formally reintroduces his amendment to the East-West trade relations bill to "block trade concessions until free emigration [is] assured."

March 20. Export-Import Loan Agreements. The Soviet Union Foreign Trade Bank is granted its first loan from the Export-Import Bank. The Soviet Union receives $101.2 million in direct loans, while American banks promise another $101.2 million for the purchase of U.S. industrial equipment.

April 27. Politburo Shake-Up. In a move viewed as bolstering General Secretary Brezhnev's authority, the Central Committee endorses the ouster from the Politburo of two of his conservative critics—Petr Shelest and Gennady Voronov. The Central Committee simultaneously grants full Politburo membership to Andrei Grechko, defense minister; Andrei Gromyko, foreign minister; and Yuri Andropov, chairman of the KGB.

May 18-22. Brezhnev in Bonn. General Secretary Brezhnev visits West Germany and holds extensive talks with Chancellor Willy Brandt. They sign several accords May 19, including a ten-year economic cooperation agreement.

June 7. Helsinki Preparatory Talks Close. Six months of preparatory talks for the Conference on Security and Cooperation in Europe (CSCE) close in Helsinki after the agenda is finalized. The conference agenda includes European security and scientific cooperation. The United States receives reluctant agreement from the Soviet delegation for the inclusion of discussions on "freer exchange of people, ideas, and information."

June 16-25. Summit in United States. General Secretary Brezhnev arrives in Washington for talks with President Nixon. The two leaders sign agreements providing for cooperation on the development of atomic energy and for the exchange of information on agriculture, transportation, oceanography, and commerce. They also pledge to

accelerate the SALT talks with the goal of completing a new treaty by the end of 1974.

July 3-7. Opening of CSCE in Helsinki. The first session of the Conference on Security and Cooperation in Europe (CSCE) opens in Helsinki. Thirty-three European nations plus the United States and Canada send representatives. Foreign Minister Gromyko represents the USSR.

August 21. Sakharov Warnings. In a discussion with Western media, Andrei Sakharov, a well-known Soviet dissident and physicist, warns of the dangers of accepting détente on Soviet terms. He says the Jackson-Vanik amendment to the East-West Trade Relations Act does not go far enough to pressure the Kremlin to improve its human rights policies.

September 9. Reaction to Anti-Sakharov Letters. In response to a Soviet press campaign against Andrei Sakharov, the U.S. National Academy of Sciences says that American scientists will not continue joint research projects with their Soviet counterparts unless the harassment is stopped. The Soviet campaign, which consists of a series of accusatory letters in Soviet publications, began August 29 with a letter written by thirty-nine academicians of the Soviet Academy of Sciences, of which Sakharov is a member. The letter accuses Sakharov of joining "the most reactionary imperialist circles."

September 29. Nixon-Gromyko Talks. President Nixon and Foreign Minister Gromyko meet in Washington. Nixon is believed to have assured Gromyko that he would continue to pressure Congress to grant the Soviet Union most-favored-nation status. They also discuss mutual balanced force reductions and SALT II.

October 1-3. Shultz in Moscow. Treasury Secretary Shultz notes at the conclusion of talks on bilateral trade in Moscow that expanded trade with the Soviet Union is held up by Congress's refusal to grant most-favored-nation status to the Soviet Union as well as by the Soviets' unwillingness to make further concessions on Jewish emigration.

October 6. War in the Middle East. On the Jewish High Holy Day of Yom Kippur Egyptian forces attack Israeli units across the Suez Canal and Syria attacks the Golan Heights. Israeli forces counterattack on October 7. They push the Syrians back but are forced to retreat in the Sinai.

October 15. Resupply Efforts. The United States announces that it is resupplying Israel with military equipment to counterbalance a "massive airlift" to Egypt by the Soviet Union. Meanwhile, Israeli forces have recaptured lost territory in the Sinai and driven deep into Syrian territory.

October 17. Sadat's Peace Proposal. Egyptian president Anwar Sadat, in an open letter to President Nixon, proposes an immediate cease-fire with Israel on the condition that Israel withdraw to pre-1967 boundaries.

October 18. Arab Oil Embargo. After President Nixon

asks Congress to appropriate $2.2 billion in emergency military aid to Israel, Libya cuts off all oil shipments to the United States. On October 20 Saudi Arabia cuts off all oil exports to the United States. By October 21 all other Arab oil exporters join the boycott.

October 20. Kissinger in Moscow. Secretary of State Henry A. Kissinger arrives in Moscow for talks with Brezhnev on restoring peace to the Middle East.

October 21. U.S.-Soviet Joint UN Resolution. The United States and the Soviet Union present a joint resolution to the UN Security Council calling for a cease-fire in the Middle East and for implementation of a Security Council resolution calling for Israeli withdrawal from lands it has occupied since the 1967 war. The proposal, formulated during Secretary of State Kissinger's trip to Moscow, is adopted by the Security Council October 22.

October 22. Cease-fire in the Middle East. A cease-fire takes effect on the Egyptian-Israeli front, but sporadic fighting continues.

October 23. Security Council Vote. The UN Security Council votes to reaffirm the Middle East cease-fire, requests Egypt and Israel to return to the cease-fire line established the day before, and asks that UN observers be stationed along the Israeli-Egyptian cease-fire line.

October 24. Sadat Appeal. Egyptian president Anwar Sadat asks the United States and the Soviet Union to send troops for supervision of the cease-fire. The White House announces it will not send forces.

October 25. Military Alert. President Nixon orders a worldwide U.S. military alert as tension mounts over whether the Soviet Union will intervene in the Middle East crisis. Secretary of State Kissinger says in a news conference that the U.S. move is inspired by intelligence reports that the Soviet Union may attempt to airlift troops into Egypt, ostensibly as a peace-keeping force. To avert a U.S.-USSR confrontation in the Middle East, the UN Security Council votes to establish an emergency supervisory force to observe the cease-fire.

October 27. Direct Negotiations. The United States announces that Egypt and Israel have agreed to negotiate directly on implementing the cease-fire.

November 11. Cease-fire Signed. Israel and Egypt sign a cease-fire accord, drawn up by Secretary of State Kissinger and Egyptian president Anwar Sadat November 7 in Cairo.

December 11. Trade Bill Passes. The House passes the foreign trade bill, which includes the Jackson-Vanik amendment "barring most-favored-nation treatment for any nation that restricts emigration" for its citizens. The amendment is included over the objections of President Nixon, who had virtually assured the Soviet Union of most-favored-nation status. The Senate has yet to act on the bill.

December 21. Mideast Peace Conference. The first Arab-Israeli peace conference opens in Geneva, with Is-rael, Egypt, Jordan, the United States, and the Soviet Union taking part. Syria boycotts the conference.

1974

January 2. Gulag Archipelago *Condemned.* Tass responds with virulent criticism after Alexander Solzhenitsyn's book *The Gulag Archipelago, 1918-1956* is published in the West. In late December, the *New York Times* had published excerpts of the book, which describes the secret police and labor camp systems in the Soviet Union.

January 17. Suez Disengagement Pact Signed. Israel and Egypt sign accords on a disengagement of forces in the Suez. According to the agreement, the Egyptian and Israeli forces along the Suez Canal will be separated to specific disengagement zones. The pullback is to be completed in forty days, with a UN truce force acting as a buffer.

February 13. Solzhenitsyn Deported. Soviet author Alexander Solzhenitsyn is stripped of his Soviet citizenship and deported to West Germany following his arrest in Moscow. Soviet authorities take action after the widely publicized appearance of Solzhenitsyn's book *The Gulag Archipelago, 1918-1956* in the West.

March 11. Credits to Soviet Union Halted. A legal technicality causes a temporary cutoff of Export-Import Bank credits to the Soviet Union, Poland, Romania, and Yugoslavia. The action coincides with continuing controversy in the United States over whether to link favorable trade treatment for the Soviets with the Jewish emigration issue.

March 24-28. Kissinger in Moscow. Secretary of State Kissinger holds talks with Soviet leaders in Moscow in anticipation of President Nixon's upcoming visit to the Soviet Union. The talks reportedly fail to achieve Kissinger's aim of "concrete progress" on SALT II and East-West mutual troop reductions.

April 7. Nixon Meets Podgorny in Paris. President Nixon and Soviet president Nikolai Podgorny discuss the forthcoming Moscow summit and SALT II. Both are in Paris attending the funeral of French president Georges Pompidou.

April 12. Gromyko in Washington. After an appearance at the United Nations, Foreign Minister Gromyko visits Washington. His discussions with President Nixon and Secretary of State Kissinger focus on the Middle East and SALT II.

April 18. Egyptian Arms. President Anwar Sadat announces that Egypt no longer will rely solely on the Soviet Union for arms. Egypt had restored diplomatic relations with the United States February 28 after a seven-year break.

May 15. Sino-Soviet Trade Agreement. Despite an increase in the verbal hostility between the Soviet Union and China, the two nations sign a trade agreement that calls for a 12 percent increase in trade for 1974.

May 18. India Nuclear Test. After a successful detonation of a nuclear device, India denies any intention to use nuclear technology for military purposes. Prime Minister Indira Gandhi declares, "We are firmly committed only to the peaceful uses of atomic energy."

June 27-July 3. Third Summit. President Nixon and General Secretary Brezhnev sign a series of limited agreements on nuclear weapons in Moscow during their third summit meeting. They also issue a joint communiqué that states their commitment to negotiate a new interim strategic arms pact. In a Moscow press conference Secretary of State Kissinger blames the Watergate scandal for preventing substantial negotiations between the two leaders. He charges that Nixon's effectiveness as a leader is being impaired. Nixon returns to the United States July 3.

July 15. Cyprus Crisis. The Cypriot National Guard commanded by Greek officers overthrows the president of Cyprus, Archbishop Makarios. The new regime reaffirms a desire for an independent Cyprus, and there is no indication that a union of Cyprus with Greece will be attempted. Turkey, however, claims the coup threatens the well-being of the Turkish Cypriot minority. The Soviet Union supports the Turkish position. On July 20 Turkey invades Cyprus by sea and air. After Turkish forces gain control of part of the island, a UN cease-fire backed by Great Britain and the United States begins July 22.

August 8. Nixon Resigns. In a dramatic television address Richard Nixon announces his resignation from the presidency. Vice President Gerald R. Ford is sworn in as the thirty-eighth president the next day. Soviet reaction emphasizes that U.S.-Soviet relations will continue unchanged. Nixon is portrayed in an August 10 Moscow television program as a victim of political maneuvering and vicious media attacks.

October 23. Kissinger in Moscow. Secretary of State Kissinger visits Moscow as part of a three-week, worldwide diplomatic tour. Kissinger discusses arms limitation, trade, and the Middle East and reports some progress despite key differences. The Soviets are annoyed at U.S. publicity surrounding Soviet assurances to increase Jewish emigration. They also are resentful over the cancellation and only partial restoration of a recent grain deal with the United States. President Ford October 4 postponed a sales agreement for the shipment of 3.2 million tons of grain. On October 19 the Treasury Department announced a new agreement that allowed Moscow to purchase 2.2 million tons of U.S. grain through June 1975.

November 23-24. Vladivostok Summit. President Ford travels to the Soviet Union to sign a tentative agreement to limit the number of all U.S. and Soviet offensive nuclear weapons through 1985. The unexpected agreement provides guidelines to SALT negotiators who are to resume talks in January. Secretary of State Kissinger goes to China November 25 to brief Chinese leaders on the talks.

November 26. Soviets Reject Chinese Offer. Speaking at a rally in Ulan Bator, Mongolia, General Secretary Brezhnev rejects the Chinese offer to negotiate a resolution of the Sino-Soviet border dispute if the Soviets withdraw their troops from regions near the border.

December 20. Foreign Trade Bill Clears. Congress clears the foreign trade bill, which extends greater trade privileges to the Soviet Union in exchange for increased Jewish emigration. The bill clears despite a December 18 Tass statement denying any agreement by the Kremlin to allow freer emigration. The bill passed in the House December 11, 1973, and in the Senate December 13, 1974. President Ford signs the bill into law (PL 93-618) January 3, 1975.

December 30. Brezhnev Cancels Mideast Trip. General Secretary Brezhnev calls off a January visit to the Middle East. No official reason is given. Western speculation about the cause of the cancellation ranges from Brezhnev's health to diplomatic differences between Cairo and Moscow.

1975

January 14. Soviets Cancel Trade Pact. Secretary of State Kissinger announces the Soviet Union's cancellation of the 1972 trade agreement with the United States. The Kremlin objects to recent U.S. legislation that limits credits to the Soviets and grants trade privileges only if the Soviet Union permits freer Jewish emigration. As a result, the Soviet Union will not pay its World War II lend-lease debts, and it will not receive most-favored-nation trade status or Export-Import Bank loans from the United States.

February 18. Egypt Buys Soviet Arms. Egypt confirms it is receiving Soviet arms for the first time since the 1973 Arab-Israeli war.

March 18. Brezhnev Overture. General Secretary Brezhnev reaffirms the Soviet desire for increased international détente. Speaking in Hungary, he emphasizes the need for a successful outcome of the upcoming Conference on Security and Cooperation in Europe (CSCE).

April 16. Removal of Shelepin. Alexander Shelepin, former head of the KGB, is removed from the Politburo. At one time considered a possible challenger to Brezhnev's authority, his influence had diminished since his demotion from the Secretariat in 1967.

April 30. South Vietnam Surrenders. The Vietnam War ends as the South Vietnamese government surrenders to Communist forces, and Viet Cong and North Vietnamese troops enter Saigon.

May 12-14. Mayaguez Incident. The Cambodian government May 12 seizes the American merchant ship *Mayaguez* in the Gulf of Siam. President Ford May 14 sends two hundred U.S. Marines to Cambodia, who rescue the ship and its crew. Tass describes the U.S. action as "a military intervention to rescue the spy ship *Mayaguez* seized earlier in Cambodian waters."

June 10. Schlesinger on Soviet Military. Secretary of Defense James R. Schlesinger at a Senate Armed Services Committee hearing accuses the Soviet Union of building naval facilities in the Somalian port of Berbera on the Gulf of Aden. It is thought the base will facilitate Soviet naval exercises in the Indian Ocean. Tass denies June 12 that the Soviets are building such a facility. On June 20 Schlesinger announces that, according to U.S. intelligence, the Soviet Union has recently deployed intercontinental ballistic missiles (ICBMs) armed for the first time with multiple independently targetable warheads.

June 30. Solzhenitsyn in Washington. In a speech to the AFL-CIO in Washington, Soviet author Alexander Solzhenitsyn warns of the dangers of détente and of making too many concessions to the Soviets. President Ford declines to meet with Solzhenitsyn July 2 because of a busy White House schedule. In a news conference July 16 Secretary of State Kissinger discloses that he and other White House aides believed the meeting would damage U.S.-Soviet relations.

July 10-11. Kissinger-Gromyko Meeting. Secretary of State Kissinger and Foreign Minister Gromyko meet in Geneva to discuss U.S.-Soviet relations, in particular the issues that have stalled SALT II negotiations.

July 17. Apollo-Soyuz Mission. The first joint Soviet-U.S. space exploration project (called the Apollo-Soyuz Test Project), which was initiated by President Nixon and General Secretary Brezhnev at the 1972 Moscow summit, is capped by the successful rendezvous in space of the Apollo and Soyuz spacecrafts.

July 31-August 1. Helsinki Summit. The Conference on Security and Cooperation in Europe (CSCE) holds the largest summit conference in European history in Helsinki. Preparatory talks for the summit began in 1972. The conference culminates August 1 with the signing of a hundred-page declaration (known as the Final Act) by leaders of the thirty-five participating nations. The Final Act's provisions express a desire for cooperation between nations, a permanent peace for Europe, and respect for the boundaries within the European continent. The Final Act is nonbinding and does not have treaty status. Both General Secretary Brezhnev and President Ford participate in the conference. The Helsinki meeting sparks controversy in the West, primarily because opponents consider the Final Act too conciliatory toward the Soviet Union.

August 14. Superpowers on Portugal. In a speech in Birmingham, Alabama, Secretary of State Kissinger objects to Soviet support of the Portuguese premier Vasco Goncalves and the Communist party, which are attempting to impose a Communist-led government. Kissinger states, "The Soviet Union should not assume it has the option, either directly or indirectly, to influence events contrary to the right of the Portuguese people to determine their own future." An August 19 *Pravda* article emphasizes "massive solidarity" with the Communist party in Portugal. On August 29, however, Goncalves is ousted, and a November coup attempt by Communist forces fails. A moderate Socialist, Gen. Antonio Ramalho Eanes, is elected president in June 1976.

September 1. Sinai Pact Signed. In separate ceremonies in Jerusalem and Alexandria, Israeli and Egyptian leaders initial a new Sinai Pact, which provides for Israeli withdrawal from areas of the Sinai and the stationing of U.S. technicians in key locations to monitor the peace.

October 9. Sakharov Wins Nobel. Andrei Sakharov, a leading Soviet physicist and dissident, is awarded the Nobel Peace Prize. The action inspires press attacks on Sakharov in the Soviet Union. Moscow denies Sakharov a visa to attend the ceremonies in Oslo, Norway. Sakharov's wife, Yelena Bonner, participates in the Oslo ceremonies December 10 and accepts the Nobel Prize in his name.

October 20. Soviets Purchase U.S. Grain. A five-year agreement providing for the Soviet purchase of six million to eight million tons of American grain annually is announced by the White House. Four days later three U.S. grain corporations announce separate deals, bringing the total amount of grain sales to approximately 11.5 million tons in 1975.

November 12. Soviets Deny Ideological Détente. In an attempt to explain Soviet actions in Portugal and Angola, an article in the Soviet military newspaper *Krasnaya Zvezda* states that despite gains toward détente in the political/military sphere, ideological détente between the United States and the Soviet Union is not possible.

November 24. United States on Angola. Secretary of State Kissinger protests Soviet and Cuban military involvement in the ongoing Angolan civil war, claiming that Soviet actions have created "an increasingly skeptical administration view of the Soviet Union's sincerity in improving relations with the United States." President Ford adds December 16 that Soviet and Cuban military involvement in Angola is "not helpful" to détente. Kissinger states in a December 23 news conference that the Soviets have not directly responded to U.S. requests to end their involvement in Angola and that "there is no question that the United States will not accept Soviet military expansion of any kind." Kissinger expresses his support for continued U.S. aid to the anti-Soviet forces in Angola.

1976

January 21-23. Kissinger in Moscow. Secretary of

State Kissinger cites "significant progress" on SALT II during his discussions with Soviet officials in Moscow. Kissinger says that he will return to the United States with new Soviet proposals. Kissinger also discusses the Angolan situation, but no agreements are achieved. Kissinger states in congressional testimony January 30 that the Ford administration will not ask Congress to reduce restrictions on U.S. trade with the Soviet Union until Moscow ends its involvement in Angola.

February 10. U.S. Embassy Radiation Warning. The State Department confirms that the U.S. embassy in Moscow has warned its employees about potentially dangerous radiation in the building caused by Soviet electronic eavesdropping devices. The State Department reports July 7 that the Soviets have reduced the level of radiation but not eliminated it entirely.

February 11. MPLA Recognized. The Popular Movement for the Liberation of Angola (MPLA), supported by thousands of Cuban troops, is judged by the Organization of African States to have established sufficient control over Angola and is recognized as its legitimate government. Many West European nations intend to recognize the MPLA by the end of the month.

February 24-March 5. Soviet Party Congress. The Twenty-fifth Congress of the Communist Party of the Soviet Union convenes in Moscow and, like the Twenty-fourth Congress, supports the program of General Secretary Brezhnev. Brezhnev reaffirms the Soviet commitment to détente as well as to an ideological struggle with the West. He states Soviet willingness to end the arms race and defends the Soviet role in Angola as one faithful to "our revolutionary conscience." Brezhnev also reproaches Chinese leaders for "frantic efforts to torpedo détente." Two leaders are appointed to full membership in the Politburo—Grigory Romanov, head of the Leningrad Communist Party Committee, and Dmitry Ustinov, Central Committee secretary responsible for the defense industry.

March 14. Sadat Abrogates Treaty. President Anwar Sadat proposes that Egypt abrogate its 1971 Treaty of Cooperation and Friendship with the Soviet Union. The Egyptian People's Assembly overwhelmingly approves the proposal March 15. Sadat cites Moscow's refusal to provide Egypt with arms or to reschedule Egypt's debts as reasons for his action.

April 2. Soviet Concern Over Détente Slowdown. Americanologist and director of the Soviet Union's Institute for the Study of the USA and Canada Georgy Arbatov warns in a Tass commentary that "deep-rooted enemies [in the United States] of the improvement in relations" could damage the political atmosphere between the two superpowers. He criticizes President Ford's recent usage of the phrase "peace through strength" instead of détente.

April 11. SALT Deadlocked. The *New York Times*

reports that SALT II negotiations are at a stalemate. President Ford states April 29 that the "slowdown" in SALT negotiations is responsible for his decision to continue Minuteman III missile production, which originally was scheduled to end June 30.

April 29. Ustinov Succeeds Grechko. Dmitry Ustinov is appointed defense minister upon the death of his predecessor, Marshal Andrei Grechko.

May 28. Nuclear Explosions Pact Signed. In joint ceremonies in Washington and Moscow, President Ford and Soviet party chief Brezhnev sign the Peaceful Nuclear Explosions Treaty. The agreement prohibits nuclear blasts greater than 150 kilotons for excavation and other peaceful purposes.

June 2. Philippines, USSR Establish Ties. President Nikolai Podgorny and Philippines president Ferdinand E. Marcos sign a document in Moscow establishing diplomatic ties between the two nations.

June 29-30. European Communists Meet. Twenty-nine West and East European Communist party leaders, including General Secretary Brezhnev, meet in East Berlin. On June 30 the conference issues a document that denies a dominant role for the Soviet Communist party in the international communist movement. Instead, the document says that each party may follow its own path to socialism.

September 9. Mao Zedong Dies. Chinese Communist party chairman Mao Zedong dies at age eighty-two. The Soviet Communist party sends a telegram to its Chinese counterpart—the first in more than a decade—expressing its "deep condolences." Beijing rejects the telegram September 14.

September 21. SALT Talks Resume. SALT negotiators return to the bargaining table in Geneva after a recess. The issue of how to deal with Soviet long-range bombers and U.S. cruise missiles remains troublesome. Despite an October 2 meeting between Foreign Minister Gromyko and President Ford, no progress on SALT is expected until after the U.S. presidential election.

October 6. Ford-Carter Second Debate. In the second of a series of debates between the two main U.S. presidential candidates, President Ford defends his record and the U.S.-Soviet relationship by stating that "there is no Soviet domination of Eastern Europe and there never will be under a Ford administration." Democratic challenger Jimmy Carter later calls the statement a "very serious blunder." Ford tries several times after the debate to clarify his statement but admits October 12 that he misspoke. Carter is elected November 2 by a small margin.

November 21. U.S. Pact with Romania. Secretary of Commerce Elliot L. Richardson signs a ten-year trade and economic cooperation pact with Romania in Bucharest. It is the most comprehensive agreement that the United States has negotiated with an East European nation.

November 28. Sino-Soviet Border Talks Resume. Leonid Ilyichev, Soviet deputy foreign minister, arrives in Beijing to resume the Sino-Soviet border talks that were suspended eighteen months before. Western experts, however, expect little progress.

November 30. Brezhnev on SALT. General Secretary Brezhnev tells U.S. businessmen attending the U.S.-USSR Trade and Economic Council in Moscow that SALT should be a top-priority concern of the new Carter administration. President-elect Carter, reportedly in response to Brezhnev's appeal, responds December 3 with a promise to move "aggressively" to conclude an agreement.

December 27. Carter to Meet Brezhnev. President-elect Carter announces that a summit meeting to discuss SALT with Brezhnev is a "likely prospect" before September 1977. Tass reports December 29 that Brezhnev also favors such a summit.

1977

January 25. Sakharov Warned. Soviet dissident Andrei Sakharov is warned by the Soviet deputy chief prosecutor to cease "hostile and slanderous" activities. The warning comes after Sakharov accuses the KGB of exploding a bomb in the Moscow subway to create a pretense for a crackdown on Soviet dissidents. The State Department issues a statement January 27 in defense of Sakharov. The action marks the first time the United States has publicly championed a Soviet dissident. On January 28 Sakharov writes President Carter, urging him to continue his efforts against human rights violations in the Soviet Union. Carter writes Sakharov February 17 to assure him that the United States is firm in its commitment to human rights.

February 8. Carter on U.S.-Soviet Relations. The main topic of President Carter's first news conference is an appeal to the Soviet Union to cooperate on SALT II and to discuss other arms issues. Carter states his intention to speak out against human rights violations but emphasizes that his administration will refrain from "linking" progress on SALT to human rights.

February 28. Sino-Soviet Talks Break Off. Soviet officials negotiating Sino-Soviet border talks depart for Moscow, marking the end of three months of negotiations. No progress is reported.

March 1. Carter Receives Bukovsky. At the White House President Carter receives exiled Soviet dissident Vladimir Bukovsky despite protests from Moscow.

March 15. Shcharansky Arrested. Prominent Jewish dissident Anatoly Shcharansky is arrested after being refused permission to emigrate. Soviet authorities accuse him of working for the CIA. Shcharansky's arrest seems to be part of a Soviet campaign against dissidents begun in February. Alexander Ginzburg, an outspoken dissident, was arrested February 4; Ukrainian dissidents Mikola

Rudenko and Olexy Tikhy were arrested February 7; and Yuri Orlov, leader of a group unofficially monitoring Soviet compliance with the Helsinki accords, was arrested February 10.

March 21. Brezhnev Criticizes Carter. In a speech in Moscow, General Secretary Brezhnev calls President Carter's recent support of Soviet dissidents "unwarranted interference in our internal affairs." The same day Carter asks Congress for twenty-eight additional radio transmitters to extend the range of the Voice of America and Radio Free Europe-Radio Liberty broadcasts.

March 31. USSR-Mozambique Treaty Signed. During a week-long tour of Africa, Soviet president Nikolai Podgorny signs a Treaty of Friendship and Cooperation with the government of Mozambique. Podgorny also visits Tanzania, Zambia, and Somalia.

May 16. U.S.-Soviet Trade. A report by the U.S. Commercial Office in London states that trade between the two superpowers is down 25 percent in early 1977.

May 18-21. Vance-Gromyko Meeting. Secretary of State Cyrus R. Vance and Foreign Minister Gromyko meet in Geneva to discuss SALT II. Vance states afterward that progress was made toward breaking the deadlock, but Gromyko cautions that "major, serious difficulties remain."

May 24. Podgorny Ousted. Soviet president Nikolai Podgorny is removed from the Politburo. Western experts speculate that he was forced out because he opposed Brezhnev on foreign policy issues and the new Soviet constitution.

June 1. Shcharansky Charged. Soviet dissident Anatoly Shcharansky is charged with treason. The White House expresses its concern June 2.

June 4. New Soviet Constitution Published. The draft of the new Soviet constitution is published. The new charter, the fourth in Soviet history, replaces the 1936 document promulgated under Joseph Stalin.

June 16. Vance on Jackson-Vanik. In a press conference Secretary of State Vance expresses the Carter administration's hope that Congress will repeal the Jackson-Vanik amendment. That amendment bars the granting of most-favored-nation trade status and Export-Import Bank credits to communist countries that do not permit freedom of emigration.

June 16. Brezhnev Elected President. The Supreme Soviet elects Leonid Brezhnev to the largely ceremonial post of president. He succeeds Nikolai Podgorny, whose retirement is announced the same day. Brezhnev is the first Soviet leader to hold the positions of party general secretary and president at the same time.

June 23. Computer Sale Canceled. The Department of Commerce cancels a planned sale of Cyber 76 computers to the Soviet Union. The sale had been opposed earlier by sixty-five members of Congress because of the possibility that the Soviet Union could use the computers' advanced technology for military purposes.

July 4. Toon Speech Canceled. Malcolm Toon, U.S. ambassador to the Soviet Union, is not allowed to deliver his traditional Fourth of July speech on Soviet television because of a reference in the text to human rights. Toon protests the decision in a meeting with President Brezhnev the following day.

August 16. Unrest in Ethiopia. Following an escalation of fighting in the Ogaden region of Ethiopia, *Izvestia* states that Ethiopia is the "victim of an armed invasion." Somali military units had invaded the region in July in support of ethnic Somali rebels living in the Ogaden who are fighting the Ethiopian government in an attempt to unite their region with Somalia. The Soviet Union supplies both sides with arms but supports Ethiopia in the current crisis. Western observers August 21 report the arrival of Soviet military aid in Ethiopia.

August 29. Soviets on South Africa Bomb. Tass says South Africa is close to testing a nuclear bomb and accuses NATO and Israel of helping Pretoria develop nuclear weapons. It is disclosed August 28 that President Brezhnev sent a letter to President Carter August 6 saying that the Soviet Union had reason to believe South Africa was preparing to test a nuclear weapon in the Kalahari Desert. Brezhnev requested Western action to stop the test.

September 23. SALT I Extended. The United States announces its intention to continue observing the 1972 SALT I agreement, which is scheduled to expire October 3. Responding September 25, the Soviet Union also promises to abide by the treaty.

October 1. Joint U.S.-Soviet Statement. The United States and the Soviet Union issue a joint declaration on a new Middle East peace conference in Geneva, suggesting that talks include discussion of "the legitimate rights of the Palestinian people." On October 2 Israel rejects the statement as "unacceptable." Israel and the United States October 5 announce agreement on procedures for reconvening the Geneva conference.

October 4. Belgrade Meeting Opens. Delegates from nations that signed the 1975 Helsinki accords meet in Belgrade for the first formal conference to review the Helsinki Final Act.

November 2-7. Bolshevik Revolution Anniversary. President Brezhnev addresses the Central Committee and the Supreme Soviet as part of a weeklong celebration of the sixtieth anniversary of the Bolshevik Revolution. Brezhnev stresses Soviet support for détente and the need for better economic performance at home.

November 13. Moscow Loses African Ally. The government of Somalia abrogates its 1974 treaty of friendship with the Soviet Union, breaks diplomatic relations with Moscow, bars Soviet ships from using the naval facility at Berbera, and orders all Soviet advisers to leave the country. The actions are a response to Soviet and Cuban military support of Ethiopia and Moscow's refusal to sell arms to Somalia.

November 29. Soviets Attack Sadat. Foreign Minister Gromyko announces that the USSR will not attend talks in Cairo to arrange a conference in Geneva on a Mideast settlement. Gromyko's statement follows the historic visit of President Anwar Sadat of Egypt to Israel November 19-21. During the visit Sadat had declared his intention to seek peace with Israel. Gromyko says Egypt has departed "from the common Arab front and sacrifices the interests of the Arab states as a whole." Sadat also had invited the United States and all Middle East countries, including Israel, to attend the meeting in Cairo.

December 5. Egypt Severs Arab Ties. Egypt severs diplomatic relations with Syria, Iraq, Libya, Algeria, and South Yemen, citing attempts by the hard-line Arab states to disrupt President Sadat's recent peace efforts. The action follows conclusion of a December 2 meeting in Tripoli, Libya, at which the Arab states declared a new "front for resistance and opposition" to thwart Egypt's peace initiatives. Egypt also closes several Soviet cultural centers and consulates in Cairo because of the Soviet Union's endorsement of the Tripoli Declaration.

December 14. Cairo Conference Opens. The Cairo conference to discuss procedures for reconvening the Geneva Middle East peace talks opens. Delegates from Egypt, Israel, and the United States participate; a UN representative attends as an observer.

1978

January 6. Crown Returned to Hungary. Secretary of State Vance visits Budapest and formally returns the crown of St. Stephen to Hungary. The crown, a Hungarian national treasure, had been in U.S. possession since 1945. The Carter administration returned the crown to symbolize the improvement of U.S.-Hungarian relations. The United States grants Hungary most-favored-nation trading status March 3.

January 11. Syrian-Soviet Arms Deal. Syria and the Soviet Union sign an arms deal under which Damascus will receive shipments of Soviet planes, tanks, and advanced air-defense missiles.

January 22. Ethiopian Offensive. Ethiopian forces, aided by Cuban troops and large amounts of Soviet arms, launch an offensive designed to clear Ethiopia's Ogaden region of invading Somali forces. Secretary of State Vance announces February 10 that Moscow has assured the United States that Ethiopian troops would not cross the Somali border once the Ogaden region had been recaptured.

February 24. ICBM Deployment Halt. The United States announces an agreement with Moscow to halt all land-based ICBM deployments until September 1980. The agreement would be superseded by a SALT II agreement if one is concluded.

February 28. USSR Compliance Satisfactory. The State Department releases a Senate Foreign Relations Committee study that finds Soviet compliance with the 1972 SALT treaty satisfactory.

March 6-9. Tito in United States. Yugoslavian president Josip Broz Tito, on a goodwill visit to the United States, requests U.S. arms.

March 9. Somali Forces Begin Pullout. President Carter announces that Somalia, under pressure from a Soviet-backed Ethiopian offensive, has begun a troop pullout from the Ogaden region of Ethiopia, raising hopes for the possible conclusion of the eight-month war.

March 9. Belgrade Conference Ends. The Belgrade Conference on Security and Cooperation in Europe (CSCE) ends with the adoption of summary documents and a pledge for a second review conference in Madrid in 1980. Western diplomats admit to being unable to obtain concrete improvements in human rights in the East Bloc.

March 17. Carter at Wake Forest. In a speech at Wake Forest University in North Carolina President Carter warns the Soviet Union about its arms buildup and its military involvement in regional disputes. He cites Soviet activity in the Horn of Africa as an example. Carter vows that the United States will not fall behind in military capabilities. Tass publishes a response the same day, scoring the United States for abandoning cooperative efforts and endorsing "a course of threats and a buildup of tension."

March 29. U.S.-Soviet Trade Declines. The U.S. embassy in Moscow reports that U.S.-Soviet trade declined 26.5 percent in 1977 (from $2.5 billion in 1976 to $1.9 billion in 1977). It is the first decline since the expansion of U.S.-Soviet trade in 1972.

April 7. Neutron Bomb Deferred. President Carter announces he has "decided to defer production" of the neutron bomb, stating that the issue's final outcome depends on Soviet restraint in arms production and deployment.

April 10. Shevchenko Defects. Arkady Shevchenko, UN under secretary general for political and Security Council affairs, defects to the United States. Shevchenko is considered the most important Soviet diplomat to defect to date.

April 20-22. Vance in Moscow. Secretary of State Vance meets in Moscow with Foreign Minister Gromyko and President Brezhnev to discuss SALT II. After the discussions both U.S. and Soviet officials report "some progress" in narrowing differences impeding agreement.

April 27. Afghanistan Coup. In a military coup in Afghanistan, President Muhammad Daoud, a neutralist, is killed. His government is replaced by a Marxist regime headed by Nur Muhammad Taraki.

May 28. Brzezinski on Zaire. U.S. national security adviser Zbigniew Brzezinski in a television interview accuses the Soviet Union, Cuba, and East Germany of involvement in Zaire's Shaba province, where secessionist rebels attacked Zairian troops on May 18. *Pravda* May 30 denies military participation in Zaire and calls Brzezinski an "enemy of détente."

June 7. Carter in Annapolis. President Carter, in a commencement address at the U.S. Naval Academy in Annapolis, Maryland, criticizes Soviet foreign and domestic policies. Carter is careful to point out progress in U.S.-Soviet relations on issues such as SALT II but states: "The Soviet Union can choose either confrontation or cooperation. The United States is adequately prepared to meet either choice."

June 8. Solzhenitsyn's Harvard Address. Nobel laureate and Soviet dissident Alexander Solzhenitsyn delivers a commencement address at Harvard on the "decline of courage" in the West.

June 29. Vietnam Joins Comecon. At an East bloc summit in Bucharest, Vietnam is admitted as the tenth full member of the Council for Mutual Economic Assistance (Comecon), the bloc's economic organization.

July 12-13. Vance, Gromyko Discuss SALT. Secretary of State Vance and Foreign Minister Gromyko meet in Geneva to discuss the remaining obstacles to a SALT II agreement: the Soviet Backfire bomber and the testing and deployment of missile systems.

July 13-14. Ginzburg and Shcharansky Sentenced. Alexander Ginzburg is sentenced July 13 to eight years in a labor camp for "anti-Soviet agitation and propaganda." Fellow dissident Anatoly Shcharansky is sentenced July 14 to three years in prison and ten years in a labor camp following his conviction for treason, espionage, and "anti-Soviet agitation." The trial, which began July 10 under heavy secrecy, focused on Shcharansky's association with *Los Angeles Times* reporter Robert Toth, who was accused by the Soviet Union of being a spy. Shcharansky defended himself after refusing a court-appointed lawyer. Congress adopts resolutions against the trials amid calls for suspending SALT, abrogating business deals, and moving the 1980 Olympic games from Moscow. On July 11, UN ambassador Andrew Young added to the furor by asserting that "there are hundreds, perhaps thousands of political prisoners in the United States." The White House protests the convictions July 18 by canceling the sale of sophisticated Sperry-Univac computers and further limiting the sale of oil technology to the Soviet Union.

August 12. Sino-Japanese Treaty. After three years of intermittent negotiations, China and Japan sign a treaty of peace and friendship in Tokyo. The Japanese previously had resisted signing a treaty with China that the Soviet Union might find offensive. Tass asserts August 12 that the treaty endangers Soviet-Japanese relations.

August 16. Hua in Romania. Chinese Communist party chairman Hua Guofeng arrives in Romania for an unofficial visit that draws worldwide attention and is generally seen as a challenge to Soviet claims of exclusive influence in Eastern Europe. After leaving Romania August 21, Hua flies to Yugoslavia for a nine-day visit. On August 24, *Pravda* attacks the Sino-Japanese peace treaty and Chairman Hua's visit to Eastern Europe.

September 5-17. Camp David Summit. Egyptian president Anwar Sadat, Israeli premier Menachem Begin, and President Carter meet in Camp David, Maryland, for a summit on the deadlocked Middle East peace negotiations. Tass denounces the summit September 6 as a "trick" to facilitate greater U.S. influence in the Middle East. After thirteen days of negotiations Carter announces the signing of two pacts that offer a framework for a "durable settlement" of Middle East problems. Brezhnev September 22 calls the agreements "a deal worked out behind the backs of the Arabs."

November 3. Soviet Treaty with Vietnam. The Soviet Union and Vietnam sign a twenty-five-year treaty of friendship and cooperation with Vietnam.

November 19. Brezhnev on Iran. In response to growing domestic unrest in Iran, *Pravda* publishes a statement by President Brezhnev warning the United States not to interfere in Iranian affairs and reminding the United States that Iran borders the Soviet Union.

November 20. Soviet-Ethiopian Agreement. President Brezhnev and Ethiopian head of state Mengistu Haile Mariam sign a twenty-year friendship and cooperation pact in Moscow, climaxing a two-year improvement in relations that saw increased Soviet involvement in the Ethiopian war against Somalia and secessionist rebels in Eritrea and Ogaden. The pact promises military "consultation" instead of overt assistance.

December 5. Soviet-Afghan Agreement. President Brezhnev and Afghan premier Nur Muhammad Taraki sign a twenty-year treaty of friendship and cooperation in Moscow. The agreement provides for "mutual economic, military and technical assistance" and notes that the Soviet Union "respects the policy of non-alignment" of the Afghan government.

December 15. United States Recognizes PRC. The governments of the People's Republic of China (PRC) and the United States issue a joint communiqué announcing the establishment of diplomatic relations as of January 1, 1979. On December 19 Brezhnev sends President Carter a note that Carter describes as "very positive in tone." Tass December 21 disputes Carter's interpretation, disclosing that Moscow has deep reservations about normalization and particularly about the inclusion of a phrase in the December 15 communiqué condemning "hegemony," a word the Chinese have often used to criticize the Soviet Union.

December 21-23. SALT II Agreement Nears. Meeting in Geneva, Secretary of State Vance and Foreign Minister Gromyko announce agreement on "most issues," but a

SALT treaty is not completed.

December 25. Vietnam Invades Cambodia. After months of border fighting, Vietnam launches a massive offensive into Cambodia. Western observers regard the Soviet-Vietnamese treaty signed in November as a measure taken by the Vietnamese to deter the Chinese from intervening on behalf of the pro-Beijing Khmer Rouge regime in Cambodia. Vietnamese forces capture Phnom Penh January 7.

1979

January 1. China, U.S. Establish Ties. The United States and China formally open full diplomatic relations.

January 6. New Government in Iran. Amidst growing domestic unrest the shah of Iran installs a new civilian government headed by Shahpur Bakhtiar. Shah Mohammed Reza Pahlavi leaves the country January 16 for a vacation that proves to be permanent exile.

January 8. Khmer Rouge Ousted in Cambodia. The Vietnamese-sponsored United Front for National Salvation announces the overthrow of the Khmer Rouge government and the formation of a People's Revolutionary Council. Heng Samrin becomes president of the new Cambodian government. On January 9 the Soviet Union sends a congratulatory telegram to Samrin.

January 15. Soviet Veto. The Soviet Union vetoes a UN Security Council resolution demanding the withdrawal of Vietnamese forces from Cambodia.

January 28. Deng in United States. Vice Premier Deng Xiaoping arrives in Washington for a nine-day visit, the first ever to the United States by a senior Chinese Communist leader. *Pravda* criticizes the U.S. government February 4 for allowing Deng to repeatedly denounce the Soviet Union during the visit. *Pravda* states that "the Soviet public cannot close its eyes to the fact" that Deng "was given a wide podium for slander on the USSR."

February 5. Soviet Buildup Reported. Japan reports that the Soviet Union is building bases and increasing its troop strength on the southernmost Kuril Island, adjacent to the northernmost Japanese island of Hokkaido. Both countries claim the Kuril Islands.

February 9-11. Revolution in Iran. Armed revolutionaries and army supporters of Ayatollah Ruhollah Khomeini overthrow the government of Shahpur Bakhtiar in Iran. Khomeini, who returned to Iran February 1 from exile in France, installs Mehdi Barzagan as premier of a provisional government. The Soviet Union recognizes the new government February 12.

February 17. China Invades Vietnam. In an action described by the Chinese as a "counterattack" brought on by repeated Vietnamese border incursions, Chinese troops invade Vietnam. Moscow vigorously protests and aids Vietnam with supplies and intelligence. However, the Kremlin does not offer armed support, and Soviet troops in Asian military districts are neither reinforced nor put on alert. On March 5 China begins withdrawing its forces after both sides suffer heavy casualties.

March 4. Podgorny Excluded. The political career of Nikolai Podgorny, former president of the Soviet Union (1965-1977), ends when he is not reelected to the Supreme Soviet.

March 26. Egyptian-Israeli Peace Treaty. Israeli prime minister Menachem Begin and Egyptian president Anwar Sadat sign a peace treaty that formally ends the state of war between their two countries. The ceremony, witnessed by President Carter, takes place on the White House lawn. Tass March 22 declares the treaty "a betrayal" of Arab interests.

April 27. Soviet Dissidents Exchanged for Spies. In the first exchange of its kind, five Soviet dissidents are flown to New York's Kennedy Airport and exchanged for two convicted Soviet spies. One of the dissidents released is Alexander Ginzburg, whose conviction in 1978 prompted worldwide protests. The other dissidents are Mark Dymshits and Eduard Kuznetsov, two Soviet Jews convicted of plotting to hijack a plane to Sweden; Valentin Moroz, a historian who advocates Ukrainian independence; and Georgy Vins, convicted for religious activities in Ukraine.

May 9. SALT II Draft Treaty Completed. Secretary of State Vance announces the completion of a SALT II draft treaty with the Soviet Union, thereby clearing the path for a summit meeting between presidents Brezhnev and Carter. On May 11 the White House announces that a summit will be held June 16-18 in Vienna.

June 2. Pope Visits Poland. Pope John Paul II makes a historic nine-day visit to his native Poland to mark the 900th anniversary of the martyrdom of St. Stanislaus, Poland's patron saint. It is the first time a Catholic pope has visited a communist country. A Soviet television broadcast states that "some circles in the Polish church are trying to use [the visit] for anti-state purposes."

June 16-18. Vienna Summit. Presidents Carter and Brezhnev meet for the first time at a U.S.-Soviet summit meeting in Vienna. The conference agenda includes five negotiating sessions and ends with the signing of the second strategic arms limitation treaty between the United States and the Soviet Union. Carter returns to the United States June 18 and asks a joint session of Congress to approve the SALT II treaty, which he says is "the most detailed, far-reaching, comprehensive treaty in the history of arms control."

June 25. Gromyko Warns Senate. Soviet foreign minister Gromyko warns the U.S. Senate against amending the SALT II treaty, stating that it "would be the end of negotiations . . . no matter what amendments would be made."

July 9. SALT Hearings Begin. The Senate Foreign Relations Committee opens three months of hearings on the SALT II treaty. Similar hearings in the Senate Armed Services Committee begin July 23.

July 17. Somoza Resigns. Nicaraguan president Anastasio Somoza resigns and flies to the United States. Two days later rebel Sandinista troops overcome disorganized national guard forces and take control of Managua.

August 31. Soviet Troops in Cuba. The State Department acknowledges the presence of a 2,000-3,000-man Soviet combat brigade in Cuba. President Carter claims the troops do not threaten U.S. security. Frank Church, D-Idaho, chairman of the Senate Foreign Relations Committee, states September 5 that he sees "no likelihood that the Senate would ratify the SALT II treaty as long as Soviet combat troops remain stationed in Cuba." In a nationally televised speech September 7, President Carter calls the presence of combat troops in Cuba "a very serious matter" but asks for "calm and a sense of proportion." On September 8 Carter says that Soviet troops in Cuba should not influence the Senate debate over ratification of SALT II, maintaining that the treaty should be judged "on its own merits."

September 10. Moscow on Cuba. In the first Soviet comments on the issue, a *Pravda* editorial denies the presence of Soviet combat troops in Cuba, while Tass states that there has been a training center in Cuba for seventeen years, and that its purpose (of training Cuban forces) has not changed.

September 16. New Government in Afghanistan. Premier Hafizullah Amin replaces Nur Muhammad Taraki as president of Afghanistan. Officially, Taraki is said to have resigned because of ill health, but it appears that he may have been killed during a government upheaval. Taraki's death is confirmed October 9, but the cause is given as "a severe and prolonged illness."

September 23. Sino-Soviet Talks. A Chinese negotiating team arrives in Moscow to begin talks aimed at easing Sino-Soviet tensions. It is the first Chinese diplomatic delegation to visit Moscow since 1964.

October 1. Carter on Cuba. In a nationally televised speech President Carter announces a comprehensive U.S. intelligence effort to survey Cuba and monitor military activity in the Caribbean. Carter stresses that "the brigade issue is certainly no reason for a return to the Cold War" and continues to press for SALT II ratification.

October 3. Record Grain Sale Approved. The largest Soviet purchase of U.S. grain to date is approved by the Agriculture Department. The sale will involve up to twenty-five million metric tons of grain in the next year.

October 25. South Yemen-USSR Pact. Officials of the Soviet Union and South Yemen sign a twenty-year friendship pact in Moscow.

November 4. Crisis in Iran. Demanding the return of the shah, Iranian students seize the U.S. embassy in Tehran and take sixty-six Americans hostage. Thirteen are freed November 19-20.

November 9. Committee Approves SALT. The Senate Foreign Relations Committee votes 9-6 to recommend the SALT II treaty for ratification.

November 27. Politburo Changes. Deputy Prime Minister Nikolai Tikhonov is promoted to full membership in the Soviet Politburo. Mikhail S. Gorbachev is made a candidate (nonvoting) member, becoming the youngest participant at age forty-eight.

December 4. United Nations Votes on Iran. The UN Security Council votes to demand an immediate release of the remaining fifty-three American hostages in Iran. In a *Pravda* article December 5, Moscow supports the UN vote but, citing U.S. naval maneuvers in the Arabian Sea, accuses the United States of attempting to "blackmail Iran by massing forces on its borders" instead of returning the shah.

December 12. NATO Dual-Track Policy. NATO members agree to deploy 108 Pershing II and 464 land-based cruise missiles in Europe by 1983. The agreement calls for simultaneously engaging Moscow in arms control talks aimed at reducing nuclear weapons in Europe.

December 20. Committee Rejects SALT. The Senate Armed Services Committee votes 10-0 to recommend rejection of the SALT II treaty as "not in the national security interest of the United States."

December 24-27. Soviets Invade Afghanistan. The Soviet Union begins airlifting troops and supplies into Afghanistan under the guise of a military exercise. On December 27 about twenty thousand Soviet ground troops invade the country. That day Afghan president Hafizullah Amin is killed during fighting between Afghan units loyal to him and invading Soviet forces. He is succeeded as president by Babrak Karmal. By December 31 Soviet troops fan through the country to contain a rebellion by Moslem tribesmen who oppose Marxist rule. Moscow issues a series of statements December 28-30 supporting the new government and promising it aid. The first admission of the intervention comes December 30 in a *Pravda* article that states the troops will withdraw when they no longer are needed. By December 31 Soviet troops in Afghanistan reportedly number fifty thousand.

December 31. Carter on Afghanistan. In a televised interview President Carter states that the Soviet intervention in Afghanistan has changed his opinion of the Soviets more dramatically than any other event during his administration.

1980

January 3. Carter Asks SALT Delay. Senate Majority Leader Robert C. Byrd, D-W.Va., receives a letter from President Carter formally requesting the Senate to delay further consideration of the SALT II treaty in light of the Soviet invasion of Afghanistan.

January 4. U.S. Response to Afghanistan. In a nation-

ally televised address, President Carter describes the Soviet intervention in Afghanistan as "an extremely serious threat to peace" and announces a series of retaliatory measures. These include an embargo on the sale of grain and high technology items to the USSR, restraint of Soviet fishing privileges in U.S. waters, delayed construction of new Soviet and U.S. embassies, and a possible U.S. boycott of the Olympic games to be held in Moscow later in the year. Soviet sources January 5 call these responses a "flagrant violation" of détente and a return to cold war policies.

January 6. Deng on Afghan Crisis. Chinese vice premier Deng Xiaoping calls the Soviet invasion of Afghanistan "a grave step," repeats Beijing's "firm demand" that the troops be withdrawn, and declares that China will "work together with the Afghan people, and all countries and people . . . to frustrate Soviet acts of aggression and expansion."

January 12. Brezhnev on Afghanistan. President Brezhnev makes his first official statement on the Afghanistan invasion, stating that "aggressive external forces of reaction" necessitated intervention.

January 13. USSR Vetoes Iran Resolution. A U.S.-proposed UN Security Council resolution urging economic sanctions against Iran for the taking of American hostages is vetoed by the Soviet Union. The Soviet Union justifies its decision on the grounds that sanctions would have "dealt a blow to the Iranian revolution."

January 14. U.S. Offers Pakistan Military Aid. The State Department announces that the United States plans to provide Pakistan with $400 million in economic and military aid because of the Soviet intervention in neighboring Afghanistan.

January 14. United Nations on Afghanistan. The UN General Assembly approves 104-18 a resolution condemning the Soviet intervention in Afghanistan and demanding a troop withdrawal.

January 20. Carter Sees Danger. Speaking on NBC's "Meet the Press," President Carter calls the Soviet invasion of Afghanistan the "most serious threat to peace since the Second World War."

January 22. Sakharov Exiled. Soviet authorities send Nobel prize-winning scientist and human rights activist Andrei Sakharov and his wife into internal exile in the city of Gorky. The Presidium of the Supreme Soviet strips Sakharov of his honors. Tass charges that Sakharov "has been conducting subversive activities against the Soviet Union for a number of years." The exiling apparently was prompted by Sakharov's protests against the Soviet invasion of Afghanistan and his support for a Western boycott of the Moscow Olympics.

January 23. Carter Doctrine. In what becomes known as the "Carter Doctrine," President Carter in his third State of the Union message declares that the United States will "use any means necessary, including force," to repel any attacks on the oil-producing Persian Gulf region.

January 29. Senate on Olympics. The Senate votes 88-4 to support a U.S. boycott of the Summer Olympics in Moscow. A similar resolution was adopted by the House January 24.

February 12. IOC Reaffirms Moscow. The International Olympic Committee (IOC) decides to retain Moscow as the site of the Summer Olympics despite pressure from the U.S. Olympic Committee to move the games.

February 22. Brezhnev on Afghanistan. President Brezhnev states that the need for Soviet involvement in Afghanistan would "cease to exist" if the governments of the United States, Pakistan, and China would end their alleged subversion of the Kabul government.

March 6. Soviets on Poison Gas. Moscow denies accusations made by Afghan refugees in Pakistan that Soviet troops are using poison gas on Afghan rebels.

April 24-25. Failed Rescue Mission. A U.S. commando mission to rescue American hostages in Iran is aborted in the Iranian desert because of equipment failures. Eight commandos are killed in a helicopter-airplane accident that occurs as the rescue team is about to take off. Tass comments April 25 that "the present master of the White House could not care less about his fellow citizens and is prepared to sacrifice their lives for his election interests."

May 4. Tito Dies. President Josip Broz Tito of Yugoslavia dies in Ljubljana after a long illness. Moscow, in response to Tito's death, makes no mention of the historically stormy relations between the two nations and does not dwell on Tito's expulsion from the international communist movement in 1948. Instead, the official statement praises Tito as "a leading figure of the international Communist and workers' movement."

May 9. Carter on SALT II. President Carter tells the World Affairs Council that he will seek the approval of SALT II "at the earliest opportune time" and that "we intend to abide by the treaty's terms as long as the Soviet Union, as observed by us, complies with those terms as well."

May 16. Gromyko and Muskie in Vienna. Secretary of State Edmund S. Muskie meets Foreign Minister Gromyko in Vienna in the first high-level U.S.-Soviet meeting since the Afghan invasion. The private meeting produces no conclusive agreements.

June 30-July 1. Schmidt in Moscow. West German chancellor Helmut Schmidt confers with President Brezhnev in Moscow. Schmidt proposes unconditional negotiations on medium-range missiles in Europe and appeals for the Soviet withdrawal of forces in Afghanistan. The two leaders conclude an economic agreement and make preliminary plans for a natural gas pipeline project from western Siberia to West Germany.

July 19. Moscow Olympics. The first Olympics held in a communist country open in Moscow. The games are boycotted by sixty-four countries. Of those, fifty-five reportedly refused to attend to protest the Afghanistan invasion.

August 5. Presidential Directive 59. The *New York Times* reports that the previous week President Carter signed Presidential Directive (PD) 59, detailing U.S. strategy against the Soviet Union in the event of a nuclear war. PD 59 emphasizes the destruction of the Soviet Union's strategic weapons and its command, control, and communications structure. The document also stresses the need for limited nuclear options and preparations for protracted nuclear war. Tass August 11 calls the document "insanity" developed by persons "who have lost all touch with reality and are prepared to push the world" into nuclear war.

August 14. Workers Strike in Poland. A labor crisis in Poland intensifies as seventeen thousand workers go on strike at the Lenin Shipyard in Gdansk. The strike spreads and by August 22 a strikers' committee representing 120,000 Polish workers from northern Poland delivers a request for political and economic reform to the Polish government. On August 21-22, the government arrests twenty-four leaders of the striking workers.

August 20. Moscow Jams VOA. The Soviet Union begins jamming Voice of America (VOA) broadcasts to the USSR, reportedly to prevent news of the labor crisis in Poland from reaching the Soviet population.

August 23. Concessions to Workers. The Polish government agrees to negotiate with representatives of the strikers. On August 24, Polish premier Edward Babiuch is ousted as part of a strike-inspired government shake-up. Despite a government promise of concessions, the strike reportedly swells to three hundred thousand workers.

August 27. Moscow on Poland. After strike leaders in Gdansk reject Polish government concessions, the Soviet Union, in its first direct response to the unrest in Poland, accuses "antisocialist forces" of attempting to disrupt Poland's socialist system.

September 3. Polish Workers Return. Most of the striking Polish workers return to their jobs by September 3 after the government announces an agreement allowing free trade unions and the right to strike. The agreement was concluded August 31. On August 21, coal miners in Silesia began their own strike, which lasted in most places until September 3.

September 6. Gierek Replaced. Polish Communist party secretary Edward Gierek, reportedly suffering from heart trouble, is replaced by Stanislaw Kania. The Kania government is expected to honor the concessions Gierek made to Polish workers.

September 20. Outbreak of Iran-Iraq War. A dispute between Iraq and Iran escalates into full-scale war. Both sides bomb oil fields; Iraqi forces invade Iran and threaten to block the strategic Strait of Hormuz. The

United States and the Soviet Union September 23 pledge neutrality in the war.

September 24. Solidarity Formed. Poland's new independent trade unions register in a Warsaw court as a single nationwide organization called "Solidarity." Solidarity draft statutes are presented by the union's new leader, Lech Walesa.

October 8. Soviet-Syrian Treaty. President Brezhnev and Syrian president Hafez Assad sign a twenty-year friendship pact.

October 21. Gorbachev Promoted. Mikhail Gorbachev is promoted from candidate member of the Politburo to full member.

October 23. Kosygin Resigns. Aleksei Kosygin resigns as Soviet premier on grounds of ill health. Nikolai Tikhonov, an economic planner and Brezhnev protégé, becomes premier. Brezhnev tells the Supreme Soviet that Kosygin also wishes to be excused from his Politbureau duties.

November 4. Reagan Elected. In a landslide election, Ronald Reagan defeats Jimmy Carter for the presidency. Premier Nikolai Tikhonov cautiously expresses Moscow's hopes that Reagan will assume "a constructive approach" in the area of U.S.-Soviet relations.

November 11. CSCE Opens in Madrid. The Conference on Security and Cooperation in Europe (CSCE) meets in Madrid to review the 1975 Helsinki accords. The Soviet Union and its East European allies protest discussion of the human rights issue, preferring more talk on a European disarmament conference. The first phase of the meeting closes December 19.

November 21. Polish Shake-Up. In a major reorganization of the Polish Communist party and government, four cabinet ministers lose their jobs. The move ousts a conservative faction of the leadership that had resisted cooperation with the Polish trade union movement. East European allies of the Soviet Union attack Polish authorities for their inability to control Solidarity.

December 5. Summit on Poland. Leaders of the Soviet Union and East Europe attend an emergency summit in Moscow to discuss the crisis in Poland. Polish Communist party secretary Stanislaw Kania attends and proclaims Polish loyalty "to the Socialist commonwealth." Simultaneously, reports of Warsaw Pact troop movements increase Western fears that the Soviets will invade Poland.

December 17. Kosygin Dies. Former Soviet premier Aleksei Kosygin dies of cardiac arrest. His death is not disclosed by Tass until December 20, after the seventy-fourth birthday celebrations (December 19) for Leonid Brezhnev.

1981

January 20. Iran Frees U.S. Hostages. Iran releases the remaining fifty-two American hostages after U.S. and Iranian negotiators reach an agreement on the return of Iran's frozen assets in the United States. The hostages, who spent 444 days in captivity, fly out of Iran minutes after Ronald Reagan is inaugurated as the fortieth U.S. president.

January 29. Reagan on Détente. In his first news conference as president, Reagan maintains that "so far, détente's been a one-way street the Soviet Union has used to pursue its own aims," which the president describes as "the promotion of world revolution and a one-world ... Communist state." Reagan also says that in pursuit of their goals the Soviets reserve the "right to commit any crime, to lie, to cheat."

February 9. Polish Government Shake-Up. Poland's defense minister, Gen. Wojciech Jaruzelski, is named premier following the dismissal of Josef Pinkowski. The government shuffle occurs amid continuing strikes in Poland.

February 14. Moscow Denies Aid to El Salvador. The Soviet Union denies U.S. allegations that it is supplying arms to Communist rebels in El Salvador but concedes that it has no restrictions on sending arms to Cuba or Ethiopia, two countries that allegedly provide the El Salvadoran rebels with arms. State Department sources February 23 claim "definite evidence" that Cuba and other communist countries have supplied the rebels with military equipment.

February 23-March 3. Soviet Party Congress. In an opening speech to the Twenty-sixth Congress of the Communist Party of the Soviet Union, President Brezhnev proposes a summit meeting with President Reagan. Secretary of State Alexander M. Haig, Jr., tells reporters that the United States is "very interested" in a summit, but that the idea should be considered "very, very carefully." Brezhnev announces at the end of the congress March 3 that the entire Politburo has been reelected, the first time a party congress has witnessed no change among the top leadership.

March 19. Soyuz 81 Maneuvers. Poland reports the beginning of Warsaw Pact maneuvers, code-named Soyuz 81, in Poland, the German Democratic Republic, the Soviet Union, and Czechoslovakia. The maneuvers are extended March 26 after Solidarity announces a warning strike for March 27, to be followed by a general strike. The general strike is subsequently canceled.

April 7. Brezhnev on Poland. Speaking in Prague, President Brezhnev states that it is not necessary for Moscow to solve Poland's problems. The Soyuz 81 Warsaw Pact maneuvers end the same day, but Western concern over Soviet intentions in Poland continues.

April 24. Reagan Ends Grain Embargo. President Reagan announces in a closed cabinet session that he will honor a campaign promise and lift the embargo on grain sales to the Soviet Union. President Carter imposed the embargo in January 1980 in response to the invasion of

Afghanistan by the Soviet army.

May 17. Reagan at Notre Dame. In a commencement speech at Notre Dame University in South Bend, Indiana, President Reagan declares that "The West will not contain Communism; it will transcend Communism. We will not bother to denounce it; we'll dismiss it as a sad, bizarre chapter in human history whose last pages are even now being written."

July 14-20. Polish Emergency Congress. Poland's Communist party convenes an emergency congress to discuss the political and economic crises buffeting the country. The congress is a watershed because it allows open criticism of party policies and voting by secret ballot. The Soviet Union protests the inclusion of democratic methods into congress procedures and sends a less important Politburo member, Viktor Grishin, as its representative. The meeting results in a large turnover of Polish Central Committee members and the reelection of Party boss Stanislaw Kania and Premier Wojciech Jaruzelski. Moscow gives the Polish congress perfunctory approval July 21, as Brezhnev sends a cool telegram asserting that the meeting has "set the task of stabilizing" the crisis in Poland. The message warns that internal and external subversive forces are "providing complications in Poland's relations with its true neighbors."

July 15. Soviet-Brazilian Trade Accord. Soviet and Brazilian officials sign a $6 billion trade accord in Moscow calling for the Soviet purchase of soybeans and the Brazilian purchase of Soviet oil.

September 5-October 7. Solidarity Congress. In an unprecedented action the Solidarity National Congress calls for free parliamentary elections in Poland. The Soviet Union immediately denounces the congress as an "anti-socialist, anti-Soviet orgy." The congress voted September 9 to urge other East European countries to encourage the development of independent trade unions. Lech Walesa is narrowly reelected as chairman. Polish authorities accuse the trade union September 16 of developing into an opposition movement that could push Poland into a "new national tragedy."

September 24. Haig and Gromyko Meeting. Secretary of State Haig and Foreign Minister Gromyko announce that negotiations on the limitation of medium-range nuclear weapons in Europe will begin November 30 in Geneva. The announcement comes on the second day of a two-day meeting in New York, the first high-level U.S.-Soviet contact of the Reagan administration.

October 6. Sadat Assassinated. President Anwar Sadat of Egypt is assassinated while reviewing a military parade. Vice President Hosni Mubarak is elected president October 13.

October 16. Reagan on Nuclear War. In a news conference President Reagan implies that it may be possible to use tactical nuclear weapons in a confrontation on European soil without igniting a full-scale nuclear war. Rea-

gan's remarks cause a furor over apparent U.S. insensitivity to the fate of Western Europe. The statements cause a stir in Europe, where the antinuclear movement is gathering momentum.

October 18. Kania Dismissed. Polish Communist party head Stanislaw Kania is dismissed and replaced by Premier Wojciech Jaruzelski. Kania's removal comes amidst worsening economic conditions and increasing strikes. Kania was criticized for being too soft on Solidarity. Jaruzelski holds supreme power as first secretary of the party, commander of the armed forces, premier, and defense minister.

October 27. CSCE Reconvenes. The thirty-five-nation Conference on Security and Cooperation in Europe (CSCE) reconvenes in Madrid to review the 1975 Helsinki accords. The session opens with a tirade against the Soviet Union as European delegates repeat earlier accusations of accord violations in the human rights area and condemn Moscow for intervening in Afghanistan and conducting Warsaw Pact maneuvers around Poland. The session ends in a deadlock December 18.

November 2. Brezhnev Interview. President Brezhnev discusses the East-West balance of power, disarmament, and détente in an interview for the German publication *Der Spiegel.* The interview follows widespread demonstrations in Europe October 24-25 protesting NATO plans to deploy medium-range nuclear weapons in Europe. Brezhnev criticizes U.S. foreign policy as the main factor behind world tension.

November 16. Brezhnev on Food Supply. In his address to a Central Committee Plenum, President Brezhnev declares that the Soviet food supply is "economically and politically the central problem of the five-year plan." He pledges development of a new food program that will include more decentralized decision making in the agricultural economy, more incentives for local initiatives, and expanded use of private plots.

November 18. Reagan's "Zero Option" Plan. In a televised speech to the National Press Club, President Reagan announces that he will cancel plans for deployment of intermediate-range nuclear weapons in Europe if the Soviet Union will dismantle its intermediate-range missiles already in place. Tass calls the plan a "propaganda ploy designed to stalemate disarmament talks."

November 22-25. Brezhnev in Bonn. President Brezhnev visits West Germany and holds extensive talks with Chancellor Helmut Schmidt on economic and security issues.

November 30. Arms Talks Begin. Negotiations on the limitation of theater nuclear forces in Europe begin in Geneva. The negotiating teams headed by Paul H. Nitze for the United States and Yuli Kvitsinsky for the Soviet Union impose a news blackout. The United States bargaining position is Reagan's "zero option" plan forgoing deployment of medium-range missiles if the Soviets dismantle their comparable missiles already in place. The Soviet team proposes a freeze on medium-range missile deployment. The session recesses December 17.

December 10. Sakharov Hunger Strike Ends. Soviet officials confirm the end of a hunger strike by Soviet dissident Andrei Sakharov and his wife, Yelena Bonner. The Sakharovs began a fast November 22 to protest Moscow's refusal to allow their daughter-in-law, Lisa Alekseyeva, to join her husband, Alexsei Semyonov, in the United States. *Izvestia* announced December 4 that the Sakharovs had been hospitalized to prevent "complications in the state of their health." The Soviet Union made what is considered an unusual concession by allowing Alekseyeva to emigrate. She arrived in the United States December 20.

December 13. Martial Law in Poland. Premier Wojciech Jaruzelski declares a state of emergency in Poland and imposes martial law. The decree interrupts the operations of Solidarity and curtails the civil rights of Polish citizens. Jaruzelski's announcement follows a December 12 decision by Solidarity to call for a nationwide referendum to decide whether to maintain a communist system of government if Polish authorities do not agree to a new series of demands. Imposition of martial law includes a raid on Solidarity headquarters, detention of Lech Walesa and other Solidarity leaders, a news blackout, and the deployment of troops to ensure control. Tass December 14 calls events in Poland an "internal matter."

December 23. U.S. Economic Sanctions. President Reagan announces U.S. economic sanctions against Poland that include suspension of civil aviation and fishing rights and restriction of Export-Import Bank credits, high-technology exports, and exports of food products. Reagan places "a major share of the blame" on Moscow for the imposition of martial law. Despite Soviet denials of interference in Poland's internal affairs, the United States December 29 imposes economic sanctions against Moscow for the crackdown in Poland. These include the suspension of Aeroflot flights to the United States, a moratorium on renewals of scientific exchange agreements, and an increase in restrictions on the export of U.S. oil and natural gas equipment to the Soviet Union. The reaction of U.S. allies is mixed. West Germany in particular questions whether Moscow is indeed the prime mover behind the imposition of martial law in Poland.

1982

January 11. NATO on Poland. Foreign ministers of NATO countries meet in emergency session in Brussels and condemn the Soviet Union for its participation in "the system of repression in Poland." In contrast to the previous stance of West European leaders, the ministers call for Europe to join the United States in imposing economic sanctions against the Soviet Union. Great Britain on Feb-

ruary 5 becomes the first NATO country to do so.

January 12. Arms Talks Reconvene. U.S. and Soviet negotiators return to Geneva to continue discussions on limiting medium-range missiles in Europe.

January 25. Suslov Dies. Influential Politburo member and chief Soviet ideologist Mikhail Suslov dies "after a brief illness."

January 26. Gromyko and Haig in Geneva. Secretary of State Haig and Foreign Minister Gromyko meet in Geneva. Haig calls the talks "beneficial" but says the Polish crisis casts "a long, dark shadow over all East-West issues."

March 8. Chemical Warfare. In testimony before the Senate Foreign Relations Committee, Deputy Secretary of State Walter J. Stoessel, Jr., states that Soviet troops have been using extensive chemical warfare in Afghanistan.

March 16. Brezhnev on SS-20s. President Brezhnev announces that the Soviet Union will not deploy any new SS-20 intermediate-range missiles targeted on Europe. The ban is to stay in effect unless NATO begins its planned deployments of Pershing II and cruise missiles. The Reagan administration dismisses the move as part of Moscow's propaganda campaign against NATO's nuclear missile program.

March 24. Brezhnev on China. President Brezhnev delivers a conciliatory speech on Sino-Soviet relations in Tashkent, Uzbekistan. He calls for border negotiations and emphasizes Moscow's desire to normalize relations with Beijing.

April 2. Falkland Islands Crisis. Argentine troops seize control of Great Britain's Falkland Islands in the South Atlantic. British prime minister Margaret Thatcher orders a thirty-five-ship naval force to steam to the islands. Moscow declares its neutrality April 7, but subsequent Soviet statements support Argentina. British forces land on the islands May 21 and secure the surrender of the Argentine garrison June 14.

April 4-5. Gromyko in Yugoslavia. Soviet foreign minister Gromyko meets in Belgrade with Yugoslav officials. It is the first visit by a high-level Soviet official since President Tito's death two years before.

May 9. Reagan's START Proposal. President Reagan outlines a strategic arms reduction proposal in a speech at his alma mater, Eureka College, in Illinois. His plan calls for a one-third reduction in total warheads, with no more than half being deployed in ICBMs. He also proposes a total ceiling of 850 ICBMs and submarine-launched ballistic missiles (SLBMs) and limits on throw-weight. Reagan makes no mention of possible cuts in bombers and cruise missiles. President Brezhnev welcomes Reagan's interest in negotiations May 18 but rejects the specifics of his proposal as "one-sided."

May 10. Soviet Aid to Nicaragua. Following a visit to the Soviet Union by Nicaraguan president Daniel Ortega, the Soviets announce a five-year, $166.8 million economic and technical aid package for Nicaragua.

May 24. Brezhnev Presents Food Program. In a widely publicized speech to the Central Committee, President Brezhnev outlines an expensive new food program designed to ensure reliable supplies of foodstuffs for the Soviet Union through the 1980s.

May 26. Andropov Leaves KGB for Secretariat. Following his promotion to the Secretariat May 24, Yuri Andropov resigns as head of the KGB. He is succeeded by Vitaly Fedorchuk.

June 2-11. Reagan in Europe. President Reagan travels to Europe for an economic summit in Versailles, France, June 4-6. The leaders of the seven major industrial democracies agree to "limit their government export credits" to the Eastern bloc, with no specific credit ceiling agreed upon. Following the summit, Reagan visits Rome, Great Britain, Bonn, and Berlin. In separate speeches to the British and West German parliaments June 8 and 9, he criticizes Soviet aggression and suppression of democracy, but he expresses U.S. desires for arms control and East-West cooperation.

June 6. Israel Invades Lebanon. The Israeli army launches a major invasion into southern Lebanon, ostensibly to eliminate Palestine Liberation Organization (PLO) bases. By June 10 Israeli units are within a few miles of Beirut and are engaging in sporadic battles with Syrian troops. On June 9 and 10 the Israeli air force effectively cripples Syria's air defenses by destroying its Soviet-supplied surface-to-air missile batteries and shooting down large numbers of Syrian fighters. Israel and Syria agree to a cease-fire June 11, but Israel and the PLO continue to fight. The Soviet Union June 14 demands that Israel withdraw from Lebanon and warns that developments in the Middle East "cannot help affecting the interests of the USSR."

June 15. Gromyko Renounces First Use. At the UN General Assembly's special session on disarmament, Foreign Minister Gromyko pledges that the Soviet Union will not be the first nation to use nuclear weapons. Two days later President Reagan addresses the special session but does not comment on Gromyko's speech. He emphasizes the U.S. commitment to arms control and accuses the Soviets of being insincere and pursuing a massive military buildup.

June 18. U.S. Widens Pipeline Sanctions. As a further response to martial law in Poland, President Reagan broadens sanctions aimed at delaying progress of the European-Siberian natural gas pipeline. The new measures prohibit foreign subsidiaries and licensees of U.S. companies from selling equipment for the pipeline. Previous sanctions enacted in December 1981 barred only the sale of American-made equipment. The European Economic Community unanimously opposes the U.S. move.

June 29. START Talks Begin. The opening round of the Strategic Arms Reduction Talks (START) begins in Geneva, with Edward L. Rowny heading the U.S. negotiating team and Victor Karpov heading the Soviet delegation.

July 16. "Walk-in-the-Woods" Plan. After weeks of unofficial conversations, U.S. arms negotiator Paul Nitze and his Soviet counterpart at the Geneva talks on intermediate nuclear forces (INF), Yuli Kvitsinsky, jointly develop a European arms control package for their respective governments to consider. The package, drawn up during a private walk in the Jura Mountains near Geneva, subsequently is rejected by both governments.

July 20. U.S. Withdraws from Test Ban Talks. President Reagan ends U.S. participation in talks on a comprehensive nuclear test ban until verification measures are improved. The three-way negotiations between Great Britain, the Soviet Union, and the United States had been suspended since November 1980. Great Britain and many members of the U.S. Congress oppose Reagan's decision. On July 21 Tass accuses Reagan of using verification problems as an excuse to sabotage the talks.

August 20. U.S.-Soviet Grain Deal Extension. The Soviet Union renews for another year the one-year grain sale agreement with the United States due to expire September 30. The extension follows a July 30 proposal by President Reagan to continue the current arrangement.

September 15. Brezhnev's Middle East Peace Plan. In a Kremlin speech President Brezhnev offers a six-point plan for achieving peace in the Middle East. It calls for an Israeli withdrawal to its pre-1967 borders and a UN-guaranteed settlement providing for the establishment of a Palestinian state. The plan is similar to one adopted by the Arab League September 9. Brezhnev attacks a September 1 peace proposal by President Reagan for its failure to advocate a completely independent Palestinian state and to recognize the Palestine Liberation Organization as the sole legitimate representative of the Palestinian people.

October 5. Sino-Soviet Talks. Formal "consultations" between Soviet and Chinese deputy foreign ministers begin in Beijing. It is the first official high-level meeting between the countries since China suspended talks in 1980 after the Soviet invasion of Afghanistan. The talks end October 21, but, as previously agreed, no official statement is released. The parties do agree to hold further meetings.

October 8. Solidarity Banned. The Polish parliament votes to ban Solidarity and all other existing Polish labor organizations. President Reagan responds by announcing October 9 that he plans to end Poland's most-favored-nation trading status.

November 8. Pope to Visit Poland. Polish authorities announce that Pope John Paul II will visit Poland in June 1983. The trip previously had been scheduled for August 26, 1982, but was canceled by Polish leaders, who claimed a papal visit could disrupt national stability.

November 10. Brezhnev Dies. Soviet president and Communist party general secretary Leonid I. Brezhnev dies of a heart attack at age seventy-five. His death is not announced in the Soviet media until the following day. A four-day period of mourning is declared.

November 11. Walesa Freed. The Polish government announces the imminent release of Lech Walesa, leader of the banned Solidarity labor union. A government spokesman says Walesa would be free to "do whatever he wants." Walesa had been interned under martial law since December 1981. He arrives home in Gdansk November 14, where he says his future conduct "will be courageous but also prudent."

November 12. Andropov Named General Secretary. The Central Committee unanimously elects Yuri V. Andropov to succeed Leonid Brezhnev as general secretary. Andropov, a Politburo member and Central Committee secretary, is nominated by Brezhnev associate Konstantin Chernenko, himself considered a candidate for the top post. Andropov does not immediately assume the titular position of president, which Brezhnev also held.

November 13. Reagan Lifts Pipeline Sanctions. President Reagan ends sanctions designed to prevent U.S. and foreign companies from selling equipment to the Soviet Union for use in the construction of the European-Siberian natural gas pipeline. The sanctions (imposed December 1981 and widened June 1982) had caused considerable friction between the United States and its European allies. Reagan maintains the sanctions are no longer necessary because of the allies' new agreement concerning economic strategy toward the Soviet Union "that provides for stronger and more effective measures." However, French president François Mitterrand November 15 asserts France has not been a party to any such agreement.

November 15. Brezhnev's Funeral. The body of Leonid Brezhnev is buried between the Lenin Mausoleum and the Kremlin wall following a nationally televised ceremony attended by many foreign dignitaries. Yuri Andropov delivers the first eulogy. After the funeral Andropov briefly meets with Vice President George Bush, the leader of the U.S. delegation. Bush describes the talks as "frank, cordial, and substantive." Andropov also meets with other world leaders in Moscow for Brezhnev's funeral, including Indian prime minister Indira Gandhi, Pakistani leader Zia ul-Haq, Cuban president Fidel Castro, and Afghan leader Babrak Karmal.

November 16. Gromyko-Huang Discussions. Soviet foreign minister Gromyko meets with Chinese foreign minister Huang Hua, who had attended Brezhnev's funeral the day before. It is the first time the countries' foreign ministers have met since the 1960s.

November 22. Andropov Speech. Yuri Andropov delivers his first policy speech as general secretary to the Central Committee. Andropov advocates more independence for manufacturing and agricultural enterprises and incentives to make workers more productive. He also expresses his support for détente with the West and improved relations with China.

December 6. Ustinov on MX Deployment. Soviet defense minister Dmitry Ustinov states the USSR will counter the MX missile with a new missile of its own, if the MX is deployed. On November 22 President Reagan had announced his support for an MX missile system deployed in a "dense pack" basing mode.

December 17. Chebrikov to Head KGB. Vitaly Fedorchuk moves from his post as head of the KGB to become minister of internal affairs. Fedorchuk replaces Nikolai Shchelokov, a Brezhnev ally who is demoted. Viktor Chebrikov replaces Fedorchuk as KGB head.

December 21. Andropov Missile Proposal. General Secretary Andropov proposes a reduction in the number of Soviet intermediate-range missiles targeted on Europe to 162 if NATO cancels its planned Pershing II and cruise missile deployments. The proposed figure is equal to the number of missiles deployed by Great Britain and France, which, along with the United States, immediately reject the offer.

1983

January 12. Podgorny Dies. Nikolai Podgorny, Soviet president from 1965 until 1977, dies in Moscow at the age of seventy-nine. Podgorny had been retired since 1979.

January 17. Soviet Missiles in Syria. American intelligence officials report that Moscow has provided new surface-to-air missiles to Syria. The long-range SA-5 missiles are expected to significantly improve Syria's air defense capabilities, which were devastated by Israeli warplanes in June 1982.

February 23. Andropov Urges Economic Reforms. In an article in the party journal *Kommunist*, General Secretary Andropov says he plans to introduce wage incentives in an effort to increase productivity. He also advocates expanding the limits of local initiative.

March 6. Kohl Wins Elections. Chancellor Helmut Kohl and his Christian Democratic party are reelected in West Germany's national parliamentary elections. Their success is regarded as a victory for NATO's current "dual-track" approach to nuclear arms that advocates the deployment of Pershing II and cruise missiles in Europe if an arms control agreement is not reached with the USSR. Kohl supported the dual-track strategy, while his opponent, Social Democrat Hans-Jochen Vogel, criticized it.

March 8. Reagan's "Evil Empire" Speech. In a speech to a convention of Protestant evangelicals in Orlando, Florida, President Reagan denounces a nuclear freeze and urges the audience not to "ignore the facts of history and the aggressive impulses of an evil empire [the Soviet Union]." Reagan also calls Soviet communism "the focus of evil in the modern world." Tass comments March 9 that the speech shows the Reagan administration "can think only in terms of confrontation and bellicose, lunatic anticommunism."

March 23. Reagan Calls for ABM Development. In a nationally televised speech President Reagan warns of the Soviet military buildup and defends his record $280.5 billion defense budget request. He then calls on American scientists to develop an advanced antiballistic missile (ABM) defense system that would render nuclear ballistic missiles "impotent and obsolete." Reagan's speech leads to the establishment of the Strategic Defense Initiative (SDI), a long-term research and development program focusing on space-based ABM weapons. General Secretary Andropov claims March 26 that Reagan's ABM development plans threaten to fuel the arms race.

May 3. Andropov Offers to Limit Warheads. General Secretary Andropov proposes limiting the warheads, missiles, and bombers of the Warsaw Pact and NATO (including French and British forces) to equitable levels. American officials welcome the Soviets' new willingness to discuss limitations on warheads but object to Andropov's continued inclusion of French and British nuclear weapons as part of NATO's nuclear arsenal.

May 4. Iran Disbands Communist Party. The government of Iran bans the Iranian Communist Tudeh party after the party's head confesses to espionage and treason charges. The government also says Soviet embassy personnel interfered in Iran "by using and establishing links with mercenaries and traitors to the republic" and expels eighteen Soviet diplomats.

May 9. Andropov Heads Defense Council. Defense Minister Dmitry Ustinov discloses in a *Pravda* article that General Secretary Andropov functions as the chairman of the Defense Council.

May 16-23. Gorbachev Visits Canada. Politburo member and Central Committee secretary Mikhail Gorbachev travels across Canada as leader of a Soviet agricultural delegation. He meets with Prime Minister Pierre Trudeau in Ottawa May 18.

June 9. British Conservatives Reelected. The Conservative party, headed by Prime Minister Margaret Thatcher, is decisively returned to power in Great Britain's national parliamentary elections. The Conservative victory ensures that NATO's scheduled deployments of cruise missiles in Great Britain will occur.

June 16. Andropov Elected President. The Supreme Soviet formally elects General Secretary Andropov as president (chairman of the Presidium of the Supreme Soviet). Andropov becomes the only Soviet leader other than Leonid Brezhnev to be president and general secretary simultaneously.

June 16-23. Pope Visits Poland. Pope John Paul II travels to his native Poland for a visit that had been postponed by Polish leaders in 1982. In a brief televised

speech the pope calls for social reform based on the August 1980 agreements that brought about the Solidarity union. The same day he meets for two hours with Wojciech Jaruzelski, the leader of the Polish regime. In subsequent speeches to huge crowds, the pope continues to emphasize Polish nationalism and social reform. He holds a private audience with Solidarity leader Lech Walesa June 23 before leaving for Rome.

June 26. Pentecostals to Emigrate. Seven Soviet Pentecostals who had been living in the U.S. embassy in Moscow since 1978 are granted permission to emigrate by Soviet authorities.

July 4-7. Kohl Visits Soviet Union. West German chancellor Helmut Kohl meets President Andropov in Moscow. Andropov reportedly tells Kohl that deployment of NATO missiles in West Germany would harm Soviet-West German relations. Kohl stops in Kiev July 7 before returning to Bonn.

July 21. Poland Ends Martial Law. Martial law is formally lifted in Poland after nineteen months. The government also extends amnesty to many political prisoners. However, the Polish Parliament enacts a series of laws that permits the government to tightly control Poland's economy and social programs.

July 26. Experimental Economic Reforms. The Soviet Union announces economic "experiments" designed to relax central bureaucratic controls. The plan gives factory managers in selected industries greater autonomy over budgets, investment, wages, and incentive bonuses. It is scheduled to begin January 1, 1984. President Andropov had publicly supported such reforms on several occasions.

August 18. Andropov on ASAT Weapons. At a Kremlin meeting with nine visiting U.S. Democratic senators, President Andropov declares a unilateral moratorium on the deployment of Soviet antisatellite (ASAT) weapons. He also asks the United States to agree to a treaty "on the elimination of the existing antisatellite systems and the prohibition of the development of new ones."

August 25. U.S.-Soviet Grain Deal. A five-year grain sale agreement is signed in Moscow by representatives of the United States and USSR. The pact obligates the Soviet Union to buy nine million tons of American grain during each of the next five years. The Soviets have the option to buy an additional three million tons annually without obtaining further U.S. government approval.

September 1. Soviets Down Korean Airliner. A Soviet warplane shoots down Korean Air Lines flight 007 over the Sea of Japan near Sakhalin Island. The Boeing 747, with 269 people on board, had strayed into Soviet airspace for unknown reasons. The Soviets do not admit until September 6 that they shot down the plane. Moscow claims the jetliner was spying for the United States and did not respond to warnings. Chief of the Soviet General Staff Marshal Nikolai Ogarkov tells foreign reporters September 9 that the order to shoot down the plane was "not an accident or an error." Many nations condemn the attack and temporarily restrict civil aviation with the USSR in protest. The Reagan administration suspends a U.S.-Soviet transportation agreement and talks on opening a U.S. consulate in Kiev.

September 15. Soviet UN Delegation Blocked. In response to the Soviet destruction of a Korean airliner, the governors of New Jersey and New York refuse to allow the Soviet delegation to the United Nations to land at New York area commercial airports. The governors also question whether they can ensure the Soviet delegation's security. The Reagan administration offers the Soviets the option of landing at a U.S. military airfield. Foreign Minister Gromyko cancels the Soviet visit September 17 and attacks the United States for failing to meet its host-country obligations.

September 26. Reagan's UN Speech. In a speech to the UN General Assembly, President Reagan calls on the USSR to accept global limits on intermediate-range missiles and offers to discuss limits on aircraft and a reduction in U.S. Pershing II deployments. Despite Reagan's tone of compromise concerning intermediate-range nuclear force talks, he attacks the USSR for human rights and arms control violations. President Andropov denounces Reagan's UN speech September 28 in a strongly worded Tass statement. He calls Reagan's arms control proposals "mere declarations" and accuses the United States of following "a militant course." Andropov also defends the downing of the Korean airliner and repeats Soviet accusations that the plane was on a spy mission.

October 5. Walesa Awarded Peace Prize. The head of the outlawed Polish Solidarity union, Lech Walesa, is awarded the Nobel Peace Prize. Walesa announces he will donate the prize money to a charity for Poland's farmers. The Polish government denounces the prize October 6. *Izvestia*, the Soviet government newspaper, calls Walesa a "low-grade hustler" October 8 but does not mention his Nobel Peace Prize.

October 21. Sino-Soviet Trade Agreement. The Soviets and Chinese conclude an agreement to increase annual trade from $800 million to more than $1.6 billion. They also agree to increase cultural, sports, and student exchanges.

October 23. Antinuclear Rallies. Demonstrations in European cities against NATO's upcoming missile deployments collectively draw more than two million protesters.

October 25. Grenada Invasion. U.S. troops aided by forces from six Caribbean nations invade Grenada, an independently governed island near Venezuela. President Reagan says the United States was acting in response to a "formal request" by the Organization of Eastern Caribbean States to help restore order in Grenada. Reagan also cites concern for the safety of American citizens on the island. American troops overcome resistance by local militias and well-armed Cuban "construction workers." The pro-Cuban, hard-line Marxist regime is deposed. The United States declares an end to the fighting November 2. Many nations, including close U.S. allies, criticize the invasion. The Soviet Union condemns it as "direct, unprovoked aggression."

October 26. Soviet INF Concessions. In a *Pravda* interview Andropov announces that the USSR is willing to reduce the number of SS-20s aimed at Europe to "about 140" and to be more flexible in negotiating limits on medium-range bombers if NATO cancels its upcoming missile deployments. The Soviets previously had offered to reduce their SS-20 force to 162. Andropov also warns that the Soviets will leave the INF negotiations in Geneva if NATO begins deploying missiles. The State Department rejects Andropov's concessions as "vague" and says they were intended to influence Western European public opinion.

November 7. Andropov Misses Parade. President Andropov, who has not been seen in public since August 18, fails to appear at the annual parade in Moscow commemorating the Bolshevik Revolution. Kremlin spokesmen maintain Andropov has a "bad cold," but many Western analysts contend he would have attended the ceremonies were he not seriously ill.

November 14. Missiles Arrive in Great Britain. The first sixteen cruise missiles scheduled for deployment arrive at Greenham Common Air Base in England.

November 22. West Germany Accepts Missiles. Following a stormy two-day debate, the West German Bundestag (parliament) votes 286-226 to allow NATO missiles to be deployed in West Germany. The first nine Pershing II missiles arrive in the country the next day.

November 23. Soviets Leave Talks. At a brief, final meeting, Yuli Kvitsinsky, head of the Soviet delegation, announces that the USSR is withdrawing indefinitely from the INF negotiations in Geneva to protest NATO's missile deployments. Kvitsinsky's American counterpart, Paul Nitze, says "the U.S. is prepared to continue the negotiations at any time."

November 24. Soviet Countermeasures. Andropov issues a statement condemning NATO missile deployments and announcing probable Soviet countermeasures. He says the USSR will end its moratorium on additional SS-20 missile deployments in Europe, accelerate the timetable for introducing new tactical nuclear missiles into Czechoslovakia and East Germany, and deploy submarines equipped with cruise missiles or depressed-trajectory ballistic missiles closer to U.S. shores.

December 7. Wu on Sino-Soviet Talks. Chinese Foreign Minister Wu Xueqian states that Sino-Soviet talks on normalizing relations are making no progress because of the Soviets' refusal to discuss their military presence in Afghanistan, their support of Vietnam's aggression against Cambodia, and their military maneuvers along the

Chinese border.

December 8. START Talks End. The Soviet delegation to the START negotiations in Geneva refuses to set a date for further talks. The Soviets say they must reexamine their positions in the wake of NATO's intermediate-range missile deployments. The Warsaw Pact also refuses to set a date for resumption of the Mutual and Balanced Force Reduction (MBFR) talks before these negotiations adjourn in Vienna December 15.

December 26. Kremlin Leadership Changes. A Central Committee plenum approves promotions of candidate Politburo members Vitaly Vorotnikov and Mikhail Solomentsev to full membership. Although Andropov does not attend the plenum and has not been seen in public since August, many Western observers regard the promotions as evidence that Andropov is still in control. The plenum also approves the appointments of Yegor Ligachev to the Central Committee Secretariat and KGB head Viktor Chebrikov to candidate member status on the Politburo.

1984

January 10. Chemical Weapons Talks Proposed. The USSR proposes that NATO and the Warsaw Pact hold negotiations on banning chemical weapons in Europe. Western officials welcome the offer but express doubts that Moscow would agree to adequate verification measures.

January 12. Negotiators Trade Accusations. In a *New York Times* article, Yuli Kvitsinsky, chief Soviet negotiator at the INF talks, blames the United States and Paul Nitze, chief U.S. negotiator, for the failure of the talks. Nitze in a January 19 *New York Times* article disputes Kvitsinsky's version of events, including the "walk-in-the-woods" negotiating session of July 1982. Nitze says for Kvitsinsky "the truth or falsity of any statement is only of secondary interest."

January 16. Reagan on East-West Relations. President Reagan calls for a resumption of arms negotiations in an address notable for its conciliatory tone. He says the principles of "realism, strength, and dialogue" should determine U.S. policy toward the Soviet Union.

January 17. Stockholm Conference Opens. The thirty-five-nation Conference on Confidence- and Security-Building Measures and Disarmament in Europe opens in Stockholm. Secretary of State George P. Shultz proposes a six-point NATO plan to reduce the chances of military confrontation. He attacks the Soviet Union's human rights record and its imposition of "an artificial barrier" dividing Europe. In a harshly worded speech January 18, Foreign Minister Gromyko says "the aggressive foreign policy of the United States is the main threat to peace." Shultz and Gromyko meet the same day, but Shultz says January 19 that they made no progress toward resumption of arms control talks.

January 22. MBFR Talks to Resume. Secretary of State Shultz announces that the United States has accepted a Soviet proposal to reopen the Mutual and Balanced Force Reduction (MBFR) talks in Vienna March 16.

January 23. Soviet Arms Violations. President Reagan sends a classified report to Congress describing alleged Soviet arms control violations. The infractions described in an unclassified synopsis include Soviet use of chemical weapons in Afghanistan; construction of an illegally positioned phased-array radar near Krasnoyarsk, Siberia; and development of a second new ICBM prohibited by the unratified SALT II treaty. A January 29 Soviet statement dismisses the accusations and charges the United States with violations of its own.

January 24. Andropov on East-West Relations. In a *Pravda* interview carried in advance by Tass, President Andropov responds to President Reagan's January 16 speech. Andropov criticizes Reagan for insisting on negotiating from a position of strength instead of on "an equal footing." Andropov calls on the United States to take "concrete steps" to improve relations. The interview's tone, however, is moderate compared with recent anti-American rhetoric. Western speculation is that the interview was actually a Politburo policy statement issued in the name of Andropov, who is rumored to be seriously ill.

February 9. Andropov Dies. Soviet leader Yuri V. Andropov dies at age sixty-nine in Moscow of complications caused by acute kidney problems. A bulletin issued February 10 announces Andropov's death and states that he had been receiving kidney dialysis therapy for the last year. Since August 18, 1983, when Andropov was last seen in public, Soviet officials had insisted that he was not ill.

February 13. Chernenko Chosen General Secretary. Konstantin U. Chernenko, a close ally of Leonid Brezhnev, is unanimously elected general secretary by the Communist Party Central Committee. The seventy-two-year-old Chernenko is the oldest man to become general secretary. Chernenko tells the Central Committee that recent economic reforms should continue. He also calls for "peaceful coexistence of states with different social systems" but warns the West against trying to upset the current military balance. No successor is named to fill the post of president, which Andropov also occupied.

February 14. Andropov's Funeral. Yuri Andropov's body is buried behind the Lenin Mausoleum following a televised ceremony in Red Square. General Secretary Chernenko, Defense Minister Ustinov, and Foreign Minister Gromyko deliver eulogies. Numerous foreign leaders attend the funeral, including Vice President George Bush, who meets with Chernenko for thirty minutes.

February 23. Chernenko Heads Defense Council. Western military attachés say Marshal Nikolai Ogarkov, chief of the Soviet general staff, referred to General Secretary Chernenko as head of the Defense Council at a Soviet Armed Forces Day reception. Andropov also led the small body, which is believed to direct defense policy.

March 2. Chernenko Address. Prior to the upcoming Supreme Soviet elections, Chernenko delivers his first policy address as general secretary. He endorses Andropov's economic and anticorruption programs, expresses Soviet desires to normalize relations with China, and calls for improved East-West relations backed up by new arms control agreements. However, Chernenko seemed to indicate that intermediate-range nuclear force and strategic arms reduction talks would not resume unless NATO reversed its decision to deploy intermediate-range missiles.

March 21. Collision at Sea. While surfacing in the Sea of Japan, a Soviet nuclear-powered submarine strikes the U.S. aircraft carrier *Kitty Hawk*. The submarine had been routinely trailing the carrier. The Defense Department accuses the submarine of violating several international navigation laws.

April 11. Chernenko Elected President. The Supreme Soviet names Chernenko president (chairman of the Presidium of the Supreme Soviet). The titular post had been vacant since Andropov's death. Politburo member Mikhail Gorbachev formally nominates Chernenko.

April 26-May 1. Reagan Visits China. Chinese leaders cordially receive President Reagan during his six-day visit to the People's Republic of China. Several protocols are signed, including a peaceful nuclear cooperation agreement. Reagan is allowed to appear on Chinese television twice, but his implied criticism of the Soviet Union is deleted. During the visit the Soviet press attacked China for its cooperation with the United States.

May 2. Sakharov Hunger Strike. Soviet dissident Andrei Sakharov begins a hunger strike to pressure the government to allow his wife, Yelena Bonner, to receive medical treatment in the West. Bonner reports that Sakharov had been taken to an unknown location by authorities May 7. The Sakharovs' treatment brings widespread condemnation from the West.

May 7. Soviets Withdraw from Olympics. The Soviet National Olympic Committee announces that the Soviet team will not attend the summer games in Los Angeles because of "inadequate security." The statement says "chauvinistic sentiments and anti-Soviet hysteria are being whipped up" in the United States. All Soviet-bloc nations but Romania also pull out of the games.

June 21. Naval Base Explosion. American intelligence sources say a huge explosion occurred in mid May at the Soviet northern fleet naval base at Severomorsk. The blast reportedly killed more than two hundred people and destroyed large stocks of ammunition and conventional missiles. The following day the Kremlin denies knowledge of the explosion.

June 29. Space Weapons Talks Proposed. The Soviet government sends a formal note to the United States proposing U.S.-Soviet negotiations on banning weapons in space. The United States responds the same day by offering to engage in talks on space weapons if they are linked to negotiations on limiting strategic and intermediate-range nuclear weapons. The Soviets reject the U.S. proposal July 1 but repeat their call for talks on space weapons.

July 5. Molotov Reinstated. Ninety-four-year-old Viacheslav Molotov is readmitted to the Soviet Communist party. Molotov, who had served as prime minister and foreign minister under Joseph Stalin, was removed from power in 1957 by Nikita Khrushchev.

July 11. Kuwait Buys Soviet Weapons. Kuwait announces it will buy $327 million in weapons from the Soviet Union. The sale includes surface-to-air missiles intended to protect Persian Gulf shipping from attacks related to the Iran-Iraq war. The deal follows a U.S. refusal to sell Kuwait Stinger antiaircraft missiles.

July 17. Hot Line Improved. Soviet and U.S. officials sign an agreement to modernize the crisis hot line between Washington and Moscow. The new hot line will transmit words three times faster than the current sixty-four-words-per-minute teleprinters.

July 21. Poland Frees Political Prisoners. The Polish government announces that 652 political prisoners will be released as part of a larger amnesty for criminals serving short sentences. On August 3 the United States lifts some of the sanctions imposed against Poland in 1981.

August 11. Reagan Joke. During a "voice check" before his regular weekly radio broadcast, President Reagan says, "My fellow Americans, I'm pleased to tell you today that I've signed legislation that will outlaw Russia forever. We begin bombing in five minutes." Although the remark is made off the record as a joke, it prompts a wave of criticism from U.S. allies and Reagan's political opponents. Moscow sharply condemns Reagan's statement as "unprecedentedly hostile toward the USSR and dangerous to the cause of peace."

August 18. Friendship '84 Games Begin. The Soviet Union's sports festival for nations that had pulled out of the Summer Olympics opens in Moscow.

September 4. Honecker Visit Postponed. East German Communist party leader Erich Honecker indefinitely postpones his scheduled visit to West Germany, which would have been the first visit to that country by an East German leader. The Soviet Union, which recently had intensified its verbal attacks against the West German government and the growing détente between the two Germanys, appeared to have pressured Honecker into the postponement.

September 6. Ogarkov Removed. Marshal Nikolai Ogarkov is removed as chief of the Soviet general staff and reassigned to unspecified duties. He is succeeded by

Marshal Sergei Akhromeev, his deputy. Tass in announcing the move gives no reason for Ogarkov's apparent demotion.

September 21-22. Gromyko-Wu Talks. The foreign ministers of the Soviet Union and China, Andrei Gromyko and Wu Xueqian, meet while in New York for the opening of the UN General Assembly. The talks are described by both sides as positive.

September 24. Reagan's UN Speech. President Reagan omits direct criticism of the Soviet Union from his address to the UN General Assembly. He calls for an overall improvement in U.S.-Soviet relations and negotiations on arms control, regional conflicts, and the militarization of space.

September 26-28. Gromyko Meetings. Foreign Minister Gromyko and Secretary of State Shultz talk for three hours in New York September 26. In an address to the United Nations September 27, Gromyko attacks U.S. foreign policy and accuses the Reagan administration of deliberately undermining arms control negotiations. On September 28 Gromyko travels to Washington for a three-and-a-half-hour meeting with President Reagan. It is the first time the president has met with a Soviet leader. No concrete results are reported.

November 6. Reagan Reelected. Ronald Reagan overwhelmingly defeats Democratic candidate Walter Mondale to win a second term as president.

November 14. Dobrynin on Arms Talks. Anatoly Dobrynin, the Soviet ambassador to the United States, tells reporters his government is interested in an American proposal made months before to begin talks that would address every aspect of the nuclear arms race.

November 22. Arms Talks Announced. The Soviet Union and the United States announce that Secretary of State Shultz and Foreign Minister Gromyko will meet in Geneva January 7-8, 1985, to lay the groundwork for future arms control negotiations.

December 15-21. Gorbachev in Great Britain. Politburo member Mikhail Gorbachev and his wife, Raisa, make a highly publicized trip to Great Britain. Gorbachev meets with Prime Minister Margaret Thatcher, who says December 17, "I like Mr. Gorbachev—we can do business together." Gorbachev criticizes the Reagan administration's Strategic Defense Initiative (SDI)—an effort to develop a space-based antiballistic missile system—but speaks positively about the prospects for arms control. He returns to Moscow December 21, a day earlier than planned, after personally announcing to the West that Defense Minister Dmitry Ustinov had died.

December 20. Ustinov Dies. Soviet defense minister and Politburo member Dmitry Ustinov dies at age seventy-six. Many Western observers expected Ustinov to be succeeded by Politburo member and Central Committee secretary Grigory Romanov, but Marshal Sergei Sokolov is appointed defense minister. President Chernenko is

absent from Ustinov's December 24 funeral.

December 21-29. Arkhipov in Beijing. First Deputy Premier Ivan Arkhipov travels to Beijing for an official visit that had been postponed since May. Arkhipov and Chinese leaders sign accords on economic, scientific, and technological cooperation. They also agree to begin talks on a trade pact covering the period from 1986 to 1990. China calls the accords "the most substantial agreements since relations between our two countries were strained in the 1960s."

December 27. Chernenko Appears. President Chernenko, who had missed Dmitry Ustinov's funeral and was believed to be ill, awards several Soviet authors medals for literature. The Soviet media give the ceremony unusually prominent coverage.

1985

January 7-8. Gromyko and Shultz in Geneva. Foreign Minister Gromyko and Secretary of State Shultz meet in Geneva to discuss the resumption of arms control negotiations. They agree to hold umbrella talks divided into three subgroups: strategic nuclear weapons, intermediate-range nuclear weapons, and weapons in space. The date and site are to be determined later.

January 13. Gromyko Interview. In a Soviet television interview, Foreign Minister Gromyko asserts that the Strategic Defense Initiative could be used to "blackmail and pressure" the Soviet Union. He says that without movement toward preventing the militarization of space no progress can be made on limiting strategic weapons.

January 24. Soviet Economic Statistics. The Soviet government reports that the economy grew by 2.6 percent in 1984. Although the West considers Soviet economic statistics to be inflated, the announcement is viewed as significant since the increase is the lowest reported since World War II. The Soviets indicate that the poor performance of the agricultural sector held down overall growth.

January 26. Arms Talks Set. The Soviet Union and the United States announce that arms negotiations will begin March 12 in Geneva. The Soviet Foreign Ministry also says Viktor Karpov, Yuli Kvitsinsky, and Aleksei Obukhov will be the chief Soviet negotiators. The United States had announced its negotiators—Max Kampelman, John Tower, and Maynard Glitman—January 18. Karpov and Kampelman will lead the delegations.

February 11-14. Papandreou in Moscow. Greek premier Andreas Papandreou is warmly received during a four-day visit to the Soviet Union. He and Soviet leaders sign several economic accords. Papandreou's scheduled February 12 meeting with President Chernenko is canceled, fueling speculation that Chernenko is ill.

February 20. Thatcher Endorses SDI. During a three-day visit to the United States, Prime Minister Margaret

Thatcher of Great Britain endorses President Reagan's SDI in a speech before a joint session of Congress. Her support is preceded by West German chancellor Helmut Kohl's qualified endorsement February 9.

February 21. Soviets Allow Inspections. The USSR signs a nuclear safeguards accord with the International Atomic Energy Agency, which provides for the opening of some Soviet civilian nuclear power plants to international inspection. Western officials praise Moscow's action.

February 24. Chernenko Appears. A frail President Chernenko, supported by an aide, appears briefly before television cameras to cast a ballot at a Moscow polling place. It is the first time Chernenko has been seen in public in more than eight weeks. Meanwhile, Politburo member Mikhail Gorbachev arrives at another polling place accompanied by his family. He jokes with reporters in front of Western cameras.

February 25-March 1. Gromyko Trip. Foreign Minister Gromyko repeatedly attacks SDI during state visits to Italy and Spain. In Rome February 27, Gromyko holds his first meeting with Pope John Paul II since 1979.

March 7-10. Shcherbitsky in United States. Politburo member and Ukrainian Communist party leader Vladimir Shcherbitsky visits the United States as head of a parliamentary delegation. Shcherbitsky is the first Soviet Politburo member other than Foreign Minister Gromyko to visit the United States since 1973. Shcherbitsky returns early to the USSR March 10, apparently after receiving word of Chernenko's death.

March 10. Chernenko Dies. President Konstantin U. Chernenko dies in Moscow of heart failure at age seventy-three. He had been weakened by a variety of ailments including emphysema, hepatitis, and cirrhosis of the liver. His death is not announced until March 11.

March 11. Gorbachev Chosen General Secretary. The Central Committee elects fifty-four-year-old Mikhail S. Gorbachev to replace Konstantin Chernenko as general secretary of the Communist party within hours of the announcement of Chernenko's death. Western observers regard the unusual speed of the succession as evidence that Soviet leaders had agreed to Gorbachev's selection before Chernenko died. In his acceptance speech, Gorbachev promises to continue the policies of the two previous general secretaries, Chernenko and Andropov, and says economic improvement is his most important goal.

March 12. Arms Talks Begin. Despite Chernenko's death, the Geneva arms negotiations begin on schedule. Chief Soviet negotiator Viktor Karpov tells reporters that General Secretary Gorbachev "presided over the Politburo meeting that approved the instructions" for the Soviet negotiating team. Both sides agree to keep the substance of their talks confidential.

March 13. Chernenko's Funeral. The body of Konstantin Chernenko is buried near the Kremlin wall following a Red Square ceremony. General Secretary Gorbachev eu-

logizes Chernenko as a "steadfast fighter for noble communist ideals." Against the advice of several aides, President Reagan does not go to Moscow but instead sends Vice President Bush. However, Reagan does invite Gorbachev to the United States in a letter presented to him by Bush. Gorbachev also meets with many other foreign dignitaries, including Chinese vice premier Li Peng.

March 20. Belgium Accepts Missiles. The Belgian parliament approves the deployment of NATO cruise missiles in Belgium by a 116-93 vote.

March 24. American Officer Killed. U.S. Army Maj. Arthur Nicholson, Jr., is shot by a Soviet guard while observing a Soviet military installation in East Germany. Soviet officials claim Nicholson was in a restricted area and failed to heed a warning shot. The United States says he was conducting routine, sanctioned observations in a nonrestricted area in accordance with a 1947 agreement allowing such observations. President Reagan condemns the shooting as an "unwarranted act of violence."

March 28. MX Funds Appropriated. Following an intense White House lobbying effort, the House of Representatives appropriates $1.5 billion for the production of twenty-one MX missiles by a 217-210 vote. The Senate had approved the funding earlier in the month, 55-45. The administration had argued that the Soviet Union would be unlikely to agree to equitable arms cuts if Congress did not support the MX.

April 7. Soviet Missile Moratorium. General Secretary Gorbachev announces Moscow has suspended deployment of intermediate-range missiles in Europe until November and asks NATO to halt its missile deployments. Gorbachev also states he is agreeable to a summit with President Reagan in the near future. The Reagan administration says that Gorbachev's freeze would not affect the scheduled deployments.

April 23. Politburo Promotions. Central Committee secretaries Nikolai Ryzhkov and Yegor Ligachev are promoted to full Politburo status along with KGB head Viktor Chebrikov. The Ryzhkov and Ligachev promotions represent dramatic advancements, since they bypassed the traditional step of candidate Politburo membership. Defense Minister Sergei Sokolov is elevated to candidate Politburo status. Viktor Nikonov is named to the Central Committee Secretariat with responsibility for agriculture.

April 25-26. Warsaw Pact Summit. Leaders of the seven Warsaw Pact nations meet in Warsaw and approve a twenty-year extension of the treaty April 26. Gorbachev attends the summit, making his first foreign trip since becoming general secretary. He stays in Warsaw April 27 for talks with Polish leader Wojciech Jaruzelski.

April 28-29. Ortega in Moscow. Nicaraguan president Daniel Ortega visits Moscow to discuss Soviet economic assistance. He meets with General Secretary Gorbachev April 29. Although no specific aid is announced, Tass quotes Gorbachev as having promised to continue economic, political, and diplomatic support of Nicaragua.

May 1. U.S. Embargo. President Reagan places an embargo on trade with Nicaragua and bans Nicaraguan shipping and air traffic from the United States. In a letter to Congress he says the growing Nicaraguan threat to Central American and U.S. security prompted his action.

May 1. Reagan in Europe. President Reagan arrives in Europe for a ten-day visit that includes an economic summit in Bonn May 2-4 and a controversial May 5 stop at a military cemetery in Bitburg, West Germany, where a number of Nazi SS troops are buried. General Secretary Gorbachev and Reagan deliver speeches May 8, the fortieth anniversary of the surrender of Nazi Germany. In Moscow, Gorbachev condemns U.S. "state terrorism" against Nicaragua and aid to Afghan rebels. He also criticizes Reagan's visit to Bitburg Cemetery, saying there were political figures at the recent Western summit who were "ready to forget or even justify the SS cutthroats and, moreover, pay homage to them." Despite the attacks, Gorbachev calls for a return to détente. Reagan, speaking before the European Parliament in Strasbourg, France, accuses the Soviets of "undermining stability and the basis for nuclear deterrence" by proceeding with plans to deploy a new mobile intercontinental ballistic missile.

May 16. Anti-alcoholism Program. The Soviet government announces new measures designed to combat drunkenness and alcoholism. Beginning June 1 the legal drinking age will be raised from eighteen to twenty-one, liquor store hours will be shortened, and alcohol production will be gradually reduced.

May 20. Walker Arrested. The FBI arrests John Walker, Jr., a retired U.S. Navy warrant officer, on charges of selling military secrets to the Soviet Union. The case widens during the following two weeks as three other people, including Walker's son and brother, are arrested for spying.

May 22. Indo-Soviet Economic Pacts. Prime Minister Rajiv Gandhi of India and General Secretary Gorbachev sign an agreement that provides for $1.2 billion in Soviet credits for construction of industrial and energy projects in India. They also agree to a new fifteen-year economic and technological cooperation agreement.

June 10. United States to Abide by SALT II. President Reagan says that the United States will stay within restrictions established by the unratified SALT II treaty. He says that when the next Trident submarine is deployed the Navy will dismantle an older Poseidon submarine to stay within the treaty's 1,200 multiple warhead missile limit.

June 11. Gorbachev Calls for Reforms. Speaking before top Soviet officials, General Secretary Gorbachev criticizes the draft of the 1986-1990 Five-Year Plan and several government ministers. He calls for increased production of quality consumer goods, enhancement of the role of local factory managers, curtailment of central planning in day-to-day factory affairs, and greater emphasis on market forces.

July 1-2. Soviet Leadership Shuffle. The Central Committee announces that Grigory Romanov, who had been a rival to Gorbachev for the general secretary post, has resigned from the Politburo for health reasons. Western analysts generally agree Romanov was ousted. The Central Committee also promotes Georgian Communist party leader Eduard Shevardnadze to full Politburo status. On July 2 Shevardnadze is named foreign minister, replacing Andrei Gromyko, who is elected to the vacant ceremonial office of president (chairman of the Presidium of the Supreme Soviet).

July 2. Summit Announced. American officials say the Soviets have agreed to a summit conference between President Reagan and General Secretary Gorbachev in Geneva November 19-20.

July 10. Sino-Soviet Trade Pact. Chinese and Soviet representatives sign an agreement that will sharply increase bilateral trade to $14 billion over the five-year period from 1986 to 1990. Annual trade between the countries is expected to rise to $3.5 billion by 1990, compared with a projected $1.8 billion in 1985.

July 17. Ogarkov Reappointed. Reports emerge that Nikolai Ogarkov, who was removed as military chief of staff in September 1984, has been appointed commander in chief of Warsaw Pact forces.

July 29. Nuclear Test Proposals. General Secretary Gorbachev declares a unilateral Soviet moratorium on nuclear tests to begin August 6. The moratorium is to continue until the end of the year and will be indefinitely extended if the United States also stops its nuclear tests. U.S. officials quickly reject the proposal, citing a recent spurt of Soviet testing. President Reagan instead invites Soviet experts to observe a U.S. nuclear test explosion. The Soviets decline but say they will proceed with their unilateral moratorium.

July 30-August 1. Helsinki Accords Anniversary. The representatives of thirty-five nations meet in Helsinki to mark the tenth anniversary of the Helsinki accords. In speeches July 30, Secretary of State Shultz criticizes the Soviet Union's human rights record, while Foreign Minister Shevardnadze asserts that the USSR, unlike Western countries, protects its people from poverty, unemployment, and discrimination. The two leaders meet July 31 to discuss the upcoming Reagan-Gorbachev summit.

August 21. Tracking Dust Allegation. The United States accuses the Soviet Union of using a chemical dust thought to be carcinogenic to track American diplomats in Moscow. The Soviets deny the allegation as "absurd" August 22.

August 26. Gorbachev Interview. In an interview published in *Time* magazine September 9, General Secretary Gorbachev says he regrets that U.S.-Soviet relations are not improving. He criticizes the Reagan administration for downplaying the upcoming summit and portraying Moscow's arms control proposals as propaganda.

September 10. Gorbachev on Chemical Arms. General Secretary Gorbachev proposes establishing a chemical weapons-free zone in central Europe. The Reagan administration immediately rejects the proposal, saying it wants a "comprehensive verifiable ban" on chemical weapons.

September 12. Defection Prompts Expulsions. Great Britain announces that the top KGB agent in Britain, Oleg Gordievsky, has defected. He had been a political counselor at the Soviet embassy in London. Great Britain expels twenty-five Soviets, including diplomats, journalists, and trade representatives, whom Gordievsky is said to have named as spies. The Soviet Union retaliates by expelling twenty-five British citizens September 14. London expels six additional Soviets September 16; Moscow responds by expelling six Britons September 18.

September 13. ASAT Test. An American F-15 fighter plane launches an antisatellite weapon that destroys a U.S. satellite orbiting 290 miles above Earth. The missile test had been announced August 20. On September 4 Tass had warned that if the test took place the Soviet Union would "consider itself free of its unilateral commitment" not to deploy ASATs in space.

September 17. Reagan on SDI. President Reagan says in a press conference that he would not negotiate limits on the development and testing of SDI to achieve an arms control agreement with the Soviets.

September 23-24. UN Speeches. Secretary of State Shultz and Foreign Minister Shevardnadze speak on arms control at the opening of the UN General Assembly. Shultz accuses the USSR September 23 of pursuing "the world's most active military space program," while simultaneously objecting to U.S. research on space weapons. On September 24 Shevardnadze portrays SDI as a U.S. attempt to gain military superiority and says the USSR is ready to negotiate an arms control agreement that would bring "truly radical reductions" in nuclear arms. After his UN visit Shevardnadze meets with President Reagan in Washington September 27 and delivers a new Soviet arms control proposal.

September 26. KGB Agent Defects. U.S. officials confirm that Vitaly Yurchenko, a high-ranking KGB agent, has defected. Yurchenko, a counselor with the Soviet Foreign Ministry in Rome, had been taken to Washington for debriefing following his defection. He reportedly provided information about Soviet double agents.

September 27. Ryzhkov Replaces Tikhonov. Nikolai Tikhonov retires as premier, citing health reasons. He is succeeded by Nikolai Ryzhkov, who had been appointed to the Politburo in April. Ryzhkov resigns October 15 from his post as a Central Committee secretary.

September 30. Soviet Arms Proposal. The Soviets formally present a plan at the Geneva arms control talks to substantially cut the nuclear arsenals of both superpow-ers. Foreign Minister Shevardnadze had outlined the offer during his September 27 meeting with President Reagan. The plan's main feature is a 50 percent reduction in the strategic weapons of both sides. Reagan said September 28 that he welcomed the Soviet offer and hoped it would provide a basis for discussion. However, senior U.S. administration officials express dissatisfaction with many aspects of the plan.

September 30. Soviets Kidnapped. In two coordinated incidents four Soviet diplomats are kidnapped in West Beirut. The Islamic Liberation Organization (ILO) issues photographs of the Soviet hostages October 1 and threatens to kill them unless the USSR pressures Syria to halt an offensive by Syrian-backed leftist militias against Moslem fundamentalists in Tripoli, Lebanon. One of the hostages is found dead October 2. The Soviet Union evacuates families and nonessential personnel from its West Beirut embassy October 4. In response to Soviet requests for help in resolving the crisis, Syria negotiates a truce between the warring factions in Tripoli. Syrian troops enter the city October 6 to enforce a cease-fire. The ILO releases the remaining three Soviet hostages unharmed October 30.

October 2-5. Gorbachev in France. Gorbachev travels to France for his first visit to the West since becoming general secretary. He proposes October 3 that France and Great Britain join the Soviet Union in talks on nuclear weapons in Europe, separate from the Geneva negotiations. France and Great Britain decline the invitation October 4. Gorbachev says his discussions with President François Mitterrand were "fruitful and constructive." Western observers point out, however, that the visit did not produce a joint Soviet-French communiqué denouncing SDI, as Gorbachev may have hoped.

October 15. Gorbachev Presents Programs. General Secretary Gorbachev presents drafts of new economic and political programs to the Central Committee. The economic program calls for a 150 percent increase in labor productivity and 100 percent increases in national income and industrial output by the year 2000.

October 22. Weinberger on Soviet Missile. Defense Secretary Caspar W. Weinberger says the Soviet Union has begun deploying the SS-25, a new mobile ICBM. He claims its deployment violates the SALT II treaty because the Soviets also have tested the new SS-24 ICBM. The treaty allows each side to develop only one new type of ICBM. Moscow maintains the new missiles are merely permissible modifications of older missile types.

October 24. Reagan, Shevardnadze Speak. At the United Nations' fortieth anniversary celebration, President Reagan calls for a "fresh start" in U.S.-Soviet relations and asks the Soviets to join the United States in finding ways to end regional conflicts in Afghanistan, Cambodia, Ethiopia, Angola, and Nicaragua. Foreign Minister Shevardnadze says the arms race must be stopped "from spreading to space."

October 31. Reagan Interview. Four Soviet journalists interview President Reagan in Washington, D.C. The interview, which focuses on superpower relations and the U.S. role in world affairs, is published November 4 in *Izvestia.* Several of Reagan's responses are censored, however, and the interview is accompanied by a rebuttal.

November 1. Netherlands Accepts Missiles. Dutch prime minister Ruud Lubbers, citing increases in the Soviet SS-20 arsenal, announces that the Netherlands will accept forty-eight U.S. cruise missiles in 1988. In June 1984 the Dutch government said it would accept the missiles November 1, 1985, unless the Soviets had reduced the number of SS-20s.

November 4. Yurchenko Reversal. Vitaly Yurchenko, whose defection to the West was announced September 26, declares in a press conference at the Soviet embassy in Washington that he had been kidnapped in Rome by American agents and held in the United States until his recent escape. U.S. officials say Yurchenko defected voluntarily. Yurchenko November 5 meets with State Department officials, who determine he freely decided to return to the USSR. Yurchenko reportedly left a Washington restaurant, where he was dining with a CIA agent, and went to the Soviet embassy.

November 16. Weinberger Letter. The *New York Times* and *Washington Post* report that Defense Secretary Weinberger gave President Reagan a letter November 13 advising him not to make an agreement at the Geneva summit affirming a restrictive interpretation of the ABM treaty or committing the United States to adhere to the SALT II treaty. The letter is attached to a Pentagon report on Soviet arms control violations.

November 19-21. Geneva Summit. President Reagan and General Secretary Gorbachev meet in Geneva for the first summit between U.S. and Soviet leaders since 1979. They achieve no breakthroughs on major issues such as arms control, human rights, or regional conflicts, but both men indicate the meeting was useful. In addition to negotiating sessions with aides present, they spend about five hours in private conversation, accompanied only by their interpreters. They sign bilateral agreements November 21 that provide for the establishment of consuls in New York and Kiev, resumption of civil aviation ties, improved air safety over the northern Pacific, and cultural and scientific exchanges. At the end of the summit they issue a joint communiqué stating their intention to accelerate the arms control process. The statement also says both sides favor a 50 percent reduction in nuclear weapons and an interim agreement on intermediate-range nuclear weapons. Reagan and Gorbachev announce they plan to meet again, beginning with a tentative trip to the United States by Gorbachev in 1986. Before leaving Geneva November 21 the general secretary attacks Reagan's inflexibility on SDI and says the USSR would counter a U.S. space-based ABM system.

December 2. Bonner Travels to West. Yelena Bonner, wife of Soviet dissident Andrei Sakharov, leaves the Soviet Union on a three-month exit visa for medical treatment in the West. She promised Soviet authorities she would not make public statements during her trip. Bonner officially received permission to go abroad October 24. She arrives in the United States December 7, after seeing doctors in Rome.

December 10. Rights Vigil Broken Up. An American television camera crew and Soviet citizens are assaulted and twelve are arrested by Soviet police as they gather in Moscow's Pushkin Square in a silent vigil commemorating UN Human Rights Day.

December 13. Foreign Minister Exchange. Soviet officials in Beijing announce that Chinese foreign minister Wu Xueqian will visit Moscow in May 1986 and Soviet foreign minister Shevardnadze will go to Beijing later that year. It will be the first time in twenty years that the countries have exchanged foreign ministers.

December 15-16. Shultz in East Europe. During a tour of six European nations, Secretary of State Shultz stops in Romania and Hungary. Shultz warns Romanian president Nicolae Ceausescu December 15 that the United States might revoke Romania's most-favored-nation trading status if he fails to improve its human rights record. In Hungary December 16 Shultz speaks optimistically about the development of U.S.-Hungarian relations.

December 19. Soviet Inspections Offer. The Reagan administration discloses that General Secretary Gorbachev December 5 offered in a letter to allow U.S. technicians to inspect some Soviet nuclear test facilities if the United States joined the USSR in an extended moratorium on nuclear tests. The White House rejects Gorbachev's call for a moratorium but says December 23 that Reagan sent a message to Gorbachev welcoming his inspection offer.

December 20. Libyan Missiles. The State Department discloses that the USSR has sold Libya long-range, surface-to-air SA-5 missiles that could threaten aircraft over the Mediterranean. The Egyptian newspaper *Al Ahram* reports December 31 that about two thousand Soviet advisers arrived in Libya in late December.

December 23. Reagan on SALT II. President Reagan reports to Congress that the United States will continue to observe the unratified SALT II treaty despite a "continuing pattern of Soviet noncompliance" with arms control agreements.

December 24. Grishin Removed. Viktor Grishin is replaced as first secretary of the Moscow City party committee by Central Committee secretary Boris Yeltsin. Western analysts regard the move as part of General Secretary Gorbachev's drive to retire older officials who might obstruct his reforms. Grishin loses his seat on the Politburo January 10, 1986.

1986

January 1. Gorbachev, Reagan Messages. General Secretary Gorbachev and President Reagan deliver five-minute speeches shown on television in each other's country. Both men express their hopes for peace and say the Geneva summit began a movement toward better superpower relations. The United States had proposed the exchange before the summit; Moscow accepted the idea December 20, 1985.

January 13. Civil War in South Yemen. An attempt by President Ali Nasser Muhammad to have rival South Yemen Politburo members assassinated precipitates a coup against his rule, which leads to civil war. Thousands of foreigners are evacuated by British and Soviet ships. Western sources report as many as ten thousand killed. Both sides declare their allegiance to Moscow. Radical Marxist opponents of the president gain the upper hand after almost two weeks of fighting. Prime Minister Haider Abu Bakr al-Attas, who was in New Delhi when the fighting erupted, returns to Aden January 25 and is named provisional president in a Marxist coalition government. Ali Nasser Muhammad reportedly flees the country.

January 15. Gorbachev Arms Plan. Mikhail Gorbachev proposes a comprehensive global ban on nuclear weapons to be achieved in stages by the year 2000. He says the United States must stop development of ASATs (antisatellite weapons) and SDI (the Strategic Defense Initiative) before the plan can be implemented. President Reagan says the United States will study the proposal. Other U.S. officials say that much of Gorbachev's offer is not new, but they praise Gorbachev's willingness to cooperate on verification. Gorbachev also calls for a ban on the production of chemical weapons and announces a three-month extension of the Soviet nuclear test moratorium.

January 15-19. Shevardnadze in Tokyo. Eduard Shevardnadze becomes the first Soviet foreign minister to visit Japan since 1976. He signs several cultural and trade accords and presses the Japanese not to participate in SDI research. Shevardnadze says that he discussed the issue of Soviet control of the Japanese-claimed Kuril Islands with Japanese leaders, but neither side reports progress.

January 28. Challenger Explodes. The U.S. space shuttle *Challenger* explodes in flight after takeoff, killing all seven crew members. General Secretary Gorbachev sends a warm message of condolence to President Reagan that is printed on the front page of *Pravda*. Subsequent articles in the Soviet press, however, cite the disaster as an example of the risks of militarizing space.

February 2-4. Soviet-Iranian Talks. Soviet first deputy premier Georgy Kornienko travels to Tehran for a three-day visit, which both sides call successful. Kornienko invites the Iranian foreign minister to Moscow and signs an agreement to resume Aeroflot flights to Tehran.

February 3. France Expels Soviets. The French government expels four Soviet diplomats after accusing them of being Soviet military intelligence agents. Moscow retaliates by expelling four French diplomats.

February 6. Gorbachev Arms Shift. In Moscow, General Secretary Gorbachev tells visiting U.S. senator Edward M. Kennedy, D-Mass., that the only preconditions for reducing intermediate-range nuclear forces (INF) in Europe are a freeze on the expansion of British and French nuclear forces and a pledge by the United States not to transfer nuclear weapons to other nations. Gorbachev surprises U.S. officials by not mentioning progress in talks on strategic and space weapons as a requirement for an INF accord.

February 11. Chemical Arms Plan Rejected. The United States dismisses a Soviet proposal for a multilateral agreement that would ban the spread of chemical weapons. General Secretary Gorbachev offered the proposal in his January 15 arms control speech as an interim step toward the elimination of chemical weapons. The Gorbachev plan would bar the transfer of chemical arms between states and their deployment on the soil of other states. U.S. officials say guarantees that chemical weapons production will be stopped and existing stockpiles destroyed are needed before an agreement can be reached.

February 15. Sakharov Letter Revealed. A letter dated October 15, 1984, from Soviet dissident Andrei Sakharov to Anatoly Aleksandrov, president of the Soviet Academy of Sciences, is made public in the West after being smuggled out of the Soviet Union. It details the forced feeding and other mental and physical abuses that KGB agents inflicted on Sakharov during his four-month incarceration in a Gorky hospital in 1984. Sakharov's relatives and friends in the United States say the letter is authentic. A London newspaper, the *Observer*, publishes the letter February 16.

February 24. Reagan Arms Response. President Reagan formally responds to General Secretary Gorbachev's January 15 nuclear arms control proposal by offering two optional three-year timetables for the removal of U.S. and Soviet intermediate-range missiles from Europe and Asia. He says Gorbachev's plan to eliminate all nuclear weapons by the end of the century is "clearly not appropriate for consideration at this time."

February 25-March 6. Soviet Party Congress. More than five thousand Soviet delegates attend the Twenty-seventh Congress of the Communist Party of the Soviet Union in Moscow. General Secretary Gorbachev delivers a five-and-a-half-hour televised keynote address February 25. He indirectly criticizes the policies of the Brezhnev era and calls for numerous economic reforms, including increased autonomy for local managers, revision of the pricing system, and new incentives to increase agricultural production. Gorbachev also advocates a peaceful coexistence policy with the West but denounces President Reagan's February 24 arms control proposal. On March 5 the party congress ratifies the fifteen-year economic and political programs written under Gorbachev's guidance. Many leadership changes are announced, including the promotions of Central Committee secretary Lev Zaikov to full Politburo membership and longtime ambassador to the United States Anatoly Dobrynin to the Central Committee Secretariat.

March 6. Soviet Probes Study Comet. The unmanned Soviet spacecraft *Vega 1* takes pictures and gathers data as it passes near Halley's comet. A second Soviet craft, *Vega 2*, flies even closer to the comet March 9. The *Vega* probes carry equipment designed by scientists of other nations, and the Soviets participated extensively in the international effort to study Halley's comet.

March 7. Soviet UN Staff Cuts. The White House orders the Soviet Union to reduce the combined staffs of the Soviet, Belorussian, and Ukrainian missions to the United Nations from 275 to 170 officials. Under a 1945 agreement, the Soviet Union gained UN representation for the Belorussian and Ukrainian republics. The White House says the large number of Soviet staff members engaged in espionage increases the security threat to the United States. The USSR March 11 protests the action as "unlawful." Reductions in Soviet personnel begin in October 1986.

March 13. Gorbachev on Nuclear Testing. General Secretary Gorbachev announces that the USSR will extend indefinitely its seven-month nuclear testing moratorium set to expire March 31, if the United States joins the halt. The White House rejects the offer and indicates that a nuclear test scheduled for March 22 in Nevada will be conducted on schedule.

March 13. Mir *Space Mission.* Two Soviet cosmonauts blast off in a *Soyuz* spacecraft that carries them to a mission aboard *Mir*, the orbiting Soviet space station launched February 20. The liftoff is broadcast live on Soviet television—a departure from Moscow's past practice of televising only space missions in which astronauts of other nations are participating.

March 14. Reagan Verification Proposals. President Reagan announces proposals aimed at enhancing verification of nuclear testing limitations. Reagan asks for talks on improving verification methods, invites Soviet scientists to witness a nuclear test in the United States in April, and offers the Soviets advanced monitoring technology. The same day the White House outlines an ambitious plan for verifying any future treaties limiting intermediate-range missiles. The proposal includes an exchange of inspectors who would count weapons and monitor their production. Tass denounces the verification proposals March 15 as "a political maneuver."

March 20. Reagan Declines Bonner Meeting. President Reagan decides not to meet with Yelena Bonner, wife of Soviet dissident Andrei Sakharov. Bonner's visa, which had been set to expire in early March, had been extended by the Soviet government until June. White House officials say the president was concerned that a meeting could jeopardize Bonner's reentry into the Soviet Union and the future release of Soviet citizens seeking to emigrate.

March 24-25. U.S.-Libyan Clash. U.S. ships and warplanes retaliate against Libyan targets after Libya launches Soviet-made missiles at elements of the Sixth Fleet conducting maneuvers in the Gulf of Sidra. American missiles damage or destroy several Libyan ships and a surface-to-air missile radar site near the Libyan coast. General Secretary Gorbachev denounces the U.S. actions as "provocative and threatening" and proposes the withdrawal of all Soviet and U.S. military ships from the Mediterranean. Washington rejects the proposal.

March 29. Test Ban Summit Proposal. General Secretary Gorbachev offers to meet President Reagan in Europe to discuss a nuclear test ban. In spite of the United States' March 22 nuclear test, Gorbachev says the Soviet Union would continue its halt of nuclear testing until the United States conducted another test. President Reagan rejects Gorbachev's summit proposal, saying a meeting should "deal with the entire range" of U.S.-Soviet relations. Moscow says April 1 that a test ban summit would not necessarily replace a more comprehensive meeting.

April 8. Dobrynin Farewell Meeting. Departing Soviet ambassador to the United States Anatoly Dobrynin and President Reagan discuss a possible 1986 summit. Following the discussions, Secretary of State Shultz says he and Foreign Minister Shevardnadze will hold talks in mid-May to prepare for a summit meeting.

April 11. Soviets to End Test Halt. In response to a U.S. nuclear test conducted April 10, Moscow says it will end its eight-month moratorium on nuclear testing.

April 14. United States Bombs Libya. U.S. Sixth Fleet naval aircraft and bombers based in England launch a massive coordinated air strike against Libya. President Reagan says the bombing was in retaliation for Col. Muammar Qaddafi's involvement in recent terrorist activities. In response to the attack, Moscow April 15 cancels the summit planning meeting scheduled for May 14-16 between Foreign Minister Shevardnadze and Secretary of State Shultz. The Soviet action renders a summer 1986 summit unlikely.

April 16. Alliluyeva Returns to United States. Joseph Stalin's daughter, Svetlana Alliluyeva, returns to the United States and renounces her Soviet citizenship. She defected to the United States in 1967 but returned to the USSR in 1984. She says Mikhail Gorbachev aided her efforts to leave.

April 16-22. Gorbachev in East Germany. General Secretary Gorbachev attends the East German Communist Party Congress in East Berlin. In an address April 18 he offers to negotiate troop and arms reductions in Europe.

April 26. Chernobyl Nuclear Accident. Just after 1:00 a.m. a fire starts in the Soviet nuclear power station at Chernobyl, eighty miles north of Kiev. Complications from the fire quickly cause a meltdown to begin in the reactor's core. Hydrogen gas forms in the overheated reactor and explodes, blowing a hole in the reinforced concrete roof. Huge quantities of radiation escape into the atmosphere. The Soviets delay disclosure of the accident. Not until the next afternoon do they evacuate nearly fifty thousand people from a 6.2-mile radius around the plant.

April 28. Nuclear Accident Revealed. Abnormally high levels of radiation are detected in Sweden. Stockholm demands an explanation from Soviet officials after atmospheric analysis reveals the radiation is coming from the USSR. Tass announces several hours later that a nuclear accident had taken place but says only that "measures are being taken to eliminate the consequences of the accident. Aid is being given to those affected."

April 29-May 29. Nuclear Disaster Unfolds. Radioactivity levels rise throughout much of Europe as Soviet workers attempt to contain the effects of the nuclear meltdown. The Soviets say April 29 that two people were killed at Chernobyl. Some early Western estimates of the dead go as high as two thousand, but later these are proved wrong. By May 29 Moscow reports twenty-one people had died. Dr. Robert Gale, a U.S. physician, performs bone marrow transplants in Moscow on victims and predicts the death toll will continue to rise. Premier Nikolai Ryzhkov, Central Committee secretary Yegor Ligachev, and Ukrainian party leader Vladimir Shcherbitsky visit the disaster area May 3. The next day the evacuation zone is widened to eighteen miles around the reactor. Numerous countries criticize the Soviets for not announcing the disaster immediately. Eventually Moscow releases films and pictures of the reactor and agrees to provide the International Atomic Energy Agency with more information. Many East and West European governments warn of health hazards from food and rainwater affected by the Chernobyl radiation. The European Community May 10 temporarily bans all fresh food imports from the Soviet Union and six East European countries.

May 4. Karmal Replaced. Najibullah becomes general secretary of the Afghanistan Communist party when Babrak Karmal resigns citing poor health. Najibullah formerly headed the Afghan secret police.

May 13. Shcharansky Meets Reagan. Recently freed Soviet Jewish dissident Anatoly Shcharansky meets with President Reagan in Washington. White House spokesmen say the president will continue to use quiet diplomacy to advance human rights in the USSR.

May 14. Gorbachev on Chernobyl. General Secretary Gorbachev gives a televised address on the Chernobyl nuclear disaster. He says 9 people have died and 299 are hospitalized, but "the worst has passed." He attacks the West for using the accident for anti-Soviet propaganda purposes and denies the USSR withheld timely information on the disaster. Gorbachev renews his offer to meet President Reagan to discuss a nuclear test ban and extends the Soviet moratorium on nuclear testing until August 6.

May 20. Dubinin Named Ambassador. Tass reports that Yuri Dubinin will become the next Soviet ambassador to the United States. The fifty-five-year-old diplomat had served as the Soviet envoy to the United Nations since March 1986. Dubinin had been ambassador to Spain for seven years before his UN assignment. A European specialist, he speaks little English and had never been to the United States before 1986. Dubinin's selection surprises Western observers, who expected an American specialist to fill the post.

May 24. Bonner Leaves for Soviet Union. Yelena Bonner leaves the United States to return home after a six-month trip to the West for medical treatment.

May 27. SALT II Limits to Be Observed. President Reagan announces that the United States will dismantle two nuclear missile submarines to stay within the SALT II treaty's limits on multiple warhead launchers. He warns, however, that in the future the Soviet military buildup may force the United States to abandon observation of the treaty. At the Geneva arms talks May 29, the Soviets offer to cut their offensive nuclear arsenal if the United States agrees to negotiate more precise definitions of the activities prohibited by the ABM treaty and pledges not to withdraw from the treaty for fifteen to twenty years. On June 11 Soviet negotiators at the START talks in Geneva expand on the proposal, offering to drop their previous demand that U.S. forward-based bombers and sea-launched cruise missiles be eliminated.

June 19. Reagan Delivers Conciliatory Speech. Speaking at a high school graduation in Glassboro, New Jersey, where a 1967 U.S.-Soviet summit was held, President Reagan says the Soviet Union is making a "serious effort" to negotiate on arms control.

June 30. Gorbachev Attacks U.S. Policies. In a speech to the Polish Communist Party Congress, General Secretary Gorbachev says Washington is obstructing progress on arms control and undermining the SALT II treaty.

July 28. Gorbachev Announces Troop Withdrawals. During a speech on Soviet relations with Asia delivered in Vladivostok, General Secretary Gorbachev announces the impending withdrawal of six Soviet regiments from Afghanistan. Gorbachev also calls for closer Sino-Soviet ties and says the withdrawal of some Soviet troops from Mongolia is being examined.

August 18. Test Moratorium Extended. General Secretary Gorbachev announces that the Soviet Union again will extend its unilateral nuclear test moratorium, this time until January 1, 1987.

August 18. Soviet-Israeli Talks. Soviet and Israeli diplomats meet in Helsinki to discuss the establishment of consulates. The talks are the first formal diplomatic contact between the two countries in nineteen years. The Soviets say the move does not signify any basic change in policy toward Israel.

August 21. Chernobyl Report. The Soviets release a 382-page report on the Chernobyl nuclear disaster. The report blames the accident primarily on human error and estimates that 5,300 will die from direct exposure over the next seventy years.

August 23. Zakharov Arrested. Gennady Zakharov, a Soviet physicist who is employed by the United Nations, is arrested in New York after he pays undercover agents for three classified documents.

August 30. Daniloff Affair. Soviet authorities arrest Nicholas Daniloff, a correspondent for *U.S. News and World Report,* on charges of espionage. Daniloff was arrested after being handed a package containing top secret maps by an acquaintance in a Moscow park. The United States charges that Daniloff was framed to provide the Soviets with a pawn to gain the release of Gennady Zakharov, a Soviet arrested in New York for spying a week before. On September 5, President Reagan sends a letter to General Secretary Gorbachev giving him his personal assurance that Daniloff is not a spy. Daniloff is formally charged September 7 with espionage; Zakharov is indicted on three counts of espionage two days later. Zakharov and Daniloff are released to the custody of their respective embassies in Washington and Moscow September 12 pending their trials. On September 18, Gorbachev calls Daniloff a "spy who was caught red-handed." The same day, Foreign Minister Shevardnadze arrives in Washington for talks with Secretary of State Shultz on plans for a superpower summit. The Daniloff case dominates their discussions, and Shevardnadze also meets with Reagan. The Soviets release Daniloff and drop all charges against him September 29. Zakharov is released one day later after pleading no contest to charges of spying. As part of the arrangement, Moscow also allows dissident Yuri Orlov and his wife, Irina Valitova, to emigrate to the United States.

September 1. Soviet Ships Collide. The 17,053-ton Soviet passenger ship *Admiral Nakhimov* and the Soviet freighter *Pyotr Vasov* collide in the Black Sea, eight miles from the port of Novorossisk. The *Admiral Nakhimov* sinks, resulting in the deaths of 398 people. Details of the accident are swiftly announced by the Soviet government.

September 17. Soviets Expelled. The Reagan administration expels twenty-five members of the Soviet delegation to the United Nations for alleged espionage activities. The White House denies the expulsions are linked to the Daniloff affair. All twenty-five leave by October 14.

September 22. New Security Pact. The Conference on Confidence- and Security-Building Measures in Europe approves a new European security pact designed to reduce the risk of accidental war. The agreement provides for prior notification and verification of troop movements by the NATO and Warsaw Pact alliances. It takes effect January 1, 1987.

September 30. Iceland Summit Announced. President Reagan announces that he and General Secretary Gorbachev will meet in Iceland in October.

October 3. Soviet Nuclear Sub Sinks. An explosion and fire aboard a Soviet Yankee-class nuclear missile submarine patrolling in the Atlantic kills three Soviet sailors. The disabled sub sinks while in tow about six hundred miles from Bermuda.

October 11-12. Iceland Summit. President Reagan and General Secretary Gorbachev meet in Reykjavik, Iceland, for talks intended to set the agenda for a full summit in early 1987. Initially, the two leaders and their aides make substantial progress toward an arms control agreement. They agree to limit the number of warheads on their intermediate-range missiles to one hundred and ban these weapons from being deployed in Europe. They also agree on a 50 percent reduction in strategic weapons. In a major concession, Gorbachev agrees to exclude sea-launched cruise missiles from the warhead count. However, Gorbachev refuses to approve these arms control measures unless the United States agrees to adhere to a strict interpretation of the 1972 ABM treaty for ten years. Reagan rejects Gorbachev's position because it would prohibit testing of SDI outside the laboratory. The talks break down amid mutual recriminations. No date is set for a future summit. On October 17, Secretary of State Shultz releases the texts of Reagan's main arms control proposals to dispel claims that Reagan had agreed in principle to eliminate all nuclear forces. But on October 22, Gorbachev insists on Soviet television that Reagan had expressed support for his proposal to seek the elimination of all nuclear arms within ten years.

October 19-22. Diplomats Expelled. The Soviet Union expels five U.S. diplomats for engaging in "impermissible activities," in retaliation for Washington's expulsion of twenty-five Soviet UN personnel in September. The United States expels fifty-five more Soviet diplomats October 21. The Soviets expel five more American diplomats the following day and announce that the United States will lose the services of the 260 Soviet employees working at the U.S. Moscow embassy and Leningrad consulate.

November 8. Molotov Dies. Viacheslav Molotov, who served as foreign minister under Joseph Stalin, dies in Moscow at the age of ninety-six.

November 19. Private Enterprise Legislation. The Supreme Soviet passes a law that sanctions some types of small-scale private enterprise. The law takes effect May 1987.

November 28. SALT II Limits Exceeded. The United

States exceeds the limitations of the unratified SALT II treaty by deploying its 131st B-52 bomber capable of carrying cruise missiles. The Soviet Union announces December 5 that it will continue to comply with the treaty but no longer considers itself obligated to do so. Reagan administration officials accuse the Soviets of hypocrisy, saying the Soviets have been violating the treaty for years.

December 16. Kunaev Loses Position. Politburo member Dinmukhamed Kunaev, an ethnic Kazakh, is replaced as party leader of Kazakhstan by Gennady Kolbin, who is an ethnic Russian. The next day riots erupt in Alma-Ata, the capital of Kazakhstan, in response to the move.

December 18. Soviets End Test Moratorium. The Soviet government announces that it will end its unilateral moratorium on nuclear weapons testing when the United States conducts its first nuclear test in 1987.

December 19. Sakharov and Bonner Freed. Physicist and Nobel Peace Prize winner Andrei Sakharov's banishment to the city of Gorky is lifted by the Soviet government. Sakharov's wife, Yelena Bonner, receives a pardon the same day. Sakharov reveals that General Secretary Gorbachev had personally phoned him to inform him of his release.

1987

January 10. Marine Guard Scandal. The Marine Corps announces the detention of Sgt. Clayton Lonetree, a former guard at the U.S. embassy in Moscow who confessed to supplying the KGB with secret information after being seduced by a female agent. Lonetree is formally charged on January 31. A second former embassy guard, Cpl. Arnold Bracey, is arrested on March 24 on similar charges, but they are dropped June 12. Lonetree is convicted on thirteen counts of espionage August 21 and is sentenced to thirty years in prison.

January 15. Export Ban Lifted. The Commerce Department lifts a nine-year ban on the export of oil-drilling equipment to the Soviet Union.

January 27. Central Committee Plenum. General Secretary Gorbachev opens a Central Committee plenum with a speech calling for major political reforms. He outlines new procedures to elect party officials that include secret balloting and a choice of candidates for voters in general elections. Dinmukhamed Kunaev is removed from the Politburo, while Aleksandr Yakovlev is appointed a candidate member of the body. Anatoly Lukyanov and Nikolai Sliunkov are appointed to the Secretariat.

February 10. Political Prisoners Released. The Soviet Foreign Ministry announces that 140 persons convicted of subversive activities have been pardoned. The release of 150 more dissidents is announced February 17. Three days later, the Soviets also release prominent Jewish dissident Joseph Begun.

February 14. Peace and Disarmament Forum. The Soviet Union hosts an international peace and disarmament forum that is attended by more than seven hundred artists, scientists, business leaders, and officials from around the world. Dissident Andrei Sakharov speaks at the gathering and calls for democratic reform. In an address to the forum, General Secretary Gorbachev says the Soviet Union desires international stability so that it can pursue domestic reform.

February 19. Reagan Lifts Polish Sanctions. President Reagan removes all remaining U.S. economic sanctions against Poland, saying the move was a response to Polish governmental reform.

February 26. Test Moratorium Ends. The USSR ends an eighteen-month unilateral moratorium on nuclear testing by conducting an underground nuclear test in Kazakhstan.

February 28. Gorbachev Separates SDI and INF. General Secretary Gorbachev announces that he is willing to sign an agreement eliminating U.S. and Soviet intermediate-range nuclear forces in Europe without regard to progress on limiting space-based ABM weapons.

March 28. Thatcher Visits Moscow. British prime minister Margaret Thatcher meets with General Secretary Gorbachev in Moscow. They discuss arms control and Soviet human rights policies. The leaders sign four bilateral protocols on March 31 providing for diplomatic, scientific, cultural, and educational cooperation.

April 2. France Expels Soviets. France expels three Soviet diplomats after learning of Soviet participation in a spy ring designed to obtain secrets concerning the European space program. The Soviets April 4 expel two French businessmen in retaliation.

April 6. New U.S. Embassy in Moscow Bugged. Rep. Olympia J. Snowe, R-Maine, and Rep. Daniel A. Mica, D-Fla., tour the Moscow embassy building and pronounce it "fully compromised" by electronic listening devices. The president and the State Department order separate studies of the situation the following day.

April 9. Gorbachev Visits Prague. Czechoslovak president Gustav Husak and General Secretary Gorbachev meet in Prague. In a speech April 10, Gorbachev says the USSR does not demand that Czechoslovakia and other Eastern European countries adopt Soviet-style reforms, but he claims the restructuring of the Soviet Union is "in accordance with the very essence of socialism."

April 13. Shultz in Moscow. Secretary of State Shultz visits Moscow for extensive talks with Foreign Minister Shevardnadze on arms control, human rights, and Soviet espionage at the U.S. embassy in Moscow. On April 14, Shultz meets with General Secretary Gorbachev, who proposes the elimination from Europe of nuclear weapons having an approximate range of three hundred to six hundred miles.

April 23. Honecker Rejects Reform. Speaking before a trade union congress, East German leader Erich Honecker says that reforms initiated in the Soviet Union should not be implemented in East Germany.

April 30. Wheat Sale. Agriculture Secretary Richard Lyng announces that the Soviet Union will buy four million metric tons of subsidized American wheat to be delivered by the end of September.

May 8. Draft START Treaty Unveiled. The United States offers a draft treaty that would cut U.S. and Soviet strategic nuclear arsenals by 50 percent over seven years. Under the plan, both sides would be left with 1,600 delivery vehicles and 6,000 warheads. The Soviets criticize the plan for failing to curtail the development of space weapons.

May 19. Asian Missile Offer. In a speech in Moscow, General Secretary Gorbachev says the Soviet Union would be willing to eliminate its intermediate-range missiles based in Asia if the United States withdrew its nuclear weapons from Japan, South Korea, and the Philippines and withdrew its naval forces in the Pacific "behind agreed lines."

May 23. Voice of America Jamming Stopped. For the first time since 1980, the Soviet Union stops jamming Voice of America radio broadcasts, although it continues to jam other Western radio networks.

May 25. Gorbachev in Romania. General Secretary Gorbachev begins a three-day visit to Romania, where he receives a polite but cool reception. In a speech before a meeting of five thousand Communist party officials, he outlines his reform program to an unreceptive audience.

May 29. Teen Pilot Lands in Red Square. Mathias Rust, a West German teenager, flies a small plane from Helsinki to Moscow, landing in Red Square. The incident leads to the removal of Soviet defense minister Sergei Sokolov and commander of Soviet air defenses Aleksandr Koldunov May 30. Dmitry Yazov replaces Sokolov as defense minister.

June 8. Schlesinger Embassy Report. James R. Schlesinger, head of a special State Department panel studying the Moscow embassy, holds a news conference in the embassy at the end of his committee's ten-day investigation. He confirms reports that the nearly completed Moscow embassy is riddled with electronic listening devices and recommends that the building be partly dismantled and rebuilt by American laborers using U.S.-made components. Schlesinger also suggests that an adjacent annex be built to house the embassy's most secret activities.

June 8-14. Pope Visits Poland. Pope John Paul II makes his third visit to his native Poland as pope. During his visit he meets with both Lech Walesa, leader of the Solidarity labor union, and President Wojciech Jaruzelski.

June 12. Reagan in West Berlin. In a speech in West Berlin at the Brandenburg Gate during celebrations of the 750th anniversary of the city, President Reagan chal-

lenges Gorbachev to "tear down" the Berlin Wall.

June 16. INF Proposal. The United States formally proposes a global ban on all intermediate-range nuclear missiles with ranges between 500 and 3,400 miles.

June 25. Gorbachev on Economic Reform. At a Central Committee plenum, General Secretary Gorbachev calls for economic reforms that would further decentralize the Soviet economy. He proposed, among other measures, that state-owned enterprises become self-financing and that central control over prices and distribution decrease. The Central Committee approves the plan June 26. Aleksandr Yakovlev, Nikolai Sliunkov, and Viktor Nikonov each are promoted to full membership in the Politburo, while Defense Minister Yazov is given candidate status.

July 15. Ukrainian Party Shake-Up. Aleksandr Lyashko retires as Ukrainian premier amid a party shake-up involving at least eight other top officials. Vitaly Masol is named to replace Lyashko. Politburo member Vladimir Shcherbitsky remains first secretary of the Ukrainian Communist party.

July 22. Gorbachev Accepts Global INF Ban. In an interview in an Indonesian newspaper, General Secretary Gorbachev says the Soviets would be willing to accept the global elimination of all intermediate-range nuclear missiles. Gorbachev thus dropped the earlier Soviet demand that the USSR be allowed to keep some intermediate-range missiles in Asia. Soviet negotiators at the INF talks in Geneva adopt this position July 23.

July 27. NATO Calls for New Talks. NATO proposes to replace the Mutual and Balanced Force Reduction talks with a new forum on conventional force reductions to be conducted within the framework of the Conference on Security and Cooperation in Europe. The new talks would not include representatives of neutral nations.

July 31. Soviet Draft Treaty. Soviet negotiators at Geneva present a draft treaty for a START agreement that links 50 percent cuts in strategic weapons to an agreement to limit development of space-based ABM weapons.

August 11. Soviets Deploy SS-24s. The Soviet Union confirms that it has begun deployment of the SS-24 intercontinental ballistic missile.

August 26. Bonn Offers to Scrap Missiles. The West German government announces that it would dismantle its seventy-two Pershing IA missiles if the superpowers concluded a treaty banning intermediate-range nuclear missiles. The United States controls the nuclear warheads for the missiles.

September 1. Honecker Visits West Germany. East German leader Erich Honecker holds talks with West German chancellor Helmut Kohl in Bonn. Honecker is the first East German head of state ever to visit West Germany. The two leaders announce agreements on a range of issues.

September 18. Tentative Agreement on INF Treaty.

After three days of talks between Foreign Minister Shevardnadze and Secretary of State Shultz in Washington, President Reagan announces that a tentative agreement has been reached on a treaty eliminating intermediate-range nuclear missiles. Reagan says the two sides were in the process of arranging a summit meeting for late 1987 at which the treaty would be signed.

October 15. Soviets to Pay UN Debts. The Soviet government announces that it will pay all its outstanding debts (about $245 million) to the United Nations.

October 21. Aliyev Removed from Politburo. The Central Committee removes Geidar Aliyev as a full member of the Politburo.

October 22-30. Summit Dispute. Secretary of State Shultz travels to the Soviet Union for talks intended to finalize the INF treaty and prepare for a summit. He meets October 23 with General Secretary Gorbachev, who unexpectedly refuses to set a summit date because of Soviet objections to SDI. Shultz leaves Moscow October 24. The Soviets reverse their position October 27, requesting consultations on arranging a summit meeting. Foreign Minister Shevardnadze arrives in Washington October 29, where he meets with Shultz and President Reagan. The next day Reagan announces that Gorbachev will come to Washington for a summit in December.

November 2. Gorbachev Speech. In a speech beginning the celebration of the seventieth anniversary of the Bolshevik Revolution, General Secretary Gorbachev revives the reputations of Nikita Khrushchev and Nikolai Bukharin and says Joseph Stalin was guilty of "enormous and unforgivable" crimes. Gorbachev also defends perestroika and asserts that the era of conflict between communism and capitalism was giving way to a new spirit of cooperation.

November 9. New Geneva Talks Begin. The superpowers begin talks in Geneva on banning underground nuclear tests.

November 11. Yeltsin Dismissed. Boris Yeltsin is removed as Moscow party chief. At a Central Committee meeting October 21, he had denounced the slow pace of reform. He is named deputy director of the State Committee for Construction November 18.

November 22. Shultz and Shevardnadze in Geneva. Secretary of State Shultz and Foreign Minister Shevardnadze meet in Geneva to resolve remaining disagreements over the INF treaty. They also develop an agenda for the Washington summit.

November 29. Polish Reforms Defeated. A referendum on political and economic reform is defeated in Poland. The Solidarity movement opposed the government's reform plan and had asked Poles to boycott the referendum, which asked citizens if they were willing to accept hardships in pursuit of radical economic reform and if they supported a "profound democratization of political life." Because of a low voter turnout, neither question received

the support of 50 percent of eligible voters—the amount required for passage.

November 30. Gorbachev Interview. Tom Brokaw of NBC News interviews General Secretary Gorbachev for one hour on national television. Gorbachev calls for a 50 percent mutual reduction in strategic nuclear arms and indicates that the USSR is prepared to counter any U.S. deployment of SDI with a similar system of its own.

December 7-10. Washington Summit. General Secretary Gorbachev and President Reagan hold a summit meeting in Washington, D.C. On December 8, they sign the INF treaty, which provides for the elimination of U.S. and Soviet intermediate-range nuclear missiles. The treaty is accompanied by a thirteen-year verification agreement that includes on-site inspections. Gorbachev meets with members of Congress at the Soviet embassy December 9. Later in the day Reagan and Gorbachev discuss Afghanistan and proposals to reduce strategic nuclear weapons. Gorbachev insists that any strategic arms treaty be accompanied by limits on SDI research. Gorbachev holds meetings with Vice President Bush and President Reagan December 10 before leaving the United States. The same day NATO foreign ministers call on the U.S. Senate to ratify the INF treaty.

December 17. Husak Resigns. Gustav Husak resigns as Czechoslovak Communist party leader. He is replaced by Milos Jakes.

1988

January 6. Shevardnadze on Afghanistan. Foreign Minister Shevardnadze says in an interview in Kabul that the USSR hopes to withdraw all its forces from Afghanistan by the end of 1988. He maintains that withdrawal of Soviet troops does not depend on a friendly government remaining in power in Afghanistan.

February 1. Poles Protest Price Increases. The Polish government implements an economic reform plan that increases the price of basic foods, alcoholic beverages, and other items by more than 40 percent. The price increases are accompanied by a 16 percent devaluation in the nation's currency. The Solidarity labor movement denounces the price increases but urges restraint on the part of the population. Nevertheless, thousands of Poles demonstrate against the price increases.

February 6. Talyzin Replaced as Gosplan Chief. Nikolai Talyzin, head of the State Planning Committee (Gosplan), is replaced by his first deputy chairman, Yuri Maslyukov. General Secretary Gorbachev had criticized Talyzin for failing to implement economic reforms.

February 8. Gorbachev Troop Withdrawal Proposal. In a statement broadcast on Soviet television, General Secretary Gorbachev says that if a settlement of the Afghanistan conflict can be reached in March at UN-sponsored peace talks in Geneva, the Soviet Union would begin withdrawing troops from Afghanistan by May 15. He asserts that the withdrawal could be completed within ten months.

February 11. Armenians Demonstrate. Thousands of Armenians living in the predominantly Armenian Nagorno-Karabakh autonomous region of Azerbaijan republic hold demonstrations to demand reunification with the Armenian republic. Rallies attended by tens of thousands of protesters begin February 20 in Armenia in support of the Armenians in Nagorno-Karabakh. On February 26, General Secretary Gorbachev calls for a restoration of order. Armenian leaders agree to a temporary suspension of the demonstrations the following day.

February 18. Yeltsin Removed. Former Moscow party chief Boris Yeltsin is removed from candidate status in the Politburo at a Central Committee plenum. Georgy Razumovsky and Yuri Maslyukov are named candidate members of the Politburo.

February 26. Romania Loses MFN Status. The United States announces that it is withdrawing Romania's most-favored-nation (MFN) trading status because of human rights violations by the Romanian government.

February 28. Ethnic Riots in Sumgait. Riots in the Azerbaijan city of Sumgait reportedly result in the deaths of at least thirty-two people. Soviet troops are sent to the city to enforce a dusk-to-dawn curfew. During the following weeks reports in the Soviet press suggest that the violence may have been more serious. Several Soviet journalists and officials maintain that the riots were pogroms against the Armenian minority in Sumgait that left hundreds dead.

March 6. Soviet Embassy in Tehran Attacked. An Iranian mob, angered by Soviet sales of missiles to Iraq, attacks the Soviet embassy in Tehran with rocks and Molotov cocktails. No Soviet personnel are killed, but the incident damages Soviet-Iranian relations.

March 13. Gorbachev Criticized in Soviet Press. The newspaper *Sovietskaya Rossiya* publishes a letter by Leningrad schoolteacher Nina Andreyeva critical of General Secretary Gorbachev's "leftist-liberal" policies. She calls for a return to the more disciplined line followed by Joseph Stalin. Authority for publishing the letter is traced to second-ranking Kremlin figure Yegor Ligachev.

April 14. Afghan Agreements Signed. The governments of Afghanistan and Pakistan sign accords in Geneva mandating the withdrawal of Soviet forces from Afghanistan, the neutrality of the Afghan state, and the repatriation of Afghan refugees. The Soviet Union and United States sign a separate accord that commits them to guarantee the Afghan agreements.

April 19. Politburo Rift. The Politburo reportedly orders Yegor Ligachev to take a two-month vacation after he clashes with General Secretary Gorbachev over policy.

April 25. Labor Upheaval in Poland. Hundreds of transportation workers in Bydgoszcz go on strike and are granted a pay increase the following day. During the next few days, workers strike at a steel mill in Nowa Huta and at shipyards in Gdansk, demanding higher wages and recognition of the Solidarity labor movement. Demonstrators and police clash on May 3 in Warsaw, Krakow, Lublin, and Lodz. Police crack down on the strikers May 5 when the government and workers fail to negotiate an agreement. On May 10, 2,500 workers who had been sealed inside a Gdansk shipyard give up their protest.

May 7-9. Soviet Opposition Drafts Charter. More than one hundred Soviet opposition leaders meet in Moscow, where they draft the charter of the Democratic Union, an independent political party. Five members of the group, including Sergei Grigoryants, editor of the journal *Glasnost*, are arrested May 9 and ordered to leave Moscow.

May 15. Soviets Begin Afghanistan Withdrawal. The Soviet Union begins to withdraw its 115,000 troops from Afghanistan. The withdrawal is scheduled to be completed February 15, 1989. On May 25 the Soviet Union for the first time releases Soviet casualty figures related to the fighting in Afghanistan. According to the Ministry of Defense, 13,310 Soviet troops had been killed as of May 1 and 35,478 had been wounded.

May 22. Kadar Removed in Hungary. Janos Kadar is replaced as general secretary of the Hungarian Communist party by Karoly Grosz.

May 27. INF Treaty Ratified. The Senate ratifies the INF treaty by a vote of 93-5.

May 27. Private Cooperatives Approved. The Supreme Soviet passes a law legalizing private cooperatives. More than twenty thousand cooperatives already have been formed by Soviet citizens, in anticipation of the law's passage.

May 29-June 2. Moscow Summit. President Reagan travels to Moscow to meet with General Secretary Gorbachev. Although no major arms control breakthroughs are achieved, meetings between the two leaders are held in a jovial atmosphere, and they sign nine bilateral agreements. During the visit, Reagan raises the issue of human rights in public speeches, in meetings with refuseniks, and in his talks with Gorbachev. The Soviets retaliate by sponsoring a Moscow press conference for American Indians who claim they are discriminated against by the Reagan administration. On June 1 Reagan and Gorbachev exchange the formal documents of ratification of the INF treaty.

June 5-12. Millennium Celebrated. With the support of the Soviet government, the Russian Orthodox Church observes the one thousandth anniversary of the establishment of Christianity in Russia.

June 6. Lenin Criticized. Soviet founding father V. I. Lenin, long considered beyond reproach in Soviet political and journalistic circles, is criticized in the monthly magazine *Novy Mir*. The author of the article, historian Vasily

Selyunin, faults Lenin for having initiated the systematic use of terror to intimidate enemies of the Bolshevik party and eliminate "potential opponents."

June 15. Armenia Requests Nagorno-Karabakh. The Armenian Supreme Soviet officially asks that Nagorno-Karabakh, the Armenian enclave within the borders of neighboring Azerbaijan, be reunited with Armenia.

June 21. Canada Announces Expulsions. Canadian prime minister Brian Mulroney reveals that eight Soviet diplomats had been expelled June 14 for attempting to obtain defense technology secrets. He also says that nine diplomats currently outside Canada would be denied reentry. The Soviets retaliate by expelling five Canadian diplomats June 22, and Canada responds with two more expulsions.

June 27. Hungarians Protest Romanian Program. Tens of thousands of Hungarians protest in Budapest against a Romanian plan to "systematize" seven thousand Romanian villages, mainly in the ethnically Hungarian region of Transylvania, by replacing them with five hundred agro-industrial complexes.

June 28-July 1. Nineteenth Party Conference. In his opening speech to the first all-union party conference since 1941, General Secretary Gorbachev calls for restructuring the Soviet government. He proposes creating a more democratic national legislature—the Congress of People's Deputies (CPD). The 2,250-seat body would consist of 1,500 deputies elected in multicandidate elections and 750 appointed by various organizations. Under the proposal, the CPD, which would meet semiannually, would select a standing Supreme Soviet of about 450 members and a strong president. Gorbachev also calls for more authority for local soviets, multicandidate elections, and a ban on interference in the economy by local party organizations. The conference July 1 adopts resolutions supporting Gorbachev's government reorganization plan, legal reform, and greater independence for national regions.

July 9. Bukharin Rehabilitated. Soviet revolutionary figure Nikolai Bukharin, who was executed by the regime of Joseph Stalin in 1937, is posthumously reinstated to membership in the Communist party.

July 11-16. Gorbachev in Poland. In a speech to the parliament at the beginning of a six-day visit to Poland, General Secretary Gorbachev denounces Joseph Stalin's deportation of thousands of Poles to the Soviet Union after World War II. Warsaw Pact leaders convene in Warsaw on July 15-16 and call for a moratorium on nuclear weapons testing and chemical weapons production and separate talks with NATO on tactical nuclear arms.

August 15. Polish Unrest. Coal miners strike in Jastrzebie following a clash between Polish police and pro-Solidarity protesters in Gdansk the previous day. The strikes quickly spread across Poland. The government August 23 rejects Solidarity's call for direct negotiations. Many of the strikes collapse by August 25.

August 17. Joint Nuclear Test. The United States and the Soviet Union conduct a joint nuclear test in Nevada. The test is intended to advance verification of test ban agreements by comparing U.S. and Soviet methods of measuring a nuclear detonation.

August 21. Prague Demonstration. An estimated ten thousand people demonstrate in Prague to commemorate the twentieth anniversary of the Soviet invasion of Czechoslovakia. Riot police use tear gas to disperse the gathering.

August 31. Kiszczak Meets with Walesa. Interior Minister Czeslaw Kiszczak meets with Solidarity leader Lech Walesa to discuss Poland's labor unrest. It is the first official meeting between the government and Solidarity since 1982. The two sides announce progress toward an agreement on holding round-table discussions. The government says it would be willing to discuss the legalization of Solidarity. After the meeting, Walesa calls for an end to strikes.

September 16. Gorbachev on Radar. During a visit to Krasnoyarsk, Siberia, General Secretary Gorbachev offers to turn the controversial Krasnoyarsk radar station into a space research facility and place it under international control. The Reagan administration says the radar must be dismantled unconditionally. Gorbachev also offers to close the Soviet Cam Rahn Bay naval base in Vietnam if the United States abandons its bases in the Philippines.

September 19. Polish Leadership Resigns. Premier Zbigniew Messner and his cabinet resign in response to parliamentary criticism of their economic policy. Messner is succeeded by Mieczyslaw Rakowski September 27.

September 30. Leadership Shake-up at Plenum. At a Central Committee plenum, Yegor Ligachev, leader of the conservative wing of the Politburo, is transferred from his position as party secretary for ideology to the less important post of secretary for agriculture. He retains his seat on the Politburo. Vadim Medvedev, a close associate of General Secretary Gorbachev, is given responsibility for ideology as well as propaganda. Aleksandr Yakovlev replaces Anatoly Dobrynin as secretary for foreign affairs. Mikhail Solomentsev is retired from the Politburo and from the chairmanship of the Party Control Committee. The following day, at a meeting of the Supreme Soviet, President Andrei Gromyko is retired, and Gorbachev is confirmed as the new president (chairman of the Presidium of the Supreme Soviet). Viktor Chebrikov, who was named secretary in charge of legal affairs the previous day, is replaced as head of the KGB by Vladimir Kryuchkov, a career KGB officer. Anatoly Lukyanov is confirmed as Soviet vice president.

October 24-27. Kohl Visits Moscow. West German chancellor Helmut Kohl meets with Soviet president Gorbachev in Moscow. Kohl asserts October 26 that the Kremlin had promised to release all political prisoners by the end of 1988. The Soviet Foreign Ministry refuses to confirm the report.

October 27. Soviets Admit Budget Deficit. Finance Minister Boris Gostev says that in the past Moscow has hidden Soviet budget deficits. He estimates that the budget deficit for 1988 will be about $58 billion.

October 31. Lenin Shipyard Controversy. The Polish government announces its intention to close Gdansk's Lenin Shipyard, where the Solidarity labor movement was founded in 1980. The action is to occur in stages beginning December 1. The government maintains the shipyard must be closed because it is losing money. Solidarity leader Lech Walesa November 6 threatens to call a strike if the decision is not reversed. After shipyard officials assure Solidarity representatives November 7 that the shutdown will be spread over two or three years and shipyard workers will be guaranteed jobs in the Gdansk area, Walesa withdraws the threat of an immediate strike. He vows, however, to fight in the coming year to keep the shipyard open.

November 15. Soviets Launch Space Shuttle. The first flight of a Soviet space shuttle is successful. The unmanned *Buran* spacecraft completes two orbits before returning to earth.

November 16. Estonian Constitutional Conflict. The Estonian Supreme Soviet passes an amendment to its constitution that allows Estonian officials to give precedence to Estonian laws that conflict with USSR laws. The Presidium of the Soviet Union declares the Estonian amendment unconstitutional November 26.

November 18-20. Gorbachev in India. President Gorbachev visits India, where he meets with Prime Minister Rajiv Gandhi. Gorbachev discusses the Soviet withdrawal from Afghanistan with Indian officials and assures them that recent efforts by Moscow to improve relations with China will not affect Soviet-Indian relations.

November 22. Violence in Azerbaijan. Anti-Armenian riots in Baku and several other Azerbaijani cities leave eight dead and more than one hundred injured.

December 1. Supreme Soviet Amends Constitution. The Supreme Soviet amends the Soviet Constitution, adopting the recommendations of the Nineteenth Party Conference for a revamped legislature and presidency.

December 1. School Bus Hijacking. Four Soviets hijack a school bus in the Caucasus Mountains. Soviet officials give the hijackers money and a cargo plane. The hijackers order the plane's crew to fly to Tel Aviv. After landing, the hijackers, who are neither Jews nor dissidents, are arrested by Israeli authorities and returned to the Soviet Union.

December 2. Sino-Soviet Summit Announced. Officials in Moscow and Beijing announce that President Gorbachev will meet with Chinese leader Deng Xiaoping during the first half of 1989.

December 6-8. Gorbachev in United States. President Gorbachev arrives in New York to address the United Nations and meet with President Reagan and President-elect Bush. In his historic speech to the UN General Assembly December 7, Gorbachev announces a unilateral military cut of five hundred thousand troops. He also says 50,000 troops will be withdrawn from Eastern Europe during the next two years, along with 10,000 tanks, 8,500 artillery pieces, and 800 combat aircraft. He asserts that the Soviet military will operate under a defensive military doctrine. After his speech, Gorbachev meets Reagan and Bush. Gorbachev cancels the rest of his trip and returns to the Soviet Union December 8 in response to a severe earthquake in Armenia the previous day.

December 7. Armenian Earthquake. An earthquake registering 6.9 on the Richter scale devastates Armenia. At least twenty-five thousand people are killed. The town of Spitak is completely leveled, and the larger cities of Leninakan and Kirovakan sustain severe damage. President Gorbachev tours the area December 10-11.

December 7. Akhromeev Retires. Soviet chief of staff and deputy defense minister Marshal Sergei Akhromeev retires amid unconfirmed rumors that he had opposed President Gorbachev's military reforms and troop cuts.

December 13. Soviets to Dismantle Radar Sites. The Soviet Union announces that it will dismantle a radar site near Moscow and one near Gomel that the United States maintains are in violation of the ABM treaty.

1989

January 8. Shevardnadze on Chemical Arms. Foreign Minister Shevardnadze announces at a 149-nation conference in Paris on chemical weapons that the Soviet Union will begin reducing its stocks of chemical arms unilaterally.

January 15. Helsinki Accords Enhanced. The thirty-five countries of the Conference on Security and Cooperation in Europe agree in Vienna on an enhancement of the 1975 Helsinki Final Act. The new accord specified freedoms that should be protected and outlined measures for assuring human rights.

January 15. Protest in Czechoslovakia. An estimated two thousand protesters demonstrate in Prague to commemorate the twentieth anniversary of a suicide committed by a Czechoslovak student in protest of the 1968 Soviet invasion. Police break up the demonstration. Dissident playwright Vaclav Havel is arrested the following day and charged with inciting the riots. Havel is released from prison on May 17, after serving nearly half of his nine-month sentence.

February 11. Multiple Parties in Hungary. The Central Committee of the Hungarian Communist party sanctions the establishment of independent political parties.

February 15. Afghan Pullout Completed. The final Soviet troops remaining in Afghanistan cross the border into the Soviet Union, thereby completing the nine-month Soviet withdrawal on schedule.

February 18-27. Shevardnadze Tours Middle East. Foreign Minister Shevardnadze visits Syria, Jordan, Egypt, Iraq, and Iran during a ten-day visit to the Middle East. At separate meetings in Cairo February 22, he confers with Israeli foreign minister Moshe Arens and PLO leader Yasir Arafat. Shevardnadze's trip is seen as an effort by Moscow to improve relations with Middle Eastern states following completion of the Soviet troop withdrawal from Afghanistan. During the trip Shevardnadze reiterates Soviet support for a UN-sponsored Middle East peace conference.

March 6. CFE Talks Open. The Conventional Forces in Europe (CFE) talks open in Vienna. They replace the Mutual and Balanced Force Reduction talks, which close permanently in Vienna by mutual agreement March 2. The CFE talks are attended by the members of the NATO and Warsaw Pact alliances and are intended to achieve cuts in conventional weapons in Europe.

March 5. Yeltsin Supporters Demonstrate. Five thousand supporters of Boris Yeltsin's candidacy for the Congress of People's Deputies demonstrate in Moscow. On March 19, ten thousand people march on the Moscow city hall to protest a Central Committee investigation of whether Yeltsin broke party discipline by calling for open parliamentary elections.

March 16. Farm Plan Backed. The Central Committee endorses President Gorbachev's plan to invigorate Soviet agriculture. Among other features, the plan sanctions the leasing of land from collective farms, abolishes the government's central agriculture agency (Gosagroprom), and allocates more resources to improve rural life.

March 26. Nationwide Elections Held. Multicandidate elections are held for 1,500 seats in the 2,250-seat Congress of People's Deputies. The Communist party's candidates win a large majority of the seats, as expected, but a surprisingly large number of party officials are defeated by reformists and nationalist figures. Yuri Solovev, the first secretary of Leningrad, is rejected when he fails to receive 50 percent of the vote, despite running unopposed. Boris Yeltsin is elected to the Moscow at-large seat with 89 percent of the vote. Nationalists win a majority of the seats in the Baltic republics. Final results of the elections are made public March 31.

April 2-7. Gorbachev Trip. President Gorbachev travels to Cuba and Great Britain. He canceled visits to these countries in December 1988, when the earthquake in Armenia forced him to remain home. Despite Cuba's resistance to Soviet-style reform, Gorbachev is received warmly in Havana April 2. Gorbachev arrives in London April 5. He and British prime minister Thatcher discuss Soviet economic reform, arms control, and regional con-

flicts. On April 7 Gorbachev delivers a speech at London's Guildhall and meets with Queen Elizabeth II, whom he invites to the Soviet Union.

April 5. Polish Reform Agreement. Negotiations between Solidarity and government officials result in agreement on major political and economic reforms. The two sides agree to replace the present unicameral legislature with a bicameral system consisting of a 460-seat lower house and 100-seat upper house. The Communists and their allies are to be guaranteed 65 percent of the seats in the lower house. All seats in the upper house and the remaining seats in the lower house are to be popularly elected. The two also agree to strengthen the presidency, legalize Solidarity, and lift price controls on privately grown farm produce.

April 7. Soviet Nuclear Sub Sinks. A Soviet nuclear-powered submarine catches fire and sinks near Norway. The Soviets report the following day that the submarine's reactors had been shut down before it sank. Forty-two of the crew's sixty-nine members are killed.

April 9. Soldiers Attack Georgian Protesters. In Tbilisi, Soviet soldiers attack a crowd of more than ten thousand Georgian protesters, who had been calling for annexation of the autonomous republic of Abkhazia into Georgia. The Soviet government says twenty demonstrators were killed. Georgian party leader Dzhumber Patiashvili resigns. A Georgian newspaper subsequently charges that the Soviet army used poison gas against the crowd. The Politburo authorizes an investigation of the incident April 21. New Georgian Communist party leader Givi Gumbaraidze says April 24 that poison gas was responsible for the deaths of some protesters. Politburo member Vadim Medvedev says April 25 that the authority to break up the protest came from Georgian party leaders, not the Kremlin.

April 25. Central Committee Purge. President Gorbachev engineers a purge of the Central Committee. Seventy-four full members and twenty-four candidate members of the Central Committee and twelve members of the Central Oversight Commission are forcibly retired. Most are former high-ranking officials from the Brezhnev era. Andrei Gromyko, Geidar Aliyev, Mikhail Solomentsev, Sergei Sokolov, and Boris Ponomarev all lose their Central Committee seats.

April 25. Conventional Reductions Begin. The Soviet Union withdraws one thousand tanks from Hungary, the first step in the unilateral conventional force reductions in Eastern Europe announced by President Gorbachev in December 1988.

May 2. Hungary Ruptures Iron Curtain. The Hungarian government begins dismantling the barbed wire fence separating it from Austria. Because Hungarians already can travel to Western Europe, no flood of Hungarian refugees is expected. The government says border patrols will continue to discourage citizens of other Eastern European countries visiting Hungary from crossing the border into Austria. East Germany, Hungary, and Romania protest the removal of the fence.

May 10-11. Baker Visits Moscow. James A. Baker makes his first trip to Moscow as secretary of state. He and Foreign Minister Shevardnadze agree to resume the START talks, which have been suspended since November 1988. He meets May 11 with President Gorbachev, who announces that the Soviet Union will unilaterally withdraw five hundred nuclear warheads from Europe. Gorbachev also presents Baker with a proposal to cut conventional forces in Europe that would equalize the two sides' forces by 1997. In a commencement address May 12 at Texas A & M University, President Bush says it is "time to move beyond containment" in dealings with the Soviet Union.

May 15-18. Sino-Soviet Summit. President Mikhail Gorbachev makes the first trip to China by a Soviet leader since 1959. On May 16 he meets with Deng Xiaoping, and they formally announce the normalization of relations between their two countries. Gorbachev reportedly proposes easing the confrontational military posture along the Sino-Soviet border. His visit is upstaged by massive prodemocracy protests in Beijing's Tiananman Square that swell to one million people May 17. The Chinese government announces martial law May 20 in an attempt to end the protests. The Chinese army violently crushes the prodemocracy movement June 3-4.

May 25. Congress Convenes in Moscow. The new Congress of People's Deputies convenes in Moscow. The congress elects a 542-seat Supreme Soviet dominated by conservatives. Mikhail Gorbachev is elected to the strengthened position of chairman of the Supreme Soviet (president) with 95.6 percent of the deputies' votes. Moscow liberal Boris Yeltsin narrowly misses being elected to the Supreme Soviet. In response to protests in Moscow over Yeltsin's exclusion, Gorbachev says that Yeltsin may have a Supreme Soviet seat if someone else gives one up. A member yields his seat to Yeltsin May 29. The same day Anatoly Lukyanov is elected vice president after being nominated for the post by Gorbachev. The congress's shockingly candid debates on previously taboo subjects are followed closely on television by the Soviet population. Debate topics include the role of the KGB, the recent ethnic unrest in the Caucasus, and defense spending.

May 29. Bush Conventional Forces Proposal. At a NATO summit in Brussels, President Bush attempts to seize the arms control initiative from Moscow by outlining a detailed plan for reducing conventional forces in Europe. His plan calls for ceilings on tanks, armored personnel carriers, artillery pieces, helicopters, and fighter aircraft. It also proposes that the Soviet Union and United States reduce their troop strength in Europe to 275,000 soldiers each.

June 3-15. Rioting in Uzbekistan. Ethnic rioting be-

tween Uzbeks and Meskhetians in Uzbekistan leaves nearly one hundred dead. Soviet troops are sent to the region June 4.

June 4. Polish Elections Held. Elections are held in Poland for the new legislature. Solidarity dominates the voting, winning virtually every contested seat. Although Communist candidates run unopposed for 299 of the 460 seats in the Sejm (assembly), only five candidates receive the requisite 50 percent of the vote. President Jaruzelski June 6 asks Solidarity to form a coalition government with the communists and their allies, but he is rejected. After runoff elections June 18, Solidarity holds 99 of 100 Senate seats and all 161 opposition seats in the Sejm. Communist party candidates fill the other 294 Sejm seats only after a rule change allows unopposed candidates to win a seat with less than 50 percent of the vote. Jaruzelski announces June 30 that he will not run for president, even though his election to that office had been part of the agreement between the government and Solidarity. The Polish parliament convenes July 4.

June 12-14. Gorbachev in West Germany. President Gorbachev travels to Bonn for meetings with Chancellor Kohl. The two leaders sign a joint declaration supporting national self-determination, arms reductions, and the development of a "common European home."

June 16. Nagy Reburied. Imre Nagy, who served as prime minister of Hungary and was executed in 1958 for his role in the 1956 Hungarian uprising, is reburied as a national hero amidst a great outpouring of Hungarian nationalist sentiment.

June 27. Ministerial Nominations Rejected. For the first time ever, the USSR Supreme Soviet rejects ministerial nominations. Six of Prime Minister Nikolai Ryzhkov's fifty-seven nominees for the Council of Ministers are rejected, forcing him to withdraw the nominations.

July 1. Gorbachev on Ethnic Violence. In a nationally televised speech, President Gorbachev warns Soviet citizens that ethnic violence and nationalism threaten his reform program and the Soviet Union as a whole.

July 7. Warsaw Pact Summit. Leaders of the Warsaw Pact nations meet in Bucharest, Romania. President Gorbachev calls for "independent solutions of national problems."

July 9-13. Bush Visits Eastern Europe. President Bush travels to Poland and Hungary. On July 10 he addresses the Polish parliament and outlines the U.S. aid program for Poland. He meets with Lech Walesa in Gdansk July 11. Walesa presents Bush with a plan calling for $10 billion in U.S. aid (compared with Bush's proposal of $115 million). Bush goes to Budapest July 12, where he meets with Hungarian leaders.

July 10. Soviet Coal Miners Strike. Miners in the western Siberian town of Mezhdurechensk strike to protest low wages, poor working and living conditions, shortages of basic products, and environmental destruction.

The strike quickly spreads to mining towns throughout the Kuznetsky Basin and threatens the entire Soviet economy. Negotiations between strikers and government officials begin July 17. The same day miners at eight coal mines in Ukraine's Donetsk Basin go on strike, touching off a widespread walkout in that region. Siberian miners agree July 19 to return to work after the government promises them higher wages, improved living and working conditions, and greater control over mine operations. Strikes in Ukraine dissipate by July 26, after the government makes similar promises to miners there.

July 19. Jaruzelski Elected President. The Polish parliament elects Gen. Wojciech Jaruzelski president. He runs unopposed but receives only the minimum number of votes necessary for election. Jaruzelski, who had previously said he would not run, announced his candidacy the day before the vote.

July 30. Inter-Regional Group Formed. About three hundred members of the Congress of People's Deputies form the Inter-Regional Group, an opposition bloc within the congress.

August 7. East Germans in West German Missions. The East German government protests Bonn's refusal to expel 130 East Germans who sought refuge in its Berlin mission. Another 180 East Germans take refuge at the West German embassy in Budapest. On August 24, the Budapest refugees are flown to West Germany. During August growing numbers of East Germans cross the border from Hungary to Austria.

August 18. Nazi-Soviet Protocols Revealed. Politburo member Aleksandr Yakovlev admits that the Soviet Union signed secret protocols to the 1939 Nazi-Soviet Nonaggression Pact, which called for the partition of Poland and allowed the Soviet Union to dominate the Baltic states. On August 22, the Lithuanian Supreme Soviet declares the 1940 Soviet annexation of Lithuania illegal.

August 24. Mazowiecki Becomes Premier. The Polish Sejm confirms Solidarity member Tadeusz Mazowiecki as premier. The Polish Communist party had been unable to form a government. President Jaruzelski agreed August 17 to allow Solidarity to put together a ruling coalition under the condition that Communists head the ministries of defense and interior. President Gorbachev had encouraged the Polish Communists to join the ruling coalition in an August 22 phone call to party leader Mieczyslaw Rakowski.

September 4. Hungary on Refugees. The Hungarian government says that East German refugees will not be allowed to cross into Austria until East and West Germany conclude an agreement on their status. Thousands of East German tourists, hoping to flee to Austria, have been piling up in Hungary, creating a crisis for the Hungarian government, trapped between the competing demands of East and West Germany.

September 9. Yeltsin Visits the United States. Boris Yeltsin arrives in New York for an eight-day speaking tour that includes stops in Washington, Baltimore, and Chicago. He meets briefly with President Bush at the White House September 12. On September 14 an Italian newspaper accuses Yeltsin of drunken behavior while in the United States. *Pravda* reprints the report on September 18.

September 10. Hungary Opens Border. The Hungarian government opens the border to Austria to unrestricted emigration by East Germans. Within two days more than ten thousand East Germans cross into Austria on their way to West Germany. In response, East Germany sharply restricts travel to Hungary.

September 12. Polish Cabinet Formed. A twenty-three-member cabinet is nominated by Premier Mazowiecki and approved by vote of the Sejm the same day. Eleven Solidarity members, four Communists, and eight representatives of smaller parties make up the cabinet. The Communists are assigned the ministries of defense and interior, as promised, as well as the transportation and foreign trade ministries.

September 19-20. Politburo Purge. At a Central Committee plenum, Vladimir Shcherbitsky, Viktor Chebrikov, and Viktor Nikonov are ousted from the Politburo. The plenum promotes KGB head Vladimir Kryuchkov and Gosplan chairman Yuri Maslyukov to full Politburo status. Shcherbitsky is replaced as first secretary of the Ukrainian party September 28 by Vladimir Ivashko.

September 21. Shevardnadze in United States. Foreign Minister Shevardnadze visits Washington and delivers a letter to President Bush from President Gorbachev. In the letter, Gorbachev agrees to destroy the Krasnoyarsk radar station, which the United States claims violates the ABM treaty. Shevardnadze and Secretary of State Baker meet September 22 in Jackson Hole, Wyoming. They agree to tentative plans for a 1990 summit meeting. The following day, Baker and Shevardnadze sign agreements concerning prior notification of nuclear tests and exchange of information on nuclear and chemical weapons stockpiles.

September 30. East German Refugee Agreement. The East German government agrees to transport 5,500 East Germans to West Germany who have taken refuge in the West German embassy in Prague. After the announcement another five thousand East Germans enter the Prague embassy. Responding to a flood of East Germans into Czechoslovakia, the East German government October 3 restricts travel to that country. On October 4, eleven thousand East Germans board trains in Prague bound for West Germany. Thousands of East Germans jam the tracks along the trains' route through East Germany, hoping to climb on board the refugee trains.

October 6. Fortieth Anniversary of East Germany. In a speech in East Berlin on the occasion of the German Democratic Republic's fortieth anniversary, President

Gorbachev says that East Germany should adopt Soviet reforms. Large demonstrations break out in several East German cities October 7-9.

October 9. Law on Strikes Passed. The Supreme Soviet passes a law legalizing strikes under limited conditions. Strikes by workers in the transportation, communication, defense, and power industries continue to be forbidden.

October 12. Polish Economic Reform. The Polish Solidarity-led government announces an economic program designed to combat inflation. Among other measures, state subsidies are cut and the indexing of wages to inflation is limited.

October 18. Krenz Replaces Honecker. Egon Krenz replaces Erich Honecker as leader of the East German Communist party and head of state. Honecker reportedly is forced out by his colleagues, who regard his hard-line approach to upheaval in Eastern Europe as impractical. On October 16, one hundred thousand people demonstrated in Leipzig for reforms. Demonstrations continue during the following weeks, including a rally by as many as three hundred thousand protesters in Leipzig on October 23.

October 18. Hungary Amends Constitution. The Hungarian National Assembly changes the name of the country from "People's Republic of Hungary" to "Republic of Hungary." It also amends the constitution to allow for the establishment of political parties and the strengthening of civil rights guarantees.

October 23. Shevardnadze Speech. In a speech to the Supreme Soviet, Foreign Minister Shevardnadze concedes that the Krasnoyarsk radar station violates the ABM treaty. He also says the 1979 Soviet invasion of Afghanistan was an illegal act.

October 28. Protests in Prague. On the seventy-first anniversary of the founding of the Czechoslovak Republic, about ten thousand people gather in Prague's Wenceslas Square. Police charge the crowd, beating and arresting hundreds of protesters.

October 31. Krenz Visits Moscow. Egon Krenz meets with President Gorbachev in Moscow. On his return to East Germany November 1, Krenz declares his complete support for the policy of perestroika.

October 31. Malta Summit Announced. President Bush announces that he and President Gorbachev will meet on ships off the coast of Malta December 2-3.

November 1. Upheaval in East Germany. In response to continuing protests, the East German government opens its border with Czechoslovakia, precipitating a flood of refugees into that country who are hoping to reach the West. Five East German Politburo members are removed November 3, and six more are ousted November 8. Half a million people demonstrate in East Berlin for political reforms November 4. Huge crowds also gather in Dresden, Leipzig, and other East German cities. Prime Minister Willi Stoph and the entire cabinet resign No-

vember 7. The following day Hans Modrow, reformer from Dresden, is named premier.

November 4. Kryuchkov Admits KGB Mistakes. In a televised speech, KGB head Vladimir Kryuchkov says that the KGB once served as a tool of Stalinist repression. He promises that the KGB will never serve such a function again.

November 9. East Germany Opens Borders. The East German government announces that East Germans will be free to travel to West Germany or West Berlin without receiving special permission. The order effectively throws open the nation's borders to unrestricted travel and emigration. Thousands of jubilant East and West Berliners hold a spontaneous celebration at the Berlin Wall that lasts for two days.

November 11. Protest Held in Bulgaria. Amidst growing protests in Bulgaria, General Secretary Todor Zhivkov unexpectedly resigns and is replaced by Foreign Minister Petar Mladenov.

November 14. Gorbachev Warning. In a commentary published in *Pravda,* President Gorbachev warns the West not to interfere in Eastern Europe.

November 15. Walesa Asks for Marshall Plan. During a visit to the United States, Polish Solidarity leader Lech Walesa addresses a joint session of Congress and exhorts U.S. policy makers to embark on a new Marshall Plan that would rebuild the economies of Eastern Europe. President Bush awarded Walesa the Medal of Freedom at the White House November 13.

November 17. Uprising in Czechoslovakia. A rally in Prague commemorating an anti-Nazi protest held fifty years ago draws twenty thousand people and turns into an antigovernment demonstration. Police break up the demonstration, arresting more than a hundred protesters. One student is rumored to have been killed. The next day two thousand people gather in Prague to protest the student's death. On November 19, Vaclav Havel and other dissidents form the opposition Civic Forum. A peaceful crowd of two hundred thousand demands the resignation of party leader Milos Jakes November 20. Alexander Dubcek, a symbol of the 1968 reform movement, addresses a crowd of two hundred thousand in Prague November 24. The same day, Jakes and the entire Politburo submit their resignations. Karel Urbanek is appointed the new general secretary. Havel warns a massive crowd in Prague estimated at eight hundred thousand not to be fooled by the leadership shuffle, because many hard-liners remain in power. On November 25, Prime Minister Ladislav Adamec announces his resignation but stays on as caretaker. Millions of Czechoslovaks stage a two-hour nationwide strike to demand further liberal changes from the government. Adamec opens negotiations with the Civic Forum on November 28.

November 17. Modrow Names Cabinet. East German premier Hans Modrow names a new cabinet. Eleven of twenty-seven members are noncommunists. He also promises to reform the feared Stasis security police force.

November 30. Gorbachev on Common European Home. While in Rome on his way to the Malta summit, President Gorbachev delivers a speech in which he outlines his vision of a common European home, where all nations are independent and cooperate economically. He meets with Pope John Paul II December 1, and they agree to work toward establishing diplomatic relations.

December 2-3. Malta Summit. President Bush and President Gorbachev travel to Malta for a shipboard summit that is held in a cordial atmosphere despite bad weather that forces changes in the summit agenda. The two leaders discuss the changes in Eastern Europe and agree to accelerate negotiations on chemical weapons and strategic nuclear forces with the intention of concluding arms control treaties sometime in 1990. They also agree to begin talks on a new trade pact that will be contingent on Soviet emigration policy. The summit concludes December 3 with a joint news conference.

December 2. East German Corruption. A special parliamentary committee finds that Erich Honecker and other East German leaders engaged in embezzlement, bribe taking, and currency speculation. On December 3, Honecker and eleven other Communist party leaders are expelled from the party. All members of the Politburo, including General Secretary Egon Krenz and Premier Hans Modrow, resign their party positions. Honecker and the other implicated officials are placed under house arrest December 5. Krenz resigns as president December 6 and is replaced by Manfred Gerlach, head of the Liberal Democratic party, which is allied with the Communists.

December 6. Lithuanian Communist Monopoly Ended. The Lithuanian Supreme Soviet votes to end the Communist party's monopoly on political power. The following day, a similar vote legalizes opposition groups.

December 8. Pravda on Article 6. A commentary in *Pravda* hints that Article 6 of the USSR Constitution, which guarantees the leading role of the party in Soviet society, could eventually be revoked. President Gorbachev tells the Congress of People's Deputies, which opens on December 12, that it is too soon to discuss Article 6. The Congress votes to delay consideration of the matter.

December 10. New Czechoslovak Government. President Gustav Husak resigns after swearing in a new cabinet. Negotiations between outgoing prime minister Ladislav Adamec and the opposition Civic Forum had resulted in agreement on the composition of a new government. Communist reformer Marian Calfa becomes premier. He heads a twenty-one-member cabinet consisting of ten Communists and eleven noncommunists. Parliament is to select an interim president in the near future, and the new government will serve until free parliamentary elections are held. Millions of Czechoslovaks join in a nationwide celebration of the new government on December 11.

December 13. East European Aid Discussed. The foreign ministers of twenty-four Western nations meet in Brussels to discuss emergency funding for East Europe. The group approves a $1 billion emergency stabilization fund for Poland and a $1 billion loan to Hungary.

December 14. Sakharov Dies. Soviet physicist and leading opposition figure Andrei Sakharov suffers a heart attack and dies in Moscow.

December 15-25. Revolution in Romania. Crowds in Timisoara prevent Romanian police from arresting the Reverend Laszlo Tokes, who had been active in promoting the rights of ethnic Hungarians. Gatherings to protect Tokes turn into prodemocracy demonstrations December 16. Army and security police (Securitate) forces attack demonstrators in Timisoara December 17. At least several hundred and perhaps thousands of citizens are killed and wounded in the assault. On December 20, fifty thousand people in Timisoara rally in protest, causing President Nicolae Ceausescu to return from a state visit to Iran. On December 21, Ceausescu is shouted down as he delivers a speech from the balcony of his Bucharest palace. Violence erupts between crowds of demonstrators in Bucharest and the Securitate forces. The Securitate is unable to control the rebellion, and the army joins the population December 22. A virtual civil war rages in the capital throughout the day. By evening the anti-Ceausescu forces have captured the Royal Palace and most strategic locations in Bucharest. Radio Bucharest announces that a coalition of dissidents, intellectuals, military officers, and former Communists had formed the National Salvation Front to take control of the country. Fighting continues for more than a week between the army and remnants of the Securitate. Ceausescu and his wife, who had disappeared when the fighting began, are captured by the army and executed after a swift military trial on December 25. The Soviet government December 22 hails the overthrow of the Ceausescu regime. The United States moves to recognize the new government on December 26.

December 17. Polish Economic Measures. The Polish government announces an austerity program designed to combat inflation. Both houses of parliament subsequently approve the plan, which includes wage ceilings.

December 19. Czechoslovak Elections Scheduled. The Czechoslovak parliament schedules elections for June 1990 and votes to reconstruct the country's social and economic systems. Premier Calfa meets with President Gorbachev in Moscow on December 20. They agree to open negotiations on the withdrawal of Soviet troops from Czechoslovakia.

December 20. Lithuanian Communist Declaration. The Lithuanian Communist party declares itself independent of the Communist party of the Soviet Union. Lithuanian party leader Algirdas Brazauskas announces that his party supports the creation of "an independent democratic Lithuanian state." President Gorbachev condemns the action.

December 24. Nazi-Soviet Pact Condemned. The Congress of People's Deputies declares that the Soviet Union illegally conspired in 1939 with Nazi Germany to occupy independent nations, including those of the Baltic region. The congress asserts that the Nazi-Soviet nonaggression pact was "invalid."

December 28. Dubcek, Havel Elected. The Czechoslovak parliament unanimously elects Alexander Dubcek as its chairman. The next day, the parliament unanimously elects playwright Vaclav Havel interim president.

1990

January 7. Troops Sent to Georgia. The Soviet government announces that troops have been sent to Georgia to prevent fighting between Georgian nationalists and members of the Ossetian ethnic group.

January 9. Ryzhkov Proposal to CMEA. Prime Minister Ryzhkov formally proposes to the members of the Council for Mutual Economic Assistance (CMEA) that the organization begin basing trade on hard currency and market prices in 1991.

January 11-13. Gorbachev in Lithuania. Gorbachev makes a three-day visit to Lithuania in an effort to persuade Communist party officials there to rescind their break with Moscow. Gorbachev is received politely, but Lithuanian leaders and citizens convey their intention to continue seeking independence.

January 15. State of Emergency in Azerbaijan. Widespread fighting between Armenians and Azerbaijanis prompts the Presidium of the Supreme Soviet to decree a state of emergency in parts of Azerbaijan. President Gorbachev dispatches eleven thousand Soviet troops to the region January 16. They raise the total Soviet troop strength in Azerbaijan to sixteen thousand. Azerbaijanis in Baku carried out a pogrom January 13-14 against Armenians in the city that resulted in the deaths of about thirty people. Both sides had responded to the killings by forming volunteer militias. Prime Minister Ryzhkov, in a radio interview, says that the Kremlin had to intervene with armed force to prevent a civil war between Armenia and Azerbaijan. The Bush administration gives its support to the Soviet action, characterizing it is as a necessary step to maintain order and protect citizens, not as a move to suppress dissent. The Soviet government reveals January 18 that it is calling up reservists from Slavic republics to support troops in the Caucasus. Widespread protests against the move, however, cause the government to abandon the call-up order December 19.

January 20-21. Soviet Troops Occupy Baku. Soviet troops break past barricades and enter Baku during a coordinated nighttime attack. President Gorbachev claims the raid, which was spearheaded by tanks, was necessary as a means of stopping a threatened coup by the Azerbaijani Popular Front and restoring order in Baku. The Azerbaijani legislature condemns the Soviet occupation January 22 and threatens to call for a national referendum on secession from the USSR unless all Soviet troops are withdrawn within forty-eight hours. The same day Soviet troops seal the border with Iran to cut off the flow of weapons into Soviet Azerbaijan.

January 31. Bush Troop Proposal. In his State of the Union address, President Bush proposes that the Soviet Union and the United States cut their forces in Europe to just 195,000 each.

February 2. Armenian-Azerbaijani Peace Talks. Representatives of Armenia and Azerbaijan meet in Riga, Latvia, for peace talks. The two groups will discuss humanitarian issues raised by the conflict in the Caucasus, but they will not address the key issue of control over Nagorno-Karabakh. At the outset, the two groups agree to condemn Moscow's use of troops in the region.

February 4. Moscow Rally Backs Democratization. More than a hundred thousand people participate in a prodemocracy rally in Moscow. It is the largest unofficial demonstration since the Bolshevik Revolution. A reformist member of the Supreme Soviet maintains February 5 that President Gorbachev was behind the rally, which he hoped would strengthen his position on the eve of a Central Committee plenum.

February 6. Monetary Unification Plan. The West German government proposes unifying the currencies of the two Germanys as a step toward reunification. West German chancellor Helmut Kohl and East German premier Hans Modrow agree February 13 to begin talks on monetary unification.

February 6-11. Baker in Eastern Europe. Secretary of State Baker embarks on a five-day tour of Eastern Europe. On February 6 he meets with Czechoslovak president Vaclav Havel. They discuss a U.S. assistance package for Czechoslovakia. Baker arrives in Moscow February 7 for a series of meetings with Soviet officials. He meets with President Gorbachev February 9, and they report progress on arms control issues. On February 10 Baker becomes the first U.S. official to testify before a Soviet parliamentary committee, fielding questions from members of the International Affairs Committee of the Supreme Soviet. Baker flies to Sofia that evening and meets with Bulgarian president Petar Mladenov. He then travels to Bucharest February 11, where he promises Romanian leaders $93.5 million in U.S. emergency food aid.

February 7. Party Renounces Power Monopoly. After three days of contentious debate, the Central Committee approves a platform renouncing the Communist party's monopoly on power encoded in Article 6 of the USSR Constitution. The plenum also endorses Gorbachev's proposal to create a Western-style executive presidency.

February 8. Soviet Arms to Afghanistan. Gen. H. Norman Schwarzkopf of the U.S. Army tells the Senate Armed Services Committee that the Soviet Union is "pouring" arms and equipment into Afghanistan at a higher rate than when the Soviets were still occupying the country.

February 9. Soviets Announce Czech Withdrawal. The Soviet government announces that it will begin to withdraw its troops from Czechoslovakia within the month and will have withdrawn the "fundamental part" of the Soviet combat force by the end of May. The Czechoslovak government had demanded a substantial Soviet withdrawal before elections scheduled for June.

February 10. Kohl Visits Moscow. West German chancellor Helmut Kohl meets with President Gorbachev in Moscow. Kohl says after the meeting that Gorbachev had agreed that reunification was a matter for Germans to decide. During the meeting, Gorbachev emphasizes the security interests of Germany's European neighbors.

February 12. Violence in Tajikistan. Soviet Interior Ministry troops move into the city of Dushanbe in an attempt to quell three days of anti-Armenian rioting in the Central Asian republic of Tajikistan. Rioting in the city left 37 dead and 108 wounded.

February 12. U.S.-Soviet Trade Talks. Representatives of the United States and the Soviet Union open talks on normalizing trade relations. The talks are designed to produce an agreement that could be signed by President Bush and President Gorbachev at the summit being planned for June in the United States.

February 16. Shcherbitsky Dies. Former Ukrainian party chief and Politburo member Vladimir Shcherbitsky dies after a long illness.

February 21. Poles Request Soviet Presence. Polish prime minister Tadeusz Mazowiecki says that Soviet troops should remain in Poland until ambiguities concerning the border between a reunified German state and Poland are resolved.

February 24. Lithuanian Elections. The Communist party is soundly defeated in Lithuanian elections, capturing only seven of the republic's ninety Supreme Soviet seats contested. The Sajudis nationalist movement wins an overwhelming majority of the seats.

February 26. Soviet Troop Withdrawal. President Gorbachev and Czechoslovak president Havel sign an agreement on removing Soviet troops from Czechoslovakia. The withdrawal is to begin immediately and be completed in stages by July 1, 1991.

March 4. Elections in Slavic Republics. Reformist and nationalist candidates dominate voting in elections to republic legislatures and other local offices in Russia, Belorussia, and Ukraine.

March 11-13. Lithuania Declares Independence. The Supreme Soviet of Lithuania votes 124-0 (with six abstentions) to declare the republic an independent nation. The body elects Vytautas Landsbergis president. Conservative Politburo member Yegor Ligachev says March 12 that force will not be used against Lithuania. President Gorbachev March 13 calls the Lithuanian declaration "illegitimate and invalid" and rules out negotiations.

March 13-15. Congress Revamps Presidency. The Congress of People's Deputies votes to strengthen the USSR presidency in accordance with a plan put forward at the February 1990 Central Committee plenum. The same day the congress repeals Article 6 of the USSR Constitution, which guarantees the Communist party's monopoly on power. On March 14 the congress votes to elect the first executive president itself for the first five-year term, then have the president chosen by popular vote beginning in 1995. The following day Mikhail Gorbachev runs unopposed for the new presidency and is elected by a 1,329-495 vote in a secret ballot. Almost four hundred deputies abstain. The new presidential office gives Gorbachev broad executive powers. Many deputies had criticized the restructured presidency as concentrating too much power in one person. The president will have the power to veto legislation, declare war "in case of attack," command the armed forces and the KGB, negotiate all international treaties, issue executive orders, declare martial law, and dissolve the legislature.

March 18. East German Elections. A coalition of parties allied with West German chancellor Helmut Kohl's conservative Christian Democratic party scores a clear victory in East German elections. The coalition favors a rapid reunification with West Germany.

March 18. Moscow Pressures Lithuania. Soviet forces begin large-scale maneuvers in Lithuania as part of a campaign to pressure Lithuanian leaders into revoking their declaration of independence. President Gorbachev issues a decree March 21 prohibiting the sale of guns in Lithuania and ordering the KGB to tighten security around Lithuania's borders.

March 24-26. Presidential Council Appointed. President Gorbachev appoints a sixteen-member Presidential Council in accordance with legislation passed earlier in the month by the Congress of People's Deputies. The council will advise the president and formulate national policy.

March 25. Communist Headquarters Seized. Despite denials by Moscow that it will use military force in Lithuania, Soviet troops occupy the headquarters of the Lithuanian Communist party in Vilnius. Troops also raid a psychiatric hospital in Vilnius March 27 and remove twenty-three Lithuanian military deserters given refuge there.

March 31. Gorbachev Warning. President Gorbachev warns Lithuanian leaders to renounce their independence declaration or face "grave consequences." Lithuanian president Landsbergis says April 2 that the republic's move to independence was intended to be gradual and its timing could be negotiated. He repeats an earlier call for negotiations with Moscow on the crisis.

April 5. Summit Announced. During talks in Washington, Secretary of State Baker and Foreign Minister Shevardnadze announce agreement on holding a U.S.-Soviet summit in the United States from May 30 to June 3. The two men also discuss the situation in Lithuania. Baker reportedly emphasized that superpower relations would be damaged if Moscow used force against Lithuania.

April 18. Oil Shipments to Lithuania Stopped. The Soviet leadership orders that Lithuania's oil supply be cut off to force the republic's leaders to rescind their declaration of independence. Natural gas pipelines supplying Lithuania are closed the following day. On April 13 President Gorbachev had threatened an economic embargo against Lithuania if it did not rescind its independence declaration.

April 24. Bush Avoids Imposing Sanctions. President Bush April 24 delays consideration of sanctions against the Soviet Union for its conduct toward Lithuania. He says U.S. sanctions could hurt Lithuania's cause and the progress of reform in the Soviet Union. Lithuanian president Vytautas Landsbergis denounces Bush's decision.

May 1. May Day Protest. President Gorbachev and other Soviet leaders are jeered by protesters at the yearly May Day parade in Moscow. Traditionally the parade in Red Square had been a well-orchestrated affair supporting the Kremlin's political line, but the Soviet leadership had decided that for the first time unofficial marchers would be allowed to participate. After the organized parade passes through the square, thousands of demonstrators march in, shouting slogans and holding banners that denounce Gorbachev, the Communist party, and Marxist-Leninist ideology. Gorbachev and the leadership watch the display from the top of Lenin's Mausoleum for about twenty-five minutes before leaving.

May 2. West German President Affirms Border. During a visit to Warsaw, West German president Richard von Weizsaecker declares that current Polish borders are "inviolable." The East and West German parliaments approve a resolution guaranteeing Poland's borders on June 21.

May 3. Bush Meets Lithuanian Prime Minister. Prime Minister Kazimiera Prunskiene of Lithuania meets with President Bush at the White House. Bush rejects her suggestion that the United States could mediate the dispute between Lithuania and Moscow.

May 4. Latvia Moves for Independence. Defying warnings from Moscow, the Latvian parliament announces the beginning of a transition period leading to the republic's independence. Mindful of Moscow's economic blockade against Lithuania, the Latvians proceed more cautiously, declaring that the USSR Constitution and most Soviet laws would be applicable in the republic until independence, which would come only after negotiations with Moscow.

May 5. German Reunification Talks Open. Talks on German reunification between the four victorious powers from World War II and the two Germanys open in Bonn. Foreign Minister Shevardnadze states that the Soviet Union will accept a united Germany but will not allow it to be a member of NATO.

May 12. Baltics Agree to Coordination. The presidents of the three Baltic republics meet and agree to coordinate their domestic and foreign policies in an effort to regain their independence from the Soviet Union.

May 16. USSR Granted GATT Observer Status. At the urging of the Bush administration, the Soviet Union is granted observer status in GATT (General Agreement on Tariffs and Trade). At the Malta summit, Bush had promised to remove American obstacles to Soviet participation.

May 17. Gorbachev Meets with Prunskiene. President Gorbachev meets with Prime Minister Kazimiera Prunskiene of Lithuania in the Kremlin. It is Gorbachev's first face-to-face meeting with a representative of the new Lithuanian government. The day before, the Lithuanian parliament had agreed to suspend all laws implementing its declaration of independence, although not the act itself. However, Gorbachev continues to insist that suspension of the declaration is a precondition to beginning formal negotiations.

May 18. Baker Negotiates Arms Pact in Moscow. Secretary of State Baker announces that after four days of intensive negotiations in Moscow, major differences on cruise missiles have been resolved, so that a general statement of principles on the strategic arms reduction treaty can be signed at the upcoming Washington summit. Progress also is made on a chemical weapons agreement.

May 21. Ruling Front Wins in Romania. Romanians go against the anticommunist electoral tide in Eastern Europe by giving the ruling National Salvation Front, which is dominated by former Communists, 73 percent of the vote, and electing Ion Iliescu as president with 89 percent of the vote. Foreign observers noted that, despite some local irregularities, the elections were generally free and fair.

May 21. Law on Presidential Insult Passed. The Supreme Soviet passes a law making insulting the Soviet president a crime punishable by a prison term, but only if the insults are expressed "in an indecent way."

May 24. Ryzhkov Economic Plan. Prime Minister Ryzhkov introduces a plan in the Supreme Soviet to double food prices as a first step in economic reform. The price increases would be subject to a public referendum. Ryzhkov sets a "regulated market economy" as his goal. The announcement triggers panic buying in Moscow stores, and sales of certain items are restricted to legal residents of Moscow. Ryzhkov's plan is harshly criticized by legislators.

May 29. Yeltsin Elected Russian President. Maverick populist Boris Yeltsin is elected president of the Russian republic, defeating Gorbachev's ally, Aleksandr Vlasov.

May 31-June 3. Washington Summit. At a summit in Washington, President Bush and President Gorbachev sign an agreement outlining mutual reductions in their countries' strategic nuclear arsenals. The agreement is to serve as a basis for a formal treaty that the leaders indicate could be concluded by the end of the year. They also sign a treaty providing for major reductions in chemical weapons. Bush unexpectedly signs a trade treaty with the Soviet Union, even though a Soviet law formally codifying the removal of restrictions on emigration has not yet been passed. Congress had declared passage of the law to be a precondition to normal U.S.-Soviet trade. To avoid a confrontation with Congress, Bush says he will not submit the treaty for congressional approval until the Soviets pass the law. After leaving Washington, Gorbachev visits Minnesota June 3 and San Francisco June 4, where he meets with South Korean leader Roh Tae Woo.

June 8. Russian Republic Declares Sovereignty. The Russian Supreme Soviet declares that its laws take precedence over Soviet laws. The move is considered a victory for new Russian president Boris Yeltsin, even though the vote falls short of the two-thirds majority needed to amend the Russian constitution.

June 8. Elections in Czechoslovakia. President Vaclav Havel's Civic Forum and its Slovak counterpart, Public Against Violence, win a broad majority in the national parliament, reflecting popular enthusiasm for Havel's management of the government.

June 10. Soviets Intervene in Central Asia. Soviet troops intervene to break up violence between Kyrgyz and Uzbeks after the death toll rises to at least 107.

June 12. Supreme Soviet Passes Press Law. A law on freedom of the press is approved, forbidding government censorship and allowing any citizen eighteen years or older to open a newspaper. Supporters hail the law as a major step in expanding glasnost but complain that the government still is able to control the nation's publishing through its power to allocate the limited supplies of newsprint.

June 12. Gorbachev Concession on Germany. In a speech to the Supreme Soviet, Gorbachev hints that German membership in NATO might be acceptable if Germany retained "associate membership" in the Warsaw Pact. This formulation is considered a concession to the Western position that a united Germany must be a member of NATO. West Germany welcomes the shift as positive but insists that it does not want dual membership.

June 14. Government Economic Plan Rejected. Responding to popular concern, the Supreme Soviet rejects the government's proposal to increase food prices by a

vote of 319 to 33. The Supreme Soviet approves a plan to develop joint stock companies and a commercial banking system.

June 18. Bulgarian Communists Win Election. Election results are released showing that Bulgaria's former Communist party (renamed the Socialist party) has won a majority of the seats in the country's new parliament, based on runoffs in the first free multiparty elections in Bulgaria in forty-five years. Although charges of intimidation and fraud were raised after the first round, international observers called the elections generally free and fair.

June 19-23. Russian Party Congress. The newly formed Russian wing of the Communist party holds its first congress. The meeting is dominated by conservatives who criticize President Gorbachev and his program. Gorbachev defends his record, saying the hard-liners had "lost touch with reality long ago." Angered by the criticism, he hints that he might resign his post as general secretary at the upcoming Twenty-eighth Party Congress. Conservative Ivan Polozkov, a doctrinaire Leninist and critic of Gorbachev, is elected Russian party leader.

June 21. Two Germanys Approve Economic Union. The parliaments of the two Germanys approve a treaty on economic and monetary union. According to the treaty, the two economies will be merged on July 1.

June 29. Lithuania Delays Independence. The Lithuanian parliament agrees to suspend its declaration of independence for a hundred days in exchange for negotiations with Moscow and the lifting of economic sanctions. Moscow reopens the oil pipeline to Lithuania June 30. The end of the embargo is formally announced in a brief telephone call to the Lithuanian government from the Ministry of Petroleum and Gas Industry.

July 1. East and West German Economies Merge. The East and West Germany economic systems are united. East Germans trade their currency for deutschemarks. East German shops are immediately stocked with Western goods. Fears of inflation fueled by massive East German spending prove unwarranted, and the deutschemark remains steady on international currency markets.

July 2-14. Soviet Party Congress. The Twenty-eighth Congress of the Communist Party of the Soviet Union opens in Moscow with a speech by President Gorbachev defending his policies and pleading for party unity. July 2 the congress rejects a demand by a conservative delegate for the entire leadership to resign. On July 7 Gorbachev is able to reverse a decision by the delegates to subject each member of the leadership to an individual vote of confidence. The same day, the Ukrainian Supreme Soviet calls home deputies who are members of the body to discuss a proposal for Ukrainian sovereignty. Gorbachev responds to critics of his reform program in a blunt speech delivered July 10. After the address he is overwhelmingly reelected general secretary. On July 12 the congress elects

Gorbachev's candidate, Vladimir Ivashko, to the post of deputy general secretary. Ivashko defeats leading conservative Politburo member Yegor Ligachev. Later that day, Russian president Boris Yeltsin announces that he is resigning from the party. During the next two days dozens of other liberal delegates follow his example and resign. On July 14 the congress selects members for a reorganized and expanded Politburo that includes only Gorbachev and Ivashko from the old Politburo. The new Politburo contains twenty-four members, including the first secretaries of all fifteen republics. Western observers say the expansion of the Politburo will reduce its influence and facilitate the ongoing transfer of power from party to government institutions.

July 5. Havel Reelected President. Vaclav Havel is elected president of Czechoslovakia by a 234-50 vote of the parliament for an initial two-year term. He had been elected president for an interim period, which began December 29, 1989.

July 5-6. NATO Leaders Meet. In a historic meeting, NATO leaders gather in London and declare that the cold war is over. They announce a new defensive doctrine that would use nuclear forces as "weapons of last resort" and propose that NATO, the Warsaw Pact, and other European states join in a "commitment to nonaggression." Gorbachev is invited to address the NATO leaders in Brussels. The language of the declaration is clearly intended to bolster Gorbachev by addressing his concerns about NATO.

July 15-16. Gorbachev Accepts Germany in NATO. On the second day of talks between President Gorbachev and Chancellor Helmut Kohl, the two sides announce agreement on all major issues relating to German unification. The Soviet Union will renounce all restrictions on German sovereignty. These include allowing Germany to join any alliance it chooses. West German leaders have stated their intention to make a united Germany a full member of NATO. In exchange for Soviet approval of German unification on German terms, Kohl promises to negotiate a treaty with the Soviet Union covering political, economic, military, scientific, and cultural relations. The Soviet Union agrees to withdraw its approximately 380,000 troops from East Germany within three or four years. West Germany will help pay the costs of their maintenance and withdrawal. In addition the agreement limits the size of the united Germany's military to 370,000 troops. Currently, the German armies combined have 667,000 troops.

July 16. Ukrainians Declare Sovereignty. The Communist-controlled Ukrainian parliament passes a motion of sovereignty, 355-4, but stops short of declaring full independence. Ukraine is the tenth republic to pass some type of sovereignty declaration. The measure asserts that Ukraine has the right to mint its own currency, organize its own military, and establish citizenship requirements.

July 16. Reunification Issues Resolved. President Gorbachev and West German chancellor Helmut Kohl announce that they have resolved all major issues related to German reunification.

July 20. Union Treaty Talks Begin. Negotiations in Moscow on a new union treaty begin with a meeting between Presidential Council, consisting of Gorbachev advisers, and the Federation Council, consisting of the top leaders of the fifteen union republics.

July 23. Kravchuk Chosen as President. The Ukrainian parliament elects Leonid Kravchuk president of the republic. He replaces Vladimir Ivashko.

July 28. Baltic Republics Decline to Join Talks. The presidents of Latvia, Lithuania, and Estonia issue a joint statement stating that the Baltic republics will not take part in the negotiations on a new union treaty between the republics of the Soviet Union.

August 2. Iraq Invades Kuwait. Iraqi forces massed on the border of Kuwait invade the sheikdom and quickly seize control of most strategic locations. Kuwait's ruler, Sheik Jaber al-Ahmed al-Sabah, flees to Saudi Arabia. President Bush denounces the invasion, and the governments of the United States, Great Britain, and France freeze Iraqi assets in their countries. The Soviet Union cuts off arms deliveries to Iraq. The UN Security Council votes 14-0 (with Yemen abstaining) to condemn the invasion and threatens to impose mandatory economic sanctions if Iraq does not withdraw immediately from Kuwait.

August 3. Baker-Shevardnadze Statement. Foreign Minister Shevardnadze and Secretary of State Baker issue a joint statement in Moscow condemning the Iraqi invasion of Kuwait and calling for an international arms embargo against Iraq.

August 6. UN Imposes Sanctions. The UN Security Council passes Resolution 661, imposing mandatory economic sanctions on Iraq.

August 25. Armenia Declares Independence. The Armenian republic's parliament votes 183-2 to declare independence and to begin in taking steps to implement the declaration.

August 29. Gorbachev and Yeltsin Discuss Reform. Presidents Gorbachev and Yeltsin meet in Moscow to discuss economic reform. After the meeting Yeltsin's aides say Gorbachev has agreed to support the "Shatalin plan," an economic reform blueprint developed by a thirteen-member working group of Yeltsin and Gorbachev's economic advisers and chaired by economist Stanislav S. Shatalin. The plan aims at ending central government economic control and instituting private property rights and other liberal economic reforms.

August 30-31. Economic Summit. The Federation Council and Presidential Council hold a joint meeting chaired by President Gorbachev to discuss economic reform. At the close of the meeting, Gorbachev indicates that he is not ready to push ahead with the Shatalin reform plan. He announces that another economic reform commission will meet to develop an approach based on both the Shatalin plan and the much less radical Ryzhkov plan, previously developed by Prime Minister Ryzhkov.

September 1. Yeltsin Calls on Ryzhkov to Resign. President Yeltsin says at a Moscow press conference that USSR prime minister Nikolai Ryzhkov is an impediment to economic reform and should resign. Yeltsin also denounces President Gorbachev's intention to try to merge the Ryzhkov plan and the Shatalin plan. Yeltsin says December 3 that the Russian Federation would proceed with the Shatalin plan regardless of what the Soviet government decided to do.

September 9. Helsinki Summit. Presidents Bush and Gorbachev hold a one-day summit in Helsinki. In a joint statement, they condemn Iraq's invasion of Kuwait and say the aggression "must not be tolerated." In the statement, the United States also recognizes for the first time a legitimate Soviet role in the Middle East peace process.

September 11. Ryzhkov Threatens to Resign. Prime Minister Ryzhkov tells the Supreme Soviet that he would resign if the Shatalin economic reform plan is adopted. After Ryzhkov's speech, President Gorbachev says that he prefers the Shatalin plan to other alternatives. But on September 14, he outlines a modified version of the Shatalin plan that would preserve central authority of banking, currency, foreign exchange, and taxes.

September 12. Treaty on Germany Signed. The United States, Soviet Union, Great Britain, France, and East and West Germany sign the Final Settlement with Respect to Germany in Moscow. The treaty ends the remaining responsibility of the four victorious World War II allies over German affairs. The treaty is the culmination of the "two-plus-four talks" between the six nations, and it opens the way for German reunification set for October 3.

September 24. Gorbachev Granted Expanded Powers. The Supreme Soviet votes overwhelmingly to give President Gorbachev expanded powers of decree that would extend to March 31, 1992. Gorbachev had requested the move September 21, saying the expanded powers were necessary for economic reform and to preserve order.

September 25. Shevardnadze UN Speech. Foreign Minister Shevardnadze tells the UN General Assembly that his government would back military action sanctioned by the United Nations to force Iraq's withdrawal from Kuwait, if Iraq refused to leave peacefully.

October 1. Religious Freedom Granted. The Supreme Soviet votes 341-2 for a law that guarantees religious freedom for all Soviet citizens.

October 3. Germany Reunited. East and West Germany are officially reunited as the Federal Republic of Germany.

October 5. Primakov Meets Hussein. On the second day of a visit to Baghdad, Yevgeny Primakov, a Middle East expert and adviser to President Gorbachev, meets with Saddam Hussein. Primakov gives Hussein a message from Gorbachev urging the Iraqi leader to comply with the UN resolutions. Primakov also seeks and receives assurances from Hussein that 5,000 Soviet citizens in Iraq will be allowed to leave.

October 15. Gorbachev to Receive Nobel. President Gorbachev is named the winner of the 1990 Nobel Peace Prize.

October 16. Gorbachev Presents Economic Plan. President Gorbachev unveils a new economic plan based on the "President's plan" he outlined on September 14. Though it calls for the achievement of a free market, the plan seeks to preserve far more central government control over the economy than the Shatalin plan, and it drops the Shatalin plan's strict timetable. President Yelsin denounces the "Gorbachev plan," but the Supreme Soviet approves it October 19 by a 333-12 vote.

October 24. Competing Sovereignty Laws Passed. The USSR Supreme Soviet passes a law invalidating legislation passed by individual republics that claims to supersede federal laws. Later in the day, the parliaments of Russia and Ukraine counter the move by passing measures requiring that they approve all federal legislation before it takes effect in their respective republics.

October 26. Gorbachev Decree on Foreign Investment. President Gorbachev issues a decree permitting foreign firms to operate wholly owned subsidiaries in the Soviet Union and lease Soviet real estate.

October 31. Russia to Pursue Shatalin Plan. The Russian Supreme Soviet votes to implement a 500-day radical economic reform plan based on the Shatalin plan, despite the USSR's decision to implement a much more moderate plan.

November 9. Gorbachev in Bonn. President Gorbachev meets with Chancellor Kohl in Bonn. They sign treaties of friendship and nonaggression and a pact outlining arrangements for Soviet troop withdrawals from eastern Germany. Kohl also agrees to increase German purchases of Soviet natural gas, but does not commit to a substantial increase in German aid to the Soviet Union.

November 16. Gorbachev Speech to Supreme Soviet. The Supreme Soviet proclaims a crisis session and asks President Gorbachev to address the body. In a seventy-minute speech he accuses unnamed persons of a plot to discredit him. He calls on the republics to sign a new union treaty. On November 17, Gorbachev proposes that the executive branch undergo an extensive reorganization that would include the elimination of the premiership, the Council of Ministers, and the Presidential Council. The proposal would increase the power of the Federation Council made up of the leaders of the fifteen republics. Later in the day, the Supreme Soviet votes to give preliminary approval to the reorganization.

November 19-21. CSCE Summit. The Conference on Security and Cooperation in Europe holds a summit in

Paris attended by the leaders of the United States, Canada, and every European nation except Albania. Leaders sign the Conventional Forces in Europe (CFE) treaty November 19, which limits the number of troops and conventional arms that can be deployed by the NATO and Warsaw Pact alliances. On November 21, they also sign the Charter of Paris for a New Europe, which proclaims an end to a divided Europe and outlines fundamental political and individual freedoms.

November 23. Gorbachev Unveils Union Treaty Draft. President Gorbachev presents a draft of a new union treaty to the Supreme Soviet. The treaty, which would have to be ratified by all the republics, would retain central USSR control over military and foreign policy, while granting substantial autonomy over economic and domestic policy to the republics. Among other items, republics would be granted full control over the organization of their government, their natural resources, and their language policies.

November 29. Security Council Authorizes Force. The UN Security Council passes Resolution 678 by a 12-2 vote, with the Soviet Union voting in favor and China abstaining. The resolution authorizes coalition forces in the Persian Gulf region to use "all means necessary" to expel Iraq from Kuwait if Iraq does not withdraw by January 15.

December 2. Boris Pugo Named Interior Minister. Boris Pugo is appointed to replace Vadim Bakatin as interior minister.

December 4. Iraq Permits Soviets to Leave. After Moscow reportedly threatens to use military force against Iraq, the Iraqi government announces that the more than 3,000 Soviet citizens still in Iraq may leave.

December 9. Walesa Elected Polish President. Lech Walesa wins a runoff election for the Polish presidency with nearly 75 percent of the vote. He is sworn in December 22.

December 12. Bush on Loan Guarantees. President Bush approves up to $1 billion in loan guarantees aimed at helping the Soviet Union buy U.S. food.

December 20. Shevardnadze Resigns. In a dramatic speech to the Congress of People's Deputies, Foreign Minister Shevardnadze denounces conservative attacks on his diplomatic efforts. He warns against the growing threat of a return to dictatorship in the Soviet Union and announces his surprise resignation.

December 25. Presidential Power Expanded. The Congress of People's Deputies votes to further expand the power of the Soviet presidency.

December 27. Yanayev Confirmed as Vice President. President Gorbachev's choice for the vice presidency, Gennady Yanayev fails by a 31-vote margin in the Congress of People's Deputies to win confirmation. After Gorbachev requests a second vote and calls on the body to back his choice, Yannayev is confirmed 1,237-563.

1991

January 7. Soviet Troop Deployments. The Soviet Defense Ministry announces that paratroops will be deployed to the Baltics, Armenia, Georgia, Moldavia, and parts of Ukraine to enforce the draft.

January 11. Soviet Troops Seize Strategic Sites. Soviet troops occupy key buildings in Vilnius, the Lithuanian capital. A "National Salvation Committee" created by pro-Moscow Lithuanian communists claims it will take over responsibility for governing the republic.

January 13. Vilnius Crackdown. At about 2:00 a.m. local time Soviet troops and tanks attack a large group of Lithuanian protestors who had encircled the central broadcast facility and transmission tower in Vilnius to prevent their seizure by the troops. The Soviets kill 15 people and wound more than 150 others before taking control of the facility. The attack is part of a wider military crackdown against the Lithuanian independence movement. President Bush cautiously condemns the attack. President Yeltsin travels to Estonia where he expresses his support for the Baltics and signs a mutual security pact between Russia and the three Baltic states.

January 14. Gorbachev Denies Ordering Attack. President Gorbachev tells the Supreme Soviet that he did not order the military crackdown in Lithuania. He contends that the Soviet military commander in Lithuania, Maj. Gen. Vladimir Uskhochnik, ordered the attack on his own authority. After returning from Estonia, President Yeltsin delivers a radio address in which he condemns the crackdown in the Baltics and suggests that Russia might form its own defense force to protect its interests against the central government.

January 14. Supreme Soviet Confirms Officials. The Supreme Soviet confirms Finance Minister Valentin Pavlov as the new prime minister. On January 15, it confirms Aleksandr Bessmertnykh, who had been ambassador to the United States, as foreign minister.

January 17. Coalition Forces Attack Iraq. At 12:50 a.m. in Saudi Arabia (4:50 p.m. EST, January 16) the allied coalition launches an air war against Iraqi targets in Iraq and Kuwait.

January 20. Assault in Latvia. Elite "Black Beret" Soviet Interior Ministry troops seize the headquarters of the Latvian interior ministry building killing four people. After the attack, a crowd numbering at least 100,000 marches in Moscow to protest the Baltic crackdown. The European Community suspends $1 billion in emergency food aid to the Soviet Union the next day.

January 22. Currency Reform Decree. President Gorbachev issues a decree initiating a process of currency reform. The decree declares that 50- and 100-ruble notes will no longer have any value and gives Soviet citizens until January 25 to redeem them for smaller notes. However, the maximum number of rubles that can be redeemed is 1,000. The decree also limits the number of rubles a citizen can withdraw from a savings account in a given month to 500. The action leads to panic in many Soviet cities as people attempt to dispose of high-denomination bills that they have hoarded. Some republics and locations defy Moscow by loosening the restrictions placed on redeeming the bills. The decree is intended to stem corruption, counterfeiting, and black market activities.

January 28. Summit Postponed. Secretary of State Baker and Foreign Minister Bessmertnykh announce during a meeting in Washington, D.C., that a summit between presidents Bush and Gorbachev planned for February 11-13 in Moscow has been postponed. They say the summit was delayed because of the Persian Gulf War and the failure of U.S.-Soviet talks to produce a final treaty on strategic nuclear weapons reductions. Neither side mentions U.S. concerns about Moscow's recent crackdown on Baltic pro-independence demonstrators.

February 6. Gorbachev Urges Support for Union. In a televised address, President Gorbachev urges Soviet citizens to support the continuation of a union in the upcoming national referendum scheduled for March 17.

February 9. Lithuanian Referendum. Lithuania holds a nonbinding referendum on the question of independence. More than 90 percent of those voting support the statement: "Do you want a democratic, independent Lithuania?"

February 18. Soviets Propose Peace Plan. President Gorbachev presents a peace plan to Iraqi foreign minister Tariq Aziz during a meeting in Moscow. Aziz returns to Baghdad, where the Revolutionary Command Council considers the plan on February 20. After being informed of the plan's contents, President Bush says February 19 that it "falls well short" of coalition requirements to end the war.

February 21. Iraq Backs Soviet Plan. Soviet officials announce that Iraq has agreed to withdraw unconditionally from Kuwait under the terms of a Soviet six-point plan. The White House announces that President Bush told Gorbachev that he has "serious concerns" about the plan.

February 24. Coalition Launches Ground War. After Iraq fails to obey an ultimatum to withdraw from Kuwait, the U.S.-led coalition opens a massive ground offensive. Iraqi resistance is quickly overwhelmed and Kuwait is liberated on February 26. The U.S. announces a cease-fire at 8:00 a.m., February 28, Saudi time.

March 1. Coal Miners Strike. About 120,000 coal miners in Ukraine stage a one-day strike to agitate for higher pay. The strike sparks a series of walkouts of indefinite duration by miners in other parts of the Soviet Union. Miners expand their demands to include political reforms. Some call for President Gorbachev's resignation.

March 3. Latvia and Estonia Plebiscites. Latvia and Estonia hold nonbinding referendums on independence. According to reports, 77.8 percent of Estonian voters and 73.6 percent of Latvian voters favor independence.

March 10. Crowd Marches in Support of Yeltsin. A huge crowd of more than 100,000, but estimated by some to be as much as five times larger, marches in Moscow. The protesters urge opposition to the referendum on preserving the Soviet Union to be held a week later. The crowd also supports President Yeltsin, and speakers echo Yeltsin's February 19 call for Gorbachev to resign.

March 17. Union Referendum. The Soviet Union holds a national referendum on preserving the union. The three Baltic states, plus Armenia, Georgia, and Moldavia boycott the election. The question posed in the referendum is: "Do you consider it necessary to preserve the Union of Soviet Socialist Republics as a renewed federation of equal sovereign republics, in which the rights and freedoms of people of any nationality will be fully guaranteed?" In Azerbaijan, Uzbekistan, and Kazakhstan the question is worded differently. In Russia, 71 percent of voters favor the union. In Ukraine 70 percent are in favor. Throughout Central Asia, more than 90 percent of those voting favor the union. However, the results are not entirely positive for President Gorbachev, as votes on other questions on the ballot in some republics indicate strong support for republic independence. In Russia, 70 percent of voters favor establishing popular elections for the Russian presidency, a step that Gorbachev had opposed. In Ukraine, 83 percent of voters agree that Ukraine's participation in the union should be based on its declaration of national sovereignty.

March 25. Gorbachev Bans Protests in Moscow. President Gorbachev issues a decree banning public demonstrations in Moscow through April 15. A crowd estimated at 100,000 defies the ban by staging a pro-Yeltsin rally March 28.

April 2. Price Increases Implemented. Price increases on many consumer items are implemented throughout the Soviet Union. President Gorbachev had issued a decree March 19 establishing the increases. Prices remain controlled by the government, but they more closely reflect the costs of production.

April 5. Russian Congress Expands Yeltsin's Power. The Russian Congress of People's Deputies votes 607-228 with 100 abstentions to pass President Yeltsin's legislative package. It contains a provision granting Yeltsin the power to issue decrees.

April 9. Georgia Declares Independence. The Supreme Soviet of the republic of Georgia votes unanimously to declare its independence from the Soviet Union. On March 31 a popular referendum had overwhelmingly supported independence. The Supreme Soviet unanimously elects Zviad Gamsakhurdia president April 14.

April 17-18. Gorbachev in Tokyo. President Gorbachev discusses investment and the status of the Kuril Islands with Japanese leaders in Tokyo. It is the first time that any top Soviet leader has visited Japan. Gorbachev and Japanese prime minister Toshiki Kaifu fail to achieve a breakthrough on the Kuril issue.

April 23. Nine Plus One Accord Signed. Gorbachev and leaders of nine republics sign the "nine plus one" accord that calls for negotiations between the central Soviet government and nine participating republics aimed at producing a new union treaty. The accord also provides for an increase in the republics' decision-making role.

April 25. Gorbachev Offers to Resign. After numerous speakers at a Communist party Central Committee plenum sharply criticize President Gorbachev's leadership, he abruptly offers to resign. The Central Committee, however, rejects the offer 323-13 with 14 abstentions.

May 6. Mines Shifted to Russian Control. The Soviet government agrees to transfer authority over coal mines in the Russian republic to Boris Yeltsin's Russian government. Striking miners had demanded the transfer. The move is a victory for Yeltsin in his efforts to wrest control of the Russian economy from the Soviet government. In the wake of the transfer and Yeltsin's promises of increased pay and benefits to miners, many miners return to work.

May 16. Sino-Soviet Border Agreement Signed. Soviet and Chinese representatives sign an agreement in Moscow that settles some of the border disputes between the two countries.

May 20. Free Emigration Law Enacted. The Supreme Soviet votes 320 to 37 (with 32 abstentions) to approve a law granting citizens the right of free travel and emigration. January 1, 1993, was designated as a target date for full implementation of the law. President Bush responds by extending a waiver of the Jackson-Vanik amendment, which restricted trade with the Soviet Union.

May 22. Gorbachev Asks for Aid. At a news conference in Moscow President Gorbachev calls on the West to provide financial aid to the Soviet Union. He also asks to attend the Group of Seven summit scheduled for mid July in London. He is extended an invitation June 13.

May 26. Gamsakhurdia Elected Georgian President. Zviad Gamsakhurdia is elected president of Georgia with more than 86 percent of the popular vote. It is the first popularly contested election of a republic president.

June 1. Conventional Arms Questions Settled. Secretary of State Baker and Foreign Minister Bessmertnykh resolve remaining points of disagreement over the Conventional Forces in Europe (CFE) treaty at talks in Lisbon. The resolution paves the way for a summer summit.

June 3. Kremlin Report on Lithuania Killings. Soviet prosecutor general, Nikolai Trubin, issues a report that exonerates Soviet troops of responsibility in the January 13 killing of thirteen unarmed demonstrators in Vilnius. The report is sharply contradicted by reports of independent observers, and Lithuanian officials denounce it as propaganda.

June 4. Strauss Appointed Ambassador. President Bush appoints Robert S. Strauss to be U.S. ambassador to the Soviet Union. Strauss replaces Jack Matlock, who is retiring.

June 6. Gorbachev Calls for Western Support. In a speech given in Oslo at the occasion of his reception of the 1990 Nobel Peace Prize, President Gorbachev asks the West to support his efforts to reform the Soviet Union.

June 12. Yeltsin Elected Russian President. Boris Yeltsin is elected president of Russia with more than 60 percent of the popular vote. Former Soviet prime minister Nikolai Ryzhkov finishes second with just 20 percent.

June 17. Union Treaty Progress. President Gorbachev and leaders of seven republics sign a draft of a new union treaty. The draft is sent to the legislatures of the republics for debate and consideration. Tajikistan and Uzbekistan state their intention to sign the treaty at a future date.

June 20. Bush Meets Yeltsin. President Bush meets with Boris Yeltsin at the White House. After the meeting Bush praises Yeltsin's drive toward greater democracy, but emphasizes that the United States will continue to build on its positive relationship with the Gorbachev government. Yeltsin meets with other officials in Washington before ending his U.S. trip June 21 in New York.

June 21. Gorbachev Overcomes Pavlov Challenge. The Supreme Soviet votes 262 to 24 against considering a proposal by Premier Valentin Pavlov that would have transferred some of the president's powers to the premier. Before the vote Gorbachev had stridently denounced Pavlov's proposal and conservative attempts to undermine reform.

July 1. Opposition Group Formed. A group of liberal Soviet leaders announce the formation of the Movement of Democratic Reforms, an opposition group aimed at unifying opposition to the Communist party. Founding members include former foreign minister Eduard Shevardnadze, Gorbachev adviser Aleksandr Yakovlev, Moscow mayor Gavril Popov, and Leningrad mayor Anatoly Sobchack.

July 10. Yeltsin Inaugurated. Boris Yeltsin is sworn in as Russia's first popularly elected president in a Kremlin ceremony attended by President Gorbachev. Yeltsin receives a blessing from Alexei II, the patriarch of the Russian Orthodox Church.

July 15. USSR Applies for Membership. The Soviet Union formally applies for full membership in the International Monetary Fund (IMF).

July 17. G-7 Summit; START Agreement Reached. President Gorbachev appeals for Western financial aid at the end of a G-7 summit meeting in London. The leaders of the United States, France, Great Britain, Germany, Japan, Italy, and Canada offer a package of technical assistance and cooperation to the Soviet Union, but they decline to promise Gorbachev large-scale financial aid.

They also state their support for the USSR to receive associate member status in the IMF. The same day in London, Gorbachev meets separately with President Bush. After the meeting they announce that they have reached final agreement on the Strategic Arms Reduction Treaty (START), which provides for significant cuts in the strategic nuclear arsenals of the United States and the Soviet Union.

July 26. Central Committee Backs Platform. A plenary session of the Communist party's Central Committee gives preliminary approval to a platform submitted by President Gorbachev. The platform endorses freedom of religion, a pluralistic political system, and private property. Contrary to expectations, conservative party members avoid a confrontation with Gorbachev over the liberal platform.

July 30-31. Moscow Summit. Presidents Bush and Gorbachev sign the completed START treaty July 31 at a summit in Moscow. That day they also issue a statement calling for joint U.S.-Soviet sponsorship of a Middle East peace conference in October. On July 30 Bush had promised Gorbachev that he would submit for congressional approval a 1990 agreement that would extend most-favored-nation trading status to the Soviet Union. After leaving Moscow Bush stops in Ukraine August 1 before returning to the United States. In a speech delivered in Kiev, Bush backs President Gorbachev's efforts to implement a new union treaty.

August 6. Treaty to be Signed. The Soviet government announces that the new union treaty will be signed on August 20.

August 16. Yakovlev Resigns from Communist Party. Aleksandr Yakovlev, an important adviser to President Gorbachev who had become increasingly vocal about his disaffection with communism, announces his resignation from the Communist party. Yakovlev warns that Stalinist reactionaries are plotting a coup.

August 18. Gorbachev Detained. In the evening President Gorbachev and his family are detained at their vacation home in the Crimea, and all means of communication with the outside world are severed. A delegation representing the leaders of a coup meet with Gorbachev, but he reportedly refuses to resign or cooperate with the coup.

August 19. Soviet Coup. At 6:00 a.m. the Soviet news agency Tass announces that President Gorbachev is incapacitated and an eight-member "State Committee for the State of Emergency" has assumed power and declared a state of emergency. The Emergency Committee consists of Vice President Gennady Yanayev, KGB chairman Vladimir Kryuchkov, Defense Minister Dmitry Yazov, Premier Valentin Pavlov, Interior Minister Boris Pugo, Communist party secretary Oleg Baklanov, and two lesser party officials, Vasily Starodubtsev and Aleksandr Tizyakov. The Emergency Committee also establishes a curfew and bans demonstrations and all news operations not under their control. Tanks are deployed at strategic points in Moscow. The committee members hold a press conference that evening. Yanayev serves as chief spokesperson for the committee. He announces that he has assumed the title of acting president. Gorbachev, he says, is receiving medical treatment and may return to his duties sometime in the future. Russian president Boris Yeltsin sharply denounces the coup and rallies support against it. He calls for a general strike. Thousands of Muscovites rush to the Russian republic's parliament building, nicknamed the Russian White House, to defend it against a military assault. Some military units defect to Yeltsin and join the defense of the Russian White House.

August 20. Coup Leaders Waiver. Opposition to the coup leaders grows in Moscow and elsewhere in the Soviet Union. Yeltsin talks by phone to President Bush and British prime minister John Major who assure him of their support. Numerous foreign governments denounce the coup as an illegal attempt to overthrow the legitimate Soviet government. Premier Pavlov claims to be ill and resigns from the Emergency Committee. At 8:00 p.m. the chief of staff of the Soviet armed forces, Gen. Mikhail Moiseyev, orders troops advancing on the Russian White House to halt.

August 21. Coup Collapses. Troops in Moscow begin withdrawing to their bases as evidence of the weakening position of the coup plotters grows. Several coup leaders fly to the Crimea in the hopes of arranging a deal with Gorbachev, but he refuses to negotiate with them. Yeltsin announces to the Russian parliament that the coup plotters have attempted to flee Moscow. Tass and Soviet television report at 8:00 p.m. that the coup has failed and President Gorbachev is back in control of the country. Emergency Committee member Boris Pugo commits suicide August 22.

August 22. Gorbachev Returns to Moscow. President Gorbachev returns to Moscow where he holds a televised press conference. He describes his detention and his refusal to cooperate with the coup plotters. Nevertheless, he admits to having placed mistaken trust in the coup leaders, most of whom he had promoted. Gorbachev commends President Yeltsin and the Soviet people for resisting the coup.

August 23. Russian Supreme Soviet Meeting. Presidents Gorbachev and Yeltsin address a session of the Russian Supreme Soviet. Members are hostile toward Gorbachev, accusing him of failing to outlaw the Communist party. Yeltsin humiliates Gorbachev by forcing him to read the minutes from a Council of Ministers session at which Gorbachev's appointees had expressed support for the coup. At Yeltsin's insistence, Gorbachev appoints Gen. Yevgeny Shaposhnikov as defense minister and Vadim Bakatin as head of the KGB. Gorbachev also fires Foreign Minister Bessmertnykh, whose role in the coup was uncertain. Boris Pankin is appointed foreign minister August 28.

August 24. Gorbachev Quits as General Secretary. President Gorbachev resigns as general secretary of the Communist party and issues orders limiting party activities. He retains his party membership, however, and says many Communists opposed the coup.

August 24. Republics Declare Independence. The Ukrainian Supreme Soviet declares Ukrainian independence. Other republic parliaments vote for independence in the coming weeks. The three Baltic states had declared their independence August 20-21 during the failed coup attempted.

August 28. Plotters Charged with Treason. Thirteen former officials, including the seven surviving members of the Emergency Committee, are charged with treason.

August 29. Communist Party Activities Banned. The USSR Supreme Soviet votes to ban all Communist party activities indefinitely.

September 2. U.S. Recognizes Baltic States. President Bush announces that the United States is extending diplomatic recognition to Latvia, Lithuania, and Estonia.

September 5. Interim Government Approved. The Congress of People's Deputies creates interim government structures headed by President Gorbachev. The new structures represent a significant shift of power from Moscow to the republics. A new State Council consisting of the USSR president and the top leaders of each of the republics is given executive power. The interim arrangement is to function until the central government and the republics come to agreement on permanent government structures.

September 6. USSR Recognizes Baltic States. The State Council of the USSR recognizes the independence of Latvia, Lithuania, and Estonia.

September 12. Gorbachev to Withdraw Brigade. President Gorbachev tells Secretary of State Baker at a Kremlin meeting that he will begin negotiations with Cuba on the withdrawal of the Soviet brigade deployed in that country.

September 13. Afghan Military Aid Agreement. The United States and the Soviet Union agree to suspend all shipments of military aid to Afghanistan as of January 1, 1992.

September 27. Bush Announces Arms Cuts. President Bush announces that the United States will unilaterally eliminate thousands of nuclear warheads and take other actions to reduce the chance of nuclear war. Among other steps, Bush says he will order the U.S. short-range nuclear weapons in Europe destroyed and nuclear-armed cruise missiles deployed on ships removed. Bush also stops efforts to deploy rail-based MX missiles. He calls on President Gorbachev to take similar measures.

October 3. Gorbachev Reciprocates on Arms Cuts. President Gorbachev announces sweeping arms reduc-

tions and relaxations in deployment in response to President Bush's September 27 announcement. Among other steps, 503 Soviet intercontinental ballistic missiles covered by the START treaty were to be deactivated and short-range nuclear weapons carried on naval vessels and aircraft were to be removed. In addition, Gorbachev announces a one-year moratorium on nuclear testing.

October 18. Eight Republics Sign Economic Union. The leaders of eight Soviet republics and President Gorbachev sign a framework agreement that provides for an economic union based on a plan developed by economist Grigory Yavlinsky. Twenty-five specific protocols on specific aspects of the plan must be negotiated by the participants. Ukraine, Georgia, Moldavia, and Azerbaijan decline to sign the agreement. The refusal of Ukraine to sign places the future of the pact in doubt. Under pressure from Western nations, Ukraine signs the agreement November 6.

October 22. Ukraine Creates Military. The Ukrainian parliament votes to create an independent Ukrainian military.

October 29. Debt-Sharing Agreement. The twelve Soviet republics agree on an arrangement for jointly assuming responsibility for the debts of the Soviet Union.

October 30. Madrid Peace Conference Opens. A Middle East peace conference sponsored by the United States and the Soviet Union opens in Madrid. Presidents Gorbachev and Bush open the talks. The two leaders held talks October 29, prior to the opening of the conference.

November 1. Yeltsin's Powers Expanded. The Russian congress of people's deputies votes to give President Yeltsin broad powers to direct economic reform by decree. He uses these powers during November to establish Russian control over Soviet resources, reduce trade restrictions, and prepare for the implementation of his economic transformation plan set to begin in January 1992.

November 19. Shevardnadze Becomes Foreign Minister Again. President Gorbachev reappoints Eduard Shevardnadze foreign minister of the Soviet Union. Boris Pankin leaves the post to become ambassador to Great Britain.

November 25. Union Treaty Rejected. Seven republic leaders refuse to accept President Gorbachev's draft of a treaty that would establish a political confederation.

November 26. Congress Backs Aid for Soviets. The U.S. Congress approves the Nunn-Lugar Amendment, which makes available $400 million in previously appropriated Defense Department funds to help the Soviet Union dismantle its nuclear weapons.

November 30. Russia to Finance Soviet Payroll. In a further sign of the declining relevance of the Soviet government, President Yeltsin announces that Russia will temporarily finance the Soviet payroll.

December 1. Ukrainians Choose Independence. In a national referendum, Ukrainians vote overwhelmingly to seek independence. Leonid Kravchuk is elected president with more than 61 percent of the vote. The Russian government recognizes Ukrainian independence December 2.

December 8. CIS Established. Russia, Ukraine, and Belarus declare the Soviet Union defunct and announce the formation of a Commonwealth of Independent States (CIS). President Gorbachev claims December 9 that the leaders of the three republics have no right to dissolve the union, but he is unable to rally support for his union treaty.

December 21. CIS Expanded. Eleven former Soviet republics formally join to create the CIS at a meeting in Alma Ata. The three Baltic states and Georgia decline to join the CIS.

December 25. Gorbachev Resigns. Mikhail Gorbachev delivers a television speech in which he resigns as Soviet president, marking the end of the Soviet Union. He transfers control of the Soviet nuclear arsenal to President Yeltsin.

December 30. CIS Agrees to Joint Weapons Control. Commonwealth of Independent States leaders agree to maintain joint control of Soviet nuclear weapons.

1992

January 2. Russia Frees Prices. The Yeltsin government begins implementation of its radical economic reform plan by freeing prices on many consumer goods. In an effort to increase the incentives to engage in entrepreneurship, reduce the state budget deficit, undermine black market activity, create competition, and encourage producers to bring their goods to market, about 90 percent of prices are freed of government control. The government also increases the price of those goods remaining under control—mainly energy and transport—three to five times. Prices in the key area of housing remain under substantial state control.

January 4. Kravchuk Demands Allegiance Oath. President Kravchuk announces that all military personnel on Ukrainian territory, including the naval personnel of the Black Sea Fleet, must take an oath of allegiance to Ukraine. More than a thousand soldiers from other republics refuse to take the oath and leave Ukraine for Russia or their home states.

January 6. Gamsakhurdia Loses Struggle. After months of factional fighting, President Zviad Gamsakhurdia of Georgia abandons Tbilisi, allowing a rebel coalition to assume power. Gamsakhurdia's headquarters had come under intense shelling by opposition groups. He flees to Armenia, where he requests asylum. On January 2, the opposition "Military Council" had appointed Tengiz Sigua, a former prime minister fired by Gamsakhurdia in August 1991, to head of a provisional government.

January 8. Yeltsin on Black Sea Fleet. President Yeltsin says that the Black Sea Fleet should remain under CIS command. In a speech the next day, however, he tells an audience of Russian workers that "the Black Sea Fleet was, is, and will be Russia's." On January 11, Russia and Ukraine agree to pursue a negotiated settlement of their dispute over the fleet. Yeltsin says Ukraine would receive a share of the fleet that would be determined through negotiations.

January 18. Yeltsin Meets with Officers. President Yeltsin attends a meeting of about 5,000 military officers in the Kremlin's Palace of Congresses. Nursultan Nazarbayev, the president of Kazakhstan, and Marshal Shaposhnikov, the commander of the CIS military, also attend. The officers voice complaints about housing, benefits, pay, and the declining prestige of the military. They demand that the military of the former Soviet Union remain unified. Yeltsin states his support for a unified military, but says if other former Soviet states create their own militaries, Russia will have to do the same.

January 16. Gamsakhurdia Returns to Georgia. Ousted Georgian president Zviad Gamsakhurdia returns to western Georgia where he encourages followers to wage war against the provisional government.

January 22-23. Soviet Aid Conference. Representatives of forty-seven nations attend a conference in Washington, D.C., aimed at coordinating international assistance to the former Soviet Union. On the first day of the conference President Bush delivers an address in which he announces a $645 million aid package (subject to the approval of Congress) for the former Soviet states. At the end of the conference Secretary of State Baker announces that the United States will begin an emergency military airlift of food and medicine to the former Soviet Union.

January 31. UN Security Council Summit. The leaders of the fifteen nations on the UN Security Council meet in New York. In a speech to the gathering, President Yeltsin proposes that the United States and Russia cooperate to develop a global antimissile shield. He also calls for deeper cuts in nuclear arsenals. On his way to New York, Yeltsin had stopped in London to meet with Prime Minister John Major January 30.

February 1. Yeltsin and Bush Meet. President Yeltsin meets informally with President Bush at Camp David. They discuss an array of matters related to arms control and U.S. assistance to Russia.

February 5-7. Yeltsin Visits France. President Yeltsin travels to Paris for a three days of meeting with French officials, including President Francois Mitterrand. On February 7 the two presidents sign a bilateral treaty of friendship and cooperation.

February 11-18. Baker Tours Former Soviet Union. Secretary of State Baker travels to Armenia, Azerbaijan, Moldova, Tajikistan, Turkmenistan, and Uzbekistan, before stopping in Moscow for two days of talks. He discusses the establishment of relations with the leaders of those states, who pledge to respect the conditions for recognition laid out by the United States. In Moscow Baker and Russian leaders discuss accelerating progress on arms control. They agree to hold a summit between presidents Bush and Yeltsin in Washington, D.C., in July. Yeltsin and Baker announce in a joint statement February 17 the creation of an international science center that will employ nuclear scientists from the former Soviet Union.

February 12. Bomber Crews Defect. The Russian crews of six SU-24 bombers stationed in Ukraine defect with their planes to Russia.

February 14. CIS Fails to Agree on Joint Military. At a CIS summit meeting in Minsk, the leaders of Ukraine, Moldova, and Azerbaijan refuse to agree to participate in a common CIS defense force. The three republics state their intention to establish their own defense forces.

February 26. Civilians Killed at Khojaly. Armenian forces kill a disputed number of Azeri civilians in the town of Khojaly in the disputed Nagorno-Karabakh enclave. Armenia denies the killings took place, but independent observers confirm that some Azeri civilians were killed and mutilated. The Azerbaijani government puts the death toll at 200. The incident is part of a bloody escalation in the fighting between Armenia and Azerbaijan.

March 2. Eight CIS States Admitted to UN. The United Nations admits Armenia, Azerbaijan, Moldova, and the five Central Asian states as members. The action leaves Georgia as the only former Soviet republic without a seat at the United Nations.

March 6. Mutalibov Resigns. Ayaz Mutalibov, the president of Azerbaijan resigns under pressure from large protests in Baku against his leadership. Many Azeris had accused Mutalibov of being too conciliatory toward Armenia. Yakub Mamedov becomes acting president.

March 8. Troops Withdrawn from Nagorno-Karabakh. The last CIS troops remaining in the disputed Nagorno-Karabakh region are withdrawn at the insistence of Armenia and Azerbaijan.

March 10. Shevardnadze Invited to Head Georgia. Georgian Military Council asks former Soviet foreign minister Eduard Shevardnadze to chair a new State Council. Shevardnadze agrees to serve as head of state pending elections that are scheduled for the fall.

March 15. Armenia-Azerbaijan Agreement Signed. Representatives of Armenia and Azerbaijan sign a truce agreement in Tehran that is brokered by the Iranian government. However, fighting continues unabated in the following days.

March 20. CIS Summit Fails. A summit between the leaders of the CIS states in Kiev fails to produce progress on key economic, military, or ethnic issues.

March 31. Russian Federation Treaty Signed. Eighteen of the twenty former autonomous Soviet socialist republics and autonomous oblasts sign a new Russian federation treaty. The treaty grants additional autonomy to Russia's constituent parts. Tatarstan and Chechen-Ingushetia decline to sign the agreement. The Russian Congress of People's Deputies ratifies the treaty April 10.

April 1. Western Aid Package Announced. President Bush and West German chancellor Helmut Kohl separately announce that the Group of Seven (G-7) industrialized nations have agreed to a $24 billion financial aid package for Russia. Part of the aid package is a $6 billion ruble stabilization fund. Much of the rest is made up of IMF loans, export credits, and humanitarian and technical assistance.

April 6. No-Confidence Vote Fails. The Russian Congress of People's Deputies opens its first session since the collapse of the Soviet Union. The body votes 447-412 with 70 abstentions to defeat a motion to bring a no-confidence vote against Yeltsin to the floor. The motion was supported by Vice President Aleksandr Rutskoy.

April 9. Black Sea Fleet Talks Set. Presidents Kravchuk and Yeltsin agree in a phone conversation to suspend all decrees related to the Black Sea Fleet and to begin negotiations on its status. The talks begin April 29.

April 13. Cabinet Resigns. President Yeltsin's entire cabinet submits its resignation to protest antireform efforts of the Russian Congress of People's Deputies. On April 11, the Russian Congress had passed a resolution placing restrictions on economic reform. President Yeltsin declines to accept the resignations.

April 15. Congress Backs Reform Measure. President Yeltsin's economic team and the Russian Congress reach a compromise on economic reform. By a vote of 578-203, the Congress passes a nonbinding resolution stating its conditional support for a continuation of Yeltsin's reform program. Yeltsin's team had argued that Western aid would be jeopardized if the reform process were slowed.

April 27. Russia Approved for IMF Membership. The International Monetary Fund (IMF) and the World Bank approve of granting most of the states of the former Soviet Union full membership. The IMF had endorsed the Russian economic reform plan March 31. Russia receives a 3 percent share of IMF capital. Temporary problems with Azerbaijan's application delay the approval of its membership in the IMF and similar technical problems delay Azerbaijan's and Turkmenistan's admittance to the World Bank. Both are expected to be approved in the near future. Russia is formally admitted to the IMF June 1.

April 28. Rebels Capture Kabul. Afghan rebels capture Kabul. The Communist government is forced to relinquish power to a rebel commission.

May 5. Crimean Independence Question. The parliament of the Crimean Autonomous Oblast votes 118-28 in favor of a declaration of independence from Ukraine. The Crimean parliament rescinds the declaration May 20 after the Ukrainian parliament authorizes the use of "all necessary means" to retain the Crimea as part of Ukraine.

May 6. Kravchuk Meets Bush. President Kravchuk travels to Washington for a meeting with President Bush. Kravchuk pledges to Bush that Ukraine will abide by the START treaty signed in July 1991. He also promises to sign the Nuclear Non-Proliferation Treaty and eventually make Ukraine a nuclear-free state.

May 7. Yeltsin Creates Russian Military. President Yeltsin signs a decree creating a Russian defense ministry. Yeltsin assumes the role of commander in chief an appoints Col. Gen. Pavel Grachev as acting defense minister.

May 15. Collective Security Pact Signed. At a CIS summit in Tashkent, the leaders of Russia, Armenia, Kazakhstan, Tajikistan, Turkmenistan, and Uzbekistan sign a mutual security treaty that pledges them to come to each other's aid if attacked. The other five members of the CIS refuse to sign the accord. The security agreement is a tacit recognition of the CIS's failure to construct a single defense policy.

May 18. Kazakhstan, Chevron Sign Deal. Kazakhstan and Chevron, a U.S. oil company, sign a pact providing for the development of Kazakhstan's huge Tengiz oilfield.

May 21. Supreme Soviet Nullifies Crimea Transfer. The Russian Supreme Soviet votes to nullify the 1954 transfer of the Crimea from Russia to Ukraine.

May 23. START Protocols Signed. Russia, Ukraine, Belarus, and Kazakhstan (the four former Soviet states in possession of nuclear weapons) and the United States sign protocols to the START treaty. The protocols pledge the four states to meet Soviet obligations under the treaty. They also commit Ukraine, Belarus, and Kazakhstan to transferring the strategic nuclear arms on their soil to Russia or destroying them.

June 5. Revised CFE Treaty Signed. Twenty-nine nations, including eight states of the CIS, sign a revised Conventional Forces in Europe (CFE) Treaty in Oslo. The revised treaty includes an agreement among CIS nations on the division of the forces permitted to the Soviet Union under the original treaty.

June 7. Elchibey Elected President of Azerbaijan. Abulfaz Elchibey is elected president of Azerbaijan with about 60 percent of the vote. Elchibey, the leader of the Azerbaijani Popular Front, had vowed during his campaign not to give up the disputed enclave of Nagorno-Karabakh.

June 15. Yeltsin on American POWs. In a presummit statement, President Yeltsin maintains that some American servicemen taken prisoner during the Vietnam War had been held in the Soviet Union, and that some of these men could still be alive. Previously, Yeltsin had said in a June 12 letter to the U.S. Senate Select Committee on POW-MIA Affairs that the Soviet Union had held and released 716 U.S. troops during World War II, had in-

terrogated 56 American prisoners of Communist forces during the Korean War, and had incarcerated as late as August 1953 twelve U.S. spy plane crew members. President Bush subsequently appoints former U.S. ambassador to the Soviet Union Malcolm Toon to investigate the information. Toon finds no evidence of live American MIAs in Russia.

June 16-17. Washington Summit. At the first formal Russian-American summit in Washington, presidents Bush and Yeltsin agree in principle June 16 to far-reaching cuts in strategic arms that go beyond cuts mandated by the START treaty. Under the tentative agreement, the U.S. nuclear arsenal would be cut to 3,500 warheads and Russia's would be cut to 3,000 warheads. These levels were less than half of the total allowed by the START agreement. On June 17 Yeltsin delivers a stirring speech to a joint session of Congress that emphasizes U.S.-Russian friendship. He asks legislators to approve an aid package for Russia.

July 5. IMF Releases Some Aid. The IMF agrees to release to Russia an initial installment of about $1 million in aid.

July 8. Yeltsin Addresses Western Summit. President Yeltsin emphasizes Russia's need for aid in an address to Western leaders at a G-7 summit in Munich. The leaders restate their commitment to aiding Russia and indicate that they will back a major rescheduling of Russian debt.

July 14. Russian-Georgian Peacekeeping Effort. A joint Russian-Georgian peacekeeping force of about 1,200 troops is deployed between warring Georgians and South Ossetian separatists. The latter were seeking to split the South Ossetia region from Georgia and unite it with the adjacent North Ossetia region inside Russia. Georgia and Russia had agreed to the peacekeeping operation on June 24.

July 16. Joint Space Projects Announced. The United States and Russia announce plans for joint space projects beginning in 1993. Among other cooperative endeavors, a Russian would travel on the U.S. space shuttle and an American would work in the Russian space station *Mir.*

July 17. Reform Opponent to Head Central Bank. The Russian Supreme Soviet chooses Viktor Gerashchenko to succeed Georgy Matyukhin as head of the central bank. The appointment is considered a setback for Yeltsin, as Gerashchenko is an outspoken opponent of radical economic reform.

July 21. Moldovan Peacekeeping Established. Russia and Moldova agree on terms of a joint peacekeeping effort to control conflict between Moldovans and ethnic Russians in Moldova.

July 23. Abkhazia Declares Sovereignty. The parliament of the autonomous region of Abkhazia in Georgia declares its sovereignty. The Georgian State Council nullifies the declaration July 25.

August 3. Black Sea Fleet Accord Signed. Presidents

Yeltsin and Kravchuk meet at Mukhalatka on the Black Sea coast to discuss the Black Sea Fleet. They agree to remove the fleet from CIS control and place it under a joint Russian-Ukrainian command for three years. The two leaders each will appoint a co-commander of the fleet. The agreement also voids the oath of allegiance to Ukraine taken by Russian sailors at the insistence of the Ukrainian government. In 1995 talks were to open on the division of the fleet.

August 6. Congress Passes Freedom Support Act. The U.S. House of Representatives passes the Freedom Support Act by a vote of 255-164. It provides more than $400 million in assistance to the former Soviet Union and authorizes a $12.3 billion increase in the U.S. contribution to the IMF. The Senate had passed a similar version of the bill 76-20 on July 2.

August 11. Abkhazian Conflict Escalates. Rebels kidnap the Georgian interior minister and other officials during truce talks between the Georgian government and forces loyal to ousted president Zviad Gamsakhurdia. In response the Georgian government August 14 launches a major offensive against Abkhazian separatists who are reported to be cooperating with Gamsakhurdia. The interior minister is freed that day. Georgian forces seize the Abkhazian capital of Sukhumi August 18, but fighting continues.

September 7. Nabiyev Resigns. Tajik president Rakhman Nabiyev resigns after he is captured by opposition troops at the Dushanbe airport. Nabiyev's resignation follows months of unrest and factional fighting. Tajikistan's parliament had passed a no-confidence resolution against Nabiyev September 2. Akbar Shah Iskandarov, the speaker of the parliament, is named acting president.

September 9. Yeltsin Postpones Japan Trip. President Yeltsin postpones a trip to Japan scheduled for September 13 because of disputes over the status of the Kuril Islands. Yeltsin had come under increasing pressure from conservatives not to return the islands or make concessions to the Japanese.

September 25. Russian Missiles Still Target U.S. Marshal Shaposhnikov reveals in a speech in Moscow that Russian missiles are still aimed at U.S. targets. He indicates that this practice would end only if the United States ceased targeting Russia.

October 1. START Ratified. The U.S. Senate ratifies the START treaty 93-6. The treaty had been signed in July 1991.

October 1. Russia Launches Privatization Effort. The Russian government begins implementing a privatization plan by distributing vouchers to its citizens that can be redeemed for shares in Russian enterprises. Each Russian receives a voucher worth 10,000 rubles (about $60). The vouchers also can be traded or sold.

DOCUMENTS

Following are texts of selected documents, speeches, and letters that have figured prominently in Soviet and post-Soviet affairs since the end of World War II. The texts are arranged in chronological order.

Winston Churchill's "Iron Curtain" Speech

Following are excerpts from Winston Churchill's "Iron Curtain" speech, delivered March 5, 1946, at Westminster College, Fulton, Missouri. The text is excerpted from The Sinews of Peace: Post-war Speeches by Winston S. Churchill, ed. Randolph S. Churchill (Boston: Houghton Mifflin, 1949).

... The United States stands at this time at the pinnacle of world power. It is a solemn moment for the American Democracy. For with primacy in power is also joined an awe-inspiring accountability to the future. If you look around you, you must feel not only the sense of duty done but also you must feel anxiety lest you fall below the level of achievement. Opportunity is here now, clear and shining for both our countries. To reject it or ignore it or fritter it away will bring upon us all the long reproaches of the after-time. It is necessary that constancy of mind, persistency of purpose, and the grand simplicity of decision shall guide and rule the conduct of the English-speaking peoples in peace as they did in war....

When American military men approach some serious situation they are wont to write at the head of their directive the words "over-all strategic concept". There is wisdom in this, as it leads to clarity of thought. What then is the over-all strategic concept which we should inscribe today? It is nothing less than the safety and welfare, the freedom and progress, of all the homes and families of all the men and women in all the lands.... To give security to these countless homes, they must be shielded from the two giant marauders, war and tyranny.... The awful ruin of Europe, with all its vanished glories, and of large parts of Asia glares us in the eyes.... When I stand here, this quiet afternoon I shudder to visualise what is actually happening to millions now and what is going to happen in this period when famine stalks the earth. None can compute what has been called "the unestimated sum of human pain". Our supreme task and duty is to guard the homes of the common people from the horrors and miseries of another war. We are all agreed on that.

Our American military colleagues, after having proclaimed their "over-all strategic concept" and computed available resources, always proceed to the next step—namely, the method. Here again there is widespread agreement. A world organisation has already been erected for the prime purpose of preventing war. UNO [United Nations Organization], the successor of the League of Nations, with the decisive addition of the United States and all that that means, is already at work. We must make sure that its work is fruitful, that it is a reality and not a sham, that it is a force for action, and not merely a frothing of words, that it is a true temple of peace in which the shields of many nations can some day be hung up, and not merely a cockpit in a Tower of Babel. Before we cast away the solid assurances of national armaments for self-preservation we must be certain that our temple is built, not upon shifting sands or quagmires, but upon the rock. Anyone can see with his eyes open that our path will be difficult and also long, but if we persevere together as we did in the two world wars—though not, alas, in the interval between them—I cannot doubt that we shall achieve our common purpose in the end.

I have, however, a definite and practical proposal to make for action. Courts and magistrates may be set up but they cannot function without sheriffs and constables. The United Nations Organisation must immediately begin to be equipped with an international armed force.... I propose that each of the Powers and States should be invited to delegate a certain number of air squadrons to the service of the world organisation. These squadrons would be trained and prepared in their own countries, but would move around in rotation from one country to another. They would wear the uniform of their own countries but with different badges. They would not be required to act against their own nation, but in other respects they would be directed by the world organisation. This might be started on a modest scale and would grow as confidence grew. I wished to see this done after the first world war, and I devoutly trust it may be done forthwith.

It would nevertheless be wrong and imprudent to entrust the secret knowledge or experience of the atomic bomb, which the United States, Great Britain, and Canada now share, to the world organisation, while it is still in its infancy. It would be criminal madness to cast it adrift in this still agitated and un-united world. No one in any country has slept less well in their beds because this knowledge, and the method and the raw materials to apply it, are at present largely retained in American hands. I do not believe we should all have slept so soundly had the position been reversed and if some Communist or neo-Fascist State monopolised for the time being these dread agencies. The fear of them alone might easily have been used to enforce totalitarian systems upon the free democratic world, with consequences appalling to human imagination. God has willed that this shall not be and we have at least a breathing space to set our house in order before this peril has to be encountered: and even then, if no effort is spared, we should still possess so formidable a superiority as to impose effective deterrents upon its employment, or threat of employment, by others. Ultimately, when the essential brotherhood of man is truly embodied and expressed in a world organisation with all the necessary practical safeguards to make it effective, these powers would naturally be confided to that world organisation.

Now I come to the second danger of these two marauders which threatens the cottage, the home, and the ordinary people—namely, tyranny. We cannot be blind to the fact that the liberties enjoyed by individual citizens throughout the British Empire are not valid in a considerable number of countries, some of which are very powerful. In these States control is enforced upon the common people by various kinds of all-embracing police governments. The power of the State is exercised without restraint, either by dictators or by compact oligarchies operating through a privileged party and a political police. It is not our duty at this time when difficulties are so numerous to interfere forcibly in the internal affairs of countries which we have not conquered in war. But we must never cease to proclaim in fearless tones the great principles of freedom and the rights of man which are the joint inheritance of the English-speaking world and which through Magna Carta, the Bill of Rights, the Habeas Corpus, trial by jury, and the English common law find their most famous expression in the American Declaration of Independence.

"Title Deeds of Freedom." ... Here are the title deeds of freedom which should lie in every cottage home. Here is the message of the British and American peoples

to mankind. Let us preach what we practise—let us practise what we preach.

I have now stated the two great dangers which menace the homes of the people: War and Tyranny. I have not yet spoken of poverty and privation which are in many cases the prevailing anxiety. But if the dangers of war and tyranny are removed, there is no doubt that science and co-operation can bring in the next few years to the world, certainly in the next few decades newly taught in the sharpening school of war, an expansion of material well-being beyond anything that has yet occurred in human experience. Now, at this sad and breathless moment, we are plunged in the hunger and distress which are the aftermath of our stupendous struggle; but this will pass and may pass quickly, and there is no reason except human folly or sub-human crime which should deny to all the nations the inauguration and enjoyment of an age of plenty....

Now, while still pursuing the method of realising our overall strategic concept, I come to the crux of what I have travelled here to say. Neither the sure prevention of war, nor the continuous rise of world organisation, will be gained without what I have called the fraternal association of the English-speaking peoples. This means a special relationship between the British Commonwealth and Empire and the United States.... Fraternal association requires not only the growing friendship and mutual understanding between our two vast but kindred systems of society, but the continuance of the intimate relationship between our military advisers, leading to common study of potential dangers.... The United States has already a Permanent Defence Agreement with the Dominion of Canada, which is so devotedly attached to the British Commonwealth and Empire. This Agreement is more effective than many of those which have often been made under formal alliances. This principle should be extended to all British Commonwealths with full reciprocity. Thus, whatever happens, and thus only, shall we be secure ourselves and able to work together for the high and simple causes that are dear to us and bode no ill to any. Eventually there may come—I feel eventually there will come—the principle of common citizenship, but that we may be content to leave to destiny, whose outstretched arm many of us can already clearly see....

A shadow has fallen upon the scenes so lately lighted by the Allied victory. Nobody knows what Soviet Russia and its Communist international organisation intends to do in the immediate future, or what are the limits, if any, to their expansive and proselytising tendencies. I have a strong admiration and regard for the valiant Russian people and for my wartime comrade, Marshal Stalin. There is deep sympathy and goodwill in Britain—and I doubt not here also—towards the peoples of all the Russias and a resolve to persevere through many differences and rebuffs in establishing lasting friendships. We understand the Russian need to be secure on her western frontiers by the removal of all possibility of German aggression. We welcome Russia to her rightful place among the leading nations of the world. We welcome her flag upon the seas. Above all, we welcome constant, frequent and growing contacts between the Russian people and our own people on both sides of the Atlantic. It is my duty, however, for I am sure you would wish me to state the facts as I see them to you, to place before you certain facts about the present position in Europe.

"An Iron Curtain Has Descended." From Stettin in the Baltic to Trieste in the Adriatic, an iron curtain has descended across the Continent. Behind that line lie all the capitals of the ancient states of Central and Eastern Europe. Warsaw, Berlin, Prague, Vienna, Budapest, Belgrade, Bucharest and Sofia, all these famous cities and the populations around them lie in what I must call the Soviet sphere, and all are subject in one form or another, not only to Soviet influence but to a very high and, in many cases, increasing measure of control from Moscow. Athens alone—Greece with its immortal glories—is free to decide its future at an election under British, American and French observation. The Russian-dominated Polish Government has been encouraged to make enormous and wrongful inroads upon Germany, and mass expulsions of millions of Germans on a scale grievous and undreamed of are now taking place. The Communist parties, which were very small in all these Eastern States of Europe, have been raised to pre-eminence and power far beyond their numbers and are seeking everywhere to obtain totalitarian control. Police governments are prevailing in nearly every case, and so far, except in Czechoslovakia, there is no true democracy.

Turkey and Persia are both profoundly alarmed and disturbed at the claims which are being made upon them and at the pressure being exerted by the Moscow Government. An attempt is being made by the Russians in Berlin to build up a quasi-Communist party in their zone of Occupied Germany by showing special favours to groups of left-wing German leaders. At the end of the fighting last June, the American and British Armies withdrew westwards, in accordance with an earlier agreement, to a depth at some points of 150 miles upon a front of nearly four hundred miles, in order to allow our Russian allies to occupy this vast expanse of territory which the Western Democracies had conquered.

If now the Soviet Government tries, by separate action, to build up a pro-Communist Germany in their areas, this will cause new serious difficulties in the British and American zones, and will give the defeated Germans the power of putting themselves up to auction between the Soviets and the Western Democracies. Whatever conclusions may be drawn from these facts—and facts they are—this is certainly not the Liberated Europe we fought to build up. Nor is it one which contains the essentials of permanent peace.

The safety of the world requires a new unity in Europe, from which no nation should be permanently outcast. It is from the quarrels of the strong parent races in Europe that the world wars we have witnessed, or which occurred in former times, have sprung. Twice in our own lifetime we have seen the United States, against their wishes and their traditions, against arguments, the force of which it is impossible not to comprehend, drawn by irresistible forces, into these wars in time to secure the victory of the good cause, but only after frightful slaughter and devastation had occurred. Twice the United States has had to send several millions of its young men across the Atlantic to find the war; but now war can find any nation, wherever it may dwell between dusk and dawn. Surely we should work with conscious purpose for a grand pacification of Europe, within the structure of the United Nations and in accordance with its Charter. That I feel is an open cause of policy of very great importance.

"Other Causes for Anxiety." In front of the iron curtain which lies across Europe are other causes for anxiety. In Italy the Communist Party is seriously hampered by having to support the Communist-trained Marshal Tito's claims to former Italian territory at the head of the Adriatic. Nevertheless the future of Italy hangs in the balance. Again one cannot imagine a regenerated Europe without a strong France. All my public life I have worked for a strong France and I never lost faith in her destiny, even in the darkest hours. I will not lose faith now. However, in a great number of countries, far from the Russian frontiers and throughout the world, Communist fifth columns are established and work in complete unity and absolute obedience to the directions they receive from the Communist centre. Except in the British Commonwealth and in the United States where Communism is in its infancy, the Communist parties or fifth columns constitute a growing challenge and peril to Christian civilisation. These are sombre facts for anyone to have to recite on the morrow of a victory gained by so much splendid comradeship in arms and in the cause of freedom and democracy; but we should be most unwise not to face them squarely while time remains.

The outlook is also anxious in the Far East and especially in Manchuria. The Agreement which was made at Yalta, to which I was a party, was extremely favourable to Soviet Russia, but it was made at a time when no one could say that the German war might not extend all through the summer and autumn of 1945 and when the Japanese war was expected to last for a further 18 months from the end of the German war. In this country you are all so well-informed about the Far East, and such devoted friends of China, that I do not need to expatiate on the situation there....

In those days [of the Versailles Treaty] there were high hopes and unbounded confidence that the wars were over, and that the League of Nations would become all-powerful. I do not see or feel that same confidence or even the same hopes in the haggard world at the present time.

On the other hand I repulse the idea that a new war is inevitable; still more that it is imminent. It is because I am sure that our fortunes are still in our own hands and that we hold the power to save the future, that I feel the duty to speak out now that I have the occasion and the opportunity to do so. I do not believe that Soviet Russia desires war. What they desire is the fruits of war and the indefinite expansion of their power and doctrines. But what we have to consider here to-day while time remains, is the permanent prevention of war and the establishment of conditions of freedom and democracy as rapidly as possible in all countries. Our difficulties and dangers will not be removed by closing our eyes to them. They will not be removed by mere waiting to see what happens; nor will they be removed by a policy of appeasement. What is needed is a settlement, and the longer this is delayed, the more difficult it will be and the greater our dangers will become.

From what I have seen of our Russian friends and Allies during the war, I am convinced that there is nothing they admire so much as strength, and there is nothing for which they have less respect than for weakness, especially military weakness. For that reason the old doctrine of a balance of power is unsound. We cannot afford, if we can help it, to work on narrow margins, offering temptations to a trial of strength. If the Western Democracies stand together in strict adherence to the principles of the United Nations Charter, their influence for furthering those principles will be immense and no one is likely to molest them. If however they become divided or falter in their duty and if these all-important years are allowed to slip away then indeed catastrophe may overwhelm us all.

"The Sinews of Peace." . . . There never was a war in all history easier to prevent by timely action than the one which has just desolated such great areas of the globe. It could have been prevented in my belief without the firing of a single shot, and Germany might be powerful, prosperous and honoured to-day; but no one would listen and one by one we were all sucked into the awful whirlpool. We surely must not let that happen again. This can only be achieved by reaching now, in 1946, a good understanding on all points with Russia under the general authority of the United Nations Organisation and by the maintenance of that good understanding through many peaceful years, by the world instrument, supported by the whole strength of the English-speaking world and all its connections. There is the solution which I respectfully offer to you in this Address to which I have given the title "The Sinews of Peace."

Let no man underrate the abiding power of the British Empire and Commonwealth. . . . If the population of the English-speaking Commonwealths be added to that of the United States with all that such co-operation implies in the air, on the sea, all over the globe and in science and in industry, and in moral force, there will be no quivering, precarious balance of power to offer its temptation to ambition or adventure. On the contrary, there will be an overwhelming assurance of security. If we adhere faithfully to the Charter of the United Nations and walk forward in sedate and sober strength seeking no one's land or treasure, seeking to lay no arbitrary control upon the thoughts of men; if all British moral and material forces and convictions are joined with your own in fraternal association, the highroads of the future will be clear, not only for us but for all, not only for our time, but for a century to come.

The "Secret Speech" of Nikita Khrushchev

Following are excerpts from the "Secret Speech" delivered by Nikita S. Khrushchev on February 24, 1956, at the Twentieth Soviet Communist Party Congress, text as supplied by the U.S. Department of State. (Note: Remarks in parentheses describe audience reaction. Explanations and identifying notes in brackets were added by Congressional Quarterly.)

Comrades! In the report of the Central Committee of the party at the 20th Congress, in a number of speeches by delegates to the congress, as also formerly during the plenary CC/CPSU [Central Committee/Communist Party of the Soviet Union] sessions, quite a lot has been said about the cult of the individual and about its harmful consequences.

After Stalin's death the Central Committee of the party began to implement a policy of explaining concisely and consistently that it is impermissible and foreign to the spirit of Marxism-Leninism to elevate one person, to transform him into a superman possessing supernatural characteristics akin to those of a god. Such a man supposedly knows everything, sees everything, thinks for everyone, can do anything, is infallible in his behavior.

Such a belief about a man, and specifically about Stalin, was cultivated among us for many years. . . .

The great modesty of the genius of the revolution, Vladimir Ilyich Lenin, is known. Lenin had always stressed the role of the people as the creator of history, the directing and organizational role of the party as a living and creative organism, and also the role of the Central Committee.

Marxism does not negate the role of the leaders of the workers' class in directing the revolutionary liberation movement.

While ascribing great importance to the role of the

leaders and organizers of the masses, Lenin at the same time mercilessly stigmatized every manifestation of the cult of the individual, inexorably combated the foreign-to-Marxism views about a "hero" and a "crowd" and countered all efforts to oppose a "hero" to the masses and to the people.

Lenin taught that the party's strength depends on its indissoluble unity with the masses, on the fact that behind the party follow the people—workers, peasants and intelligentsia. "Only he will win and retain the power," said Lenin, "who believes in the people, who submerges himself in the fountain of the living creativeness of the people."...

During Lenin's life the Central Committee of the party was a real expression of collective leadership of the party and of the nation. Being a militant Marxist-revolutionist, always unyielding in matters of principle, Lenin never imposed by force his views upon his co-workers. He tried to convince; he patiently explained his opinions to others. Lenin always diligently observed that the norms of party life were realized, that the party statute was enforced, that the party congresses and the plenary sessions of the Central Committee took place at the proper intervals.

In addition to the great accomplishments of V. I. Lenin for the victory of the working class and of the working peasants, for the victory of our party and for the application of the ideas of scientific communism to life, his acute mind expressed itself also in this, that he detected in Stalin in time those negative characteristics which resulted later in grave consequences. Fearing for the future fate of the party and of the Soviet nation, V. I. Lenin made a completely correct characterization of Stalin, pointing out that it was necessary to consider the question of transferring Stalin from the position of the secretary general because of the fact that Stalin is excessively rude, that he does not have a proper attitude toward his comrades, that he is capricious and abuses his power.

In December 1922 in a letter to the Party Congress Vladimir Ilyich wrote: "After taking over the position of secretary general Comrade Stalin accumulated in his hands immeasurable power and I am not certain whether he will be always able to use this power with the required care."

This letter—a political document of tremendous importance, known in the party history as Lenin's "testament"—was distributed among the delegates to the 20th Party Congress. You have read it, and will undoubtedly read it again more than once. You might reflect on Lenin's plain words, in which expression is given to Vladimir Ilyich's anxiety concerning the party, the people, the state, and the future direction of party policy....

This document of Lenin's was made known to the delegates at the 13th Party Congress [May 1924], who discussed the question of transferring Stalin from the position of secretary general. The delegates declared

themselves in favor of retaining Stalin in this post, hoping that he would heed the critical remarks of Vladimir Ilyich and would be able to overcome the defects which caused Lenin serious anxiety.

Comrades! The Party Congress should become acquainted with two new documents, which confirm Stalin's character as already outlined by Vladimir Ilyich Lenin in his "testament." These documents are a letter from Nadezhda Konstantinovna Krupskaya [Lenin's wife] to [Lev B.] Kamenev, who was at that time head of the Political Bureau, and a personal letter from Vladimir Ilyich Lenin to Stalin.

I will now read these documents:

"Lev Borisovich!

"Because of a short letter which I had written in words dictated to me by Vladimir Ilyich by permission of the doctors, Stalin allowed himself yesterday an unusually rude outburst directed at me. This is not my first day in the party. During all these thirty years I have never heard from any comrade one word of rudeness. The business of the party and of Ilyich are not less dear to me than to Stalin. I need at present the maximum of self-control. What one can and what one cannot discuss with Ilyich—I know better than any doctor, because I know what makes him nervous and what does not, in any case I know better than Stalin. I am turning to you and to Grigory [Zinoviev] as to much closer comrades of V. I. and I beg you to protect me from rude interference with my private life and from vile invectives and threats. I have no doubt as to what will be the unanimous decision of the Control Commission, with which Stalin sees fit to threaten me; however, I have neither the strength nor the time to waste on this foolish quarrel. And I am a living person and my nerves are strained to the utmost.

"N. Krupskaya"

Nadezhda Konstantinovna wrote this letter on December 23, 1922. After two and a half months, in March 1923, Vladimir Ilyich Lenin sent Stalin the following letter:

"To Comrade Stalin:

"Copies for: Kamenev and Zinoviev.

"Dear Comrade Stalin!

"You permitted yourself a rude summons of my wife to the telephone and a rude reprimand of her. Despite the fact that she told you that she agreed to forget what was said, nevertheless Zinoviev and Kamenev heard about it from her. I have no intention to forget so easily that which is being done against me, and I need not stress here that I consider as directed against me that which is being done against my wife. I ask you, therefore, that you weigh carefully whether you are agreeable to retracting your words and apologizing or whether you prefer the severance of relations between us.

"Sincerely:
"Lenin

"March 5, 1923"
(Commotion in the hall)

Comrades! I will not comment on these documents. They speak eloquently for themselves. Since Stalin could behave in this manner during Lenin's life, could thus behave toward Nadezhda Konstantinovna Krupskaya, whom the party knows well and values highly as a loyal friend of Lenin and as an active fighter for the cause of the party since its creation—we can easily imagine how Stalin treated other people. These negative characteristics of his developed steadily and during the last years acquired an absolutely insufferable character.

As later events have proven, Lenin's anxiety was justified: in the first period after Lenin's death Stalin still paid attention to his [Lenin's] advice, but later he began to disregard the serious admonitions of Vladimir Ilyich.

"Grave Abuse of Power by Stalin." When we analyze the practice of Stalin in regard to the direction of the party and of the country, when we pause to consider everything which Stalin perpetrated, we must be convinced that Lenin's fears were justified. The negative characteristics of Stalin, which, in Lenin's time, were only incipient, transformed themselves during the last years into a grave abuse of power by Stalin, which caused untold harm to our party.

We have to consider seriously and analyze correctly this matter in order that we may preclude any possibility of a repetition in any form whatever of what took place during the life of Stalin, who absolutely did not tolerate collegiality in leadership and in work, and who practiced brutal violence, not only toward everything which opposed him, but also toward that which seemed to his capricious and despotic character contrary to his concepts.

Stalin acted not through persuasion, explanation, and patient cooperation with people, but by imposing his concepts and demanding absolute submission to his opinion. Whoever opposed this concept or tried to prove his viewpoint, and the correctness of his position, was doomed to removal from the leading collective and to subsequent moral and physical annihilation. This was especially true during the period following the 17th Party Congress [January-February 1934], when many prominent party leaders and rank-and-file party workers, honest and dedicated to the cause of communism, fell victim to Stalin's despotism.

We must affirm that the party had fought a serious fight against the Trotskyites, rightists and bourgeois nationalists, and that it disarmed ideologically all the enemies of Leninism. This ideological fight was carried on successfully, as a result of which the party became strengthened and tempered. Here Stalin played a positive role.

The party led a great political ideological struggle against those in its own ranks who proposed anti-Leninist theses, who represented a political line hostile to the party and to the cause of socialism.... Let us consider for a moment what would have happened if in 1928-1929 the political line of right deviation had prevailed among us, or orientation toward "cotton-dress industrialization," or toward the kulak [wealthy peasants], etc. We would not now have a powerful heavy industry, we would not have the *kolkhozes* [collective farms], we would find ourselves disarmed and weak in a capitalist encirclement....

Worth noting is the fact that even during the progress of the furious ideological fight against the Trotskyites, the Zinovievites, the Bukharinites and others, extreme repressive measures were not used against them. The fight was on ideological grounds. But some years later when socialism in our country was fundamentally constructed, ... when the ideological opponents of the party were long since defeated politically—then the repression directed against them began.

It was precisely during this period (1935-1937-1938) that the practice of mass repression through the government apparatus was born, first against the enemies of Leninism—Trotskyites, Zinovievites, Bukharinites, long since politically defeated by the party, and subsequently also against many honest communists, against those party cadres who had borne the heavy load of the civil war and the first and most difficult years of industrialization and collectivization, who actively fought against the Trotskyites and the rightists for the Leninist party line.

Stalin originated the concept "enemy of the people." This term automatically rendered it unnecessary that the ideological errors of a man or men engaged in a controversy be proven; this term made possible the usage of the most cruel repression, violating all norms of revolutionary legality, against anyone who in any way disagreed with Stalin, against those who were only suspected of hostile intent, against those who had bad reputations. This concept, "enemy of the people," actually eliminated the possibility of any kind of ideological fight or the making of one's views known on this or that issue, even those of a practical character. In the main, and in actuality, the only proof of guilt used, against all norms of current legal science, was the "confession" of the accused himself; and, as subsequent probing proved, "confessions" were acquired through physical pressures against the accused. This led to glaring violations of revolutionary legality, and to the fact that many entirely innocent persons, who in the past had defended the party line, became victims.

We must assert that in regard to those persons who in their time had opposed the party line, there were often no sufficiently serious reasons for their physical annihilation. The formula, "enemy of the people," was specifically introduced for the purpose of physically annihilating such individuals.

It is a fact that many persons, who were later annihilated as enemies of the party and people, had worked with

Lenin during his life. Some of these persons had made errors during Lenin's life, but, despite this, Lenin benefited by their work, he corrected them and he did everything possible to retain them in the ranks of the party; he induced them to follow him. . . .

"Violence, Mass Repressions, and Terror." An entirely different relationship with people characterized Stalin. Lenin's traits—patient work with people; stubborn and painstaking education of them; the ability to induce people to follow him without using compulsion, but rather through the ideological influence on them of the whole collective—were entirely foreign to Stalin. He discarded the Leninist method of convincing and educating; he abandoned the method of ideological struggle for that of administrative violence, mass repressions, and terror. He acted on an increasingly larger scale and more stubbornly through punitive organs, at the same time often violating all existing norms of morality and of Soviet laws. . . .

Let us recall some historical facts.

In the days before the October Revolution two members of the Central Committee of the Bolshevik Party—Kamenev and Zinoviev—declared themselves against Lenin's plan for an armed uprising. In addition, on October 18 [1917], they published in the Menshevik newspaper, *Novaya Zhizn,* a statement declaring that the Bolsheviks were making preparations for an uprising and that they considered it adventuristic. Kamenev and Zinoviev thus disclosed to the enemy the decision of the Central Committee to stage the uprising, and that the uprising had been organized to take place within the very near future.

This was treason against the party and against the revolution. In this connection, V. I. Lenin wrote: "Kamenev and Zinoviev revealed the decision of the Central Committee of their party on the armed uprising to [Duma president Mikhail] Rodzyanko and [Aleksandr F.] Kerensky [head of the provisional government from July to October 1917]. . . ." He put before the Central Committee the question of Zinoviev's and Kamenev's expulsion from the party.

However, after the Great Socialist October Revolution, as is known, Zinoviev and Kamenev were given leading positions. Lenin put them in positions in which they carried out most responsible party tasks and participated actively in the work of the leading party and Soviet organs. It is known that Zinoviev and Kamenev committed a number of other serious errors during Lenin's life. In his "testament" Lenin warned that "Zinoviev's and Kamenev's October episode was of course not an accident." But Lenin did not pose the question of their arrest and certainly not their shooting.

Or, let us take the example of the Trotskyites. At present, after a sufficiently long historical period, we can speak about the fight with the Trotskyites with complete calm and can analyze this matter with sufficient objectiv-

ity. After all, around Trotsky were people whose origin cannot by any means be traced to bourgeois society. Part of them belonged to the party intelligentsia and a certain part were recruited from among the workers. We can name many individuals who in their time joined the Trotskyites; however, these same individuals took an active part in the workers' movement before the revolution, during the Socialist October Revolution itself, and also in the consolidation of the victory of this greatest of revolutions. Many of them broke with Trotskyism and returned to Leninist positions. Was it necessary to annihilate such people? We are deeply convinced that had Lenin lived such an extreme method would not have been used against many of them.

Such are only a few historical facts. But can it be said that Lenin did not decide to use even the most severe means against enemies of the revolution when this was actually necessary? No, no one can say this. Vladimir Ilyich demanded uncompromising dealings with the enemies of the revolution and of the working class and when necessary resorted ruthlessly to such methods. You will recall only V. I. Lenin's fight with the Socialist Revolutionary organizers of the anti-Soviet uprising, with the counter-revolutionary kulaks in 1918 and with others, when Lenin without hesitation used the most extreme methods against the enemies. Lenin used such methods, however, only against actual class enemies and not against those who blunder, who err, and whom it was possible to lead through ideological influence, and even retain in the leadership. . . .

Stalin, on the other hand, used extreme methods and mass repressions at a time when the revolution was already victorious, when the Soviet state was strengthened, when the exploiting classes were already liquidated and socialist relations were rooted solidly in all phases of national economy, when our party was politically consolidated and had strengthened itself both numerically and ideologically.

It is clear that here Stalin showed in a whole series of cases his intolerance, his brutality and his abuse of power. Instead of proving his political correctness and mobilizing the masses, he often chose the path of repression and physical annihilation, not only against actual enemies, but also against individuals who had not committed any crimes against the party and the Soviet government. Here we see no wisdom but only a demonstration of the brutal force which had once so alarmed V. I. Lenin.

"A Very Ugly Picture." Lately, especially after the unmasking of the [Lavrenty] Beria gang, the Central Committee has looked into a series of matters fabricated by this gang. This revealed a very ugly picture of brutal willfulness connected with the incorrect behavior of Stalin. As facts prove, Stalin, using his unlimited power, allowed himself many abuses, acting in the name of the

Central Committee, not asking for the opinion of the committee members nor even of the members of the Central Committee's Political Bureau; often he did not inform them about his personal decisions concerning very important party and government matters.

Considering the question of the cult of an individual we must first of all show everyone what harm this caused to the interests of our party. . . .

Collegiality of leadership flows from the very nature of our party, a party built on the principles of democratic centralism. "This means," said Lenin, "that all party matters are accomplished by all party members—directly or through representatives—who without any exceptions are subject to the same rules; in addition, all administrative members, all directing collegia, all holders of party positions are elective, they must account for their activities and are recallable.". . .

During Lenin's life Party Congresses were convened regularly; always, when a radical turn in the development of the party and the country took place, Lenin considered it absolutely necessary that the party discuss at length all the basic matters pertaining to internal and foreign policy and to questions bearing on the development of party and government. . . .

Were our party's holy Leninist principles observed after the death of Vladimir Ilyich?

Whereas during the first few years after Lenin's death Party Congresses and Central Committee plenums took place more or less regularly, later, when Stalin began increasingly to abuse his power, these principles were brutally violated. This was especially evident during the last 15 years of his life. Was it a normal situation when over 13 years elapsed between the 18th [March 1939] and 19th [October 1952] Party Congresses, years during which our party and our country had experienced so many important events? These events demanded categorically that the party should have passed resolutions pertaining to the country's defense during the Patriotic War [World War II] and to peacetime construction after the war. Even after the end of the war a Congress was not convened for over seven years. Central Committee plenums were hardly ever called. It should be sufficient to mention that during all the years of the Patriotic War not a single Central Committee plenum took place. It is true that there was an attempt to call a Central Committee plenum in October 1941, when Central Committee members from the whole country were called to Moscow. They waited two days for the opening of the plenum, but in vain. Stalin did not even want to meet and to talk to the Central Committee members. This fact shows how demoralized Stalin was in the first months of the war and how haughtily and disdainfully he treated the Central Committee members.

In practice Stalin ignored the norms of party life and trampled on the Leninist principle of collective party leadership. . . .

Having at its disposal numerous data showing brutal willfulness toward party cadres, the Central Committee has created a party commission under the control of the Central Committee Presidium; it was charged with investigating what made possible the mass repressions against the majority of the Central Committee members and candidates elected at the 17th Congress of the All-Union Communist Party (Bolsheviks).

The commission has become acquainted with a large quantity of materials in the NKVD [People's Commissariat of Internal Affairs, the name of the secret police from 1934 to 1943] archives and with other documents and has established many facts pertaining to the fabrication of cases against communists, to false accusations, to glaring abuses of socialist legality—which resulted in the death of innocent people. It became apparent that many party, Soviet and economic activists who were branded in 1937-1938 as "enemies" were actually never enemies, spies, wreckers, etc., but were always honest communists; they were only so stigmatized, and often, no longer able to bear barbaric tortures, they charged themselves (at the order of the investigative judges—falsifiers) with all kinds of grave and unlikely crimes. . . .

"98 Persons . . . Arrested and Shot." It was determined that of the 139 members and candidates of the party's Central Committee who were elected at the 17th Congress, 98 persons, i.e., 70 percent, were arrested and shot (mostly in 1937-1938). (Indignation in the hall.)

The same fate met not only the Central Committee members but also the majority of the delegates to the 17th Party Congress. Of 1,966 delegates with either voting or advisory rights, 1,108 persons were arrested on charges of anti-revolutionary crimes, i.e., decidedly more than a majority. This very fact shows how absurd, wild and contrary to common sense were the charges of counter-revolutionary crimes made out, as we now see, against a majority of participants at the 17th Party Congress. (Indignation in the hall.). . .

We should recall that the 17th Party Congress is historically known as the Congress of Victors. Delegates to the Congress were active participants in the building of our socialist state; many of them suffered and fought for party interests during the pre-Revolutionary years in the conspiracy and at the civil war fronts; they fought their enemies valiantly and often nervelessly looked into the face of death.

How then can we believe that such people could prove to be "two-faced" and had joined the camps of the enemies of socialism during the era after the political liquidation of Zinovievites, Trotskyites and rightists and after the great accomplishments of socialist construction? This was the result of the abuse of power by Stalin, who began to use mass terror against the party cadres. . . .

After the criminal murder of S. M. Kirov [Leningrad

party boss assassinated December 1, 1934], mass repressions and brutal acts of violation of socialist legality began. On the evening of December 1, 1934, on Stalin's initiative (without the approval of the Political Bureau—which was passed two days later, casually) the Secretary of the Presidium of the Central Executive Committee, [Abel Sofronovich] Yenukidze, signed the following directive:

"1. Investigative agencies are directed to speed up the cases of those accused of the preparation or execution of acts of terror.

"2. Judicial organs are directed not to hold up the execution of death sentences pertaining to crimes of this category in order to consider the possibility of pardon, because the Presidium of the Central Executive Committee [of the] USSR does not consider as possible the receiving of petitions of this sort.

"3. The organs of the Commissariat of Internal Affairs [NKVD] are directed to execute death sentences against criminals of the above-mentioned category immediately after the passage of sentences."

This directive became the basis for mass acts of abuse against socialist legality. During many of the fabricated court cases the accused were charged with "the preparation" of terroristic acts; this deprived them of any possibility that their cases might be re-examined, even when they stated before the court that their "confessions" were secured by force, and when, in a convincing manner, they disproved the accusations against them....

It must be asserted that to this day the circumstances surrounding Kirov's murder hide many things which are inexplicable and mysterious and demand a most careful examination. There are reasons for the suspicion that the killer of Kirov, [Leonid V.] Nikolayev, was assisted by someone from among the people whose duty it was to protect the person of Kirov.

A month and a half before the killing, Nikolayev was arrested on the grounds of suspicious behavior, but he was released and not even searched. It is an unusually suspicious circumstance that when the Chekist [secret police agent] assigned to protect Kirov was being brought for an interrogation, on December 2, 1934, he was killed in a car "accident" in which no other occupants of the car were harmed. After the murder of Kirov, top functionaries of the Leningrad NKVD were given very light sentences, but in 1937 they were shot. We can assume that they were shot in order to cover the traces of the organizers of Kirov's killing. (Movement in the hall.)

Mass repressions grew tremendously from the end of 1936 after a telegram from Stalin and [Stalin supporter Andrei] Zhdanov, dated from Sochi on September 25, 1936, was addressed to [Lazar] Kaganovich, [Viacheslav] Molotov and other members of the Political Bureau. The content of the telegram was as follows:

"We deem it absolutely necessary and urgent that Comrade [Nikolai] Yezhov be nominated to the post of People's Commissar for Internal Affairs. [Secret police head Genrikh] Yagoda has definitely proved himself to be incapable of unmasking the Trotskyite-Zinovievite bloc. The OGPU [Unified State Political Administration, the name of the secret police from 1922 until 1934] is four years behind in this matter. This is noted by all party workers and by the majority of the representatives of the NKVD."

Strictly speaking we should stress that Stalin did not meet with and therefore could not know the opinion of party workers.

This Stalinist formulation that the "NKVD is four years behind" in applying mass repression and that there is a necessity for "catching up" with the neglected work directly pushed the NKVD workers on the path of mass arrests and executions....

Stalin's report at the February-March Central Committee Plenum in 1937, "Deficiencies of party work and methods for the liquidation of the Trotskyites and of other two-facers," contained an attempt at theoretical justification of the mass terror policy under the pretext that as we march forward toward socialism, class war must allegedly sharpen. Stalin asserted that both history and Lenin taught him this.

Actually Lenin taught that the application of revolutionary violence is necessitated by the resistance of the exploiting classes, and this referred to the era when the exploiting classes existed and were powerful. As soon as the nation's political situation had improved, when in January 1920 the Red Army took Rostov and thus won a most important victory over [White Russian forces led by General Anton] Deniken, Lenin instructed [Felix] Dzerzhinsky [first head of the secret police] to stop mass terror and to abolish the death penalty....

Stalin deviated from these clear and plain precepts of Lenin. Stalin put the party and the NKVD up to the use of mass terror when the exploiting classes had been liquidated in our country and when there were no serious reasons for the use of extraordinary mass terror....

Mass arrests of party, Soviet, economic and military workers caused tremendous harm to our country and to the cause of socialist advancement....

Only because our party has at its disposal such great moral-political strength was it possible for it to survive the difficult events in 1937-1938 and to educate new cadres. There is, however, no doubt that our march forward toward socialism and toward the preparation of the country's defense would have been much more successful were it not for the tremendous loss in the cadres suffered as a result of the baseless and false mass repressions in 1937-1938. We are justly accusing [NKVD chief Nikolai] Yezhov for the degenerate practices of 1937. But we have to answer these questions:

Could Yezhov have arrested Kossior, for instance, without the knowledge of Stalin? Was there an exchange of opinions or a Political Bureau decision concerning this?

No, there was not, as there was none regarding other cases of this type.

Could Yezhov have decided such important matters as the fate of such eminent party figures?

No, it would be a display of naivete to consider this the work of Yezhov alone. It is clear that these matters were decided by Stalin, and that without his orders and his sanction Yezhov could not have done this....

"Stalin Was ... Sickly Suspicious." Facts prove that many abuses were made on Stalin's orders without reckoning with any norms of party and Soviet legality. Stalin was a very distrustful man, sickly suspicious; we knew this from our work with him. He could look at a man and say: "Why are your eyes so shifty today" or "Why are you turning so much today and avoiding to look me directly in the eyes?" The sickly suspicion created in him a general distrust even toward eminent party workers whom he had known for years. Everywhere and in everything he saw "enemies," "two-facers" and "spies.".....

When Stalin said that one or another should be arrested, it was necessary to accept on faith that he was an "enemy of the people." Meanwhile, Beria's gang, which ran the organs of state security, outdid itself in proving the guilt of the arrested and the truth of materials which it falsified. And what proofs were offered? The confessions of the arrested, and the investigative judges accepted these "confessions." And how is it possible that a person confesses to crimes which he has not committed? Only in one way—because of application of physical methods of pressuring him, tortures, bringing him to a state of unconsciousness, deprivation of his judgment, taking away of his human dignity. In this manner were "confessions" acquired....

The power accumulated in the hands of one person, Stalin, led to serious consequences during the Great Patriotic War [World War II].

When we look at many of our novels, films and historical "scientific studies," the role of Stalin in the Patriotic War appears to be entirely improbable. Stalin had foreseen everything. The Soviet Army, on the basis of a strategic plan prepared by Stalin long before, used the tactics of so-called "active defense," i.e., tactics which, we know, allowed the Germans to come up to Moscow and Stalingrad. Using such tactics the Soviet Army, supposedly thanks only to Stalin's genius, turned to the offensive and subdued the enemy. The epic victory gained through the armed might of the land of the Soviets, through our heroic people, is ascribed in this type of novel, film and "scientific study" as being completely due to the strategic genius of Stalin....

During the war and after the war Stalin put forward the thesis that the tragedy which our nation experienced

in the first part of the war was the result of the "unexpected" attack of the Germans against the Soviet Union. But, Comrades, this is completely untrue. As soon as Hitler came to power in Germany he assigned to himself the task of liquidating Communism. The fascists were saying this openly; they did not hide their plans....

Documents which have now been published show that by April 3, 1941, Churchill, through his ambassador to the USSR, [Sir Stafford] Cripps, personally warned Stalin that the Germans had begun regrouping their armed units with the intent of attacking the Soviet Union....

However, Stalin took no heed of these warnings. What is more, Stalin ordered that no credence be given to information of this sort, in order not to provoke the initiation of military operations.

We must assert that information of this sort concerning the threat of German armed invasion of Soviet territory was coming in also from our own military and diplomatic sources; however, because the leadership was conditioned against such information, such data was dispatched with fear and assessed with reservation.

Thus, for instance, information sent from Berlin on May 6, 1941, by the Soviet military attaché ... stated: "Soviet citizen Bozer ... communicated to the deputy naval attaché that according to a statement of a certain German officer from Hitler's Headquarters, Germany is preparing to invade the USSR on May 14 through Finland, the Baltic countries and Latvia. At the same time Moscow and Leningrad will be heavily raided and paratroopers landed in border cities...."

In his report of May 22, 1941, the deputy military attaché in Berlin ... communicated that "...the attack of the German army is reportedly scheduled for June 15, but it is possible that it may begin in the first days of June...."

A cable from our London Embassy dated June 18, 1941, stated: "As of now Cripps is deeply convinced of the inevitability of armed conflict between Germany and the USSR which will begin not later than the middle of June. According to Cripps, the Germans have presently concentrated 147 divisions (including air force and service units) along the Soviet borders...."

Despite these particularly grave warnings, the necessary steps were not taken to prepare the country properly for defense and to prevent it from being caught unawares.

Did we have time and the capabilities for such preparations? Yes, we had the time and the capabilities....

Had our industry been mobilized properly and in time to supply the army with the necessary matériel, our wartime losses would have been decidedly smaller. Such mobilization had not been, however, started in time. And already in the first days of the war it became evident that our army was badly armed, that we did not have enough artillery, tanks and planes to throw the enemy back....

In this connection we cannot forget, for instance, the

following fact: Shortly before the invasion of the Soviet Union by the Hitlerite army, . . . [the] Chief of the Kiev Special Military District (he was later killed at the front) wrote to Stalin that the German armies were at the Bug River, were preparing for an attack and in the very near future would probably start their offensive. In this connection . . . [he] proposed that a strong defense be organized, that 300,000 people be evacuated from the border areas and that several strong points be organized there: antitank ditches, trenches for the soldiers, etc.

Moscow answered this proposition with the assertion that this would be a provocation, that no preparatory defensive work should be undertaken at the borders, that the Germans were not to be given any pretext for the initiation of military action against us. Thus, our borders were insufficiently prepared to repel the enemy. . . .

And what were the results of this carefree attitude, this disregard of clear facts? The result was that already in the first hours and days the enemy had destroyed in our border regions a large part of our air force, artillery and other military equipment; he annihilated large numbers of our military cadres and disorganized our military leadership; consequently we could not prevent the enemy from marching deep into the country.

Very grievous consequences, especially in reference to the beginning of the war, followed Stalin's annihilation of many military commanders and political workers during 1937-1941 because of his suspiciousness and through slanderous accusations. During these years repressions were instituted against certain parts of military cadres beginning literally at the company and battalion commander level and extending to the higher military centers; during this time the cadre of leaders who had gained military experience in Spain and in the Far East was almost completely liquidated.

The policy of large-scale repression against the military cadres led also to undermined military discipline, because for several years officers of all ranks and even soldiers in the party and Komsomol cells were taught to "unmask" their superiors as hidden enemies. (Movement in the hall.) It is natural that this caused a negative influence on the state of military discipline in the first war period. . . . All this brought about the situation which existed at the beginning of the war and which was the great threat to our Fatherland.

"This Was the End." It would be incorrect to forget that after the first severe disaster and defeats at the front, Stalin thought that this was the end. In one of his speeches in those days he said: "All that which Lenin created we have lost forever."

After this Stalin for a long time actually did not direct the military operations and ceased to do anything whatever. He returned to active leadership only when some members of the Political Bureau visited him and told him

that it was necessary to take certain steps immediately in order to improve the situation at the front.

Therefore, the threatening danger which hung over our Fatherland in the first period of the war was largely due to the faulty methods of directing the nation and the party by Stalin himself.

However, we speak not only about the moment when the war began, which led to serious disorganization of our army and brought us severe losses. Even after the war began, the nervousness and hysteria which Stalin demonstrated, interfering with actual military operations, caused our army serious damage.

Stalin was very far from an understanding of the real situation which was developing at the front. This was natural because during the whole Patriotic War he never visited any section of the front or any liberated city except for one short ride on the Mozhaisk Highway during a stabilized situation at the front. To this incident were dedicated many literary works full of fantasies of all sorts and so many paintings. Simultaneously, Stalin was interfering with operations and issuing orders which did not take into consideration the real situation at a given section of the front and which could not help but result in huge personnel losses.

I will allow myself in this connection to bring out one characteristic fact which illustrates how Stalin directed operations at the fronts. There is present at this Congress Marshal [Ivan] Bagramyan who was once the chief of operations in the headquarters of the southwestern front and who can corroborate what I tell you.

When there developed an exceptionally serious situation for our Army in 1942 in the Kharkov region, we had correctly decided to drop an operation whose objective was to encircle Kharkov, because the real situation at that time would have threatened our Army with fatal consequences if this operation were continued. . . .

Contrary to common sense, Stalin rejected our suggestion and issued the order to continue the operation aimed at the encirclement of Kharkov, despite the fact that at this time many Army concentrations were themselves actually threatened with encirclement and liquidation. . . .

And what was the result of this? The worst that we had expected. The Germans surrounded our Army concentrations and consequently we lost hundreds of thousands of our soldiers. This is Stalin's military "genius"; this is what it cost us. (Movement in the hall.). . .

The tactics on which Stalin insisted without knowing the essence of the conduct of battle operations cost us much blood until we succeeded in stopping the opponent and going over to the offensive.

The military know that already by the end of 1941 instead of great operational maneuvers flanking the opponent and penetrating behind his back, Stalin demanded incessant frontal attacks and the capture of one village after another.

Because of this we paid with great losses—until our generals, on whose shoulders rested the whole weight of conducting the war, succeeded in changing the situation and shifting to flexible-maneuver operations, which immediately brought serious changes at the front favorable to us.

All the more shameful was the fact that after our great victory over the enemy which cost us so much, Stalin began to downgrade many of the commanders who contributed so much to the victory over the enemy, because Stalin excluded every possibility that services rendered at the front should be credited to anyone but himself. . . .

In the same vein, let us take, for instance, our historical and military films and some literary creations; they make us feel sick. Their true objective is the propagation of the theme of praising Stalin as a military genius. Let us recall the film, *The Fall of Berlin.* Here only Stalin acts; he issues orders in the hall in which there are many empty chairs and only one man approaches him and reports something to him—that is [A. N.] Poskrebyshev [Stalin's secretary and trusted aide], his loyal shield-bearer. (Laughter in the hall.)

And where is the military command? Where is the Political Bureau? Where is the Government? What are they doing and with what are they engaged? There is nothing about them in the film. Stalin acts for everybody; he does not reckon with anyone; he asks no one for advice. Everything is shown to the nation in this false light. Why? In order to surround Stalin with glory, contrary to the facts and contrary to historical truth.

The question arises: And where are the military on whose shoulders rested the burden of the war? They are not in the film; with Stalin in, no room was left for them.

Not Stalin, but the party as a whole, the Soviet government, our heroic Army, its talented leaders and brave soldiers, the whole Soviet nation—these are the ones who assured the victory in the Great Patriotic War. (Tempestuous and prolonged applause.). . .

The main role and the main credit for the victorious ending of the war belongs to our Communist Party, to the armed forces of the Soviet Union, and to the tens of millions of Soviet people raised by the party. (Thunderous and prolonged applause.)

Comrades, let us reach for some other facts. The Soviet Union is justly considered as a model of a multinational state because we have in practice assured the equality and friendship of all nations which live in our great Fatherland.

"Mass Deportations." All the more monstrous are the acts whose initiator was Stalin and which are rude violations of the basic Leninist principles of the nationality policy of the Soviet state. We refer to the mass deportations from their native places of whole nations, together with all Communists and Komsomols without any exception; this deportation action was not dictated by any military considerations.

Thus, already at the end of 1943, when there occurred a permanent breakthrough at the fronts of the Great Patriotic War benefiting the Soviet Union, a decision was taken and executed concerning the deportation of all the Karachai from the lands on which they lived.

In the same period, at the end of December 1943, the same lot befell the whole population of the Autonomous Kalmyk Republic. In March 1944 all the Chechen and Ingush peoples were deported and the Chechen-Ingush Autonomous Republic was liquidated. In April 1944, all Balkars were deported to faraway places from the territory of the Kabardino-Balkar Autonomous Republic and the Republic itself was renamed the Autonomous Kabardin Republic.

The Ukrainians avoided meeting this fate only because there were too many of them and there was no place to which to deport them. Otherwise, he would have deported them also. (Laughter and animation in the hall.). . .

After the conclusion of the Patriotic War, the Soviet nation stressed with pride the magnificent victories gained through great sacrifices and tremendous efforts. The country experienced a period of political enthusiasm. The party came out of the war even more united; in the fire of the war party cadres were tempered and hardened. Under such conditions nobody could have even thought of the possibility of some plot in the party.

And it was precisely at this time that the so-called "Leningrad affair" was born. As we have now proven, this case was fabricated. Those who innocently lost their lives included Comrades [Nikolai A.] Voznesensky, [A. A.] Kuznetsov, [Mikhail I.] Rodinov, [Pyotr S.] Popkov, and others.

As is known, Voznesensky and Kuznetsov were talented and eminent leaders. Once they stood very close to Stalin. It is sufficient to mention that Stalin made Voznesensky first deputy to the chairman of the Council of Ministers and Kuznetsov was elected Secretary of the Central Committee. The very fact that Stalin entrusted Kuznetsov with the supervision of the state security organs shows the trust which he enjoyed.

How did it happen that these persons were branded as enemies of the people and liquidated?

Facts prove that the "Leningrad affair" is also the result of willfulness which Stalin exercised against party cadres. Had a normal situation existed in the party's Central Committee and in the Central Committee Political Bureau, affairs of this nature would have been examined there in accordance with party practice, and all pertinent facts assessed; as a result such an affair as well as others would not have happened.

We must state that after the war the situation became even more complicated. Stalin became even more capricious, irritable and brutal; in particular his suspicion grew. His persecution mania reached unbelievable dimensions. Many workers were becoming enemies before his very eyes. After the war Stalin separated himself from the collective even more. Everything was decided by him alone without any consideration for anyone or anything.

This unbelievable suspicion was cleverly taken advantage of by the abject provocateur and vile enemy, Beria, who had murdered thousands of Communists and loyal Soviet people. The elevation of Voznesensky and Kuznetsov alarmed Beria. As we have now proven, it had been precisely Beria who had "suggested" to Stalin the fabrication by him and by his confidants of materials in the form of declarations and anonymous letters, and in the form of various rumors and talks.

The party's Central Committee has examined this so-called "Leningrad affair"; persons who innocently suffered are now rehabilitated and honor has been restored to the glorious Leningrad party organization. [Victor S.] Abakumov [minister of state security, 1947-1951] and others who had fabricated this affair were brought before a court; their trial took place in Leningrad and they received what they deserved.

The question arises: Why is it that we see the truth of this affair only now, and why did we not do something earlier, during Stalin's life, in order to prevent the loss of innocent lives? It was because Stalin personally supervised the "Leningrad affair," and the majority of the Political Bureau members did not, at that time, know all of the circumstances in these matters, and could not therefore intervene....

The willfulness of Stalin showed itself not only in decisions concerning the internal life of the country but also in the international relations of the Soviet Union.

The July plenum of the Central Committee studied in detail the reasons for the development of conflict with Yugoslavia. It was a shameful role which Stalin played here. The "Yugoslav affair" contained no problems which could not have been solved through party discussions among comrades. There was no significant basis for the development of this "affair"; it was completely possible to have prevented the rupture of relations with that country. This does not mean, however, that the Yugoslav leaders did not make mistakes or did not have shortcomings. But these mistakes and shortcomings were magnified in a monstrous manner by Stalin, which resulted in a break of relations with a friendly country....

You see to what Stalin's mania for greatness led. He had completely lost consciousness of reality; he demonstrated his suspicion and haughtiness not only in relation to individuals in the USSR, but in relation to whole parties and nations.

We have carefully examined the case of Yugoslavia and have found a proper solution which is approved by the peoples of the Soviet Union and of Yugoslavia as well as by the working masses of all the people's democracies and by all progressive humanity. The liquidation of the abnormal relationship with Yugoslavia was done in the interest of the whole camp of socialism, in the interest of strengthening peace in the whole world.

"Affair of the Doctor-Plotters."   Let us also recall the "affair of the doctor-plotters." (Animation in the hall.) Actually there was no "Affair" outside of the declaration of the woman doctor, [Lydia] Timashuk, who was probably influenced or ordered by someone (after all, she was an unofficial collaborator of the organs of state security) to write Stalin a letter in which she declared that doctors were applying supposedly improper methods of medical treatment.

Such a letter was sufficient for Stalin to reach an immediate conclusion that there were doctor-plotters in the Soviet Union. He issued orders to arrest a group of eminent Soviet medical specialists. He personally issued advice on the conduct of the investigation and the method of interrogation of the arrested persons. He said that the academician [A. I.] Vinogradov should be put in chains, another one should be beaten. Present at this Congress as a delegate is the former Minister of State Security, Comrade [S. D.] Ignatiev. Stalin told him curtly, "If you do not obtain confessions from the doctors we will shorten you by a head." (Tumult in the hall.)

Stalin personally called the investigative judge, gave him instructions, advised him on which investigative methods should be used; these methods were simple— beat, beat and, once again, beat.

Shortly after the doctors were arrested we members of the Political Bureau received protocols with the doctors' confessions of guilt. After distributing these protocols Stalin told us, "You are blind like young kittens; what will happen without me? The country will perish because you do not know how to recognize enemies."

The case was so presented that no one could verify the facts on which the investigation was based. There was no possibility of trying to verify facts by contacting those who had made the confessions of guilt.

We felt, however, that the case of the arrested doctors was questionable. We knew some of these people personally because they had once treated us. When we examined this "case" after Stalin's death, we found it to be fabricated from beginning to end.

This ignominious "case" was set up by Stalin; he did not, however, have the time in which to bring it to an end (as he conceived that end), and for this reason the doctors are still alive. Now all have been rehabilitated; they are working in the same places they were working before; they treat top individuals, not excluding members of the government; they have our full confidence; and they execute their duties honestly, as they did before....

"The Cult of the Individual." Comrades: The cult of the individual acquired such monstrous size chiefly because Stalin himself, using all conceivable methods, supported the glorification of his own person. This is supported by numerous facts. One of the most characteristic examples of Stalin's self-glorification and his lack of even elementary modesty is the edition of his *Short Biography,* which was published in 1948....

We need not give here examples of the loathsome adulation filling this book. All we need to add is that they all were approved and edited by Stalin personally and some of them were added in his own handwriting to the draft text of the book.

What did Stalin consider essential to write into this book? Did he want to cool the ardor of his flatterers who were composing his *Short Biography?* No! He marked the very places where he thought that the praise of his services was insufficient.

Here are some examples characterizing Stalin's activity, added in Stalin's own hand:

"In this fight against the skeptics and capitulators, the Trotskyites, Zinovievites, Bukharinites and Kamenevites, there was definitely welded together, after Lenin's death, that leading core of the Party ... that upheld the great manner of Lenin, rallied the Party behind Lenin's behests, and brought the Soviet people into the broad road of industrializing the country and collectivizing the rural economy. The leader of this core and the guiding force of the Party and the State was Comrade Stalin."

Thus writes Stalin himself! Then he adds:

"Although he performed his task of leader of the Party and the people with consummate skill and enjoyed the unreserved support of the entire Soviet people, Stalin never allowed his work to be marred by the slightest hint of vanity, conceit or self-adulation."

Where and when could a leader so praise himself? Is this worthy of a leader of the Marxist-Leninist type? No. Precisely against this did Marx and Engels take such a strong position. This also was always sharply condemned by Vladimir Ilyich Lenin....

Stalin recognized as the best a text of the national anthem of the Soviet Union which contains not a word about the Communist Party; it contains, however, the following unprecedented praise of Stalin: *"Stalin brought us up in loyalty to the people. He inspired us to great toil and acts."*

In these lines of the anthem is the whole educational, directional and inspirational activity of the great Leninist party ascribed to Stalin. This is, of course, a clear deviation from Marxism-Leninism, a clear debasing and belittling of the role of the party. We should add for your information that the Presidium of the Central Committee has already passed a resolution concerning the composition of a new text of the anthem, which will reflect the role of the people, and the role of the party. (Loud, prolonged applause.)

And was it without Stalin's knowledge that many of the largest enterprises and towns were named after him? Was it without his knowledge that Stalin monuments were erected in the whole country—these "memorials to the living"? It is a fact that Stalin himself had signed on July 2, 1951, a resolution of the USSR Council of Ministers concerning the erection on the Volga-Don Canal of an impressive monument to Stalin; on September 4 of the same year he issued an order making 33 tons of copper available for the construction of this impressive monument. Anyone who has visited the Stalingrad area must have seen the huge statue which is being built there, and that on a site which hardly any people frequent. Huge sums were spent to build it at a time when people of this area had lived since the war in huts. Consider yourself, was Stalin right when he wrote in his biography that "... he did not allow in himself ... even a shadow of conceit, pride, or self-adoration"?

At the same time Stalin gave proofs of his lack of respect for Lenin's memory. It is not a coincidence that, despite the decision taken over 30 years ago to build a Palace of Soviets as a monument to Vladimir Ilyich, this palace was not built, its construction was always postponed, and the project allowed to lapse.

We cannot forget to recall the Soviet Government resolution of August 14, 1925, concerning "the founding of Lenin prizes for educational work." This resolution was published in the press, but until this day there are no Lenin prizes. This, too, should be corrected. (Tumultuous, prolonged applause.)

During Stalin's life, thanks to known methods which I have mentioned, and quoting facts, for instance, from the *Short Biography* of Stalin—all events were explained as if Lenin played only a secondary role, even during the October Socialist Revolution. In many films and in many literary works, the figure of Lenin was incorrectly presented and inadmissibly depreciated.

Stalin loved to see the film *The Unforgettable Year of 1919,* in which he was shown on the steps of an armored train and where he was practically vanquishing the foe with his own saber. Let Kliment Yefremovich [Voroshilov, chairman of the Presidium of the Supreme Soviet, 1953-1960], our dear friend, find the necessary courage and write the truth about Stalin; after all, he knows how Stalin had fought. It will be difficult for Comrade Voroshilov to undertake this, but it would be good if he did it. Everyone will approve of it, both the people and the party. Even his grandsons will thank him. (Prolonged applause.)

In speaking about the events of the October Revolution and about the civil war, the impression was created that Stalin always played the main role, as if everywhere and always Stalin had suggested to Lenin what to do and how to do it. However, this is slander of Lenin. (Prolonged applause.)

I will probably not sin against the truth when I say that 99 percent of the persons present here heard and knew very little about Stalin before the year 1924, while Lenin was known to all; he was known to the whole party, to the whole nation, from the children up to the graybeards. (Tumultuous, prolonged applause.)

All this has to be thoroughly revised, so that history, literature, and the fine arts properly reflect V. I. Lenin's role and the great deeds of our Communist Party and of the Soviet people—the creative people. (Applause.)

Comrades! The cult of the individual has caused the employment of faulty principles in party work and in economic activity; it brought about rude violation of internal party and Soviet democracy, sterile administration, deviations of all sorts, covering up of shortcomings and varnishing of reality. Our nation gave birth to many flatterers and specialists in false optimism and deceit.

We should also not forget that due to the numerous arrests of party, Soviet and economic leaders, many workers began to work uncertainly, showed over-cautiousness, feared all which was new, feared their own shadows and began to show less initiative in their work. . . .

Stalin's reluctance to consider life's realities and the fact that he was not aware of the real state of affairs in the provinces can be illustrated by his direction of agriculture.

All those who interested themselves even a little in the national situation saw the difficult situation in agriculture, but Stalin never even noted it. Did we tell Stalin about this? Yes, we told him, but he did not support us. Why? Because Stalin never traveled anywhere, did not meet city and *kolkhoz* workers; he did not know the actual situation in the provinces.

He knew the country and agriculture only from films. And these films had dressed up and beautified the existing situation in agriculture. . . .

Vladimir Ilyich Lenin looked at life differently; he was always close to the people; he used to receive peasant delegates, and often spoke at factory gatherings; he used to visit villages and talk with the peasants.

Stalin separated himself from the people and never went anywhere. This lasted tens of years. The last time he visited a village was in January 1928 when he visited Siberia in connection with grain deliveries. How then could he have known the situation in the provinces? . . .

Comrades! If we sharply criticize today the cult of the individual which was so widespread during Stalin's life and if we speak about the many negative phenomena generated by this cult which is so alien to the spirit of Marxism-Leninism, various persons may ask: How could it be? Stalin headed the party and the country for 30 years and many victories were gained during his lifetime. Can we deny this? In my opinion, the question can be asked in this manner only by those who are blinded and hopelessly hypnotized by the cult of the individual, only by those who do not understand the essence of the revolution and of the Soviet state, only by those who do not understand, in a Leninist manner, the role of the party and of the nation in the development of the Soviet society.

The Socialist Revolution was attained by the working class and by the poor peasantry with the partial support of middle-class peasants. It was attained by the people under the leadership of the Bolshevik Party. Lenin's great service consisted of the fact that he created a militant party of the working class, but he was armed with Marxist understanding of the laws of social development and with the science of proletarian victory in the fight with capitalism, and he steeled this party in the crucible of revolutionary struggle of the masses of the people.

During this fight the party consistently defended the interests of the people, became its experienced leader, and led the working masses to power, to the creation of the first socialist state. . . .

Our historical victories were attained thanks to the organizational work of the party, to the many provincial organizations, and to the self-sacrificing work of our great nation. These victories are the result of the great drive and activity of the nation and of the party as a whole; they are not at all the fruit of the leadership of Stalin, as the situation was pictured during the period of the cult of the individual. . . .

In the last years, when we managed to free ourselves of the harmful practice of the cult of the individual and took several proper steps in the sphere of internal and external policies, everyone saw how activity grew before their very eyes, how the creative activity of the broad working masses developed, how favorably all this acted upon the development of economy and of culture. (Applause.)

Where Was the Political Bureau? Some comrades may ask us: Where were the members of the Political Bureau of the Central Committee? Why did they not assert themselves against the cult of the individual in time? And why is this being done only now?

First of all we have to consider the fact that the members of the Political Bureau viewed these matters in a different way at different times. Initially, many of them backed Stalin actively because Stalin was one of the strongest Marxists and his logic, his strength and his will greatly influenced the cadres and party work.

It is known that Stalin, after Lenin's death, especially during the first years, actively fought for Leninism against the enemies of Leninist theory and against those who deviated. Beginning with Leninist theory, the party, with its Central Committee at the head, started on a great scale the work of socialist industrialization of the country, agricultural collectivization and the cultural revolution.

At that time Stalin gained great popularity, sympathy and support. The party had to fight those who attempted to lead the country away from the correct Leninist path; it had to fight Trotskyites, Zinovievites and rightists, and the bourgeois nationalists. This fight was indispensable.

Later, however, Stalin, abusing his power more and more, began to fight eminent party and government leaders and to use terroristic methods against honest Soviet people. . . .

It is clear that such conditions put every member of the Political Bureau in a very difficult situation. And when we also consider the fact that in the last years the Central Committee plenary sessions were not convened and that the sessions of the Political Bureau occurred only occasionally, from time to time, then we will understand how difficult it was for any member of the Political Bureau to take a stand against one or another unjust or improper procedure, against serious errors and shortcomings in the practices of leadership. . . .

Let us consider the first Central Committee Plenum after the 19th Party Congress when Stalin, in his talk at the Plenum, characterized Vyacheslav Mikhailovich Molotov and Anastas Ivanovich Mikoyan and suggested that these old workers of our party were guilty of some baseless charges. It is not excluded that had Stalin remained at the helm for another several months, Comrades Molotov and Mikoyan would probably have not delivered any speeches at this Congress.

Stalin evidently had plans to finish off the old members of the Political Bureau. He often stated that Political Bureau members should be replaced by new ones.

His proposal, after the 19th Congress, concerning the selection of 25 persons to the Central Committee Presidium, was aimed at the removal of the old Political Bureau members and the bringing in of less experienced persons so that these would extol him in all sorts of ways.

We can assume that this was also a design for the future annihilation of the old Political Bureau members and in this way a cover for all shameful acts of Stalin, acts which we are now considering.

Comrades! In order not to repeat errors of the past, the Central Committee has declared itself resolutely against the cult of the individual. We consider that Stalin was excessively extolled. However, in the past Stalin doubtless performed great services to the party, to the working class, and to the international workers' movement.

This question is complicated by the fact that all this which we have just discussed was done during Stalin's life under his leadership and with his concurrence; here Stalin was convinced that this was necessary for the defense of the interests of the working classes against the plotting of the enemies and against the attack of the imperialist camp.

He saw this from the position of the interest of the working class, of the interest of the laboring people, of the interest of the victory of socialism and communism. We cannot say that these were the deeds of a giddy despot. He considered that this should be done in the interest of

the party; of the working masses, in the name of the defense of the revolution's gains. In this lies the whole tragedy! . . .

We should in all seriousness consider the question of the cult of the individual. We cannot let this matter get out of the party, especially not to the press. It is for this reason that we are considering it here at a closed Congress session. We should know the limits; we should not give ammunition to the enemy; we should not wash our dirty linen before their eyes. I think that the delegates to the Congress will understand and assess properly all these proposals. (Tumultuous applause.)

Comrades: We must abolish the cult of the individual decisively, once and for all; we must draw the proper conclusions concerning both ideological-theoretical and practical work. It is necessary for this purpose:

First, in a Bolshevik manner to condemn and to eradicate the cult of the individual as alien to Marxism-Leninism and not consonant with the principles of party leadership and the norms of party life, and to fight inexorably all attempts at bringing back this practice in one form or another.

To return to and actually practice in all our ideological work the most important theses of Marxist-Leninist science about the people as the creator of history and as the creator of all material and spiritual good of humanity, about the decisive role of the Marxist party in the revolutionary fight for the transformation of society, about the victory of communism.

In this connection we will be forced to do much work in order to examine critically from the Marxist-Leninist viewpoint and to correct the widely spread erroneous views connected with the cult of the individual in the sphere of history, philosophy, economy and of other sciences, as well as in literature and the fine arts. It is especially necessary that in the immediate future we compile a serious textbook of the history of our party which will be edited in accordance with scientific Marxist objectivism, a textbook of the history of Soviet society, a book pertaining to the events of the civil war and the Great Patriotic War.

Secondly, to continue systematically and consistently the work done by the party's Central Committee during the last years, a work characterized by minute observation in all party organizations, from the bottom to the top, of the Leninist principles of party leadership, characterized, above all, by the main principle of collective leadership, characterized by the observation of the norms of party life described in the statutes of our party, and finally, characterized by the wide practice of criticism and self-criticism.

Thirdly, to restore completely the Leninist principles of Soviet socialist democracy, expressed in the Constitution of the Soviet Union, to fight willfulness of individuals abusing their power. The evil caused by acts violating revolutionary socialist legality which have accumulated during a long time as a result of the negative influence of the cult of the individual has to be completely corrected.

Comrades! The 20th Congress of the Communist Party of the Soviet Union has manifested with a new strength the unshakable unity of our party, its cohesiveness around the Central Committee, its resolute will to accomplish the great task of building communism. (Tumultuous applause.)

And the fact that we present in all their ramifications the basic problems of overcoming the cult of the individual which is alien to Marxism-Leninism, as well as the problem of liquidating its burdensome consequences, is an evidence of the great moral and political strength of our party. (Prolonged applause.)

We are absolutely certain that our party, armed with the historical resolutions of the 20th Congress, will lead the Soviet people along the Leninist path to new successes, to new victories. (Tumultuous, prolonged applause.)

Long live the victorious banner of our party—Leninism! (Tumultuous, prolonged applause ending in ovation. All rise.)

"Kitchen Debate" of Nixon and Khrushchev

Following are excerpts from an exchange between Vice President Richard Nixon and Soviet premier Nikita S. Khrushchev at a U.S. trade exhibition in Moscow, July 24, 1959, as published in The Challenges We Face, *edited and compiled from the speeches and papers of Richard Nixon (New York: McGraw-Hill, 1980).*

Khrushchev: "Americans have lost their ability to trade. Now you have grown older and you don't trade the way you used to. You need to be invigorated."

Nixon: "You need to have goods to trade."

Nixon: "There must be a free exchange of ideas. . . ."

Khrushchev: "We want to live in peace and friendship with Americans because we are the two most powerful countries, and if we live in friendship, then other countries will also live in friendship. But if there is a country that is too war-minded we could pull its ears a little and say, 'Don't you dare; fighting is not allowed now.' This is a period of atomic armament; some foolish one could start a war and then even a wise one couldn't finish the war. Therefore, we are governed by this idea in our policy, internal and foreign. How long has America existed? Three hundred years?"

Nixon: "More than one hundred and fifty years."

Khrushchev: "More than one hundred and fifty years? Well, then, we will say America has been in existence for 150 years and this is the level she has reached. We have existed not quite forty-two years and in another seven

years we will be on the same level as America.

"When we catch you up, in passing you by, we will wave to you. Then if you wish we can stop and say: Please follow up. Plainly speaking, if you want capitalism you can live that way. That is your own affair and doesn't concern us. We can still feel sorry for you, but since you don't understand us, live as you do understand.

"We are all glad to be here at the Exhibition with Vice President Nixon. I personally, and on behalf of my colleagues, express my thanks for the President's message. I have not as yet read it but I know beforehand that it contains good wishes. I think you will be satisfied with your visit and if—I cannot go on without saying it—if you would not take such a position [captive nations resolution passed by Congress July 17] which has not been thought out thoroughly, as was approved by Congress, your trip would be excellent. But you have churned the water yourselves—why this was necessary God only knows.

"What happened? What black cat crossed your path and confused you? But that is your affair; we do not interfere with your problems." (Wrapping his arms about a Soviet workman.) "Does this man look like a slave laborer?" (Waving at others.) "With men with such spirit how can we lose?"

Nixon (pointing to American workmen): "With men like that we are strong. But these men, Soviet and American, work together well for peace, even as they have worked together in building this Exhibition. This is the way it should be.

"Your remarks are in the tradition of what we have come to expect—sweeping and extemporaneous. Later on we will both have an opportunity to speak, and consequently I will not comment on the various points that you raised, except to say this—this color television is one of the most advanced developments in communication that we have.

"I can say that if this competition in which you plan to outstrip us is to do the best for both of our peoples and for peoples everywhere, there must be a free exchange of ideas. After all, you don't know everything. . . ."

Khrushchev: "If I don't know everything, you don't know anything about communism except fear of it."

Nixon: "There are some instances where you may be ahead of us; for example, in the development of the thrust of your rockets for the investigation of outer space; there may be some instances in which we are ahead of you—in color television, for instance."

"We Have Bested You." Khrushchev: "No, we are up with you on this too. We have bested you in one technique and also in the other."

Nixon: "You see, you never concede anything."

Khrushchev: "I do not give up."

Nixon: "Wait till you see the picture. Let's have far more communication and exchange in this very area that we speak of. We should hear you more on our television. You should hear us more on yours."

Khrushchev: "That's a good idea. Let's do it like this. You appear before our people. We will appear before your people. People will see and appreciate this."

Nixon: "There is not a day in the United States when we cannot read what you say. When [Soviet first deputy premier Frol R.] Kozlov was speaking in California about peace, you were talking here in somewhat different terms. This was reported extensively in the American press. Never make a statement here if you don't want it to be read in the United States. I can promise you every word you say will be translated into English."

Khrushchev: "I doubt it. I want you to give your word that this speech of mine will be heard by the American people."

Nixon (shaking hands on it): "By the same token, everything I say will be translated and heard all over the Soviet Union?"

Khrushchev: "That's agreed."

Nixon: "You must not be afraid of ideas."

Khrushchev: "We are telling you not to be afraid of ideas. We have no reason to be afraid. We have already broken free from such a situation."

Nixon: "Well, then, let's have more exchange of them. We are all agreed on that. All right? All right?"

Khrushchev: "Fine." (Aside.) "Agreed to what? All right, I am in agreement. But I want to stress what I am in agreement with. I know that I am dealing with a very good lawyer. I also want to uphold my own miner's flag so that the coal miners can say, 'Our man does not concede.' "

Nixon: "No question about that."

Khrushchev: "You are a lawyer for capitalism and I am a lawyer for communism. Let's compete."

Nixon: "The way you dominate the conversation you would make a good lawyer yourself. If you were in the United States Senate you would be accused of filibustering."

Khrushchev: "If your reporters will check on the time, they will see who has talked more."

"You Do All the Talking." Nixon: "You do all the talking and do not let anyone else talk."

Khrushchev (referring to American model home): "You think the Russian people will be dumbfounded to see this? But I tell you all our modern homes have equipment of this sort, and to get a flat you have only to be a Soviet visitor, not a citizen."

Nixon: "We do not claim to astonish the Russian people. We hope to show our diversity and our right to choose. We do not wish to have decisions made at the top by government officials who say that all homes should be built in the same way. Would it not be better to compete in the relative merits of washing machines than in the strength of rockets? Is this the kind of competition you want?"

Khrushchev: "Yes, that's the kind of competition we want, but your generals say we must compete in rockets. Your generals say they are so powerful they can destroy us. We can also show you something so that you will know the Russian spirit. We are strong; we can beat you. But in this respect we can also show you something."

Nixon: "To me you are strong and we are strong. In some ways, you are stronger than we are. In others, we are stronger, but to me it seems that in this day and age to argue who is the stronger completely misses the point. We are both strong, not only from the standpoint of weapons but also from the standpoint of will and spirit.

"No one should ever use his strength to put another in the position where he in effect has an ultimatum. For us to argue who is the stronger misses the point. If war comes we both lose."

Khrushchev: "For the fourth time I have to say I cannot recognize my friend Mr. Nixon. If all Americans agree with you, then who don't we agree [with]? This is what we want."

Nixon: "Anyone who believes the American government does not reflect the people is not an accurate observer of the American scene. I hope the Prime Minister understands all the implications of what I have just said. When you place either one of the powerful nations or any other nations in a position so that they have no choice but to accept dictation or fight, then you are playing with the most destructive thing in the world.

"This is very important in the present world context. It is very dangerous. When we sit down at a conference table it cannot all be one way. One side cannot put an ultimatum to another. It is impossible. But I shall talk to you about this later."

Khrushchev: "Who is raising an ultimatum?"

Nixon: "We will discuss that later."

Khrushchev: "If you have raised the question, why not go on with it now while the people are listening? We know something about politics, too. Let your correspondents compare watches and see who is filibustering. You put great emphasis on *diktat* [dictation]. Our country has never been guided by *diktat*. *Diktat* is a foolish policy."

Nixon: "I am talking about it in the international sense."

No Threats. Khrushchev: "It sounds to me like a threat. We, too, are giants. You want to threaten—we will answer threats with threats."

Nixon: "That's not my point. We will never engage in threats."

Khrushchev: "You wanted indirectly to threaten me. But we have the means to threaten too."

Nixon: "Who wants to threaten?"

Khrushchev: "You are talking about implications. I

have not been. We have the means at our disposal. Ours are better than yours. It is you who want to compete. *Da, da, da.*"

Nixon: "We are well aware that you have the means. To me who is best is not material."

Khrushchev: "You raised the point. We want peace and friendship with all nations, especially with America."

Nixon: "We want peace, too, and I believe that you do also."

Khrushchev: "Yes, I believe that."

Nixon: "I see that you want to build a good life. But I don't think that the cause of peace is helped by reminders that you have greater strength than we do, because this is a threat, too."

Khrushchev: "I was answering your words. You challenged me. Let's argue fairly."

Nixon: "My point was that in today's world it is immaterial which of the two great countries at any particular moment has the advantage. In war, these advantages are illusory. Can we agree on that?"

Khrushchev: "Not quite. Let's not beat around the bush."

Nixon: "I like the way he talks."

Khrushchev: "We want to liquidate all bases from foreign lands. Until that happens we will speak different languages. One who is for putting an end to bases on foreign lands is for peace. One who is against it is for war. We have liquidated our bases, reduced our forces, and offered to make a peace treaty and eliminate the point of friction in Berlin. Until we settle that question, we will talk different languages."

Nixon: "Do you think it can be settled at Geneva?"

Khrushchev: "If we considered it otherwise, we would not have incurred the expense of sending our Foreign Minister to Geneva. [Andrei] Gromyko is not an idler. He is a very good man."

Nixon: "We have great respect for Mr. Gromyko. Some people say he looks like me. I think he is better-looking. I hope it [the Geneva Conference] will be successful."

Khrushchev: "It does not depend on us."

Nixon: "It takes two to make an agreement. You cannot have it all your own way."

Khrushchev: "These are questions that have the same aim. To put an end to the vestiges of war, to make a peace treaty with Germany—that is what we want. It is very bad that we quarrel over the question of war and peace."

Nixon: "There is no question but that your people and you want the government of the United States to be for peace—anyone who thinks that our government is not for peace is not an accurate observer of America. In order to have peace, Mr. Prime Minister, even in an argument between friends, there must be sitting-down around a table. There must be discussion. Each side must find areas where it looks at the other's point of view. The world

looks to you today with regard to Geneva. I believe it would be a grave mistake and a blow to peace if it were allowed to fail."

Khrushchev: "This is our understanding as well."

Nixon: "So this is something. The present position is stalemate. Ways must be found to discuss it."

Khrushchev: "The two sides must seek ways of agreement."

Kennedy, Khrushchev on Cuban Missile Crisis

Following are the texts of President Kennedy's October 22, 1962, television address about Soviet offensive missiles in Cuba and Kennedy's October 27 message to Soviet premier Nikita S. Khrushchev, and excerpts from Khrushchev's October 27 and October 28 messages to Kennedy and Kennedy's October 28 reply.

Kennedy's October 22 Speech

Good evening, my fellow citizens:

This Government, as promised, has maintained the closest surveillance of the Soviet military buildup on the island of Cuba. Within the past week, unmistakable evidence has established the fact that a series of offensive missile sites is now in preparation on that imprisoned island. The purpose of these bases can be none other than to provide a nuclear strike capability against the Western Hemisphere.

Upon receiving the first preliminary hard information of this nature last Tuesday morning at 9 a.m., I directed that our surveillance be stepped up. And having now confirmed and completed our evaluation of the evidence and our decision on a course of action, this Government feels obliged to report this new crisis to you in fullest detail.

The characteristics of these new missile sites indicate two distinct types of installations. Several of them include medium range ballistic missiles, capable of carrying a nuclear warhead for a distance of more than 1,000 nautical miles. Each of these missiles, in short, is capable of striking Washington, D.C., the Panama Canal, Cape Canaveral, Mexico City, or any other city in the southeastern part of the United States, in Central America, or in the Caribbean area.

Additional sites not yet completed appear to be designed for intermediate range ballistic missiles—capable of traveling more than twice as far—and thus capable of striking most of the major cities in the Western Hemisphere, ranging as far north as Hudson Bay, Canada, and as far south as Lima, Peru. In addition, jet bombers, capable of carrying nuclear weapons, are now being uncrated and assembled in Cuba, while the necessary air bases are being prepared.

This urgent transformation of Cuba into an important strategic base—by the presence of these large, long-range, and clearly offensive weapons of sudden mass destruction—constitutes an explicit threat to the peace and security of all the Americas, in flagrant and deliberate defiance of the Rio Pact of 1947, the traditions of this Nation and hemisphere, the joint resolution of the 87th Congress, the Charter of the United Nations, and my own public warnings to the Soviets on September 4 and 13. This action also contradicts the repeated assurances of Soviet spokesmen, both publicly and privately delivered, that the arms buildup in Cuba would retain its original defensive character, and that the Soviet Union had no need or desire to station strategic missiles on the territory of any other nation.

The size of this undertaking makes clear that it has been planned for some months. Yet only last month, after I had made clear the distinction between any introduction of ground-to-ground missiles and the existence of defensive antiaircraft missiles, the Soviet Government publicly stated on September 11 that, and I quote, "the armaments and military equipment sent to Cuba are designed exclusively for defensive purposes," that, and I quote the Soviet Government, "there is no need for the Soviet Government to shift its weapons . . . for a retaliatory blow to any other country, for instance Cuba," and that, and I quote their government, "the Soviet Union has so powerful rockets to carry these nuclear warheads that there is no need to search for sites for them beyond the boundaries of the Soviet Union." That statement was false.

Only last Thursday, as evidence of this rapid offensive buildup was already in my hand, Soviet Foreign Minister Gromyko told me in my office that he was instructed to make it clear once again, as he said his government had already done, that Soviet assistance to Cuba, and I quote, "pursued solely the purpose of contributing to the defense capabilities of Cuba," that, and I quote him, "training by Soviet specialists of Cuban nationals in handling defensive armaments was by no means offensive, and if it were otherwise," Mr. Gromyko went on, "the Soviet Government would never become involved in rendering such assistance." That statement also was false.

Neither the United States of America nor the world community of nations can tolerate deliberate deception and offensive threats on the part of any nation, large or small. We no longer live in a world where only the actual firing of weapons represents a sufficient challenge to a nation's security to constitute maximum peril. Nuclear weapons are so destructive and ballistic missiles are so swift, that any substantially increased possibility of their use or any sudden change in their deployment may well be regarded as a definite threat to peace.

For many years, both the Soviet Union and the United States, recognizing this fact, have deployed strategic nuclear weapons with great care, never upsetting the precarious status quo which insured that these weapons would not be used in the absence of some vital challenge. Our own strategic missiles have never been transferred to the territory of any other nation under a cloak of secrecy and deception; and our history—unlike that of the Soviets since the end of World War II—demonstrates that we have no desire to dominate or conquer any other nation or impose our system upon its people. Nevertheless, American citizens have become adjusted to living daily on the bull's-eye of Soviet missiles located inside the U.S.S.R. or in submarines.

In that sense, missiles in Cuba add to an already clear and present danger—although it should be noted the nations of Latin America have never previously been subjected to a potential nuclear threat.

But this secret, swift, and extraordinary buildup of Communist missiles—in an area well known to have a special and historical relationship to the United States and the nations of the Western Hemisphere, in violation of Soviet assurances, and in defiance of American and hemispheric policy—this sudden, clandestine decision to station strategic weapons for the first time outside of Soviet soil—is a deliberately provocative and unjustified change in the status quo which cannot be accepted by this country, if our courage and our commitments are ever to be trusted again by either friend or foe.

The 1930's taught us a clear lesson: aggressive conduct, if allowed to go unchecked and unchallenged, ultimately leads to war. This nation is opposed to war. We are also true to our word. Our unswerving objective, therefore, must be to prevent the use of these missiles against this or any other country, and to secure their withdrawal or elimination from the Western Hemisphere.

Our policy has been one of patience and restraint, as befits a peaceful and powerful nation, which leads a worldwide alliance. We have been determined not to be diverted from our central concerns by mere irritants and fanatics. But now further action is required—and it is under way; and these actions may only be the beginning. We will not prematurely or unnecessarily risk the costs of worldwide nuclear war in which even the fruits of victory would be ashes in our mouth—but neither will we shrink from that risk at any time it must be faced.

Acting, therefore, in the defense of our own security and of the entire Western Hemisphere, and under the authority entrusted to me by the Constitution as endorsed by the resolution of the Congress, I have directed that the following *initial* steps be taken immediately:

First: To halt this offensive buildup, a strict quarantine on all offensive military equipment under shipment to Cuba is being initiated. All ships of any kind bound for Cuba from whatever nation or port will, if found to contain cargoes of offensive weapons, be turned back.

This quarantine will be extended, if needed, to other types of cargo and carriers. We are not at this time, however, denying the necessities of life as the Soviets attempted to do in their Berlin blockade of 1948.

Second: I have directed the continued and increased close surveillance of Cuba and its military buildup. The foreign ministers of the OAS [Organization of American States], in their communique of October 6, rejected secrecy on such matters in this hemisphere. Should these offensive military preparations continue, thus increasing the threat to the hemisphere, further action will be justified. I have directed the Armed Forces to prepare for any eventualities; and I trust that in the interest of both the Cuban people and the Soviet technicians at the sites, the hazards to all concerned of continuing this threat will be recognized.

Third: It shall be the policy of this Nation to regard any nuclear missile launched from Cuba against any nation in the Western Hemisphere as an attack by the Soviet Union on the United States, requiring a full retaliatory response upon the Soviet Union.

Fourth: As a necessary military precaution, I have reinforced our base at Guantanamo, evacuated today the dependents of our personnel there, and ordered additional military units to be on a standby alert basis.

Fifth: We are calling tonight for an immediate meeting of the Organ of Consultation under the Organization of American States, to consider this threat to hemispheric security and to invoke articles 6 and 8 of the Rio Treaty in support of all necessary action. The United Nations Charter allows for regional security arrangements—and the nations of this hemisphere decided long ago against the military presence of outside powers. Our other allies around the world have also been alerted.

Sixth: Under the Charter of the United Nations, we are asking tonight that an emergency meeting of the Security Council be convoked without delay to take action against this latest Soviet threat to world peace. Our resolution will call for prompt dismantling and withdrawal of all offensive weapons in Cuba, under the supervision of U.N. observers, before the quarantine can be lifted.

Seventh and finally: I call upon Chairman Khrushchev to halt and eliminate this clandestine, reckless, and provocative threat to world peace and to stable relations between our two nations. I call upon him further to abandon this course of world domination, and to join in an historic effort to end the perilous arms race and to transform the history of man. He has an opportunity now to move the world back from the abyss of destruction—by returning to his government's own words that it had no need to station missiles outside its own territory, and withdrawing these weapons from Cuba—by refraining from any action which will widen or deepen the present crisis—and then by participating in a search for peaceful and permanent solutions.

This Nation is prepared to present its case against the Soviet threat to peace, and our own proposals for a peaceful world, at any time and in any forum—in the OAS, in the United Nations, or in any other meeting that could be useful—without limiting our freedom of action. We have in the past made strenuous efforts to limit the spread of nuclear weapons. We have proposed the elimination of all arms and military bases in a fair and effective disarmament treaty. We are prepared to discuss new proposals for the removal of tensions on both sides—including the possibilities of a genuinely independent Cuba, free to determine its own destiny. We have no wish to war with the Soviet Union—for we are a peaceful people who desire to live in peace with all other peoples.

"An Atmosphere of Intimidation." But it is difficult to settle or even discuss these problems in an atmosphere of intimidation. That is why this latest Soviet threat—or any other threat which is made either independently or in response to our actions this week—must and will be met with determination. Any hostile move anywhere in the world against the safety and freedom of peoples to whom we are committed—including in particular the brave people of West Berlin—will be met by whatever action is needed.

Finally, I want to say a few words to the captive people of Cuba, to whom this speech is being directly carried by special radio facilities. I speak to you as a friend, as one who knows of your deep attachment to your fatherland, as one who shares your aspirations for liberty and justice for all. And I have watched and the American people have watched with deep sorrow how your nationalist revolution was betrayed—and how your fatherland fell under foreign domination. Now your leaders are no longer Cuban leaders inspired by Cuban ideals. They are puppets and agents of an international conspiracy which has turned Cuba against your friends and neighbors in the Americas—and turned it into the first Latin American country to become a target for nuclear war—the first Latin American country to have these weapons on its soil.

These new weapons are not in your interest. They contribute nothing to your peace and well-being. They can only undermine it. But this country has no wish to cause you to suffer or to impose any system upon you. We know that your lives and land are being used as pawns by those who deny your freedom.

Many times in the past, the Cuban people have risen to throw out tyrants who destroyed their liberty. And I have no doubt that most Cubans today look forward to the time when they will be truly free—free from foreign domination, free to choose their own leaders, free to select their own system, free to own their own land, free to speak and write and worship without fear or degradation. And then shall Cuba be welcomed back to the society of free nations and to the associations of this hemisphere.

My fellow citizens: let no one doubt that this is a difficult and dangerous effort on which we have set out. No one can foresee precisely what course it will take or what costs or casualties will be incurred. Many months of sacrifice and self-discipline lie ahead—months in which both our patience and our will will be tested—months in which many threats and denunciations will keep us aware of our dangers. But the greatest danger of all would be to do nothing.

The path we have chosen for the present is full of hazards, as all paths are—but it is the one most consistent with our character and courage as a nation and our commitments around the world. The cost of freedom is always high—but Americans have always paid it. And one path we shall never choose, and that is the path of surrender or submission.

Our goal is not the victory of might, but the vindication of right—not peace at the expense of freedom, but both peace *and* freedom, here in this hemisphere, and, we hope, around the world. God willing, that goal will be achieved.

Thank you and good night.

Khrushchev's October 27 Message

...I understand your concern for the security of the United States, Mr. President, because this is the first duty of the president. However, these questions are also uppermost in our minds. The same duties rest with me as chairman of the USSR Council of Ministers. You have been worried over our assisting Cuba with arms designed to strengthen its defensive potential—precisely defensive potential—because Cuba, no matter what weapons it had, could not compare with you since these are different dimensions, the more so given up-to-date means of extermination.

Our purpose has been and is to help Cuba, and no one can challenge the humanity of our motives aimed at allowing Cuba to live peacefully and develop as its people desire. You want to relieve your country from danger and this is understandable. However, Cuba also wants this. All countries want to relieve themselves from danger. But how can we, the Soviet Union and our government, assess your actions which, in effect, mean that you have surrounded the Soviet Union with military bases, surrounded our allies with military bases, set up military bases literally around our country, and stationed your rocket weapons at them? This is no secret. High-placed American officials demonstratively declare this. Your rockets are stationed in Britain and in Italy and pointed at us. Your rockets are stationed in Turkey.

You are worried over Cuba. You say that it worries you because it lies at a distance of 90 miles across the sea from the shores of the United States. However, Turkey lies next to us. Our sentinels are pacing up and down and watching each other. Do you believe that you have the right to demand security for your country and the removal of such weapons that you qualify as offensive, while not recognizing this right for us?

You have stationed devastating rocket weapons, which you call offensive, in Turkey literally right next to us. How then does recognition of our equal military possibilities tally with such unequal relations between our great states? This does not tally at all.

It is good, Mr. President, that you agreed for our representatives to meet and begin talks, apparently with the participation of U.N. Acting Secretary General U Thant. Consequently, to some extent, he assumes the role of intermediary, and we believe that he can cope with the responsible mission if, of course, every side that is drawn into this conflict shows good will.

I think that one could rapidly eliminate the conflict and normalize the situation. Then people would heave a sigh of relief, considering that the statesmen who bear the responsibility have sober minds, an awareness of their responsibility, and an ability to solve complicated problems and not allow matters to slide to the disaster of war.

This is why I make this proposal: We agree to remove those weapons from Cuba which you regard as offensive weapons. We agree to do this and to state this commitment to the United Nations. Your representatives will make a statement to the effect that the United States, on its part, bearing in mind the anxiety and concern of the Soviet state, will evacuate its analogous weapons from Turkey. Let us reach an understanding on what time you and we need to put this into effect.

After this, representatives of the U.N. Security Council could control on-the-spot the fulfillment of these commitments. Of course, it is necessary that the Governments of Cuba and Turkey would allow these representatives to come to their countries and check fulfillment of this commitment, which each side undertakes. Apparently, it would be better if these representatives enjoyed the trust of the Security Council and ours—the United States and the Soviet Union—as well as of Turkey and Cuba. I think that it will not be difficult to find such people who enjoy the trust and respect of all interested sides.

We, having assumed this commitment in order to give satisfaction and hope to the peoples of Cuba and Turkey and to increase their confidence in their security, will make a statement in the Security Council to the effect that the Soviet Government gives a solemn pledge to respect the integrity of the frontiers and the sovereignty of Turkey, not to intervene in its domestic affairs, not to invade Turkey, not to make available its territory as a place d'armes for such invasion, and also will restrain those who would think of launching an aggression against Turkey either from Soviet territory or from the territory of other states bordering on Turkey.

The U.S. Government will make the same statement in

the Security Council with regard to Cuba. It will declare that the United States will respect the integrity of the frontiers of Cuba, its sovereignty, undertakes not to intervene in its domestic affairs, not to invade and not to make its territory available as place d'armes for the invasion of Cuba, and also will restrain those who would think of launching an aggression against Cuba either from U.S. territory or from the territory of other places bordering on Cuba.

Of course, for this we would have to reach agreement with you and to arrange for some deadline. Let us agree to give some time, but not to delay, two or three weeks, not more than a month.

The weapons on Cuba, that you have mentioned and which, as you say, alarm you, are in the hands of Soviet officers. Therefore any accidental use of them whatsoever to the detriment of the United States of America is excluded. These means are stationed in Cuba at the request of the Cuban Government and only in defensive aims. Therefore, if there is no invasion of Cuba, or an attack on the Soviet Union, or other of our allies then, of course, these means do not threaten anyone and will not threaten. For they do not pursue offensive aims.

If you accept my proposal, Mr. President, we would send our representatives to New York, to the United Nations, and would give them exhaustive instructions in order to come to terms sooner. If you would also appoint your men and give them appropriate instructions, this problem could be solved soon.

Why would I like to achieve this? Because the entire world is now agitated and expects reasonable actions from us. The greatest pleasure for all the peoples would be an announcement on our agreement, on nipping in the bud the conflict that has arisen. I attach a great importance to such understanding because it might be a good beginning and, specifically, facilitate a nuclear test ban agreement. The problem of tests could be solved simultaneously, not linking one with the other, because they are different problems. However, it is important to reach an understanding to both these problems in order to make a good gift to the people, to let them rejoice in the news that a nuclear test ban agreement has also been reached and thus there will be no further contamination of the atmosphere. Your and our positions on this issue are very close.

All this, possibly, would serve as a good impetus to searching for mutually acceptable agreements on other disputed issues, too, on which there is an exchange of opinion between us. These problems have not yet been solved but they wait for an urgent solution which would clear the international atmosphere. We are ready for this.

These are my proposals, Mr. President.

Respectfully yours,

Nikita Khrushchev
October 27, 1962

Kennedy's October 27 Response

Dear Mr. Chairman:

I have read your letter of October 26th [not made public] with great care and welcomed the statement of your desire to seek a prompt solution to the problem. The first thing that needs to be done, however, is for work to cease on offensive missile bases in Cuba and for all weapons systems in Cuba capable of offensive use to be rendered inoperable, under effective United Nations arrangements.

Assuming this is done promptly, I have given my representatives in New York instructions that will permit them to work out this weekend—in cooperation with the Acting Secretary General and your representative—an arrangement for a permanent solution to the Cuban problem along the lines suggested in your letter of October 26th. As I read your letter, the key elements of your proposals—which seem generally acceptable as I understand them—are as follows:

1. You would agree to remove these weapons systems from Cuba under appropriate United Nations observation and supervision; and undertake, with suitable safeguards, to halt the further introduction of such weapons systems into Cuba.

2. We, on our part, would agree—upon the establishment of adequate arrangements through the United Nations to ensure the carrying out and continuation of these commitments—(a) to remove promptly the quarantine measures now in effect and (b) to give assurances against an invasion of Cuba. I am confident that other nations of the Western Hemisphere would be prepared to do likewise.

If you will give your representative similar instructions, there is no reason why we should not be able to complete these arrangements and announce them to the world within a couple of days. The effect of such a settlement on easing world tensions would enable us to work toward a more general arrangement regarding "other armaments," as proposed in your second letter which you made public. I would like to say again that the United States is very much interested in reducing tensions and halting the arms race; and if your letter signifies that you are prepared to discuss a detente affecting NATO and the Warsaw Pact, we are quite prepared to consider with our allies any useful proposals.

But the first ingredient, let me emphasize, is the cessation of work on missile sites in Cuba and measures to render such weapons inoperable, under effective international guarantees. The continuation of this threat, or a prolonging of this discussion concerning Cuba by linking these problems to the broader questions of European and world security, would surely lead to an intensification of the Cuban crisis and a grave risk to the peace of the world. For this reason I hope we can quickly agree along the lines outlined in this letter and in your letter of October 26th.

John F. Kennedy

Khrushchev's October 28 Message

Dear Mr. President: I have received your message of 27 October. I express my satisfaction and thank you for the sense of proportion you have displayed and for realization of the responsibility which now devolves on you for the preservation of the peace of the world. . . .

In order to eliminate as rapidly as possible the conflict which endangers the cause of peace, to give an assurance to all people who crave peace, and to reassure the American people, who, I am certain, also want peace, as do the people of the Soviet Union, the Soviet Government, in addition to earlier instructions on the discontinuation of further work on weapons construction sites, has given a new order to dismantle the arms which you described as offensive, and to crate and return them to the Soviet Union.

Mr. President, I should like to repeat what I had already written to you in my earlier messages—that the Soviet Government has given economic assistance to the Republic of Cuba, as well as arms, because Cuba and the Cuban people were constantly under the continuous threat of an invasion of Cuba. . . .

The Cuban people want to build their life in their own interests without external interference. This is their right, and they cannot be blamed for wanting to be masters of their own country and disposing of the fruits of their own labor. The threat of invasion of Cuba and all other schemes for creating tension over China are designed to strike the Cuban people with a sense of insecurity, intimidate them, and prevent them from peacefully building their new life.

Mr. President, I should like to say clearly once more that we could not remain indifferent to this. The Soviet Government decided to render assistance to Cuba with means of defense against aggression—only with means for defense purposes. We have supplied the defense means which you describe as offensive means. We have supplied them to prevent an attack on Cuba—to prevent rash acts.

I regard with respect and trust the statement you made in your message of 27 October 1962 that there would be no attack, no invasion of Cuba, and not only on the part of the United States, but also on the part of other nations of the Western Hemisphere, as you said in your same message. Then the motives which induced us to render assistance of such a kind to Cuba disappear.

It is for this reason that we instructed our officers—these means as I had already informed you earlier are in the hands of the Soviet officers—to take appropriate measures to discontinue construction of the aforementioned facilities, to dismantle them, and to return them to the Soviet Union. As I had informed you in the letter of 27 October, we are prepared to reach agreement to enable U.N. representatives to verify the dismantling of these means. Thus in view of the assurances you have given and our instructions on dismantling, there is every condition for eliminating the present conflict. . . .

In conclusion, I should like to say something about a detente between NATO and the Warsaw Treaty countries that you have mentioned. We have spoken about this long since and are prepared to continue to exchange views on this question with you and to find a reasonable solution.

We should like to continue the exchange of views on the prohibition of atomic and thermonuclear weapons, general disarmament, and other problems relating to the relaxation of international tension. . . .

We are confident that the people of all countries, like you, Mr. President, will understand me correctly. We are not threatening. We want nothing but peace. Our country is now on the upsurge. Our people are enjoying the fruits of their peaceful labor. They have achieved tremendous successes since the October Revolution, and created the greatest material, spiritual, and cultural values. Our people are enjoying these values; they want to continue developing their achievements and insure their further development on the way of peace and social progress by their persistent labor.

I should like to remind you, Mr. President, that military reconnaissance planes have violated the borders of the Soviet Union. . . .

[O]n 28 October, . . . one of your reconnaissance planes intruded over Soviet borders in the Chukotka Peninsula area in the north and flew over our territory. The question is, Mr. President: How should we regard this? What is this, a provocation? One of your planes violates our frontier during this anxious time we are both experiencing, when everything has been put into combat readiness. Is it not a fact that an intruding American plane could be easily taken for a nuclear bomber, which might push us to a fateful step; and all the more so since the U.S. Government and Pentagon long ago declared that you are maintaining a continuous nuclear bomber patrol?

Therefore, you can imagine the responsibility you are assuming; especially now, when we are living through such anxious times.

I should also like to express the following wish; it concerns the Cuban people. You do not have diplomatic relations. But through my officers in Cuba, I have reports that American planes are making flights over Cuba.

We are interested that there should be no war in the world, and that the Cuban people should live in peace. And besides, Mr. President, it is no secret that we have our people on Cuba. Under a treaty with the Cuban Government we have sent there officers, instructors, mostly plain people: specialists, agronomists, zoo technicians, irrigators, land reclamation specialists, plain workers, tractor drivers, and others. We are concerned about them.

I should like you to consider, Mr. President, that violation of Cuban airspace by American planes could also lead to dangerous consequences. And if you do not want this to happen, it would be better if no cause is given for a dangerous situation to arise. We must be careful now and refrain from any steps which would not be useful to the defense of the states involved in the conflict, which could only cause irritation and even serve as a provocation for a fateful step. Therefore, we must display sanity, reason, and refrain from such steps.

We value peace perhaps even more than other peoples because we went through a terrible war with Hitler. But our people will not falter in the face of any test. Our people trust their government, and we assure our people and world public opinion that the Soviet Government will not allow itself to be provoked. But if the provocateurs unleash a war, they will not evade responsibility and the grave consequences a war would bring upon them. But we are confident that reason will triumph, that war will not be unleashed, and peace and the security of the peoples will be insured. . . .

N. Khrushchev
28 October 1962

Kennedy's October 28 Reply

. . . I consider my letter to you of October twenty-seventh and your reply of today as firm undertakings on the part of both our governments which should be promptly carried out. I hope that the necessary measures can at once be taken through the United Nations, as your message says, so that the United States in turn will be able to remove the quarantine measures now in effect. I have already made arrangements to report all these matters to the Organization of American States, whose members share a deep interest in a genuine peace in the Caribbean area.

You referred in your letter to a violation of your frontier by an American aircraft in the area of the Chukotskiy Peninsula. I have learned that this plane, without arms or photographic equipment, was engaged in an air sampling mission in connection with your nuclear tests. . . . I regret this incident and will see to it that every precaution is taken to prevent recurrence.

Mr. Chairman, both of our countries have great unfinished tasks and I know that your people as well as those of the United States can ask for nothing better than to pursue them free from the fear of war. Modern science and technology have given us the possibility of making labor fruitful beyond anything that could have been dreamed of a few decades ago.

I agree with you that we must devote urgent attention to the problem of disarmament, as it relates to the whole world and also to critical areas. Perhaps now, as we step back from danger, we can together make real progress in this vital field. I think we should give priority to questions relating to the proliferation of nuclear weapons, on earth and in outer space, and to the great effort for a nuclear test ban. But we should also work hard to see if wider measures of disarmament can be agreed and put into operation at an early date. The United States Government will be prepared to discuss these questions urgently, and in a constructive spirit, at Geneva or elsewhere.

John F. Kennedy

Chinese Rejection of Invitation to Moscow

Following are excerpts from a March 23, 1966, letter sent to Moscow by the Chinese declining an invitation to attend the Twenty-third Party Congress. The Chinese rejection was a formal acknowledgment of the serious rift that had developed between the two former allies.

In normal circumstances it would be considered an indication of friendship for one party to invite another fraternal party to send a delegation to its Congress. But around the time you sent this invitation, you distributed an anti-Chinese document in the Soviet Union, both inside and outside the party, and organized a whole series of anti-Chinese reports from top to bottom, right down to the basic units, whipping up hysteria against China.

Moreover, you sent an anti-Chinese letter to other parties, instigating them to join you in opposing China. You wantonly vilified the Communist Chinese party as being "bellicose" and "pseudo-revolutionary," as "refusing to oppose imperialism" and "encouraging United States imperialist aggression," and as being guilty of "adventurism," "splitism," "Trotskyism," "nationalism," "great power chauvinism," "dogmatism," and so on and so forth.

You have also been spreading rumors alleging that China "is obstructing aid to Vietnam" and that "China has been encroaching on Soviet territory." You have gone so far as to state that "China is not a Socialist country.". . . In these circumstances, how can the Chinese Communist party, which you look upon as an enemy, be expected to attend your Congress?

The Chinese Communist party has attended many of the Congresses of the CPSU. Also, we sent delegations to your 20th, 21st and 22nd Congresses, after the Khrushchev revisionist group usurped the leadership of the CPSU. But at the 20th Congress of the CPSU you suddenly lashed out at Stalin. Stalin was a great Marxist-Leninist.

In attacking Stalin, you were attacking Marxism-Leninism, the Soviet Union, Communist parties, China, the people and all the Marxist-Leninists of the world. At the 22nd Party Congress you adopted an out-and-out revisionist program, made a wild public attack on Albania and reproached the Chinese Communist party, so that the head of our delegation had to leave for home while the Congress was only half way through. . . .

Over the last years, we have made a series of efforts in the hope that you would return to the path of Marxism-Leninism. Since Khrushchev's downfall, we have advised the new leaders of the CPSU on a number of occasions to make a fresh start. We have done everything we could, but you have not shown the slightest repentance.

Since coming to power, the new leaders of the CPSU have gone farther and farther down the road of revisionism, splitism and great power chauvinism. . . .

Despite the tricks you have been playing to deceive people, you are pursuing United States-Soviet collaboration for the domination of the world with your heart and soul. In mouthing a few words against United States imperialism and making a show of supporting anti-imperialist struggles, you are conducting only minor attacks on United States imperialism while rendering it major help.

. . . Your clamor for "united action," especially on the Vietnam question, is nothing but a trap for the purpose of deceiving the Soviet people and the revolutionary people of the world. You have all along been acting in coordination with the United States in its plot for peace talks, vainly attempting to sell out the struggle of the Vietnamese people against United States aggression and for national salvation and to drag the Vietnam question into the orbit of Soviet-United States collaboration.

You have worked hand in glove with the United States in a whole series of dirty deals inside and outside the United Nations. In close coordination with the counterrevolutionary "global strategy" of United States imperialism, you are now actively trying to build a ring of encirclement around socialist China. Not only have you excluded yourself from the international united front of all peoples against United States imperialism and its lackeys, you have even aligned yourselves with United States imperialism, the main enemy of the people of the world, and established a holy alliance against China, against the movement and against the Marxist-Leninists. . . .

We are confident that in all parts of the world, including the Soviet Union, the masses of the people, who constitute more than 90 percent of the population, are for revolution and against imperialism and its lackeys. In the ranks of the international Communist movement, including the Communist party of the Soviet Union, more than 90 percent of the Communists and cadres will eventually march along the path of Marxism-Leninism.

. . . The Soviet people may rest assured that once the Soviet Union meets with imperialist aggression and puts up resolute resistance, China will definitely stand side by side with the Soviet Union and fight against the common enemy.

With fraternal greetings.

Brezhnev Doctrine of Limited Sovereignty

Following are excerpts from Soviet leader Leonid I. Brezhnev's November 13, 1968, speech to the Fifth Congress of the Polish United Workers' Party and his October 28, 1969, address to visiting Czech officials.

Speech to Poles

. . . The experience of struggle and realistic stocktaking of the situation obtaining in the world with utmost clarity shows that it is vitally necessary for the Communists of the socialist countries to carry high the banner of socialist internationalism, constantly to strengthen the cohesion and solidarity of the countries of socialism. Therein lies one of the main conditions for the successful construction of socialism and communism in each of our countries and the successful struggle of the world system of socialism against imperialism.

The interests of the defence of each socialist country, the interests of its economic, scientific and cultural advance, all this calls for broadest cooperation between the fraternal countries, the all-round development of various contacts between them, genuine internationalism. . . .

The socialist states stand for strict respect for the sovereignty of all countries. We emphatically oppose interference into the affairs of any states, violations of their sovereignty.

At the same time the establishment and defence of the sovereignty of states which have embarked upon the road of building socialism is of particular significance for us, Communists. The forces of imperialism and reaction seek to deprive the people now of . . . their sovereign right . . . to ensure the prosperity of their country, the well-being and happiness of the broad mass of the working people through building a society free from any oppression and exploitation. . . .

It is common knowledge that the Soviet Union has done much for the real strengthening of the sovereignty and independence of the socialist countries. The CPSU [Communist Party of the Soviet Union] has always advocated that each socialist country determine the specific forms of its development along the road of socialism with consideration of its specific national conditions. However, it is known, Comrades, that there are also common laws governing socialist construction, a deviation from which might lead to a deviation from socialism as such.

And when the internal and external forces hostile to socialism seek to revert the development of any socialist country towards the restoration of the capitalist order, when a threat to the cause of socialism in that country, a threat to the security of the socialist community as a whole emerges, this is no longer only a problem of the people of that country but also a common problem, concern of all socialist countries.

It goes without saying that such an action as military aid to a fraternal country to cut short the threat to the socialist order is an extraordinary, enforced step, it can be sparked off only by direct actions of the enemies of socialism inside the country and beyond its boundaries, actions creating a threat to the common interests of the camp of socialism. . . .

Let all those who are inclined to forget the lessons of history and who would like to engage again in recarving the map of Europe know that the frontiers of Poland, the German Democratic Republic, Czechoslovakia, just as any other member-country of the Warsaw Treaty, are immutable and inviolable. These frontiers are defended by the entire armed might of the socialist community. We advise all who like to encroach upon other peoples' frontiers to remember this well! . . .

Speech to Czechs

. . . Comrades! For almost a year and a half now, the thoughts and feelings of Soviet Communists and all Soviet people, as well as those of people in other socialist countries, have been focused on the events in Czechoslovakia. We had to experience a great deal in this period—anxiety for the destiny of socialism in a fraternal country subjected to the onslaught of the joint forces of internal and external reaction, sentiments of combat solidarity with the principled and staunch Marxists-Leninists in the Communist Party of Czechoslovakia who courageously rose to struggle for the cause of socialism and, last but not least, pride in the successes scored by Czechoslovakia's Communists in this hard struggle. . . .

Hardly can anyone deny now that the forces of socialism have stood this test—test by practice, test by struggle—with honor. The principled stand of Communists, the unity of socialist countries and their international solidarity proved to be stronger than those who wanted to reverse the history of Czechoslovak society and to wrest state power from the hands of the working class, and from the hands of working people. . . .

The CPSU [Communist Party of the Soviet Union] and our entire people had faith that this would be so. We, the allies of Czechoslovakia, did our internationalist duty. . . .

[T]he struggle against the anti-socialist, counter-revolutionary forces in Czechoslovakia raised in all sharpness the question of international responsibility of the Communists for the fate of socialism. There can be only one reply to the attempts of external and internal reaction to weaken the positions of socialism, to impair the socialist community, and that reply is still greater cohesion of the fraternal countries on the basis of socialist internationalism, and mutual support in the struggle against the intrigues of imperialism and for the consolidation of the socialist system.

Our common stand on this issue is clearly expressed in the well-known Bratislava Statement of the fraternal Parties of six socialist countries [issued after an August 3, 1968, meeting of Eastern-bloc nations]. It says there, that the support, strengthening and defence of the gains of socialism "are the common international duty of all the socialist countries." And the summing-up document of the recent International Conference of Communist Parties says: "The defence of socialism is the international duty of the Communists." Our invincible strength lies in the close solidarity of the fraternal socialist countries, in the unity of the national detachments of Communists. . . .

Nixon-Brezhnev 1972 Summit Statements

Following are the texts of the declaration of basic principles of relations between the United States and the Soviet Union signed May 29, 1972, by President Richard Nixon and Communist party leader Leonid I. Brezhnev and a joint communiqué issued by Nixon and Soviet leaders on May 29. The Moscow summit, which produced the documents, was the result of efforts by the Nixon administration and the Kremlin to establish a détente between the superpowers. Earlier in the summit Nixon and Brezhnev had signed the SALT I Treaty, providing for limits on the strategic nuclear arsenals of both countries.

Declaration of Principles

The United States of America and the Union of Soviet Socialist Republics,

Guided by their obligations under the Charter of the United Nations and by a desire to strengthen peaceful relations with each other and to place these relations on the firmest possible basis,

Aware of the need to make every effort to remove the threat of war and to create conditions which promote the reduction of tensions in the world and the strengthening of universal security and international cooperation,

Believing that the improvement of US-Soviet relations and their mutually advantageous development in such areas as economics, science and culture, will meet these objectives and contribute to better mutual understanding and business-like cooperation, without in any way prejudicing the interests of third countries.

Conscious that these objectives reflect the interests of the peoples of both countries.

Have agreed as follows:

First. They will proceed from the common determination that in the nuclear age there is no alternative to conducting their mutual relations on the basis of peaceful coexistence. Differences in ideology and in the social systems of the USA and the USSR are not obstacles to the bilateral development of normal relations based on the principles of sovereignty, equality, non-interference in internal affairs and mutual advantage.

Second. The USA and the USSR attach major importance to preventing the development of situations capable of causing a dangerous exacerbation of their relations. Therefore, they will do their utmost to avoid military confrontations and to prevent the outbreak of nuclear war. They will always exercise restraint in their mutual relations, and will be prepared to negotiate and settle differences by peaceful means. Discussions and negotiations on outstanding issues will be conducted in a spirit of reciprocity, mutual accommodations and mutual benefit.

Both sides recognize that efforts to obtain unilateral advantage at the expense of the other, directly or indirectly, are inconsistent with these objectives. The prerequisites for maintaining and strengthening peaceful relations between the USA and the USSR are the recognition of the security interests of the Parties based on the principle of equality and the renunciation of the use or threat of force.

Third. The USA and the USSR have a special responsibility, as do other countries which are permanent members of the United Nations Security Council, to do everything in their power so that conflicts or situations will not arise which would serve to increase international tensions. Accordingly, they will seek to promote conditions in which all countries will live in peace and security and will not be subject to outside interference in their internal affairs.

Fourth. The USA and the USSR intend to widen the juridical basis of their mutual relations and to exert the necessary efforts so that bilateral agreements which they have concluded and multilateral treaties and agreements to which they are jointly parties are faithfully implemented.

Fifth. The USA and the USSR reaffirm their readiness to continue the practice of exchanging views on problems of mutual interest and, when necessary, to conduct such exchanges at the highest level, including meetings between leaders of the two countries.

The two governments welcome and will facilitate an increase in productive contacts between representatives of the legislative bodies of the two countries.

Sixth. The Parties will continue their efforts to limit armaments on a bilateral as well as on a multilateral basis. They will continue to make special efforts to limit strategic armaments. Whenever possible, they will conclude concrete agreements aimed at achieving these purposes.

The USA and the USSR regard as the ultimate objective of their efforts the achievement of general and complete disarmament and the establishment of an effective system of international security in accordance with the purposes and principles of the United Nations.

Seventh. The USA and the USSR regard commercial and economic ties as an important and necessary element

in the strengthening of their bilateral relations and thus will actively promote the growth of such ties. They will facilitate cooperation between the relevant organizations and enterprises of the two countries and the conclusion of appropriate agreements and contracts, including long-term ones.

The two countries will contribute to the improvement of maritime and air communications between them.

Eighth. The two sides consider it timely and useful to develop mutual contacts and cooperation in the fields of science and technology. Where suitable, the USA and the USSR will conclude appropriate agreements dealing with concrete cooperation in these fields.

Ninth. The two sides reaffirm their intention to deepen cultural ties with one another and to encourage fuller familiarization with each other's cultural values. They will promote improved conditions for cultural exchanges and tourism.

Tenth. The USA and the USSR will seek to ensure that their ties and cooperation in all the above-mentioned fields and in any others in their mutual interest are built on a firm and long-term basis. To give a permanent character to these efforts, they will establish in all fields where this is feasible joint commissions or other joint bodies.

Eleventh. The USA and the USSR make no claim for themselves and would not recognize the claims of anyone else to any special rights or advantages in world affairs. They recognize the sovereign equality of all states.

The development of US-Soviet relations is not directed against third countries and their interests.

Twelfth. The basic principles set forth in this document do not affect any obligations with respect to other countries earlier assumed by the USA and the USSR.

Moscow, May 29, 1972

For the United States of America	For the Union of Soviet Socialist Republics
Richard Nixon President of the United States of America	Leonid I. Brezhnev General Secretary of the Central Committee, CPSU

USA-USSR Joint Communiqué

By mutual agreement between the United States of America and the Union of Soviet Socialist Republics, the President of the United States and Mrs. Richard Nixon paid an official visit to the Soviet Union from May 22 to May 30, 1972. The President was accompanied by Secretary of State William P. Rogers, assistant to the President Dr. H. A. Kissinger, and other American officials. During his stay in the U.S.S.R. President Nixon visited, in addition to Moscow, the cities of Leningrad and Kiev.

President Nixon and L. I. Brezhnev, general secretary of the Central Committee of the Communist Party of the

Soviet Union, N. Podgorny, chairman of the Supreme Soviet of the U.S.S.R., and A. N. Kosygin, chairman of the Council of Ministers of the U.S.S.R., conducted talks on fundamental problems of American-Soviet relations and the current international situation.

Also taking part in the conversations were:

On the American side: William P. Rogers, secretary of state, Jacob D. Beam, American ambassador to the U.S.S.R., Dr. Henry A. Kissinger, assistant to the President for national security affairs, Peter M. Flanigan, assistant to the President, and Martin J. Hillenbrand, assistant secretary of state for European affairs.

On the Soviet side: A. A. Gromyko, minister of foreign affairs of the U.S.S.R., N. S. Patolichev, minister of foreign trade, V. V. Kuznetsov, deputy minister of foreign affairs of the U.S.S.R., A. F. Dobrynin, Soviet ambassador to the U.S.A., A. M. Aleksandrov, assistant to the general secretary of the Central Committee, C.P.S.U., G. M. Korniyenko, member of the collegium of the Ministry of Foreign Affairs of the U.S.S.R.

The discussions covered a wide range of questions of mutual interest and were frank and thorough. They defined more precisely those areas where there are prospects for developing greater cooperation between the two countries, as well as those areas where the positions of the two sides are different.

I. Bilateral Relations

Guided by the desire to place U.S.-Soviet relations on a more stable and constructive foundation, and mindful of their responsibilities for maintaining world peace and for facilitating the relaxation of international tension, the two sides adopted a document entitled: "Basic Principles of Mutual Relations Between the United States of America and the Union of Soviet Socialist Republics," signed on behalf of the U.S. by President Nixon and on behalf of the U.S.S.R. by General Secretary Brezhnev.

Both sides are convinced that the provisions of that document open new possibilities for the development of peaceful relations and mutually beneficial cooperation between the U.S.A. and the U.S.S.R.

Having considered various areas of bilateral U.S.-Soviet relations, the two sides agreed that an improvement of relations is possible and desirable. They expressed their firm intention to act in accordance with the provisions set forth in the above-mentioned document.

As a result of progress made in negotiations which preceded the summit meeting, and in the course of the meeting itself, a number of significant agreements were reached. This will intensify bilateral cooperation in areas of common concern as well as in areas relevant to the cause of peace and international cooperation.

Limitation of Strategic Armaments. The two sides gave primary attention to the problem of reducing the danger of nuclear war. They believe that curbing the competition in strategic arms will make a significant and tangible contribution to this cause.

The two sides attach great importance to the treaty on the limitation of anti-ballistic missile systems and the interim agreement on certain measures with respect to the limitation of strategic offensive arms concluded between them.

These agreements, which were concluded as a result of the negotiations in Moscow, constitute a major step towards curbing and ultimately ending the arms race.

They are a concrete expression of the intention of the two sides to contribute to the relaxation of international tension and the strengthening of confidence between states as well as to carry out the obligations assumed by them in the Treaty on the Nonproliferation of Nuclear Weapons Article VI. Both sides are convinced that the achievement of the above agreements is a practical step toward saving mankind from the threat of the outbreak of nuclear war. Accordingly, it corresponds to the vital interests of the American and Soviet peoples as well as to the vital interests of all other peoples.

The two sides intend to continue active negotiations for the limitation of strategic offensive arms and to conduct them in a spirit of good will, respect for each other's legitimate interests and observance of the principle of equal security.

Both sides are also convinced that the agreement on measures to reduce the risk of outbreak of nuclear war between the U.S.A. and the U.S.S.R. signed in Washington Sept. 30, 1971, serves the interest not only of the Soviet and American peoples, but of all mankind.

Commercial and Economic Relations. Both sides agreed on measures designed to establish more favorable conditions for developing commercial and other economic ties between the U.S.A. and the U.S.S.R. They agree that realistic conditions exist for increasing economic ties. These ties should develop on the basis of mutual benefit and in accordance with generally accepted international practice.

Believing that these aims would be served by conclusion of a trade agreement between the U.S.A. and the U.S.S.R., the two sides decided to complete in the near future the work necessary to conclude such an agreement. They agreed on the desirability of credit arrangements to develop mutual trade and of early efforts to resolve other financial and economic issues. It was agreed that a lend-lease settlement will be negotiated concurrently with a trade agreement.

In the interests of broadening and facilitating commercial ties between the two countries, and to work out specific arrangements, the two sides decided to create a U.S.-Soviet joint commercial commission. Its first meeting will be held in Moscow in the summer of 1972.

Each side will promote the establishment of effective working arrangements between organizations and firms of both countries and encouraging the conclusion of long-term contracts.

Maritime Matters, Incidents at Sea.   The two sides agreed to continue the negotiations aimed at reaching an agreement on maritime and related matters. They believe that such an agreement would mark a positive step in facilitating the expansion of commerce between the United States and the Soviet Union.

An agreement was concluded between the two sides on measures to prevent incidents at sea and in air space over it between vessels and aircraft of the U.S. and Soviet navies. By providing agreed procedures for ships and aircraft of the two navies operating in close proximity, this agreement will diminish the chances of dangerous accidents.

Cooperation in Science and Technology.   It was recognized that the cooperation now under way in areas such as atomic energy research, space research, health and other fields benefits both nations and has contributed positively to their over-all relations. It was agreed that increased scientific and technical cooperation on the basis of mutual benefit and shared effort for common goals is in the interest of both nations and would contribute to a further improvement in their bilateral relations. For these purposes the two sides signed an agreement for cooperation in the fields of science and technology. A U.S.-Soviet joint commission on scientific and technical cooperation will be created for identifying and establishing cooperative programs.

Cooperation in Space.   Having in mind the role played by the U.S. and the U.S.S.R. in the peaceful exploration of outer space, both sides emphasized the importance of further bilateral cooperation in this sphere. In order to increase the safety of man's flights in outer space and the future prospects of joint scientific experiments, the two sides agreed to make suitable arrangements to permit the docking of American and Soviet spacecraft and stations. The first joint docking experiment of the two countries' piloted spacecraft, with visits by astronauts and cosmonauts to each other's spacecraft, is contemplated for 1975. The planning and implementation of this flight will be carried out by the U.S. National Aeronautics and Space Administration and the U.S.S.R. Academy of Sciences, according to principles and procedures developed through mutual consultations.

Cooperation in the Field of Health.   The two sides concluded an agreement on health cooperation which marks a fruitful beginning of sharing knowledge about,

and collaborative attacks on, the common enemies, disease and disability. The initial research efforts of the program will concentrate on health problems important to the whole world—cancer, heart diseases, and the environmental health sciences.

This cooperation subsequently will be broadened to include other health problems of mutual interest. The two sides pledged their full support for the health cooperation program and agreed to continue the active participation of the two governments in the work of international organizations in the health field.

Environmental Cooperation.   The two sides agreed to initiate a program of cooperation in the protection and enhancement of man's environment. Through joint research and joint measures, the United States and the U.S.S.R. hope to contribute to the preservation of a healthful environment in their countries and throughout the world. Under the new agreement on environmental cooperation there will be consultations in the near future in Moscow on specific cooperative projects.

Exchanges in the Fields of Science, Technology, Education, and Culture.   Both sides note the importance of the agreement on exchanges and cooperation in scientific, technical, educational, cultural, and other fields in 1972-1973, signed in Moscow on April 11, 1972. Continuation and expansion of bilateral exchanges in these fields will lead to better understanding and help improve the general state of relations between the two countries. Within the broad framework provided by this agreement the two sides have agreed to expand the areas of cooperation, as reflected in new agreements concerning space, health, the environment and science and technology.

The U.S. side, noting the existence of an extensive program of English-language instruction in the Soviet Union, indicated its intention to encourage Russian-language programs in the United States.

II. International Issues

Europe.   In the course of the discussions on the international situation, both sides took note of favorable developments in the relaxation of tensions in Europe.

Recognizing the importance to world peace of developments in Europe, where both world wars originated, and mindful of the responsibilities and commitments which they share with other powers under appropriate agreements, the U.S.A. and the U.S.S.R. intend to make further efforts to ensure a peaceful future for Europe, free of tensions, crises and conflicts.

They agree that the territorial integrity of all states in Europe should be respected.

Both sides view the Sept. 3, 1971, quadripartite agreement relating to the western sectors of Berlin as a good example of fruitful cooperation between the states concerned, including the U.S.A. and the U.S.S.R. The two sides believe that the implementation of that agreement in the near future, along with other steps, will further improve the European situation and contribute to the necessary trust among states.

Both sides welcomed the treaty between the U.S.S.R. and the Federal Republic of Germany signed on Aug. 12, 1970. They noted the significance of the provisions of this treaty as well as of other recent agreements in contributing to confidence and cooperation among the European states.

The U.S.A. and the U.S.S.R. are prepared to make appropriate contributions to the positive trends on the European continent toward a genuine detente and the development of relations of peaceful cooperation among states in Europe on the basis of the principles of territorial integrity and inviolability of frontiers, non-interference in internal affairs, sovereign equality in independence and renunciation of the use or threat of force.

The U.S. and U.S.S.R. are in accord that multilateral consultations looking toward a conference on security and cooperation in Europe could begin after the signature of the final quadripartite protocol of the agreement of Sept. 3, 1971. The two governments agree that the conference should be carefully prepared in order that it may concretely consider specific problems of security and cooperation and thus contribute to the progressive reduction of the underlying causes of tension in Europe. This conference should be convened at a time to be agreed by the countries concerned, but without undue delay.

Both sides believe that the goal of ensuring stability and security in Europe would be served by a reciprocal reduction of armed forces and armaments, first of all in central Europe. Any agreement on this question should not diminish the security of any of the sides. Appropriate agreement should be reached as soon as practicable between the states concerned on the procedures for negotiations on this subject in a special forum.

The Middle East. The two sides set out their positions on this question. They reaffirm their support for a peaceful settlement in the Middle East in accordance with Security Council Resolution 242.

Noting the significance of constructive cooperation of the parties concerned with the special representative of the U.N. secretary general, Ambassador Jarring, the U.S. and the U.S.S.R. confirm their desire to contribute to his mission's success and also declare their readiness to play their part in bringing about a peaceful settlement in the Middle East. In the view of the U.S. and the U.S.S.R., the achievement of such a settlement would open prospects for the normalization of the Middle East situation and would permit, in particular, consideration of further

steps to bring about a military relaxation in that area.

Indochina. Each side set forth its respective standpoint with regard to the continuing war in Vietnam and the situation in the area of Indochina as a whole.

The U.S. side emphasized the need to bring an end to the military conflict as soon as possible and reaffirmed its commitment to the principle that the political future of South Vietnam should be left for the South Vietnamese people to decide for themselves, free from outside interference.

The U.S. side explained its view that the quickest and most effective way to attain the above-mentioned objectives is through negotiations leading to the return of all Americans held captive in the region, the implementation of an internationally supervised, Indochina-wide cease-fire and the subsequent withdrawal of all American forces stationed in South Vietnam within four months, leaving the political questions to be resolved by the Indochinese peoples themselves.

The United States reiterated its willingness to enter into serious negotiations with the North Vietnamese side to settle the war in Indochina on a basis just to all.

The Soviet side stressed its solidarity with the just struggle of the peoples of Vietnam, Laos and Cambodia for their freedom, independence and social progress. Firmly supporting the proposals of the DRV (North Vietnam) and the Provisional Revolutionary Government of the Republic of South Vietnam, which provide a realistic and constructive basis for settling the Vietnam problem, the Soviet Union stands for a cessation of bombings of the DRV, for a complete and unequivocal withdrawal of the troops of the U.S.A. and its allies from South Vietnam, so that the people of Indochina would have the possibility to determine for themselves their fate without any outside interference.

Disarmament Issues. The two sides note that in recent years their joint and parallel actions have facilitated the working out and conclusion of treaties which curb the arms race or ban some of the most dangerous types of weapons. They note further that these treaties were welcomed by a large majority of the states in the world, which became parties to them.

Both sides regard the convention on the prohibition of the development, production and stockpiling of bacteriological, biological and toxic weapons and on their destruction, as an essential disarmament measure. Along with Great Britain, they are the depositories for the convention which was recently opened for signature by all states. The U.S.A. and U.S.S.R. will continue their efforts to reach an international agreement regarding chemical weapons.

The U.S.A. and the U.S.S.R., proceeding from the need to take into account the security interests of both countries on the basis of the principle of equality, and without prejudice to the security interests of third countries, will actively participate in negotiations aimed at working out new measures designed to curb and end the arms race. The ultimate purpose is general and complete disarmament, including nuclear disarmament, under strict international control. A world disarmament conference could play a role in this process at an appropriate time.

Strengthening the United Nations. Both sides will strive to strengthen the effectiveness of the United Nations on the basis of strict observance of the U.N. charter.

They regard the United Nations as an instrument for maintaining world peace and security, discouraging conflicts, and developing international cooperation. Accordingly, they will do their best to support United Nations efforts in the interests of international peace.

Both sides emphasized that agreements and understandings reached in the negotiations in Moscow, as well as the contents and nature of these negotiations, are not in any way directed against any other country. Both sides proceed from the recognition of the role, the responsibility and the prerogatives of other interested states, existing international obligations and agreements, and the principles and purposes of the U.N. charter.

Both sides believe that positive results were accomplished in the course of the talks at the highest level. These results indicate that despite the differences between the U.S.A. and the U.S.S.R. in social systems, ideologies, and policy principles, it is possible to develop mutually advantageous cooperation between the peoples of both countries, in the interests of strengthening peace and international security.

Both sides expressed the desire to continue close contact on a number of issues that were under discussion. They agreed that regular consultations on questions of mutual interest, including meetings at the highest level, would be useful.

In expressing his appreciation for the hospitality accorded him in the Soviet Union, President Nixon invited General Secretary L. I. Brezhnev, Chairman N. V. Podgorny and Chairman A. N. Kosygin to visit the United States at a mutually convenient time. This invitation was accepted.

1977 Soviet Constitution

Following are excerpts from the constitution ratified by the Supreme Soviet on October 7, 1977.

Constitution of the Soviet Union

The Soviet people, guided by the ideas of scientific communism and remaining true to their revolutionary traditions, resting on the great social, economic and political achievements of socialism, striving to further develop socialist democracy, taking into account the international position of the USSR as part of the world socialist system and conscious of their international responsibility, preserving the continuity of the ideas and principles of the 1918 Constitution of the RSFSR, the 1924 Constitution of the USSR and the 1936 Constitution of the USSR, proclaim the aims and principles, define the foundations of the organization of the socialist state of the whole people, and formalize them in this Constitution. . . .

The Political System.   Article 1. The Union of Soviet Socialist Republics is a socialist state of the whole people, expressing the will and interests of the working class, the peasantry and the intelligentsia, of all the nations and nationalities in the country.

Article 2. All power in the USSR shall be vested in the people.

The people shall exercise state power through the Soviets of People's Deputies, which constitute the political foundation of the USSR.

All other organs of state shall be under the control of and accountable to the Soviets.

Article 3. The Soviet state shall be organized and shall function in accordance with the principle of democratic centralism: electivity of all organs of state power from top to bottom, their accountability to the people, and mandatory fulfillment of the decisions of higher organs by lower organs. Democratic centralism shall combine single leadership with local initiative and creative activity, with the responsibility of each state organ and each official for the work at hand.

Article 4. The Soviet state, in all its organs, shall function on the basis of socialist legality and ensure the protection of law and order, the interests of society and the rights of citizens. State institutions, public organizations and officials shall observe the Constitution of the USSR and Soviet laws. . . .

Article 6. The Communist Party of the Soviet Union is the leading and guiding force of Soviet society and the nucleus of its political system, of all state and public organizations. The CPSU exists for the people and serves the people.

Armed with the Marxist-Leninist (body of) teaching, the Communist Party shall determine the general perspective of society's development and the guidelines for the internal and external policy of the USSR, give guidance to the great creative endeavor of the Soviet people, and place their struggle for the triumph of communism on a planned, scientific basis. . . .

The Economic System.   Article 9. Socialist ownership of the means of production shall be the foundation of the economic system of the USSR. Socialist ownership shall comprise: state property (belonging to the whole people), property of collective farms and other cooperative organizations (collective farm-cooperative property), and property of trade unions and other public organizations.

The state shall protect socialist property and create the conditions for augmenting it.

No one shall have the right to use socialist property for personal gain.

Article 10. State property, i.e., property belonging to the whole people, shall be the principal form of socialist ownership.

The land, its minerals, waters and forests shall be the exclusive property of the state. The state shall be in possession of the basic means of production: industrial, building and agricultural enterprises, means of transport and communication, and also the banks, distributive enterprises and community services and the bulk of urban housing....

Article 13. The free labor of Soviet people shall be the basis of the growth of social wealth and the welfare of the people, of every Soviet citizen.

The state shall control the measure of labor and consumption in accordance with the principle: "From each according to his ability, to each according to his work." It shall determine the rates of the income tax and establish the level of wages exempted from taxes.

Socially useful work and its results shall determine a citizen's status in society. By combining material and moral incentives the state shall help turn labor into the prime need in the life of every Soviet citizen....

Article 15. The economy of the USSR shall be an integral economic complex embracing all the elements of social production, distribution and exchange on the territory of the USSR.

The economy shall be managed on the basis of state plans for economic, social and cultural development with due account taken of the branch and territorial principles, and combining centralized leadership with the economic independence and initiative of enterprises, associations and other organizations. Here active use shall be made of cost accounting, profit and production costs....

Social Development and Culture. Article 19. The Soviet state shall create the conditions for enhancing society's social homogeneity, erasing the essential distinctions between town and countryside and between mental and manual labor, and further developing and drawing together all the nations and nationalities of the USSR.

Article 20. In accordance with the communist ideal, "the free development of each is the condition for the free development of all," the Soviet state shall pursue the aim of expanding the actual possibilities for citizens to develop and apply their creative strength, abilities and talents, for the all-around development of the individual....

Foreign Policy. Article 28. The Soviet state shall consistently pursue the Leninist policy of peace and stand for the consolidation of the security of peoples and broad international cooperation.

The foreign policy of the USSR shall be aimed at ensuring favorable international conditions for the building of communism in the USSR, at strengthening the positions of world socialism, supporting the struggle of peoples for national liberation and social progress, preventing wars of aggression, and consistently implementing the principle of peaceful coexistence of states with different social systems.

In the USSR war propaganda shall be prohibited by law.

Article 29. The relations of the USSR with other states shall be based on the observance of the principle of mutual renunciation of the use or threats of force, and of the principles of sovereign equality, inviolability of frontiers, territorial integrity of states, peaceful settlement of disputes, non-interference in internal affairs, respect for human rights and basic freedoms, equality and the right of peoples to decide their own destiny, cooperation between states, scrupulous fulfillment of commitments emanating from universally recognized principles and norms of international law, and the international treaties signed by the USSR.

Article 30. As part of the world socialist system, of the socialist community, the Soviet Union shall promote and strengthen friendship, cooperation and comradely mutual assistance with the other socialist countries on the basis of socialist internationalism, and shall actively participate in economic integration and in the international socialist division of labor....

The State and the Individual. Article 33. Soviet citizenship shall be uniform for the whole Union of Soviet Socialist Republics. Every citizen of a Union Republic shall be a citizen of the USSR.

The grounds and procedure of acquiring or losing Soviet citizenship shall be established by the law of the USSR.

Citizens of the USSR living abroad shall have the protection and guardianship of the Soviet state.

Article 34. Citizens of the USSR shall be equal before the law, irrespective of origin, social and property status, nationality or race, sex, education, language, attitude to religion, type or character of occupation, domicile, or other particulars.

Equality of rights of citizens of the USSR shall be ensured in all fields of economic, political, social, and cultural life.

Article 35. In the USSR women shall have equal rights with men.

Exercise of these rights shall be ensured by according to women equal opportunities (with men) for education and professional training, for employment, remuneration and promotion, for social, political and cultural activity, and likewise by special measures for the protection of the labor and health of women; by legal protection, material and moral support of mother and child, including paid leaves and other benefits to mothers and expectant mothers, and state aid to unmarried mothers.

Article 36. Soviet citizens of different nationalities and races shall have equal rights.

The exercise of these rights shall be ensured by the policy of all-around development and drawing together of all nations and nationalities of the USSR, education of citizens in the spirit of Soviet patriotism and socialist internationalism, and the opportunity for using their mother tongue as well as the languages of the other peoples of the USSR.

Any and all direct or indirect restrictions of the rights of, or the establishment of direct or indirect privileges for, citizens on grounds of race or nationality, and likewise any advocacy of racial or national exclusiveness, hostility or contempt, shall be punishable by law.

Article 37. In the USSR citizens of other countries and stateless persons shall be guaranteed the rights and freedoms provided for by law, including the right of instituting proceedings in law courts and other state organs in protection of personal, proprietary, family and other rights accorded to them by law.

On the territory of the USSR, citizens of other countries and stateless persons shall be obliged to respect the Constitution of the USSR and to observe Soviet laws.

Article 38. The USSR shall afford the right of asylum to foreign nationals persecuted for upholding the interests of the working people and the cause of peace, or for participating in a revolutionary or national liberation movement, or for progressive social, political, scientific or other creative activity.

Rights, Freedoms, and Duties. Article 39. Citizens of the USSR shall enjoy in their entirety the social, economic, political and personal rights and freedoms proclaimed and guaranteed by the Constitution of the USSR and Soviet laws. The socialist system shall ensure extension of rights and freedoms and unintermittent improvement of the conditions of life of citizens relative to the fulfillment of programs of social, economic and cultural development.

Exercise by citizens of rights and freedoms must not injure the interests of society and the state, or the rights of other citizens.

Article 40. Citizens of the USSR shall have the right to work, that is, to guaranteed employment and remuneration for their work in accordance with its quantity and quality, including the right to choice of profession, type of occupation and employment, in accordance with their vocation, abilities, training, education, and with due ac-

count taken of the needs of society....

Article 41. Citizens of the USSR shall have the right to rest and leisure....

Article 42. Citizens of the USSR shall have the right to health protection....

Article 43. Citizens of the USSR shall have the right to maintenance in old age, in the event of sickness, and likewise in the event of complete or partial disability or loss of breadwinner....

Article 44. Citizens of the USSR shall have the right to housing. This right shall be ensured by the development and protection of state and public housing, assistance to co-operative and individual house-building, fair distribution under public control of housing, allotted with reference to the implementation of the housing program, and likewise by low rent.

Article 45. Citizens of the USSR shall have the right to education....

Article 46. Citizens of the USSR shall have the right to make use of the achievements of culture....

Article 47. Citizens of the USSR shall have the right to take part in the administration of state and public affairs....

Article 49. Every citizen of the USSR shall have the right to submit to state organs and public organizations proposals for improving their activity, to criticize shortcomings in their work. Officials shall be bound, within terms established by law, to examine proposals and requests made by citizens, reply to them and take due action.

Persecution for criticism shall be prohibited.

Article 50. In conformity with the interests of the working people and for the purpose of strengthening the socialist system, citizens of the USSR shall be guaranteed freedom of speech, press, assembly, meetings, street processions and demonstrations. Exercise of these political freedoms shall be ensured by putting at the disposal of the working people and their organizations public buildings, streets and squares, by broad dissemination of information, and by the opportunity to use the press, television and radio....

Article 52. Freedom of conscience, that is, the right to profess any religion and perform religious rites, or not to profess any religion and to conduct atheistic propaganda, shall be recognized for all citizens of the USSR. Incitement of hostility and hatred on religious grounds shall be prohibited.

The church in the USSR shall be separated from the state, and the school from the church.

Article 53. The family shall be under the protection of the state.

Marriage shall be entered into with the free consent of the intending spouses; spouses shall be completely equal in their matrimonial relations....

Article 54. Citizens of the USSR shall be guaranteed

inviolability of the person. No person shall be subjected to arrest other than by decision of a court of law, or with the sanction of a prosecutor.

Article 55. Citizens of the USSR shall be guaranteed inviolability of the home. No person shall without lawful grounds enter a home against the will of the persons residing in it.

Article 56. The privacy of citizens, of correspondence, telephone conversations and telegraphic messages shall be protected by law.

Article 57. Respect for the individual and protection of the rights and freedoms of Soviet citizens shall be the duty of all state organs, public organizations and officials....

Article 58. Citizens of the USSR shall have the right to lodge complaints against actions of officials in state organs and public organizations. These complaints shall be examined in the manner and within the terms defined by law....

Citizens of the USSR shall have the right to compensation for damage inflicted by unlawful actions of state institutions and public organizations, and likewise by officials in the performance of their duties, in the manner and within the limits defined by law.

Article 59. Exercise of rights and freedoms shall be inseparable from the performance by citizens of their duties....

Article 62. The citizens of the USSR shall be obliged to safeguard the interests of the Soviet state, to contribute to the strengthening of its might and prestige.

Defense of the socialist motherland shall be the sacred duty of every citizen of the USSR.

High treason shall be the gravest crime against the people....

Article 64. It shall be the duty of every citizen of the USSR to respect the national dignity of other citizens, to strengthen the friendship of the nations and nationalities of the Soviet multinational state....

Article 67. Citizens of the USSR shall be obligated to protect nature, to safeguard its wealth.

Concern for the preservation of historical monuments and other cultural values shall be the duty of citizens of the USSR.

Article 68. It shall be the internationalist duty of citizens of the USSR to further the development of friendship and cooperation with the peoples of other countries and the maintenance and consolidation of world peace....

The USSR—A Federal State. Article 69. The Union of Soviet Socialist Republics is an integral federal multinational state formed on the basis of the free self-determination of nations and the voluntary union of equal Soviet Socialist Republics.

The USSR embodies the state unity of the Soviet people and brings all the nations and nationalities together

for the joint building of communism....

Article 71. Every Union Republic shall retain the right freely to secede from the USSR....

The Soviets of People's Deputies. Article 88. The Soviets of People's Deputies—the Supreme Soviet of the USSR, the Supreme Soviets of the Union Republics, the Supreme Soviets of the Autonomous Republics, the Territorial and Regional Soviets of People's Deputies, the Soviets of People's Deputies of Autonomous Regions and Autonomous Areas, and the city, district, city district, township and village Soviets of People's Deputies—shall comprise an integral system of organs of state power....

Article 101. Deputies shall be authorized representatives of the people in the Soviets of People's Deputies.

By participating in the work of the Soviets, deputies shall resolve matters related to state, economic, social and cultural development, organize the execution of the decisions of the Soviets, and exercise control over the work of state organs, enterprises, institutions and organizations....

Article 103. A deputy shall have the right to address an inquiry to the appropriate state organs and officials, who shall be obliged to reply to the inquiry at a session of the Soviet.

Deputies shall have the right to address an inquiry to any state or public organ, enterprise, institution or organization on questions within their terms of reference as deputies and to take part in considering the questions thus raised. The heads of the respective state or public organs, enterprises, institutions or organizations shall be obliged to receive deputies without delay and consider their recommendations within the period established by law.

Article 104. Deputies shall be assured conditions for the unobstructed and effective exercise of their rights and duties.

The immunity of deputies, as well as other guarantees of their functions as deputies, shall be defined in the Law on the Status of Deputies and other legislation of the USSR and of the Union and Autonomous Republics....

The Supreme Soviet. Article 106. The Supreme Soviet of the USSR shall be the highest organ of state power in the USSR.

The Supreme Soviet of the USSR shall be empowered to deal with all matters placed within the jurisdiction of the Union of Soviet Socialist Republics by the present Constitution.

The adoption of the Constitution of the USSR and amendments to it, the admission of new Republics to the USSR, approval of the formation of new Autonomous Republics and Autonomous Regions, endorsement of state plans of economic, social and cultural development and of the State Budget of the USSR, and of reports on their execution, and the formation of organs of the USSR accountable to it shall be the exclusive competence of the Supreme Soviet of the USSR.

Laws of the USSR shall be enacted solely by the Supreme Soviet of the USSR.

Article 107. The Supreme Soviet of the USSR shall consist of two chambers: the Soviet of the Union and the Soviet of Nationalities.

The two chambers of the Supreme Soviet of the USSR shall have equal rights.

Article 108. The Soviet of the Union and the Soviet of Nationalities shall have an equal number of deputies.

The Soviet of the Union shall be elected by constituencies with equal populations.

The Soviet of Nationalities shall be elected on the basis of the following quotas: 32 deputies from each Union Republic, 11 deputies from each Autonomous Republic, 5 deputies from each Autonomous Region, and one deputy from each Autonomous Area.

Upon representation by the credentials commissions elected by them, the Soviet of the Union and the Soviet of Nationalities shall recognize the credentials of deputies, and in cases where the election law has been violated, declare the election of individual deputies invalid. . . .

Article 111. The right to initiate legislation in the Supreme Soviet of the USSR shall be exercised by the Soviet of the Union and the Soviet of Nationalities, the Presidium of the Supreme Soviet of the USSR, the Council of Ministers of the USSR, the Union Republics represented by their higher organs of state power, the commissions of the Supreme Soviet of the USSR and the Standing commissions of its chambers, deputies of the Supreme Soviet of the USSR, the Supreme Court of the USSR, and the Prosecutor-General of the USSR.

The right to initiate legislation shall be enjoyed also by mass public organizations represented by their all-Union organs. . . .

Article 117. The Supreme Soviet of the USSR at a joint sitting of the two chambers shall elect the Presidium of the Supreme Soviet of the USSR, the continuously functioning organs of the Supreme Soviet of the USSR accountable to it in all its activities.

Article 118. The Presidium of the Supreme Soviet of the USSR shall be elected from among deputies and shall consist of a President, a First Vice President, 15 Vice Presidents, i.e., one from each Union Republic, a Secretary of the Presidium, and 21 members of the Presidium of the Supreme Soviet of the USSR. . . .

The Council of Ministers of the USSR. Article 127. The Council of Ministers of the USSR—the Government of the USSR—shall be the highest executive and administrative organ of state power in the USSR.

Article 128. The Council of Ministers of the USSR shall be formed by the Supreme Soviet of the USSR at a joint sitting of the Soviet of the Union and the Soviet of Nationalities and consist of: the Chairman of the Council of Ministers of the USSR, First Vice-Chairmen and Vice-Chairmen of the Council of Ministers of the USSR, the Ministers of the USSR, the Chairmen of state committees of the USSR.

The Council of Ministers of the USSR shall include, by virtue of their office, the Chairmen of the Councils of Ministers of Union Republics.

Upon submission by the Chairman of the Council of Ministers of the USSR, the Supreme Soviet of the USSR may include in the Government of the USSR leaders of other organs and organizations of the USSR.

Article 129. The Council of Ministers of the USSR shall be responsible and accountable to the Supreme Soviet of the USSR, and between sessions of the Supreme Soviet of the USSR to the Presidium of the Supreme Soviet of the USSR, to which it shall be accountable.

The Council of Ministers of the USSR shall regularly report on its work to the Supreme Soviet of the USSR. . . .

Article 131. The Presidium of the Council of Ministers of the USSR, consisting of the Chairman of the Council of Ministers of the USSR and the First Vice-Chairmen and Vice-Chairmen of the Council of Ministers of the USSR, shall function as a permanent organ of the Council of Ministers of the USSR for the purpose of dealing with matters related to the administration of the economy and to other questions of state administration. . . .

Courts of Law and Arbitration. Article 150. In the USSR justice shall be administered exclusively by courts of law.

In the USSR the court system shall consist of the following: the Supreme Court of the USSR, Supreme Courts of Union Republics, Supreme Courts of Autonomous Republics, territorial, regional and city courts, courts of Autonomous Regions, courts of Autonomous Areas, district (city) people's courts, and military tribunals in the Armed Forces.

Article 151. All courts in the USSR shall be formed on the principle of electivity of judges and people's assessors. . . .

The Prosecutor's Office. Article 163. Supreme supervisory power over the precise and uniform execution of laws by all ministries, state committees and departments, enterprises, institutions and organizations, executive and administrative organs of local Soviets of People's Deputies, collective farms, cooperative and other public organizations, officials and citizens, shall be exercised by the Prosecutor General of the USSR and prosecutors subordinate to him.

Article 164. The Prosecutor General of the USSR shall be appointed by the Supreme Soviet of the USSR and shall be responsible and accountable to it, or between sessions of the Supreme Soviet to the Presidium of the

Supreme Soviet of the USSR, to which he is accountable. . . .

Amendment of the Constitution of the USSR. Article 172. The Constitution of the USSR shall have supreme legal force. All laws and other acts of state organs shall be issued on the basis of, and in conformity with, the Constitution of the USSR.

The Constitution of the USSR shall be effective from the time of its adoption.

Article 173. Amendment of the Constitution of the USSR shall be by decision of the Supreme Soviet of the USSR, adopted by a majority of not less than two-thirds of the total number of deputies of each of its chambers.

Gorbachev UN Speech

Following are excerpts from Soviet leader Mikhail S. Gorbachev's December 7, 1988, speech to the UN General Assembly.

Esteemed Mr. President,
Esteemed Mr. Secretary-General,
Distinguished delegates,

We have come here to show our respect for the United Nations, which increasingly has been manifesting its ability to act as a unique international center in the service of peace and security.

We have come here to show our respect for the dignity of this organization which is capable of accumulating the collective wisdom and will of mankind.

Recent events have been making it increasingly clear that the world needs such an organization, and that the organization itself needs the active involvement of all of its members, their support for its initiatives and actions and their potential and original contributions that enrich its activity. . . .

The role played by the Soviet Union in world affairs is well-known and, in view of the revolutionary perestroika under way in our country, which contains a tremendous potential for peace and international cooperation, we are now particularly interested in being properly understood.

That is why we have come here to address this most authoritative world body and to share our thoughts with it. We want it to be the first to learn of our new important decisions.

I

What will mankind be like when it enters the twenty-first century? People are already fascinated by this not too distant future. We are looking ahead to it with hopes for the best and yet with a feeling of concern.

The world in which we live today is radically different from what it was at the beginning or even in the middle of this century. And it continues to change as do all its components.

The advent of nuclear weapons was just another tragic reminder of the fundamental nature of that change. A material symbol and expression of absolute military power, nuclear weapons at the same time revealed the absolute limits of that power.

The problem of mankind's survival and self-preservation came to the fore. . . .

Today the preservation of any kind of "closed" societies is hardly possible. This calls for a radical review of approaches to the totality of the problems of international cooperation as a major element of universal security.

The world economy is becoming a single organism, and no state, whatever its social system or economic status, can normally develop outside it. . . .

Today, further world progress is only possible through a search for universal human consensus as we move forward to a new world order.

We have come to a point when the disorderly play of elemental forces leads into an impasse. The international community must learn how it can shape and guide developments in such a way as to preserve our civilization, to make it safe for all and more conducive to normal life. . . .

Efforts to solve global problems require a new scope and quality of interaction of states and sociopolitical currents, regardless of ideological or other differences.

Of course, radical changes and revolutionary transformations will continue to occur within individual countries and social structures. This is how it was and how it will be.

But here too, our time marks a change. Internal transformations no longer can advance their national goals if they develop just along "parallel courses" with others, without making use of the achievements of the outside world and of the potential inherent in equitable cooperation.

In these circumstances, any interference in those internal developments, designed to redirect them to someone's liking, would have all the more destructive consequences for establishing a peaceful order. . . .

It is obvious, for instance, that the use or threat of force no longer can or must be an instrument of foreign policy. This applies above all to nuclear arms, but that is not the only thing that matters. All of us, and primarily the stronger of us, must exercise self-restraint and totally rule out any outward-oriented use of force. . . .

After all, it is now quite clear that building up military power makes no country omnipotent. What is more, one-sided reliance on military power ultimately weakens other components of national security.

It is also quite clear to us that the principle of freedom of choice is mandatory. Its nonrecognition is fraught with extremely grave consequences for world peace. . . .

This objective fact calls for respect for the views and

positions of others, tolerance, a willingness to perceive something different as not necessarily bad or hostile, and an ability to learn to live side-by-side with others while remaining different and not always agreeing with each other....

What we are talking about, therefore, is unity in diversity. If we assert this politically, if we reaffirm our adherence to freedom of choice, then there is no room for the view that some live on earth by virtue of divine will while others are here quite by chance....

The new phase also requires de-ideologizing relations among states. We are not abandoning our convictions, our philosophy or traditions, nor do we urge anyone to abandon theirs.

But neither do we have any intention to be hemmed in by our values. That would result in intellectual impoverishment, for it would mean rejecting a powerful source of development—the exchange of everything original that each nation has independently created.

In the course of such exchange, let everyone show the advantages of their social system, way of life or values—and not just by words or propaganda, but by real deeds.

That would be a fair rivalry of ideologies. But it should not be extended to relations among states. Otherwise, we would simply be unable to solve any of the world's problems, such as:

• Developing wide-ranging, mutually beneficial and equitable cooperation among nations;
• Making efficient use of the achievement of scientific and technological revolution;
• Restructuring the world economy and protecting the environment;
• Overcoming backwardness, eliminating hunger, disease, illiteracy and other global scourges.

Nor, of course, shall we then be able to eliminate the nuclear threat and militarism....

In short, the understanding of the need for a period of peace is gaining ground and beginning to prevail. This has made it possible to take the first real steps in creating a healthier international environment and in disarmament....

I am referring to the process of negotiations on nuclear arms, conventional weapons and chemical weapons, and to the search for political approaches to ending regional conflicts.

Of course, I am referring above all to political dialogue—a more intense and open dialogue pointed at the very heart of the problems instead of confrontation, at an exchange of constructive ideas instead of recriminations. Without political dialogue the process of negotiations cannot advance.

We regard prospects for the near and more distant future quite optimistically.

Just look at the changes in our relations with the United States. Little by little, mutual understanding has started to develop and elements of trust have emerged, without which it is very hard to make headway in politics.

In Europe, these elements are even more numerous. The Helsinki process is a great process. I believe that it remains fully valid. Its philosophical, political, practical and other dimensions must all be preserved and enhanced, while taking into account new circumstances.

Current realities make it imperative that the dialogue that ensures normal and constructive evolution of international affairs involve, on a continuous and active basis, all countries and regions of the world, including such major powers as India, China, Japan and Brazil and other countries—big, medium and small....

II

In this specific historical situation, we face the question of a new role for the United Nations....

The recent reinvigoration of its peace-making role has again demonstrated the United Nations' ability to assist its members in coping with the daunting challenges of our time and working to humanize their relations.

Regrettably, shortly after it was established, the organization went through the onslaught of the cold war. For many years, it was the scene of propaganda battles and continuous political confrontation.

Let historians argue who is more and who is less to blame for it. What political leaders today need to do is to draw lessons from that chapter in the history of the United Nations which turned out to be at odds with the very meaning and objectives of our organization.

One of the most bitter and important lessons lies in the long list of missed opportunities. As a result, at a certain point the authority of the United Nations diminished and many of its attempts to act failed.

It is highly significant that the reinvigoration of the role of the United Nations is linked to an improvement in the international climate....

What is needed here is joining the efforts and taking into account the interests of all groups of countries, something that only this organization, the United Nations, can accomplish....

I would like to join the voice of my country in the expressions of high appreciation for the significance of the universal declaration of human rights adopted forty years ago on December 19, 1948.

Today, this document retains its significance. It, too, reflects the universal nature of the goals and objectives of the United Nations.

The most fitting way for a state to observe this anniversary of the declaration is to improve its domestic conditions for respecting and protecting the rights of its own citizens.

Before I inform you on what specifically we have undertaken recently in this respect, I would like to say the following.

Our country is going through a period of truly revolutionary uplifting.

The process of perestroika is gaining momentum. We began with the formulation of the theoretical concept of perestroika. We had to evaluate the nature and the magnitude of problems, to understand the lessons of the past and express that in the form of political conclusions and programs. This was done....

For our society to participate in efforts to implement the plans of perestroika, it had to be democratized in practice. Under the sign of democratization, perestroika has now spread to politics, the economy, intellectual life, and ideology.

We have initiated a radical economic reform. We have gained experience. At the start of next year the entire national economy will be redirected to new forms and methods of operation. This also means profoundly reorganizing relations of production and releasing the tremendous potential inherent in socialist property.

Undertaking such bold revolutionary transformations, we realized that there would be mistakes and also opposition, that new approaches would generate new problems. We also foresaw the possibility of slowdowns....

But the guarantee that the overall process of perestroika will steadily move forward and gain strength lies in a profound democratic reform of the entire system of power and administration.

With the recent decisions by the USSR Supreme Soviet on amendments to the Constitution and the adoption of the law on elections we have completed the first stage of the process of political reform.

Without pausing, we have begun the second stage of this process with the main task of improving the relationship between the center and the republics, harmonizing inter-ethnic relations on the principles of Leninist internationalism that we inherited from the great revolution, and at the same time reorganizing the local system of Soviet power....

We have become deeply involved in building a socialist state based on the rule of law. Work on a series of new laws has been completed or is nearing completion.

Many of them will enter into force as early as 1989, and we expect them to meet the highest standards from the standpoint of ensuring the rights of the individual.

Soviet democracy will be placed on a solid normative base. I am referring, in particular, to laws on the freedom of conscience, glasnost, public associations and organizations, and many others.

In places of confinement there are no persons convicted for their political or religious beliefs.

Additional guarantees are to be included in the new draft laws that rule out any form of persecution on those grounds.

Naturally, this does not apply to those who committed actual criminal offenses or state crimes such as espionage, sabotage, terrorism, etc., whatever their political or ideological beliefs....

The problem of exit from and entry to our country, including the question of leaving it for family reunification, is being dealt with in a humane spirit.

As you know, one of the reasons for refusal to leave is a person's knowledge of secrets. Strictly warranted time limitations on the secrecy rule will now be applied. Every person seeking employment at certain agencies or enterprises will be informed of this rule. In case of disputes there is a right of appeal under the law.

This removes from the agenda the problem of the so-called "refuseniks."

We intend to expand the Soviet Union's participation in the United Nations and CSCE [Conference on Security and Cooperation in Europe] human rights monitoring arrangements. We believe that the jurisdiction of the International Court of Justice at the Hague as regards the interpretation and implementation of agreements on human rights should be binding on all states.

We regard as part of the Helsinki process the cessation of jamming of all foreign radio broadcasts beamed at the Soviet Union....

III

Now let me turn to the main issue—disarmament, without which none of the problems of the coming century can be solved....

Tomorrow marks the first anniversary of the signing of the INF Treaty [for the reduction of intermediate-range nuclear weapons in Europe]. I am therefore particularly pleased to note that the implementation of the treaty—the elimination of missiles—is proceeding normally, in an atmosphere of trust and businesslike work....

The Soviet leadership has decided to demonstrate once again its readiness to reinforce this healthy process not only by words but also by deeds.

Today, I can report to you that the Soviet Union has taken a decision to reduce its armed forces.

Within the next two years their numerical strength will be reduced by 500,000 men. The numbers of conventional armaments will also be substantially reduced. This will be done unilaterally, without relation to the talks on the mandate of the Vienna meeting.

By agreement with our Warsaw Treaty allies, we have decided to withdraw by 1991 six tank divisions from the German Democratic Republic, Czechoslovakia and Hungary, and to disband them.

Assault landing troops and several other formations and units, including assault crossing units with their weapons and combat equipment, will also be withdrawn from the groups of Soviet forces stationed in those countries.

Soviet forces stationed in those countries will be reduced by 50,000 men and their armaments, by 5,000 tanks.

All Soviet divisions remaining, for the time being, in the territory of our allies are being reorganized. Their structure will be different from what it is now; after a major cutback of their tanks it will become clearly defensive.

At the same time, we shall reduce the numerical strength of the armed forces and the numbers of armaments stationed in the European part of the USSR.

In total, Soviet armed forces in this part of our country and in the territories of our European allies will be reduced by 10,000 tanks, 8,500 artillery systems and 800 combat aircraft.

Over these two years we intend to reduce significantly our armed forces in the Asian part of our country, too. By agreement with the government of the Mongolian People's Republic a major portion of Soviet troops temporarily stationed there will return home.

In taking this fundamental decision the Soviet leadership expresses the will of the people, who have undertaken a profound renewal of their entire socialist society.

We shall maintain our country's defense capability at a level of reasonable and reliable sufficiency so that no one might be tempted to encroach on the security of the USSR and our allies.

By this action, and by all our activities in favor of demilitarizing international relations, we wish to draw the attention of the international community to yet another pressing problem—the problem of transition from the economy of armaments to an economy of disarmament.

Is conversion of military production a realistic idea? I have already had occasion to speak about this. We think that, indeed, it is realistic.

For its part, the Soviet Union is prepared:

- In the framework of our economic reform we are ready to draw up and make public our internal plan of conversion; in the course of 1989 to draw up, as an experiment, conversion plans for two or three defense plants;
- To make public our experience in providing employment for specialists from military industry and in using its equipment, buildings and structures in civilian production.

It is desirable that all states, in the first place major military powers, should submit to the United Nations their national conversion plans.

It would also be useful to set up a group of scientists to undertake a thorough analysis of the problem of conversion as a whole and as applied to individual countries and regions and report to the Secretary-General of the United Nations and, subsequently, to have this matter considered at a session of the General Assembly.

IV

And finally, since I am here on American soil, and also for other obvious reasons, I have to turn to the subject of our relations with this great country. I had a chance to appreciate the full measure of its hospitality during my memorable visit to Washington exactly a year ago....

[I]n the last few years the entire world could breathe a sigh of relief thanks to the changes for the better in the substance and the atmosphere of the relationship between Moscow and Washington....

The USSR and the United States have built the largest nuclear and missile arsenals. But it is those two countries that, having become specifically aware of their responsibility, were the first to conclude a treaty on the reduction and physical elimination of a portion of these armaments which posed a threat to both of them and to all others.

Both countries possess the greatest and the most sophisticated military secrets. But it is those two countries that have laid a basis for and are further developing a system of mutual verification both of the elimination of armaments and of the reduction and prohibition of their production.

It is those two countries that are accumulating the experience for future bilateral and multilateral agreements.

We value this. We acknowledge and appreciate the contribution made by President Ronald Reagan and by the members of his administration, particularly Mr. George Shultz.

All this is our joint investment in a venture of historic importance. We must not lose this investment, or leave it idle.

The next U.S. Administration headed by President-elect George Bush will find in us a partner who is ready—without long pauses or backtracking—to continue the dialogue in a spirit of realism, openness and goodwill, with a willingness to achieve concrete results working on the agenda which covers the main issues of Soviet-U.S. relations and world politics.

I have in mind, above all:

- Consistent movement toward a treaty on 50 percent reductions in strategic offensive arms while preserving the ABM Treaty;
- Working out a convention on the elimination of chemical weapons—here, as we see it, prerequisites exist to make 1989 a decisive year;
- And negotiations on the reduction of conventional arms and armed forces in Europe.

We also have in mind economic, environmental and humanistic problems in their broadest sense....

I am concluding my first address to the United Nations with the same feeling that I had when I began it—a feeling of responsibility to my own people and to the world community.

We are meeting at the end of a year which has meant so much for the United Nations and on the eve of a year from which we all expect so much.

I would like to believe that our hopes will be matched by our joint effort to put an end to an era of wars, confrontation and regional conflicts, to aggressions against nature, to the terror of hunger and poverty as well as to political terrorism.

This is our common goal and we can only reach it together.

Thank you.

Party Renunciation of Monopoly on Power

Following are excerpts from the Communist Party Central Committee Platform published February 13, 1990, in Pravda. The platform was adopted February 7 at the end of a Central Committee plenum. In addition to outlining party positions on many issues, the document renounced the Communist party's monopoly on power codified in Article 6 of the USSR Constitution.

At this sharp turning point, the party will be able to retain its vanguard positions and to pursue the cause which it has launched and which enjoys the people's support provided it radically restructures itself.

The authoritarian regime had an extremely negative effect on the party, its role in society, and its work methods. In practice a party-state structure of power developed. In terms of internal party life, relations between primary organizations and leadership organs were deformed, communists were isolated from the shaping of party policy and had hardly any influence on the activity of higher-ranking party committees. Great harm was done by supercentralization, the stifling of free thought, and the repressions. The party's prestige suffered tremendous damage as a result of cases of ideological and moral degeneration.

Nonetheless, the broad party masses retained a commitment to Lenin's ideals, selflessness, and self-sacrifice in serving the people. The CPSU [Communist Party of the Soviet Union] always had active living forces, and this is precisely why it managed to overcome the inertia of Stalinism and stagnation, headed the revolutionary turnabout, and thus proved again its ability to play a vanguard role.

The scale and newness of the tasks which emerged urgently raised the question of the need to fundamentally change the CPSU's position in society, to abandon the claims to infallibility and political monopolism. Moreover, the dynamics of changes in society dictate the fast pace of the party's transformation—otherwise it runs the risk of

being forced onto the sidelines of political life. The party masses are acutely aware of this situation: The question of reforming the party and profoundly restructuring it is being raised with growing persistence.

The CPSU is a self-managing sociopolitical organization, a voluntary union of like-mined communists. We conceive the renewed CPSU as a party of socialist choice which expresses the interests of the working class and all working people and builds its policy on the basis of scientific analysis of new realities, creatively developing the legacy of Marx, Engels, and Lenin in the context of all social thought and historical experience of the 20th century.

In its theory and practice, the CPSU relies on the democratic and humanist traditions of all peoples in the Soviet Union. Organically combining national and international principles, the party is implacable toward chauvinism, nationalism, and racism and toward any other manifestations of reactionary ideology and obscurantism. It is cleansing its ranks of those who reject its ideopolitical and organizational foundations and those who participate in antisocialist, nationalist, and anti-Soviet organizations and actions.

The CPSU's position and role in a society undergoing renewal. The CPSU will pursue its policy and will struggle to retain the position of a ruling party within the framework of the democratic process, gaining in elections the voters' votes so as to obtain the people's mandate for shaping leadership organs at the center, in the republics, and at local level.

The CPSU, just like other sociopolitical organizations and mass movements, participates in the management of state and social affairs and nominates its representatives for soviets of people's deputies and other state organs. The party does not take on any powers of state authority. Its role is to be the democratically recognized political leader, acting through communists without claiming an advantage or the enshrining of its special status in the USSR Constitution. In this context, the party deems it necessary to exercise the right of legislative initiative and to submit to the Congress of USSR People's Deputies an appropriate proposal concerning Article 6 of the country's Fundamental Law.

The CPSU, based on the principles of Marxism-Leninism, engages in ideopolitical work among the masses to propagandize its policy and program objectives, to disseminate the humanist values of socialism, and to agitate for the achievement of perestroika's goals.

By casting off duties that are alien to its nature, the CPSU will be able to concentrate its efforts on the elaboration of theory and action programs, on organizational and educational work, on the implementation of the party's cadre policy, and on the resolution of the tasks of society's consolidation along the paths of its revolutionary renewal. Therein lies the main essence of its vanguard role. This will dominate its new relations with all socio-political organizations operating within the framework of the USSR Constitution—relations of dialogue, debate, cooperation, and partnership. . . .

The party initiated the affirmation of glasnost in the country. It will continue to do everything to ensure that glasnost becomes the natural environment for shaping public opinion, a powerful means of the people's direct influence on policy and of citizens' participation in all affairs of state and society, a factor of perestroika's ir-reversibility and dynamization. Taking into account the mass media's important role in society's life, primarily in the implementation of glasnost, the party will assist their activity by all possible means and will exercise its ideolog-ical influence on them on a democratic basis. The CPSU will struggle against disinformation, against the mass me-dia being used to promote selfish personal and group interests, to fan interethnic dissension, or to propagandize ideas which are alien to humane and democratic social-ism.

This is how we perceive the party's new role in society. This does not mean that everything in the future is clear. The unfolding of reforms will make it possible to amplify the answers to numerous specific questions.

Shevardnadze Resignation Speech

Following are excerpts from Eduard A. Shevardnad-ze's speech to the Congress of People's Deputies in Mos-cow, December 20, 1990, announcing his resignation as Soviet foreign minister, as transcribed and translated by the Foreign Broadcast Information Service.

Comrade deputies: I have perhaps the shortest and the most difficult speech of my life. . . .

I would like to make a short statement, comprising two parts.

The first part: Yesterday there were speeches by some comrades—they are our veterans—who raised the ques-tion of the need for a declaration to be adopted forbidding the president and the country's leadership from sending troops to the Persian Gulf. That was the approximate content, and this was not the first or the second occasion. There are many such notes and items in the press, on television, and so on.

These speeches yesterday, comrades, overfilled the cup of patience, to put it bluntly. What, after all, is happening with the Persian Gulf? On about 10 occasions both within the country and outside the country's borders I have had to speak and explain the attitude and the policy of the Soviet Union toward this conflict. This policy is serious, well considered, sensible, and in accordance with all stan-dards, present standards, of civilized relations between states. We have friendly relations with the state of Iraq.

They have been built up over years. These relations are being preserved, but we have no moral right at all to reconcile ourselves to aggression and the annexation of a small, defenseless country. In that case we would have had to strike through everything that has been done in recent years by all of us, by the whole country, and by the whole of our people in the field of asserting the principles of the new political thinking. This is the first thing.

Second, I have been repeatedly explaining—and Mikhail Sergeevich [Gorbachev] spoke of this in his speech at the Supreme Soviet—that the Soviet leadership does not have any plans—I do not know, maybe someone else has some plans, some group—but official bodies, the Defense Ministry—and they are now accusing the foreign minister of having such a plan, a plan to land troops in the Persian Gulf, in that region. I have been explaining and saying that there are no plans like this, they do not exist in practice. Nobody is planning to send even one serviceman in a military uniform, even one representative of the Armed Forces of the Soviet Union. This was said. But someone needed to raise this issue, this problem again. I know what is happening in the corridors of the congress.

The third issue. I said there and I confirm and state it publicly that if the interests of Soviet people are en-croached upon, if just one person suffers—wherever it could happen, in any country, not just in Iraq but in any other country—yes, the Soviet Government, the Soviet side will stand up for the interests of its citizens. I think that deputies should back up, should back up the Soviet leadership in this. [applause] I would like to raise another question. Excuse me, is it all accidental? Is it an accident that two members of the legislature made a statement saying that the minister of internal affairs was removed successfully and the time has come to settle accounts with the foreign minister?

This statement has been circulated literally throughout the world press and in our newspapers. Are they such daredevils, these lads—I will call them that, age permits me to because they are really young, in a colonel's shoulderboards—to address such statements to a minister, to a member of the government? Look in the newspaper, I will not name a single name today. What is surprising, I believe one must think seriously about this: Who stands behind these comrades, and what sort of thing is this? Why does no one deny it and say that this is not so, that there are no such plans? Perhaps there are such plans?

In this connection permit me to say a few words about the personal worth of the man, about his personal sufferings, because many people think that the ministers who sit there or the members of the government or the president or someone else are hired, are being hired and that they can do what they like with them. I think that is impermissible. In this connection I remember that party congress. Was this really a chance phenomenon? Because at the congress a real struggle developed, a most acute struggle, between the reformers and—I will not say conservatives, I respect the conservatives because they have their own views which are acceptable to society—but the reactionaries, precisely the reactionaries. [applause] Furthermore, this battle, it must be stated bluntly, was won with merit by the progressive section, by the progressive members, delegates, by the progressively-minded delegates to the congress. I would like to recall that it was against my will, without being consulted, that my name, I, my candidacy, was included for secret voting, and I had 800 against; 800 delegates voted against. What then: Is this random, or on purpose? Is the Foreign Ministry's policy not good enough? Or am I personally undesirable? This is a serious matter, more than serious. I say that, all the same, this is not a random event. Excuse me, I am now going to recall the Supreme Soviet session. At Comrade Lukyanov's initiative, literally just before the start of the sitting, a serious matter was included on the agenda about the treaties with the German Democratic Republic. As it happened, I was on my travels, and they called in deputies, and people found themselves in an utterly stupid position, and the issue was a flop. I myself had to speak the following week. How did it turn out? Those same people who are now speaking as the authors came out with serious accusations against the foreign minister, of unilateral concessions, of incompetence, lack of skills, and so on and so forth. Not one person could be found, including the person in the chair, to reply and say simply that this was dishonorable, that this is not the way, not how things are done in civilized states. I find this deeply worrying.

Things went as far as personal insults. I endured that, too. Comrades, a hounding is taking place. I will not name the publications, all manner of publications, the Pamyat society—I add the Pamyat society to these publications—what expressions: Down with the Gorbachev clique! They also add Shevardnadze and several other names. Who are they, the so-called reformers? I will put it bluntly, comrades: I was shaken; I was shaken by the events of the first day, the start of the work of our congress. By the pressing of a button, the fate not only of the president but of perestroyka and democratization was decided. Is that normal? Democrats, I will put it bluntly: comrade democrats, in the widest meaning of this word, you have scattered. The reformers have gone to seed. Dictatorship is coming; I state this with complete responsibility. No one knows what kind of dictatorship this will be and who will come—what kind of dictator—and what the regime will be like.

I want to make the following statement: I am resigning. Let this be—and do not respond, and do not curse me—let this be my contribution, if you like, my protest against the onset of dictatorship.

I express profound gratitude to Mikhail Sergeyevich Gorbachev. I am his friend. I am a fellow thinker of his. I have always supported, and will support to the end of my days, the ideas of perestroyka, the ideas of renewal, the ideas of democracy, of democratization. We have done great things in the international arena. But, I think that it is my duty, as a man, as a citizen, as a Communist; I cannot reconcile myself to the events taking place in our country and to the trials awaiting our people. I nevertheless believe, I believe that the dictatorship will not succeed, that the future belongs to democracy and freedom.

Thank you very much. [applause]

Strategic Arms Reduction Treaty Signing

Following are remarks by presidents George Bush and Mikhail S. Gorbachev at the signing of the Strategic Arms Reduction Treaty in Moscow, July 31, 1991:

Gorbachev: Mr. President, ladies and gentlemen, comrades. In a few moments the President of the United States and I will put our signatures under the treaty on the reduction of strategic offensive arms. This completes many years of efforts that required hard work and patience on the part of government leaders, diplomats, and military officials. They required will, courage, and the rejection of outdated perceptions of each other. They required trust.

This is also a beginning—the beginning of voluntary reduction of the nuclear arsenals of the U.S.S.R. and the United States, a process with unprecedented scope and objectives. It is an event of global significance, for we are imparting to the dismantling of the infrastructure of fear that has ruled the world, a momentum which is so powerful that it will be hard to stop.

In both countries we face the complex process of the ratification of the new treaty. There will be critics. Here in Moscow some will point to our unilateral concessions, while in Washington there will be talk about concessions made to the Soviet Union. Some will say the new treaty does not really fulfill the promise of a peace dividend since considerable resources will be required to destroy the missiles. And if the missiles are not destroyed, critics will say they're obsolete and must be replaced with new ones, and that will be even more expensive.

Sharp criticism is to be expected also from those who want to see faster and more ambitious steps toward abolishing nuclear weapons. In other words, the treaty will have to be defended. I'm sure we have achieved the best that is now possible and that is required to continue progress.

Tremendous work has been done and unique experience has been gained of cooperating in this enormously complex area. It is important that there is a growing realization of the absurdity of overarmament now that the world has started to move toward an era of economic interdependence, and that the information revolution is making the indivisibility of the world ever more evident.

But the policymakers have to bear in mind that as we move toward that era we will have to make new, immense efforts to remove the dangers inherited from the past and newly emerging dangers, to overcome various physical, intellectual, and psychological obstacles. Normal human thinking will have to replace the kind of militarized political thinking that has taken root in the minds of men. That will take time. A new conceptual foundation of security will be a great help. Doctrines of war fighting must be abandoned in favor of concepts of preventing war. Plans calling for a crushing defeat of the perceived enemy must be replaced with joint projects of mutual stability and defense sufficiency.

The document before us marks a moral achievement [and] major breakthrough in our country's thinking and behavior. Our next goal is to make full use of this breakthrough to make disarmament an irreversible process. So, as we give credit to what has been achieved, let us express our appreciation to those who have contributed to this treaty—their talent and their intellectual and numerous resources—and let us get down to work again for the sake of our own and global security.

Mr. President, we can congratulate each other. We can congratulate the Soviet and American people and the world community on the conclusion of this agreement.

Thank you.

Bush: Thank you, Mr. President. To President Gorbachev and members of the Soviet Government, and all the honored guests here: May I salute you.

The treaty that we sign today is a most complicated one—the most complicated of contracts governing the most serious of concerns. Its 700 pages stand as a monument to several generations of U.S. and Soviet negotiators, to their tireless efforts to carve out common ground from a thicket of contentious issues—and it represents a major step forward for our mutual security and the cause of world peace.

And may I, too, thank everybody who worked on this treaty—the military, State Department arms control negotiators—really on both sides. And I would like to say that many are here today; some, like my predecessor, President Reagan, is not here. But I think all of us recognize that there are many who are not in this room that deserve an awful lot of credit on both the Soviet side and the United States side.

The START treaty vindicates an approach to arms control that guided us for almost a decade: the belief that we could do more than merely halt the growth of our nuclear arsenals. We could seek more than limits on the number of arms. In our talks we sought stabilizing reductions in our strategic arsenals.

START makes that a reality. In a historic first for arms control, we will actually reduce U.S. and Soviet strategic nuclear arsenals. But reductions alone are not enough. So, START requires even deeper cuts of the most dangerous and destabilizing weapons.

The agreement itself is exceedingly complex, but the central idea at the heart of this treaty can be put simply: Stabilizing reductions in our strategic nuclear forces reduce the risk of war.

But these promises to reduce arms levels cannot automatically guarantee success. Just as important are the treaty's monitoring mechanisms so we know that the commitments made are being translated into real security. In this area, START builds on the experience of earlier agreements—but goes far beyond them in provisions to ensure that we can verify this treaty effectively.

Mr. President, in the warming relations between our nations, this treaty stands as both cause and consequence. Many times during the START talks, reaching agreement seemed all but impossible. In the end, the progress that we made in the past year's time—progress in easing tensions and ending the cold war—changed the atmosphere at the negotiating table, and paved the way for START's success.

Neither side won unilateral advantage over the other. Both sides committed themselves instead to achieving a strong, effective treaty—and securing the mutual stability that a good agreement would provide.

Mr. President, by reducing arms, we reverse a half-century of steadily growing strategic arsenals. But more than that, we take a significant step forward in dispelling a half-century of mistrust. By building trust, we pave a path to peace.

We sign the START treaty as testament to the new relationship emerging between our two countries—in the promise of further progress toward lasting peace.

Thank you very much.

Yeltsin on the Collapse of the Coup

Following are excerpts from President Boris Yeltsin's speech to the Russian Supreme Soviet on August 22, 1991, the day after the collapse of the coup attempt by Communist party hard-liners:

Dear Muscovites, dear Russians, compatriots:

Last night, major events occurred. . . . The group of adventurists who tried to seize power has been arrested. The attempt to change the direction of the development of our country, to cast it into the abyss of violence and lawlessness, has failed. On the third day, the anti-people, anti-constitutional rebellion was eliminated.

During the extremely short existence of the Dictatorship of the Eight, it became exceedingly clear what would await the country and its citizens if the putschists won victory and seized power. From the first minutes of the dictatorship, brute force was the main means of carrying out the anti-people policy.... A malicious attempt was made to smother freedom and democracy, to revive the wolf law of a totalitarian system; within a few hours the country was drowned in a sea of lies, starting with the imaginary illness of the deposed president....

Yes, within a few hours glasnost had been trampled on. Even during the days of Stalinism there was none of the rigid censorship introduced by the putschists....

During those days and nights, many thousands of Muscovites demonstrated steadfastness, citizenship and heroism. It was they who halted the advance of reaction and inflicted a crushing blow against it.... Your weapon was the enormous will to defend the ideals of freedom, democracy and human worth.... I express profound gratitude to the thousands of servicemen and personnel of the law enforcement bodies, the security bodies and the true patriots of Russia who came to its aid in its hour of destiny. The active stance of the inhabitants of many cities and villages of the country ... of people of various ages and professions, men and women, played an inestimable role in breaking the mutiny. The miners, the church and others had a large say in the defense of the sovereign rights of Russia.

Our joint efforts have been crowned with success, and a major victory over the forces of reaction has been won. The activities of the so-called Committee for the State of Emergency were in flagrant contradiction not only with the laws, the constitution and the declaration of the state sovereignty of the republics, but also with elementary moral norms....

A most grave state crime has been committed, and the criminals—traitors to the motherland—must be handed over to the courts.... Retribution for what has been perpetrated must follow, and not for the sake of vengeance, but for the sake of the highest human justice so that such a thing should never be repeated in our country.

All of us have to draw serious lessons from the past. Once again we have seen how fragile freedom is in our society, and how vulnerable democracy and glasnost are. Once again we have seen that the reforms being carried out in the country have not yet become irreversible....

This is a lesson for us all, including the country's president—Gorbachev. At the same time, it has again been shown how great are the powers of the people. The political course of Russia, the honor and virtue of its highest bodies of authority, of its leadership, were defended by unarmed, peaceful citizens. It is symbolic that among those who became the defense of the constitution, the law, and human worth, there were a great many young people. This means that the future course of this reform is ensured.

The past days make it necessary to draw a number of conclusions: Today, the lagging of reforms in the center behind the transformation in the republics is extremely dangerous. The putsch has shown once again that the union structures remain conservative, impermissibly cumbersome, and they work first and foremost on an each-for-himself basis. At any moment they will seek to restore their dictatorship over the republics. Their immediate and resolute transformation is necessary.

The formation of a government of national accord can no longer be postponed. It should be mobile, effective, rationally structured, and the republics forming the union should have the decisive word in its formation. Adjustments in the matter of the union treaty are also necessary. The coup d'etat disrupted its signing, but it is impermissible to postpone this procedure for an indefinite period.

At the same time, Russia, but not it alone, has become convinced that some of the articles of the last version of the treaty have proven, bluntly, to be weak, and they have to be corrected. And, of course, on the other hand, this document should take account of the experience we have acquired over these past three black days.

Life has again shown us that Russia cannot feel itself secure without its own national guard ... [and] we intend to adopt a more principled stand with regard to ensuring the economic sovereignty of Russia. The Russian republic must have a full-blown economy, and yesterday a decree was signed transferring union property on the territory of Russia to the jurisdiction of Russia, all enterprises.

The days of rule by the notorious committee showed that the mass media were extremely vulnerable. In the very shortest time, it is essential to adopt resolute measures to strengthen the mass media system in the republic. The stability of freedom of speech is a most important condition of progress in Russian society. The appropriate decree has been drawn up and was signed last night. Other measures are also being prepared....

Support for the illegal and anti-constitutional actions on the part of whoever carried them out cannot remain unpunished. Yesterday, the Russian parliament instructed me to conduct a reorganization of staff in those regions where the leaders supported the illegal Committee for the State of Emergency. Even before, those people were, in effect, in a state of cold war with the leadership of Russia. Now they must leave their jobs. The decree on their dismissal was signed last night.

Esteemed fellow citizens, the situation in the country is getting back to normal. The shameful days of the appearance of the gang of high-ranking adventurists is receding into the past, but too high a price has been paid for this—the irreplaceable loss of human life, of people killed during the putsch, huge losses in the economy. Still, the main thing is that the coup failed. The country is emerging from the crisis foisted upon it. The forces that organized [the coup] are historically doomed, and first and foremost because the people have already made their choice and do not intend to reject it. The people have already freed themselves from the fear of former years.

In the name of national unity, I call on all my fellow citizens to embark on creative work directed at the regeneration and renewal of Russia. For the victory of democracy over reaction, and as always in Russia, in conclusion: Hoorah! Hoorah!

Gorbachev Press Conference on Coup Attempt

Following are excerpts from President Mikhail Gorbachev's press conference on August 22, 1991, in which he described his captivity during the three-day coup.

Today's press conference is taking place after events which more than anything I hope are not repeated, and that similar press conferences on this topic will not have to take place.

We made it through. As I want to be accurate—did we make [it] all the way through or not—yes we did—the most difficult test in all the years in the reformation of our society since 1985.

We faced a real, without any exaggeration, anti-constitutional coup organized by reactionary forces, which appeared to be in the leadership, in the very center of the leadership, people which I advanced, believed in and trusted, who appeared to be not only the participants but the organizers of this coup, against the president, against the constitution, against perestroika and against democracy.

On August 18, 10 minutes to 5 p.m., my head guard told me that a group of people had arrived demanding a meeting with me. I told them that I was not expecting anybody, had invited nobody, and that nobody notified me in advance. . . .

I decided to clarify who sent them here, and as far as I had [available] all sorts of communications [at my disposal]—ordinary, governmental, strategic and satellite—I was working in my office, picked up the one telephone, it didn't work. I lifted the second, the third, the fourth, the fifth—nothing. Then I tried the house phone and realized nothing worked and I was cut off. . . .

Then I went to another place, called the family, my wife, daughter, and said that an event had taken place. I didn't need any new information, I knew that a very serious event was going on, that they would either blackmail me or there would be attempts to arrest me or take me away somewhere. Basically, anything could happen.

I told Raisa Maximovna and Irina Anatoleyevna [Gorbachev's wife and daughter] that if we talk about the main thing, about politics, the course of politics, that I will stick to my position to the end and that I would not step back, not under any pressure, blackmail or threats. I would neither change nor take up new positions.

All the family—I thought it was important to tell them, you understand why—because I realized that anything could happen, especially to the members of my family. This we also know. The family told me that I, this should be my decision and that [they] would go with me through this to the end. This was the end of our conversation.

Then I went to invite them, but by that time they had already come in, they didn't stand on ceremony, with the head of the presidential apparatus [chief of staff Valery] Boldin, ahead of them. They gave the president an ultimatum: to transfer all power to the vice president.

I told them that before I answered, I wanted to know who had sent them, what committee. They said the State Committee for the State of the Emergency in the country. Who created it? I didn't create it, the Supreme Soviet didn't create it.

They told me that people had already united and they needed a presidential decree, either you issue this decree and stay here or transfer your powers to the vice president. They said the situation in the country was such, that it was nearing catastrophe, and that we should take measures, a state of emergency, other measures won't do, we shouldn't daydream anymore. . . .

I told them that I knew the situation in the country better than anyone, politically, economically, and the life of people and all the difficulties they were facing, and that we had come to the phase where we need to do everything as fast and decisive as we can to live better.

I told them that I was always an opponent of such methods, not only because of political and moral reasons, but because in the history of our country they have always led to the death of hundreds, thousands and millions of deaths. And we need to get away from that, and to refuse it forever. If we do differently, we are not behaving like ourselves, and everything that we started we'll have to bury forever. We should agree that we are going in a bloody circle.

Then I told them that you and those who sent you are adventurists, you will kill yourselves, but the hell with you, it's your problem, do what you want to do, but you will also kill the country, everything that we are doing. . . .

Only those who want to commit suicide can now suggest to lead a totalitarian regime in the country.

They demanded that I resign. You won't get that from me, not one or the other. Tell that to the people who sent you here.

Well, after that everything developed according to the logic of confrontation. Full isolation from land and sea. Thirty-two security people stayed with me, to the end, as they say, they decided to stay. They divided up all the spheres of defense, including my family, divided all the locations, and decided to stand until the end.

When it became known . . . they said I was ill, seriously, and that in general, I understood, that I was not capable of returning to a normal life, then it became clear to me that what would follow was that reality would soon be synchronized to this statement.

This is why—it was understood the same way by security—decision was taken to refuse all ordered food and live on only what we already had at hand. I was sure, I was positive, and absolutely calm, although I was struck to the bones and indignant with the political blindness and irresponsibility of these criminals.

It won't last long, and it won't succeed. Basically, that's how it was. Seventy-two hours of total isolation and struggle. I think everything was done to psychologically break the president down. It is difficult, it's also difficult to talk about it here. Every day, morning and evening, I put forth demands, and passed them on.

The demands were that communications of the president be re-established, that a plane was sent immediately to take me to Moscow, back to work, and after the [Yanayev] press conference, I added to the demands that they publish the refutation of this announcement made in front of you about the condition of my health....

... I want to tell you that I, all of us, have indeed seen the truth, that these six years in this country that we have gone through have not been wasted. And with difficulty, and often painfully, we have looked for the path to move forward. This society—and now we can now speak about this—has rejected the putschists. They turned out to be isolated. They weren't able to direct the army, the army made contact with the people, and nothing could be done about it. It became clear to them that they failed.

The republics took a negative position, and here I want to pay tribute and put in first place the principled position of our Russian parliament, Russian deputies, Russian government officials, and the outstanding role of the president of Russia, Boris Nikolayevich Yeltsin [applause]. I have to say that we also have to pay tribute to the principled positions of Muscovites and Leningraders, as well as people from many other regions....

Basically, when it became clear, when Russia, its leadership, the republics and the people took such an irreconcilable position, that the army didn't go, they began to look for an exit in panic. They told me that the group of conspirators have arrived in the Crimea on the presidential plane, to talk to the president and to take him to Moscow. When they arrived, I said to put them in the house, detain them, and tell them my demands: I won't talk to any of them until all the governmental communications are reestablished.... So the communications were turned back on, and I began to speak with the country. I spoke first with Boris Nikolayevich Yeltsin. I called [Kazakh President Nursultan] Nazarbayev, [Ukraine President Leonid] Kravchuk, [Byelorussian President Nikolai] Dementei, [Uzbek President Islam] Karimov.... I started to work. I gave [Soviet chief of staff Gen. Mikhail] Moiseyev orders to take over the leadership of Defense Ministry, and he was also summoned from the

Crimea and taken there. I gave troops orders to go back immediately to the places where they were located, to their barracks, and to announce that Yazov will be dismissed and arrested. All that was done.... Basically I started calling to the most important points, to block everything at once. Because everything was still dangerous and they could have destroyed me on my way [to Moscow] or anywhere. I decided not to go until—then they told me that the plane of the Russian delegation was coming and I said I would receive them first of all. I got in touch with [Civil Aviation Minister Boris] Panyukov, with Moiseyev and told them to land not in Simferopol, which would have meant they would get to me in three hours, but at the military airport where I usually land. Then I gave the orders to meet them there, to organize the transport to bring them here. So the work started. The delegation arrived, we all sat down, came to great understanding. I think what we had suffered through has contributed not only to our experience but also to our understanding, the difference between a united democratic force and a divided one....

Then I had to issue more instructions. Then [Communist party deputy general secretary Vladimir] Ivanskho and [Supreme Soviet speaker Anatoly] Lukyanov arrived separately—they didn't give them transport—and I received them. I didn't receive the conspirators, I didn't see them, and I don't want to see them. We put them into different planes, brought them to Moscow, and getting off the plane they were arrested and interned. I gave an order to the Kremlin not to let anyone in who cooperated with that "Commandant." And so forth, that is, so to say, the work has begun. I planned a meeting tomorrow with the leaders of the nine republics that signed the [Union] treaty—who worked out the treaty and prepared it to be signed.

Tomorrow we will meet and we should discuss everything. These were hard lessons, for me it has been the most difficult, it's simply a hard trauma for me. I think that tomorrow we will come close to discussing, seriously thinking about and developing the positions on the main questions of moving forward and what new steps to take. We have to think about this, we have to see not only the great sorrow that occurred, but also we have to see what an enormous chance this event opened up to us, how it showed the true position of the people. In conversations with foreign leaders, the leaders of foreign governments, they all drew attention to this fact, that the position of the people and the army showed that the Soviet Union has already gone through changes that were irreversible. For that reason they hope will take advantage of all opportunities, and they all said that they will cooperate with us, and that this cooperation should take more active forms, more decisive ones....

About the decisions that were made: I issued a decree that annulled the decrees.... [I]t looked like they could destroy or do anything . . . to my family, to me, to everyone who was with me, and tell [the people] that the president has such and such a position. Moreover, they could say that they were acting on orders from him. For that reason, at the [Emergency Committee] press conference I saw all this craftiness, though a primitive one, crude. As one of the comrades in the Russian Federation said, "They can't even do this properly, like the other things they do."

I decided to immediately make four tapes . . . and we started to look for channels whom we could trust to send them. Here is the tape, one of them [holds up a tape], the others may appear because they have, in any case, gone. The doctor wrote his opinion, several copies, and we gave them out, I distributed them so that the people knew the actual state of the condition of the health of the president. And I finally put forward the first four points in written form, I wrote some things by hand so that people could see that it was I who wrote it . . . and I signed it.

Point One: The fact that [Vice President Gennady] Yanayev took over the responsibilities of president on the pretext of my illness and inability to fulfill responsibilities is a deception of the people, and given this, can only be considered a governmental coup.

Point Two: This means that all the actions that followed are illegal. Neither the president nor the Congress of People's Deputies delegated such responsibility to Yanayev.

Point Three: I ask to tell [parliament speaker Anatoly] Lukyanov my demand to immediately convene a meeting of the Supreme Soviet and the Congress of People's Deputies to consider the situation that emerged. They and only they, having considered the emerging situation, have the right to solve the problems of taking and putting into effect necessary government measures.

Point Four: I demand immediately to freeze the actions of the State Committee of the State of Emergency until the Supreme Soviet or the Congress of People's Deputies pass the aforementioned decisions.

The continuation of these actions, the further escalation of the measures taken by the State Committee for the State of Emergency, could turn out to be a tragedy for all the peoples, to exacerbate the situation and even completely destroy the consensual work of the center and the republics that has already begun to find a way out of the crisis.

[Remark: When was the document written? The 20th?] Yes, the 20th. . . . The prosecutor's office, the prosecutor of the Russian Federation, reported to me that yesterday he began criminal proceedings, and we agreed that the group should include both Russian and Soviet investigators.

Temporary decisions were adopted in cases wherein certain agencies [where] people could not be trusted, not even for a single day. Tomorrow when we meet with the leaders of the republics, we'll start to think over the disposition of forces among other problems, that's the most important thing, so that the authorities acted, and the consensual actions built a momentum. We cannot lose. We have a program, we have to move and solve the problems, this is the most important thing. But enough for the introduction.

Gorbachev Resignation as General Secretary

Following is President Mikhail Gorbachev's statement of August 24, 1991, as translated by the Tass news agency, declaring his resignation as general secretary of the Communist party of the Soviet Union:

The secretariat [and] the Politburo failed to stand against the coup d'etat, the Central Committee proved unable to take a resolute position of condemnation and opposition to the coup, it didn't urge Communists to fight against the suppression of constitutional legality. Members of the party leadership were among the conspirators, a number of party committees and mass media organs supported the actions of the state criminals. This put millions of Communists into an ambiguous position. Many party members refused to collaborate with the conspirators, [they] condemned the coup and joined the fight against it. Nobody has a moral right to blame all Communists indiscriminately, and I, as President, consider it my duty to defend them as citizens from unsubstantiated accusations.

In this situation, the Communist Party Central Committee should take the difficult but honest decision to dissolve itself. The republic Communist parties and local party organizations will decide their own fate.

I don't think it's possible for me to continue to fulfill the functions of general secretary of the Communist Party of the Soviet Union, and I'm relinquishing the corresponding powers. I believe that democratic-minded Communists loyal to constitutional lawfulness, to the course of renewal of society, will stand up for creation on a new basis of a party capable of joining in the ongoing radical democratic transformations along with all progressive forces in the interests of the working people.

Commonwealth Pact

Following is the agreement signed by Russia, Ukraine, and Belarus in Moscow, December 8, 1991, establishing the Commonwealth of Independent States. Eight other former Soviet republics signed a protocol to this agreement and joined the Commonwealth on December 21, 1991.

We, the Republic of Byelorussia [Belarus], the Russian Federation and Ukraine, as founding members of the Union of Soviet Socialist Republics, having signed the Union Treaty of 1922 and hereafter referred to as the agreeing parties, state that the Union of Soviet Socialist Republics, as a subject of international law and geopolitical reality, is ceasing its existence.

Based on historical commonalities of our peoples and on ties that were set up between them, considering bilateral agreements signed between the agreeing parties,

Striving to found democratic legal states and intending to develop our relations on the basis of mutual recognition and the respect of state sovereignty, the integral right to self-determination, the principles of equality and non-interference in internal affairs, the refusal to use force or pressure by economic or other means, the settlement of controversial problems through agreement, other common principles and norms of international law,

Taking into account that the further development and strengthening of relations of friendship, good-neighborliness and mutually beneficial cooperation between our states is consistent with the basic national interests of their people and serves in the interests of peace and security,

Confirming our commitment to the goals and principles of the United Nations Charter, the Helsinki Final Act and other documents from the Conference on Security and Cooperation in Europe,

Obliging to observe common international norms on human and national rights,

We agree on the following:

Article 1. The agreeing parties are founding a Commonwealth of Independent States.

Article 2. The agreeing parties guarantee their citizens, regardless of nationality or other differences, equal rights and freedoms. Each of the agreeing parties guarantees citizens of other parties and also people without citizenship who reside on its territory, regardless of nationality or other differences, civil, political, social, economic and cultural rights and freedoms in accordance with common international norms on human rights.

Article 3. The agreeing parties that wish to found unique ethno-cultural regions to contribute to the manifestation, preservation and development of ethnic, cultural, linguistic and religious distinctions of national minorities residing on their territories, will take them under their own protection.

Article 4. The agreeing parties will develop equal and mutually beneficial cooperation of their peoples and states in the spheres of politics, economics, culture, education, health care, environmental protection, science, trade, and humanitarian and other spheres, and will contribute to the wide exchange of information and will fully and strictly observe mutual obligations.

The parties consider it necessary to conclude agree-ments on cooperation in the above-mentioned spheres.

Article 5. The agreeing parties recognize and respect each other's territorial integrity, and the integrity of each other's borders in the framework of the commonwealth. They guarantee openness of borders, and the freedom for citizens to travel and exchange information within the framework of the commonwealth.

Article 6. Members of the commonwealth will cooperate to insure international peace and security and to carry out effective measures on limiting weapons and military expenditures. They are striving to liquidate all nuclear armaments, to have total and complete disarmament under strict international control.

The parties will respect each other's striving to achieve the status of a nuclear-free zone and neutral state.

Members of the commonwealth will preserve and support common military and strategic space under a common command, including common control over nuclear armaments, which will be regulated by special agreement.

They also mutually guarantee necessary conditions for the deployment, functioning, material and social maintenance of strategic armed forces. The parties are obliged to pursue consensual policy on questions of social protection and pensions for military personnel and their families.

Article 7. The parties recognize that the spheres of their mutual activities conducted on a mutual basis through common coordinating institutions of the commonwealth embrace:

Coordination of foreign policy.
Cooperation in forming and developing a common economic space, common European and Eurasian markets, in the sphere of customs policy.
Cooperation to develop transport and communications systems.
Cooperation on the sphere of environmental protection, participation in creating of the all-encompassing international system of ecological security.
Questions of migration policy.
The fight against organized crime.

Article 8. The parties are aware of the universal character of the Chernobyl disaster and are obliged to unite and coordinate their efforts to minimize and overcome its consequences.

They agreed to sign a special agreement on this matter, taking the consequences of the catastrophe into consideration.

Article 9. Disputes relating to the interpretation and usage of the norms of the current agreement are subject to be solved through negotiations between corresponding organs, and at the state and government level if necessary.

Article 10. Each party reserves the right to suspend the current agreement or its individual articles by notifying the agreement's participants a year in advance.

The current agreement can be supplemented or

changed according to mutual consent of the agreeing parties.

Article 11. From the moment the current agreement is signed, the laws of third states, including the Union of Soviet Socialist Republics, are not valid on the territories of states which signed the current agreement.

Article 12. The parties guarantee the fulfillment of international obligations, treaties and agreements of the former Union of Soviet Socialist Republics, coming from these obligations.

Article 13. The current agreement does not concern obligations of the agreeing parties in relation to third states.

The current agreement is open to all state members of the former Union of Soviet Socialist Republics, and also to other states that share the goals and principles of the current agreement.

Article 14. The official location to station the coordinating organs of the Commonwealth is the city of Minsk.

The activities of the organs of the former Union of Soviet Socialist Republics on the territories of state members of the Commonwealth are stopped.

Finalized in three copies in the Byelorussian, Russian and Ukrainian languages in the city of Minsk, Dec. 8, 1991. All three copies bear equal weight.

Gorbachev's Resignation as President

Following is the text of Mikhail Gorbachev's December 25, 1991, televised speech, in which he announces his resignation as president of the USSR:

Dear compatriots, fellow citizens: As a result of the newly formed situation, creation of the Commonwealth of Independent States, I cease my activities in the post of USSR president.

I am making this decision out of considerations based on principle. I have firmly stood for independence, self-rule of nations, for the sovereignty of the republics, but at the same time for preservation of the union state, the unity of the country.

Events went a different way. The policy prevailed of dismembering this country and disuniting the state, with which I cannot agree. And after the Alma-Ata meeting and the decisions made there, my position on this matter has not changed. Besides, I am convinced that decisions of such scale should have been made on the basis of a popular expression of will.

Yet I will continue to do everything in my power so that agreements signed there should lead to real accord in the society [and] facilitate the escape from the crisis and the reform process.

Addressing you for the last time in the capacity of president of the USSR, I consider it necessary to express my evaluation of the road we have traveled since 1985, especially as there are a lot of contradictory, superficial and subjective judgments on that matter.

Fate had it that when I found myself at the head of the state it was already clear that all was not well in the country. There is plenty of everything: land, oil and gas, other natural riches, and God gave us lots of intelligence and talent, yet we lived much worse than developed countries and keep falling behind them more and more.

The reason could already be seen. The society was suffocating in the vise of the command-bureaucratic system, doomed to serve ideology and bear the terrible burden of the arms race. It had reached the limit of its possibilities. All attempts at partial reform, and there had been many, had suffered defeat, one after another. The country was losing perspective. We could not go on living like that. Everything had to be changed radically.

That is why not once—not once—have I regretted that I did not take advantage of the post of [Communist party] general secretary to rule as a czar for several years. I considered it irresponsible and amoral. I realized that to start reforms of such scale in a society such as ours was a most difficult and even a risky thing. But even today I am convinced of the historic correctness of the democratic reforms that were started in the spring of 1985.

The process of renovating the country and radical changes in the world community turned out to be far more complicated than could be expected. However, what has been done ought to be given its due. This society acquired freedom, liberated itself politically and spiritually, and this is the foremost achievement—which we have not yet understood completely, because we have not learned to use freedom.

However, work of historic significance has been accomplished. The totalitarian system that deprived the country of an opportunity to become successful and prosperous long ago has been eliminated. A breakthrough has been achieved on the way to democratic changes. Free elections, freedom of the press, religious freedoms, representative organs of power, a multi-party [system] became a reality. Human rights are recognized as the supreme principle.

The movement to a diverse economy has started, equality of all forms of property is becoming established, people who work on the land are coming to life again in the framework of land reform, farmers have appeared, millions of acres of land are being given over to people who live in the countryside and in towns.

Economic freedom of the producer has been legalized, and entrepreneurship, shareholding, privatization are gaining momentum. In turning the economy toward a market, it is important to remember that all this is done for the sake of the individual. At this difficult time, all should be done for his social protection, especially for senior citizens and children.

We live in a new world. The Cold War has ended; the arms race has stopped, as has the insane militarization that mutilated our economy, public psyche and morals. The threat of a world war has been removed. Once again I want to stress that on my part everything was done during the transition period to preserve reliable control of nuclear weapons.

We opened ourselves to the world, gave up interference into other people's affairs, the use of troops beyond the borders of the country, and trust, solidarity and respect came in response. We have become one of the main foundations for the transformation of modern civilization on peaceful democratic grounds.

The nations and peoples [of this country] gained real freedom of self-determination. The search for a democratic reformation of the multinational state brought us to the threshold of concluding a new union treaty. All these changes demanded immense strain. They were carried out with sharp struggle, with growing resistance from the old, the obsolete forces: for former party-state structures, the economic apparatus, as well as our habits, ideological superstitions, the psychology of sponging and leveling everyone out.

They stumbled on our intolerance, low level of political culture, fear of change. That is why we lost so much time. The old system collapsed before the new one had time to begin working, and the crisis in the society became even more acute. I am aware of the dissatisfaction with the present hard situation, of the sharp criticism of authorities at all levels including my personal activities. But once again I'd like to stress that radical changes in such a vast country, and a country with such a heritage, cannot pass painlessly without difficulties and shake-up.

The August coup brought the general crisis to its ultimate limit. The most damaging thing about this crisis is the breakup of the state. And today I am worried by our people's loss of the citizenship of a great country. The consequences may turn out to be very hard for everyone.

I think it is vitally important to preserve the democratic achievements of the last years. They have been paid for by the suffering of our whole history, our tragic experience. They must not be given up under any circumstances or any pretext, otherwise all our hopes for the better will be buried. I am saying all this straight and honestly. It is my moral duty.

Today, I'd like to express my gratitude to all citizens who supported the policy of renovating the country, got involved in the implementation of democratic reforms. I am grateful to statesmen, public and political figures, millions of people abroad, those who understood our concepts and supported them, turned to us, started sincere cooperation with us.

I am leaving my post with apprehension, but also with hope, with faith in you, your wisdom and force of spirit.

We are the heirs of a great civilization, and its rebirth into a new, modern and dignified life now depends on one and all.

I wish to thank you with all my heart all those who have stood together with me all these years for a fair and good cause. Some mistakes could surely have been avoided; many things could have been done better. But I am convinced that sooner or later our common efforts will bear fruit, our nations will live in a prosperous and democratic society.

I wish all the best to all of you.

Yeltsin Speech to U.S. Congress

Following is the Reuter transcript of President Boris Yeltsin's speech to a joint session of the U.S. Congress on June 17, 1992, delivered through an interpreter:

Mr. Speaker, Mr. President, members of Congress, ladies and gentlemen:

It is indeed a great honor for me to address the Congress of the great land of freedom as the first-ever, over 1,000 years of history of Russia, popularly elected president, as a citizen of the great country which has made its choice in favor of liberty and democracy.

For many years, our two nations were the two poles, the two opposites. They wanted to make us implacable enemies. That affected the destinies of the world in a most tragic way.

The world was shaken by the storms of confrontation. It was close to exploding; close to perishing beyond salvation.

That evil scenario is becoming a thing of the past. Reason begins to triumph over madness. We have left behind the period when America and Russia looked at each other through gun sights, ready to pull the trigger at any time.

Despite what we saw in the well-known American film, "The Day After," it can be said today, tomorrow will be a day of peace, less of fear and more of hope for the happiness of our children.

The world can sigh in relief. The idol of communism, which spread everywhere social strife, animosity and unparalleled brutality, which instilled fear in humanity, has collapsed.

It has collapsed never to rise again. I am here to assure you, we will not let it rise again in our land.

I am glad that the people of Russia have found strength to shake off the crushing burden of the totalitarian system. I am proud that I am addressing you on behalf of the great people whose dignity is restored.

I admire ordinary Russian men and women who, in spite of severe trials, have preserved their intellectual integrity and are enduring tremendous hardships for the sake of the revival of their country.

Russia has made its final choice in favor of a civilized way of life, common sense and universal human heritage. I am convinced that our people will reach that goal. There is no people on this earth who could be harmed by the air of freedom. There are no exceptions to that rule.

Liberty sets the mind free, fosters independence and unorthodox thinking and ideas. But it does not offer instant prosperity or happiness and wealth to everyone. This is something that politicians in particular must keep in mind. Even the most benevolent intentions will inevitably be abandoned and committed to oblivion if they are not translated into everyday efforts.

Our experience of the recent years has conclusively pointed that out. Liberty will not be fooled. There can be no coexistence between democracy and a totalitarian state system. There can be no coexistence between market economy and powers who control everything and everyone.

There can be no coexistence between a civic society, which is pluralist by definition, and communist intolerance to dissent. The experience of the past decade has taught us: Communism has no human face. Freedom and communism are incompatible.

You will recall August 1991, when for three days Russia was under the dark cloud of dictatorship.

I addressed the Muscovites who were defending the White House of Russia. I addressed all the people of Russia. I addressed them standing on top of the tank whose crew had disobeyed criminal orders.

I will be candid with you: At that moment, I feared. But I had no fear for myself. I feared for the future of democracy in Russia and throughout the world. Because I was aware what could happen if we failed to win.

Citizens of Russia upheld their freedom and did not allow the continuation of the 75 years of nightmare. From this high rostrum I want to express our sincere thanks and gratitude to President Bush and to the American people for their invaluable moral support for the just cause of the people of Russia.

Last year citizens of Russia passed another difficult test of maturity. We chose to forgo vengeance and the intoxicating craving for summary justice over the fallen colossus known under the name of the CPSU [Communist Party of the Soviet Union].

There was no replay of history. The Communist Party citadel, next to the Kremlin, the Communist Bastille, was not destroyed. There was not a hint of violence against Communists in Russia. People simply brushed off the venomous dust of the past and went about their business.

There were no lynch law trials in Russia. The doings of the Communist Party over many years have been referred to the constitutional court of the Russian Federation. I am confident that its verdict will be fair.

Russia has seen for itself that any delay in strengthen-

ing the foundations of freedom and democracy can throw the society far back. For us the ominous lesson of the past is relevant today as never before. It was precisely in a devastated country, with an economy in near paralysis, that Bolshevism succeeded in building a totalitarian regime, creating a gigantic war machine and an insatiable military-industrial complex.

Economic and Political Reforms. This must not be allowed to happen again. That is why economic and political reforms are the primary tasks for Russia today. We are facing the challenges that no one has ever faced before at any one time.

We must carry through unprecedented reforms in the economy, which over the seven decades has been stripped of all market infrastructure; lay the foundations for democracy; and restore the rule of law in the country that for scores of years was poisoned with political strife and political oppression.

We have no right to fail in this most difficult endeavor, for there will be no second try, as in sports. Our predecessors have used them all up. The reforms must succeed.

I am given strength by the support of the majority of the citizens of Russia. The people of Russia are aware that there is no alternative to reform, and that this is very important.

My job, as everybody else's in Russia, is not an easy one. But in everything I do, I have the reliable and invaluable support of my wife, and of my entire large family.

Today I am telling you what I tell my fellow countrymen: I will not go back on the reforms. And it is practically impossible to topple Yeltsin in Russia. I am in good health, and I will not say "uncle" before I make the reforms irreversible.

We realize our great responsibility for the success of our changes, not only toward the people of Russia but also toward the citizens of America and of the entire world.

Today the freedom of America is being upheld in Russia. Should the reforms fail, it will cost hundreds of billions to upset that failure.

New Arms Treaty. Yesterday we concluded an unprecedented agreement on cutting down strategic offensive arsenals. They will be reduced radically in two phases, not by 30 or 40 percent, as negotiated previously over 15 years. They will be slashed to less than one-third of today's strength—from 21,000 nuclear warheads on both sides down to 6,000 to 7,000 by the year 2000. And it has taken us only five months to negotiate. And I fervently hope that George Bush and myself will be there in the year 2000 to preside over that.

We have simply no right to miss this unique opportunity, the more so that arms and the future of Russian reforms designed to make impossible any restoration of the totalitarian dictatorship in Russia are so dramatically interrelated.

I am here to say that we have the firm determination and the political will to move forward. We have proved that by what we have done.

It is Russia that has put an end to the imperial policies and was the first to recognize the independence of the Baltic republics.

Russia is a founding member of the Commonwealth of Independent States, which has averted uncontrolled disintegration of the former empire and the threat of a general interethnic blood bath.

Russia has granted tangible powers to its autonomous republics. The treaty of federation has been signed, and our nation has escaped the fate of the Soviet Union.

Russia has preserved its unity. It was Russia that substantially slowed down the flywheel of militarization and is doing all it can to stop it altogether.

I am formally announcing that, without waiting for the treaty to be signed, we have begun taking off alert the heavy SS-18 missiles targeted on the United States of America.

And the defense minister of Russia is here in this room to confirm that.

Russia has brought its policies toward a number of countries in line with its solemn declarations of the recent years. We have stopped arms deliveries to Afghanistan, where the senseless military adventure has taken thousands of Russian and hundreds of thousands of Afghan lives.

With external props removed, the puppet regime collapsed.

We have corrected the well-known imbalances in relations with Cuba. At present that country is one of our Latin American partners. Our commerce with Cuba is based on universally accepted principles and world prices.

An End to Double Standards. It is Russia that once and for all has done away with double standards in foreign policy. We are firmly resolved not to lie any more, either to our negotiating partners, or to the Russian or American or any other people.

There will be no more lies—ever.

The same applies to biological weapons experiments and the facts that have been revealed about American prisoners of war, the KAL 007 flight and many other things. That list could be continued.

The archives of the KGB and the Communist Party Central Committee are being opened.

Moreover, we are inviting the cooperation of the United States and other nations to investigate these dark pages.

I promise you that each and every document in each and every archive will be examined in order to investigate the fate of every American unaccounted for. As president of Russia, I assure you that even if one American has been detained in my country, and can still be found, I will find him; I will get him back to his family. (Sustained applause.)

I thank you for the applause. I could see everybody rise.

Some of you who have just risen here to applaud me have also written in the press that until Yeltsin gets things done and gets all the jobs done, there should be no Freedom Support Act passing through the Congress.

Well, I don't really quite understand you, ladies and gentlemen. This matter has been investigated, and is being investigated. Yeltsin has already opened the archives, and is inviting you to join us in investigating the fate of each and every unaccounted American.

So now you are telling me, first, do the job, and then we shall support you in passing that act? I don't quite understand you.

We have made tangible moves to make contact between Russia and foreign business communities much easier. Under the recent legislation, foreign nationals who privatize a facility or a building in Russia are given property rights to the plot of land on which they are located.

Legislation on bankruptcy has been recently enacted.

Mandatory sale of foreign currency to the state, at an artificially low rate of exchange, has been ended.

We are ready to bring our legal practice, as much as possible, in line with world standards, of course on the basis of symmetry with each country.

We are inviting the private sector of the United States to invest in the unique and untapped Russian market. And I am saying: Do not be late.

U.S. Policy. Now that the period of global confrontation is behind us, I call upon you to take a fresh look at the current policy of the United States toward Russia, and also to take a fresh look at the longer-term prospects of our relations.

Russia is a different country today. Sometimes the obsolete standards brought into being by a different era are artificially imposed on new realities.

True, that equally applies to us. Let us together, therefore, master the art of reconciling differences on the basis of partnership, which is the most efficient and democratic way.

This would come naturally both for the Russians and the Americans. If this is done, many of the problems which are now impeding mutual advantageous cooperation between Russia and the United States will become irrelevant, and I mean legislative frameworks too.

It will not be a wasteful endeavor. On the contrary, it will promote a more efficient solution of your problems, as well as of ours. And of course it will create new jobs, in Russia as well as in the United States.

History is giving us a chance to fulfill President [Woodrow] Wilson's dream, namely, to make the world safe for democracy.

More than 30 years ago, President [John F.] Kennedy addressed these words to humanity: "My fellow citizens of the world, ask not what America can do for you, but what together we can do for the freedom of man."

I believe that his inspired call for working together toward a democratic world is addressed above all to our two peoples, to the people of America and to the people of Russia.

Partnership and friendship of our two largest democracies, in strengthening democracy, is indeed a great goal.

Joining the world community, we wish to preserve our identity, our own image and history, promote culture, strengthen moral standards of our people.

We find relevant the warning of the great Russian philosopher, Berdyaev, who said to negate Russia in the name of humankind is to rob humankind.

At the same time, Russia does not aspire to change the world in its own image. It is the fundamental principle of the new Russia to be generous and to share experience, moral values and emotional warmth, rather than to impose and curse.

It is the tradition of the Russian people to repay kindness with kindness. This is the bedrock of the Russian lifestyle, the underlying truth revealed by the great Russian culture.

Free and democratic Russia will remain committed to this tenet. Today, free and democratic Russia is extending its hand of friendship to the people of America. Acting on the will of the people of Russia, I am inviting you, and through you, the people of the United States, to join us in partnership in the quest for freedom and justice in the 21st century.

The Russo-American dialogue has gone through many a dramatic moment. But the peoples of Russia and America have never gone to war against each other. Even in the darkest periods, our affinity prevailed over our hatred.

In this context, I would like to recall something that took place 50 years ago. The unprecedented war, world war, was waging. Russia, which was bleeding white, and all our people were looking forward to the opening of the second front. And it was opened, first and foremost, thanks to the active stance taken by President [Franklin D.] Roosevelt and by the entire American people.

Sometimes I think that if today, like during that war, a second but peaceful front could be opened to promote democratic market reforms, their success would be guaranteed early.

The passing by Congress of the Freedom Support Act could become the first step in that direction.

Today legislation promoting reforms is much more important than appropriation of funds.

May I express the hope that the United States Congress, as the staunch advocate of freedom, will remain faithful to its strategic course on this occasion as well.

Members of Congress, every man is a man of his own time. No exception is ever made for anyone, whether an ordinary citizen or the president. Much experience has been gained; many things have been reassessed.

I would like now to conclude my statement with the words from a song by Irving Berlin, an American of Russian descent: God bless America, to which I add, and Russia.

BIBLIOGRAPHY

CHAPTER 1
Imperial Russia and the Revolution

Books

Bain, Robert N. *First Romanovs, 1613-1725*. New York: Russell & Russell, 1967.

Ball, Alan M. *Russia's Last Capitalists: The Nepmen, 1921-1929*. Berkeley and Los Angeles: University of California Press, 1987.

Bashkina, Nina N., ed. *The United States and Russia: The Beginning of Relations, 1765-1815*. Washington, D.C.: Government Printing Office, 1980.

Berlin, Isaiah. *Karl Marx: His Life and Environment*. New York: Oxford University Press, 1959.

Billington, James H. *The Icon and the Axe*. New York: Random House, 1970.

Browder, Robert P., and Alexander F. Kerensky, eds. *The Russian Provisional Government Documents*. 3 vols. Stanford, Calif.: Stanford University Press, 1961.

Budurowycz, Bohdan B. *Polish-Soviet Relations, 1917-1921*. Cambridge, Mass.: Harvard University Press, 1969.

Carr, Edward H. *A History of Soviet Russia*. 3 vols. New York: Macmillan, 1953.

Chernov, Victor M. *The Great Russian Revolution*. Translated and abridged by Philip E. Moseley. New Haven, Conn.: Yale University Press, 1936.

Clarkson, Jesse D. *History of Russia*. New York: Random House, 1969.

Crankshaw, Edward. *The Shadow of the Winter Palace: The Drift to Revolution, 1825-1917*. New York: Penguin, 1976.

Curtiss, John S. *The Russian Army under Nicholas I*. Durham, N.C.: Duke University Press, 1965.

Deutscher, Isaac. *The Prophet Armed: Trotsky, 1879-1921*. New York: Oxford University Press, 1954.

Dukes, P. *Catherine the Great and the Russian Nobility*. New York: Cambridge University Press, 1968.

Fedyshyn, Oleh S. *Germany's Drive to the East and the Ukrainian Revolution, 1917-1918*. New Brunswick, N.J.: Rutgers University Press, 1971.

Field, Daniel. *Rebels in the Name of the Tsar*. Boston: Houghton Mifflin, 1976.

Freeze, Gregory L. *From Supplication to Revolution: A Documentary Social History of Imperial Russia*. New York: Oxford University Press, 1988.

Graham, Stephen. *Tsar of Freedom: The Life and Reign of Alexander II*. Hamden, Conn.: Shoe String Press, 1968.

Hingley, Ronald. *Tsars: From Ivan the Terrible to Nicholas II, 1533-1917*. Urbana-Champaign: University of Illinois Press, 1968.

Hunt, R. N. Carew. *The Theory and Practice of Communism*. New York: Macmillan, 1957.

Johnson, Robert E. *Peasant and Proletarian: The Working Class of Moscow at the End of the 19th Century*. New Brunswick, N.J.: Rutgers University Press, 1979.

Kahan, Arcadius. *Russian Economic History: The Nineteenth Century*. Chicago: University of Chicago Press, 1989.

Kenez, Peter. *Civil War in South Russia, 1919-1920: The Defeat of the Whites*. Berkeley and Los Angeles: University of California Press, 1977.

Kerensky, Alexander. *The Catastrophe*. New York: Appleton-Century-Crofts, 1929.

Kettle, Michael. *Road to Intervention: March-November 1918*. New York: Routledge, 1988.

Kochan, Miriam L. *The Last Days of Imperial Russia: 1910-1917*. New York: Macmillan, 1976.

_____. *Life in Russia under Catherine the Great*. New York: Putnam, 1969.

Koenker, Diane, William G. Rosenberg, and Ronald Grigor Suny, eds. *Party, State and Society in the Russian Civil War: Explorations in Social History*. Bloomington: Indiana University Press, 1989.

Lane, David. *The Roots of Russian Communism: A Social and Historical Study of Russian Social Democracy, 1898-1907*. University Park: Pennsylvania State University Press, 1975.

Lawrence, John. *A History of Russia*. New York: New American Library, 1978.

Leggett, George. *The Cheka: Lenin's Secret Police*. New York: Oxford University Press, 1981.

Lenin, V. I. *Selected Works*. 12 vols. New York: International Publishers, 1938.

Lewin, Moshe. *Lenin's Last Struggle*. New York: Monthly Review Press, 1978.

Lyons, Marvin. *Nicholas II: The Last Tsar*. New York: St. Martin's, 1975.

Massie, Robert P. *Nicholas and Alexandra*. New York: Atheneum, 1967.

_____. *Peter the Great*. New York: Random House, 1981.

McCauley, Martin, and Peter Waldron. *The Emergence of the Modern Russian State, 1855-1881*. Basingstoke (Eng.): Macmillan, 1988.

Medvedev, Roy A. *The October Revolution*. New York: Columbia University Press, 1979.

Mosse, Werner E. *Alexander the Second and the Modernization of Russia*. New York: Macmillan, 1962.

Offord, Derek. *The Russian Revolutionary Movement in the 1880's*. New York: Cambridge University Press, 1986.

Pares, Bernard. *The Fall of the Russian Monarchy: A Study of the Evidence*. New York: Knopf, 1939.

_____. *A History of Russia*. New York: Knopf, 1953.

Pipes, Richard, ed. *Revolutionary Russia*. Cambridge, Mass.: Harvard University Press, 1968.

Presniakov, Alexander E. *Emperor Nicholas the First of Russia: The Apogee of Autocracy, 1825-1855*. Gulf Breeze, Fla.: Academic International, 1974.

Riasanovsky, Nicholas V. *A History of Russia*. 3d ed. New York: Oxford University Press, 1977.

Rywkin, Michael, ed. *Russian Colonial Expansion to 1917*. New York: Mansell, 1988.

Saul, Norman E. *Sailors in Revolt: The Russian Baltic Fleet in 1917*. Lawrence: University of Kansas Press, 1978.

Seton-Watson, Hugh. *The Decline of Imperial Russia, 1855-1914*. New York: Praeger, 1952.

_____. *Russian Empire, 1801-1917*. New York: Oxford University Press, 1967.

Shanin, Teodor. *Russia, 1905-1907: Revolution as a Moment of Truth*. New Haven: Yale University Press, 1986.

Smith, Edward E. *The Young Stalin: The Early Years of an Elusive Revolutionary*. New York: Farrar, Strauss & Giroux, 1967.

Sokol, Edward D. *The Revolt of 1916 in Russian Central Asia*. New York: AMS Press, 1978.

Szamuely, Tibor. *The Russian Tradition*. New York: McGraw-Hill, 1975.

Thomas, Benjamin P. *Russo-American Relations, 1815-1867*. New York: AMS Press, 1978.

Troyat, Henri. *Catherine the Great*. New York: E. P. Dutton, 1980.

Tucker, Robert C., ed. *The Lenin Anthology*. New York: W. W. Norton, 1975.

Ulam, Adam B. *The Bolsheviks*. New York: Collier, 1968.

Vernadsky, George. *A History of Russia*. 6th ed. New Haven, Conn.: Yale University Press, 1969.

Von Laue, Theodore H. *Why Lenin? Why Stalin? A Reappraisal of the Russian Revolution*. New York: Harper & Row, 1971.

Wolfe, Bertram D. *Three Who Made a Revolution*. New York: Dial, 1964.

Yanov, Alexander. *The Origins of Autocracy: Ivan the Terrible in Russian History*. Berkeley and Los Angeles: University of California Press, 1981.

CHAPTER 2
Stalin Era

Books

Antonov-Ovseyenko, Anton. *The Time of Stalin: Portrait of a Tyranny*. New York: Harper & Row, 1982.

Bialer, Seweryn, ed. *Stalin and His Generals: Soviet Military Memoirs of World War II*. New York: Pegasus, 1969.

Brzezinski, Zbigniew. *The Permanent Purge: Politics of Soviet Totalitarianism*. Cambridge, Mass.: Harvard University Press, 1956.

Clark, Alan. *Barbarossa: The Russian-German Conflict, 1941-45*. New York: William Morrow, 1965.

Clemens, Diane Shaver. *Yalta*. New York: Oxford University Press, 1970.

Conquest, Robert. *The Great Terror: Stalin's Purge of the Thirties*. New York: Macmillan, 1968.

_____. *The Great Terror: A Reassessment*. New York: Oxford University Press, 1990.

Dallin, David J. *Soviet Russia's Foreign Policy: 1939-1942*. New Haven, Conn.: Yale University Press, 1942.

Davis, Lynn E. *The Cold War Begins*. Princeton, N.J.: Princeton University Press, 1974.

Deane, John R. *The Strange Alliance: The Story of Our Efforts at Wartime Cooperation with Russia*. New York: Viking, 1947.

Dedjer, Vladimir. *The Battle Stalin Lost: Memoirs of Yugoslavia, 1948-1953*. New York: Viking, 1971.

Deutscher, Isaac. *Stalin: A Political Biography*. 2d ed. New York: Oxford University Press, 1966.

Djilas, Milovan. *Conversations with Stalin*. Translated by Michael B. Petrovich. New York: Harcourt, Brace & World, 1962.

Druks, Herbert. *Harry S. Truman and the Russians, 1945-1953.* New York: Speller & Sons, 1967.

Feis, Herbert. *Churchill, Roosevelt, Stalin: The War They Waged and the Peace They Sought.* Princeton, N.J.: Princeton University Press, 1957.

Fischer, George. *Soviet Opposition to Stalin: A Case Study in World War II.* Cambridge, Mass.: Harvard University Press, 1952.

Fleming, D. F. *The Cold War and Its Origins: 1917-1960.* 2 vols. Garden City, N.Y.: Doubleday, 1961.

Gaddis, John Lewis. *The United States and the Origins of the Cold War, 1941-1947.* New York: Columbia University Press, 1972.

Gormly, James L. *The Collapse of the Grand Alliance, 1945-1948.* Baton Rouge: Louisiana State University Press, 1987.

Hahn, Werner G. *Postwar Soviet Politics: The Fall of Zhdanov and the Defeat of Moderation.* Ithaca, N.Y.: Cornell University Press, 1982.

Kennan, George F. *Soviet Foreign Policy, 1917-1941.* New York: Van Nostrand, 1960.

Levytsky, Borys. *The Stalinist Terror in the Thirties.* Stanford, Calif.: Hoover Institution Press, 1974.

McNeal, Robert Hatch. *Stalin: Man and Ruler.* New York: New York University Press, 1988.

Medvedev, Roy A. *All Stalin's Men: Six Who Carried Out the Bloody Policies.* Garden City, N.Y.: Anchor, 1985.

____. *Let History Judge.* Rev. ed. New York: Columbia University Press, 1989.

Neumann, William L. *After Victory: Churchill, Roosevelt, Stalin and the Making of the Peace.* New York: Harper & Row, 1967.

Resis, Albert. *Stalin, the Politburo, and the Onset of the Cold War.* Pittsburgh: University of Pittsburgh Press, 1988.

Salisbury, Harrison E. *Moscow Journal: The End of Stalin.* Chicago: University of Chicago Press, 1961.

____. *900 Days: The Siege of Leningrad.* New York: Harper & Row, 1969.

Seabury, Paul. *The Rise and Decline of the Cold War.* New York: Basic Books, 1967.

Solzhenitsyn, Alexander. *The Gulag Archipelago, 1918-1956: An Experiment in Literary Investigation.* 2 vols. New York: Harper & Row, 1974.

Sontag, Raymond J., and James S. Beddie, eds. *Nazi-Soviet Relations, 1939-1941: Documents from Archives of German Foreign Office.* Westport, Conn.: Greenwood, 1976.

Stalin, J. V. *On the Great Patriotic War of the Soviet Union.* Moscow: Foreign Languages Publishing House, 1945.

Stettinius, Edward R., Jr. *Roosevelt and the Russians: The Yalta Conference.* Garden City, N.Y.: Doubleday, 1949.

Taubman, William. *Stalin's American Policy: From Entente to Détente to Cold War.* New York: W. W. Norton, 1982.

Trotsky, Leon. *Trotsky's Diary in Exile, 1935.* Cambridge, Mass.: Harvard University Press, 1959.

Tucker, Robert C. *Stalin as Revolutionary, 1879-1929: A Study in History and Personality.* New York: W. W. Norton, 1973.

Ulam, Adam B. *Stalin: The Man and His Era.* New York: Viking, 1973.

Voznesensky, Nicholas. *Economy of the USSR during World War II.* Washington, D.C.: Public Affairs Press, 1948.

Wittlin, Thaddeus. *Commissar: The Life and Death of Lavrenty Pavlovich Beria.* New York: Macmillan, 1972.

Wolin, Simon, and Robert M. Slusser, eds. *The Soviet Secret Police.* New York: Praeger, 1957.

CHAPTER 3
Khrushchev Era

Books

Allison, Graham T. *Essence of Decision: Explaining the Cuban Missile Crisis.* Boston: Little, Brown, 1971.

Armstrong, John A. *The Politics of Totalitarianism.* New York: Random House, 1961.

Bialer, Seweryn. *Stalin's Successors: Leadership, Stability, and Change in the Soviet Union.* New York: Cambridge University Press, 1980.

Breslauer, George W. *Khrushchev and Brezhnev as Leaders: Building Authority in Soviet Politics.* Winchester, Mass.: Allen & Unwin, 1982.

Brzezinski, Zbigniew, and Samuel P. Huntington. *Political Power: USA/USSR.* New York: Viking, 1964.

Crankshaw, Edward. *Khrushchev: A Career.* New York: Penguin, 1966.

Dallin, Alexander, ed. *Soviet Conduct in World Affairs.* New York: Columbia University Press, 1960.

Dinerstein, Herbert S. *The Making of a Missile Crisis: October 1962.* Baltimore: Johns Hopkins University Press, 1976.

Dornberg, John. *The New Tsars: Russia under Stalin's Heirs.* Garden City, N.Y.: Doubleday, 1972.

Garthoff, Raymond L. *Soviet Strategy in the Nuclear Age.* New York: Praeger, 1958.

Gehlen, Michael P. *The Politics of Coexistence: Soviet Methods and Motives.* Bloomington: Indiana University Press, 1967.

Goldman, Eric. *The Crucial Decade and After, 1945-1960.* New York: Vintage, 1960.

Horelick, Arnold L., and Myron Rush. *Strategic Power*

and Soviet Foreign Policy. Chicago: University of Chicago Press, 1965.

Hyland, William, and Richard W. Shryock. *The Fall of Khrushchev*. New York: Funk & Wagnalls, 1968.

Jones, Goronwy J. *From Stalin to Khrushchev*. London: Linden, 1960.

Kennedy, Robert F. *Thirteen Days: A Memoir of the Cuban Missile Crisis*. New York: W. W. Norton, 1971.

Linden, Carl A. *Khrushchev and the Soviet Leadership, 1957-1964*. Baltimore: Johns Hopkins University Press, 1966.

McClosky, Herbert, and John E. Turner. *The Soviet Dictatorship*. New York: McGraw-Hill, 1960.

Overstreet, Harry A., and Bonaro Overstreet. *War Called Peace: Khrushchev's Communism*. New York: W. W. Norton, 1961.

Schecter, Jerrold L., ed. and trans. *Khrushchev Remembers: The Glasnost Tapes*. Boston: Little, Brown, 1991.

Smolansky, Oles. *The Soviet Union and the Arab East under Khrushchev*. Lewisburg, Pa.: Bucknell University Press, 1974.

Talbott, Strobe, ed. *Khrushchev Remembers*. Boston: Little, Brown, 1970.

———. *The Last Testament*. Boston: Little, Brown, 1974.

CHAPTER 4
Brezhnev Era

Books

Amalrik, Andrei. *Will the Soviet Union Survive until 1984?* New York: Harper & Row, 1970.

Dallin, Alexander, and Thomas H. Larson, eds. *Soviet Politics since Khrushchev*. Englewood Cliffs, N.J.: Prentice-Hall, 1968.

Dawisha, Karen. *Kremlin and the Prague Spring*. Berkeley: University of California Press, 1984.

Dornberg, John. *Brezhnev: The Masks of Power*. New York: Basic Books, 1974.

Dzirkals, Lilita, Thane Gustafson, and A. Ross Johnson. *The Media and Intra-Elite Communication in the USSR*. Santa Monica, Calif.: Rand Corporation, 1982.

Edmonds, Robin. *Soviet Foreign Policy 1962-1973: The Parody of Super Power*. New York: Oxford University Press, 1975.

Eidlin, Fred. *The Logic of Normalization: The Soviet Intervention in Czechoslovakia of 21 August 1968 and the Czechoslovakia Response*. New York: Columbia University Press, 1980.

Gelman, Harry. *The Brezhnev Politburo and the Decline of Détente*. Ithaca, N.Y.: Cornell University Press, 1984.

Hough, Jerry F. *Soviet Leadership in Transition*. Washington, D.C.: Brookings Institution, 1977.

———. *The Soviet Prefects*. Cambridge, Mass.: Harvard University Press, 1969.

Kelley, Donald R., ed. *Soviet Politics in the Brezhnev Era*. New York: Praeger, 1980.

Levesque, Jacques. *The USSR and the Cuban Revolution: Soviet Ideological and Strategic Perspectives, 1959-77*. New York: Praeger, 1981.

London, Kurt, ed. *The Soviet Union in World Politics*. Boulder, Colo.: Westview, 1980.

Nixon, Richard. *RN: The Memoirs of Richard Nixon*. New York: Grosset & Dunlap, 1978.

Pipes, Richard. *U.S.-Soviet Relations in the Era of Détente*. Boulder, Colo.: Westview, 1981.

Simes, Dimitri K. *Détente and Conflict: Soviet Foreign Policy, 1972-1977*. Beverly Hills, Calif.: Sage, 1977.

Simis, Konstantin M. *USSR: The Corrupt Society (The Secret World of Soviet Capitalism)*. New York: Simon and Schuster, 1982.

Simon, Jeffrey. *Ruling Communist Parties and Détente: A Documentary History*. Washington, D.C.: American Enterprise Institute for Public Policy Research, 1975.

Stoessinger, John G. *Nations in Darkness: China, Russia and America*. New York: Random House, 1981.

Strong, John W. *Soviet Union under Brezhnev and Kosygin: The Transition Years*. New York: Van Nostrand Reinhold, 1971.

Tatu, Michel. *Power in the Kremlin from Khrushchev to Kosygin*. New York: Macmillan, 1969.

Ulam, Adam B. *Dangerous Relations: The Soviet Union in World Politics, 1970-1982*. New York: Oxford University Press, 1983.

Valenta, Jiri. *Soviet Intervention in Czechoslovakia, 1968*. Baltimore: Johns Hopkins University Press, 1979.

Yanov, Alexander. *Détente after Brezhnev: The Domestic Roots of Soviet Foreign Policy*. Berkeley: Institute of International Studies, University of California, 1977.

Zeman, Z. A. B. *Prague Spring: A Report on Czechoslovakia*. Baltimore: Penguin, 1969.

Articles

Arbatov, Georgii. "The Great Lie of the Opponents of Détente." *Pravda,* February 5, 1977.

Aspaturian, Vernon V. "The Aftermath of the Czech Invasion." *Current History* (November 1968): 263-267.

Blumenfeld, Yorick. "Russia's Diplomatic Offensive." *Editorial Research Reports*, April 5, 1972, 253-270.

Borisov, A. "A Chronicle of Soviet Foreign Policy." *International Affairs* (January 1981): 88-92.

Campbell, John C. "Soviet-American Relations: Conflict and Cooperation." *Current History* (October 1967): 193-202.

Cohen, Stephen F. "The Friends and Foes of Change:

Reformism and Conservatism in the Soviet Union." *Slavic Review* (June 1979): 197-202.

Conquest, Robert. "The Limits of Détente." *Foreign Affairs* (Summer 1968): 733-742.

_____. "A New Russia? A New World?" *Foreign Affairs* (Spring 1975): 482-497.

Costello, Mary. "Russia after Détente." *Editorial Research Reports,* February 6, 1981, 83-104.

Deans, Ralph C. "Trends in U.S.-Soviet Relations." *Editorial Research Reports,* May 25, 1973, 399-416.

Gilison, Jerome M. "New Factors of Stability in Soviet Collective Leadership." *World Politics* (July 1967): 563-581.

Gitelman, Zvi. "The Politics of Socialist Restoration in Hungary and Czechoslovakia." *Comparative Politics* (January 1981): 187-210.

Gray, Colin. "The Most Dangerous Decade: Historic Mission, Legitimacy, and Dynamics of the Soviet Empire in the 1980s." *Orbis* (Spring 1981): 13-28.

Hough, Jerry. "The Soviet Elite: In Whose Hands the Future?" *Problems of Communism* (March-April 1967): 18-25.

Laqueur, Walter. "Reagan and the Russians." *Commentary* (January 1982): 19-26.

Legvold, Robert. "The Nature of Soviet Power." *Foreign Affairs* (Fall 1977): 49-71.

Leonhard, Wolfgang. "The Domestic Politics of the New Soviet Foreign Policy." *Foreign Affairs* (Fall 1973): 59-74.

Liska, George. "Russia and the West: The Next to the Last Phase." *SAIS Review* (Summer 1981): 141-153.

Meissner, Boris. "The Soviet Union under Brezhnev and Kosygin." *Modern Age* (Winter 1966-1967): 7-23.

Nitze, Paul H. "Strategy in the Decade of the 1980s." *Foreign Affairs* (Fall 1980): 82-101.

Pennar, Jaan. "The Arabs, Marxism and Moscow: A Historical Survey." *Middle East Journal* (September 1968): 433-447.

Pick, Otto. "Reacting to Reagan: Soviet Fears and Opportunities." *World Today* (July/August 1981): 262-291.

Ploss, Sidney. "Politics in the Kremlin." *Problems of Communism* (May-June 1970): 1-14.

Salisbury, Harrison E. "Russia vs. China: Global Conflict?" *Antioch Review* (Winter 1967-1968): 425-439.

Shulman, Marshall D. "Toward a Western Philosophy of Coexistence." *Foreign Affairs* (Fall 1973): 35-58.

Sorensen, Theodore C. "Most-Favored-Nation and Less Favorite Nations." *Foreign Affairs* (Winter 1973-1974): 273-286.

Spechler, Dina Rome. "The USSR and Third World Conflicts: Domestic Debate and Soviet Policy in the Middle East, 1967-1973." *World Politics* (April 1986): 435-461.

Tucker, Robert C. "Swollen State, Spent Society: Stalin's Legacy to Brezhnev's Russia." *Foreign Affairs* (Winter 1981-1982): 414-435.

CHAPTER 5
Gorbachev Comes to Power

Books

Beichman, Arnold, and M. S. Bernstam. *Andropov: New Challenge to the West.* New York: Stein & Day, 1983.

Bialer, Seweryn. *The Soviet Paradox: External Expansion, Internal Decline.* New York: Knopf, 1986.

Brown, Archie, and Michael Kaser, eds. *Soviet Policy for the 1980s.* Bloomington: Indiana University Press, 1983.

Butson, Thomas G. *Gorbachev: A Biography.* New York: Stein & Day, 1985.

Byrnes, Robert F., ed. *After Brezhnev: Sources of Soviet Conduct in the 1980s.* Bloomington: Indiana University Press and Georgetown University Center for Strategic and International Studies, 1983.

Colton, Timothy J. *The Dilemma of Reform in the Soviet Union.* New York: Council of Foreign Relations, 1986.

Dallin, Alexander, and Condoleezza Rice, eds. *The Gorbachev Era.* Stanford, Calif.: Stanford University Press, 1986.

Davies, Robert Will. *Soviet History in the Gorbachev Revolution.* Basingstoke (Eng.): Macmillan, 1989.

Desai, Padma. *Perestroika in Perspective: The Design and Dilemmas of Soviet Reform.* Princeton, N.J.: Princeton University Press, 1989.

Dizard, Wilson, and S. Blake Swensrud. *Gorbachev's Information Revolution: Controlling Glasnost in a New Electronic Age.* Boulder, Colo.: Westview, 1987.

Doder, Dusko. *Shadows and Whispers: Power Politics inside the Kremlin from Brezhnev to Gorbachev.* New York: Random House, 1986.

Dyker, David A., ed. *The Soviet Union under Gorbachev: The Real Prospects for Reform.* London: Croom Helm, 1987.

Ebon, Martin. *The Andropov File.* New York: McGraw-Hill, 1983.

Goldman, Marshall I. *Gorbachev's Challenge: Economic Reform in the Age of High Technology.* New York: W. W. Norton, 1987.

Gorbachev, Mikhail S. *Perestroika: New Thinking for Our Country and the World.* New York: Harper & Row, 1987.

_____. *A Time for Peace.* New York: Richardson & Steirman, 1986.

Gunlicks, Arthur B., and John D. Treadway, eds. *Soviet*

Union under Gorbachev: Assessing the First Year. New York: Praeger, 1987.

Hazan, Barukh. *From Brezhnev to Gorbachev: Infighting in the Kremlin.* Boulder, Colo.: Westview, 1987.

Hough, Jerry F. *Russia and the West: Gorbachev and the Politics of Reform.* New York: Simon and Schuster, 1988.

Kerblay, Basile H. *Gorbachev's Russia.* New York: Pantheon, 1989.

Laqueur, Walter. *The Long Road to Freedom: Russia and Glasnost.* London: Unwin Hyman, 1989.

Lerner, Lawrence, and Donald Treadgold, eds. *Gorbachev and the Soviet Future.* Boulder, Colo.: Westview, 1988.

McCauley, Martin, ed. *The Soviet Union under Gorbachev.* New York: St. Martin's, 1987.

Medvedev, Zhores A. *Andropov.* New York: W. W. Norton, 1983.

———. *Gorbachev.* New York: W. W. Norton, 1986.

Miller, William Green, ed. *Toward a More Civil Society?: The USSR under Mikhail Sergeyevich Gorbachev.* New York: Harper & Row, 1989.

Shlapentokh, Vladimir. *Soviet Ideologies in the Period of Glasnost: Responses to Brezhnev's Stagnation.* New York: Praeger, 1988.

Smith, Gordon B. *Soviet Politics: Continuity and Contradiction.* New York: St. Martin's, 1988.

Solovyov, Vladimir, and Elena Klepikova. *Yuri Andropov: A Secret Passage into the Kremlin.* New York: Macmillan, 1983.

Tarasulo, Isaac J., ed. *Gorbachev and Glasnost: Viewpoints from the Soviet Press.* Wilmington, Del.: Scholarly Resources, 1989.

Zamascikov, Sergei. *Gorbachev and the Soviet Military.* Santa Monica, Calif.: Rand Corporation, 1988.

Zemtsov, Ilya. *Chernenko: The Last Bolshevik: The Soviet Union on the Eve of Perestroika.* New Brunswick, N.J.: Transaction, 1989.

———, and John Farrar. *Gorbachev: The Man and the System.* New Brunswick, N.J.: Transaction, 1989.

Articles

Bialer, Seweryn, and Joan Afferica. "Gorbachev's World." *Foreign Affairs* (America and the World, 1985): 605-644.

Bilinsky, Yaroslav. "Nationality Policy in Gorbachev's First Year." *Orbis* (Summer 1986): 331-342.

Brown, Archie. "Andropov: Discipline *and* Reform." *Problems of Communism* (January-February 1983): 18-31.

Caldwell, Lawrence, and Robert Legvold. "Reagan through Soviet Eyes." *Foreign Policy* (Fall 1983): 3-21.

Connor, Walter D. "Social Policy under Gorbachev."

Problems of Communism (July-August 1986): 31-46.

Cooper, Mary H. "Gorbachev's Challenge." *Editorial Research Reports,* February 14, 1986, 107-124.

Epstein, Edward Jay. "The Andropov File." *New Republic,* February 7, 1983, 18-21.

Gati, Charles. "Soviet Empire: Alive but Not Well." *Problems of Communism* (March-April 1985): 73-86.

Gelb, Leslie H. "What We Really Know about Russia." *New York Times Magazine,* December 28, 1984, 22-25.

Griffiths, Franklyn. "The Sources of American Conduct: Soviet Perspectives and Their Policy Implications." *International Security* (Fall 1984): 3-50.

Gustafson, Thane, and Dawn Mann. "Gorbachev's First Year: Building Power and Authority." *Problems of Communism* (May-June 1986): 1-19.

Hahn, Werner. "Electoral Choice in the Soviet Bloc." *Problems of Communism* (March-April 1987): 29-39.

Houslohner, Peter. "Gorbachev's Social Contract." *Soviet Economy* (January-March 1987): 54-89.

Katsenelinboigen, Aron. "Will Glasnost Bring the Reactionaries to Power?" *Orbis* (Spring 1988): 217-230.

Lyne, Roderic. "Making Waves: Mr. Gorbachev's Public Policy, 1985-1986." *International Affairs* (Spring 1987): 205-224.

Parrott, Bruce. "Soviet National Security under Gorbachev." *Problems of Communism* (November-December 1988): 1-36.

Ploss, Sidney I. "A New Soviet Era?" *Foreign Policy* (Spring 1986): 46-60.

Powell, David E. "Soviet Glasnost: Definitions and Dimensions." *Current History* (October 1988): 321-324.

Rumer, Boris. "The Consequences of Chernobyl." *Problems of Communism* (November-December 1986): 1-58.

Sherlock, Thomas. "Politics and History under Gorbachev." *Problems of Communism* (May-August 1988): 16-42.

Simes, Dimitri. "America's New Edge." *Foreign Policy* (Fall 1984): 24-43.

———. "National Security under Andropov." *Problems of Communism* (January-February 1983): 32-39.

———. "The New Soviet Challenge." *Foreign Policy* (Summer 1984): 113-131.

Wall, Josephine. "Glasnost and Soviet Culture." *Problems of Communism* (November-December 1989): 40-50.

Zagoria, Donald. "The Moscow-Beijing Détente." *Foreign Affairs* (Spring 1983): 853-873.

Zelnick, Robert C. "The Foundering Soviets." *Foreign Policy* (Winter 1984-1985): 92-107.

Zlotnik, Marc D. "Chernenko Succeeds." *Problems of Communism* (March-April 1984): 17-31.

CHAPTER 6
The Second Russian Revolution

Books

Allison, Graham T., and Grigory Yavlinsky. *Window of Opportunity: The Grand Bargain for Democracy in the Soviet Union*. New York: Pantheon, 1991.

Clark, Susan L. *Gorbachev's Agenda*. Boulder, Colo.: Westview, 1989.

Doder, Dusko, and Louise Branson. *Gorbachev: Heretic in the Kremlin*. New York: Viking, 1990.

Goldman, Marshall. *What Went Wrong with Perestroika?* New York: Norton, 1991.

Gorbachev, Mikhail S. *The August Coup: The Truth and the Lessons*. New York: HarperCollins, 1991.

Gwertzman, Bernard, and Michael Kaufman. *The Collapse of Communism*. New York: New York Times, 1992.

Kaiser, Robert. *Why Gorbachev Happened: His Triumphs, His Failure, and His Fall*. New York: Simon and Schuster, 1991.

Lewin, Moshe. *The Gorbachev Phenomenon: An Historical Interpretation*. Berkeley and Los Angeles: University of California Press, 1991.

Tarasulo, Isaac J., ed. *Perils of Perestroika: Viewpoints from the Soviet Press 1989-1991*. Wilmington, Del.: Scholarly Resources, 1992.

Taubman, William, and Jane Taubman. *Moscow Spring*. New York: Summit, 1989.

Woodby, Sylvia. *Gorbachev and the Decline of Ideology*. Boulder, Colo.: Westview, 1989.

Articles

Alksnis, Viktor. "Suffering from Self-Determination." *Foreign Policy* (Fall 1991): 61-71.

Avineri, Shlomo. "The Return to History: The Breakup of the Soviet Union." *Brookings Review* (Spring 1992): 30-33.

Bialer, Seweryn. "The Death of Soviet Communism." *Foreign Affairs* (America and the World 1991-1992): 166-181.

Breslauer, George. "Reflections on the Anniversary of the August 1991 Coup." *Soviet Economy* (April-June 1992): 164-174.

Brudny, Yitzhak M. "The Heralds of Opposition to Perestroyka." *Soviet Economy* (April-June 1989): 162.

Colton, Timothy J. "The Resignation of Mikhail Gorbachev." *Soviet Economy* (October-December 1991): 277-280.

Gooding, John. "Perestroika as Revolution from Within: An Interpretation." *Russian Review* (January 1992): 36-57.

Mandelbaum, Michael. "Coup de Grace: The End of the Soviet Union." *Foreign Affairs* (America and the World 1991-1992): 164-183.

Miller, Stephen. "The Soviet Coup and the Benefits of Breakdown." *Orbis* (Winter 1992): 69-85.

Meyer, Stephen. "How the Threat (and the Coup) Collapsed." *International Security* (Winter 1991/92): 5-38.

Sturua, Melor. "The Real Coup." *Foreign Policy* (Winter 1991): 63-72.

Swoboda, Victor. "Was the Soviet Union Really Necessary?" *Soviet Studies*, no. 5 (1992): 761-784.

CHAPTER 7
The Commonwealth

Books

Alexis, Alexander R., and S. Enders Wimbush, eds. *Ethnic Minorities in the Red Army: Asset or Liability?* Boulder, Colo.: Westview, 1988.

Amalrik, Andrei. *Will the Soviet Union Survive until 1984?* New York: Harper & Row, 1970.

Bialer, Seweryn, ed. *Politics, Society and Nationality inside Gorbachev's Russia*. Boulder, Colo.: Westview, 1989.

Billington, James. *Russia Transformed: The Breakthrough to Hope*. New York: Free Press, 1992.

Conquest, Robert, ed. *The Last Empire: Nationality and the Soviet Future*. Stanford, Calif.: Hoover Institution Press, 1986.

Currie, Kenneth. *Soviet Military Politics: Contemporary Issues*. New York: Paragon House, 1992.

Karklins, Rasma. *Ethnic Relations in the USSR: The Perspective from Below*. Boston: Allen & Unwin, 1986.

Kozlov, Viktor I. *The Peoples of the Soviet Union*. Bloomington: Indiana University Press, 1988.

Lebov, Oleg, and John Crowfoot, eds. *The Soviet Empire: Its Nations Speak Out*. New York: Harwood, 1989.

Motyl, Alexander J. *Will the Non-Russians Rebel?* Ithaca, N.Y.: Cornell University Press, 1987.

Pankhurst, Jerry G., and Michael Paul Sacks. *Contemporary Soviet Society: Sociological Perspectives*. New York: Praeger, 1980.

Pushkarev, Sergei, Vladimir Rusak, and Gleb Yakunin. *Christianity and Government in Russia and the Soviet Union*. Boulder, Colo.: Westview, 1989.

Sacks, Michael Paul, and Jerry G. Pankhurst, eds. *Understanding Soviet Society*. Boston: Allen & Unwin, 1988.

Steeves, Paul. *Keeping the Faiths: Religion and Ideology in the Soviet Union*. New York: Holmes & Meier, 1989.

Articles

Armstrong, John A. "Nationalism in the Former Soviet Empire." *Problems of Communism* (January-April 1992): 121-133.

Brzezinski, Zbigniew. "Post-Communist Nationalism." *Foreign Affairs* (Winter 1989-1990): 1-25.

Cockburn, Patrick. "Dateline USSR: Ethnic Tremors." *Foreign Policy* (Spring 1989): 168-184.

Cole, John P., and Igor V. Filatotchev. "Some Observations on Migration within and from the Former USSR in the 1990s." *Post-Soviet Geography* (September 1992): 432-453.

Cullen, Robert B. "Soviet Jewry." *Foreign Affairs* (Winter 1986-1987): 252-266.

Dunlop, John B. "Soviet Cultural Politics." *Problems of Communism* (November-December 1987): 34-56.

Gitelman, Zvi. "Glasnost, Perestroika and Antisemitism." *Foreign Affairs* (Spring 1991): 141-159.

Goble, Paul. "Forget the Soviet Union." *Foreign Policy* (Spring 1992): 56-65.

Hajda, Lubomyr. "The Nationalities Problem in the Soviet Union." *Current History* (October 1988): 325-328.

Hopf, Ted. "Managing Soviet Disintegration: A Demand for Behavioral Regimes." *International Security* (Summer 1992): 44-75.

Lapidus, Gail W. "Gorbachev's Nationalities Problem." *Foreign Affairs* (Fall 1989): 92-108.

Odom, William E. "Soviet Politics and After: Old and New Concepts." *World Politics* (October 1992): 66-98.

Ozerov, Michael V. "Is a Commonwealth of Nations Possible in the USSR?" *Round Table* (January 1992): 19-22.

Rubinstein, Alvin Z. "The USSR in Turmoil: Views from the Right, Center, and Left." *Orbis* (Spring 1991): 267-284.

CHAPTER 8
The Economy

Books

Aslund, Anders. *Gorbachev's Struggle for Economic Reform: The Soviet Reform Process*. Ithaca, N.Y.: Cornell University Press, 1989.

_____, ed. *The Post-Soviet Economy: Soviet and Western Perspectives*. New York: St. Martin's, 1992.

Becker, Abraham Samuel. *Soviet Central Decision Making and Economic Growth*. Santa Monica, Calif.: Rand Corporation, 1986.

_____. *Gorbachev's Program for Economic Modernization and Reform*. Santa Monica, Calif.: Rand Corporation, 1987.

Berliner, Joseph. *Soviet Industry from Stalin to Gorbachev*. Ithaca, N.Y.: Cornell University Press, 1988.

Bornstein, Morris. *The Soviet Economy: Continuity and Change*. Boulder, Colo.: Westview, 1981.

Caldwell, Lawrence T., and William Diebold. *Soviet-American Relations in the 1980s: Superpower Politics and East-West Trade*. New York: McGraw-Hill, 1981.

Chadwick, Margaret. *Soviet Oil Exports*. Oxford, England: Oxford University Press, 1987.

Cooper, Leo. *The Political Economy of Soviet Military Power*. Basingstoke (Eng.): Macmillan, 1989.

Davies, Robert W. *The Soviet Economy in Turmoil*. Cambridge, Mass.: Harvard University Press, 1989.

Desai, Padma. *The Soviet Economy: Problems and Prospects*. Oxford, England: Blackwell, 1987.

Feshbach, Murray, and Alfred Friendly. *Ecocide in the USSR: Health and Nature Under Siege*. New York: Basic Books, 1992.

Hahn, Werner G. *The Politics of Soviet Agriculture, 1960-1970*. Baltimore: Johns Hopkins University Press, 1972.

Hewett, Ed A. *Energy, Economics, and Foreign Policy in the Soviet Union*. Washington, D.C.: Brookings Institution, 1984.

_____. *Reforming the Soviet Economy*. Washington, D.C.: Brookings Institution, 1988.

Hough, Jerry F. *Opening Up the Soviet Economy*. Washington, D.C.: Brookings Institution, 1988.

Ioffe, Olimpiad. *Gorbachev's Economic Dilemma: An Insider's View*. St. Paul: Merrill/Mangus, 1989.

Johnson, D. Gale, and Karen McConnell Brooks. *Prospects for Soviet Agriculture in the 1980s*. Bloomington: Indiana University Press, 1983.

Kanet, Roger, and Donna Bahry, eds. *Soviet Economic and Political Relations with the Developing World*. New York: Praeger, 1975.

Liebowitz, Ronald D., ed. *Gorbachev's New Thinking: Prospects for Joint Ventures*. Cambridge, Mass.: Ballinger, 1988.

Linz, Susan, and William Moskoff, eds. *Reorganization and Reform in the Soviet Economy*. Armonk, N.Y.: M. E. Sharpe, 1988.

Sokoloff, Georges. *The Economy of Détente*. New York: St. Martin's, 1987.

Articles

Aganbegyan, Abel G. "Basic Directions of Perestroyka." *Soviet Economy* (October-December 1987): 277-297.

Aslund, Anders. "Gorbachev's Economic Advisors." *Soviet Economy* (July-September 1987): 246-269.

Blank, Stephen. "Dangers from Russia's Military-Industrial Complex: New Strategists Who Demand the Old Economy." *Orbis* (Summer 1992): 365-378.

Bond, Daniel. "Impact on Soviet Trade of a Sharp Decline in Oil Prices." Vol. 5, no. 79-80. Washington, D.C.: Wharton Econometrics Centrally Planned Economies Current Analysis, October 29, 1985.

Chapman, Janet G. "Gorbachev's Wage Reform." *Soviet Economy* (October-December 1988): 338-365.

Colton, Timothy J. "Approaches to the Politics of Systematic Reform in the Soviet Union." *Soviet Economy* (April-June 1987): 145-170.

Cooper, Julian. "Military Cuts and Conversion in the Defense Industry." *Soviet Economy* (April-June 1991): 121-142.

Cooper, Mary H. "Communist Reformers Look West." *Editorial Research Reports,* March 4, 1988, 110-123.

Costello, Mary. "Soviet Economic Dilemma." *Editorial Research Reports,* February 19, 1982, 127-146.

Goldman, Marshall I. "Gorbachev the Economist." *Foreign Affairs* (Spring 1990): 28-44.

_____ and Merle Goldman. "Soviet and Chinese Economic Reform." *Foreign Affairs,* no. 3 (1988): 551-573.

Gregory, Paul R., and Irwin L. Collier, Jr. "Unemployment in the Soviet Union: Evidence from the Soviet Interview Project." *American Economic Review* (September 1988): 613-632.

Hewett, Ed A. "Perestroyka and the Congress of People's Deputies." *Soviet Economy* (January-March 1989): 47-69.

Hough, Jerry F. "The Politics of Successful Economic Reform." *Soviet Economy* (January-March 1989): 3-46.

Kaser, Michael. "One Economy, Two Systems: Parallels Between Soviet and Chinese Reform." *International Affairs* (Summer 1987): 395-412.

Kostakov, Vladimir G. "Labor Problems in Light of Perestroyka." *Soviet Economy* (January-March 1988): 95-101.

Lavoie, Louis. "The Limits of Soviet Technology." *Technology Review* (November-December 1985): 69-75.

Noren, James. "The Russian Economic Reform: Progress and Prospects." *Soviet Economy* (January-March 1992): 3-41.

Nove, Alec. "A Review of Soviet Economic Progress." *National Institute Economic Review* (November 1959): 37-47.

Ofer, Gur. "Budget Deficit, Market Disequilibrium and Soviet Economic Reforms." *Soviet Economy* (April-June 1989): 107-161.

Roucek, Libor. "Private Enterprise in Soviet Political Debates." *Soviet Studies* (January 1988): 46-63.

Sagers, Mathew J. "Regional Industrial Structures and Economic Prospects in the Former USSR." *Post-Soviet Geography* (October 1992): 487-515.

Schroeder, Gertrude E. "Soviet Economic Reforms: A Study in Contradictions." *Soviet Studies* (July 1988): 1-21.

Schwartz, Charles A. "Economic Crime in the USSR: A Comparison of the Khrushchev and Brezhnev Eras." *International Comparative Law Quarterly* (April 1981): 281-296.

Staar, Richard F. "The High-Tech Transfer Offensive of the Soviet Union." *Strategic Review* (Spring 1989): 32-39.

Toumanoff, Peter. "Economic Reform and Industrial Performance in the Soviet Union: 1954-1984." *Comparative Economic Studies* (Winter 1987): 128-149.

Weickhardt, George G. "The Soviet Military Industrial Complex and Economic Reform." *Soviet Economy* (July-September 1986): 193-227.

CHAPTER 9
Foreign Policy

Books

Bradsher, Henry S. *Afghanistan and the Soviet Union.* 2d ed. Durham, N.C.: Duke University Press, 1983.

Breslauer, George W. *Soviet Strategy in the Middle East.* Boston: Unwin Hyman, 1990.

Campbell, Kurk M., and S. Neil Macfarlane. *Gorbachev's Third World Dilemmas.* New York: Routledge, 1989.

Clark, Susan L., ed. *Gorbachev's Agenda: Changes in Soviet Domestic and Foreign Policy.* Boulder, Colo.: Westview, 1989.

Clemens, Walter C. *Can Russia Change? The USSR Confronts Global Interdependence.* Boston: Unwin Hyman, 1990.

Congressional Research Service. *The Soviet Union in the Third World, 1980-1985: An Imperial Burden or Political Asset?* Report prepared for the Committee on Foreign Affairs of the U.S. House of Representatives. September 23, 1985.

Connor, Walter D. *Socialism's Dilemmas: State and Society in the Soviet Bloc.* New York: Columbia University Press, 1988.

Dawisha, Adeed, and Karen Dawisha. *The Soviet Union in the Middle East: Perspectives and Policies.* New York: Holmes & Meier, 1982.

Edmonds, Robin. *Soviet Foreign Policy: The Brezhnev Years.* New York: Oxford University Press, 1983.

Eusebio, Mujal-Leon. *The USSR and Latin America: A Developing Relationship.* Boston: Unwin Hyman, 1989.

Freedman, Robert O. *Soviet Policy toward the Middle East since 1970.* 3d ed. New York: Praeger, 1982.

Fukuyama, Francis. *The Tenth Period of Soviet Third World Activity.* Santa Monica, Calif.: Rand Corporation, 1987.

Gelman, Harry. *Gorbachev's Policies toward Western*

Europe: A Balance Sheet. Santa Monica, Calif.: Rand Corporation, 1987.

Golan, Galia. *The Soviet Union and the National Liberation Movements in the Third World.* Boston: Allen & Unwin, 1988.

Hammond, Thomas T. *Red Flag over Afghanistan: The Communist Coup, the Soviet Invasion, and the Consequences.* Boulder, Colo.: Westview, 1984.

Haslam, Jonathan. *The Soviet Union and the Politics of Nuclear Weapons in Europe, 1969-1987.* Basingstoke (Eng.): Macmillan, 1989.

Hoffmann, Erik P., and Frederick Fleron, eds. *The Conduct of Soviet Foreign Policy.* Hawthorne, N.Y.: Aldine, 1980.

Holden, Gerard. *The Warsaw Pact: Soviet Security Policy and Bloc Politics.* New York: Blackwell, 1989.

Horak, Stephan. *Russia, the USSR, and Eastern Europe.* Littleton: Libraries Unlimited, 1987.

Hough, Jerry. *The Struggle for the Third World: Soviet Debates and American Options.* Washington, D.C.: Brookings Institution, 1985.

Jacobsen, Carl G., ed. *Soviet Foreign Policy: New Dynamics, New Themes.* New York: St. Martin's, 1989.

Kaplan, Stephen S. *Diplomacy of Power: Soviet Armed Forces as a Political Instrument.* 2d ed. Washington, D.C.: Brookings Institution, 1985.

Karsh, Efraim. *Soviet Policy towards Syria since 1970.* New York: St. Martin's, 1991.

Katz, Mark N. *Gorbachev's Military Policy in the Third World.* New York: Praeger, 1989.

Kolodziej, Edward A., and Roger E. Kanet, eds. *Limits of Soviet Power in the Developing World.* Baltimore: Johns Hopkins University Press, 1989.

Korbonski, Andrzej, and Francis Fukuyama, eds. *The Soviet Union and the Third World: The Last Three Decades.* Ithaca, N.Y.: Cornell University Press, 1987.

Laird, Robbin F., and Susan L. Clark. *The USSR and the Western Alliance.* Boston: Unwin Hyman, 1990.

Leiken, Robert, ed., *Central America: Anatomy of Conflict.* Elmsford, N.Y.: Pergamon, 1984.

Low, Alfred D. *The Sino-Soviet Confrontation since Mao Zedong.* Boulder, Colo.: Westview, 1987.

Lynch, Allen. *Gorbachev's International Outlook.* Boulder, Colo.: Westview, 1989.

Menon, Rajan, and Daniel N. Nelson. *Limits to Soviet Power.* Lexington, Mass.: Lexington Books, 1989.

Miller, Nicola. *Soviet Relations with Latin America, 1959-1987.* New York: Cambridge University Press, 1989

Nogee, Joseph L., and Robert H. Donaldson. *Soviet Foreign Policy since World War II.* 2d ed. Elmsford, N.Y.: Pergamon, 1984.

Porter, Bruce D. *The USSR in Third World Conflicts.*

New York: Cambridge University Press, 1984.

Robertson, Myles. *Soviet Policy toward Japan.* New York: Cambridge University Press, 1988.

Rozman, Gilbert. *Japan's Response to the Gorbachev Era 1985-1991: A Rising Superpower Views a Declining One.* Princeton, N.J.: Princeton University Press, 1992.

Rubinstein, Alvin Z. *Moscow's Third World Strategy.* Princeton, N.J.: Princeton University Press, 1988.

Shemesh, Haim. *Soviet-Iraqi Relations, 1968-1988: In the Shadow of the Iran-Iraq Conflict.* Boulder, Colo: Lynne Rienner, 1992.

Smith, Wayne, ed. *The Russians Aren't Coming: New Soviet Policy in Latin America.* Boulder: Lynne Rienner, 1991.

Sodaro, Michael. *Moscow, Germany, and the West from Khrushchev to Gorbachev.* Ithaca, N.Y.: Cornell University Press, 1990.

Staar, Richard F. *USSR Foreign Policies after Détente.* Stanford, Calif.: Hoover Institution Press, 1987.

Ulam, Adam B. *Expansion and Coexistence: Soviet Foreign Policy, 1917-73.* 2d ed. New York: Praeger, 1974.

Zacec, Jane Shapiro, ed. *The Gorbachev Generation: Issues in Soviet Foreign Policy.* New York: Paragon, 1988.

Zagoria, Donald S., ed. *Soviet Policy in East Asia.* New Haven, Conn.: Yale University Press, 1982.

Articles

Banjaree, Jyotirmoy. "Moscow's Indian Alliance." *Problems of Communism* (January-February 1987): 1-12.

Clement, Peter. "Moscow and Southern Africa." *Problems of Communism* (March-April 1985): 29-50.

Deudney, Daniel, and G. John Ikenberry. "The International Sources of Soviet Change." *International Security* (Winter 1991-92): 74-118.

Fukuyama, Francis. "Gorbachev and the Third World." *Foreign Affairs* (Spring 1986): 715-731.

Gati, Charles. "Gorbachev and Eastern Europe." *Foreign Affairs* (Summer 1987): 958-975.

Golan, Galia. "Moscow and the Third World National Liberation Movements: The Soviet Role." *Journal of International Affairs* (Spring 1987): 303-323.

_____. "Gorbachev's Difficult Time in the Gulf." *Political Science Quarterly* (Summer 1992): 213-230.

Goldstein, Steven M. "Diplomacy amid Protest: The Sino-Soviet Summit." *Problems of Communism* (September-October 1989): 49-71.

Goodman, Melvin A., and Carolyn McGiffert Ekedahl. "Gorbachev's 'New Directions' in the Middle East." *Middle East Journal* (Autumn 1988): 571-586.

Hamilton, Daniel. "Dateline East Germany: The Wall Behind the Wall." *Foreign Policy* (Fall 1989): 176-197.

Haslam, Jonathan. "The UN and the Soviet Union: New Thinking." *International Affairs* (Autumn 1989): 677-684.

Heuser, Beatrice. "What Nuclear Strategy for Post-Cold War Europe?" *Orbis* (Spring 1992): 211-225.

Howe, Geoffrey. "Soviet Foreign Policy under Gorbachev." *World Today* (March 1989): 40-45.

Hunter, Robert E. "The United States, Japan, and the Future of Russia." *SAIS Review* (Summer-Fall 1992): 65-71.

Keegan, John. "The Ordeal of Afghanistan." *Atlantic Monthly,* November 1985, 94-105.

Kramer, Mark N. "Soviet Arms Transfers to the Third World." *Problems of Communism* (September-October 1987): 52-68.

Kull, Steven. "Burying Lenin." *Foreign Policy* (Spring 1990): 172-191.

Leighton, Marian, and Robert Rudney. "Non-Offensive Defense: Toward a Soviet-German Security Partnership." *Orbis* (Summer 1991): 377-394.

Leiken, Robert. "Fantasies and Facts: The Soviet Union and Nicaragua." *Current History* 83 (October 1984): 314-317.

Lukin, Vladimir. "Our Security Predicament." *Foreign Policy* (Fall 1992): 57-75.

Macfarlane, S. Neil. "The Soviet Union and Southern African Security." *Problems of Communism* (March-June 1989): 71-89.

Menon, Rajan. "New Thinking and Northeast Asian Security." *Problems of Communism* (March-June 1989): 1-29.

_____. "Soviet Arms Transfers to the Third World: Characteristics and Consequences." *Journal of International Affairs* (Summer 1986): 59-76.

Schopflin, George. "Why Communism Collapsed." *International Affairs* (January 1990): 3-16.

Segal, Gerald. "Sino-Soviet Relations: The New Agenda." *World Today* (June 1988): 95-99.

Sestanovich, Stephen. "Gorbachev's Foreign Policy: A Diplomacy of Decline." *Problems of Communism* (January-February 1988): 1-15.

Szayna, Thomas S. "Addressing 'Blank Spots' in Polish-Soviet Relations." *Problems of Communism* (November-December 1988): 37-61.

Valenta, Jiri. "From Prague to Kabul: The Soviet Style of Invasion." *International Security* (Fall 1980): 114-141.

Wettig, Gerhard. "New Thinking on Security and East-West Relations." *Problems of Communism* (March-April 1988): 1-14.

Zubok, Vladislav. "Tyranny of the Weak: Russia's New Foreign Policy." *World Policy Journal* (Spring 1992): 191-217.

CHAPTER 10
Relations with the United States

Books

Allison, Graham T., William L. Ury, and Bruce Allyn, eds. *Windows of Opportunity.* Cambridge, Mass.: Ballinger, 1989.

Barkenbus, Jack N. *U.S.-Soviet Relations: An Agenda for the Future.* Baltimore: Johns Hopkins University Press, 1988.

Barnet, Richard J. *The Giants: Russia and America.* New York: Simon and Schuster, 1977.

Bialer, Seweryn, and Michael Mandelbaum. *Global Rivals.* New York: Knopf, 1988.

_____, eds. *Gorbachev's Russia and American Foreign Policy.* Boulder, Colo.: Westview, 1988.

Blacker, Coit D. *Reluctant Warriors: The U.S. and the Soviet Union and Arms Control.* New York: W. H. Freeman, 1987.

Browder, Robert P. *The Origins of the Soviet-American Diplomacy.* Princeton, N.J.: Princeton University Press, 1953.

Brzezinski, Zbigniew. *Game Plan: The Geostrategic Framework for the Conduct of the U.S.-Soviet Contest.* Boston: Atlantic Monthly Press, 1986.

Calingaert, Daniel. *Soviet Nuclear Policy under Gorbachev: A Policy of Disarmament.* New York: Praeger, 1991.

Carvounis, Chris, and Brinda Z. Carvounis. *U.S. Commercial Opportunities in the Soviet Union.* New York: Quorum, 1989.

Freedman, Robert Owen. *The Soviet Union and the Carter Administration.* Pittsburgh: University of Pittsburgh Press, 1989.

Gaddis, John Lewis. *The Long Peace: Inquiries into the History of the Cold War.* New York: Oxford University Press, 1987.

Galbraith, John Kenneth, and Stanislav Menshikov. *Capitalism, Communism, and Coexistence: From the Bitter Past to the Better Prospect.* Boston: Houghton Mifflin, 1988.

Garthoff, Raymond. *Détente and Confrontation: American-Soviet Relations from Nixon to Reagan.* Washington, D.C.: Brookings Institution, 1985.

George, Alexander L., Philip Farley, and Alexander Dallin, eds. *U.S.-Soviet Security Cooperation.* New York: Oxford University Press, 1988.

Gordon, Lincoln. *Integrating Economic and Security Factors in East-West Relations.* Washington, D.C.: Atlantic Council, 1988.

Greenwald, G. Jonathan, and Leonard Sullivan. *The Western Stake in the Future of the Soviet Economy.* Washington, D.C.: Atlantic Council, 1987.

Griffith, William E. *The Super Powers and Regional Tensions: The USSR and the U.S. and Europe.* Lexington, Mass.: Lexington Books, 1981.

Harriman, William Averell. *America and Russia in a Changing World: A Half Century of Personal Observation.* Garden City, N.Y.: Doubleday, 1971.

Horelick, Arnold Lawrence. *U.S.-Soviet Relations: The Next Phase.* Ithaca, N.Y.: Cornell University Press, 1986.

Hyland, William G. *Mortal Rivals: Superpower Relations from Nixon to Reagan.* New York: Random House, 1987.

Jervis, Robert, and Seweryn Bialer, eds. *Soviet-American Relations after the Cold War.* Durham, N.C.: Duke University Press, 1991.

Kalb, Marvin, and Bernard Kalb. *Kissinger.* Boston: Little, Brown, 1974.

Kissinger, Henry. *White House Years.* Boston: Little, Brown, 1979.

Legvold, Robert. *Gorbachev's Foreign Policy: How Should the U.S. Respond?* New York: Foreign Policy Association, 1988.

Libbey, James K. *American-Russian Economic Relations.* Claremont, Calif.: Regina, 1989.

Litwak, Robert, and Samuel Wells, eds. *Superpower Competition and Security in the Third World.* Cambridge, Mass.: Ballinger, 1988.

Mandelbaum, Michael, and Strobe Talbott. *Reagan and Gorbachev.* New York: Vintage, 1987.

Mandelbaum, Michael, ed. *The Rise of Nations in the Soviet Union: American Foreign Policy and the Disintegration of the USSR.* New York: Council on Foreign Relations Press, 1991.

McNamara, Robert S. *Out of the Cold.* New York: Simon and Schuster, 1989.

Oberdorfer, Don. *The Turn: From the Cold War to a New Era: The United States and the Soviet Union, 1983-1990.* New York: Poseidon, 1991.

Parrott, Bruce. *The Soviet Union and Ballistic Missile Defense.* Boulder, Colo.: Westview, 1987.

Payne, Samuel B. *The Soviet Union and SALT.* Cambridge, Mass.: MIT Press, 1980.

Potter, William C., ed. *Verification and SALT: The Challenge of Strategic Deception.* Boulder, Colo.: Westview, 1980.

Seaborg, Glenn T. et al. *Kennedy, Khrushchev and the Test Ban.* Berkeley and Los Angeles: University of California Press, 1981.

Sherr, Alan B. *The Other Side of Arms Control: Soviet Objectives in the Gorbachev Era.* Boston: Unwin Hyman, 1988.

Sherr, James. *Soviet Power: The Continuing Challenge.* Basingstoke (Eng.): Macmillan, 1987.

Sivachev, Nikolai, and Nikolai Yakovlev. *Russia and the United States.* Chicago: University of Chicago Press, 1979.

Smith, Gerard. *Doubletalk: The Story of the First Strategic Arms Limitation Talks.* Garden City, N.Y.: Doubleday, 1980.

Smith, Raymond F. *Negotiating with the Soviets.* Bloomington: Indiana University Press, 1989.

Talbott, Strobe. *Deadly Gambits.* New York: Random House, 1984.

_____. *Endgame: The Inside Story of SALT II.* New York: Harper & Row, 1980.

Ulam, Adam B. *The Rivals: America and Russia since World War II.* New York: Viking, 1971.

Vance, Cyrus. *Hard Choices: Critical Years in America's Foreign Policy.* New York: Simon & Schuster, 1983.

Weber, Steve. *Cooperation and Discord in U.S.-Soviet Arms Control.* Princeton, N.J.: Princeton University Press, 1991.

Wolfe, Thomas W. *The SALT Experience.* Cambridge, Mass.: Ballinger, 1979.

Articles

Bertram, Christoph. "The German Question." *Foreign Affairs* (Spring 1990): 45-62.

Blight, James G. et al. "The Cuban Missile Crisis Revisited." *Foreign Affairs* (Fall 1987): 170-188.

Brzezinski, Zbigniew. "The U.S.-Soviet Relationship: Paradoxes and Prospects." *Strategic Review* (Spring 1987): 11-18.

Bundy, McGeorge. "From Cold War toward Trusting Peace." *Foreign Affairs* (America and the World 1989-1990): 51-69.

Chase, James. "A New Grand Strategy." *Foreign Policy* (Spring 1988): 3-25.

Cooper, Mary H. "Soviet Trade: In America's Best Interest?" *Editorial Research Reports,* February 10, 1989, 74-87.

Fessler, Pamela. "Yeltsin Charges onto Capitol Hill, Charms the Life out of Cold War." *Congressional Quarterly Weekly Report* (June 20, 1992): 1813-1818.

Fuller, Graham. "Moscow and the Gulf War." *Foreign Affairs* (Summer 1991): 55-76.

Gaddis, John Lewis. "The Long Peace: Elements of Stability in the Postwar International System." *International Security* (Spring 1986): 99-142.

Haley, P. Edward. "You Could Have Said Yes: Lessons from Reykjavik." *Orbis* (Spring 1987): 75-98.

Horelick, Arnold L. "U.S.-Soviet Relations: The Threshold of a New Era." *Foreign Affairs* (America and the World 1989-1990): 51-69.

Husband, William B. "Soviet Perspectives of U.S. 'Positions-of-Strength' Diplomacy in the 1970s." *World Politics* (July 1979): 495-517.

Hyland, William G. "U.S.-Soviet Relations: The Long

Road Back." *Foreign Affairs* (America and the World 1981): 525-550.

Kennan, George F. "Containment Then and Now." *Foreign Affairs* (Spring 1987): 885-890.

Larrabee, F. Stephen, and Allen Lynch. "Gorbachev: The Road to Reykjavik." *Foreign Policy* (Winter 1986-1987): 3-28.

Marantz, Paul. "Soviet 'New Thinking' and East-West Relations." *Current History* (October 1988): 309-312.

May, Michael, et al. "Strategic Arsenals after START: The Implications of Deep Cuts." *International Security* (Summer 1988): 90-133.

McConnell, James M. "SDI, the Soviet Investment Debate and Soviet Military Policy." *Strategic Review* (Winter 1988): 47-62.

Potter, William C. "Exodus: Containing the Spread of Soviet Nuclear Weapons." *Harvard International Review* (Spring 1992): 26-29.

Rogov, Sergey M. "Detente Is Not Enough." *Foreign Policy* (Spring 1989): 86-102.

Schlesinger, Arthur M., Jr. "Origins of the Cold War." *Foreign Affairs* (Fall 1967): 22-52.

Seabury, Paul, and Brian Thomas. "Cold War Origins." *Journal of Contemporary History* (January 1968): 169-198.

Slater, Jerome. "The Eleventh Hour of the Cuban Missile Crisis." *International Security* (Winter 1987-1988): 5-92.

CHAPTER 11
The Baltic States

Books

Clemens, Walter. *Baltic Independence and Russian Empire.* New York: St. Martin's, 1991.

Hiden, John, and Patrick Salmon. *The Baltic Nations and Europe: Estonia, Latvia and Lithuania in the Twentieth Century.* New York: Longman, 1991.

Raun, Toivo. *Estonia and the Estonians.* Stanford, Calif.: Hoover Institution Press, 1991.

Tarulis, Albert N. *Soviet Policy Toward the Baltic States 1918-1940.* South Bend, Ind.: University of Notre Dame Press, 1959.

Trapans, Jan Arveds. *Toward Independence: The Baltic Popular Movements.* Boulder, Colo.: Westview, 1991.

U.S. Congress. Commission on Security and Cooperation in Europe. *Implementation of the Helsinki Accords: Hearing Before the CSCE 102nd Congress, First session, the Soviet Crackdown on the Baltic States, January 17, 1991.* Washington, D.C.: Government Printing Office, 1991.

Van Arkadie, Brian, and Mats Karlsson. *Economic Survey of the Baltic States.* New York: New York University Press, 1992.

Von Rauch, George. *The Baltic States, the Years of Independence: Estonia, Latvia, Lithuania 1917-1940.* Berkeley and Los Angeles: University of California Press, 1974.

Articles

Burant, S. R. "Polish-Lithuanian Relations: Past, Present, and Future." *Problems of Communism* (May-June 1991): 67-84.

Dreifelds, Juris. "Immigration and Ethnicity in Latvia." *Journal of Soviet Nationalities* (Winter 1990-1991): 43-81.

Olcott, Martha Brill. "The Lithuanian Crisis." *Foreign Affairs* (Summer 1990): 30-46.

Taagepera, Rein. "Building Democracy in Estonia." *PS* (September 1991): 478-481.

Trapans, Jan A. "Averting Moscow's Baltic Coup." *Orbis* (Summer 1991): 427-439.

Uibopuu, Henn-Juri. "Dealing with the Minorities: A Baltic Perspective." *World Today* (June 1992): 108-112.

Vardys, V. Stanley. "Lithuanian National Politics." *Problems of Communism* (July-August 1989): 53-76.

CHAPTER 12
The Central Asian States

Books

Allworth, Edward, ed. *Central Asia: 120 Years of Russian Rule.* Durham, N.C.: Duke University Press, 1989.

_____. *The Modern Uzbeks: From the Fourteenth Century to the Present: A Cultural History.* Stanford, Calif.: Hoover Institution Press, 1990.

Bacon, Elizabeth. *Central Asians under Russian Rule: A Study in Cultural Change.* Ithaca, N.Y.: Cornell University Press, 1980.

Critchlow, James. *Nationalism in Uzbekistan: A Soviet Republic's Road to Sovereignty.* Boulder, Colo.: Westview, 1991.

Dienes, Leslie. *Soviet Asia, Economic Development and National Policy Choices.* Boulder, Colo.: Westview, 1987.

Fierman, William, ed. *Soviet Central Asia: The Failed Transformation.* Boulder, Colo.: Westview, 1991.

Fuller, Graham. *Central Asia: The New Geopolitics.* Santa Monica, Calif.: Rand Corporation, 1992.

Gross, Jo-Ann. *Muslims in Central Asia: Expressions of Identity and Change.* Durham, N.C.: Duke University

Press, 1992.

Jukes, Geoffrey. *The Soviet Union in Asia.* Berkeley and Los Angeles: University of California Press, 1973.

Olcott, Martha Brill. *The Kazakhs.* Stanford, Calif.: Hoover Institution Press, 1987.

Park, Alexander G. *Bolshevism in Turkestan 1917-1927.* New York: Columbia University Press, 1957.

Rumer, Boris Z. *Soviet Central Asia: "A Tragic Experiment."* Boston: Unwin Hyman, 1989.

Rywkin, Michael. *Moscow's Muslim Challenge: Soviet Central Asia.* Armonk, N.Y.: M. E. Sharpe, 1990.

Taheri, Amir. *Crescent in a Red Sky: The Future of Islam in the Soviet Union.* London: Hutchinson, 1989.

Articles

Imart, Guy G. "Kirgizia-Kazakhstan: A Hinge or a Faultline?" *Problems of Communism* (September-October, 1990): 1-13.

Olcott, Martha Brill. "Central Asia's Catapult to Independence." *Foreign Affairs* (Summer 1992): 108-130.

———. "Central Asia's Post-Empire Politics." *Orbis* (Spring 1992): 253-268.

Roi, Yaacov. "The Islamic Influence on Nationalism in Soviet Central Asia." *Problems of Communism* (July-August 1990): 49-64.

Rupert, James. "Dateline Tashkent: Post-Soviet Central Asia." *Foreign Policy* (Summer 1992): 175-195.

CHAPTER 13
The Transcaucasian States

Books

Altstadt, Audrey. *The Azerbaijani Turks: Power and Identity under Russian Rule.* Stanford, Calif.: Hoover Institution Press, 1992.

Henze, Paul. *The Transcaucus in Transition.* Santa Monica, Calif.: Rand Corporation, 1991.

Rost, Yuri. *Armenian Tragedy.* New York: St. Martin's, 1990.

Walker, Christopher. *Armenia: The Survival of a Nation.* New York: St. Martin's, 1990.

U.S. Congress. Commission on Security and Cooperation in Europe. *Implementation of the Helsinki Accords: Hearing Before the CSCE 102nd Congress, First session, the Nagorno-Karabakh Crisis, Prospects for Resolution, October 23, 1991.* Washington, D.C.: Government Printing Office, 1991.

Articles

Carney, James. "Carnage in Karabakh." *Time* (April 13,

1992): 40-42.

Cullen, Robert. "Roots." *New Yorker* (April 15, 1991): 55-76

Hiro, Dilip. "The Question of Azerbaijan." *The Nation* (September 14, 1992): 241-243

MacKenzie, Kenneth. "Azerbaijan and the Neighbors." *The World Today* (January 1992): 1-2.

Quinn-Judge, Paul. "Revenge Tragedy." *The New Republic* (April 1992): 11-12.

Saroyan, Mark. "The 'Karabakh Syndrome' and Azerbaijani Politics." *Problems of Communism* (September-October 1990): 14-29.

Slider, D. "The Politics of Georgia's Independence." *Problems of Communism* (November-December): 1991.

CHAPTER 14
The Western States

Books

Dima, Nicholas. *From Moldavia to Moldova: The Soviet-Romanian Dispute.* New York: Columbia University Press, 1991.

Forsyth, James. *A History of the Peoples of Siberia: Russia's North Asian Colony.* Cambridge: Cambridge University Press, 1992.

Hubbs, Joanna. *Mother Russia: The Feminine Myth in Russian Culture.* Bloomington: Indiana University Press, 1988.

Kaiser, Robert G. *Russia: The People and Power.* New York: Washington Square Press, 1984.

Little, David. *Ukraine: The Legacy of Intolerance.* Washington, D.C.: United States Institute of Peace, 1991.

Marples, David. *Ukraine under Perestroika: Ecology, Economics, and the Workers' Revolt.* New York: St. Martin's, 1991.

Miller, Wright. *Who Are the Russians? A History of the Russian People.* New York: Taplinger, 1973.

Solchanyk, Roman, ed. *Ukraine from Chernobyl to Sovereignty: A Collection of Interviews.* New York: St. Martin's, 1992.

Subtelny, Orest. *Ukraine: A History.* Toronto: University of Toronto Press, 1988.

Swearingen, Rodger, ed. *Siberia and the Soviet Far East.* Stanford, Calif.: Hoover Institution Press, 1987.

Articles

Crowther, William. "The Politics of Mobilization: Nationalism and Reform in Soviet Moldavia." *Russian Review* (April 1991): 183-202.

Dima, Nicholas. "The Soviet Political Upheaval of the

1980s: The Case of Moldavia." *Journal of Social, Political, and Economic Studies* (Spring 1991): 39-58.

Karatnycky, Adrian. "The Ukrainian Factor." *Foreign Affairs* (Summer 1992): 90-107.

Korotich, Vitaly. "The Ukraine Rising." *Foreign Policy* (Winter 1991): 73-82.

Kozyrev, Andrei. "Russia: A Chance for Survival." *Foreign Affairs* (Spring 1992): 1-16.

Malcolm, Neil. "Reconstructing Russia." *World Today* (October 1992): 183-187.

Marples, David R. "Post-Soviet Belarus and the Impact of Chernobyl." *Post-Soviet Geography* (September 1992): 419-431.

McFaul, Michael. "Russia's Emerging Political Parties." *Journal of Democracy* (January 1992): 25-40.

Radvanyi, Jean. "And What If Russia Breaks Up." *Post-Soviet Geography* (February 1992): 69-77.

Simon, Gerhard. "The Ukraine and the End of the Soviet Union." *Aussen Politik* (First Quarter 1992): 62-71.

Smart, Christopher. "Dangers from Russia's Military-Industrial Complex: Amid the Ruins, Arms Makers Raise New Threats." *Orbis* (Summer 1992): 349-364.

Szporluk, Roman. "Dilemmas of Russian Nationalism." *Problems of Communism* (July-August 1989): 15-35.

Urban, M. E. "Boris Yeltsin, Democratic Russia, and the Campaign for the Russian Presidency." *Soviet Studies,* no. 2 (1992): 187-207.

General Readings

Books

Arbatov, Georgy. *The System: An Insider's Guide to Soviet Politics.* New York: Random House, 1992.

Bialer, Seweryn. *The Soviet Paradox: External Expansion, Internal Decline.* New York: Knopf, 1986.

Black, Cyril Edwin. *Understanding Soviet Politics: The Perspective of Russian History.* Boulder, Colo.: Westview, 1986.

Brown, Archie, ed. *Political Leadership in the Soviet Union.* Bloomington: Indiana University Press, 1990.

Central Intelligence Agency. Directorate of Intelligence. *The Republics of the Former Soviet Union and the Baltic States: An Overview.* 1992.

Colton, Timothy J., and Thane Gustafson, eds. *Soldiers and the Soviet State: Civil-Military Relations from Brezhnev to Gorbachev.* Princeton, N.J.: Princeton University Press, 1990.

Conquest, Robert. *The Soviet Political System.* New York: Praeger, 1968.

Cracraft, James, ed. *The Soviet Union Today: An Interpretive Guide.* Chicago: University of Chicago Press, 1988.

Dmytryshyn, Basil. *USSR: A Concise History.* 4th ed. New York: Charles Scribner's Sons, 1984.

Foreign Broadcast Information Service. *Daily Report: Soviet Union.*

Haupt, Georges, and Jean-Jacques Marie. *Makers of the Russian Revolution: Biographies of Soviet Leaders.* Ithaca, N.Y.: Cornell University Press, 1974.

Hough, Jerry F., and Merle Fainsod. *How the Soviet Union Is Governed.* Cambridge, Mass.: Harvard University Press, 1979.

Kanet, Roger E., ed. *The Behavioral Revolution and Communist Studies.* New York: Free Press, 1971.

Medish, Vadim. *The Soviet Union.* 2d ed. Englewood Cliffs, N.J.: Prentice-Hall, 1985.

Morrison, John. *Boris Yeltsin: From Bolshevik to Democrat.* New York: Dutton, 1991.

Potichnyj, Peter, ed. *The Soviet Union: Party and Society.* New York: Cambridge University Press, 1988.

Richelson, Jeffrey T. *Sword and Shield: Soviet Intelligence and Security Apparatus.* Cambridge, Mass.: Ballinger, 1986.

Rudolph, Richard, and David Good. *Nationalism and Empire: The Habsburg Empire and the Soviet Union.* New York: St. Martin's, 1992.

Sakharov, Andrei. *Memoirs.* Translated by Richard Lourie. New York: Knopf, 1990.

Scott, Harriet Fast, and William F. Scott. *The Armed Forces of the USSR.* 3d ed. Boulder, Colo.: Westview, 1984.

Shevardnadze, Eduard. *The Future Belongs to Freedom.* London: Sinclair-Stevenson, 1991.

Shlapentokh, Vladimir. *Public and Private Life of the Soviet People: Changing Values in Post-Stalin Russia.* New York: Oxford University Press, 1989.

Steeves, Paul. *The Communists: A Story of Power and Lost Illusions, 1948-1991.* New York: Macmillan, 1992.

Thompson, John M. *Russia and the Soviet Union: An Historical Introduction.* New York: Charles Scribner's Sons, 1986.

Ulam, Adam B. *A History of Soviet Russia.* New York: Praeger, 1976.

Utechin, S. V. *A Concise Encyclopaedia of Russia.* New York: Dutton, 1964.

Westwood, J. N. *Endurance and Endeavor: Russian History, 1812-1980.* New York: Oxford University Press, 1981.

INDEX